VISIONS OF ANTIQUITY

William Stukeley's frontispiece to the minutes of the Society of Antiquaries (drawn 1717, though the first minute dates from 1 January 1718) shows three Roman knights clasping hands over an altar, with a banner showing Julius Caesar, King Alfred and Charles I. The clubbable motto comes from Sallust's *Bellum Jugurthinum*. In the original, the phrase *Concordia res parvae crescent*, 'small matters grow large through unity', is balanced by the words *discordia maximae dilabuntur*, 'the largest fall apart through disunity'.

Photograph: Society of Antiquaries of London.

VISIONS OF ANTIQUITY

The Society of Antiquaries of London
1707–2007

EDITED BY SUSAN PEARCE

BEING VOLUME 111 OF ARCHAEOLOGIA
THE SOCIETY OF ANTIQUARIES OF LONDON
2007

First published 2007
by
The Society of Antiquaries of London
Burlington House
Piccadilly
London W1J 0BE

www.sal.org.uk

ISBN 978-0-85431-287-0
ISSN 0261-3409

British Library Cataloguing in Publication Data
A CIP catalogue record for this book is available from the British Library.

Edited and produced by The Dial House Partnership Ltd
Designed and laid out by Libanus Press, Marlborough, Wiltshire
Printed and bound in Great Britain by Cambridge University Press, Cambridge

CONTENTS

List of illustrations   vi
List of tables   ix
Acknowledgements   x
Foreword by HRH The Duke of Gloucester   xi

CHAPTER ONE   Visions of Antiquity: Introduction *by Susan Pearce*   1

CHAPTER TWO   Images of the Antiquary in Seventeenth-Century England *by Daniel Woolf*   11

CHAPTER THREE   Forming an Identity: The Early Society and its Context, 1707–51 *by Arthur MacGregor*   45

CHAPTER FOUR   The Incorporated Society and its Public Role *by Rosemary Sweet*   75

CHAPTER FIVE   The Society of Antiquaries and the Graphic Arts: George Vertue and his Legacy *by Martin Myrone*   99

CHAPTER SIX   Art and Antiquity in the Long Nineteenth Century *by Sam Smiles*   123

CHAPTER SEVEN   Antiquaries and the Interpretation of Ancient Objects, 1770–1820 *by Susan Pearce*   147

CHAPTER EIGHT   The Society, its Council, the Membership and Publications, 1820–50 *by Richard Hingley*   173

CHAPTER NINE   The Development of the Library *by Bernard Nurse*   199

CHAPTER TEN   Prehistory in the Nineteenth Century *by C Stephen Briggs*   227

CHAPTER ELEVEN   'Delineating Objects': Nineteenth-Century Antiquarian Culture and the Project of Archaeology *by Christopher Evans*   267

CHAPTER TWELVE   Fabric, Form and Function: The Society and 'the Restoration Question' *by Rick Turner*   307

CHAPTER THIRTEEN   Breathing the Future: The Antiquaries and Conservation of the Landscape, 1850–1950 *by Richard Morris*   329

CHAPTER FOURTEEN   The Grand Excavation Projects of the Twentieth Century *by Michael Fulford*   353

CHAPTER FIFTEEN   Changing Roles and Agendas: the Society of Antiquaries and the Professionalization of Archaeology, 1950–2000 *by Graeme Barker*   383

CHAPTER SIXTEEN   'A Tree with Many Branches': The Fellowship at the Start of the Twenty-First Century *by David Gaimster*   415

EPILOGUE   'Society of Antiquaries?' *by Eric Fernie*   430

List of contributors   436
Index   438

ILLUSTRATIONS

		page
Frontispiece	William Stukeley's frontispiece to the minutes of the Society of Antiquaries (1717)	ii
1	'The reception of a new member at the Society of Antiquaries' (1782), by Thomas Rowlandson	xii
2	Samuel Gale (artist unknown)	10
3	John Dodderidge (artist unknown)	25
4	John Weever: line engraving in *Ancient Funerall Monuments* (1631), by Thomas Cecill	27
5	William Camden: portrait by Robert White from *Remains* (1674 edition)	27
6	William Camden: portrait from Sylvanus Morgan, *The Sphere of Gentry* (1661)	28
7	John Speed: engraving from *A Prospect of the Most Famous Parts of the World* (1631 edition), by Salomon Savery	29
8	William Burton: line engraving by Francis Delaram from *Description of Leicester Shire* (1622)	30
9	John Selden: engraved portrait by Robert White from *Titles of Honor* (3rd edn, 1672)	30
10	John Selden: portrait from *Contextio gemmarum* (Oxford, 1658)	30
11	Thomas Hearne: portrait (1723) by George Vertue	31
12	Sir William Dugdale: engraved portrait by Wenceslaus Hollar from *Antiquities of Warwickshire* (1656)	31
13	Elias Ashmole: portrait (1682) attributed to John Riley	32
14	Charles Leigh: portrait by William Faithorne from *Naturall History of Lancashire, Cheshire, and the Peak, in Derbyshire* (Oxford, 1700)	33
15	Humfrey Wanley: portrait (1711) by Thomas Hill	34
16	The earliest surviving minutes of the Society, 5 and 12 December 1707	44
17	Cross-sectional view showing the method of excavation of Royston Cave	58
18	Mosaic from a Romano-British villa at Stonesfield, Oxfordshire, engraved by George Vertue, 1712	60
19	Tesserae recovered from a Romano-British villa at Stonesfield, Oxfordshire, and exhibited on 7 December 1721	60
20	Spearheads and daggers from a Bronze Age hoard discovered at Arreton Down, Isle of Wight, drawn by Charles Frederick, Director 1735/6–1741/2	61
21	Anglian urn of the type exhibited by Peter le Neve, 25 November 1719	62
22	Lamp found at St Leonard's Hill, Windsor, in 1717 and presented to the Society by Sir Hans Sloane, 1736	64
23	Engraving by John Talman, 1718 (from *Vetusta Monumenta*, I, pl I) of the lamp presented to the Society by Sir Hans Sloane in 1736	64
24	John Carter (1748–1817): a sketch portrait by Sylvester Harding	74
25	'Section of the Quadrangle designed for the British Museum, including the Royal Society, Antiquarian Society, and a Royal Academy of Painting, Sculpture and Architecture': engraving by Cornelius Johnson	77
26	Richard Gough: sketch made at the Duchess of Portland sale, 1785	81
27	Jeremiah Milles: portrait copied by Mary Black in 1785 from an original by Nathaniel Dance of unknown date	82
28	'Richard II': engraving by George Vertue (1747)	98
29	'Ulphi Cornu': engraving by George Vertue (1747)	103
30	'The Royal Family Piece': engraving by George Vertue after Hans Holbein; first published in 1742 and republished by the Society of Antiquaries in 1776	105
31	'Brass trumpets and other instruments found in Ireland, and a shield found at Hendinas in Shropshire': engraving by James Basire (1763)	112
32	'Inside view of Magdalen Chapel, near Winchester, from the west': etching and engraving by James Basire after Jacob Schnebbelie (1790)	115
33	'Magdalen Chapel near Winchester': etching and engraving by James Basire after Jacob Schnebbelie (1790)	115
34	'An antique statue of bronze, discovered in Suffolk': etching and engraving by James Basire after Richard Smirke (1807)	116

35 'A general plan of the ground occupied by the abbey of St Mary, York': lithograph (1829) — 118

36 James Basire the younger, *The Ribchester Helmet* (1799) — 122

37 William Blake, *Tomb Effigy from Westminster Abbey of Countess Aveline, First Wife of Edmund Crouchback, Earl of Lancaster* (1775) — 127

38 Thomas Girtin, *Flanged Palstave and Roman Bow Brooch* (c 1794) — 128

39 J M W Turner, *Studies of Seals from Whalley Abbey* (1799–1800) — 130

40 John Britton's 'Celtic Cabinet' (1820s) — 130

41 Frederick Sandys, *Antiquities Found at Kennett, Wiltshire* (1854) — 131

42 William Müller, *Water Tomb, Telmessus* (1844) — 132

43 Charles Alfred Stothard, *Facsimile Drawing of the Bayeux Tapestry* (c 1816) — 134

44 Benjamin West, *The First Installation of the Order of the Garter, in St George's Chapel* (1787) — 136

45 Ford Madox Brown, *Chaucer at the Court of Edward III* (1847–51) — 137

46 After Sir Lawrence Alma-Tadema, *Hadrian in England: Visiting a Romano-British Pottery* (1884) — 138

47 After Edward Burne-Jones, *The Attainment: The Vision of the Holy Grail to Sir Galahad, Sir Bors and Sir Percival* (1895–6) — 142

48 'An Arch Druid in his Judicial Habit': coloured aquatint by Robert Havell — 146

49 Late Bronze Age hammered bronze shield from Beith, Ayrshire, Scotland — 149

50 Drawing of a Middle Bronze Age gold torc added to the Minute Book for 12 December 1771 — 156

51 Plate I from Richard Gough's *Sepulchral Monuments in Great Britain* — 160

52 'Grand Conventional Festival of the Britons': coloured aquatint by Robert Havell — 164

53 Print engraved by Thomas Rowlandson (1822), showing the exhibition of Lapland life mounted at the Egyptian Hall in that year — 165

54 'The Antiquarian Society': coloured engraving by George Cruikshank (1812) — 172

55 'A Point of Antiquity': lithograph (1833) — 181

56 Papers published in *Archaeologia* from the 1820s to the 1840s by area — 188

57 Varying proportions of reports on sites/finds/documents in *Archaeologia* by decade — 189

58 'Bricks and tiles found among the Roman remains at North Stoke' (1829) — 190

59 Proportions of different types of report published in *Archaeologia*, 1820s to 1840s — 191

60 'Vestiges supposedly Druidical, on Dartmoor near Tavistock, Devon' (1829) — 192

61 'The White Horse at Uffington' (1846) — 193

62 'A Declaration for . . . drawing the great standing Lottery': printed broadside (1615) — 198

63 Plan of the Society's library and museum on the ground floor of Somerset House, 1781 — 203

64 Jousting cheque for a tournament held at the Field of the Cloth of Gold in 1520 — 205

65 *The Legend of St Etheldreda* (c 1455) — 207

66 The south elevation of the Society's library in Somerset House (c 1847) — 208

67 The library in Burlington House looking south (1921) — 216

68 The library looking north west (1984) — 220

69 'Flint implements from the valley of the Somme' (1859) — 226

70 Before and after records of a barrow excavated by the Revd Anthony Freston at Duntisbourne Abbots, Gloucestershire, in 1806 — 233

71 Before and after records of a barrow excavated by the Revd Anthony Freston at Duntisbourne Abbots, Gloucestershire, in 1806 — 233

72 Cross-section of a chamber of the megalithic tomb on L'Ancresse Common, Guernsey (1845) — 234

73 Probably the first published depiction of a co-axial field system from Britain, on Baildon Moor, Yorkshire (1846) — 235

74 Palaeolithic ovate hand-axe from Hoxne, found in 1797 (published 1800) — 245

75 A section from the Somme gravels: Boucher de Perthes, *Antiquités celtiques et antédiluviennes* (1849) — 247

76 'Before the Deluge': Penn's 1828 schematic method showing the 'vertical and lateral positions of rocks' with the Bible employed as its keystone; card published by J Reynolds, showing the geological 'progress' (and respective strata) of amphibious life-forms to dinosaurs and mammals at the Crystal Palace — 266

77 Society meetings within Somerset House: (a) the Cruikshank print of 1812; (b) detail of the same, showing misattributed antiquities; (c) detail of the 1844 Fairholt print; (d) and (e) 'Learned Society room-plans' at Somerset House — 273

78 Saxon cemeteries: Dryden's Marston St Lawrence site of 1843; Akerman's Harnham Hill plan   278
79 Nineteenth-century site graphics: (a) plan of Standlake (1857); (b) plan of barrow at   279
    Collingbourn, Wilts (1871); (c) and (d) plan and view of the Iffins Wood barrow (1844);
    (e) plan of the New Forest kiln excavations (1853); (f) Pitt-Rivers's excavation medallion
80 'A picturesque pursuit': (a) introductory view to Conyngham's Breach Down report (1844);   281
    (b) Logan's illustration of Balquhain stone circle (1829); (c) Kempe's view of the Holwood
    Hill temple (1829)
81 'Still-life' displays: 'massed' finds from Conyngham's barrow-digging 'marathon' at Breach   282
    Down in 1844; 'plinthed' grave-assemblage figure from the Youngsbury barrow (1890)
82 'The testimony of strata': (a) section across a paved building floor at Silchester (1881);   285
    (b) one of Pitt-Rivers's 'piles near London Wall' sections (1867); (c) 'perspective section'
    across the ramparts of Cissbury hillfort, with flint mine shaft below (1875)
83 Palaeolithic, Neolithic and Bronze Age implements (1860, 1872 and 1873)   297
84 Darwin's 'Tree of Evolution', from *The Origin of Species* (1859); Kroeber's 'Tree of Life' and   299
    'Tree of Knowledge' (1948)
85 The west front of Tintern Abbey Church (1899)   306
86 One bay of the Chapel of the Nine Altars, Durham Cathedral, drawn by John Carter (1795)   311
87 The west front of Durham Cathedral, drawn by John Carter (1795)   312
88 Restoration of a buttress on the west front of Tintern Abbey Church by F W Waller in 1905   317
89 Aerial photograph of Tintern Abbey following the completion of the excavation and   318
    conservation work by the Ministry of Works
90 Frontispiece of *News from Nowhere* (Kelmscott Press, 1892), drawn by C M Gere   320
91 Condition survey of Kelmscott Manor, drawn by Ailwyn Best (1965)   321
92 A Fellows' Day at Kelmscott Manor   324
93 Dust jacket from *English Villages and Hamlets* (1949 reprint) in Batsford's *Face of*   328
    Britain series
94 Clough Williams-Ellis (1883–1978), photographed by Howard Coster (1936)   333
95 Charles Bathurst, first Viscount Bledisloe (1867–1958), photographed in 1928   337
96 O G S Crawford returning from a Mediterranean holiday, probably in 1937   339
97 Major G W G Allen (1891–1940) and his aircraft (date unknown)   340
98 Kathleen Kenyon (1906–78), Jewry Wall Roman excavations, Leicester, 1936   347
99 Stonehenge: restoring a lintel to the sarsen circle (probably 1919)   352
100 The location of the Society's 'Grand Excavation Projects', 1890–1999   354
101 The directors of the Silchester Excavation Fund at Silchester in 1900   355
102 Inscription from London commemorating the procurator of Britain, Gaius Julius Alpinus   360
    Classicianus, discovered in 1935
103 Richborough, Kent: view in 1924 of the late Roman bath-building   362
104 Richborough, Kent: view in 1932 of Claudian/pre-Flavian granaries and super-imposed   362
    pre- or early Flavian timber buildings
105 Verulamium: view of the south-east 'London' gate from the north east (1936)   366
106 Verulamium: the 'triangular temple', view from the north (1936)   366
107 Maiden Castle, Dorset: southern portal of the eastern entrance of the Iron Age hillfort (1943)   367
108 Maiden Castle, Dorset: the 'war cemetery' at the eastern entrance of the Iron Age   368
    hillfort (1943)
109 Sutton Hoo, Suffolk: the excavations on their completion in 1991, looking west   374
110 Mons Porphyrites, Egypt: view of the Lykabettus quarry village (1998)   376
111 Mortimer Wheeler, President of the Society of Antiquaries of London, 1954–9   382
112 James Mann, President of the Society of Antiquaries of London, 1949–54   386
113 J N L Myres, President of the Society of Antiquaries of London, 1970–5   388
114 Barry Cunliffe, President of the Society of Antiquaries of London, 1991–5   391
115 John Evans, President of the Society of Antiquaries of London, 1984–7   402
116 President Eric Fernie admitting new Fellow Melanie Hall on 2 November 2006   414

viii

TABLES

		page
1	Number of papers published in *Archaeologia* in the period 1770–1817, scored by topic	154
2	Appendices published in *Archaeologia* in the period 1785–1817, scored by topic	155
3	Analysis of the membership of the Society of Antiquaries of London in 1817 by social categories	176
4	Membership of the Society of Antiquaries of London, 1812–52	185
5	A British 'archaeological' and socio-historical chronology	268
6	Nineteenth-century excavation reports published in *Archaeologia*	276
7	Summary table of contents of *Archaeologia*, the *Archaeological Journal* and the *Journal of the British Archaeological Association* between 1850 and 1875	290
8	Summary table of the contents of *Archaeologia*, 1800–99	291
9	Summary of the contents of *Archaeologia*, local society and anthropology and ethnology journals, 1850–75	292
10	Presidents of the Society, 1950–2000	385
11	Gold Medallists of the Society, 1950–2000, and their principal fields of expertise	385
12	Successful and unsuccessful elections to the Fellowship, 1951–95	393
13	Places of residence of candidates elected to the Fellowship, 1951–95	394
14	Fields of study of candidates elected to the Fellowship, 1951–95	395
15	Employment of candidates elected to the Fellowship, 1951–95	396
16	The Society's Research Fund allocations for archaeological research, 1950–2000	398–9
17	Distribution of archaeological papers in the *Antiquaries Journal*, 1951–95	404
18	Research Reports published by the Society, 1950–2000	408–9
19	Occasional Papers (new series) published by the Society, 1980–2000	410
20	Age profile of Fellows in 2005	417
21	Employment profile of Fellows: (a) in 2005; (b) 1999–2004	418
22	Geographical location of Fellows: (a) domicile of Fellows in 2006; (b) overseas Fellows in 2006	420–1
23	Qualifications of Fellows: (a) in 2005; (b) 1999–2004	422
24	Fellows' research interests: (a) in 2005; (b) 1999–2004	423
25	Fellows' main period interests: (a) in 2005; (b) 1999–2004	424
26	Fellows' main geographical research interests in 2005	425
27	Fellows sitting on boards of management or acting in advisory capacity in 2005	427

ACKNOWLEDGEMENTS

During 2001 Arthur MacGregor, FSA, and Dai Morgan Evans, FSA, then respectively the Director and General Secretary of the Society of Antiquaries, conceived the idea of a volume of papers to be published in 2007 in celebration of that year's tercentenary of the founding of the Society. They invited me to act as Editor, and the project progressed through discussions with the then President, Professor Rosemary Cramp, FSA, and the Society's Council. Over the next eighteen months, three seminars were held at Burlington House, through which the eventual lists of contributors and topics were established.

Since 2001, many people have helped in the shaping and production of this volume and I offer my grateful thanks to them all. I should particularly like to thank Bernard Nurse, FSA, for generously making available to all of us his profound knowledge of the Society's archive, Adrian James for helping to locate illustrations, and Geremy Butler for taking many of the photographs. I am grateful to my Research Assistant, Anna Catalani, who did valuable work towards the volume in amongst her other duties, to the University of Leicester, who provided Anna's funding, and to the Research Committee of the Society of Antiquaries for additional financial support.

To all the contributors I offer my warmest thanks for bearing with the many queries, which they answered so patiently, and I am grateful to the anonymous reviewers, whose assistance was invaluable.

On the editorial side I am very grateful to Christopher Catling, FSA, who copy-edited the papers in this volume to ensure that any rare lapse in lucidity was spotted and corrected, while Kate Owen, FSA, has provided invaluable help throughout the editorial process, not only managing the design and production side of the project, but also in checking and tracking down hundreds of references, finding pictures and obtaining copyright permissions and in giving a final reading to ensure that no spelling or grammatical error, inconsistency or repetition has been allowed to survive in the texts (except for the few that have remained at the insistence of the author!). Kate's expertise and patience have been crucial to the publication of the volume, and the warmest thanks are due to her from me, and from the Society as a whole.

Finally, I wish to thank my husband, Mac, for all his wonderful support and encouragement.

SUSAN PEARCE, FSA, EDITOR
CHRISTMAS 2006

FOREWORD

The public has a strong impression of the concept of 'the mists of time', excusing its ignorance of the distant past as a consequence of the lack of written records and the paucity of the kind of evidence for our immediate past that we can experience all around us. The Society of Antiquaries has always believed that the 'mists' that hide our past can be blown away through diligent research in the many records and archives available, and that archaeologists will continue to dig up ancient remains that prove a historic or economic point. What we find is not some polished bedrock of absolute truth but a field where firm analysis and intelligent speculation can provide many different answers to questions that will constantly rejudge our views of the past. Each generation sees the past in comparison to its own time and place, and the moral problems of its own.

L P Hartley wrote in *The Go Between* that 'the past is a foreign country', even in the course of one man's lifetime. Manners and a sense of prestige guided the conformity of behaviour in different ways. It was, for instance, unfair of Macauley to judge the Duke of Marlborough by nineteenth-century standards and condemn him for being in communication with the 'enemy'. Today's biographies have to place themselves in different moral time zones.

For many people their chief experience of the past is through costume dramas portraying historical eras that contrast with our own. The accuracy or otherwise depends on the director's understanding of events and contemporary beliefs and avoidance of anachronisms. It may well be the work of the Society that has furnished the background to provide credibility to the plot.

Perhaps the greatest influence that this Society has had is in placing the architectural monuments that are still with us in an intellectual setting, and thus by popular demand buildings well past their original usage are preserved for reasons of continuity. Unlike books and records that are portable and relatively easy to protect, buildings require maintenance and thus are threatened by either neglect and poverty or, in our venerable city centres, more usually by economic advance that demands their replacement by something more 'profitable'.

This Society has over the centuries provided a suitably pluralist approach, providing not the 'official' history that some might approve, but the various economic, social, political, industrial, literary, artistic, architectural and archaeological histories that you would expect from a vibrant, intellectually aware group of people who wanted to understand the mysteries of our forebears so as to illuminate the stories and the limitations of the future.

HRH The Duke of Gloucester, KG, GCVO
Royal Patron, Society of Antiquaries of London

CHAPTER ONE

VISIONS OF ANTIQUITY: INTRODUCTION

Susan Pearce

In 1778 a letter was published in the *Gentleman's Magazine*, under the name of Philistor, declaring that 'a visionary turn is characteristic of our Antiquaries'.[1] Philistor did not mean this kindly. He was promoting the idea of a unified 'national history', which the Society of Antiquaries was not interested in pursuing.

What some historians in the later eighteenth century and afterwards saw as wayward and individualistic in the Fellows of the Society would probably now be welcomed as many-stranded, diverse and imbued with healthy cultural obstinacy. The title of this volume, *Visions of Antiquity* – published to celebrate the tercentenary of the 1707 founding of the Society, which is itself one of the Society's several 'beginnings' – was chosen with deliberate intent. It signals the belief that many views of many kinds of pasts are equally possible and equally valid, provided that they can be sustained by reference to documented and material evidence and subjected to the scrutiny of historians and archaeologists. This is accompanied by the conviction that nothing in the past can be understood without reference to its surrounding cultural context, and that each generation should be studied in its own right, rather than as part of some putative progression or grand narrative.

This matches, of course, the current climate of research into the past, which sees not just the past itself as a field for investigation but also the ways in which that past has been investigated and presented; indeed, the two are inextricably intertwined. In its long history, the Society of Antiquaries of London as an institution – and its Fellows as individuals – have been major players in the shifting visions that have created successive ways of discovering and understanding the past, and it is these roles and their significances which this book is intended to explore.

It is in keeping with this spirit that the celebration of the Society's tercentenary in 2007 represents one of a number of possible choices made among several dates, all marking key early moments in the Society's first years. In his introduction to the first volume of *Archaeologia* (1770), Richard Gough (Director of the Society from 1771) recounts the Society's history to date. He tells the story of the Elizabethan Society using a wealth of biographical detail and then does his best to connect it with the present Society by saying: 'Some of these great men had scarce retired from the world, when the Antiquarian Society began to revive under the auspices of their worthy

Fig 1. 'The reception of a new member at the Society of Antiquaries', 1782, by Thomas Rowlandson, shows Dr Jeremiah Milles, Dean of Exeter and President of the Society 1768–84 (see also fig 27, chapter 4). *Photograph*: John Hammond; © Society of Antiquaries of London.

imitators'.[2] No evidence has appeared to suggest that Fellows tried explicitly to count the age of the Society from Elizabeth's reign,[3] although a certain wistfulness is detectable in Gough's account, and in that of Sir Arthur Evans in 1917 (see below).[4]

Gough moves immediately to 1707 and the meeting at the Bear Tavern, in the Strand, saying that: 'Mr. Talman, Mr. Bagford and Mr. Wanley met there Nov 5 that year, and agreed to do so every Friday, at six in the evening, and sit till ten at the furthest'.[5] This casual, although undoubtedly important, arrangement between three friends who shared a common interest in antiquities is presented as the fundamental gathering of the founding fathers. Gough, however, goes on to say: 'After these meetings had continued about ten years, as the number of gentlemen who composed them increased, it was resolved to form themselves into a Society, to meet every Wednesday evening'.[6] This resolution was made in 1717, but it was from 1 January 1718[7] that the formal constitution can be traced, with the election of officers, the establishment of ballots and fees, and the beginning of formal minutes, although some earlier records, now lost, may have been made. The resolution seems to have been generally regarded as the key moment in this sequence of events.

During the nineteenth century, anniversaries were relatively low-key affairs. Nothing seems to have been done in 1807 or 1817. A Centenary Dinner took place on 23 April 1851, possibly assembled by J Y Akerman, the Secretary of the day.[8] This celebrated the granting of the Royal Charter in 1751, though it seems to have been differentiated from the usual Anniversary Dinner only in that invitations were given to a few leading figures by the Society, and by Fellows to friends. In his Presidential Address earlier on that day, Viscount Mahon began with the usual obituaries and ended with a few remarks on the state of the Society:

> Your present anniversary, as the hundredth since the grant of the Royal Charter, may well suggest to your minds the retrospect of our past, and the contemplation of our future prospects . . . Much, nay everything, let me say, must depend upon the exertion of individual members. Any gentleman who applies his learning and his talents to the production of some valuable essay wherewith to animate our meetings, and enrich our *Archaeologia*, may lend us powerful aid. Any gentleman, on the contrary, who, without strong necessity, raises a discussion at any of our ordinary meetings on any other subject than those of antiquarian science, and, whenever it can be avoided, converts this apartment onto an arena for debate, may do us a great disservice.[9]

Evidently, although the hundredth anniversary of the Charter was a cause for celebration, it was also a moment for stern reflection.

As far back as 1914 some thought was given to the anniversary falling in 1917[10] but the First World War made the various suggestions impossible, and when Evans came to deliver his Presidential Address in 1917 he forcibly rejected the idea that he was speaking in a potential bicentenary year, saying: 'I cannot help feeling that it is perhaps as well that the stringency of public affairs and the preoccupations of the hour should not have been favourable to a project for a bicentenary celebration of the Society in the present year. This is . . . from a strong conviction that by attaching public importance to the date 1717 as the starting point of its activities the Society of Antiquaries would be understating its own legitimate claims to antiquity. That year . . . can hardly be taken to mark the date of its birth.'[11] He then continued with an account of the 1707 Bear Tavern meeting, concluding: 'It would really seem that the principal reason for looking about for a bicentenary celebration in 1917 was that no one seems to have thought of it in 1907.'[12] He concluded that: 'the Society will probably prefer to go back for its foundation in its present form to the select meeting of choice antiquarian spirits in the Bear Tavern'[13] and went so far as to assert: 'A certain tendency seems traceable in Stukeley's records [of the events of 1717–18] to minimise the connection of the Society in its later with its earlier shape. He doubtless wished to share the honour of an entirely new foundation.'[14] In the end, 1917 was marked with a paper by Sir Edward Brabrook, the Director, entitled 'Bicentenary Observations on Antiquarian Longevity, with a list of Fellows who could be seen as "Fathers" of the Society because they averaged 86 years of age'. This happy thought was only published in the *Proceedings*.[15]

Earlier in his delivery Evans had suggested, dismissively, that 'With as much reason [as a celebration in 1917] we might defer the consideration of such a [bicentenary celebration] until 1951, since in 1751 the Charter of Incorporation was obtained from the King.'[16] However, a book entitled *The Society of Antiquaries: notes on its history and possessions*, was published by the Society and described as 'First issued on the Occasion of the Bicentenary of the Society's Royal Charter, 2 November 1951'.[17] This was prepared by the Secretary, Rupert Bruce-Mitford, and forty-nine of its seventy-seven pages were taken up with photographs and short descriptions of objects that the Society owned. In his brief review of the Society's history, Bruce-Mitford touched upon the events of 1707 and 1717, but played down the significance of the Elizabethan Society, saying: 'It is impossible to trace any connection between the Elizabethan Society and that of 1707'.[18] Similarly, in his introduction to Joan Evans's *A History of the Society of Antiquaries*, which came out in 1956, Sir James Mann, President from 1949 to 1954, tells us: 'This book was planned as part of the celebration of the Bicentenary of the Royal Charter granted to the Society of Antiquaries of London by King George ii in 1751.'[19] Clearly, 1951 was deemed a suitable year for the Society to produce a major statement about itself.

Of course, the anniversary of the Society's Charter is not the same as the anniversary of its beginning. However, it is clear that the choice of founding date has always been driven by a mix of sentiment and notions of legitimacy and practicality. At one level this emphasizes the fact that the initiative behind antiquarian endeavours, as later archaeological ones, has tended to rest with modest private gentlemen (and gentlewomen), rather than grand, and more easily traceable and datable, alliances of sovereigns, aristocrats and public men. At another, individual Fellows (and others) could clearly select among the range of origin stories on offer, in order to pick up a theme that fitted their personal perspectives.

Throughout the Society's existence a constant theme has been the desire to assemble information about the Fellowship. *A Register-Book of the Members of the Antiquary Society* was started in January 1718 and continued until 1741, although this was compiled chiefly for administrative purposes.[20] A list of Fellows with biographical notes, based at least in part on earlier Society records, was compiled in the early nineteenth century by Mark Noble, with material relating to the Elizabethan Society and the Society of Antiquaries up to 1796, and some later notes.[21] This was continued with Sir Henry Ellis's 'Collections for Lives of Early Members of the Society of Antiquaries',[22] which brings the information up to the mid-nineteenth century, adding fresh material along the way. Arthur Gould's collection of materials towards a history of the Society focuses upon various lists of members, from the Elizabethan Society to *c* 1921.[23] This project continues with the current work being undertaken to compile an online database of information about men who were Fellows between 1770 and 1820.[24]

The Fellowship was not always at peace with itself; indeed the disruptive strength and venom of some past quarrels have entered into the Society's folklore. Viscount Mahon's blunt remarks about divisive debate on non-antiquarian topics have already been quoted. Sir James Mann, another President writing about another centenary year, also alluded to past divisions when he said, referring to Joan Evans's history of the Society: 'the first impression may be that of a tissue of disputed policies, personal quarrels, crises, and lost opportunities . . . but [the Society] could never have lasted so long or attained its present influence were it not that beneath the troubled surface the main stream of endeavour has flowed strongly onward'.[25]

Such strictures miss the point. There was (and is) never a convenient distinction between the turbulent surface and the strong, steady, progressive current below; rather, the tensions and quarrels created the energy and imaginative quality which enabled ideas to emerge, and the persistence to ensure that the enterprise continued. The ongoing efforts of the Society rested then, as now, in the determination of its Fellows, and the strength they drew from the feelings of solidarity which their association brought.

This is why the instinct to gather information about all the individual Fellows is sound. In a real way, the history of the Antiquaries since its earliest days is written in the detailed information of finds, monuments and documents sent in by its members week in, week out (with the odd thin patch) and faithfully recorded by the Society over close on 300 years; first rather spasmodically,[26] then in written minutes (from 1718), in volumes of *Archaeologia* (from 1770), in the pages of the *Proceedings of the Society of Antiquaries* (from 1843 to 1920) and now as material worked up for publication in the *Antiquaries Journal*.[27] The project of observing, drawing, planning, recording and publishing continued steadily until what had been a miscellaneous accumulation became, through its quality and reach, the crucial basis for extended analysis and intellectual ordering. It is wonderful for an archaeologist to see the first recording, usually accompanied by an excellent illustration, of a site or an object that she or he has known and argued about all her working life, with its original entry into the literature, perhaps 150 years ago, still an essential reference in the contemporary bibliography. In this way, the work of the Society and its Fellows has entered into our collective bloodstream.

As one would expect from its very nature, the Society has produced a steady stream of histories of itself, and naturally these share the same divergent character. Such accounts are very largely based on the Society's own manuscript records, particularly the Minute Books (extant since 1718; see frontispiece) of Ordinary Council and other meetings, the Audit Books (kept since 1761) and a quantity of letters and memoranda, much of which remains unpublished,[28] even though not all Fellows were careful to keep archive material.[29] Further material is held by the British Museum, the British Library, the Ashmolean Museum and the Bodleian Library.[30]

As early as 1731, Maurice Johnson read a paper on the history of the Society and its antecedents to a meeting;[31] by 1748, George North was collecting relevant historical material and consulting with George Vertue and Andrew Ducarel, who had prepared an account of the early Society by 1752; Browne Willis, William Foster and William Stukeley were also assembling their recollections. Characteristically, the effort to co-ordinate all this material was sparked off by differing claims to the credit for the 1717 revival. In 1753 John Warburton published his *Vallum Romanum*, an account of his work at Hadrian's Wall, in which he stated: 'The old Society of Antiquaries being thus broke up, the study of Roman learning lay dormant in Britain until the year 1716 . . . [when] the publication of my map of Northumberland again revived it. . . . in the year 1717 a new society of antiquaries was formed'.[32] In 1754 Ducarel read out to a meeting letters from Johnson, Willis and Vertue, whose recollections matched the account which has generally been accepted, and North was asked (but refused) to produce a comprehensive statement. Stukeley, meanwhile, had written an account of the early years, which survives as a manuscript written in 1752;[33] Arthur Evans's view of it (and of Stukeley) have already been quoted. Stukeley presented a version of this paper to the Anniversary Meeting on St George's Day, 1760, but died before he could publish it.

The first major public account was that written by Richard Gough, using material he had inherited from Stukeley, and published in 1770.[34] Gough saw the antiquarian project as part of the characteristically eighteenth-century effort 'to separate false-hood from truth, and tradition from evidence, to establish what had probability for its basis' so that by 'modern criticism' the facts of the past could be established. This required enquiry into ancient records and proofs, seen as 'unchizeled stone', as well as documents. It was in the light of this endeavour that he charted the Society's history up to his own time.[35] As part of the quarrels over reform that characterized the late 1820s and early 1830s, Sir Nicholas Harris Nicolas, disappointed by the conduct of senior Fellows, declared in 1827 that he intended to become 'The Historian of the S.A.'.[36] By this he perhaps meant that he would publish an account of how far into dullness and exclusiveness the Society had sunk, and how it might be improved. At any rate, he produced no general narrative, although the episode generated some interesting polemical publications. Perhaps warned by this, no official or quasi-official history was offered again for a long time. Brabrook produced an account of the Society's Directors in 1910,[37] and Kendrick of its Presidents in 1945,[38] but the only sustained view of the Society's past in the period from 1770 to

1956 was that offered by Arthur Evans in his Presidential Address of 1917.[39]

In 1956 Joan Evans produced the Society's only full-length official history.[40] As James Mann remarked in his introduction: 'Dr Joan Evans was the obvious choice to undertake the work. Her family has been intimately connected with the Society for more than a century. She is the daughter of one President and the sister of another, and herself holds the office of Director.'[41] A different view might suggest that these were good reasons why another person should have been chosen. Joan was the daughter, by a very late third marriage, of Sir John Evans, elected FSA in 1852 and President from 1885 to 1892, and the half-sister of Sir Arthur, President from 1914 to 1919; she was forty-two years younger than Arthur. Joan had already published *Time and Chance*,[42] a history of her family, and her *History of the Society of Antiquaries*, written in a style very similar to that of *Time and Chance*, drew in detail upon manuscript sources, many of which were also family papers. Her account of the Society's past is solid and indispensable, but in some ways uncritical. As Kenneth Garlick says: 'Joan Evans was a woman of strong family loyalties'[43] and perhaps she saw both books in a similar light. Sir John Evans's contribution to prehistoric material culture studies was undoubtedly very significant, but Arthur's reputation has not worn so well. His work at Knossos (especially his approach to dating) is now seen as debatable and his desire to uphold his chronological views apparently led sometimes to more than it should have done.[44] The complex and lengthy relationship of the whole Evans family to the Society awaits sustained investigation.

Antiquarianism and the Society of Antiquaries have also, of course, been of interest to historians concerned with understanding how the past has been constructed. This is not the place for an analysis of the views they have taken of the Society, but a few key works should be mentioned. Among British writers, Stuart Piggott did much to bring antiquarian studies to a wider audience.[45] Others followed his lead. Among more recent writers, Philippa Levine has explored the 'professionalization' of the past, as institution-based archaeologists and historians gradually achieved ascendancy over 'gentlemen of leisure',[46] while Graham Parry has illuminated the invigorating effects of humanism upon the medieval tradition.[47] Joseph Levine has made a considerable contribution to our appreciation of how the baroque age in England situated itself between antiquity and modernity.[48] Three major books have appeared since 2000. David Boyd Haycock's *William Stukeley* is an important study for all those concerned with the past of the Society;[49] Daniel Woolf's *The Social Circulation of the Past* gives a detailed account of English historical culture between 1500 and 1730;[50] and Rosemary Sweet's *Antiquaries* illuminates the internal history of the Society of Antiquaries and the roles of the Fellows in the emergence of significant historical themes.[51] All subsequent researchers in the field owe a considerable debt to these scholars.

The papers in this volume are intended to investigate the ways in which the Fellows of the Society of Antiquaries, at various moments in time, came to understand the past and their relationship to it, and to show how these are interpreted at the beginning of the twenty-first century. Sir Nicholas Harris Nicolas's attacks of 1827–9 were answered by 'Antiquarius'[52] who wrote: 'A spear head, a coin, an imperfect inscription, a fragment of painting, the remnant of a building, a rude stone, are all legitimate objects of [the antiquary's] speculation' provided he endeavours 'to weigh in equal scales the force of conflicting evidence, to reconcile discrepancies, and to draw strong conclusions out of minute facts which have escaped the general eye'.[53] Just so. In contemporary terms, the range of disciplines falling within the broad remit of the Society – and which are each supported by their own intellectual traditions – is reflected in the authors of the papers in this volume, each contributing the different styles and approaches proper to their own fields. As a result, the same piece of evidence has sometimes been used by more than one author, in order to make a range of points. Equally, many topics have been omitted; often by choice, reinforced by the knowledge that they are not currently attracting the attention of scholars.

In no sense is the volume intended to be a 'history' of the Society, although the papers are organized very broadly in chronological order. More interesting, perhaps, are the interlocking themes that emerge when each author addresses his or her topic. A key theme is how people found a way of fusing imagination, understanding and method in order to produce accounts of the past, and how they made decisions when faced with competing possibilities – the invention and subsequent development of object handling, excavation, field survey and buildings recording, of a useful language in which to discuss them, of appropriate styles for creating plans, sections, maps and illustrations, and of written narratives in which everything could be framed. This has always been inextricably bound up with the regular meetings and the daily business of the Society, always greater than the sum of its parts.

This fundamental issue has engaged all the contributors, one way or another. Woolf discusses how the antiquaries of his period felt the need to balance objects and texts, MacGregor draws attention to the significance of post-1660 club culture (fig 1) and Sweet considers the importance of individuals, such as Richard Gough. Briggs, Evans and Hingley, in their different ways, analyse how, in the first half of the nineteenth century, the mix of intellectuals of European stature, the operation of strong institutions and the social structure made possible the emergence of new branches upon the trees of knowledge. Nurse shows how the development of the Society's library became the key focus for the deployment of this knowledge, making continuity and growth possible. Morris, Barker and Fulford address the ways in which the twentieth-century Society intermeshed with other institutions of the time to shape the directions in which the emerging discipline of archaeology was moving. Gaimster turns the question outwards towards the present and the future.

A significant aspect of our presumed ability to capture the past and render it intelligible has been visualization. The development of recording techniques has already been mentioned, but equally significant was how the surviving material culture from the past began to be used to produce the 'fullness' of the past before the viewer's eyes. The ways in which antiquarians and artists approached the contextualization of the past in visual form have been considered by Myrone for the eighteenth century, with particular reference to George Vertue, and by Smiles for the nineteenth. Pearce examines the issues which arose around 1800 when taste in London (and Paris) turned towards the physical re-creation of the past. The reconstruction of the actual past, in the shape of its surviving ruins, is discussed by Turner in relation to three critical moments.

A shift in emphasis brings out the importance of the relationships between antiquaries/archaeologists, the Society and the wider community, issues which are discussed by Woolf, Sweet and Hingley, amongst others. What comes to the fore are social networks binding Fellows in town and country and across the class spectrum, itself influenced by antiquarian activity and other issues, such as gender. These papers explore the links between successive governments and the Society – Lord Aberdeen, President between 1812 and 1846, served twice as Foreign Secretary during the same period – and the genesis of key pieces of legislation. They consider the Society's relationship to cultural activities such as journalism, and to satire (of which it has always attracted its full share, and which provides a fascinating mirror).

It is satisfying that a volume of essays interested in the multiplicity of histories on offer should take the simple meeting of three people in a London tavern as its point of reference. Like all the endeavours of the Antiquaries – past, present and to come – this volume is a tract of the times. The choice of topics and their treatment reflects the temper of the present generation; in due course *Visions of Antiquity*, too, will provide material for cultural historians when future anniversaries come around.

NOTES

1. Pinkerton 1788. 'Philistor' was John Pinkerton, a Scottish antiquary, who challenged the 'Celtic' view of history: see O'Halloran 2004, 56–65, 202–3.
2. Gough 1770, xxvi.
3. Whatever the exact date was, 'About 42 years since', counted from 1614, was the closest Gough could get, giving the date as 1572, which became generally accepted. Linda van Norden (1946) considers that the foundation was in fact 1584–6.
4. *Proc Soc Antiq London*, 2nd ser, **29** (1916–17), 168: 'I say "its [the Society's] foundation in its present form", because it is impossible to keep out of the reckoning the interesting fact that the antiquaries of England had already formed a Society in the days of Elizabeth, of which considerable records have been preserved'.
5. Gough 1770, xxvi. 'Nov' here is a mistake for December. The meeting was meant to be at the Young Devil Tavern, but seems to have been changed to the Bear, although the next meetings were at the original choice: see MacGregor, this volume.
6. Ibid, xxv.
7. See MacGregor, this volume.
8. SAL, MS 833: Willetts 2000, 395.
9. *Proc Soc Antiq London*, 1st ser, **2** (1849–53), 155. On the previous 27 Feb 1851, T G Pettigrew, of mummy-unwrapping fame, 'reminded the meeting' that the grant of the Charter had been in 1751, 'making us, this year, to complete the first centenary of our Society's incorporated existence': ibid, 133; Pearce 2002.
10. At the Council Meeting held on 21 Jan 1914, Sir Hercules Read, President, had suggested a book

dealing with the various branches of English archaeology: Evans 1956, 385.
11. *Proc Soc Antiq London*, 2nd ser, **29** (1916–17), 166–7.
12. Ibid, 168.
13. Ibid, 168.
14. Ibid, 179.
15. Ibid, 67–71. It was intended 'to make a slight contribution to the history of the Society on the occurrence of the first meeting for reading papers in the 200th year after its re-organization in 1717', and gave a table analysing the Society careers of thirty-three Fellows. The minutes recorded that the paper was received with 'heavy levity'.
16. *Proc Soc Antiq London*, 2nd ser, **29** (1916–17), 168.
17. Bruce-Mitford 1951.
18. Ibid, 9–13.
19. Mann 1956, v.
20. SAL, MS 268 A: Willetts 2000, 145.
21. SAL, MS 269: ibid, 146.
22. SAL, MS 270: ibid, 146.
23. SAL, MS 678: ibid, 290.
24. Being compiled by Anna Catalani and Susan Pearce, giving biographical information, and details of collections, publications, and of material they exhibited at meetings or presented.
25. Mann 1956, v.
26. Between 1707 and 1717 some material was clearly being received and published in what was to become, broadly, the standard approach of the Society – first in *Archaeologia*, then in *Proc Soc Antiq London*, until that publication ceased in 1920 – but this process took

a while to become formalized. In 1711, for example, Wanley received a letter from Samuel Carte, a Leicester parson, describing a mosaic pavement found near the city – exactly the kind of find which would continue to be reported. However, it was published by the Royal Society: Carte 1710–12.

27. Volume 1 of the *Antiquaries Journal* appeared in January 1921. Initially it continued the practice of recording discussions about papers that had been read, publishing shorter Notes that had been received and read and, when appropriate, printing obituaries and Society proceedings.
28. Willetts 2000 gives a full account.
29. In 1769 George North, when asked for the materials he had collected, said the small remaining amount were all 'that survived his order to burn most of his papers' at a time when he was ill: Evans 1956, 109–10.
30. Willetts 2000; Evans 1956, 453–4.
31. For what follows, see Evans 1956, 108–11.
32. Warburton 1753, vi; Evans 1956, 51–2. I am grateful to Arthur MacGregor for drawing my attention to these references.
33. SAL, MS 11, 266: Willetts 2000, 8 and 144.

34. Gough 1770.
35. Ibid, i.
36. Evans 1956, 247.
37. *Proc Soc Antiq London*, 2nd ser, **23** (1909–11), 34.
38. Society of Antiquaries of London 1945.
39. *Proc Soc Antiq London*, 2nd ser, **29** (1916–17), 166–82.
40. Evans 1956.
41. Mann 1956, v; Evans was to become President herself in 1959, serving until 1964.
42. Evans 1943.
43. Garlick 2004
44. Briggs 1987–8; I am grateful to Stephen Briggs for this reference. For a recent discussion of the problems of interpretation at Knossos, see Mountjoy 2003.
45. Piggott 1978 and 1989.
46. Levine 1986.
47. Parry 1995.
48. Levine 1999.
49. Haycock 2002.
50. Woolf 2003.
51. Sweet 2004.
52. 'Antiquarius' was A Kempe: see below, p 195 n 86.
53. *Gent's Mag*, 1829, 99/2, 417.

BIBLIOGRAPHY

Briggs, C S 1987–8. 'Were there two cauldrons from Raffrey, Co. Down?', *J Ir Archaeol*, 4, 21–2

Bruce-Mitford, R 1951. *The Society of Antiquaries of London: notes on its history and possessions. First issued on the occasion of the bicentenary of the Society's Royal Charter, 2 November 1951*, London

Carte, S 1710–12. 'Part of a letter from the Reverend Mr. Samuel Carte, rector of St. Margaret's parish in Leicestershire, to Mr. Humfrey Wanley F.R.S., concerning an ancient tessellated, or mosaic work, at Leicester', *Phil Trans Roy Soc London*, B, **27** (no. 133 for 1711), 324–5

Evans, J 1943. *Time and Chance: the story of Arthur Evans and his forebears*, London

Evans, J 1956. *A History of the Society of Antiquaries*, Oxford

Garlick, K 2004. 'Evans, Dame Joan (1893–1977)', in *Oxford Dictionary of National Biography: Online Edition* (eds H C G Matthew and B Harrison), <http://www.oxforddnb.com./view/article/47612> (24 June 2006)

Gough, R 1770. 'Introduction: containing an historical account of the origin and establishment of the Society of Antiquaries', *Archaeologia*, 1 (2nd edn), i–xl

Haycock, D B 2002. *William Stukeley: science, religion and archaeology in eighteenth-century England*, Woodbridge

Levine, J 1999. *Between the Ancients and the Moderns: baroque culture in Restoration England*, New Haven

Levine, P 1986. *The Amateur and the Professional: antiquarians, historians and archaeologists in Victorian England 1838–1886*, Cambridge

Mann, J 1956. 'Introduction', in Evans 1956, v–vi

Mountjoy, P 2003. *Knossos: the South House*, Brit School Athens, supp vol 34, London

O'Halloran, C 2004. *Golden Ages and Barbarous Nations: antiquarian debate and cultural politics in Ireland c 1750–1800*, Cork

Oudit, S (ed) 2002. *Displaced Persons: conditions of exile in European culture*, Aldershot

Parry, G 1995. *The Trophies of Time*, London

Pearce, S 2002. 'Bodies in exile: Egyptian mummies in the early nineteenth century and their cultural implications', in Oudit (ed) 2002, 54–71

Piggott, S 1978. *Antiquity Depicted: aspects of archaeological illustration*, London

Piggott, S 1989. *Ancient Britons and the Antiquarian Imagination*, London

Pinkerton, J 1788. 'Letters to the people of Great Britain on their cultivation of their national history', *Gent's Mag*, **58**/2, 689

Society of Antiquaries of London 1945. *The Presidents of the Society of Antiquaries of London. With biographical notes*, Soc Antiq London Occas Pap, new ser, 2, London

Sweet, R 2004. *Antiquaries: the discovery of the past in eighteenth-century Britain*, London

van Norden, L 1946. 'The Elizabethan College of Antiquaries', unpublished doctoral thesis, University of California, Los Angeles

Warburton, J 1753. *Vallum Romanum: or the history and antiquities of the Roman wall, commonly called the Picts' wall*, London

Willetts, P 2000. *Catalogue of Manuscripts in the Society of Antiquaries of London*, Woodbridge

Woolf, D 2003. *The Social Circulation of the Past*, Oxford

CHAPTER TWO

IMAGES OF THE ANTIQUARY IN SEVENTEENTH-CENTURY ENGLAND

Daniel Woolf

Throughout its history, antiquarianism has had a good press and a bad. To many, the word 'antiquary' immediately summons up a mental image of a rather stuffy grey-bearded collector (the associated gender is surprisingly often still exclusively male) of coins or other old objects, or excited but dull-witted rural curates, or perhaps elbow-patched habitués of shops selling used and rare books – given that the most public face of the antiquarian is now the bookseller's. To those more knowledgeable about what it is that many antiquaries now do (and have been doing for five hundred years) the word conjures up a very different set of connotations: of well-trained and disciplined scholars possessing a keen devotion to the understanding, restoration and preservation of the past (not quite the same as the preservation of 'heritage'),[1] wide-ranging linguistic and technical skills, a willingness in many cases to undertake the kind of 'fieldwork' more often associated with archaeologists (who deal in many of the same materials but enjoy a more romantic reputation) and a meticulous attention to facts and minute detail. The Society of Antiquaries of London was founded three centuries ago to provide a common meeting ground for some of the best historical minds of the Augustan age, and today it remains a considerable honour for a scholar to be elected to its ranks. Some very respectable and venerable regional societies still proudly feature the word 'antiquarian' in their names.[2]

Whence came these two rather different notions, the methodical scholar and the obsessed pedant? With respect to the more commonplace, and popular, associations of antiquarianism, two nineteenth-century novelists have a great deal to answer for, though they traded in different currency. The later of the two, George Eliot, had classical scholarship in mind when she wrote *Middlemarch* rather than 'antiquarianism' as such – the word appears nowhere in that lengthy novel. Yet Edward Casaubon, the fixated but unsuccessful cleric obsessed with his doomed *magnum opus*, 'The Key to All Mythologies', behaves in ways that seem oddly familiar. With his relentless devotion to learning, severe bearing and subordination of the real world of the living to that of dead antiquity, Casaubon is the embodiment of the detached and cold scholar, 'dead from the waist down'. His vast unwritten project is a heritable burden, not unlike the legal dead hand that his will imposes on the future decisions of his idealistic young widow, Dorothea. There has been speculation that the Revd Mr

Fig 2. Samuel Gale (artist unknown: probably early eighteenth century): portrait now hanging in the Fellows' Room, Society of Antiquaries of London. *Photograph*: Society of Antiquaries of London.

11

Casaubon was loosely modelled on the Oxford scholar Mark Pattison, a friend of the author and an early advocate of universities as centres of advanced scholarship as well as teaching. Whether that is true or not, the character is very clearly named after the great early seventeenth-century philologist, of whom Pattison was the biographer, Isaac Casaubon (by most accounts a considerably more attractive man than his fictional namesake).[3] This connects Eliot's creation with one significant stream in the very early history of English antiquarianism: its philological and textual side. In Casaubon's case, this is completely divorced not only from real people in the present but also from the physical objects of the antiquarian past that would very much have interested his ecclesiastical predecessors a century or so earlier. Churchman he might be, but this unsympathetic incumbent reveals no spark of interest in the zealous pursuit of buried objects or even the study of hard-to-reach inscriptions in remote church belfries – activities now more conventionally associated with clerical antiquarianism, and connoting unbridled enthusiasm rather than chilling restraint.

Jonathan Oldbuck, the eponymous antiquary of Sir Walter Scott's novel, is an earlier caricature by several decades and represents a different species. Scott provides a more reliable paradigm for the antiquarian image, though he was reflecting on a century of Georgian activity through the not-unsympathetic lens of romanticism, rather than anticipating the systematic activities of the nineteenth century.[4] Oldbuck is cantankerous, mercurial and both unwavering and undiscerning in his devotion to the past, much to the amusement of his neighbours and retainers. Yet he is no Casaubon – Edward or Isaac. For one thing, his interests are much less focused and much more wide-ranging – embracing oral tradition, ancient balladry and that old stock-in-trade of rare coins, as well as other mementoes of the past. For another, he is a man of means and influence, the Laird of Monkbarns who, for all his detachment from most of the problems of the present, continues to live in it more clearly than his Victorian successor.

For all their differences, the impulsive Oldbuck and the phlegmatic Casaubon are still distant cousins at a few generations remove: related if one looks closely for resemblance, but springing from different branches of the antiquarian pedigree, a house divided since the early seventeenth century. On the one hand, the humanistic philological tradition of the close study of text-bound language, which weaves back via eighteenth-century classical scholarship to such great Augustans as George Hickes and Humfrey Wanley (and one half of the versatile Edward Lhuyd), through John Selden, Sir Henry Savile and the first – flesh and blood – Casaubon, to the great continental philologists of the sixteenth century: Scaliger, Baudouin, Budé and their Italian *quattrocento* predecessors, Valla and Poliziano.[5] On the other hand, there is the peripatetic antiquary for whom languages as such are but one among many tools, and for whom objects, rather than texts, are both the problem and the primary data. For this figure – whose ancestry can be traced back a respectable distance to another fifteenth-century Italian, Flavio Biondo – the road and the field, rather than the library, are the principal sites of discovery. These two forms of scholarship, each at one time associated with antiquarianism, both lie at some remove from their much more glamorous and popular cousin, 'history proper', with whom they have enjoyed sporadic hot-and-cold relations for half a millennium. Antiquaries themselves first began to diverge in the seventeenth century, and it is the object-oriented archaeo-logical cadet branch of the family that has, for most of the past three centuries, assumed stewardship of the whole estate, while philology has withdrawn to places more concerned with classical scholarship, literature, etymology, linguistics and – more recently – anthropology.

TUDOR ANTIQUARIES

In some ways, the popular notion of what an antiquary was and what he did changed remarkably little between the early seventeenth and the later eighteenth centuries. The jibes at antiquaries do not alter noticeably between the time of Ben Jonson and that of Samuel Johnson, the latter an especially harsh critic of a type of antiquarian investigation that appeared to him to possess little redeeming social value.[6] There are, however, as we shall see further on, some subtle Restoration shifts in the sorts of things with which their critics supposed antiquaries to be preoccupied.

The early modern antiquary was the counterpart of today's computer 'geek', an intelligent social oddity whose erudition was simultaneously envied and mocked. The traces of this were slow to appear. The first of the great English antiquaries, John Leland (who was once wrongly supposed to have had the title of 'king's antiquary' bestowed upon him by Henry VIII), conducted most of his research under the radar of Tudor culture, publishing relatively little in his own lifetime. Like many modern Oxbridge doctoral dissertations, neither his *Itinerary* nor his *Collectanea* was immediately suitable for print. Both, however, would circulate as much-cited manu-scripts through sixteenth- and seventeenth-century hands until Thomas Hearne, a respectable antiquary but an even more impressive editor of other men's works, finally saw them through the press in 1710 and 1715 respectively. Apart from his published poetry, the greatest prominence Leland achieved was when he, along with a number of younger scholars (principally Welsh), banded together to defend the historicity of the Galfridian inheritance from the assault of Polydore Vergil – that Italian worthy and international doubting Thomas who had two strikes against him – being both a foreigner and a papal official. He pointed out the lack of any contemporary textual authority for much, if anything, in Geoffrey of Monmouth's universe of British kings, from ancient invaders, such as Brute, right through to Arthur, the definitive British hero. Those who asserted the veracity of Geoffrey on Arthur were more or less bound to accept even his more outrageous fantasies, and Leland's friend and sometime editor, John Bale, elaborated on Geoffrey by inserting a line of pre-British 'Samothean' kings into the story in order to fill in the lineage more or less back to Noah.

The story of this *querelle* has been told many times by other historians and need not be repeated here.[7] It is sufficient to note that this was the first occasion in England when a group of scholars, acting more or less independently, combined to take a public position on a historical issue, denouncing in print the revisionism of an interloper whose methods and motives alike appeared suspect. We must be careful not to overstate the prominence that this episode gave them. No Old Bailey libel trial, attended by lurid headlines, ensued; far fewer people actually cared a great deal about the remote past – or even relatively recent history – in the first half of the sixteenth century than came to be true only a few decades later. There had to be something more concrete than an ancient king at stake and, more often than not, this was local rather than national: a prescriptive right being challenged, an ancestral perquisite threatened or a new tax imposed. Only rarely before the mid-seventeenth century did major matters of historical dispute and orthodoxy become more public, and then critically so – as in the case of a very new religion that needed to claim that it was, in fact, very old, or the Tudor monarchs' bookend efforts at the beginning and end of the sixteenth century to reinforce bad memories of the old baronial wars as a guard against rebellion, disobedience and succession challenges in their own time.

It is not until the middle of Elizabeth I's reign that we begin to see the English antiquary appearing on the intellectual stage (and, a short while later, the literal stage) as a kind of occupational category. The mid-century had seen Leland's heirs – most notably Bale – largely abandon Leland's observational methods and return to more traditional philological concerns – in particular the recovery of a history for the Protestant Church in England that could bridge back to the pure and primitive church of antiquity. This is the kind of task undertaken by Archbishop Matthew Parker's circle in recovering and editing Anglo-Saxon manuscripts, an endeavour that led to editions such as that of Bede's *Ecclesiastical History* in 1565 and Aelfric's *Testimonie of antiquitie* in 1566.[8] It was not so great a departure from Leland as it might appear. The documented travels that he had undertaken, with their useful observations of local monuments and commentary on oral traditions and local customs, had been almost an unintended by-product of Leland's work. His actual charge was the rescuing and gathering of the medieval monastic literary heritage from abbeys and other houses dissolved in the early years of the Reformation between 1536 and 1540. By nature a book-oriented humanist, Leland accidentally encouraged the roving antiquaries of William Camden's generation and, more remotely, the archaeological investigations of William Stukeley's era a century later still. But his real roots lay in the older and much more mainstream continental humanist activity of discovering long-hidden manuscript treasures and from them distilling the earliest extant and purest texts of the ancients and the Church Fathers.

The first Elizabethan 'Society' of Antiquaries was convoked in 1586, principally through the initiative of William Camden and several like-minded associates. The membership, which was never formalized, included a significant number of lawyers and heralds, both occupations well versed in dealing with records from the past and sifting what we would now call 'matters of fact' from conjecture.[9] The Society – or 'college' as it is perhaps more accurately termed in the parlance of the day – was important less for any individual or collective contribution that its members made during the intermittent meetings that occurred before 1614 than for the example they set and the framework they provided for discussion. Many of their discourses – mainly collected by their unofficial secretary, Francis Tate – make for interesting reading, and were published – once again by Hearne – in the early eighteenth century.[10] Their true significance, however, lay in establishing antiquarian enquiry as a serious activity that could be, simultaneously, a pleasant pastime (as it was for such men as William, Lord Howard of Naworth and most of the aristocrats with connections to the group) and a useful tool (as it was for Camden's politically ambitious protégé, Sir Robert Cotton, both an active parliamentarian and a rapacious landlord).[11] They also, in combination with many non-members who were now engaging in various pursuits that can collectively be called antiquarian, helped give the still nameless activity of antiquarian*ism* a profile.[12]

Although theirs were not public meetings, the college's activities gained prominence simply from the other activities of its 'star' members: John Stow, with his seemingly endless output of chronicles and his *Survey of London*; the charming Cornishman, Richard Carew; Camden's pupil, Cotton; the future King's Bench justice, John Dodderidge; and, above all, Camden himself, whose *Britannia*, first appearing in 1586, gave that amiable schoolmaster and soon-to-be Clarenceux King of Arms a prominence that he neither sought nor wanted. Camden had written *Britannia* at the behest of Abraham Ortelius, the cartographer, principally to introduce European readers to Britain's Roman (and secondarily medieval) remains, but the book quickly evolved beyond this, with the post-Domesday manorial holdings of the great families of the realm and their descents becoming a subject of importance in its own right.[13] Over two decades the audience also changed from a narrow band of colleagues in the Latin republic of letters to established and newer gentry families jostling for pride of place in the past and the present. The success of *Britannia* – measured by the number of subsequent revised and enlarged editions, the 1610 translation by the Coventry physician Philemon Holland, the great 1695 re-edition by Bishop Edmund Gibson (itself expanded into two volumes in 1722) and ultimately the final revision and updating by Richard Gough in 1789 – made Camden's book a virtual *Gray's Anatomy* for English antiquarian activity over two centuries.[14]

It is with this heightened activity at the time of the first Society that an object of satire was created. Many rural gentry had already been concerned with the muniments in their possession, if for no other reason than an understandable preoccupation with security of tenure and length of ancestry during a time of pronounced social and economic change.[15] By the end of the century, amid the 'great rebuilding' of their houses, the prosperous began to develop an interest in the random objects being turned up by their ploughboys or uncovered in the course of foundation digging. Now, in the wake of *Britannia*, a number of county-based writers began to include details of such things in their 'descriptions' and 'surveys' – a genre soon to be known as 'chorography'. A decade before Camden, William Lambarde had shown the way with his *Perambulation of Kent* (1576), as had the cleric William Harrison on a national scale with his *Description of England*, published in Holinshed's *Chronicles* in 1577.[16] They were followed by the surveyor John Norden, Staffordshire's Sampson

Erdeswicke, William Burton of Leicestershire, Cornwall's Richard Carew[17] and – perhaps most impressively – Stow in *The Survey of London* (the work that, of all works written by that generation, most conveys the nostalgia for a vanishing past commonly associated with the antiquary).[18] A respectable line of imitations, many of them unpublished until much later, fills the space between Camden and his heraldic successor, Sir William Dugdale, while the post-Restoration era would give rise to further examples (rather different in emphasis from the earlier chorographies, as we shall see) from authors such as John Aubrey and Robert Plot.[19]

Until there was a significant critical mass and a public presence, there was little need for an image, positive or negative: we would not tell lawyer jokes if lawyers were a rare breed. Indeed, the first comment that looks as if it might have been made about an antiquary cannot have been. Sir Philip Sidney, who died in the year that *Britannia* first appeared in print, had in mind a different sort of activity (probably that of chroniclers such as Grafton, Holinshed and Stow) when he spoke disparagingly in his *Apology for Poetry* of the historian 'loaden with old mouse-eaten records'.[20] It was an odd remark – almost a throwaway. The activities of the historian and the antiquary were already quite distinct, as Arnaldo Momigliano reminded us long ago,[21] though some, like Camden, eventually ended up engaged in both.[22] Sidney's comments aside, the historian offered a much more respectable character than the antiquary, one with many ancient precursors (virtually the only ancient example of an antiquary whose works were extant in the sixteenth century, and then only in fragments, was Varro). The historian told a story, even if it were cast in the form of annals or a chronicle, the dominant genre of writing about the past throughout the sixteenth century in England. At its best, history was a moral, didactic and, even, a political guide – in Cicero's famous phrase, history was *magistra vitae* ('life's teacher'). Its authors – especially the neo-humanist 'politic' historians of the very end of Elizabeth's reign and of James I's – modelled themselves on the greats of antiquity: Livy, Polybius, Thucydides and (especially) Tacitus. As Francis Bacon, the most high profile of Stuart historians (though his historical output is neither impressive in volume nor terribly significant within the context of his overall work) commented, the historian must be a man of affairs, an experienced general or a statesman, either a Thucydides or a Machiavelli. No warrior (unlike his sometime patron, the Earl of Essex), Bacon had nothing of the Athenian, but a healthy share of the Florentine – as both his own career and his eventual treatment of the reign of Henry VII demonstrate.[23]

This connection between worldly engagement and 'true' history – or 'perfect' history, as Bacon called it – stuck, and it excluded much of what the antiquaries did. Bacon himself was not very enthusiastic about the actual activity of research: the great encourager of observation and induction from examples was himself an ideas – rather than a details – man. Tweaking Cicero, Bacon asserted that history was a 'guide' to the present rather than a 'light' on the past, and he depicted the antiquary as a lesser servant of Clio, whose main function was to gather materials for the true historian to synthesize. As for the work of the conventional philologist – slave to language and acolyte of that most deadly of idols, the theatre – this was to be cast aside altogether.[24]

16

A lawyer (and ultimately Lord Chancellor), Bacon no doubt thought of the antiquary primarily as the user of Sidney's 'mouse-eaten records' rather than the kind of travelling recorder of physical monuments represented by Camden (whose own late Stuart heirs would, ironically, lay claim to 'Baconian' methods of induction and observation).[25] He may well have had in mind a Stow, or perhaps a less-familiar name such as Arthur Agarde – one of the original members of the Elizabethan college and an accomplished archivist in his capacity as deputy chamberlain of the Exchequer, whose Westminster tomb inscription proclaimed him 'Recordorum regiorum hic prope depositorum diligens scrutator'.[26] True to his convictions, the extent of Bacon's own original research for *Henry VII*, a *pièce d'occasion*, written hastily in the aftermath of his abrupt fall from power, consisted in retaining two scholars – John Selden and John Borough (the former a lawyer-philologist and parliamentarian researcher of growing reputation, the latter a keeper of archives) – to conduct a modest amount of uncredited work at the documentary coal-face.[27]

Did the antiquaries react to Sidney's condescension and Bacon's scorn? Beyond the fierce advocacy of recondite archival scholarship found in the early writings of Selden, an unusually aggressive bulldog on behalf of erudition's priority over rhetoric, there is little to suggest concern, much less resistance. On the contrary, a number of antiquaries of Camden's generation quietly bought stock in the characterization of themselves as scholars removed from the pressures of the world and the need to apply their knowledge to public affairs. Here again, the generation of Camden's pupil Cotton and of Selden himself, along with younger contemporaries, such as Sir Simonds d'Ewes, William Prynne and Sir Edward Dering, would mark a break with the Elizabethan past as they brought such knowledge to the parliamentary debates of the early Stuart era and to problems of governance and religion. A poor choice for James I's Chelsea College (a planned institute for anti-papal theological controversy), Camden's *Annales* were as close as he was ever to come to an engagement with the recent past, and even that was composed in the most cautious and the most even-handed Latin its author could muster.[28]

In his final years, Camden was also presented with a golden opportunity to improve the status of history at Oxford. He endowed a professorship in history and bestowed it on a competent (but uninspiring) classicist, Degory Wheare, rather than a solid antiquary such as Brian Twyne.[29] There is not much mystery in this. This was Camden the classicist and former schoolmaster putting his money where he thought it would do the most public good, into providing lectures to undergraduates on ancient history. Always conflict-averse (he had left others, such as his devoted deputy Augustine Vincent, to defend him against the acerbic herald Ralph Brooke's attacks on *Britannia*), Camden wished his appointees to avoid matters of controversy – including ecclesiastical history – and to shun treacherous pathways through the very recent past. But it was also the decision of Camden the antiquary and herald, whose own assessment of his activities may not have been far off Bacon's, given that he self-effacingly describes himself in *Britannia* as 'but of the lowest fourme in the schoole of Antiquity'.[30]

THE DEVELOPMENT OF THE ANTIQUARIAN IMAGE

With his usual mix of sarcasm and hyperbole, that gadfly of late Elizabethan culture, Thomas Nashe, offered the first extensive commentary on antiquarianism in 1592:

> An antiquary is an honest man, for he had rather scrape a piece of copper out of the dirt than a crown out of Plowden's standish. I know many wise gentlemen of this musty vocation who, out of love with the times wherein they live, fall a-retailing of Alexander's stirrups because, in verity, there is not such a strong piece of stretching leather made nowadays, nor iron so well tempered for any money . . . Let their mistress or some other woman give them a feather of her fan for her favour and, if one ask them what it is, they make answer 'A plume of the phoenix', whereof there is but one in all the whole world. A thousand gewgaws and toys have they in their chambers, which they heap together with infinite expense and are made believe of them that sell them that they are rare and precious things, when they have gathered them upon some dunghill, or raked them out of the kennel by chance . . . Let a tinker take a piece of brass worth a halfpenny and set strange stamps on it, and I warrant he may make it more worth to him of some fantastical fool than all the kettles that ever he mended in his life.[31]

By the middle of James I's reign – about the time the king took what Henry Spelman referred to as a 'mislike' of their activities – the jibes at antiquaries' expense became somewhat more frequent. John Donne, drawing a contrast for Queen Anne of Denmark in 1617 between the English Church and Catholicism, compared the latter to 'an Antiquaries Cabinet, full of rags and fragments of antiquity, but nothing fit for that use for which it was first made'. In a lighter tone he would rhyme:

> If in his Studie he hath so much care
> To hang all old strange things, let his wife beware.[32]

A generation later the dramatist Shakerley Marmion offered a complete portrait of the early Stuart antiquary, while further mock-definitions appeared after the Restoration.[33] The perennial wit Joseph Addison made fun of antiquaries in a deadpan dissertation on the cat-call (a cheap metal whistle then popular), for which he 'consulted' many antiquaries and a Fellow of the Royal Society, who expressed various opinions as to its antiquity and origins.[34]

Meric Casaubon, son of the great Isaac, would offer a psychological explanation of the fixation on old objects that was rapidly becoming synonymous with the antiquary:

> Antiquaries are so taken with the sight of old things; not as doting (as I take it) upon the bare either form or matter (though both oftentimes be very notable in old things); but because those visible superviving evidences of antiquities represent unto their minds former times, with as strong an impression, as if they were actually present, and in sight as it were: even as old men looke gladly upon those things, that they were wont to see, or have beene otherwise used

unto in their younger yeares, as injoying those yeares again in some sort, in those visible and palpable remembrances.[35]

The antiquary, in short, used the object as a kind of talisman to restore to his inner sight or imagination the original world of which the object was a rare survival, nostalgically recalling the human collective past in the same way that a man in his declining years gazes upon the belongings, or places, familiar to him in robust youth.

Meric Casaubon's analysis is deeply insightful, but it was not the comment on antiquarianism that enjoyed the widest circulation in the seventeenth century. Undoubtedly the most quoted of the early squibs is that by the Jacobean satirist John Earle. Unkind as they are, Earle's remarks need quotation at length since they are also more complex than is generally allowed:

[The antiquary] is a man strangely thrifty of Time past, and an enemy indeed to his Maw, whence he fetches out many things when they are now all rotten and stinking. Hee is one that hath that unnaturall disease to bee enamour'd of old age and wrinckles, and loves all things (as Dutchmen doe Cheese) the better for being mouldy and worme-eaten. He is of our Religion, because wee say it is most ancient; and yet a broken Statue would almost make him an Idolater. A great admirer hee is of the rust of old Monuments, and reades onely those Characters, where time hath eaten out the letters. Hee will goe you forty miles to see a *Saints well*, or a ruin'd Abbey, and if there be but a Crosse or stone footstoole in the way, hee'l be considering it so long, till he forget his journey. His estate consists much in shekels, and Roman Coynes, and he hath more pictures of *Caesar*, then *James*, or *Elizabeth*: Beggers cozen him with musty things which they have rak't from dunghills, and he preserves their rags for precious Reliques. He loves no Library, but where there are more Spiders volumes then Authors, and lookes with great admiration on the Antique worke of Cob-web. Printed booke, he contemnes, as a novelty of this latter age, but a *Manu-script* hee pores on everlastingly, especially if the cover be all Moth-eaten, and the dust make a *Parenthesis* betweene every Syllable. He would give all the Bookes in his study (which are rarities all) for one of the old Romane binding, or six lines of Tully, in his owne hand. His chamber is hung commonly with strange Beasts skins, and is a kinde of Charnel-house of bones extraordinary, and his discourse upon them, if you will heare them, shall last longer. His very attire is that which is the eldest out of fashion, and you may picke a *Criticisme* out of his Breeches. He never lookes up on himself til he is gray-hair'd, and then he is pleased with his owne Antiquity. His Grave do's not fright him, for he ha's bene us'd to Sepulchers, and he likes Death the better, because it gathers him to his Fathers.[36]

This was but one of seventy-eight such caricatures in the sixth edition of Earle's book, and it had not been featured in its earlier imprints. Others are just as biting, and some of the same foibles are recycled in connection with characters such as the attorney (a lover of old parchments), the herald ('a greater diver in the streames or issues of Gentry') and the 'pretender to learning', all of whose activities come close to that of the antiquary, who is certainly not singled out for special attention. It is of course an over-the-top and deliberately humorous piece, which pushes the image of the antiquary to extremes while tossing in virtually every imaginable negative association.

However indiscriminately thrown, Earle's mud stuck. In more modern times it has often been quoted – but not always completely, and rarely with very close attention to its nuances. In certain respects, Earle's description of antiquarian activities is apt, including his remarkably prescient observation of the trade between local labourers and visiting antiquaries – from which soil would grow an elaborate 'archaeological economy'.[37] Not much appeared to have changed by the century's end when another wit described an antiquary as a 'curious critick in old coins, stones, and inscriptions, in worm-eaten records, and ancient manuscripts; also one that affects and blindly doats, on relicks, ruins, old customes, phrases and fashions'.[38] Many even later descriptions adopt the same vocabulary, and Dr Johnson would add his voice in the mid-eighteenth century with the Walpolean antiquary of *Marmor Norfolciense* (1739), while his *Rambler* character Quisquilius translates as 'rubbish man'.[39] There are also some false assumptions – not least that antiquaries are universally observant Protestants because the Reformed Church is the 'oldest'. Many rejected that depiction of the Church and remained Catholic, and the fear of contemporaries that dabbling with the past in such a way could either lure a man to Rome or reinforce his Romanist inclinations was not altogether misplaced. Stow had famously been under suspicion for certain 'popish' books, and the rural recusant William Blundell, half a century later, would see the discovery of a trove of Anglo-Saxon coins as a sign from God encouraging his family's steadfastness.[40]

But just as Sidney had previously conflated antiquary and historian, Earle had really lumped together a wide array of disparate scholarly activities into a single composite that does not well reflect contemporary activity. There is, for instance, not much evidence from the early seventeenth century to support the equation of the travelling antiquary with the fervid collector of rarities. Of those known to have taken extended tours of England and to have engaged in antiquarian writing prior to 1640, only Cotton bequeathed significant collections, and those (the Cottonian manuscripts) principally acquired by other means and unconnected with his youthful expeditions. In short, the studious and the proprietary have been deliberately conflated by Earle into an introspective, hoarding and pathologically antisocial misfit that looks less like Scott's Oldbuck or Eliot's Edward Casaubon than the latter's Silas Marner.

THE VIRTUOSO AND THE ANTIQUARY

The great Elizabethan chronicler, Chaucerian and surveyor of London, John Stow, illustrates the social divide between antiquary and virtuoso; Stow was virtually the template of the ruder sort of scholar whose works were useful to his betters, but who lacked the means and station to compete with the courtly collector.[41] The latter was no threadbare grizzled ancient, and anything but an unfashionable recluse. Overt display, rather than hidden study, suited the owners of such wonders as the Arundel marbles; eloquent conversation arose from their possessions, not tedious monologue. In describing the gathering of antiquities, Henry Peacham remarked in 1634 that 'possession of such rarities, by reason of their dead costlinesse, doth properly belong to Princes, or rather to princely minds'.[42] The great collectors of the age who, in common with antiquaries, maintained an interest in the physical and literary relics of the past, are not reflected in stereotypes prior to the middle of the seventeenth century. Rather, they belong to a different social stratum, of wealthy and powerful gentry and aristocrats, generally referred to as 'virtuosi' and associated with a much-refined and tasteful collection of objects, with aesthetic quality balancing the value of oldness.[43] These were the English imitators of great continental art collectors and of early naturalists such as Ulisse Aldrovandi, and they included no less an eminence than Charles I himself.[44] To some degree this is a distinction without a difference, not unlike that which leads us to describe a maladjusted Lazarus as a lunatic and an equally odd Dives as merely 'eccentric'. But closely examined, the language points in two separate directions. Earle's description is not socially neutral: the 'estate' or property of his antiquary consists not in land but in chattels – the small objects he has recovered – and he is familiar with sepulchres only because he has visited them, not because he is possessed of a great manor house with its own marble-laid mausoleum.

By contrast, contemporary writers such as Peacham and Richard Brathwait, writing for socially ambitious court-bound gentry, stressed at virtually the same time the usefulness of many of the same activities in the hands of the privileged, powerful and affluent. Brathwait commended to his youthful reader in 1614 'the excellent study of antiquities' and praised the work of 'laborious and judicious antiquaries'.[45] Peacham's *Compleat Gentleman* was dedicated to the younger son of the Earl Marshall, Thomas Howard, Earl of Arundel, and Arundel himself was the quintessential noble patron, collector and Maecenas of Jacobean and Caroline England (and a reformed Catholic of notably Italianate tastes). Peacham's recommendations on the inculcation of civility include the reading of history and knowledge of statuary and medals (as well as other activities such as painting and music). His book is both a late version of the Renaissance courtesy book descended from Castiglione's *Book of the Courtier* and a more detailed prescription for the activity of the virtuoso, that fine figure of a discerning, tasteful and prosperous collector, the nobility of his soul reflected in the breadth of his intellectual interests and the quality of the collections displayed in his cabinet; it belongs to the same exotic world as that of the emblem book, another arena in which Peacham himself was to make significant contributions.[46] Indeed, Peacham even refers to the antiquary as a different breed of cat altogether, a kind of 'Antiques Road Show' consultant to the legitimate collector. 'Insomuch as if you bring an old rusty coyne to any reasonable Antiquary: if he can see but a nose upon it, or a peece of the face, he will give you a shrewd guesse at him, though none of the inscription be to be seene.'[47] We see the same activities similarly advocated by Edmund Bolton, the champion of a virtuoso academy of higher learning to be ruled by the powerful, assisted – in his vision – by antiquaries of straitened means such as himself.[48]

Beginning in the late Elizabethan period, antiquaries and interested noblemen, such as Arundel and John, Lord Lumley, and polymathic scholars, such as John Dee, assembled cabinets of marvels and curiosities to adjoin and adorn their private closets and receiving rooms (as well, increasingly, as exterior spaces such as gardens), symbolizing the connection between the worlds of nature, art and learning that would ultimately split into the interior spaces of three different institutions: the museum, the gallery and the library.[49] These often served more than scholarly interest, becoming pieces of furniture or decoration. The size and quality of collections became an index of power, wealth, taste and intellectual sophistication. At the time of his early death in 1612, for instance, Henry, Prince of Wales had, according to the letter-writer John Chamberlain, assembled a 'cabinet-room' filled with a collection of paintings and 'medalls or antient coins of gold' worth three thousand pounds.[50] His younger brother, Charles I, left an even more impressive collection at his execution in 1649.[51]

The distinction between the virtuoso and the antiquary is difficult to draw with any precision, and many collectors fit both labels. They shared, for a time, an interest in the *display* of artefacts and curiosities, and tastes that ran beyond those of a third type, the mere bibliophile. An instructive comparison between the latter two categories can be made by juxtaposing the fictional courtly reader satirized by Donne (who did not, for once, here intend the antiquary) at the beginning of the seventeenth century, with Sir Thomas Browne's Aldrovandi-like virtuoso a few decades later. Whereas Donne's acerbic *The Courtier's Library* (written before 1611) is filled with thirty-four quarrel-fuelling religious and legal books that offended Donne's eirenic tendencies, Browne's *Musaeum Clausum* (c 1674) is a much more heterogeneous assemblage of manuscripts, books, pictures, medals and 'rarities of several sorts'.[52]

The whole point of a cabinet of marvels is its potential as a *monstra* or 'show' to inspire admiration, a potential unrealized if its contents cannot be seen. As possessions such marvels are proprietary symbols of the same conspicuous consumption represented at large by the great houses in which they sat. On this point the genuine virtuoso had much in common with the antiquary, including an appetite for objects, such as coins and medals. He was not always possessed of the historical sense that inhered in many of the earliest antiquaries, especially those in the philological-textual tradition, who were always much less dependent on communication by 'showing'. It is especially hard to distinguish virtuoso and antiquary before 1640, other than by social status, since many antiquaries also had a wide range of interests. The separating islands of knowledge, observed John Selden (no virtuoso, but the philological oracle of Arundel's inscrutable marbles), remained an archipelago that could still be bridged, each outcrop visible from another once it had been conquered.[53] The common element was 'curiosity' itself (in the sense of a quality of mind, rather than of a particular object), which furnished the standard of appreciation for both nature and art through much of this period, just as the 'sublime' would come to do for a later age.[54]

Wherein, then, lay the difference? Many antiquaries – ignoring the increasingly pejorative sense that their title carried outside their own circles – studied (and occasionally acquired for their own use) 'artefacts', and struggled not to neglect the historical context within which they had been created. The virtuoso, by contrast, often collected 'curiosities' (those objects to which the mental outlook of curiosity applied) indiscriminately, with little attention to the contexts of time and place. The qualities of exoticism and beauty often trumped that of age, and to some virtuosi it did not especially matter that an object was old, so long as it was rare, unusual and suitable for exhibition – paintings, gems and natural objects fitting the bill as well or better than the soiled shards of a Roman burial urn.[55]

There are signs as early as the Restoration of a willingness to separate the natural from the artificial, and the antique from the modern curiosity. By this time, antiquaries were no longer alone in being lampooned by wits. By the last quarter of the seventeenth century, the generality and uselessness of virtuoso knowledge – once treated so seriously by Peacham, Sir Kenelm Digby and younger members of the Arundel circle, such as John Evelyn – was now itself being satirized in the person of Sir Nicholas Gimcrack, the title character of Shadwell's *The Virtuoso* (1676), 'a rare mechanic philosopher' modelled on members of the Royal Society. For Gimcrack, knowledge, not application, is the sole end, and 'so it be knowledge, 'tis no matter of what'.[56] Fossile, the aged protagonist of Gay's *Three Hours After Marriage* and a stand-in for the real-life Dr John Woodward, is a natural philosopher concerned with 'hermaphrodites, monstrous twins, antediluvian shells, bones and vegetables'. An ancient set of cutlery 'with the mark of Tubal Cain in Hebrew' illustrates for him 'the stature and magnitude of those antediluvians'.[57]

Gimcrack's activities are all 'inventions' and experiments, rather than book learning or antiquarian collection, quite unlike the preoccupations of Marmion's Veterano barely three decades earlier.[58] Sir Nicholas's fictitious will, published by Addison in the *Tatler*, would include everything from a female skeleton and a humming-bird's nest to a box of butterflies. While it mentions an Egyptian mummy, it is notably devoid of the usual sorts of antiquities: coins, Roman bricks and manuscripts.[59] The satirized virtuoso in Judith Drake's *An Essay in Defence of the Female Sex* (sometimes attributed to Mary Astell) is similarly a collector of seashells, not of Caesars.[60] And when Pope featured Annius the antiquary ('canker'd as his Coins') and his rival Mummius in the fourth book of the final edition of *The Dunciad*, the 'proper employment' described for the Indolents is as Virtuosos, busily engaged 'in the study of Butterflies, Shells, Birds-nests, Moss'.[61]

It is difficult to escape the impression that the *savants* of the last quarter of the seventeenth century were, like Harry Potter's new classmates, once again sorting themselves into distinct, if overlapping, houses. One group now fixed their eyes more squarely on the middle-distance past, where antiquarianism had begun a century or so earlier. There was a remarkable Augustan revival in medieval textual and linguistic studies, as practised by Thomas Rymer, Thomas Madox, Humfrey Wanley, George Hickes and Henry Wharton, among others, of the sort of manuscript-based scholarship then being tuned to a higher pitch in the realm of classical philology by the likes of Richard Bentley. This activity was now supported by the emergent ancillary sciences of palaeography, epigraphy, diplomatics and numismatics. Meanwhile, some exponents of the new natural philosophy were abandoning virtuosity in the other direction, calling for an orderly and discriminating inventory of knowledge of the natural world under various categories, and repudiating the cult of rarity in order to make knowledge not exotic and wonderful, but explicable, familiar and taxonomically organized.[62] Krzysztof Pomian has usefully described the later seventeenth century as a time during which institutional mechanisms such as journals and societies brought the era of 'curiosity' in Europe to a close.[63] So far as England is concerned, this reminds us that the interests of Augustan antiquarianism and Augustan science, themselves so often closely associated in individuals like Woodward or Lhuyd, were never quite the same.

The connections between virtuoso and antiquarian interests are, therefore, most obvious in the century between John Caius – early Elizabethan student of dogs, medicine and the antiquity of Cambridge – and John Aubrey – gossipy biographer, student of rural archaeology and early folklorist. Aubrey may well have been the last of the great seventeenth-century antiquaries to work effectively in several fields, but his *Naturall Historie of Wiltshire* has been identified by Professor Michael Hunter as the first book to depart from the older county chorographies by abandoning the place-by-place itinerary used since Leland in favour of a description and arrangement of natural and artificial objects according to type.[64] The overlap is less and less apparent as we move from the Restoration to the Georgian era, though some topics by their very nature continued to demand the attention of philologist and naturalist alike. Edward Lhuyd's interest in fossils, plants, runic inscriptions and linguistics is an excellent example – his pursuit of all of these in the field occasioned a four-year break from his post as Keeper of the Ashmolean between 1697 and 1701.[65]

THE PUBLIC FACE OF THE ANTIQUARY

So much for the idea of the early modern antiquary as conceived by contemporary satirists. How did the antiquary present himself to readers? In the sixteenth century printing brought the author out of relative obscurity and privacy and gave him a presence outside the circle of cognoscenti and noble patrons. This was as true of the antiquary as of the historian, the poet or the divine. Although Leland and Bale are both referred to approvingly by subsequent authors, it is Camden again who first gave the antiquary a public face in the first and many subsequent editions of *Britannia*. This face was literal as well as figurative. Camden is one of the rare sixteenth-century antiquaries whose physical appearance – or at least his visage – is familiar from a number of near-contemporary illustrations and from his Westminster Abbey monument (defaced in the Civil War by a marauding band of Cavaliers or Independents, depending on which side's propaganda is believed).[66] Matthew Parker's face is known through many images, but principally because of his status as primate, and the archbishop was, in any case, more patron than practitioner of antiquarian codicological study; Leland is known only through a bust based on an eighteenth-century Grignion engraving that may or may not be accurate. John Stow's portrait was engraved for the 1603 edition of the *Survey of London* from a portrait in private hands, but few extant copies of the book retain it; the sculpted monument erected by his widow at St Andrew Undershaft, Leadenhall Street, portrays him in the act of writing.[67] Lambarde is known principally from a much later portrait engraved by George Vertue for the first publication (in 1730) of his *Dictionarium Angliæ topographicum et historicum.* Sampson Erdeswicke erected a monument to himself at Sandon Church, in Staffordshire, but his *Survey of Staffordshire* remained unpublished until 1717, over a century after his death (the monument was engraved in the 1844 edition of the *Survey*). Michael Heneage was known only from a similar monument of himself and his wife recumbent, in St Paul's Cathedral. An anonymous (and posthumously painted) 1601 portrait of Laurence Nowell,[68] Lambarde's mentor in Old English, exists in Dulwich Gallery. Of mid-Tudor antiquaries – such as Robert Talbot – and of many of their Elizabethan successors – Arthur Agarde, Francis Thynne, Richard Carew, Thomas Hatcher, Francis Tate and the diplomat Daniel Rogers – we have no picture or funerary monument, and thus no visual image. Contemporaries had even less knowledge of (and less interest in) the appearance of authors than do we. Those Tudor antiquaries whose images were preserved were done in portrait only, not engraved in print, and were thus not generally publicly

Fig 3. John Dodderidge (artist unknown): oil portrait now hanging in the Meeting Room of the Society of Antiquaries of London. *Photograph*: Society of Antiquaries of London.

25

accessible at the time. They also tended to be done because the subject was famous –
like Parker or Caius – for other things than antiquarian pursuits: the portly John
Dodderidge, whose image survives in the Society of Antiquaries (fig 3), is an
ermine-gowned justice whose portrait gives no indication of his interest in English
legal antiquities.[69]

This situation changed in the seventeenth century. Apart from occasional physical
descriptions provided by near-contemporary biographers such as Aubrey (from whom
we learn that Sir Henry Spelman was 'a handsome gentleman, strong and valiant, and
wore always his sword till he was about 70 or more'), it was increasingly fashionable
for publishers to include engraved images of authors with their books.[70] In an age
that valued the more socially exclusive practices of portraiture and limning, gentle
readers were often interested in the more widely reproducible visage of the author.
Physiognomy and comportment could speak to character and seriousness, and the
engraved image offered publishers a relatively inexpensive means of capitalizing on
an author's reputation or social status in order to promote sales. For authors
themselves, representation in image as well as text played into the culture of what
Stephen Greenblatt has famously called 'Renaissance self-fashioning', permitting
them to shape a public identity for themselves.[71] Consequently, these pictures of
antiquaries deserve some attention in their own right, both for what they tell us about
the establishment of a public image of antiquarianism, and even more for what they
tell us about the way in which antiquaries themselves wished to be portrayed. Of those
seen by the present writer, only one partially approximates the Earle stereotype: that
of John Weever engraved at the age of fifty-five by Thomas Cecill for Weever's *Ancient
Funerall Monuments* (1631). This *vera effigies* (fig 4) depicts Weever in Jacobean
garb (cap and ruff), with two stacked volumes to his right and his left hand resting
upon a skull. In the unlikely event that the reader missed the point, verses comment
on the antiquary:

> Lanchashire [*sic*] gave him breath,
> And Cambridge education.
> His Studies are of Death
> Of Heaven his meditation.

The death's head was, of course, a staple of late Renaissance iconography, denoting
contemptus mundi and resignation to mortality. Yet despite the commonplace appearance of the skull in portraits of the great, it features remarkably rarely in antiquarian
frontispieces, suggesting that the kind of obsessive fixation on decay and death
of which John Earle spoke (and that Sir Thomas Browne mused on at length in
Hydriotaphia) was not an essential part of antiquaries' own self-image, whatever
the private morbidity of some, like Evelyn, who notoriously practised for his death
by sleeping in a casket. It is not an entirely satisfactory answer to say simply that
Weever's primary concern with funerary monuments associated him more closely with
death than other antiquaries.

Let us compare some others. Camden is among the most portrayed of antiquaries, so much so that his image has given an impression of him as 'active in body, of middle height, of a pleasant countenance, and . . . of a ruddy complexion'.[72] At the instigation of some of his friends, including the French virtuoso Nicolas Fabri de Peiresc, Camden had Marc Geerarts paint two portraits, one of which passed to Degory Wheare and thence to the Bodleian Library, the other to Cotton and, by way of the British Museum, to the National Portrait Gallery. A deathbed portrait was also painted, which belonged at one point to the first Earl of Clarendon. No engraved image appeared in any of Camden's own books during his lifetime; the 1657 edition of his *Remains Concerning Britain* (1674) offers an image once ascribed by Edward Maunde Thompson to John Payne (d 1647).[73] This was adapted, with very few changes, by Robert White (fig 5) for the 1674 edition of *Remains*, though the image itself was by now an antiquity in its own right, the Elizabethan-styled Clarenceux King of Arms being anachronistic in the world of Restoration fashion. The 1657 and 1674 versions of *Remains*, like Weever's book, feature a death's head, but much less prominently; it appears in the bottom right corner, almost out of the way and outside the oval, where it is opposed in the bottom left by a lantern, the illumination that

Fig 4. John Weever: line engraving in *Ancient Funerall Monuments* (1631), by Thomas Cecill. *Photograph*: Society of Antiquaries of London.

Fig 5. William Camden: portrait by Robert White from *Remains* (1674 edition). *Photograph*: Society of Antiquaries of London.

scholarship can bestow on the past. Much more obvious are the heraldic shield (top right), and the figure of an ancient (top centre) leaning on a further skull, with a surveyor's sextant. The 1691 edition of Camden's correspondence (edited by Thomas Smith) offers a variant on this portrait, with a slightly glummer-looking Camden, his surrounding oval now devoid of inscription, and death or ageing imagery totally absent, but retaining the sextant and shield at top (though now on opposite sides) and an additional royal shield (the cross of St George and a fleur-de-lis) below. Finally, a portrait of Camden appears at the end of Book I of Sylvanus Morgan's *Sphere of Gentry*, a book that Morgan dedicated to the then Garter King of Arms, Sir Edward Walker.[74] As befits the antiquary whose work had embraced all three kingdoms, the image includes Camden's inner garment bearing a Scottish lion rampant, enclosed by a cloak featuring multiple English lions passant gardant, and, in the bottom corner – symbolizing its lesser status among the kingdoms – an Irish harp, on which the English antiquary rests his arm (fig 6).

Perhaps the most interesting engraving of an early Stuart historian or antiquary is that of John Speed, who mixed with antiquaries such as Cotton and Bolton but was not really one himself. The line engraving of Speed at his desk by Salomon Savery, now in the National Portrait Gallery, was reproduced in several of Speed's works and depicts him with his left hand resting not on a skull, but on a pair of dividers, the tool of a cartographer or geographer rather than that of a historian or antiquary (fig 7).[75] The majority of engraved images are much simpler. If they feature iconography at all,

Fig 6. William Camden: portrait from Sylvanus Morgan, *The Sphere of Gentry* (1661), Book I, facing p 120. *Photograph*: reproduced by permission of the British Library (BL, 605 g.16).

28

Fig 7. John Speed: engraving from *A Prospect of the Most Famous Parts of the World* (1631 edition), by Salomon Savery. Reproduced from the copy in the library of the Society of Antiquaries of London of Speed, *Theatre of the Empire of Great Britain* (1676 edition, including the *Prospect*); note that this illustration was added to the book after publication and not included in the original 1676 printing. *Photograph*: Society of Antiquaries of London.

it tends to be armorial, befitting the genealogical preoccupations of the period up to and including Dugdale, a transitional character in the story of seventeenth-century English antiquarianism. Dugdale's Midlands predecessor, William Burton, was a lawyer who retired early to Falde in Staffordshire but who was mainly preoccupied with Leicestershire, his county of birth. Francis Delaram's oval-enclosed three-quarter-length engraving of Burton for the latter's *Description of Leicester Shire* (1622) is cornered by armorial shields, but the portrait proper features Burton standing, leaning against a desk with writing implements; again, death is no longer an overt theme (fig 8).[76]

The many printed engravings of the greatest philological antiquary of the first half of the century, John Selden (of whom a number of portraits survive by the school of Peter Lely), are severe and unadorned; a common one, based on a bust by Robert White, was repeated in a number of Selden's works such as *The Reverse or Back-face of the English Janus* (1682) (fig 9). Aubrey describes Selden as 'very tall – I guess six foot high – sharp, oval face, head not very big, long nose inclining to one side,

Fig 8. William Burton: line engraving by Francis Delaram from *Description of Leicester Shire* (1622). *Photograph*: reproduced by permission of the British Library (BL, G3495).

Fig 9. John Selden: engraved portrait by Robert White from *Titles of Honor* (3rd edn, 1672). From the copy in the Rutherford Memorial Library, University of Alberta. *Photograph*: University of Alberta.

Fig 10. John Selden: portrait from *Contextio gemmarum, sive, Eutychii patriarchae Alexandrini annales. Illustriss: Johanne Seldeno . . . chorago. Interprete Edwardo Pocockio* (Oxford, 1658). *Photograph*: reproduced by permission of the British Library (BL, E 758).

full popping eie'.[77] A more informative engraving that matches Aubrey's account, and leaves no doubt as to what kind of antiquary the great legal scholar was, is that included in the 1658 edition of Selden's study of Eutychius, the tenth-century patriarch of Alexandria (fig 10).[78] An angular Selden stands stiffly in front of shelves lined with chained books, stored spine-inward and without titles; biographical details are featured in the text below the portrait. Eight decades later, the book-oriented antiquary received a similar treatment in a 1723 engraving of Hearne (fig 11) by George Vertue. A scholar associated with the Bodleian (and with surprisingly profitable editions of medieval chronicles rather than the examination of physical antiquities), Hearne is suitably portrayed with his right hand holding an open volume and his right shoulder against a much-consulted (judging by its mismatched sizes and gaps) shelf of volumes, now with spines out in the modern fashion.

On the whole, genealogical and armorial themes dominate the images of antiquaries up to and including Dugdale. They continued with such derivative writers as Sylvanus Morgan, and such latter-day heralds as Edward Waterhouse, whose *Gentlemans Monitor* of 1665 (a commentary on social decay rather than a heraldic tract *per se*) has a plain portrait of its author with only one armorial shield and no other illustration. The most informative of all such images is that of Dugdale himself as drawn by Hollar (fig 12), an engraving included in *Antiquities of Warwickshire* and the *History of St Paul's Cathedral*. A hatted and confident Dugdale sits beside his

Fig 11. Thomas Hearne: portrait (1723) by George Vertue (following Peter Tillemans). *Photograph*: Society of Antiquaries of London.

Fig 12. Sir William Dugdale: engraved portrait by Wenceslaus Hollar from *Antiquities of Warwickshire* (1656). *Photograph*: Society of Antiquaries of London.

desk, facing outward to the world rather than downward in contemplation of his materials: this is no solitary St Jerome contemplative in his study. The sole genealogical or heraldic images are a griffon at top right and a shield at top left, both so sketchily drawn as to suggest they are virtually an afterthought. Much more impressively drawn are the tools of the antiquary – inkpot and pens foregrounded, Dugdale's right hand resting on a scrolled sheet of paper, the desk itself crowded with the output of this implied labour, two volumes of which display their titles (*Monasticon* and *Warwickshire*). Behind these stands a bookshelf crammed with manuscripts. This interesting depiction does not mean that the works to follow are devoid of genealogical and heraldic matter – as a herald, this was the world in which Dugdale lived. What it does suggest, however, is that the image of the author surrounded by the sources and the fruit of his scholarship is of equal importance in marketing the book as the reputation of any of the families contained therein.[79] The triumph of the book over the shield is even more obvious in a 1682 portrait of Elias Ashmole, whose third wife was the daughter of his friend Dugdale. Perhaps even more than his father-in-law (or that other intellectual polymath, John Aubrey), Ashmole could face both ends of the seventeenth century in comfort. A complex virtuoso-astrologer, latter-day magus, outspoken champion of the Order of the Garter and quondam Windsor Herald, he resigned that office in 1675, the year in which he began to negotiate with Oxford University for the building of his famous museum; he thereafter avoided official heraldic pursuits. Now in the Ashmolean Museum, this three-quarter length painting of Ashmole (attributed to John Riley) features only a standing bound volume in the subject's hand; heraldry is limited to a single shield, and that confined to the sumptuous Grinling Gibbons frame (fig 13).[80]

Fig 13. Elias Ashmole: portrait (1682) attributed to John Riley, with a frame by Grinling Gibbons, in the Ashmolean Museum, Oxford. *Photograph*: reproduced by permission of the Ashmolean Museum, Oxford.

By the turn of the seventeenth century, the antiquarian image has changed further still. The engraving by William Faithorne the Younger of Dr Charles Leigh, FRS, adorning the latter's *Naturall History of Lancashire, Cheshire, and the Peak, in Derbyshire* (fig 14) is devoid of all heraldry save a lion rampant below the oval, itself containing the author – now in Augustan peruke rather than Renaissance ruff and cap. Like other similarly inclined physicians (Sir Hans Sloane, for instance), Leigh saw himself as more naturalist than antiquary, and refused the latter title the way Camden had once disclaimed that of historian. Following a few lines on the ancient Brigantes at the beginning of his book – drawn from Camden – he abandons further discussion of ancient Britons 'to the Antiquaries, it being forein to this under-taking'.[81] Armorial images continue to appear throughout such natural history texts, but increasingly they are little more than a printer's decorative advice, a mark of the author's own social respectability, or a tributary symbol to those who had subscribed for a particular title, such as Leigh's. Sir Robert Sibbald's *Scotia illustrata* of 1683 (translated as *Scotland Illustrated*, 1684) has only a repeated printer's device at the start of chapters on natural objects and antiquities: a Scottish lion rampant surrounded by twin unicorns passant, or

alternately by crowned thistles. The major illustrations in Sibbald's book are all at the end, and are exclusively of plants, animals and fossils.[82] Other images are even more austere. A late engraving of the Anglo-Saxonist William Somner, in the 1693 posthumous edition of his *Treatise of the Roman Ports and Forts in Kent* (Oxford 1693), has but a single shield. A 1711 Thomas Hill portrait of Humfrey Wanley (fig 15), now in the library of the Society of Antiquaries of London, shows the great palaeographer and librarian to the Harleys seated at his desk, holding a bound Greek codex open to a page on which the words are arranged as a cross – an interesting choice on Wanley's part given his comments in other contexts on the popish 'superstition' of such practices. A medieval parchment, the 'Life of St Gunthlac', unfurls from the desk top, anchored there by two books, a quill sandwiched between the latter. There is no heraldic icon or device whatever; a former draper's apprentice and the younger son of a rural cleric, Wanley needed no display of arms to mark the intellectual respect that he had achieved, first in Oxford and then in London.[83]

By 1700, whatever their other activities might be, antiquaries and natural historians alike were putting some distance between themselves and the heraldic detail that had been bread and butter in Camden's day. Various explanations can be adduced for this, including the declining influence of the College of Arms (and the end of peripatetic visitations by its officers, the heralds), and society's greater acceptance of the notion that deeds, not descent, were the prime determinant of virtue; but the most important reason may simply have been changing intellectual tastes and the

Fig 14. Charles Leigh: portrait by William Faithorne from *Naturall History of Lancashire, Cheshire, and the Peak, in Derbyshire* (Oxford, 1700). *Photograph*: reproduced by permission of the University of California, Santa Barbara.

greater attention now being paid to tangible antiquity, and in particular to natural objects, such as fossils.[84] In short, the archaeological was rapidly displacing the armorial as the focus of antiquarian activity, just as the explicable and comparable was supplanting the mysterious and unique. We should not be surprised to see the visual style of antiquarian self-representation alter in response to these shifts in interest.

OLD SOCIETY INTO NEW

A generation further on, one of the two oil portraits of Samuel Gale now hanging in the Fellows' Room in the Society of Antiquaries (fig 2) shows the customs-office clerk turned antiquary in what must surely be among the earliest pictures of an antiquary deliberately set against an image of ruins – viewable over his shoulder. Gale (son of Thomas and brother of Roger, two other scholars of distinction, as well as brother-in-law and close friend of Stukeley) became the first treasurer of the modern Society of Antiquaries at its official foundation in 1717, an event marked by a two-night dramatic revival of Shakerley Marmion's *Antiquary*. As the present volume reminds us, however, the first meetings of the new body had already commenced a decade earlier, rather hesitantly, at the Bear Tavern and then the Young Devil Tavern.

The year 1707 is itself not without significance, since it marked the cessation of England's status as an independent kingdom and its union with Scotland within the

Fig 15. Humfrey Wanley: portrait (1711) by Thomas Hill in the library of the Society of Antiquaries of London. *Photograph*: Society of Antiquaries of London.

single United Kingdom of Great Britain.[85] Two centuries previously, with a 'British' dynasty on the throne in the shape of the Welsh Tudors, the first generation of English antiquaries necessarily fixed on maintaining the historicity of the ancient British kings, and of demonstrating the one-time unity of the island in the era of Brutus and his sons (an account from which Scots, such as Hector Boece and George Buchanan, not unsurprisingly dissented). Poets up to William Warner and Michael Drayton continued to echo these tales, but the British muse had lost its charm by the end of the sixteenth century. A brief revival of interest in matters British during the early years of the reign of James VI and I notably dwelt more on the documentable medieval than the mythical ancient past, notwithstanding such plays as *King Lear*. The best of the late Tudor and early Stuart antiquaries were now much more keenly focused on quite specific problems in Romano-British and medieval history, many of which could be quite as controversial, but which had the virtue of being supported by physical and contemporary textual evidence. The kinds of issues addressed by the Elizabethan college of antiquaries reflected both the concerns of contemporary gentry and nobility with their genealogies and coats of arms, and practical issues such as the history of the coinage or of types of land measurement; they were intended to trace the origins and linear development of things surviving in their present. So, too, did the major antiquarian published works of the first half of the seventeenth century, the majority of which were cast as chorographies. Even the rare antiquarian book that was not a chorography, such as Selden's *Historie of Tithes*, did not deviate notably from the pattern of 'discourse' practised by the first society, with chronology forming the organizational principle, just as topography did in the chorographical works.[86]

By 1707 the landscape looked very different. In the first place, the era of fixation on pedigrees and genealogies was by and large over – Dugdale's *Warwickshire* may safely be regarded as the culminating work of the heraldically focused Elizabethan and early Stuart chorographical tradition. The prominence of less magical strains of natural philosophy, and the gradual integration of 'Baconian' methods of induction and observation into what were becoming studies of 'natural history', can be seen in embryo in the works that appear from the 1660s onward (such as Plot's surveys of Oxfordshire and Staffordshire), though for a time the majority of works continued to give plenty of space to the older issues.[87] The full measure of the change is not really evident until the early eighteenth century, and can best be assessed by comparing a man such as Edward Lhuyd, who died in 1709, with Camden, of only a century earlier. Both Camden and Lhuyd were learned scholars and accomplished linguists; both undertook extensive travels and both were interested almost equally in words and objects – but there the similarities end. Where *Britannia* depicted individual examples of monuments and effigies as points of interest in a county-by-county, family-by-family travelogue, Lhuyd's catalogue of Ashmolean fossils, the *Lithophylacii Britannici ichnographia* (1699), focuses on the objects themselves, and especially on what can be gleaned from their comparison and grouping. Where Camden's *Remains* studied the etymology of particular words in a rather speculative manner, Lhuyd's extensive 1707 *Glossography* (the first volume of his projected

Archaeologica Britannica) provided a comparative vocabulary of indigenous Celtic languages, grammars and dictionaries for Cornish, Irish and Welsh; most significantly, Title VIII of the *Glossography* made detailed and systematic phonetic comparisons of Welsh with various European tongues, employing the same classificatory approach that he had earlier applied to fossils.[88] Lhuyd's earlier-announced design for this 'British Dictionary', submitted to raise funds for his five summers of travels about the island, pays lip service to the history of major families (who would be called upon to foot the bill and ultimately subscribe), but it promises a book much more concerned with the antiquities, flora and fauna of Wales, something also reflected in the parochial queries that he issued in 1697. Lhuyd was a contributor to young Edmund Gibson's 1695 rendition of *Britannia*, throughout which we find polite respect on the part of the antiquaries of the day for their early Stuart forebears, rather than either obedience or repudiation. It is probable that the shifts in interest and approach which appear more obvious to us at three centuries remove were viewed as simply a natural evolution by antiquaries of that time.

One of the twentieth century's great authorities on early modern antiquarianism, Stuart Piggott, believed that the new Society appeared just at the end of a long period of improvement in scholarship, and just prior to a precipitous decline in standards that lasted until the nineteenth century. Others such as Drs Sweet and MacGregor are better placed than this author to argue that point (as they do elsewhere in the present volume), but it must be admitted that Piggott himself had a teleological (and even positivist) view of the advancement of learning, and rather set ideas as to how it should occur. That made him occasionally harsh in judgement on those who deviated from this standard, in particular those at the tail end of the period – on nobody was he tougher than on Stukeley, the subject of his biography, for allegedly abandoning the proper 'field archaeology' he had applied to Avebury for nonsensical speculation with respect to Stonehenge and Druids more typical of Restoration charlatans, such as Aylett Sammes, or dabbling enthusiasts, such as Inigo Jones.[89] On one point, however, Piggott was dead right: the scholars who assembled in 1707 (and, in greater strength, in 1717) were no doubt conscious of their obligations to the class of 1586, but the new Society had very different purposes – among them the much greater emphasis on the dissemination of visual images of the objects that they studied.[90] If they had inherited the seventeenth-century virtuoso love of the collectable, they were less likely to think of it in connection with *virtù* than with Vertue. Stukeley and his contemporaries, as Piggott noted, did things differently and had broader interests than the chorographers of Camden's or even Dugdale's time, the much more prominent intrusion of natural history into the history of antiquities being the most obvious. So it will not do to think of the new Society as a mere revival of the old. If public perceptions of antiquaries as admirably odd hunters of a past both obscure and vanished did not evolve very much between John Earle and Sir Walter Scott, then at least the ideas that the antiquaries themselves had about how best to recapture that past had come some distance.

36

NOTES

1. Hunter 1981b, 22–32; Prince 1981, 33–49. There are now numerous general studies of early modern historical thought that include discussions of Tudor and Stuart antiquarianism: among the more recent, see Levine 1987 and Parry 1995. The present essay builds on topics I have discussed at greater length elsewhere, and repeats some examples from those earlier works (see *Bibliography*), here adduced in support of the particular argument I wish to make with respect to the image of the 17th-century antiquary. I am indebted to Susan Pearce, Arthur MacGregor and Rosemary Sweet for comments on earlier versions.

2. Piggott 1976, 171–95. On 19th-century antiquarianism, see more recently Levine 1986.

3. Nuttall 2003 offers studies of Mark Pattison and both the real and imaginary Casaubons.

4. Piggott 1976, 133–70.

5. Grafton 1983 and 1993; Kelley 1970. Budé is a critical figure: a traditional humanist focused on languages and text, he also drew early attention to the use of coins as a source of extra-textual information on the remote past. But for the fact that many English philologists of the Elizabethan period began to use old manuscripts in their linguistic and textual researches (in particular the Anglo-Saxonists associated with Archbishop Matthew Parker), the word 'antiquary' might never have become associated with philologists. Both Camden and Selden, outstanding antiquaries of their respective generations, were principally philologists and masters of language (Camden was a Greek schoolmaster in the tradition of William Grocyn) who branched out into other activities that are more legitimately seen as antiquarian – in Camden's case his heraldic studies and travelling observations, in Selden's the use of rare ancient manuscripts and obscure parliamentary archives. These kinds of pursuits lent them the title of antiquary among contemporaries and later admirers, and thus created the confusion between the two different activities.

6. Vance 1984, 62–83.

7. Kendrick 1950; Levy 1967, 130–1, for Leland's contribution; Ferguson 1993, 84–105.

8. McKisack 1971, 26–49.

9. Wright 1958, 176–212; van Norden 1946 (doctoral thesis; copy on deposit at the Society of Antiquaries, London); van Norden 1949–50, 131–60; Schoeck 1954, 417–21.

10. See especially BL, Stowe MS, 1045; Hearne 1775. Hearne's own career has now been chronicled in Harmsen 2000.

11. Manning 1990, 277–88.

12. A rather lengthy review of the early usages of cognate terms, as provided by the *Oxford English Dictionary*, is necessary at this juncture. 'Antiquary' in English (deriving from the Latin noun *antiquarius*) appears to have been first used by Richard Grafton in 1563 to describe Leland. It became the preferred term to describe persons engaged in erudite study of the past and retained this status until the 18th century, though the more modern noun 'antiquarian' puts in an early appearance in Philemon Holland's English translation of *Britannia* (Camden 1610, 6), as Camden abdicates responsibility for passing a verdict on the historicity of Brutus the Trojan, referring the matter to 'the Senate of Antiquarians' (Holland's rendering of Camden's Latin *rem integram ad antiquitatis senatum refero*: Camden 1607, 4). By the mid-18th century, 'antiquarian' appears to have displaced 'antiquary' in lay usage – the word is used for two characters in Samuel Foote's 1772 comedy, *The Nabob* – but was still rejected by practitioners themselves. Daines Barrington would write to Thomas Pennant: 'As I conclude you mean to incorporate your additions into the 2nd Ed: of your Scotch tour, give me leave to observe a trifling mistake which one who means to become a member of the Society in Chancery Lane should not persist in; You speak of an Antiquarian as a substantive which should be Antiquary: Antiquarian is the adjective from Antiquarius' (Warks County Record Office, TP 168/2: Barrington to Pennant, 25 Apr 1772). I owe this last reference to the kindness of Professor Rosemary Sweet, who confirms that 'antiquary' continued to be preferred to 'antiquarian' as a noun in the correspondence of Richard Gough and his circle in the last third of the 18th century. The endurance of 'antiquary' into the 19th century is demonstrated by the title of Sir Walter Scott's 1816 novel, *The Antiquary*. The noun 'antiquary' was also more rarely applied to a person of great age. As an adjective, 'antiquarian' seems not to have appeared before the late 18th century. However, an early variant – 'antiquarious' – was added by William Warner (Warner 1606, 'To the Reader', sig. [a2r]), with reference to the 'pen' of John Stow, who had died a year earlier. Various other derivative terms appeared in the 18th century and after, such as 'antiquarianize' (a verb describing the act of 'playing the antiquary'), 'antiquarium' (a repository of antiquities) and 'antiquarian' (the name for a new size of paper, measuring 53 by 31 inches, produced for the Society's engravings by the papermaker James Whatman in 1773).

13. Rockett 2000, 475–99, esp 496.

14. Camden 1610, 1695 and 1789; Levy 1964; Piggott 1976, 33–53.

15. Woolf 2003, chs 3 and 4.

16. Warnicke 1973.

17. Lambarde 1576; Harrison 1577; Norden 1598; Erdeswicke 1717; Burton 1622; Carew 1602.
18. Stow 1598. Stow has had a great deal of recent attention: see especially Beer 1998, 127–46; Archer 1995; Collinson 2001.
19. Reyce 1902; Westcote 1845, xvi, 449; Habington 1895; Bedwell 1631; Gray 1649; Youings 1970; Greenslade 1982, 41, 49, 54; Broadway 1999, 17–18.
20. Sidney 1973, 105.
21. Momigliano 1966, 1977 and 1990; Phillips 1996. For a further development of this theme see Woolf 1990, esp ch 7.
22. Collinson 1998.
23. Bacon, *De augmentis scientiarum*, in Bacon 1858–61, IV, 300–4, and elsewhere.
24. Bacon 1858–61, III, 334; IV, 254, 301, 303–4; Marwil 1976.
25. The connection between antiquarianism and science after the Restoration has been made by a number of scholars, perhaps sometimes rather simplistically, as in Mendyk 1989. See especially Hunter 1995, 67–98. The extended title of Joshua Childrey's *Britannia Baconica, or, The natural rarities of England, Scotland & Wales: according as they are to be found in every shire: historically related according to the precepts of the Lord Bacon . . . with observations upon them and deductions from them* (Childrey 1660) signals an explicit connection between Camden's book and the methods proposed by Bacon.
26. 'Careful investigator of the royal records deposited nearby': Stanley 1876, 380.
27. Woolf 1984.
28. Woolf 1990, 115–25; Trevor-Roper 1985.
29. Sharpe 1982; Salmon 1997.
30. Camden 1607 ('Lectori', no signature or page) refers to himself as *ex infimo antiquariorum subsellio*; translated in Camden 1610, 'To the reader' (sig. 4v).
31. Thomas Nashe, *Pierce Penniless his Supplication to the Devil* (1592), in Nashe 1964, 43–4.
32. Donne 1953–62, I, no. 5, 246 (14 Dec 1617); Donne, *Epigrams*, in Donne 2001, 91.
33. Marmion, *The Antiquary*, Act II, in Marmion 1875; cf Puckle 1711, 10–11.
34. *The Spectator*, no. 361 (24 Apr 1712), in Bond 1965, III, 351.
35. Casaubon 1638, 97.
36. Earle 1633, essay no. 9 (not paginated, following sig. C5).
37. For this term see Woolf 2003, ch 7.
38. Gent 1699, *sub* 'Antiquary'.
39. Johnson 1977, 19–51; Vance 1984, 63.
40. Beer 1998, 6; Woolf 2003, 187–97, 246–55; Woolf 1997.
41. On Stow's career and especially the social biases that gave others much of the credit for some of his work, see Pearsall 2004.

42. Peacham 1634, ch 12 (antiquities; listed in the table of contents as 'statues and medals'), 104–5.
43. Houghton 1942 remains the classic study of virtuoso activities. See also Bann 1990, 100–21, 125; Bann 1994.
44. Findlen 1994, esp ch 7.
45. Brathwait 1614, 61, 80.
46. Peacham 1634, 104–24. Neither this nor the sixth chapter, on history, appears in the 1622 or 1627 editions of the book.
47. Peacham 1634, 109.
48. Caudill 1975, 279–86.
49. The literature on museums and collecting is prodigious. Especially relevant here are Impey and MacGregor 1985, especially chapters by MacGregor (pp 147–58), Hunt (pp 193–203) and Hunter (pp 159–68); Findlen 1989; Pomian 1990, 34–44; Muensterberger 1994, 183–203 (especially on the German 'Wunderkammer'); MacGregor 1983; Sharpe 1979, chs 1–3; Brears 1989, 213–24.
50. Chamberlain to Dudley Carleton, 19 Nov 1612, in Chamberlain 1939, I, 391–3. Veterano, the aged protagonist of Shakerley Marmion's *The Antiquary*, extols the virtues of such antiquities as 'the registers, the chronicles of the age they were made in', proclaiming that they 'speak the truth of history better than a hundred of your printed commentaries': Marmion, *The Antiquary*, Act II, in Marmion 1875, 228.
51. MacGregor 1989.
52. Donne 1930, 43–53; Browne 1964, III, 109–20. The contrast between Donne and Browne is especially well drawn in Preston 2005, 155–74, and I am grateful to Dr Preston for a discussion of this issue.
53. Selden 1631, epistle dedicatory. The contrast between European intellectuals of the age of Selden's contemporary, Peiresc, and those of the later 17th century, and the greater weight acquired by science in between, is well treated in Miller 2000, 148–51.
54. Whitaker 1996, 76.
55. See the longer discussion in Woolf 2003, 173–80, 204–12.
56. *The Virtuoso*, II. ii. 303 (p 43), III. iii. 26–7 (p 69) in Shadwell 1966. For the ambivalent relations of the newer scientific community to the virtuosi, see Hunter 1981a, 66–72.
57. Gay 1961, 171–2. Woodward is expressly mentioned in the appended 'A key to the new comedy, &c', 211–12.
58. *The Antiquary*, in Marmion 1875. Houghton 1942 suggests that Marmion's antiquary is in fact a virtuoso, though his chattels are predominantly *ancient* rarities, such as the 'urn that did contain the ashes of the emperors'. This is not mistaken, but it does suggest that the terminological confusion was then (at mid-century) at its most pronounced. By 1772, when Samuel Foote presented two stage antiquaries in his *The Nabob*, one finds still a mix of naturalist and antiquarian (Act III,

scene i: Taylor 1984, 103–6). The 'Antiquarian Society' meets to discuss items as variable as a chunk of lava from Mount Vesuvius, 'bones, beetles and butterflies', the lost books of Livy, a corkscrew given by Falstaff to Henry v, the toe of Cardinal Pandulpho's slipper used to kick King John ('an excellent antidote against the progress of Popery') and 'a curious collection . . . of all the tickets of Islington turnpike, from its first institution', which the second antiquarian urges be preserved 'as they may hereafter serve to illustrate that part of English history'. Archaeological activities are noticeably absent.

59. *The Tatler*, no. 216 (26 Aug 1710), in Bond 1987, iii, 133–5; cf Lady Gimcrack's fictitious letter to Bickerstaff in no. 221 (7 Sept 1710), in Bond 1987, iii, 153–5. On the other hand, Lewis Theobald's satire on 'useless antiquaries', *The Censor*, also included the mock will of Sir Tristram Littlewit, who had mathematical instruments and air pumps with his coins, medals and broken statues: Theobald 1717, 206–13.

60. Drake 1696, 102–4. For a mid-18th-century example of antiquarian satire, see Shell 1997, 223–45.

61. From Pope, *The Dunciad*, iv, Argument and line 350, in Pope 1966, 548, 568.

62. Thomas Sprat, the great apologist for the Royal Society, was critical of the virtuoso cabinets while advocating the Society's museum; a call for comprehensiveness comes out of the botanist Nehemiah Grew's 1681 catalogue of the Society's collections: Hunter 1985, 163–4.

63. Pomian 1990, 64.

64. Hunter 1975, 192.

65. Ovenell 1986, 90. The Ashmolean, like the British Museum in the following century, was an important institution for the merging of a number of now distinct activities, such as philology, antiquarianism, natural philosophy and natural history; the critical role of the Tradescant botanical collections, once in Ashmole's hands, ensured that an able scholar such as Lhuyd could continue to take an interest in topics as seemingly divergent as fossils and the Welsh language.

66. Stanley 1876, 271.

67. Stow told John Manningham that 'a model of his picture was found in the Recorder Fleetwoods study, with this inscription or circumscription: Johannes Stow, Antiquarius Angliae, which nowe is cutt in brasse and prefixed in print to his Survey of London' (Manningham 1976, 154). The portrait is sadly absent from most extant copies of the edition, but was reprinted in the *Gentleman's Magazine* in 1837; both it and the funeral monument are printed in Beer 1998, iv, 8. For discussion of his monument see Duncan-Jones 2004.

68. Grant 1996.

69. Unlisted in the original *Dictionary of National Biography*, this portrait, probably a copy of one in the National Portrait Gallery, is now mentioned in the new article on Dodderidge in the *Oxford Dictionary of National Biography: Online Edition* (Ibbetson 2004); the painting is attributed to an unknown artist of the 'British School' *c* 1612–28 in Scharf 1865, no. 79 (typescript addendum).

70. Aubrey 1949, 281.

71. Greenblatt 1980. For the economics of history books and their publication see Woolf 2000, 202–54.

72. Thompson 1886.

73. Ibid.

74. Camden 1691; Morgan 1661.

75. This geographical emphasis is true both of the 1676 *Prospect of the Most Famous Parts of the World* (the source of the illustration reproduced here as fig 7) as of the 1650 re-edition of *The Historie of Great Britaine*, though the biographical note by the publisher, George Humble, refers to Speed as the author of both histories and sacred genealogies.

76. There is also an oil portrait of Burton in the Society of Antiquaries: Scharf 1865, no. 42.

77. Aubrey 1949, 272.

78. Selden 1658.

79. Woolf 2003, 135–7. The oil painting of Dugdale later in life (*c* 1675), by Peter Borsselaer, contains books but no heraldry at all, nor his heraldic chains of office: Evans 1956, pl iii, facing p 17.

80. Hunter 2004.

81. Leigh 1700, 1.

82. Sibbald 1684. The strength of the trend before 1700 should not be overstated. A number of Restoration works continued to feature genealogical and heraldic materials; for instance Leycester 1673. In some, such as Izacke 1677, on the city of Exeter, coats of arms predominate; in others, such as Wright 1684, on Rutland, there is extensive heraldic material, with arms accompanied by pedigrees, but also pictures of other objects, such as buildings.

83. See full description in Scharf 1865, no. 51, 42; the picture is reprinted in Evans 1956, pl iv, facing p 32. The MS has been tentatively identified as Wanley's own copy of the *Book of Specimens* (which includes his facsimile of the Covel Gospel), now Longleat MS 345: I owe this information to Bernard Nurse. Wanley commented in the catalogue of Harleian manuscripts, of BL, Harleian MS 1437, art 8 (a copy of the Jacobean antiquary William Blundell's illustration of Anglo-Saxon coins arranged as a cross), that its author showed 'more superstition than learning', but he may have distinguished between medieval arrangements and post-Reformation imitations.

84. For a lengthier discussion of the decline of genealogical and heraldic interests, see Woolf 2003, 73–137.

85. On the Society in the 18th century see Evans 1956, a rather celebratory and often uncritical account; a more

rounded and contextual view is offered by Sweet 2004, and elsewhere in the present volume.

86. On Selden's redefinition of history to comprehend antiquarian topics, see Woolf 1990, 214–35.
87. Wright 1684; Taylor 1730; Chauncy 1700; Atkyns 1712.
88. Lhuyd 1707, Title VIII, 266–89. Lhuyd's work was the Celtic counterpart to George Hickes's massive *Linguarum veterum septentrionalium thesaurus* of 1703-5, the crowning work of 17th-century Anglo-Saxon scholarship, which comprehended related languages such as Icelandic. An heir to the mid-century philological revival spearheaded by Oxford's Bishop John Fell, Hickes had a knowledge of antiquarian sources for Germanic languages, such as runes; he did not, however, share Lhuyd's interests in natural history: Douglas 1951, 86–97; Harris 1992.

89. Piggott 1976, 1–24. Piggott found reinforcement for his views in the argument of Douglas 1951, 272–84, that rigorous antiquarian and philological-historical scholarship, after peaking in the Restoration and early 18th century with the works of Hearne, Thomas Madox, Thomas Rymer, Hickes, Wanley, Henry Wharton and others, similarly declined into mediocrity for nearly a century. Piggott's own views, especially on Stukeley, have been subject to revision: Ucko *et al* 1991, 54; Haycock 2002, 7–9.
90. I have left aside the repudiation of the early Stuart chorographers' use of oral tradition as a source, another key methodological change that I have addressed at length in other places, eg Woolf 2003, ch 10.

BIBLIOGRAPHY

Archer, I 1995. 'The nostalgia of John Stow', in Smith, Strier and Bevington (eds) 1995, 17–34
Atkyns, R 1712. *The Ancient and Present State of Glostershire* (reprinted 1974), Wakefield
Aubrey, J 1949. *Brief Lives* (ed O L Dick), London
Bacon, F 1858-61. *Works* (eds J Spedding, R L Ellis and D D Heath), 7 vols, London
Bann, S 1990. *The Inventions of History: essays on the representation of the past*, Manchester and New York
Bann, S 1994. *Under the Sign: John Bargrave as collector, traveller, and witness*, Ann Arbor, Mich
Bedwell, W 1631. *A Brief Description of the Towne of Tottenham High-Crosse*, London
Beer, B L 1998. *Tudor England Observed: the world of John Stow*, Stroud
Bond, D F (ed) 1965. *The Spectator*, 5 vols, Oxford
Bond, D F (ed) 1987. *The Tatler*, 3 vols, Oxford
Brathwait, R 1614. *The Schollers Medley*, London
Brears, P C D 1989. 'Ralph Thoresby: a museum visitor in Stuart England', *J Hist Collect*, **2**, 213–24
Broadway, J 1999. *William Dugdale and the Significance of County History in Early Stuart England*, Dugdale Soc Occas Pap 39, Oxford
Browne, T 1964. 'Musaeum Clausum', in *Miscellany Tracts: the works of Sir Thomas Browne* (ed G Keynes), 4 vols, 2nd edn, London
Burton, W 1622. *The Description of Leicester Shire. Containing matters of antiquitye, historye, armorye, and genealogy*, London
Camden, W 1607. *Britannia*, London
Camden, W 1610. *Britain* (trans P Holland), London
Camden, W 1691. *V. Cl. Gulielmi Camdeni et illustrium virorum ad G. Camdenum epistolae* (ed T Smith), London

Camden, W 1695. *Camden's Britannia* (ed E Gibson), London
Camden, W 1789. *Britannia* (ed R Gough), 3 vols, London
Carew, R 1602. *The Survey of Cornwall*, London
Casaubon, M 1638. *A Treatise of Use and Custome*, London
Caudill, R W 1975. 'Some literary evidence of the development of English virtuoso activities in the seventeenth century', unpublished DPhil thesis, University of Oxford
Chamberlain, J 1939. *The Letters of John Chamberlain* (ed N E McClure), 2 vols, Philadelphia, Penn
Chauncy, H 1700. *The Historical Antiquities of Hertfordshire*, London
Childrey, J 1660. *Britannia Baconica, or, The natural rarities of England, Scotland and Wales: according as they are to be found in every shire: historically related according to the precepts of the Lord Bacon . . . with observations upon them and deductions from them*, London
Collinson, P 1998. 'One of us? William Camden and the making of history', *Trans Roy Hist Soc*, 6th ser, **8**, 139–63
Collinson, P 2001. 'John Stow and nostalgic antiquarianism', in Merritt (ed) 2001, 27–51
Donne, J 1930. *The Courtier's Library, or Catalogus librorum aulicorum incomparabilium et non vendibilium* (ed E M Simpson), London
Donne, J 1953–62. *John Donne* (eds G R Potter and E Simpson), 10 vols, Berkeley and Los Angeles
Donne, J 2001. *The Complete Poetry and Selected Prose of John Donne* (ed C M Coffin), New York
Douglas, D C 1951. *English Scholars, 1660-1730*, 2nd rev edn, London

Drake, J 1696. *An Essay in Defence of the Female Sex*, London

Duncan-Jones, K 2004. 'Afterword: Stow's Remains', in Gadd and Gillespie (eds) 2004, 157–63

Earle, J 1633. *Micro-cosmographie*, 6th edn, London

Erdeswicke, S 1717. *A Survey of Staffordshire*, London

Evans, J 1956. *A History of the Society of Antiquaries*, Oxford

Ferguson, A B 1993. *Utter Antiquity: perceptions of prehistory in Renaissance England*, Durham, NC, and London

Findlen, P 1989. 'The museum: its classical etymology and Renaissance genealogy', *J Hist Collect*, 1, 59–78

Findlen, P 1994. *Possessing Nature: museums, collecting, and scientific culture in early modern Italy*, Berkeley, Calif

Fox, L (ed) 1956. *English Historical Scholarship in the Sixteenth and Seventeenth Centuries*, London and New York

Gadd, I and Gillespie, A (eds) 2004. *John Stow (1525–1605) and the Making of the English Past*, London

Gay, J 1961. *Three Hours After Marriage* (ed J H Smith), Augustan Reprint Soc Pub 91–92, Los Angeles

Gent, B E 1699. A *New Dictionary of the Terms, Ancient and Modern, of the Canting Crew*, London

Grafton, A 1983. *Joseph Scaliger: a study in the history of classical scholarship. I: textual criticism and exegesis*, Oxford

Grafton, A 1993. *Joseph Scaliger: a study in the history of classical scholarship. II: historical chronology*, Oxford

Grant, R J S 1996. *Laurence Nowell, William Lambarde, and the Laws of the Anglo-Saxon*, Amsterdam and Atlanta, Ga

Gray, W 1649. *Chorographia, or, A survey of Newcastle upon Tine*, Newcastle

Greenblatt, S 1980. *Renaissance Self-Fashioning: from More to Shakespeare*, Chicago, Ill

Greenslade, M W 1982. *The Staffordshire Historians*, Stafford

Habington, T 1895. *A Survey of Worcestershire* (ed J Amphlett), 2 vols, Worcester

Harmsen, T 2000. *Antiquarianism in the Augustan Age: Thomas Hearne 1678–1735*, Berne

Harris, R L (ed) 1992. *A Chorus of Grammars: the correspondence of George Hickes and his collaborators on the Thesaurus linguarum septentrionalium*, Toronto

Harrison, W 1577. 'The description of Britaine', in Holinshed (ed) 1577, fols 1r–124v

Haycock, D B 2002. *William Stukeley: science, religion and archaeology in eighteenth-century England*, Woodbridge

Hearne, T (ed) 1775. *A Collection of Curious Discourses*, 2 vols, London

Hickes, G, Jónsson, R and Bernard, E 1703–5. *Linguarum vett. septentrionalium thesaurus grammatico-criticus et archæologicus*, 2 vols, Oxford

Holinshed, R (ed) 1577. *The Chronicles of England, Scotland and Ireland*, London

Houghton, W E Jr 1942. 'The English virtuoso in the seventeenth century', *J Hist Ideas*, 3, 51–73, 190–219

Hunt, A, Mandelbrote, G and Shell, A (eds) 1997. *The Book Trade and its Customers 1450–1900: historical essays for Robin Myers*, New Castle, Del, and Winchester

Hunt, J D 1985. 'Curiosities to adorn cabinets and gardens', in Impey and MacGregor (eds) 1985, 193–203

Hunter, M 1975. *John Aubrey and the Realm of Learning*, London and New York

Hunter, M 1981a. *Science and Society in Restoration England*, Cambridge and New York

Hunter, M 1981b. 'The preconditions of preservation: a historical perspective', in Lowenthal and Binney 1981, 22–32

Hunter, M 1985. 'The cabinet institutionalized: the Royal Society's "Repository" and its background', in Impey and MacGregor (eds) 1985, 159–68

Hunter, M 1995. *Science and the Shape of Orthodoxy: intellectual change in late seventeenth-century Britain*, Woodbridge and Rochester, NY

Hunter, M 2004. 'Ashmole, Elias (1617–1692)', in *Oxford Dictionary of National Biography: Online Edition* (eds H C G Matthew and B Harrison), <http://www.oxforddnb.com./view/article/764> (24 June 2006)

Ibbetson, D 2004. 'Dodderidge [Doddridge], Sir John (1555–1628)', in *Oxford Dictionary of National Biography: Online Edition* (eds H C G Matthew and B Harrison), <http://www.oxforddnb.com./view/article/7745> (24 June 2006)

Impey, O and MacGregor, A (eds) 1985. *The Origins of Museums: the cabinet of curiosities in sixteenth- and seventeenth-century Europe*, Oxford

Izacke, R 1677. *Antiquities of the City of Exeter*, London

Jardine, N, Secord, J A and Spary, E C (eds) 1996. *Cultures of Natural History*, Cambridge

Johnson, S 1977. *The Yale Edition of the Works of Samuel Johnson* (ed D J Greene), 14 vols, New Haven, Conn, and London

Josten, C H (ed) 1967. *Elias Ashmole (1617–1692): his autobiographical and historical notes, his correspondence, and other contemporary sources relating to his life and work*, 5 vols, Oxford

Kelley, D R 1970. *Foundations of Modern Historical Scholarship: language, law and history in the French Renaissance*, New York

Kelley, D R and Sacks, D H (eds) 1997. *The Historical Imagination in Early Modern Britain*, Cambridge

Kendrick, T D 1950. *British Antiquity*, London

Lambarde, W 1576. *A Perambulation of Kent*, London

Leigh, C 1700. *Naturall History of Lancashire, Cheshire, and the Peak, in Derbyshire*, Oxford

Levine, J M 1987. *Humanism and History: origins of modern English historiography*, Ithaca, NY

Levine, P 1986. *The Amateur and the Professional: antiquarians, historians and archaeologists in Victorian England, 1838-1886*, Cambridge

Levy, F J 1964. 'The making of Camden's *Britannia*', *Bibliothèque d'humanisme et renaissance*, **26**, 608-17

Levy, F J 1967. *Tudor Historical Thought*, San Marino, Calif

Leycester, P 1673. *Historical antiquities, in two books the first treating in general of Great-Brettain and Ireland: the second containing particular remarks concerning Cheshire faithfully collected out of authentick histories, old deeds, records, and evidences*, London

Lhuyd, E 1707. *Archaeologia Britannica, giving some account additional to what has hitherto been publish'd, of the languages, histories, and customs of the original inhabitants of Great Britain: from collections and observations in travels through Wales, Cornwal, Bas-Bretagne, Ireland and Scotland. Vol. I, Glossography*, Oxford

Lowenthal, D and Binney, M (eds) 1981. *Our Past Before Us: why do we save it?*, London

MacGregor, A 1983. 'Collectors and collections of rarities', in *Tradescant's Rarities: essays on the foundation of the Ashmolean Museum* (ed A MacGregor), 70-97, Oxford

MacGregor, A 1985. 'The cabinet of curiosities in seventeenth-century Britain', in Impey and MacGregor (eds) 1985, 147-58

MacGregor, A (ed) 1989. *The Late King's Goods: collections, possessions and patronage of Charles I in the light of the Commonwealth sale inventories*, London

Manning, R B 1990. 'Antiquarianism and the seigneurial reaction: Sir Robert and Sir Thomas Cotton and their tenants', *Hist Res*, **58**, 277-88

Manningham, J 1976. *The Diary of John Manningham of the Middle Temple 1602-1603* (ed R P Sorlien), Hanover, NH

Marmion, S 1875. *The Dramatic Works of Shakerley Marmion* (eds J Maidment and W H Logan), Edinburgh and London

Marwil, J 1976. *The Trials of Counsel: Francis Bacon in 1621*, Detroit, Mich

McKisack, M 1971. *Medieval History in the Tudor Age*, Oxford

Mendyk, S A E 1989. *"Speculum Britanniae": regional study, antiquarianism and science in Britain to 1700*, Toronto

Merritt, J F (ed) 2001. *Imagining Early Modern London: perceptions and portrayals of the city from Stow to Strype, 1598-1720*, Cambridge

Miller, P 2000. *Peiresc's Europe: learning and virtue in the seventeenth century*, New Haven, Conn

Momigliano, A D 1966. *Studies in Historiography*, New York

Momigliano, A D 1977. *Essays in Ancient and Modern Historiography*, Middletown, Conn

Momigliano, A D 1990. *The Classical Foundations of Modern Historiography*, Berkeley, Calif

Morgan, S 1661. *The Sphere of Gentry*, London

Muensterberger, W 1994. *Collecting, An Unruly Passion: psychological perspectives*, Princeton, NJ

Nashe, T 1964. *Selected Writings* (ed S Wells), Cambridge, Mass

Norden, J 1598. *Speculi Britan[n]iae pars: the description of Hartfordshire*, London

Nuttall, A D 2003. *Dead from the Waist Down: scholars and scholarship in literature and the popular imagination*, London and New Haven, Conn

Ovenell, R 1986. *The Ashmolean Museum 1683-1894*, Oxford

Parry, G 1995. *The Trophies of Time: English antiquarians of the seventeenth century*, Oxford

Peacham, H 1634. *The Compleat Gentleman*, rev edn, London

Pearsall, D 2004. 'John Stow and Thomas Speght as editors of Chaucer: a question of class', in Gadd and Gillespie (eds) 2004, 119-25

Phillips, M S 1996. 'Reconsiderations on history and antiquarianism: Arnaldo Momigliano and the historiography of eighteenth-century Britain', *J Hist Ideas*, **58**, 297-316

Piggott, S 1976. *Ruins in a Landscape: essays in antiquarianism*, Edinburgh

Pomian, K 1990. *Collectors and Curiosities: Paris and Venice, 1500-1800* (trans E Wiles-Portier), Cambridge

Pope, A 1966. *Poetical Works* (ed H Davis), London

Preston, C 2005. *Thomas Browne and the Writing of Early Modern Science*, Cambridge

Prince, H 1981. 'Revival, restoration, preservation: changing views about antique landscape features', in Lowenthal and Binney (eds) 1981, 33-49

Puckle, J 1711. *The Club: or a dialogue between father and son*, London

Reyce, R 1902. *Suffolk in the XVIIth Century: the Breviary of Suffolk* (ed F Hervey), London

Rockett, W 2000. '*Britannia*, Ralph Brooke, and the representation of privilege in Elizabethan England', *Renaissance Quarterly*, **53**, 475-99

Salmon, J H M 1997. 'Precept, example, and truth: Degory Wheare and the *ars historica*', in Kelley and Sacks (eds) 1997, 11-36

Scharf, G 1865. *A Catalogue of the Pictures Belonging to the Society of Antiquaries, Somerset House, London*, London

Schoeck, R J 1954. 'The Elizabethan Society of Antiquaries and men of law', *Notes Queries*, new ser, **1**, 417-21

Selden, J 1631. *Titles of Honor*, 2nd edn, London

Selden, J (ed) 1658. *Contextio gemmarum, sive, Eutychii patriarchae Alexandrini annales*, Oxford

Selden, J 1672. *Titles of Honor*, 3rd edn, London

Shadwell, T 1966. *The Virtuoso* (eds M H Nicolson and D S Rodes), Lincoln, Nebr

Sharpe, K 1979. *Sir Robert Cotton 1586–1631*, Oxford

Sharpe, K 1982. 'The foundation of the chairs of history at Oxford and Cambridge: an episode in Jacobean politics', *Hist Universities*, **2**, 127–52

Shell, A 1997. 'The antiquarian satirized: John Clubbe and the antiquities of Wheatfield', in Hunt, Mandelbrote and Shell (eds) 1997, 223–45

Sibbald, R 1684. *Scotland illustrated, or, An essay of natural history in which are exquisitely displayed the nature of the country . . . and the manifold productions of nature in its three-fold kingdom*, Edinburgh

Sidney, P 1973. *An Apology for Poetry* (ed G Shepherd), 2nd edn, Manchester

Smith, D L, Strier, R and Bevington, D (eds) 1995. *The Theatrical City: culture, theatre and politics in London, 1576–1649*, Cambridge

Stanley, A P 1876. *Historical Memorials of Westminster Abbey* (reprinted 1924), London

Stow, J 1598. *The Survey of London*, London

Sweet, R 2004. *Antiquaries: the discovery of the past in eighteenth-century Britain*, London and New York

Taylor, G (ed) 1984. *Plays by Samuel Foote and Arthur Murphy*, Cambridge

Taylor, S 1730. *The History and Antiquities of Harwich and Dovercourt, Topographical, Dynastical and Political* (ed S Dale), London

Theobald, L 1717. *The Censor*, London

Thompson, E M 1886. 'Camden, William (1551–1623)', in *Dictionary of National Biography* (eds L Stephen and S Lee), VIII, 277, London

Trevor-Roper, H R 1985. 'Queen Elizabeth's first historian: William Camden and the beginnings of English "civil" history', in *Renaissance Essays* (H R Trevor-Roper), 121–48, London and Chicago, Ill

Ucko, P J, Hunter, M, Clark, A J and David, A 1991. *Avebury Reconsidered: from the 1690s to the 1990s*, London

Vance, J A 1984. *Samuel Johnson and the Sense of History*, Athens, Ga

van Norden, L 1946. 'The Elizabethan College of Antiquaries', unpublished PhD thesis, University of California at Los Angeles

van Norden, L 1949–50. 'Sir Henry Spelman on the chronology of the Elizabethan College of Antiquaries', *Huntington Library Quarterly*, **13**, 131–60

Warner, W 1606. *A Continuance of Albion's England*, London

Warnicke, R M 1973. *William Lambarde, Elizabethan Antiquary, 1536–1601*, Chichester

Westcote, T 1845. *A View of Devonshire in 1630*, Exeter

Whitaker, K 1996. 'The culture of curiosity', in Jardine, Secord and Spary (eds) 1996, 75–90

Woolf, D R 1984. 'John Selden, John Borough, and Francis Bacon's *History of King Henry the Seventh*, 1621', *Huntington Library Quarterly*, **47**, 47–53

Woolf, D R 1990. *The Idea of History in Early Stuart England: erudition, ideology and the 'Light of Truth' from the accession of James I to the Civil War*, Toronto

Woolf, D R 1997. 'Little Crosby and the horizons of early modern historical culture', in Kelley and Sacks (eds) 1997, 93–132

Woolf, D R 2000. *Reading History in Early Modern England*, Cambridge

Woolf, D R 2003. *The Social Circulation of the Past: English historical culture 1500–1730*, Oxford

Wormald, F and Wright, C E (eds) 1958. *The English Library before 1700*, London

Wright, C E 1958. 'The Elizabethan Society of Antiquaries and the formation of the Cottonian Library', in Wormald and Wright (eds) 1958, 176–212

Wright, J 1684. *The History and Antiquities of the County of Rutland*, London

Youings, J A 1970. 'Devon's first local historians', *Devon Hist*, **1**, 5–8

Friday, 5. December. 1707.

Mr Talman, Mr Bagford, & Mr Wanley, met together, and agreed to Meet together each Friday in the evening by six of the clock upon pain of forfeiture of six pence.

Agreed that we will meet each Friday night at the Bear Tavern in the Strand till we shall Order otherwise.

~~Agreed that the Hour of Meeting shall be at five of the Clock in the Evening~~ Friday 12. December, 1707.

Agreed that the Business of this Society shall be limited to the Subject of Antiquities; and more particularly, to such things as may Illustrate or Relate to the History of Great Britain.

Agreed that by the Subject of Antiquities, and History of Great Britain, we understand such things only as shall precede the Raign of James the first King of England. Provided, that upon any now Discovery of Antient Coins, books, Sepulchres or other Remains of Antient Workmanship, which may be communicated to us, we reserve to our selves the Liberty of Conferring upon them.

Agreed that the Forfeiture of six pence upon failure of any Members meeting each Friday in the Evening by six of the Clock, shall hold no longer than till our Number be Advanced to more than Ten; unless the Society shall then think fit to continue that Order.

Agreed that the Business of this Society shall be Adjourned, or Broken off by Ten of the Clock at the furthest.

Agreed that while we meet at a Tavern, no person shall be oblig'd to pay for more than he shall Call for.

Wanley proposed Peter le Neve Esq for a Member of this Society.

CHAPTER THREE

FORMING AN IDENTITY: THE EARLY SOCIETY AND ITS CONTEXT, 1707–51

Arthur MacGregor

Notwithstanding the lapse of half a century since the publication of Dame Joan Evans's *History of the Society of Antiquaries* (1956), it remains difficult to improve on her account of the foundation and early progress of the Society. Only negligible evidence has surfaced in the meantime to cause a significantly different light to be thrown on the course of events which she documents, and merely to reiterate her narrative in summary form would scarcely do justice to this celebratory volume. Instead, the opportunity is taken here to situate the emergence of the Antiquaries against the broader background of social (or rather societal) progress in the first half of the eighteenth century, a period that saw a great burgeoning of clubs and associations embracing all manner of interests. The early Society of Antiquaries takes its place among a myriad of comparable bodies and – although undoubtedly one of the more successful – it will be seen to have shared a great many characteristics (and indeed a considerable part of its membership) with these sibling associations. In numerous ways, therefore, our understanding of the influences that shaped the genesis and early development of the Antiquaries is enhanced by reference to the experiences of these comparable bodies.

The benign social climate that proved so conducive to these developments entered its ameliorating phase at the time of the Restoration and gathered pace considerably after the Glorious Revolution of 1688. A distinct loosening of the grip of the monarchy and of government censorship of many aspects of everyday life – combined with the corresponding advances made by an increasingly independent landowning gentry and with the emergence of a vigorous professional class of physicians, lawyers and others – proved highly favourable to the development of new patterns of association in which clubs and societies came to provide important points of social intersection.[1] London led the way in this movement, but almost every provincial town participated in it and, by means of affiliation, widespread and mutually beneficial networks of like-minded members criss-crossed the country. Their respective interests were manifold: masonic lodges, economic associations, professional and trade organizations all throve in this favourable social environment; other groupings espoused common religious sentiments, national or ethnic affiliations, philosophical persuasions, musical or literary tastes and scientific interests. Although not exclusively a British

Fig 16. The earliest surviving minutes of the Society, 5 and 12 December 1707, in the hand of Humphrey Wanley (BL, Harleian MS 7055, fol 1). *Photograph*: reproduced by permission of the British Library.

phenomenon, the movement took root in Britain so successfully as to have been regarded almost as a national trait,[2] and by 1720 John Macky was to characterize London as having 'an Infinity of CLUBS, or SOCIETIES, for the Improvement of Learning and keeping up of good Humour and Mirth'.[3]

Conviviality provided a great deal of the cement that bound these institutions, and it was indeed a central factor in their successful establishment that meetings commonly took place in taverns and coffee-houses – institutions which themselves underwent a parallel phase of vigorous development at this time. The Temple Coffee House, for example, had given its name by the turn of the century to a botanical club (never formally constituted) that included many of the foremost natural historians of the day in its loose association.[4] Enterprising publicans went out of their way to cater for the lucrative trade that began to flow from meetings of this sort, setting aside appropriate accommodation – ranging from a reserved table to private rooms for societies that contracted regular agreements. It is in this milieu, in the taverns that clustered in the Fleet Street area and in the company of numerous comparable clubs and associations, that the Society of Antiquaries began to take shape from the early years of the eighteenth century.

THE SOCIETY OF 1707 AND THE SOCIETY OF 1717

While at least one oblique reference has been found to indicate that informal gatherings of certain gentlemen with a shared taste for antiquarian studies were convened in a London tavern from the opening years of the eighteenth century,[5] the anniversary marked by the present volume is that of a meeting that took place on 5 December 1707 at which three friends foregathered (evidently not for the first time) and committed to paper a succinct record of their encounter (fig 16):

> Mr Talman, Mr Bagford, & Mr Wanley, met together, and Agreed to Meet together each Friday in the evening by six of the clock upon pain of forfeiture of six pence.

> Agreed that we will meet each Friday night at [ye Young Devill Taverne, *deleted*] the Bear Tavern in the Strand till we shall Order otherwise.[6]

A further agreement that the meetings would take place at 5pm, also deleted, concludes the record of the evening, but a week later the members reassembled, solemnly undertaking to meet regularly thereafter from 6pm to 10pm at the latest and setting out their corporate aims:

> Agreed that the Business of this Society shall be limited to the subject of Antiquities; and more particularly, to such things as may Illustrate & Relate to the History of Great Britain.

> Agreed that by the Subject of Antiquities, and History of Great Britain, we understand such things only as shall precede the Raign of James the first King

46

of England. Provided, that upon any new Discovery of Antient Coins, books, Sepulchres or other Remains of Antient Workmanship, which may be communicated to us, we reserve ourselves the Liberty of Conferring upon them.[7]

Thereafter, with a break for Christmas, the records continue until 20 February, by which time the number of actual or prospective members had risen to twelve, various communications on antiquarian matters had been received and the venue had reverted to the Young Devil in Fleet Street. In Joan Evans's words: 'The manuscript ends there; and in it is all the earliest history of our Society . . . from the first scratchy notes written with a bad pen on a tavern table to relatively orderly and tidy minutes.'[8]

In spite of this premature collapse, the potential for the development of such a body had evidently been firmly grasped, as is made plain by a draft petition seemingly prepared by Humfrey Wanley at this time in the name of his influential employer, Robert Harley, first Earl of Oxford, in which a royal charter was to be sought by the earl from the sovereign, Queen Anne, on behalf of the nascent Society.[9] The future envisaged in this text looked promising indeed: the Society would meet at the palace of Whitehall[10] 'in a Convenient Apartment, with Room for a Library & Repository' – a description taken to refer to the Harleian Library itself – with the queen and Prince George as its royal sponsors. 'Eminent Persons' were to be recruited to its cause, in order to form 'a Society of nobles and Gentlemen meeting in Order to Improve and Cultivate the History and Antiquities of Great Britain; wherein many most excellent Monuments are still to be found, which for want of due Care, go more and more to decay and ruin'. Due acknowledgement is made of the successes already achieved by continental scholars in documenting remains of the past, but Wanley goes on to observe that 'the History of a man's own Country is (or should be) dearer to him than that of Foreign Regions' and that while 'most of the Great Cities and Churches of Italy, Spain, France & Germany have been described in Print . . . the English, tho' they have not been wholly Silent on these Subjects, have yet . . . publish'd less to the World than other Nations'. Since the task of remedying this situation must, says Wanley, 'be a Work of great Charge & Constant Application, and far too great for one purse, 'tis to be wish'd that a Society of Antiquaries might be sett up, from whose united endeavours, the World might receive compleat volumes Relating to Our Native Countrey, to Our Kings, Our Church, & Our People, with others of a Miscellaneous nature'. Extensive lists follow of the principal tasks that the Society would undertake in each of these areas, its far-reaching cultural concerns underscored by the last of these, the compiling of 'A Dictionary for the Fixing the English Language, as the French & Italians have done'.

In France and Italy, of course, great projects such as these were properly seen as the province of formally constituted academies, commonly under royal patronage, and it is a striking contrast in national practice that in Britain they were to be shouldered by purely voluntary societies. Even the Royal Society, despite finding early favour with the monarchy, received only modest and irregular financial support for such important projects as the establishment of longitude and nothing at all for its day-to-day expenses. Certainly the granting of a royal charter – an ambition that would preoccupy the Antiquaries for the next four decades and more – carried no commitment to, nor any expectation of, royal subvention.

The Society envisaged in the draft document, it was suggested, 'would Bring to Light and Preserve All old Monumental Inscriptions, & other pieces of Antiquite yet remaining'; the history of architecture, the fine arts and music would be investigated, 'and the Antient Methods being retrieved, perhaps many things may be used afresh to good Purpose'; also many obscurities in ancient geography would be illuminated. In order to achieve these ends it would be necessary 'to maintain a Correspondence with the Learned & curious men in each County and with the most eminent Persons abroad'. Furthermore, 'fitt Persons' would be sent out 'to Inspect the Books, Writings, and other Rarities, which the Owners will be loth to send up to Town'; they would 'take the Prospects' of ancient remains, would make drawings of monuments, stained glass, etc, and collect 'Relations of Persons of known Worth & Veracity'; if need be, they would 'buy up the most curious & useful pieces of Antiquity, of all Kinds, at the Charge of the Society'.

While this extraordinarily ambitious document reveals the currency of a remarkably comprehensive agenda with which the early eighteenth-century antiquary thought it his business to engage, the concept of an incorporated society under royal protection was to remain for the moment no more than an ideal, since plans for the charter suffered the same eclipse as the embryonic Society itself. The reasons for the abrupt interruption of the promising new body's progress had nothing to do with any slackening of antiquarian interest but can be attributed specifically to a catastrophic downturn in the fortunes of Wanley's patron, Lord Harley, whose enforced resignation from government was accepted by Queen Anne on 11 February 1708;[11] the ensuing calamity in the Harley camp no doubt accounted for the lack of a meeting of the Antiquaries two days later and, it seems, for the suspension of proceedings the following week. As the earl's librarian, Wanley, was himself in danger of being tainted by the air of treason that hung over his master, and with Talman a practising (if covert) Catholic, the little group would have been in real danger of appearing potentially seditious: a period of discreet and less regular association was clearly a wise course of action.

That the intervening years leading to the formal refounding of the Society were by no means fallow in terms of academic interest is made plain in a later recollection by Maurice Johnson, whose account of this period shows a measure of continuation of former practice. From 1709–10 onwards, he says, he met frequently 'at the Temple 'Change, and other coffee houses and Taverns about the Temple' with a considerable group of like-minded gentlemen whose interests made him 'very willingly wait on such of them, and other noblemen and gentlemen of other professions curious in their researches of antiquity, as then were used to meet and discourse on such subjects'.[12] So successful were these meetings that ambitions again arose for the establishment of a formally structured association. A degree of uncertainty surrounds the point at which matters coalesced. Stukeley has an entry (perhaps retrospective) in his own copy of the minutes, headed 'Founders of the Antiquarian Society London. July 1717',[13] but his own manuscript, 'Memoirs towards an History of the Antiquarian Society of London 1752', gives a slightly variant account:

> In 1717, or somewhat earlier, a number of gentlemen residing in and about London . . . used to meet on a Wednesday evening at the Miter tavern in Fleetstreet. Their conversation turned on matters of learning, chiefly antiqui-tys . . . In the end of the year, the ardor, which had kindled in the breast of [the Elizabethan antiquaries] reviv'd among us: and on the 1st day of the succeeding year we form'd ourselves again into one body under the style and title of the Society of Antiquarys, London.[14]

Twenty-three founding members are recorded,[15] from which number Peter le Neve[16] was elected as President, with Samuel Gale[17] as Treasurer, Stukeley[18] as Secretary and Talman[19] as Director.

THE EARLY SOCIETY AND CONTEMPORARY INSTITUTIONS

With the refounded Society formally launched, its defining characteristics may be reviewed with some reference to the similar bodies which, as already stated, were springing up in large numbers at this period: by the mid-century, close on a thousand such clubs and societies are estimated to have been established in the metropolis alone.[20] So numerous were they, indeed, that many perished after only a brief flowering: even in the uncertainty of their beginnings the Antiquaries were entirely typical of their era.

The stress laid by Wanley on the polite character of the intended Society, with its cultivated nobles and gentlemen working in unison to generate antiquarian enlight-enment, reflects with some degree of accuracy the composition that was ultimately to emerge, although he greatly overestimated the contribution that would be made by the nobility while underplaying the importance of the solid core of professional men who would dominate the membership, as well as the place that would be found for those with more talent and skill than social standing.[21] Following the loss of Lord Harley to their cause by the original company (a misfortune of the highest order), members of the refounded Society of 1717 were acutely conscious of the desirability of attracting influential members to bolster their cause; within weeks of their first meeting, it was 'proposed that such Noblemen and Persons of Quality as please to be Members of the Society may be admitted by Ballot'.[22] The aristocracy were never numerous, however: Henry Hare, who had been a member of the short-lived Society of 1707 and became a staunch supporter of its successor (and a Vice-President from 1727), succeeded as Baron Coleraine in 1708; Lord Hertford (later third Duke of Somerset) was President from 1724 and Lord Winchelsea a Vice-President from the same period, while the second Duke of Montagu and the third Earl of Burlington were elected ordinary members. At Somerset's death in 1750 he was succeeded as President by the Duke of Richmond, but Richmond survived barely a year and it was under a commoner, Martin Folkes, that the Society finally achieved its royal charter.[23]

Of the triumvirate of prime movers in 1707, John Talman was comfortably off as the son of a successful architect,[24] but Humfrey Wanley, youngest son of a Coventry draper, had never enjoyed easy financial circumstances despite his precocious rise to become a highly respected scholar of palaeography and early English.[25] John Bagford, having been brought up a shoemaker, had through his own wits acquired so intimate a knowledge of books, prints and literary curiosities that he was able to establish himself as a full-time bookseller, but his knowledge was never translated into commercial success.[26]

There would be others whose obsessions made them all too careless of worldly matters and who fell victim to the lure of antiquity. Most memorable among them was Browne Willis, born comfortably off, well educated and elected to Parliament before dedicating his life to antiquarian study. He published energetically, but somewhat at the expense of his personal fortune; so intently focused was he on his researches that he paid scant heed to himself and was said to have taken on 'more the appearance of a mumping beggar than a gentleman . . . dressed in an old slouched hat . . . a weather-beaten large wig, three or four old-fashioned coats, all tied round by a leather belt, and over all an old blue cloak, lined with black fustian'.[27] The early Antiquaries formed a church sufficiently broad that it could accommodate such vagaries (always provided members could pay their dues). To judge from the assessment of an observer from the later eighteenth century, who drew a contrast between the 'smooth faces and dainty thin shoes' that characterized the fashionable Society of his day and the 'old square toes' of earlier years, the assembled company of the first generations of Antiquaries would have differed little in character from those of living memory – a sprinkling of good-quality tweeds, business wear much in evidence, a couple of dog-collars, a dandy or two and the odd unkempt eccentric.

Not surprisingly for such a characteristic cross-section of society of the middling class, many of the ambitions espoused by the early members formed part of the common currency of other such societies, and their widely shared rhetoric would have been a natural consequence of the fact that many Antiquaries held plural memberships of a number of associations espousing broadly similar aspirations. Wanley recognized that the costliness and the scale of the Antiquaries' self-appointed task necessitated the application of their 'united endeavours' to succeed; and this was a fundamental trait of the associational movement – or at least of those clubs with scholarly rather than purely self-indulgent objectives. The principle of united endeavour was one enshrined in the way that research in the natural sciences was carried out from the middle years of the seventeenth century, when the value of collaborative rather than individual effort came to be acknowledged. In 1693, while Edmund Gibson's revised edition of Camden's *Britannia* – incorporating contributions from almost thirty specialist authors (in contrast to the solitary labour of its original begetter) – was in an advanced stage of preparation,[28] William Nicolson, Archdeacon of Carlisle, gave passionate expression to this sentiment in a letter to Ralph Thoresby, whose coin cabinet was to provide new material for Gibson's volume:

> I wish we had in this kingdom, as they have in Sweden,[29] a society for the collecting and preserving of antiquities. This would do something for us. But as long as particular men engage in burdens beyond their strength, we have millions of great matters attempted, and nothing performed to any purpose.[30]

Elsewhere, he continued:

> All the great improvements in learning are now carried on in France and Italy, by societies of persons proper for the several undertakings. I know of no reason why history and antiquities should not be this way cultivated, as well as any other Belles Lettres whatever.[31]

These advantages were well appreciated too by Stukeley, who would later write of the effectiveness of societies in being able to consider their respective corporate missions over long periods of time, how they could 'by their constant succession of members triumph over death & avoyd the common fate all things else are involved in'.[32]

As a concept, the establishment of regular correspondence with the 'learned and curious' of other nations also had a long history. Since the early decades of the seventeenth century scholars of many nationalities had acknowledged an allegiance and a mutual debt to a wider 'republic of letters', a communications network that imposed obligations of free exchange of information on its members as well as bringing them valuable benefits in the form of news and advice on a range of subjects.[33] Perhaps the most prestigious exemplar in London during the early 1700s was Sir Hans Sloane, whose position as Secretary and later President of the Royal Society, together with his huge personal collections of books, manuscripts and specimens, placed him at the very hub of this vast informal network;[34] although Sloane himself was never to join the ranks of the Antiquaries he was generous in the provision of exhibits and even gifts from his collections (see below) while a number of his amanuenses and friends were among the early members, so that the Society can scarcely have escaped his influence.[35]

Indeed, many metropolitan societies recognized a need for country or corresponding members to complement those resident in the capital and to extend their experience;[36] initially these might be found no further away than the provinces, but increasingly it was the contributions of overseas members that was particularly valued. On 20 May 1736 the minutes record an agreement 'That Foreigners of Eminent Note & Learning may be admitted as Honorary Members of this Society, without being subject to any Annual Contributions', their numbers not to be counted in the maximum of one hundred members then admitted. Anders Celsius of Sweden was at first admitted as an ordinary member and later was elected an honorary member, as were the Marchese Scipione Maffei of Verona and Francesco Algarotti of Venice – all appointed with a view to extending the Society's international links.[37] The exchange of minutes with other societies fulfilled something of the same need for news from out of town.[38]

Highly characteristic of the era too is the appeal made to the potential for improvement offered by systematic study of the arts of the ancients, with the consequence that such practices as might be revealed 'may be used afresh to good Purpose'. A conviction that recovery of the lost wisdom of the ancient world would lead to manifold benefits to society ran through much seventeenth-century scholarship, promising such advantages as the development of a universal language and the revelation of the divine geometry of Creation.[39] In painting – and more especially in sculpture – the classical tradition represented an ideal to be recaptured by contemporary artists,[40] and many of the private galleries and collections that began to enter the public domain during the eighteenth century were made available by their owners with the conviction that exposure to the most refined exemplars would inspire a great renaissance in British art, while the championing of neo-classical taste under Lord Burlington was about to change for ever the face of English architecture. 'Improvement' was of course a *mot clef* of the period of the Enlightenment, permeating the fields of husbandry, agriculture, trade and manufacturing as well as social issues, and its linkage in the Antiquaries' manifesto to the uncovering of the lost practices of antiquity would have resonated in a convincing manner.[41]

No shortage of models presented themselves to the Antiquaries for constituting their new association, but it was the Royal Society more than any other body that formed a template against which they could measure themselves and could frame their activities. Several of the most influential Antiquaries also held fellowships at the Royal Society and, indeed, until the presidency of Sir Isaac Newton (1703–27) the study of antiquity sat comfortably within the wide programme of multi-disciplinary research embraced by that society. Newton's refocusing of his society's interests on a more strictly 'mathematical' (rather than a 'literary') agenda, and his perceived antipathy to antiquarian studies in particular, were seen by Joan Evans as having provided an important catalyst for the formation of a separate body in which the subject of antiquity could be specifically addressed.[42] The emergence of the Antiquaries, however, may more accurately be seen as part of a wider trend towards the formation of more specialized societies – a phenomenon witnessed also, for example, among the medical practitioners in the Royal Society.[43] Wanley himself had previously acted as an assistant secretary to the Royal Society (and from 1702 was Secretary of the Society for the Promotion of Christian Knowledge – one of the earliest bodies with a nationwide membership), so the potential existed for importing many of the formal procedures observed in these other bodies.[44]

In addition to these comparatively powerful associations, a number of smaller provincial societies – a category that scarcely existed before the turn of the century – also played a part in shaping the character and activities of the early Antiquaries. Most noteworthy was the Gentlemen's Society of Spalding, a small circle which, from 1710, met 'to pass an hour in literary conversation and reading some new publications' and, more formally according to statutes drawn up by the members in 1712, 'for the supporting of mutual Benevolence and their Improvement in the Liberal Sciences and Polite Learning'.[45] The moving spirit and secretary of the club for many years was Maurice Johnson, a founding member of the reconstituted Antiquaries and a lawyer whose affairs at Inner Temple demanded his frequent presence during the law terms, so facilitating his regular attendance at the London society. The members of the Spalding club evinced wide-ranging interests and it functioned more properly as a satellite of the broadly based Royal Society: 'They did not confine their enquiries to Antiquities', it was said, 'but made discoveries in Natural History, and improvements in Arts and Sciences in general their objects'.[46] The club's interests were, however, sufficiently antiquarian in character for exchanges of minutes between the two societies to be organized on a regular basis. Gough and Nichols suggest of the Spalding club that 'It may even boast a principal share in the revival of the Society of Antiquaries of London [that is to say, in 1717] and it outlived the lesser Societies that surrounded it, and may be said to have merged in it.'[47] Indeed, it was further stated that the gentlemen of Spalding, 'in the true style of monastic antiquity, assumed to themselves the modest denomination of a *Cell* to that of London; at once expressing their relation and connexion with that respectable body, of which most of them were also members, and with which they kept up an uninterrupted correspondence, and Communication of their Minutes, for upwards of forty years'.[48] Undoubtedly the tireless Johnson must take the credit for its high antiquarian profile.[49] He was instrumental also in recruiting William Stukeley to the membership; on one occasion Stukeley 'gave a discourse on Ancaster, which he had prepared for a meeting of gentlemen which occasionally met there'.[50]

This reference serves to indicate how widely the practice of holding regular gatherings for mutual improvement had penetrated into provincial – even rural – society. Among other clubs recorded that were similar in character to that at Spalding (though ultimately less successful), several were to be found in the East Midlands alone: well-documented societies were established at Stamford and Peterborough, while others existed for a time at Doncaster, Boston, Lincoln, Wisbech, Market Overton and Greetham, testifying to a thriving provincial culture unknown in the 1600s.[51] The Brazenose Society at Stamford, founded by Stukeley, was close in character to the Spalding club and, indeed, the members at Spalding were entertained at times with readings from the minutes of the Stamford society, including accounts of Roman camps and tesselated pavements. On the whole, however, their interests were more readily held by aspects of natural science (the members regularly went on 'simpling' expeditions to furnish the Society's *Hortus siccus indiginarum*), meteorology and astronomy.[52]

The Peterborough Gentlemen's Society owed its foundation, on 26 August 1730, to the Revd Timothy Neve. It quickly grew to embrace twenty regular attendants and close on a hundred honorary members, from whom the Society aspired to receive regular communications that could be relayed to the company.[53] Their interests were also of a widespread nature, with papers being delivered on the nature and production of fossils, mathematical problems, magnetism and 'the unseasonable colds of recent years . . . owing to the great spots on the surface of the sun', as well as anti-quarian matters. Nevertheless, the gentlemen of Peterborough included a number of committed antiquarian scholars[54] and they clearly anticipated a special relationship with the Antiquaries in London from the outset, to judge from an occasion when Stukeley 'acquainted the Society that Mr. Jos. Sparks desir'd a Copy of our Orders, for that they had erected a Society of Antiquarys at Peterburgh, which was to be a Cell or Subordinate to ours, as that some years ago establisht at Spalding, and therefore they intended to proceed in the same Method & by the same Rules'.[55] Talks duly recorded at Peterborough include contributions on Roman lamps, mosaics, urns and coins.[56] Having flourished successfully for some years, the Society lost momentum in the later 1700s before transforming itself into the Book Society in the early nineteenth century.

In London, a number of parallel (rather than rival) antiquarian societies sprang up, catering to different interest groups. The Roman Club (founded in 1723) successfully promoted an interest in specifically Italian art and culture among its members – who were drawn from the landed and professional classes – until it was eclipsed in the early 1740s by the Society of Dilettanti.[57] As their name suggested (or has come to suggest), this was an altogether more self-indulgent body – at least in its early years when its privileged membership, bound by the common experience of having completed the Grand Tour, developed a reputation for dissolute behaviour and a veritable antipathy to corporate ambition; the Society's sponsorship of more elevated (if still lavish) antiquarian projects dates only from the second half of the eighteenth century. Perhaps significantly, the Antiquaries and the Dilettanti had not a single member in common during the early phase of their joint existence (the first with a foot in both camps was to be Sir Joseph Banks), and it was not until the era of Sir William Hamilton that any degree of identity of interest began to manifest itself between the two societies.

More closely allied were two societies in which Stukeley again played a prominent part. He was the principal begetter of the Society of Roman Knights, founded in 1722 with a mission to revive 'Roman glory' in Britain. Much brave rhetoric was addressed by Stukeley to members of the newly formed association, alluding to 'the secret emotions which kindle in your hearts, a noble flame of recording the Antiquitys of our Country, which retrieved by your labors the most envious power of Time shall not be able to extinguish'.[58] Not only were antiquities at the heart of the agenda subscribed to by the *Equites Romani* but many of the recruits – including the Earl of Winchelsea, Maurice Johnson and Roger and Samuel Gale – were already members of the Society of Antiquaries, while its patron was the Earl of Pembroke. By contrast with the Antiquaries, the Knights – characterized as 'busying themselves to restore their Gothic Remnants' – set themselves a more narrowly focused quest: 'to adorn the truly noble monuments of the Romans in Britain & give them Roman eternity'. Far from forming a mere sedentary society, members were expected to ride out and travel the countryside, in true knightly fashion, and 'never to return home without conquests, without large spoils & trophys'.[59] The zeal and level of commitment of the members – if indeed these characteristics were widely manifested beyond the person of the founder himself and if held with the degree of seriousness to which they pretended[60] – are curiously reminiscent of the spirit that was to permeate the nationalist societies of the Germanic world during the following century (although such archaeological interest as these Romantic societies manifested was directed towards 'national antiquities' and specifically not to Roman remains); they are certainly less characteristic of the rational world of Hanoverian England and, perhaps predictably, were sustained for only a few years before the society folded.[61]

Somewhat more sober was the Egyptian Society, founded at the Lebeck's Head Tavern in Chandos Street on 11 December 1742 to further 'the promoting & preserving Egyptian & other antient learning', and dissolved two years later.[62] This society was far from dull in the way it conducted itself: the President (or 'Sheich') – in the person of the first Earl of Sandwich[63] – called the fortnightly meetings to order with the rattling of a specially made *sistrum* and he was assisted by a number of officers bearing equally exotic titles (variously of Turkish or Persian origin, hinting at the rudimentary level of understanding of matters Egyptian at this time). The core members (who, together with the first tranche of invitees, were designated the Founders of the Society) were distinguished by having personally visited Egypt; this exclusive body reserved to itself the right to elect with immediate effect other members who could claim the same distinction, while ordinary candidates lacking such first-hand knowledge had to undergo more conventional election by the whole society. It seems to have started out promisingly and to have grown steadily, leading to a ceiling being set at thirty members. Persistent absentees were automatically excluded. One historian of the club (Anis) identifies only four significant papers ever being delivered – two by Stukeley (one on the *sistrum* and one on the Feast of Isis, which he attempted to link with druidical practice in Britain) and two by Richard Pococke (on the sacred ibis and on burial practices); on other occasions, he suggests, 'members of the Society actually did no more than presenting some of their curiosities' (a practice not unlike that observed at the Antiquaries), with a small core contributing regularly.[64] Indeed, a curious ruling of the Society might have contributed to its demise by penalizing the most active members, stating that 'if for the future any member of the Society shall produce three several writings . . . the said member shall never be allowed to give in anything more in writing to the Society'.[65] Its last recorded meeting took place on 16 April 1743.

Freemasonry provided a more general meeting ground for the early Antiquaries and members of other clubs (including the Egyptian Society). Prominent masons included Charles Lennox, second Duke of Richmond, briefly the Society's President from 1750 until his death the following year, Lord Coleraine and Lord Montagu, all of whom served as grand masters of the Grand Lodge; Martin Folkes was a deputy grand master by the age of thirty-five. Other masons included Stukeley, Le Neve, Francis Drake, Sir Richard Manningham and the Earl of Winchelsea.[66]

While some societies, such as the Kit-Kat Club and the Hanoverian Club, were founded for purely political ends, most other associations saw politics as the road to ruination and avoided alignment with one faction or another. Writing of the activities of the Spalding Gentlemen's Society, for example, Maurice Johnson states that '[we] exclude nothing from our conversation but politics, which would throw us all into confusion and disorder'.[67] Religious faith could be equally divisive, especially at a time when an identification between Catholicism and seditious ends could all too easily be perceived and when the Stuart dynasty, biding its time on the Continent, could still foment rebellion on a wide scale, as witnessed in 1715 and again in 1745. Despite the early recruitment of a number of Anglican bishops (and from 1751 the Archbishop of Canterbury), the Antiquaries seem to have been broadly ecumenical in temper, with several Catholic members and a number of Huguenots, not to mention at least one Jew from 1752 in the – sadly reprehensible – person of Emanuel Mendes da Costa. Indeed an optimistic clause included in Wanley's draft charter foresaw that the Society might exercise a conciliatory influence, predicting that it 'will promote the ends of the Union, since a Communication and Correspondence with the Scotch will ensue, which begets mutual Love'. While early evidence of success in this respect may be hard to find (with the notable exception of Sir John Clerk of Penicuik, a member from 1725 and a regular correspondent thereafter), the 'mislike' of the monarchy was never to be visited on the refounded Society for dangerous political or religious leanings, as had befallen its predecessor under James I.

MEETINGS, PREMISES AND ADMINISTRATION

Like so many contemporary bodies, the newly re-formed Antiquaries functioned initially as a tavern society, the early meetings taking place at the Mitre in Fleet Street, 'in the room up 2 pair of stairs'.[68] The benefits of such an arrangement have already been alluded to but, for all their advantages, such convivial surroundings also put a limit on the proceedings. As early as 1718 Stukeley is to be found writing to Maurice Johnson that 'We have thoughts of taking a room in the Temple and laying up liquor in it' – evidently aiming to enhance the ambience of the meetings without compromising their convivial appeal.[69] At the prompting of several bishops among the members, embarrassed at crossing the threshold of the tavern, accommodation was found in the sober surroundings of the Inns of Court where a room was rented in chambers at Gray's Inn. This proved both out of the way and expensive – necessitating a two-shilling per month levy – and signally failed to attract more members. When the possibility of reverting to a tavern was raised, however, several of the more temperate members (not least the President, Lord Hertford) declared their opposition, so the meetings moved to alternative chambers at King's Bench Walk in the Temple. Yet again finding no improvement in the numbers attending (not even among the bishops), the Society reinvestigated the possibility of finding shelter in a tavern. This time, encouraged by the example of Thomas Tanner, lately Bishop of St Asaph, who 'ventur'd to put his Mitred head into the Mitre Tavern which others pretended some excuse to avoid', a return to the establishment that had nourished the Society at birth was approved in 1729. Within a decade the agitators had once again embarked on a campaign to have the meetings moved, but several such attempts were seen off by those content with the congenial surroundings of the tavern.

From time to time the Antiquaries flirted with the idea of acquiring or building their own accommodation. The Royal Society had given up the premises it initially occupied at Gresham College in 1711 when an independent property was purchased at Crane Court, off Fleet Street, and there is no doubt that, for a time, Crane Court, with its meeting room, library, laboratory and repository, became something of a talisman for those with a vision of what the Antiquaries might aspire to become. As well as the Royal Society, they had before them the example of the Spalding Gentlemen's Society, whose acquisition of a permanent base in part of the former monastery in the town allowed its members to establish a library and to fit out a museum for their collections in a manner that must have been a source of envy in London.[70] By 1722 Stukeley was investigating the possibility of purchasing the site of the Whitefriars' chapel (again off Fleet Street) with a view to building a meeting hall for the Society,[71] but it quickly proved too expensive a project. Without becoming an incorporated body the Society would in any case not have been empowered to own property; it was only with the acquisition of its charter that the search was renewed.

From 1738 the membership elected to observe an annual feast day, a convention widely practised in other societies and regarded as an important mechanism for strengthening associational bonds.[72] The Egyptian Society mentioned above, for example, held an annual celebration on the 'Feast of Isis' (the winter solstice), while the Antiquaries opted appropriately enough for St George's Day, a tradition maintained in polite, but diminished, form in today's Anniversary reception.

The low turn-outs at meetings, which threatened the continuity of the Society from time to time, proved a recurring problem for many clubs of the period and indeed a number of them quickly withered away entirely. At the time of their earliest meetings in 1707 the Antiquaries, like numerous other societies, sought to encourage regular appearances by levying fines for non-attendance,[73] but it was a strategy that could easily become self-defeating, especially when, with the passage of time, members all too often fell behind with their dues. The problem in maintaining momentum might in part be explained by the patterns of attendance imposed on those members who observed law terms in London but attended to the demands of country properties at other times of year. Absence from the metropolis during the summer months on account of its general unwholesomeness was rendered all the more desirable on health grounds, and it is noteworthy that the provincial Spalding and Peterborough clubs, although smaller in size, were much less affected by these seasonal fluctuations, continuing to function successfully throughout the year.[74] In time, the Antiquaries alleviated the problem by suspending meetings for the summer. Then, on 20 November 1728, it was proposed that meetings should be moved from Wednesday to Thursday, in order to coincide with those of the Royal Society: instead of having to turn out on two evenings a week, those who belonged to both societies now found themselves able to attend the Antiquaries 'after the Royal Society had broke up', an arrangement that evidently suited a considerable number of members.[75]

In line with the increasingly standard practice of the period, responsibility for the smooth running of the Society was vested initially in its officers, who played an important role in providing stability, continuity and good management to the proceedings. Although the membership was originally capped at 100 – then increased on 24 April 1746 to 120 – and although membership was frequently at a maximum,[76] an attendance of a tenth of that number (or less) was common and meetings were, from time to time, non-quorate;[77] without the contributions of the elected officers there seems little chance that the Society could have survived these uncertain times. By the end of its first year of existence a statement of the Society's financial position was presented to and approved by the membership, a policy maintained thereafter. Occasionally we find the Society tempted into perilous financial practice, as when the sum of £10 from its funds was ventured on a lottery ticket in 1722; having failed, a further £2 was hazarded before more conventional investment practice was re-established.

The increasing burden of administration led quite naturally to the recruitment of the first paid member of staff – Alexander Gordon was appointed Secretary on 1 May

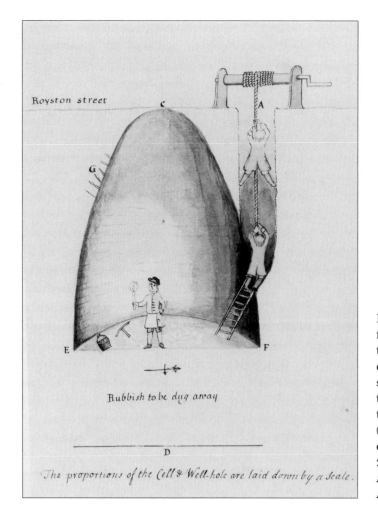

Fig 17. A rare record of field archaeology from the early eighteenth century: a cross-sectional view showing the method of excavation of Royston Cave (SAL, Minutes, IV, drawing facing p 135, 21 October 1742). *Photograph*: Society of Antiquaries of London.

1735. Rather than settling on an annual salary, Gordon was to be paid a five-shilling attendance fee for each meeting, a strategy that must have acted as a useful spur to the incumbent and a further means of ensuring that the momentum of the meetings was maintained.

Although the paucity of early reports of fieldwork of an archaeological nature has been remarked upon,[78] there were occasional exceptions – notably in 1742 when A C Ducarel reported on the opening of a barrow at Stevenage in September,[79] when a description was received in October of the excavation of a vault found at Royston, containing rudely sculptured 'figures in Basso Relievo . . . crucifixes', etc (fig 17),[80] and when the opening of a charnel-pit at 'Hackendon or Heckingdown Banks' near the North Foreland lighthouse on the Isle of Thanet was communicated in the same month.[81] Seven years later, 'Mr Baker read a pretty account of the openning of a Large Barrow or *Tumulus*, in the County of Wiltshire in a letter directed to himself, wherein was observed a dark spicy Jelly attending an Urn with burnt bones, & the mouth of the Urn sett downward.'[82]

The membership did, however, develop at an early stage a consciousness of the role it could play in the recording and preservation of antiquities in the field. Hence it was resolved in 1721 that an attempt should be made to salvage all the inscriptions from the church of St Martin-in-the-Fields and later that two oak posts should be set up at the Society's expense in order 'to secure Waltham Cross from injury by Carriages'.[83] Francis Wise suggested that the Society 'might still be made more useful, if some of the most knowing members would form themselves into parties, each party at their leisure undertaking a distinct province, and in the nature of a travelling Committee . . . give directions for such enquiries . . . and . . . receive informations, not from the vulgar inhabitants alone, but from gentlemen of learning and curiosity',[84] but such a scheme proved all too ambitious.

Reports were none the less received from time to time of newly discovered or newly surveyed field monuments, often accompanied by records made on the spot. Stukeley proved as enterprising as ever when he exhibited in 1722 'a Model wch he had made in Wood of Stonehenge, together wth some drawings of that celebrated antiquity taken upon the Spot, whence he demonstrated the true form thereof, & its avenue different from what has yet appeard',[85] while the Roman mosaic at Stonesfield, Oxfordshire, previously recorded in a detailed engraving by Vertue, was brought to attention in the form of a collection of tesserae exhibited in 1721 (figs 18 and 19).[86]

More usually it was chance finds, brought before the membership for their enlightenment and appraisal, that represented the common fare at meetings. Among the more significant of these were the spearheads, daggers and axes forming part of the Bronze Age hoard from Arreton Down on the Isle of Wight: the records of these exhibits made in the minutes,[87] together with a set of contemporary drawings produced by the Director of the day, Charles Frederick (fig 20), retain a continuing importance and have been used in recent years to help elucidate the history of this important type-site of the early British Bronze Age.[88] Other Bronze Age exhibits included a 'copper Tuba or trumpet' from St Leonard's Hill at Windsor and another

Fig 18. Mosaic from a Romano-British villa at Stonesfield, Oxfordshire, engraved by George Vertue, 1712. *Photograph*: Society of Antiquaries of London.

Fig 19. Tesserae recovered from a Romano-British villa at Stonesfield, Oxfordshire, and exhibited on 7 December 1721. *Photograph*: Society of Antiquaries of London.

from Griffinrath near Maynooth, from the collection of Sir Hans Sloane, exhibited by Cromwell Mortimer,[89] as well as innumerable 'celts'. References in the minutes to Roman objects probably outnumber all others – mostly from England but including, as early as 1718, a number of vessels from Port Mahon, exhibited by Samuel Gale.[90] Anglo-Saxon finds were naturally scarce, and even when they did appear they were not necessarily recognized as such, as when Le Neve 'brought a fine Roman Urn taken up in his presence at Elmham in Norfolk, which was opend before the Society. Nothing but Bones was found in it'.[91] The urn, a fifth-century Anglian type, was presented to the Society (fig 21).

Despite the view of some members that the Society spent too much time busying itself with 'Gothic Remnants', medieval material was less frequently exhibited. Seals formed an exception and were a subject of recurring interest. Five plates of medieval seals had already been published in the *Vetusta Monumenta* series by the time interest was channelled in a new direction in 1736 when 'Mr. Drake delivered in a Dissertation on the Use of the knowledge of Ancient Seals, being an abstract from a MS. on that Subject compiled by John Anstis . . . wherein . . . he proves that Several real Antique Seals were used by Bishops & Abbots in this Kingdom as theyr Secretum or Contr-scelle'. From this it emerged that there survived in the Duchy of Lancaster office and elsewhere 'the Impresions of many antique Seals with [later] Inscriptions and reverses, pendant to divers ancient deeds'; consequently 'it was proposed & agreed to That a Committee be Appointed to Inspect the Said Seals and make a Report, whether there are not a Sufficient Number of Curious ones to form two Plates to be engraven at the Expence of ye Society'.[92] Two plates were duly engraved by Vertue and published in 1738, followed by three more in 1741, while evidence exists for further preparatory drawings which were never engraved.[93]

From the very inception of the Society a wide-ranging programme of publications had formed a primary ambition. To the draft charter drawn up in 1708, Humfrey Wanley appended a list of topics that he anticipated would form the subject of books – many of them by their nature to be multi-volume productions – to which attention would be directed, arranged under four principal heads: 'The Countrey' opens with 'A Compleat History of Great Britain and Ireland' and 'Volumes of such of our old English Historians as have not yet been Printed', continuing with histories of various counties and manors, castles, cities and boroughs, the coinage and a 'Compleat

Fig 20. Spearheads and daggers from a Bronze Age hoard discovered at Arreton Down, Isle of Wight, drawn by Charles Frederick, Director 1735/6–1741/2. *Photographs*: Society of Antiquaries of London.

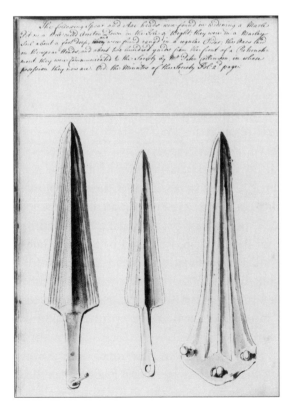
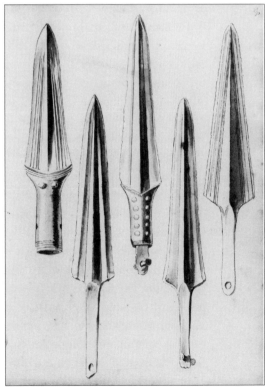

Fig 21. Urn of Anglian type, traditionally associated with Peter le Neve, now thought to be a later acquisition of the eighteenth century. *Photograph:* Society of Antiquaries of London.

Treatise, concerning the Prices of All Things (Eatable and Movable)'; under 'The King', priority is given to 'A Treatise of all the Laws, Rights and Prerogative of the Crown' followed by an 'Historical Account of the Great Officers of the Kingdom'; 'The Church' embraces surveys of monastic and ecclesiastical history together with lists of prelates of all degrees as well as saints and their days, while all the books in use in the Latin Church are called in review; the section on 'The People' envisages a need for lists and genealogies of all noble and illustrious families, an 'Historical Account of the remarkable Customs and Ceremonies used by our Ancestors', and treatises on the origin and progress of chivalry and heraldry, on manufactures and handicrafts, on 'all Weapons, Instruments and Utensils . . . with their Names and Figures', and on 'the Habits of the English, Men and Women, of all states and Degrees . . . with their Names and Proper Draughts'. Having failed to attract the lavish patronage necessary to underpin such a vast project, the Society embarked in a more modest way on a programme that would begin to fulfil the most accessible of these ambitions, establishing in the process its *bona fides* in the field of antiquarian studies and demonstrating to the wider world its title to pride of place as the national arbiter on matters of antiquity.[94]

Numismatics had always featured prominently among the Antiquaries' interests.[95] Among the books envisaged by Wanley had been a 'Historical Account of the Coin of this Realm, its Mixture, and Value, with Draughts of all the principal pieces . . .' and it was in this field that the Society was to make its first successful contribution, although it was to be a long time in coming. In 1722 plans were formally launched to publish 'a complete description and history of all the coins relating to Great Britain from the earliest times to our own', but little progress had been made by the time Martin Folkes developed an interest in the project from the 1730s, spurred by the publication of his own *Table of English Gold Coins* (1736) and later consolidated by the appearance of his *Table of English Silver Coins* (1745). In this same year he agreed with the Antiquaries that he would take on the responsibility for its projected volume of plates with explanatory text, but it remained incomplete at the time of his death and it was to be 1763 before it finally appeared, thanks to the intervention of Andrew Gifford, a talented numismatist who had been recruited to the staff of the recently formed British Museum.[96]

A great deal of the energies of the early Society went into the production of engraved illustrations rather than extensive texts.[97] One of the first proposals received by the refounded Society, on 5 February 1718, was to the effect that an engraving of the image of Richard II in Westminster Abbey should be produced; a week later it was resolved that George Vertue, a prominent member whose appointment as official engraver to the Society must have ensured that the programme remained at the forefront of the members' consciousness, should be paid two guineas for engraving the font at St James's.[98] The practice developed of publishing these prints with a view to inclusion in the handsome folio series titled *Vetusta Monumenta*. It was a project that would continue intermittently for the next two centuries, recording monuments at every scale from wax sealings to architectural complexes, and embracing both surviving treasures and those threatened with (or already having suffered) obliteration,[99] drawing the comment from Horace Walpole that 'The best merit of the Society lies in their prints'.[100] In time the presentation of sets of its prints became one of the recognized ways in which the Society could express its gratitude or support to other bodies and to favoured individuals.[101] One image from that period which continues to exert an impact today is that of the Society's symbol – its ever-burning lamp. The object itself became part of the collection in 1736, when 'Dr Mortimer brought in a present to the Society from Sr Hans Sloan Bart., of the brass Lamp which was found at St. Leonard's hill near Windsor, a print of which is prefixed to the printed Works of ye Society' (figs 22 and 23).[102]

As well as producing its own prints the Society also formed the rudiments of a collection at this time, as when Stukeley gave an engraved portrait of Sir Francis Bacon in 1717,[103] when the President presented prints of Chinese, Coptic and Turkish writing in 1723 and when on 4 April 1734 Alexander Gordon provided copies of the engravings compiled for his *Egyptian Antiquities* (judged 'a very elegant & curious performance').[104] When Talman's personal collection of prints and drawings came on the market in 1727, Vertue was asked to attend the auction and to acquire any items 'which relate to British antiquities for yᵉ use of the Society'.[105]

The provision of a working library for the benefit of members doubtless would have been seen as a major asset to the early Society as it is today, although it was an ambition that could scarcely be fulfilled before the acquisition of a permanent home. The range of publications already available and continuing to appear in print was already beyond the means of most researchers, who had to rely on the generosity of wealthy individuals or on the resources of the Cottonian library (held for the nation but difficult of access until its ultimate combination with the Harleian library and that

Fig 22. Lamp found at St Leonard's Hill, Windsor, in 1717 and presented to the Society by Sir Hans Sloane, 1736. *Photograph*: Society of Antiquaries of London.

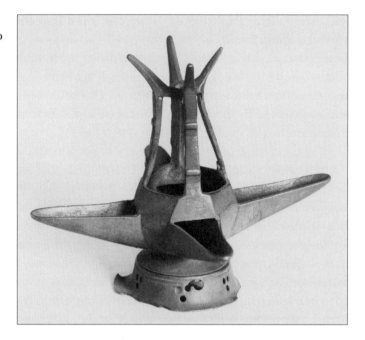

Fig 23. Engraving by John Talman, 1718 (from *Vetusta Monumenta*, I, pl I) of the lamp presented to the Society by Sir Hans Sloane in 1736. The lamp continues to serve as the Society's device to the present day. *Photograph*: Society of Antiquaries of London.

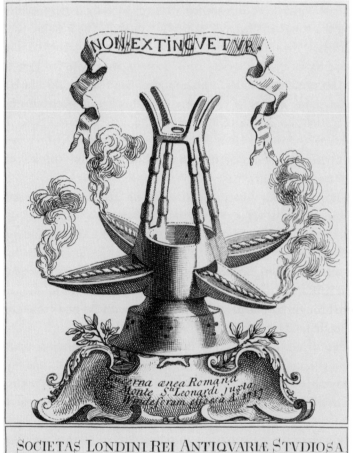

of Sir Hans Sloane to form the British Museum library, which opened to the scholarly public in 1758). Until the Society settled in its own premises, however, there were severe limits on the extent to which the collection of books could be developed and there seems to have been no special agenda for expanding it – a contrast to the practice in the Spalding and Peterborough clubs, for example, which proved enterprising in requiring new members each to present a book for the benefit of the members. Similarly, the Society's museum did not extend beyond a few items at this time.

THE ROYAL CHARTER

The advantages to the Society of chartered status had been apparent from its earliest days and in time the pressures to apply for formal incorporation became irresistible. The move was not without its opponents, however – particularly those who saw in it a device to draw the Antiquaries further within the ambit of the Royal Society. On 27 November 1729, while Sir Hans Sloane was President of the Royal Society, the Antiquaries had indeed debated whether a merging of the two bodies might be beneficial;[106] the resolution was rejected, but conspiracy theorists among the Antiquaries were constantly looking out thereafter for attempts to achieve by subterfuge what had been rejected by formal mechanism,[107] and the quest for a royal charter was seen by some in this light. The election of Martin Folkes as President of the Royal Society in 1741, assisted as Treasurer by James West – another member (and from 1749 a Vice-President) of the Antiquaries – appeared indeed to bring the identities of the two bodies closer together, much to the alarm of some members. To them the charter seemed to be 'a means of absolutely destroying, instead of establishing or perpetuating the Society'; they foresaw that 'An invidious member [i.e. Folkes] of the R[oyal] S[ociety] is most likely and able to effect it, out of resentment to a Society that has subsisted several years with at least an equal degree of reputation',[108] and numbers of them were unwilling to subscribe to the costs of procuring the charter.[109] Others (notably Stukeley) saw the dangers in quite the reverse light: wearing his Royal Society hat, he observed that 'the antiquarys by getting a charter seem to set themselves up in opposition to us: by thus dividing the languishing streams of literature among us, it seems not difficult to presage, that the glory of the Royal Society, the first of its kind in Europe, is upon the wane, along with that of learning in general'.[110]

Things were brought to a head at the end of 1749 with the news that Lord Coleraine had died, leaving a bequest to the Antiquaries of certain prints and drawings. 'By the advice of the learned in the law', however, they learned that they were not empowered to receive the donation, 'their Society being nominal only'. The event set in train the course of events that led to a formal resolution being adopted on 26 April 1750, 'That it is the opinion of the members now present, that it will be for the advantage of this Society to procure His Majesties Charter of Incorporation'.[111] The application, drawn up under Folkes and intended for presentation to the king by the Society's noble President, the Duke of Richmond, asserted the members' commitment to 'the Study of Antiquities and . . . the History of Former Times which has ever been esteemed highly commendable and Useful, not only to inform the Minds of Men, but also to incite them to Noble and Virtuous Actions and such as may hereafter render them Famous and Worthy Examples to late Posterity'. It also expressed the belief that in their new status 'several persons would give them considerable donations for their future encouragement to proceed in their said studies', benefits that were unavailable to them as a voluntary society.

Even the Duke of Richmond counselled caution on the grounds of cost, but when Richmond died on 15 November and was replaced as President two weeks later by Folkes the movement gathered an unstoppable momentum. A draft petition was drawn up by one of the members, Philip Carteret Webb, 'an attorney versed in archive lore', evidently drawing heavily for its structure and detailed character on the charter granted by Charles II to the Royal Society[112] – the only learned society to have been incorporated by that time. The petition was, it seems, submitted to the Secretary of State and quickly gained the approval of the law officers; finally, on 14 November 1751, the Society received its charter from the king, 'his Majesty being pleased to declare himself its "Founder and Patron"'. Forthwith it was incorporated with the style and title of the 'President, Council, and Fellows of the Society of Antiquaries of London', endowed with 'a body of statutes and a common seal', and empowered 'to hold in perpetuity lands, &c. to the yearly value of 1000£'.[113]

Perhaps inevitably, the achievements of the Society to this point scarcely measured up to the grandiose agenda set out by its founding members, but in constitutional terms it had undoubtedly come of age and had established a firm foundation that would stand it in good stead. The administration that had piloted the fledgling Society through its formative years had proved remarkably effective, if perilously dependent on the commitment of a few tireless individuals; although the Officers and Council designated by the charter would vary wildly in the effectiveness and energy they brought to their respective offices in years to come, the more rigorous framework of administration brought about by the process of incorporation would bring new levels of stability that would become the envy (and the model for emulation) of other societies, which increasingly sought the same levels of protection during the second half of the century.

One significant advance enshrined in the new charter concerned the stage on which the Society saw itself performing its role: gone was the restrictive declaration that the 'Antiquities and History of Great Britain' would form the exclusive focus of attention for members (indeed it had been honoured in the breach for many years by the introduction of foreign – notably Egyptian – exhibits at meetings) and in came an expectation that Fellows should be 'Excelling in the Knowledge of the Antiquities and History of this and other Nations'.[114] Henceforth the Society's activities were to be judged on an international rather than a parochial basis, and Britain had acquired at last an organization of acknowledged authority whose works could be judged alongside those of the continental institutions that had formed a source of envious comparison just half a century earlier.

ACKNOWLEDGEMENTS

Warm thanks are due to Bernard Nurse, FSA, Rosemary Sweet, FSA, and Daniel Woolf, FSA, each of whom read the above text in draft and generously made many suggestions for its improvement. I am also grateful to the late John Goodall, FSA, who, with characteristic kindness, allowed me to quote from his unpublished researches on the Society's early interest in seals.

NOTES

1. The phenomenon has recently been surveyed in exemplary fashion by Clark (2000), who traces the beginnings of clubs to the late 16th century, with a general faltering under the early Stuarts and a modest revival under the Commonwealth before renewed expansion set in during the later years of Charles II's rule.

2. In this context Evans (1956, 35–6) appositely quotes Joseph Addison, writing in 1710, who observed of the English that they 'take all occasions and pretences for forming themselves into those little nocturnal assemblies which are known by the name of clubs. When a set of men find themselves to agree in any particular, though never so trivial, they establish themselves into a kind of fraternity and meet once or twice a week on account of such a fantastic resemblance.'

3. Macky 1724, I, 269.

4. For the 'club' at the Temple Coffee House see Jessop 1989.

5. See Nichols 1812–16, III, 412; Evans 1956, 35 n 5. The tavern in question was the Bull's Head and the company included Thomas Tanner as well as Peter le Neve and Henry Hare (later third Baron Coleraine), both of whom were quickly absorbed into membership of the society discussed hereafter.

6. BL, Harleian MS 7055, fol 1.

7. Ibid.

8. Evans 1956, 36–8, where the complete text of the minutes is reproduced.

9. BL, Harleian MS 7055, fols 4–10, reproduced *in extenso* in Evans 1956, 40–4.

10. Meetings were to begin at Whitehall 'after its Rebuilt', that is to say, following the completion of its reconstruction after the disastrous fires of 1691 and 1698.

11. A number of factors seem to have contributed to Harley's downfall. He was for years widely mistrusted in government as a 'Commonwealthsman' and as a Tory sympathizer; the final crisis was precipitated by accusations that he acted treacherously in his handling of debate on the war with Spain, and by the discovery that a member of his office had acted treasonably in passing intelligence to France.

12. 'Four letters passed between Dr Ducarel, Mr Johnson, &c. relative to the revival of the Society of Antiquaries of London, 1717': Nichols 1812–16, VI, 144.

13. Evans 1956, 51.

14. BL, Add MS 6182, fol 6. Stukeley's record seems to invite us to count the foundation from 1 January 1718, although later in the same manuscript (fol 14) he himself gives 'A Catalogue of the Fellows of the Society of Antiquaries of London, from its revival in the year 1717'. For the purposes of consistency, the present volume adopts 1717 as the year when the present Society was proposed to be established, although the origins can be traced back to 1707.

15. SAL, MS 268, July 1717; the full list of names is reproduced in Evans 1956, 51–2. Of the twelve members who had formed the earlier Society constituted in 1707, three had died in the meantime and six of the remainder were included in the new body. The new Society's Articles of Association, contained in SAL, Minutes, I, 4–7, 1 Jan 1718, are reproduced in full in Evans 1956, 58–60.

16. Peter le Neve (1661–1729), by profession 'one of the Under Chamberlains of the Court of Receipts', was also a herald and from 1704 Norroy King of Arms. Parsimonious in other respects, he was a voracious collector of books and manuscripts of heraldic and genealogical interest; most famously, he owned for a time the rich literary treasure known as the Paston Letters: Woodcock 2004.

17. Samuel Gale (1682–1754), appointed 'searcher of the books and curiosities imported into this kingdom, and land surveyor of the customs', like his brother-in-law Stukeley and his friend A C Ducarel (with both of whom he made extended antiquarian outings), led a private life dedicated to study of the past. He completed *A History of Winchester Cathedral* (1715) but a similar work on York Minster remained unpublished at the time of his death: Haycock 2004.

18. William Stukeley (1687–1765) played a pivotal role in the early Antiquaries. Having graduated in medicine from Cambridge, he continued his studies in London with Richard Mead on anatomy and medicine, which he practised until being ordained in his early forties. He discoursed at length with Newton on a range of

subjects, including chronological history, and travelled widely with his friends Roger and Samuel Gale, publishing his observations in *Itinerarium Curiosum* (1724) as well as influential monographs on Avebury and Stonehenge. He founded the Brazenose Society in Stamford and belonged to several other antiquarian bodies: Piggott 1985; Haycock 2002.

19. John Talman (1677–1726), an accomplished draughtsman, had just returned from eight years in Italy in the company of William Kent and others, studying and recording architectural interiors. He built up a sizeable collection of prints and drawings (to which the rich collection of his father, William Talman, was later added). He acted as an agent for several English aristocrats in Italy and enjoyed privileged access to Vatican circles, becoming widely acknowledged as one of the leading cognoscenti in Rome: Parry 2004.

20. Clark 2000, 89. By the end of the century this number had increased three-fold: ibid, 131.

21. Had any real intention been formed of creating an over-genteel society, it seems likely that it would have led to trouble, as when Sir Joseph Banks split the Royal Society later in the century by (allegedly) attempting to boost its standing by encouraging every nobleman to apply while interfering in the election of the professional men who had come to form its backbone: see Royal Society 1784.

22. SAL, Minutes, I, 20, 11 Mar 1719.

23. In the engagement of the landed classes in societies such as the Antiquaries we may see not so much a continuation of the dominant old order but rather a novel form of interaction commonly manifested among the clubs and societies of the age in which peers and landed gentry freely engaged with the influential new professional classes to their mutual benefit; the nature of their contribution was by now seen in terms of enlightened patronage rather than the customary exercise of hereditary authority.

24. For Talman see note 19.

25. The pre-eminence of Humfrey Wanley (1672–1726) as the principal scholar of Old English of his day is all the more remarkable for his being self-taught. He was employed as an assistant at the Bodleian Library from 1695 and by 1701 had completed a catalogue of all the Anglo-Saxon manuscripts known in England. He was by now employed as Secretary of the SPCK but he entered the service of Robert (and later Edward) Harley in 1708, remaining there as librarian for the rest of his life. Many of his personal ambitions were thwarted, as were his many grandiose publishing schemes; something of the latter may be detected in the encyclopaedic programme mapped out for the early Antiquaries (see pp 47–8).

26. John Bagford (1650/1–1716) gained the respect of his antiquarian contemporaries on account of his bibliographical knowledge, acquiring in Hearne's words 'an unusual skill in the History of Printing & in our own History & Antiquities'. Strype (1720, II, appendix 23) also describes him as 'studious of Antiquities' and records his attention to animal bones, etc, little regarded by others at this time. His ambitions to publish a history of printing came to nothing, though he did contribute to Gibson's edition of Camden's *Britannia* and Strype's reworking of Stow's *Survey of London*. He died an impecunious pensioner of the Charterhouse. See Bagford 1770; Fletcher 1896–8; Nickson 1983; Harmsen 2004.

27. The Revd William Cole, in Nichols 1812–16, VI, 208.

28. For the identities of his collaborators on the revised edition of Camden's *Britannia*, see Gibson's preface to Camden 1695, 2–4.

29. The Antiquities College within the Academy (later University) of Uppsala, founded in 1666 with Olof Verelius, the Royal Antiquary, as its first professor (Klindt-Jensen 1975, 26–7), proved a particular beacon for English antiquaries. 'At Upsal, in Sweden, they have a college of antiquaries. And why should we not have the like in England?' asked Nicolson (Hunter 1832, I, 162). His particular plea seemed to be aimed at galvanizing the antiquaries into collaborative action, however, and carried no particular expectation of royal support.

30. Hunter 1832, I, 138.

31. Ibid, 162.

32. Bodleian, Eng. Misc. c. 401, fol 20. The sentiment was expressed in relation to the Society of Roman Knights, in which Stukeley played such a prominent role.

33. Ultee 1987; Goldgar 1995.

34. MacGregor 1994, 19.

35. The value of a wide network of correspondents was recognized especially by members of the smaller provincial societies discussed below, for whom news from beyond their regional horizons was their life's blood. Referring to the Peterborough Gentlemen's Society, for example, its founder bemoans the fact that: 'What we stand most in need of is a correspondence with gentlemen in distant parts of the kingdom, or the world; but as yet we are too inconsiderable to have an intercourse of that sort settled amongst us' (see 'History of the Peterborough Society'; in a letter from the Revd Dr Timothy Neve to the Revd Littleton Brown, 23 July 1741, in Nichols 1812–16, VI, 136).

36. Clark (2000, 210) notes that in 1712 the SPCK, of which Wanley was then Secretary, had only eighty residing members compared with 370 corresponding members; by the early 1740s the Peterborough Gentlemen's Society boasted 'near 20 regular members, and almost 100 honorary' ('History of the Peterborough Society', in Nichols 1812–16, VI, 136). Sweet (2004, 82) notes that the membership of the

Antiquaries was never narrowly restricted to the metropolis, and that members were indeed notably well travelled throughout England.

37. SAL, Minutes, ii, 105–6, 23 Oct 1735; ii, 109, 6 Nov 1735; ii, 182, 20 May 1736; ii, 186, 27 May 1736. Sweet (2004, 89) notes, however, that only seven foreign members were elected prior to 1751 and that it was only after the granting of the charter that the numbers began to climb.

38. Mutual exchanges of minutes took place between the Antiquaries and the Gentlemen's Society of Spalding while Stukeley and Johnson were their respective secretaries. Gough and Nichols imply that the arrangement was one more valued by the provincial society than the metropolitan one, when they say of the Antiquaries that 'with such care and exactness were their Minutes kept by some succeeding Secretaries, that scarcely a trace of these communications remains on their books, while the Spalding Minute-books, kept by their indefatigable founder, have preserved a variety of curious matter from the wreck of time' ('Some account of the Gentlemen's Society at Spalding by Mr. Gough and Mr. Nichols', in Nichols 1812–16, vi, 2). The Minute Books nevertheless contain over a dozen references to communications from the Spalding society being read to the Antiquaries between 28 Nov 1734 and 3 Dec 1747. The minutes of the Peterborough society were also read, for example on 24 May 1739.

39. Bennett and Mandelbrote 1998.

40. Among the societies to emerge in the late 17th century were the Virtuosi of St Luke, first documented *c* 1689 (its meetings were formalized and minutes kept from 1698 onwards). Like the Antiquaries, the Virtuosi began by meeting in a tavern but, by 1711, they had established an academy of painting in Great Queen Street: Clark 2000, 63.

41. The movement was to find its most eloquent expression in the Society for the Encouragement of Arts, Manufactures and Commerce, established by William Shipley in 1754: see most recently Fox 2003.

42. Evans 1965, 49. Both Rosemary Sweet and Daniel Woolf have observed in personal communications that Newton's attitudes to antiquity were over-simplified by Evans. Newton and Stukeley shared a great deal of common ground in their ideas about early religion (notably 'ye old religion of the Egyptians') and on the evolution of temple architecture. Newton in particular had speculated on the structure and plan of Solomon's Temple as a key to understanding elements of the Book of Revelations: Haycock 2002, 154–6. It remains true, however, that in a list drawn up for the Royal Society by Thomas Clerk in 1718, for 'showing what subjects seem most suitable to the ends of its institution', 'Antiquities' came at the very bottom of the list,

following 'Husbandry, Gardening and Planting': Weld 1848, I, 424–7.

43. This suggestion was first made by Evans (1956, 35, 49). For the overlap in membership and the many-stranded common interests between the Royal Society and the Antiquaries, see Hunter 1971; the Royal Society's sibling philosophical societies in Oxford and Dublin were equally frequented by those with antiquarian interests. The failure of the Royal Society to satisfy the more specialized interests of its Fellows should not be laid entirely at Newton's door: for example, the Temple Coffee House botanical club, mentioned above, was founded with a strong representation of FRSs as early as 1689; it seems to have lapsed *c* 1713 but, in a manner similar to the Antiquaries, it re-emerged as the Botanical Society in 1721, meeting at a coffee-house in Watling Street, while the Aurelian Society emerged at much the same time to cater for those with an interest in Lepidoptera: Clark 2000, 63, 74. On the other hand, narrowing the range of interest of a society ran the risk of attracting too few members, especially in the provinces, as Erasmus Darwin found when his attempt to establish a botanical society in Lichfield failed: ibid, 111.

44. A further interesting link is provided by George Vertue, who had been a pupil of the Academy founded at Kneller's studio by the Virtuosi of St Luke (see note 40) and had therefore experienced at first hand the benefits for the greater good brought about by collaborative effort.

45. The club is said to have acquired its distinctive character some years later, in 1724, and to have reached its peak around 1729: Minute Books of the Spalding Gentlemen's Society, vii.

46. 'Some account of the Gentlemen's Society at Spalding', in Nichols 1812–16, vi, 6. Topics discussed ranged from 'Danceing wrote down or drawn in characters' to the trapping of mallards on the Fens, from architectural history to bookbinding; the club also established a physic garden, made astronomical and meteorological observations and sponsored concerts and plays: Spalding Gentlemen's Society 1981, x–xiii. The importance of the energies brought to these pursuits by such dedicated members as Johnson and Stukeley were crucial to the well-being of the Spalding society, as they were to the Antiquaries, the Egyptian Society and others.

47. The influence referred to was no doubt that exerted personally by Maurice Johnson, founder of the Spalding club and an active member of the circle of antiquaries meeting in London from before the formal refounding of 1717. Our knowledge of the early history of the club stems from the extensive minutes and notes which he kept; indeed, whenever new business was lacking he supplied that too with exhibits from his

own collections or summaries from his own researches on numismatic and historical topics: Spalding Gentlemen's Society 1981, vii–ix.

48. See note 38.

49. On one occasion, for example, Johnson reported to the Antiquaries that 'the Gent[lemen] of Spalding have pursuant to his proposals to them formerly read here collected & transcribd severall sheets of Abbreviatures in Cannon L[aw] & the plagae, names, Countries & times when & where severall hundreds of eminent Statuaries Painters, Engravers, Seal cutters &c flourished' – evidently applying themselves to some of the tasks that had been anticipated as falling within the remit of the Antiquaries themselves: SAL, Minutes, I, 132, 18 Nov 1724.

50. Spalding Gentlemen's Society 1981, xiii.

51. Clark 2000, 85. The Boston club was yet another of Stukeley's foundations. It took the form of a botanical society, attracting local apothecaries and surgeons, and its activities included weekly 'simpling' expeditions.

52. Spalding Gentlemen's Society 1981, xiv–xvi; Bodleian, Eng. Misc. e. 122, fols 67–84.

53. Nichols 1812–16, VI, 136–7. See also Dack 1899.

54. One of their founding members, the Revd Robert Smyth, for example, compiled a history of Huntingdonshire (which remained unpublished) and recorded innumerable inscriptions and epitaphs throughout the surrounding counties: Dack 1899, 141.

55. SAL, Minutes, I, 70, 14 Nov 1722; see also I, 256, 17 Dec 1730.

56. Nichols 1812–16, VI, 137–9; Dack 1899, 145–55. Sweet (2004, 389 n 142) calculates that some 27 per cent of papers communicated to the Peterborough Gentlemen's Society were concerned with antiquarian matters, compared to 20 per cent at Spalding.

57. Clark (2000, 78) mentions also the Pope's Head Club as one of the successors to the Roman Club, drawing its membership from a variety of artists, gentry, booksellers and antiquaries.

58. Bodleian, Eng. Misc. c. 401, fol 15: quoted in Haycock 2002, 117.

59. Piggott 1985, 53–5; Haycock 2002, 118–20. Haycock makes the interesting suggestion that the Knights' preoccupation with Old Rome was both a reflection and an affirmation of the imperial supremacy that Britain increasingly claimed for itself in the course of the 18th century.

60. Rosemary Sweet has expressed doubt that the Roman Knights took their mission quite as seriously as we might be led to believe by their written legacy (pers comm).

61. The Roman Knights were progressive in other ways, too – not least in admitting female members on equal terms (an almost unprecedented practice at this time): the Duchess of Hertford was elected in 1724 and

Stukeley's future wife, Frances Williamson, was also a member. The Peterborough Gentlemen's Society seems later to have flirted briefly with the admission of women: on 15 April 1803 it was decided that 'such ladies as are admitted members of this Society, pay the usual sum for their ordinary', but then immediately it was 'Ordered . . . that no lady be admitted a member in future': Dack 1899, 158.

62. Dawson 1937; Anis 1952.

63. The four founding members were Sandwich, Charles Perry, Richard Pococke and Frederik Norden, all of whom had travelled in Egypt or the Near East. The associate members whom they invited to join them included (in addition to Stukeley) Charles Lennox (second Duke of Richmond), Martin Folkes, Alexander Gordon, Jeremiah Milles (Dean of Exeter), Andrew Mitchell and William Lethieullier – all influential members of the Antiquaries: Bodleian, Eng. Misc. e. 124, fols 85–105.

64. Anis 1952, 102–4.

65. Ibid.

66. Evans 1956, 55 n 2.

67. Johnson to le Neve, 1746, quoted in 'Some account of the Gentlemen's Society at Spalding', in Nichols 1812–16, VI, 7.

68. Stukeley's diary, 30 Mar 1748: Bodleian, Eng. Misc. e. 127, fol 14.

69. Both men were, of course, leading lights in the Spalding Gentlemen's Society, which acquired permanent premises at an early stage in its existence within a former monastery building: Nichols 1812–16, VI, 9.

70. Even the more modest Peterborough Gentlemen's Society had the use from 1752 onwards of a room over the town church which the treasurer was ordered to see 'fitted up' to receive the society's 'books, medals, pictures and other curiosities': Dack 1899, 157.

71. SAL, Minutes, I, 70, 14 Nov 1722.

72. Clark (2000, 265–6) regards the holding of an annual feast as one of the earliest expressions of a common associational identity, stemming from medieval guild practice.

73. Members of the Spalding Gentlemen's Society, for example, were encouraged to attend 'on pain of forfeiting two-pence a time for a fund of books &c. except those living 3 miles off from Spalding'; those who missed four meetings in a row were required to communicate 'something new or curious' to the club or pay a further fine of 6d, which would go towards the costs of the museum: Nichols 1812–16, VI, 28–31.

74. Clark 2000, 237, 239.

75. SAL, Minutes, [proposed] I, 226, 20 Nov 1728, [adopted] I, 228, 11 Dec 1728. Gough (1770, xxxviii) dates the full flourishing of the Antiquaries from the time of this change. In a similarly pragmatic move (and reflecting the very different rhythm of life in the

provinces), it was proposed on 8 Nov 1732 that the
Peterborough Gentlemen's Society should bring
forward its meetings by an hour to coincide with the
end of prayers at the cathedral at three o'clock: Dack
1899, 147. A more serious issue facing the rural
societies in particular was the difficulty that members
might encounter in finding their way home in the
dark; in Peterborough they got round this by agreeing
on 22 Nov 1762 henceforth 'to dine on the Wednesday
before the full moon' (ibid, 157) – a practice which
later gave its name to the Lunar Society of
Birmingham, whose meetings were similarly timed
from 1775 onwards: see, most recently, Uglow
2002, 264.

76. In the Minute Books for the 1740s the names of
candidates for election are regularly introduced with
the formula 'A vacancy happening in this Society
occasioned by the decease of [a], [b] was put to the
Ballot, and elected unanimously'. Potential members
were introduced in advance to the membership and,
if approved, were placed on a waiting list in turn, so
that when vacancies occurred there would be only one
pre-approved candidate.

77. See, for example, SAL, Minutes, VI, 106, 4 July 1751:
'A Rainy Day, and not Company enough to make a
Society'.

78. Evans 1956, 97.

79. SAL, Minutes, IV, 127, 9 Sept 1742.

80. SAL, Minutes, IV, 134–6, 21 Oct 1742. Pevsner (1977,
282) describes Royston Cave as 'a bottle-shaped cavern
c 28ft deep and 17ft diameter, in which are rudely
carved reliefs of the Crucifixion, St Christopher, etc.
Probably of various dates between the fourteenth and
the seventeenth century (the work of unskilled men)'.

81. SAL, Minutes, IV, 139, 11 Nov 1742.

82. SAL, Minutes, VI, 227, 13 Apr 1749. What seems to
have been another urn recovered on this occasion was
presented to the Ashmolean Museum in 1754; the
account of the discovery that accompanied it differs in
some points from that given here but relates several of
the same details: MacGregor and Hook 2006, x.

83. SAL, Minutes, I, 46, 12 July 1721.

84. Wise 1738, 6.

85. SAL, Minutes, I, 56, 14 Feb 1722. A few months later
we find him exhorting members to keep a look out for
Roman stations, roads, etc: I, 65, 20 June 1722.

86. SAL, Minutes, I, 50, 7 Dec 1721. Other mosaics
brought to members' attention with the benefit of
drawings include those from Woodchester, Glos ('in
proper colours'), on 18 Feb 1731 (I, 264), Well, Yorks,
on 12 Feb 1736 (II, 148), Cotterstock, Northants, on 26
May 1737 (III, 16–17), Chichester, West Sussex, on 5
Apr 1750 (VI, 35) and Winterton, Lincs, on 7 Feb 1750
(VI, 75), as well as one from Rome on 12 May 1737 (III,
12–13). Evans (1956, 93) mentions that, for a time in

the late 1730s, the Society harboured ambitions of
compiling an inventory of mosaics, but nothing came
of it. In a sense (though representing – as so often –
the triumph of personal, rather than corporate,
enterprise), the four-volume inventory by David Neal
and Stephen Cosh (2002–), currently under
production by the Society, represents its apotheosis.

87. SAL, Minutes, II, 128–9, 18 Dec 1735; II, 285–6,
17 Mar 1737, where the circumstances of their
discovery are transcribed from a letter addressed
to Peter Collinson by Benjamin Cooke.

88. Needham 1986 and 1989.

89. Herity 1969, 3–4; Briggs and Hawarth 1978;
MacGregor 1994, 184–5.

90. SAL, Minutes, I, 17, 24 Dec 1718.

91. SAL, Minutes, I, 27, 25 Nov 1719. A finger-ring with a
runic inscription, found at Harwood, Yorks, was also
communicated by way of drawings on 2 June 1737
(III, 18) and again on 11 Sept 1740 (IV, 17).

92. SAL, Minutes, II, 148, 12 Feb 1736.

93. Society of Antiquaries of London 1747–1896, I, pls
LIII–LIV, LVIII–LX. See also an unpublished typescript,
'A newly discovered report to the Society of Antiquaries
by a Committee established to examine seals for
publication in 1736 (BL, Lansdowne 843, fols 11–13v)',
by the late John Goodall, FSA (SAL archives,
uncatalogued typescript).

94. The perceived importance of such a publication
programme is reflected in Gough and Nichols's
reference to the Royal Society in which, they suggest,
'by uninterruptedly diffusing knowledge in its regular
publications, it has maintained a reputation proof
against the ridicule or restlessness of a few
discontented individuals': Nichols 1812–16, VI, 2.

95. On occasion the coins that were regularly exhibited
would be presented to the Society, leading to a decision
of the members in 1736 that 'propper drawers be
provided for repositing the Medals & Coins belonging
to them': SAL, Minutes, II, 133, 8 Jan 1736. When
these were duly delivered the gifts to date were
placed there, but as yet they amounted to no more
than forty-four coins: SAL, Minutes, II, 180,
20 May 1736.

96. See Pagan 2003.

97. This interest would certainly have been encouraged by
John Talman, charged in his position as the Society's
first Director to 'Superintend and regulate all the
Drawings, Prints, Plates and Books of the Society and
all their works of Printing Drawing or Engraving'.
Talman (see note 19) was both a practising draughtsman and a connoisseur of prints and drawings.

98. SAL, Minutes, I, 10, 5 Feb 1718; I, 10, 12 Feb 1718. The
proposal that the St James's font should be engraved
had in fact been aired on 6 Nov 1717: Evans 1956, 57.

99. Lolla 1999.

100. Walpole 1937–83, II, 116.
101. The Peterborough Gentlemen's Society was so honoured (SAL, Minutes, I, 279, 29 Dec 1731), as was Sir Hans Sloane (II, 80, 5 June 1735; II, 89, 26 June 1735).
102. SAL, Minutes, II, 215, 28 July 1736. Following years of uncertainty over its date, this object – which is still displayed at meetings of the Society – was recently identified as a medieval Jewish Sabbath lamp: Emanuel 2000.
103. Haycock 2002, 18. By way of comparison, the Spalding Gentlemen's Society similarly accumulated a collection of prints and drawings which, in 1735, was arranged into four portfolios according to subject matter.
104. SAL, Minutes, II, 16, 12 Apr 1733; II, 59, 13 Feb 1735.
105. SAL, Minutes, I, 208, 19 Apr 1727; £9 0s 6d was authorized for reimbursement to Vertue the following week.
106. Evans 1956, 83.
107. Richard Gough's summary history of the Society mentions that 'several attempts were made to unite it to the Royal Society, notwithstanding the obvious difference in their pursuits; the one being limited by their Institution and Charter to the Improvement of Natural Knowledge, the other to the Study of History and Antiquities': Gough 1770, xxxviii.
108. Letter from George North to A C Ducarel, reproduced in Nichols 1812–16, v, 442. See also a letter from Vertue to Johnson, dated 8 Sept 1750, setting out the need for the Antiquaries to be 'well established for

time to come, not any ways obliquely . . . engaged to another Society, but clearly and firmly attached to the foundation of this that it may stand on its own bottom, as it should do, for which reason many motions have been made proposed and projected to obtain a charter in order for the better establishing for perpetuating their meetings . . . somewhat like the . . . Royal Society – many of wch Society having joynd the Antiquarys have over grown and over shaded this poor Society' (quoted in Haycock 2000, 273). Ducarel, North and Vertue were among those most passionately opposed to the merger, while James Theobald and Cromwell Mortimer were aligned with the pro-merger faction led by Folkes and comprising mostly existing Fellows of the Royal Society.
109. North to Ducarel, 6 July 1752 (quoted in Nichols 1812–16, v, 455–6).
110. Quoted in Haycock 2002, 228.
111. Acceptance of the resolution by no means marked the end of the rearguard action by those committed to maintaining the unchartered status of the Society and who characterized moves for incorporation as a flagrant plot, hatched by 'a few designing members' for their own ends: Haycock 2000.
112. The Royal Society had received its initial charter in 1662, but it was found necessary to modify it in the following year.
113. The detailed history of the charter and of its progress through Chancery is given in Pugh 1982.
114. Society of Antiquaries of London 1984, 8.

BIBLIOGRAPHY

Anderson, R G W, Caygill, M L, MacGregor, A G and Syson, L (eds) 2003. *Enlightening the British: knowledge, discovery and the museum in the eighteenth century*, London

Anis, M 1952. 'The first Egyptian Society in London (1741–43)', *Bulletin de l'Institut Français d'Archéologie Orientale*, **50**, 99–105

Bagford, J 1770. 'A Letter to the Publisher, written by the ingenious Mr John Bagford', in Hearne (ed) 1770, I/1, lviii–lxxxvi

Bennett, J and Mandelbrote, S 1998. *The Garden, the Ark, the Tower, the Temple: Biblical metaphors of knowledge in early modern Europe*, exh cat, Museum of the History of Science, Oxford

Briggs, C S and Haworth, R G 1978. 'Dean Sankey Winter and the Bronze Age trumpet from "Manooth"', *J Roy Soc Antiq Ireland*, **108**, 111–15

Camden, W 1695. *Camden's Britannia* (ed E Gibson), London

Clark, P 2000. *British Clubs and Societies 1500–1800: the origins of an associational world*, Oxford

Dack, C 1899. 'The Peterborough Gentlemen's Society', *J Brit Archaeol Assoc*, new ser, **5**, 141–60

Dawson, W R 1937. 'The first Egyptian Society', *J Egyptian Archaeol*, **23**, 259–60

Emanuel, R R 2000. 'The Society of Antiquaries' Sabbath lamp', *Antiq J*, **80**, 308–15

Evans, J 1956. *A History of the Society of Antiquaries*, Oxford

Fletcher, W Y 1896–8. 'John Bagford and his collections', *Trans Bibliog Soc*, **4**, 185–201

Fox, C 2003. '"Utile et Dulce": applying knowledge at the Society for the Encouragement of Arts, Manufactures and Commerce', in Anderson, Caygill, MacGregor and Syson (eds) 2003, 62–7

Goldgar, A 1995. *Impolite Learning: conduct and community in the republic of letters, 1680–1750*, New Haven and London

Gough, R 1770. 'Introduction: containing an historical account of the origin and establishment of the Society of Antiquaries', *Archaeologia*, **1**, i–xl

Harmsen, T 2004. 'Bagford, John (1650/1–1716)', in *Oxford*

Dictionary of National Biography: Online Edition (eds H C G Matthew and B Harrison), <http://www.oxforddnb.com./view/article/1030> (24 June 2006)

Haycock, D B 2000. '"The cabals of a few designing members": the presidency of Martin Folkes, PRS, and the Society's first charter', *Antiq J*, **80**, 273–84

Haycock, D B 2002. *William Stukeley: science, religion and archaeology in eighteenth-century England*, Woodbridge

Haycock, D B 2004. 'Gale, Samuel (1682–1754)', in *Oxford Dictionary of National Biography: Online Edition* (eds H C G Matthew and B Harrison), <http://www.oxforddnb.com./view/article/10295> (24 June 2006)

Hearne, T (ed) 1770. *Leland's Collectanea*, 2nd edn, 5 vols, London

Herity, M 1969. 'Early finds of Irish antiquities from the minute-books of the Society of Antiquaries of London', *Antiq J*, **49**, 1–21

Hunter, J (ed) 1832. *Letters of Eminent Men, Addressed to Ralph Thoresby, FRS*, 2 vols, London

Hunter, M 1971. 'The Royal Society and the origins of British archaeology', *Antiquity*, **45**, 113–21, 187–92

Jessop, L 1989. 'The club at the Temple Coffee House: facts and supposition', *Archives Nat Hist*, **16**, 263–74

Klindt-Jensen, O 1975. *A History of Scandinavian Archaeology*, London

Lolla, M G 1999. 'Ceci n'est pas un monument: *Vetusta Monumenta* and antiquarian aesthetics', in Myrone and Pelz (eds) 1999, 15–35

MacGregor, A (ed) 1994. *Sir Hans Sloane: collector, scientist, antiquary; founding father of the British Museum*, London

MacGregor, A and Hook, M 2006. *Ashmolean Museum: catalogues of the early museum collections. Part II: The Vice-Chancellor's Consolidated Catalogue of 1695*, BAR Int Ser 1569, Oxford

Macky, J 1724. *A Journey through England. In familiar letters from a gentleman here, to his friend abroad*, 4th edn, 2 vols, London

Myrone, M and Pelz, L (eds) 1999. *Producing the Past: aspects of antiquarian culture and practice, 1700–1850*, Aldershot

Needham, S 1986. 'Towards the reconstitution of the Arreton Hoard: a case of faked provenances', *Antiq J*, **66**, 9–28

Needham, S, 1989. 'The decorated flanged axe from the Arreton Down Hoard, Isle of Wight', *Antiq J*, **69**, 315

Nichols, J 1812–16. *Literary Anecdotes of the Eighteenth Century*, 9 vols, London

Nickson, M 1983. 'Bagford and Sloane', *Brit Lib J*, **9**, 51–5

Pagan, H 2003. 'Martin Folkes and the study of the English coinage in the eighteenth century', in Anderson, Caygill, MacGregor and Syson (eds) 2003, 158–63

Parry, G 2004. 'Talman, John (1677–1726)', in *Oxford Dictionary of National Biography: Online Edition* (eds H C G Matthew and B Harrison), <http://www.oxforddnb.com./view/article/26955> (24 June 2006)

Pevsner, N 1977. *The Buildings of England: Hertfordshire*, rev edn (ed B Cherry), Harmondsworth

Piggott, S 1985. *William Stukeley: an eighteenth-century antiquary*, rev edn, London

Pugh, R B 1982. 'Our first charter', *Antiq J*, **62**, 347–55

Royal Society 1784. *An Authentic Narrative of the Dissensions and Debates in the Royal Society*, London

Society of Antiquaries of London 1747–1896. *Vetusta Monumenta*, 7 vols, London

Society of Antiquaries of London 1984. *Royal Charters and Statutes of the Society of Antiquaries of London*, London

Spalding Gentlemen's Society 1981. *The Minute-Books of the Spalding Gentlemen's Society 1712–55*, Lincoln Rec Soc 73, Lincoln

Strype, J 1720. *A Survey of the Cities of London and Westminster*, 2 vols, London

Sweet, R 2004. *Antiquaries: the discovery of the past in eighteenth-century Britain*, London

Uglow, J 2002. *The Lunar Men: the friends who made the future, 1730–1810*, London

Ultee, M 1987. 'The Republic of Letters: learned correspondence, 1680–1720', *The Seventeenth Century*, **17**, 95–112

Walpole, H 1937–83. *The Yale Edition of Horace Walpole's Correspondence*, 48 vols, New Haven

Weld, C R 1848. *A History of the Royal Society*, 2 vols, London

Wise, F 1738. *A Letter to Dr Mead concerning some Antiquities in Berkshire*, Oxford

Woodcock, T 2004. 'Le Neve, Peter (1661–1729)', in *Oxford Dictionary of National Biography: Online Edition* (eds H C G Matthew and B Harrison), <http://www.oxforddnb.com./view/article/16440> (24 June 2006)

CHAPTER FOUR

THE INCORPORATED SOCIETY AND ITS PUBLIC ROLE

Rosemary Sweet

Following the successful acquisition of its charter of incorporation in 1751, the Society of Antiquaries began to take its place as one of the leading learned societies in Europe and to establish its reputation for publishing high-quality prints and a notable series of transactions – the *Archaeologia*. Despite these considerable successes, and a dramatic expansion in membership to over 800, the Society nevertheless struggled to define a clear identity for itself. In part this was a consequence of the highly eclectic nature of eighteenth-century antiquarian studies (see chapter 2): while intellectual diversity could be seen as a strength, it also inhibited the development of a clear agenda at a time when other bodies were becoming more specialized in the scope of their enquiries. It also created room for disagreement, and the Society was periodically divided by internal disputes about the proper direction of antiquarian studies and the public role that it should adopt. Unlike many continental societies, which were established under royal patronage for the study of national history and given a clear directive as to the bent of their studies, the Society of Antiquaries of London was made up of private individuals who pursued antiquarianism out of personal or professional interest, albeit often tempered by a sense of patriotism. In this respect the Antiquaries were highly typical of their age: voluntarism of this nature was key to the formation of civil society in eighteenth- and nineteenth-century Britain. But voluntarism relied on the energy of particular individuals, and when that energy was lacking, or when it pulled in opposing directions, the coherence of the Society's ambitions could be lost.

Despite the misgivings and dissent that had surrounded negotiations over the charter, the worst fears of individuals such as George North (see chapter 3) were not realized: the Antiquaries resisted absorption by the Royal Society and avoided bankruptcy without having to raise membership fees to unaffordable levels. Rather, the act of incorporation provided a kind of institutional permanency and a public identity that ultimately enabled the Society to carry on through periods of apathy or low attendance.[1] Concerted efforts were made to place the conduct of the Society's business on a firmer footing, appropriate to its status as a public body, but much of this was simply the rhetoric of modernization: as Roger Gale pointed out somewhat tersely, nothing was suggested but what had been the usual custom of old and which

Fig 24. John Carter (1748–1817): a sketch portrait by Sylvester Harding. *Photograph*: © copyright the Trustees of the British Museum.

had simply fallen into abeyance.[2] One of the most obvious changes, however, was the expansion in foreign members. The Antiquaries had always compared their efforts to those of the Royal Society, the Académie des Inscriptions et Belles-lettres and the other learned societies of Europe; incorporation consolidated the Society's ambition to be seen as one of the leading learned societies of Europe. The importance attached to emulating their foreign counterparts is evident in the decision to acquire a copy of the plan followed by the Académie des Belles-lettres. A sharp uptake in the number of foreign honorary members to the Society is also noticeable in the years following incorporation as the Society sought to extend its continental links and to follow the example of the Royal Society. The first honorary foreign member had been Celsius, elected in 1735; he was one of only seven *sodales honarii* elected in the years up to 1751. In the following decade thirty-one Honorary Fellows were created, with a peak in 1761 when nine were added, setting a pattern of foreign correspondence and communication that would be followed for the rest of the century.

There was also a more subtle way in which incorporation had changed the Fellows' perception of their place in society more broadly conceived. As the petition for incorporation explained, the study of antiquities had 'ever been esteemed highly Commendable and Usefull, not only to inform the Minds of Men, but also to encite them to Noble and Virtuous Actions'.[3] The minutes of the Society during the 1750s suggest genuine attempts to realize the potential of the Society in its new incarnation as a public body and to secure more widespread recognition within the world of learning.[4]

There was likewise a movement within the Society to find accommodation more appropriate to the Society's newly incorporated status and the public role that it was to assume. On 9 November 1752 Josiah Colebrook submitted plans for a new house, designed by Theodore Jacobsen, but with the coffers drained from the cost of incorporation, the newly created Council was forced to reject them on grounds of cost. A year later, however, a new opportunity seemed to present itself: in November 1753 William Stukeley, one of those appointed a trustee of the British Museum,[5] attended a meeting at which the trustees were informed of a plan to accommodate Sloane's library, together with the Harleian and Cottonian collections, in Montagu House and, furthermore, to 'bring thither the Royal and Antiquarian Societies'.[6] This seemed to represent the kind of public recognition that the Antiquaries craved and a year later the Secretary, Joseph Ames, exhibited to the Society an engraving by Cornelius Johnson which showed 'a Section of the Quadrangle designed for the British Museum, including the Royal Society, Antiquarian Society, and a Royal Academy of Painting, Sculpture and Architecture' (fig 25).[7] In the event, although the museum was established at Montagu House, neither the Antiquaries nor the Royal Society found a home there. The Antiquaries were forced to take on rooms in Chancery Lane instead; their expectations of formal recognition for their importance of national cultural life were, for the time being, disappointed.

Fig 25. 'Section of the Quadrangle designed for the British Museum, including the Royal Society, Antiquarian Society, and a Royal Academy of Painting, Sculpture and Architecture': engraving by Cornelius Johnson (Middlesex Red Portfolio, vol 1, fol 11). *Photograph*: Society of Antiquaries of London.

PUBLICATIONS

Despite this setback, Philip Carteret Webb (whose legal advice had been instrumental in securing the charter) and James Theobald were determined to demonstrate the public utility of the newly incorporated body. Their efforts were to meet with mixed success. Theobald was an energetic individual who soon produced a plan for the Society to issue a questionnaire, which members would distribute during the summer recess, when they left London for the country, 'to obtain materials for compiling a compleat History as well of the Antiquities as natural Production in the Several parts of the nation'. Each gentleman was expected to compile an account of his own parish, and to distribute the queries to neighbouring gentlemen and clergy to fill in. The proposals were printed for distribution by the Fellows, but they also appeared in the pages of the *Gentleman's Magazine*, which was already becoming established as an important medium of communication on antiquarian subjects. It was never entirely clear by what means the resulting information was to be collated once the questionnaires were returned to the Society, but, as it transpired, this never posed a problem because the scheme did not meet with quite the enthusiastic reception that had been anticipated. By the end of the year no one had responded to Theobald's plan. A handful of parochial surveys trickled in over time, but it was hardly the comprehensive survey of the nation's antiquities for which he had hoped.[8]

Other projects were no more successful. Another member, Henry Baker, suggested that the Society should keep a memoranda book or 'chronological register' in which to record 'remarkable events'. What he envisaged was less a chronicle of political occurrences than a record of the changes and improvements taking place in transport, building, manufactures and sciences.[9] This attempt to broaden the Society's horizons met with even fewer responses than Theobald's project. In fact, Theobald was the only member to respond.[10] The collection of useful and instructive material which Theobald and Baker hoped would reflect honour upon the Society failed to materialize: members did not respond well to such directed activity.[11]

The attempts of Philip Carteret Webb to promote the publication of Domesday Book met with a rather better response, even if publication was ultimately delayed until 1783. Webb argued that it was incumbent upon the Society to undertake some project that would vindicate its claims to erudition and public service. If incorporation had brought the Antiquaries into closer alignment with the Royal Society (of which he was also a member), it was all the more important to establish the credentials of the Antiquaries as a body of public utility, which could advise the government on matters of importance – as the Royal Society did in drafting instructions for voyages of scientific discovery, undertaking a comparison of weights and measures or performing geophysical surveying.[12] To this end, like Theobald and Baker, he took it upon himself to galvanize the Fellows into greater activity. The Society should follow the example set by other learned bodies abroad, he suggested; during the summer recess members should collect and write up interesting materials that could then be presented at meetings over the coming year.[13]

His major project, however, was the publication of Domesday Book. He first raised the possibility of this at the end of 1755 and by 1756 he had prepared his *Short Account of Some Particulars Concerning Domesday Book*, which he circulated among the Fellowship. Through the Society he appealed for information on the whereabouts of copies, transcriptions and extracts of Domesday dispersed through England. He soon had reports from over a dozen other members across the country about copies of Domesday Book which they had tracked down locally, and the subject certainly dominated many of the meetings in the subsequent decade. It was easier, perhaps, for antiquaries to respond to a specific enquiry about one volume – Domesday Book – whose importance was undisputed, than to formulate answers to a long and open-ended set of enquiries, such as those found in Theobald's questionnaire.[14]

Some antiquaries published their papers in *Philosophical Transactions*, but it was self-evident that if the Antiquaries were to establish a separate identity as a learned society in the Republic of Letters it would be necessary to bring their transactions before a wider public.[15] Publication of papers had been mooted at several points since the official foundation in 1717, but nothing had been achieved except for the publication of prints. The only publishing project, apart from *Vetusta Monumenta*, on which any progress had been made was the table of English coinage, finally completed in 1763.[16] Incorporation eased some of the legal problems inherent in publication, as one of the obstacles in the early days of the Society had been the fact that it had no legal right of securing to itself the copyright of anything it published. Plans were therefore made to publish not just the papers but also a history of the Society's foundation and proceedings, and to 'shew the World they have neither wanted Diligence in their

Researches, Success in their Discussions nor Liberality in their Communications'.[17]

The publication of papers came to be seen as essential to the *raison d'être* of the Society, as a means of fulfilling its claims for broader public responsibility. John Ward who, like Theobald and Baker, was also a member of the Royal Society and a trustee of the British Museum to boot, sternly informed the Antiquaries that it was their duty as a public body. The public would expect many new discoveries and improvements in matters relating to British history and antiquities from a society such as theirs, particularly now that it was legally incorporated and under royal patronage.[18] Just as private gentlemen were frequently exhorted to place their collections in public repositories, rather than keeping them in personal custody where they could benefit none but the owner, it behoved the Society of Antiquaries to be less illiberal in sharing its knowledge.[19] A committee to review past papers, and to recommend those suitable for publication, was established in June 1753. It reported back with a list of eligible papers in January 1754, but executive action was repeatedly stalled until the end of the 1760s.[20]

FOREIGN RELATIONS

The broader horizons of the Society consequent upon incorporation were also apparent in the subject matter discussed at meetings. Although it was ostensibly established for the study of native antiquities, this stance had never been rigorously maintained to the exclusion of any other sort of antiquity, and antiquaries, as earlier chapters have shown, had always displayed a very varied range of interests. In the 1750s the Grand Tour was still essentially confined to the nobility; members of the aristocracy aside, few of the Fellows of the Society of Antiquaries had travelled to Italy, except for those who had done so as artists or tutors.[21] The interests of collectors such as Lyde Brown and Thomas Hollis (elected in 1752 and 1757 respectively), however, should not be discounted. By 1760 there was a discernible shift in the subject matter of papers presented at meetings away from the eclectic mix of coins, charters, drawings of churches and parochial surveys towards classical topics. For a number of years, from the late 1750s through the 1760s, Lyde Brown's name appears with great frequency in the pages of the Minute Books, as he presented drawings of antiquities, or the antiquities themselves which had been procured for him from Italy. It was the influence of Lyde Brown and Thomas Hollis, witnessed in their signatures to the testimonials, that secured the election of such individuals as Thomas Jenkins (Brown's chief agent in Rome) and James Stuart, and such artists as Piranesi and Richard Wilson who specialized in depicting the classical antique.[22] Their testimonials referred not only to the candidates' contribution to scholarship, but also to past and future services rendered to English travellers in Italy.

During the winter season of excavation in Rome, Jenkins sent the Society regular reports of the latest discoveries, often accompanied by drawings or prints of choice antiquities.[23] It would be wrong, however, to attribute the classicizing trend within the Society solely to the influence of Grand Tourists: there was a general interest and enthusiasm which the discoveries at Herculaneum in particular had done much to arouse. The first reports from the excavations were entering the public domain, generating great excitement amongst antiquaries across Europe,[24] and it was important that the Society of Antiquaries should establish itself as the body to which reports should be communicated, rather than the Royal Society. Throughout the 1750s the Society received accounts of the excavations from Neapolitan antiquaries, who were elected as honorary members, and it was to the Society of Antiquaries that Sir William Hamilton communicated his account of the antiquities excavated at Pompeii in the 1770s.[25]

THE DIRECTORSHIP OF RICHARD GOUGH

The reputation of the Society of Antiquaries was certainly more firmly established by the 1760s. It seemed to offer to an enthusiast such as the young Richard Gough (fig 26) a means by which antiquarian research could be encouraged and promoted. Information and expertise could be shared, topics of enquiry identified, assistance with publication offered. Gough's own preliminary work, a digest of antiquarian and topographical literature – *Anecdotes of British Topography* (1768) – had indicated to him both how much antiquarian activity had already achieved, and how much more work there remained to be done. In 1767 he was elected to the Society with high expectations of what might be accomplished and for the remainder of the century his was one of the most powerful voices within it. Gough's relationship with the Society was a troubled one, however, and it brings into sharp relief the paradoxical basis upon which the Antiquaries and other societies like it existed. In order to succeed they needed to attract the social elite, gentlemen of wealth and fashion who brought with them patronage and influence, but in order to achieve the ends for which they were founded it was necessary to maintain a scholarly ethos which often conflicted with the rather more superficial interests of precisely those members whom it had been necessary to attract.[26] A year after his election, Gough was writing to his friend and fellow antiquary, Foote Gower of Essex, in tones of disillusionment and disappointment. The Society, he found, was not the kind of antiquarian hot-house which he had hoped for. He ridiculed the way in which his fellow members gaped over nondescript items presented for their inspection – you would have been ashamed to number yourself among them, he told Gower. When the President, Charles Lyttelton, died in 1768, Gough was in despair; he feared that the fortunes of the Society would deteriorate further and that it would hasten along the path of fashion rather than enquiry. It was, he repeatedly told Gower, taken up with *virtù* rather than with genuine antiquarian researches.[27]

The evidence of the Minute Books gives some substance to Gough's recriminations: there were often occasions when no paper was read and no antiquities presented for discussion – all that is recorded is the presentation of a book, or the election of a new

Fig 26. Richard Gough: sketch made at the Duchess of Portland sale, 1785. *Photograph*: Julian Pooley. Reproduced by kind permission of the owner.

Fellow. During the 1750s active Fellows, such as Richard Rawlinson and George Vertue, had produced a ready supply of prints, engravings, charters, seals and other antiquities for exhibition and discussion at meetings. They had both died by 1755 and the following decade was dominated by papers relating to Webb's plans for Domesday Book or William Stukeley's over-active antiquarian imagination. The death of Stukeley in 1765 meant that even this source of papers dried up. In some instances it was frankly admitted that there was no one to take the chair, so the evening was spent in conversation instead. Attendance levels dropped, despite the fact that membership had been increased to 180.[28] The attempts to write a history of the Society floundered and plans for publishing papers continued to be stalled. The burst of enthusiasm and new ideas that had characterized the years immediately following incorporation had fizzled out and the impetus for activity seemed lost.

ARCHAEOLOGIA

Lyttelton's successor as President was his nephew, Jeremiah Milles (fig 27). Milles did not, perhaps, have the antiquarian acumen of Lyttelton, but he was at least committed to the study of British antiquities, as well as having the requisite connections of birth and education which were necessary for a President of the Society.[29] Between them Lyttelton, Milles and Gough at last launched the publication of *Archaeologia*, which first appeared in 1770 and continued to be issued at roughly two-year intervals until the early nineteenth century, with a brief interruption

Fig 27. Jeremiah Milles: this portrait was copied by Mary Black (1737–1814) in 1785 from an original by Nathaniel Dance of unknown date (Scharf 1865, no. 49). *Photograph*: Society of Antiquaries of London.

following Gough's resignation in 1797. Publication was undoubtedly a significant step towards securing the Society's wider reputation and greatly facilitated correspondence with other societies in Europe, with whom volumes of transactions could now be exchanged.[30] It also contributed to the 'imagined community' of antiquaries that existed across Britain, binding the provincial antiquaries, who were generally unable to attend meetings, more closely to the London Society. John Whitaker welcomed the long-awaited publication of the first volume in the pages of his *History of Manchester*. It was, he told his readers, a rich resource in itself, but of still greater significance were its future consequences: 'It now forms a valuable and respectable repository for the effusions of the antiquarian genius. It will peculiarly stimulate the ingenious and sensible, both in and out of the society, to remit their disquisitions to it.'[31]

The publication of *Archaeologia* rejuvenated expectations that the Society would be able to consolidate and digest the scattered researches of its members. Through its pages, enthused John Watson, another provincial member in Halifax, 'discoveries may be made to flow together as to one common centre, and such a Fund be at last acquired, as may give to Britain what the immortal Camden in vain attempted, a compleat Account of its Antiquities'.[32] There is indeed a discernible shift in emphasis away from metropolitan contributions in the Society's Minute Books in the years following 1771 and the tenor of meetings began to change. An increasing number of communications originated from provincial members who wrote about antiquities in their own locality or raised points of discussion from papers that they had read in *Archaeologia*.

Gough who, as Director of the Society from 1771, was ultimately responsible for editing the volume, did not find it an entirely straightforward procedure. Antiquaries could be vain, captious and quick to take offence, and Gough's somewhat brusque manner did not lend itself to soothing ruffled feathers. Thomas Pownall, on being informed that his paper on Irish antiquities was too long for inclusion in the forthcoming volume, demanded its return and declared that he would 'no longer incumber the learned works of the society'. Thomas Percy, meanwhile, took offence at the Council's decision to publish Samuel Pegge's criticisms of his *Reliques of Antient Poetry*. Jeremiah Milles had to intervene on this and a number of other occasions, as Fellows complained about the way in which their papers had been treated. 'I find it no small undertaking', he informed Gough, 'to reconcile the little misunderstandings and Jealousies that arise amongst our members.'[33]

For his part, Gough repeatedly bemoaned the poor quality of the papers presented for publication in his correspondence with his close friends. Whitaker's hopeful prophecy was not, in his opinion, borne out. In his personal correspondence he gave vent to his feelings of frustration and disappointment: 'I past Thursday and Friday last in town', he told his friend and fellow antiquary Michael Tyson, '& looking into the Antiq. Soc. had the mortification to find scarce a dozen persons droning over a dull paper of Antiquaries long since departed about R[oman] antiquities in the North detailed in Horsley or other printed books.'[34] He made similar complaints to the Cambridgeshire antiquary, William Cole: 'We are cruelly deficient in papers', hoping (without success) that Cole himself would contribute something for *Archaeologia*.[35] Gough also struggled with the pettiness of the contributors and the indifference of other members of the Council, who failed to respond to the suggestions he put to them for enhancing the Society's publications.[36] His own conception of what antiquarianism should involve meant that he was constantly at odds with the rather more miscellaneous approach employed by many of his fellow antiquaries, for whom the Society operated less as a forum for the investigation of antiquities than as a place for the presentation of papers on any subject upon which they were interested. Viewing the list of papers due to be published in the fifth volume of *Archaeologia*, which included an essay on poisonous snakes in Ireland and an account of patriarchal customs and manners, he feared that the antiquarian principles of the Society were in danger of becoming obscured.[37]

THE 'HISTORICAL PRINTS'

Gough's disillusionment festered through the 1770s as he witnessed the Society's reluctance to sponsor any engravings except a series of large historical prints. The first – the 'Field of the Cloth of Gold', published in 1775 – was taken from a scene decorating the Royal Apartments at Windsor. Its size was 31 by 53 inches (so large that it had to be printed on specially manufactured paper) and it had cost more than £440 to complete, including 200 guineas paid to James Basire, who had spent over two years engraving the drawing. By 1775 only 144 copies had been sold, realizing £264 8s. There was thus a shortfall of £176.[38] The Cowdray print, published in 1778, was a copy of one of the grand historical scenes in the great parlour at Cowdray, Sussex. It depicted the repulse of the French attack upon Portsmouth. Public interest would, it was hoped, be stimulated by the preparations being made at the time to repel another threatened French invasion.[39] The costs involved were similarly heavy and its dimensions, at 72 by 23 inches, slightly bigger – so large, in fact, that it had to be etched on two separate plates.[40] A third print – the embarkation of Henry VIII for Calais, taken again from a painting at Windsor Castle – was put in hand in 1779. Basire's bill was only a little less expensive, at 170 guineas, and the print was published in 1781.[41]

Taken together the prints represented an extravagant gesture and they certainly raised the profile of the Society of Antiquaries. The sheer size and richness of the prints undoubtedly caused a stir among the wider public, and seen as a public relations exercise the series was at least partially successful. In choosing to illustrate these historical scenes the Society was also showing itself to be in tune with the vogue for history painting which currently dominated at the Royal Academy, where two medals for paintings illustrating scenes of national history were awarded annually.[42] Jeremiah Milles tactfully made much of this common purpose in the speech he gave on moving into the new apartments at Somerset House where the two societies were now neighbours.[43] Scenes from history were believed to encourage patriotism and, as imperial and domestic crisis loomed at the end of the 1770s, this held considerable appeal. Lord Hardwicke wrote to the Society in February 1779 to commend them on their 'laudable and spirited Views' in publishing the prints and specifically mentioned 'the high Opinion they stood in with the Publick upon Account thereof'. They would, he hoped, undertake more engravings of the same kind from the historical paintings at Windsor or the great parlour at Cowdray.[44] The venture, therefore, pleased many Fellows, including members of the aristocracy who otherwise generally held themselves aloof; it also brought the Society to the attention of the king. Impressive though the prints were, money as a consequence was extremely scarce during the 1770s and 1780s and other projects had to be sidelined.[45] Significantly, there were no editions of *Vetusta Monumenta* during this period. The decision to go ahead with the Cowdray print only three years later was, therefore, particularly provoking for Gough, who had different views on how the Society's money should be spent. He gave public expression to his frustration at this 'ill advised venture' in the preface to *British Topography* in 1780. The Society, he fumed, had given the public two or three pieces of English history but had neglected the earlier (medieval) periods and the country still lacked anything comparable to Montfaucon's *Monumens de la monarchie françoise*.[46]

THE MOVE TO SOMERSET HOUSE

The plans to move from Chancery Lane to Somerset House, being projected at the same time, elicited further condemnation of what Gough saw as ill-conceived expenditure. He had a low opinion of most of the membership, which by this time had expanded to 180 members, and Milles's presidency, for which he had once entertained such high hopes, was a disappointment. In his frustration he drafted a letter of resignation, replete with bitter disappointment at the Society's failure to live up to his own expectations of what such a body should achieve. The Society, he wrote, was his 'Hobby horse' whose interests he had promoted with the utmost zeal, but he was compelled to withdraw as he saw it decline 'from its Meridian Glory'. The communications were no longer original, the President neglected to attend, Councils were not called, members did not pay their subscriptions. Such revenues as existed were lavished upon engravings to satisfy the whim of a private clique, while more important publications were neglected. To crown it all, the Society was on the point of moving to magnificent new apartments where they might cut a great figure, but where their chief ornament, the library, was in danger of being hidden away.[47]

Whether the Society had ever enjoyed the putative 'Meridian Glory' to which Gough referred in his letter is a moot point – securing attendance at meetings and papers of a consistent quality, as we have seen, had presented problems throughout the period of its existence. The range and quality of papers in the 1770s and 1780s was certainly no worse than in previous years. In the event Gough did not resign, reserving that ultimate expression of displeasure until the furore over James Wyatt's candidature in 1797, but his attendance at Council meetings became increasingly erratic. Gough's assessment of the Society's recent fortunes reflected his own high expectations of antiquarian scholarship and his suspicion of anything that savoured of dilettantism or fashionable superficiality. It was the removal to Somerset House that really provoked Gough's fury, as the costs involved detracted from what he perceived as the true ends for which the Society had been established. In this, however, he was in something of a minority.

The plans to move to Somerset House had first been broached in 1775 when it was announced to the Council that Parliament had decided that the old Somerset House should be taken down and new buildings for public offices erected, to be paid for with public monies. The Royal Academy was reported to have already been assigned chambers; it was also noted that the Royal Society had been allocated rooms in the building.[48] Whatever the Royal Society did, the Antiquaries had to match. They could not afford to let the larger Society overshadow them or assume a position of greater public visibility and importance. As Gough predicted, the move did involve considerable additional expense. It would be necessary, Milles informed Gough, to furnish the new rooms 'in a manner correspondent to that of the Royal Society and suitable to the Royal munificence'. Furthermore, given that the Society would now be lodged in apartments which were open to visitors and spectators, 'not to have proper conveniences and decorations, will disgrace our name'.[49]

The demands of the move did at least necessitate some reorganization of the Society's affairs. An inventory was taken of all the prints, engravings, copper plates and other items that had been amassed; the library was recatalogued and books rebound where necessary; the finances were overhauled and firmer action was to be taken against defaulters. The procedural innovations and the investment in the public persona of the Society were continued under Edward King's short-lived presidency in 1784. King was, it must be said, a better administrator than he was an antiquary; in fact he was the ultimate bureaucrat. Forms and ceremonies, he informed the Society in his speech of resignation, are undoubtedly trifling things in themselves, but 'as connected with, and conducting, and arranging, the management of all the affairs of life, they are perhaps of more real utility to the world than even the greatest abilities, or the most consummate knowledge'.[50] It was King who introduced the practice of having two secretaries 'to expedite business', and who attempted to tighten up the financial procedures for the Society. He also took the significant step of appointing a draughtsman to the Society in order to ensure that all antiquities presented at meetings were correctly recorded. Like Gough, he appreciated the importance of the visual record as a historical source.

Cumulatively, the move to Somerset House, the publication of *Archaeologia*, the increase in the size of the membership, as well as the more general broadening of interest in matters of antiquity and national history, had the effect of endowing the Society in the last decades of the century with a stronger institutional presence. Yet it still felt the want of a public role comparable to that of the Royal Society, and it was further hampered by the limited powers of patronage at its disposal. Nor had it even been possible to secure agreement among its own members as to what this role should be or even what subjects lay properly within its sphere. Edward King had offered one vision of the Society's role and function in his speech of resignation, delivered in a flight of rhetoric more suited to the pulpit than the gathering of a learned society. The principal pursuits of the Society, he declared, should be 'to bring *truth* to light; to devellop [*sic*] the true history of man; to show the gradual progress of the world from darkness and ignorance to light and perfection, through succeeding ages . . . and to ascertain the overruling hand of Providence in the whole progressive work'. Stirring stuff, but it hardly constituted an agenda for future activity.[51] The following year, more serious criticisms were levelled against the Society that went considerably further than the usual jibes at the esoteric and trivial aspects of its activities.

THE SOCIETY AND ITS PUBLIC REPUTATION

In 1788 the polemical antiquary and man of letters, John Pinkerton, writing as Philistor, took the Society to task in the pages of the *Gentleman's Magazine* for its failure to fulfil any kind of public role, comparing its activities unfavourably with the record of comparable societies in other European countries. The Society of Antiquaries, he argued, was composed of respectable men, but its transactions published in *Archaeologia* lacked any kind of profundity. They were but fugitive papers: 'The Society consists chiefly of men of fortune, exists at the expence of its members; and was not intended to serve the publick, but merely for an innocent and laudable amusement to the members themselves.'[52] Pinkerton called for a body which was more focused and disciplined in its activities; what was needed, he suggested, was an Academy of National History which would publish illustrations of the national historical monuments, promote research and engage in writing dissertations on national history. Medals, he suggested, should be awarded for the best dissertation upon a given historical subject, as was the practice in the Society for the Encouragement of Arts and Manufactures and in the continental academies. He even argued that the government should take the unprecedented measure of confining the Society to the study of history alone by the terms of its charter and allot it a revenue which would allow it to publish original writers 'in an elegant manner'.[53]

What Pinkerton was suggesting was a society much more akin to the academies established by royal fiat in France or Denmark than a modern vision of state-sponsored history. His manifesto would not have appealed to most antiquaries, who would have resisted the concept of state directives in the matter of what they should research,[54] but his argument, that the Society could and should play an important role in promoting the study of history and the preservation of national antiquities, would have struck a chord with Richard Gough and his circle. In 1785 Michael Lort, one of Gough's allies within the Society and a long-serving Vice-President, had offered Thomas Percy, by then Bishop of Drogher, some advice on establishing a new antiquarian society in Ireland.[55] Drawing on his experience of the Society of Antiquaries, Lort recommended that the membership should be limited – in the London society, he explained, the policy was too open, and anyone who applied was admitted. He also advised Percy to draw up a set of subjects and topics of enquiry for members to investigate – a measure which clearly anticipated Pinkerton's call to arms in the *Gentleman's Magazine* and which reflected Lort's own frustrations with the London Society.[56] There was, therefore, a minority at least, who had a vision of a dynamic organization; one that would do more in the way of co-ordinating research, promoting publication and establishing national history upon a sounder footing. The reality of the Society in which they found themselves, however, precluded their dreams from being realized. The Society was unable to act effectively as a body to promote the illustration of national history and antiquities, however much its members might wish to do so as individuals.[57]

DIVISIONS WITHIN THE SOCIETY

The failure of common purpose in the proceedings of the Society was a reflection of the lack of unity among the Antiquaries as a body. The Fellowship was a heterogeneous mix, and became more so as numbers expanded (see chapter 8). By the end of the eighteenth century it included some of the leading political, ecclesiastical, legal and intellectual luminaries of the day, as well as those with more serious antiquarian credentials. There were many competing interests and, like any body of that size, it was afflicted by factionalism. The Antiquaries liked to pride themselves that their dissensions were far less divisive than those of the Royal Society, but there was nevertheless scope for considerable disagreement which proved a powerful obstacle to any kind of activity that involved the commitment of time or money on the part of the members. The matter of the charter had been followed by a relatively quiet period, but in the 1770s and 1780s, as the Society became more ambitious in its publications and pretensions, the scope for disagreement opened up again. Gough's reservations over the publication of the historical prints have already been mentioned. Rising membership fees provoked unhappiness from the country members who considered that the Society was being managed in the interests of a metropolitan elite. Edward King's brief presidency had given rise to the first contested election for the presidency in the Society's history in which he lost out to Lord de Ferrers, subsequently Earl of Leicester. 'King seems to have a Party', Hayman Rooke told Samuel Pegge, 'which I am sorry for, being fearful lest the restlessness of such Party should cause a lasting, & not only a temporal Disease in the Society'.[58] Rooke's anxieties were not, in the short term at least, fulfilled. The contest was in reality more of a reflection upon Edward King's personal ambitions than of factional manoeuvrings within the Council.

The relationship with the Royal Society, which had been so contentious in the negotiations for the charter, continued to be a somewhat delicate matter. Given that a third or more of the members also belonged to the Royal Society at any one point, and given also the extent of common intellectual ground between the two societies, their interests were always going to be closely linked. The very proximity of the relationship made the Antiquaries the more conscious of a need both to preserve a separate identity and to match the Royal Society at every instance. Thus the move to Somerset House was not just a question of expediency for those who enjoyed dual membership, and who could now move effortlessly from one meeting to the other without the inconvenience of leaving the building, but also one of competition. The cohabitation was not without its difficulties; petty rivalries, expressed in territorial disputes over the common stairway and entrance hall or the provision of a porter, were a frequent occurrence. The Antiquaries' old fear – that the Royal Society might seek to absorb their own society – never died away; indeed, it acquired a new cogency during the forty-two-year period in which Sir Joseph Banks was President of the Royal Society. Banks was typical of the kind of polymathic individual who shaped the English Enlightenment before the period of disciplinary segregation and increasing specialization. Just as many antiquaries had interests in natural history, Banks too could claim that 'general antiquities has been always with me a favorite pursuit of Relaxation'. He was elected to both the Royal and the Antiquarian Societies in 1766 and moved easily between the two worlds, even if his primary interests lay in botany and natural history.[59] Any chance to excavate a barrow was seized upon with alacrity, and when in Lincolnshire at the family estates he worked upon his collections for the history and antiquities of Lincolnshire.[60]

The Banksian hegemony in the Royal Society was challenged by a faction led by the mathematician Samuel Horsley, who alleged that Banks had interfered with elections to the Council and the Fellowship of the Royal Society. Horsley demanded a more rigorously mathematical approach in the conduct of the Royal Society in place of the rule of the virtuosi, which encouraged a much broader range of subjects.[61] Much of Banks's support within the Royal Society derived from those members who, like him, belonged also to the Antiquaries. 'If my friends of the Antiquarian Society support me', he told Thomas Astle when standing for election as President of the Royal Society, 'I have not the least doubt of succeeding in a very creditable manner.'[62] Banks was never an officer of the Society of Antiquaries, but he was elected twice to the Council. Normally this did not constitute a conflict of interest, but the fact that Banks commanded such enormous patronage in the cultural world inevitably meant that a coterie of Banksites gathered around him. Among those members who had first-hand knowledge of the dissensions in the Royal Society, there was always a lingering suspicion that the divisions would spill over into the realm of the Antiquaries as well and that Banks would try to bring the other society more effectively under his sway. It was the latter point which created tensions at the end of the 1790s and into the nineteenth century.

In 1797 the architect James Wyatt – responsible for alterations at the cathedrals of Salisbury, Lichfield, Hereford and Durham – was elected to the Society, despite the vehement protests of a minority led by John Carter, Richard Gough and Sir Henry Englefield, who objected to what they regarded as his vandalism of the nation's medieval fabric.[63] Gough resigned in protest and withdrew almost all contact with the Society. Joseph Banks, who enjoyed close relations with the monarch, was always going to be a supporter of Wyatt, given the fact that Wyatt was the king's surveyor general, and, with effect from 1797, surveyor to Somerset House.[64] There were also practical reasons for supporting Wyatt: any changes to be made to the accommodation of the Royal and Antiquarian Societies, as well as the Royal Academy, would have to win Wyatt's approval and be executed under Wyatt's direction. Wyatt's supporters knew where their best interests lay. In retaliation it was Banks who called for Carter's expulsion and his party of 'anti-Gothicists', including Samuel Lysons, Thomas Astle and John Topham. It took some time for the ill feeling generated by the controversy to die down, and the veracity of Carter's allegations that Wyatt had planned to destroy the Galilee Chapel in Durham Cathedral was still being debated with some heat through the summer of 1799.[65] Carter, formerly draughtsman to the Society, found that his commissions were gradually dropped; he turned increasingly to journalism in the *Gentleman's Magazine*, while A C Pugin and Richard Smirke were employed to complete engravings of St Davids Cathedral and St Stephen's Chapel.[66] Nevertheless Carter continued to appear regularly at meetings, presenting papers and airing his grievances against Samuel Lysons (Gough's successor as Director), and the other Banksites within the Society (fig 24).

When the President, the Earl of Leicester, signalled his intention of resigning a year after these ructions had taken place in 1799, Banks saw an opportunity to secure the election of someone amenable to his own influence, such as the botanist Lord Lewisham, and the chance to defeat those who had supported Carter in the Wyatt débâcle, such as Sir Henry Englefield. The presidency was contested between Lewisham and Leicester, who decided to stand again.[67] Leicester prevailed with a majority of fifty-six.[68] The fact that Lewisham had no pretensions to being anything but a botanist, combined with the knowledge that his chief supporter was Sir Joseph Banks, seemed to Richard Gough and his followers to herald yet another attempt to subsume the Antiquaries within the Royal Society and the Banksian empire of knowledge.[69] Joseph Farington's diaries, detailing the long drawn-out campaign of meetings between Lysons and Banks and the endless canvassing of votes, indubitably confirm that Banks was the driving force behind the projected *coup d'état*. A letter to the *Gentleman's Magazine* in 1803 reiterated the same point, referring to the 'late attempt at revolution', which would have made the Society of Antiquaries dependent upon the Royal Society. The author also charged the Society with having become too fashionable, too polite and too rich to fulfil the original designs of its institution.[70] The bitter feelings provoked by the quarrel of 1797–9 festered and soured relations within the Society through the early years of the nineteenth century.

THE 'FASHIONABLE WEEKLY RENDEZVOUS'

It is actually debatable whether the Society really was too rich, given that its finances were heavily encumbered by the enormously expensive engravings of 'Cathedral Antiquities', which Gough himself had been instrumental in promoting. The retail price for these rose from £2 8s for the first volume to six guineas for the fifth, but as most of the copies were distributed free to the members there was little money to be made from their sale. Gough had carped at the costs of engraving the historical prints, but they did not begin to match the £600 charged by Basire for engraving Carter's drawings of Durham.[71] The Society was forced to increase revenue by expanding the membership even further, but it was nevertheless left with a loss of over £5,000.[72] By 1803 it numbered over 800 members and in 1807 membership stood at 849. By this time the Antiquaries had overtaken the Royal Society in terms of membership, if not in wealth – in 1800 the membership of the Royal Society numbered only 531. Its capital, however, stood at a satisfactory £11,000, whereas the Antiquaries were forced to sell some of their own investments to make up the losses sustained on their publications.[73] The value of the books and prints which the Fellows had been receiving as members (unscrupulous individuals took their copies straight to the book dealers) far exceeded the value of the admission and subscription fees, a situation which was exacerbated by chronic arrears of payment which amounted to over £1,300 by 1810.[74] As a consequence of the dire financial situation in which the Society found itself, the admission fee in 1804 was raised to eight guineas, with an annual fee of four guineas, an increase which went well beyond the rate of inflation. The cumulative effect of these developments was to heighten the aura of social exclusivity with which the Society was associated, rather than to enhance its scholarly credentials.

Social exclusivity was also written into the very structure of the Society. Even in the early years of the eighteenth century, when the son of a shoemaker such as John Bagford could be elected, the Antiquaries had never admitted quite the diversity of social backgrounds that could be found in the Royal Society. Personal knowledge of potential candidates to the Society of Antiquaries was essential: in 1773 the Council ruled that in future no candidates should be nominated unless known personally to the members making or subscribing to the nomination,[75] and family connections often weighed more heavily than mere antiquarian aptitude. Members of the aristocracy had always been welcomed as Fellows, irrespective of their interest in antiquities, and membership was automatic upon their making it known that they would welcome admission. Thus many members were drawn from London's fashionable elite, headed by the Prince of Wales and the Dukes of Gloucester and Cumberland – men not known for their antiquarian proclivities. James Douglas's observation that the Society had 'become one of our most fashionable weekly rendezvous' was more than just another ironic jibe.[76] The anonymous correspondent in the *Gentleman's Magazine* complained that the membership of the Society had become nothing more than an 'indiscriminate rabble'; wealth and rank were given preference over any ability to contribute to the study of antiquities.[77]

Some individuals professed to seek admission in order to participate in antiquarian correspondence, but for many others the prime motivation in joining the Society was to form social contacts or simply to add to their collection of engravings (which would account for the number of artists and architects who were enrolled but who scarcely ever attended the meetings). The close proximity to the Royal Academy

in Somerset House evidently facilitated social interaction between members of the
Society, and, as with the Royal Society, there was a considerable overlap in membership during these years. The blackballing inflicted upon the architect James Wyatt
in protest against his architectural innovations at Durham Cathedral was the more
pointed in that membership was being granted to other artists and architects with
increasing frequency. In addition to Joseph Farington, whose diaries provide so much
personal and anecdotal detail of the social world in which these people moved,
fashionable artists such as Benjamin West and Richard Cosway, or engravers such
as Valentine Green and Thomas Byrne, were being elected. Joseph Farington and
his ilk were part of a lively social and cultural elite who moved easily from the
drawing rooms of the nobility and artists' studios to meetings of the Royal Academy
or the Society of Antiquaries. The Antiquaries represented yet another social
forum where connections might be made, introductions effected, news exchanged
and commissions sought after. Even at the contested election in 1799, when Farington
estimated that 400 of the 800-plus members were within 'penny post' distance of
London, he predicted that only 250 would turn up.[78] Membership for many was just
an additional status symbol.

A LOSS OF DIRECTION?

'I think this Society is going fast to the D——', fumed Francis Douce in 1809. The
complaint was not a new one. Fellows had been lamenting intermittently that the
Society was no longer what it was since the 1720s. But other scholars have followed
Douce in arguing that the Society lost its way in the early nineteenth century.[79] The
very public wrangling of 1797–9 had left a perception of internecine quarrelling in
the public mind. 'The world calls us old women', complained one antiquary: 'we can
quarrel too like them.'[80] Attendance at meetings was, by some accounts, poor, but
such complaints are hard to substantiate since the names of those attending ceased
to be recorded in 1770. The only time at which the meetings were full, according
to Douce, was when there was a contested election; otherwise the room was empty,
with a dearth of papers. Again, the Minute Books show that there was some truth
in this. Samuel Lysons regaled the assembled company with 'interesting extracts'
from his *History of the Berkeley Family*, for want of alternative fare, no less than
twenty-two times between 1799 and 1801.[81] The Earl of Leicester had never been a
dynamic figure as President, and his interest in antiquities was largely limited to
heraldry and his own pedigree. After 1801 his role in the Society became increasingly
marginal, and his attendance more and more infrequent until his death in 1811.
Sir Henry Englefield was initially elected as his successor, and did at least have
claims to genuine antiquarian scholarship. But Englefield's open support for Carter
in the 1790s, and his own Catholicism, had earned him enemies among the Council
and the Earl of Aberdeen was elected in his stead. Aberdeen brought the dignity
of the peerage to the presidency, but was no more committed an antiquary than

Leicester, and even more erratic in attendance. It was not an auspicious appointment.

The other officers were hardly more suited to exercise leadership. Samuel Lysons was a more than competent antiquary, as his work at Woodchester and the unfinished *Magna Britannia* shows, but he did not use his position as Director to further the role played by the Society in sponsoring the study of antiquities in any readily discernible way.[82] Thomas Frognall Dibdin penned some caustic comments upon Lysons's record as Director: he was 'opinionated, dogmatical, and at times, over-bearing. There was only *one* dictum to which he, apparently, deferred – and *that* was the opinion of . . . Sir Joseph Banks.'[83] Lysons's energies were certainly directed towards his own publications, but he did at least ensure that *Archaeologia* continued to appear on a regular basis. The Secretary, Nicholas Carlisle, was even less active, treating the position, which came with free accommodation and a comfortable salary of £200, as little more than a sinecure, never doing more than was absolutely required of him.[84] Criticisms were expressed in the pages of the *Gentleman's Magazine*; the Council was charged with having becoming an unaccountable oligarchy, which failed to exercise responsible stewardship over the Society's resources.[85] From having been a supplement to the proceedings of the Society, the *Gentleman's Magazine* had, since the 1790s, become an arena where antiquaries aired their differences and settled scores.

There was a clear irony here. At a time when antiquarianism was enjoying greater popularity than in previous periods, and when an awareness of the importance of the preservation of buildings and the potential historical value of excavation work was becoming more widely established, the Society was not in a position to capitalize upon the situation. Individual members might take an interest in preservation or excavation, but the Society as a body did next to nothing. It failed to mobilize the growth in sentiment in favour of preservation or to assert itself in an advisory capacity to the government with respect to, for example, the Record Committees. It had still to be established where the priorities of the Society lay, and the tenor of its meetings and publications was determined by the personal agenda of whichever members were most assiduous in attendance. The refusal to take a stand over the election of Wyatt in the case of Durham Cathedral had dented its reputation as a body concerned for the preservation of antiquities. Its expansion in size had enhanced its public profile but diluted its antiquarian credentials. Perhaps unfairly, it was known for expensive high-quality engravings – but little else. Looking forward into the nineteenth century the Society would face considerable problems in meeting the challenge of ever increasing disciplinary specialization which went against the grain of the Society's traditionally eclectic approach. Other societies were established that encroached upon areas that had traditionally fallen within its scope – such as the British Archaeological Association, the Camden Society and the myriad county historical and archaeological societies. It would be some time later, and after a period of relative stagnation, that the Society of Antiquaries would acquire a firmer sense of purpose and identity.[86]

NOTES

1. Clark 2000, 97–8.
2. SAL, Minutes, VII, 60, 26 Apr 1753.
3. Evans 1956, 104.
4. SAL, Minutes, VII, 240, 2 May 1754: motion that the Society should apply for copies of the plan followed by the Académie des Inscriptions et Belles-lettres.
5. Of the 63 individuals named in Sir Hans Sloane's will as trustees of the British Museum, half were members of the Society of Antiquaries and 40 were Fellows of the Royal Society: MacGregor 1994, 48.
6. Quoted in Evans 1956, 111.
7. SAL, Minutes, VII, 286, 14 Nov 1754.
8. During the following year he received only one other parochial account, from Hopton, Norfolk. In 1756 an account of Elton in Huntingdonshire was sent in, followed by accounts from Monmouthshire in 1758 and Sherborne in 1759. The questionnaire reappeared in various guises throughout the century, however, and in another abortive proposal to co-ordinate a series of county surveys of antiquities from the members in 1771: see SAL, Council Minutes, I (not paginated), 3 Mar 1771.
9. SAL, Minutes, VII, 478, 11 Nov 1756.
10. Theobald provided accounts of the water gate at the end of Buckingham Street in York Buildings, which was soon to be dismantled; of the fate of the collection of Arundel marbles (he was able to report that one of the columns was currently in use as a roller for his bowling green at White Waltham); and of the rise and progress of the Society for the Encouragement of Arts and Manufactures, of which both he and Baker were founder members: SAL, Minutes, VIII, 66, 5 May 1757; ibid, 219, 11 May 1758; ibid, 28, 1 June 1758; see also Allan and Appleby 1996. Other antiquaries who also belonged to the Society of Arts included Thomas Brand, Gustavus Brander, Sir Henry Cheere, Thomas Hollis, the Earl of Macclesfield, James Stuart, Charles Morton and Philip Carteret Webb.
11. The pair achieved rather more success in the context of the Society of Arts, where, with the Cornish antiquary William Borlase, they were instrumental in establishing the county surveys: Harley 1963–4. Competition with France was a driving force behind this project also: there was a strong sense that Britain lagged behind France where Louis XV had commissioned a map of the whole of France upon a trigonometrical framework.
12. Lyons 1944, 163.
13. The only member who specifically responded to this was, predictably, James Theobald, who reported that he had collected addenda to Lewis's history of Thanet: SAL, Minutes, VII, 466, 24 June 1756; ibid, 489, 9 Dec 1756.
14. SAL, Minutes, VII, 438, 1 Apr 1756; VIII, 41–2, 24 Mar 1757; ibid, 110, 8 Dec 1757. See also Henry Ellis's interleaved copy of Webb 1756, which includes much of the correspondence generated from this project and the negotiations which took place over publication: BL, Add MS 38541. For the subsequent history of its publication and the Society's involvement, see Condon and Hallam 1984.
15. Bodleian, Top. London c. 2, fols 187–188.
16. Folkes 1736, 1745 and 1763.
17. Bodleian, Top. London c. 2, fol 192. George North was at work on a history of the Society in 1754 but never completed it: SAL, Minutes, VII, 221, 28 Feb 1754.
18. Evans 1956, 139.
19. William Blackstone observed that 'it were much to be wished that all gentlemen, who are possessed of similar curiosities [a copy of the Great Charter], would follow so laudable an example, by placing them in some public repository [*sic*]': Blackstone 1759, xxxv.
20. SAL, Minutes, VII, 156, 28 June 1753; ibid, 207, 24 Jan 1754.
21. By 1760 444 Fellows had been elected to the Society; excluding the Honorary Fellows, this left 419 members, of whom only 47, or just over 10 per cent, are known to have travelled to Italy: Ingamells 1998. Seven of these travellers were, or would become, members of the Society of Dilettanti.
22. Ford 1974a and 1974b.
23. Pierce 1965.
24. SAL, MS 264, fols 44–45: 'Extract of Two Letters from Signor Camillo Paderni at Rome to Mr Allan Ramsay, Painter in Covent Garden, Concerning Some Ancient Statues, Pictures and other Curiosity's Found in a Subterranean Town, Lately Discovered near Naples, Translated from the Italian by Mr Ramsay and Sent by him to Mr Ward', dated 20 Nov 1739 and 20 Feb 1740; Anon 1750; Bellicard 1753; Martyn and Lettice 1757; Hamilton 1777.
25. Don Francesco Valetta, a member of the 'Academy for explaining the antiquities of Herculaneum instituted by the King of Naples', was elected in 1756; his election was followed a few months later by that of Signor Camillo Paderni, keeper of the museum at Herculaneum.
26. Gough's influence is discussed in greater detail in Sweet 2001.
27. BL, Add MS 29944, fol 134v: Richard Gough to Foote Gower, 18 Feb 1768.
28. Average attendance in 1752 was 20, in 1762 it was 15. This does not include attendance at the meeting on 23 April, when numbers were always much higher on the occasion of the elections and the Anniversary Dinner. The resolution of 2 Mar 1769 to move the

time of meetings to 6.30pm to secure a better attendance is again indicative of the problems experienced
in securing active participation from the Fellows.

29. Milles did not publish anything of great antiquarian
significance; essays were published in *Archaeologia* and
Philosophical Transactions. Of more significance were
his unpublished collections, particularly those relating
to the history and antiquities of Devon. His reputation
in later life suffered as a consequence of the outspoken
support which he initially offered to Thomas
Chatterton in the Rowley controversy.

30. In 1773 bound copies of the second volume of
Archaeologia were presented to the Society of
Mannheim, the Society of St Petersburg and the
University of Göttingen. In 1777 volumes were
exchanged with the Imperial College and Royal
Academy of Sciences and Belles-Lettres of Brussels
and the Society of Antiquaries at Hesse Cassell (SAL,
Council Minutes, II (not paginated), 1 Dec 1777
and 3 Feb 1778).

31. Whitaker 1773, I, 136.

32. Watson 1775, v.

33. SAL, MS 447/1, fol 82: Jeremiah Milles to Richard
Gough, 17 May 1774; fol 88, Gough to Milles, 18 May
1774; fol 99v, Gough to Milles, 30 Sept 1774; fol 101,
Milles to Gough, 8 Oct 1774; fol 111, Milles to Gough,
27 Nov 1774. The paper which so offended Percy was
Pegge 1773.

34. Bodleian, Gough Gen. Top. 44, fol 458: Richard Gough
to Michael Tyson, 20 Mar 1780; Nichols 1814, 664.
Edward Hasted made similarly scathing comments to
Andrew Coltée Ducarel: 'Our Transactions of the
Antiquarian Society have done us so little credit, that
we are rather out of humour with the compilers of it':
ibid, 648, 18 Feb 1771.

35. BL, Add MS 5834, fol 105: Richard Gough to William
Cole, 22 Jan 1781.

36. See, for example, Gough's letter to Michael Lort: SAL,
MS 447/2, fols 124–126, 29 Jan 1778.

37. SAL, MS 447/2, fol 88: Richard Gough to Michael
Lort, 11 Dec 1776. The papers in question were
Barrington 1779 and Pegge 1779.

38. SAL, Council Minutes, II (not paginated), 21 June
1775.

39. SAL, MS 447/2, fol 134: Michael Lort to Richard
Gough, 26 Jan 1778.

40. SAL, Council Minutes, II (not paginated), 8 July 1778.

41. SAL, Council Minutes, II (not paginated), 23 Nov 1779.

42. Strong 1978, 13–29; Cannon-Brookes 1991.

43. 'From the judicious Investigation of ancient Science,
and Art, a more general and useful Field of Knowledge
is opened to the modern Artist. The most valuable
Hints for the Direction of his Studies are to be
collected from the Works of Antiquaries; and the
Repositories of Arts have been enriched with a Variety

of necessary Information from the same Source': SAL,
Minutes, XVII, 220, 11 Jan 1781. On the Royal Academy
see Hoock 2003, 152–3.

44. SAL, Minutes, XVI, 223, 25 Feb 1779. Michael Lort had
written to Lord Hardwicke the previous year, telling
him how a 'good puffing' description of the print had
been drawn up at the last Council meeting, 'we had
almost thought of sending Hawkers down to the
respective encampments to circulate that & Sir
Joseph's [Ayloffe] historical description, but this the
Baronet thought would be degrading his & our own
dignities': BL, Add MS 35614, fol 277, Michael Lort
to Lord Hardwicke, 9 July 1778.

45. SAL, MS 447/2, fol 59: Michael Lort to Richard
Gough, 11 May 1775.

46. Suffolk Record Office, Bury St Edmunds, E2/22/1,
unfoliated collection: Richard Gough to George Ashby;
Gough 1780, I, xli.

47. SAL, MS 447/1, fol 215: Richard Gough to Jeremiah
Milles, undated letter, *c* 1780. The text of the letter is
reproduced in Evans 1956, 180.

48. Hoock 2003, 37.

49. SAL, MS 447/1, fol 157: Jeremiah Milles to Richard
Gough, 12 Feb 1776. It was decided to have moreen
curtains in the meeting room, twelve chairs for the
library, at a cost of twenty shillings each, and a couple
of brass chandeliers. The mace had to be regilded, the
President's chair 'beautified'; the time piece and the
ballot box were both deemed to be unsuitable to the
dignity of the Society. One of the largest items of
expenditure was a marble bust of their royal patron,
costing 100 guineas.

50. King 1784, 4.

51. Ibid, 5, 11.

52. Pinkerton 1788, 1150.

53. Ibid, 1149–51.

54. Three years earlier Michael Lort had rejected the
notion of premiums of this kind, on the grounds that
'the determination of which is often unpleasant and
invidious': Nichols 1848, 469, Michael Lort to Thomas
Percy, 24 June 1785.

55. The Hibernian Society of Antiquaries (1780–3) was
founded by William Burton Conyngham, Mervyn
Archdall, Charles Vallancey, Edward Ledwich, Charles
O'Connor and William Beauford. Matters went 'very
well' at first, but the strain upon Ledwich of moderat-
ing his comments on Vallancey's wilder speculations
proved too much. 'By the lively jocular way in which
he wrote, [Ledwich] offended Colonel Valancey [*sic*],
who expatriated him from his Collectanea, and from a
Society which immediately ceased': *Gent's Mag*, 1796,
66, 528. Following the failure of the Hibernian Society,
the Royal Irish Academy, established in 1788, comprehended antiquities within its enquiries. On the latter
society see O'Raifeartaigh 1985.

56. Nichols 1848, 469: Michael Lort to Thomas Percy, 24 June 1785.
57. Nichols 1780, i–iii, drew particular attention to this failure of the Society to produce anything of note.
58. SAL, MS 891/1, unfoliated collection: Hayman Rooke to Samuel Pegge, 18 May 1785.
59. Carter 1988, 32. Two of the sponsors were the same in each case – Charles Lyttelton and Charles Morton: Gascoigne 1994, 123.
60. His correspondence with Gough on Lincolnshire history and antiquities is printed in Nichols 1822, 694–9. See also Gascoigne 1994, 124–6.
61. Lyons 1944, 212–14; Maty 1784; Kippis 1784.
62. Gascoigne 1994, 121.
63. This episode is discussed in more detail in Sweet 2004, 288–94. See also Crook 1995.
64. Crook 1973, 49–76.
65. SAL, Minutes, XXVII, 225, 335–7, 345–7, 360–6, 368. See also Garlick and Macintyre 1979, IV, 1227, 1235.
66. Evans 1956, 212. A committee was deputed to report on the state of affairs vis à vis Carter's cathedral engravings in 1799. Carter had completed Exeter, Bath and Durham (yet to be engraved) and had work in hand for Gloucester and Wells, for which he had not been paid.
67. Details of the negotiations preceding the election were recorded by Joseph Farington: see Garlick and Macintyre 1979, IV, 1161, 1163, 1168, 1169, 1173, 1174, 1176, 1182, 1185, 1187, 1188, 1191, 1192, 1193, 1204, 1208–10.
68. 'There were more violent contests in the Society of Antiquaries on St George's day. A Set of Gentlemen, who wish to remove the President and all the Officers, set up a new Candidate (Lord Lewisham) for the Chair, with an Intent to discard the Secretaries, and every other Officer in the present Establishment who did not accord with their Wishes': SAL, MS 891/1, unfoliated collection: Samuel Pegge jun. to Hayman Rooke, 8 May 1799.
69. Nichols 1831, 776–7: Samuel Denne to Richard Gough, 13 May 1799: 'I was much obliged to you for your favour received by the post on Sunday; and join heartily with you in the congratulation on the victory obtained over Magog Banks'.
70. *Gent's Mag*, 1803, **73**, 316. The letter was anonymous, but it could easily have been penned by Gough.
71. SAL, Council Minutes, III (not paginated), 30 May 1799.
72. SAL, Council Minutes, IV, 166–7, 25 May 1810, statement of accounts; Evans 1956, 214.
73. Sorrenson 1996, 30.
74. *Gent's Mag*, 1802, **72**/2, 1181; SAL, Council Minutes, IV, 128, 8 Feb 1810.
75. Evans 1956, 148.
76. James Douglas to Bryan Faussett, 4 Feb 1785, quoted in Jessup 1975, 28.
77. *Gent's Mag*, 1803, **73**/1, 125.
78. See also Garlick and Macintyre 1979, IV, 1193.
79. Evans 1956, 225–51; Levine 1986, 49–51.
80. Parker Library, Corpus Christi College, Cambridge, Kerrich MS 601, fol 123v: Edward Balme to Thomas Kerrich, 21 Nov 1803.
81. Evans 1956, 213, on the basis of the index, suggests that it was only fifteen times.
82. Lysons 1797 and 1806.
83. Evans 1956, 222.
84. Ibid, 224.
85. *Gent's Mag*, 1802, **72**, 1181–3; *Gent's Mag*, 1803, **73**, 123–5.
86. The account offered by Evans 1956, 225–51, is particularly damning, laying the blame squarely on the inefficacy of the officers who should have been responsible for a more effective use of the Society's considerable resources and who should have offered a firmer leadership.

BIBLIOGRAPHY

Allan, D G C and Appleby, J H 1996. 'James Theobald's "Missing" MS "History of the Society of Arts" and his "Chronological Register of the Present Age"', *Antiq J*, **76**, 201–14

Anon 1750. *Memoirs Concerning Herculaneum, the Subterranean City*, London

Barrington, D 1779. 'Observations on patriarchal customs and manners', *Archaeologia*, **5**, 119–36

Bellicard, J C 1753. *Observations upon the Antiquities of the Town of Herculaneum, Discovered at the Foot of Mount Vesuvius: with some reflections on the painting and sculpture of the ancients and a short description of the antiquities in the neighbourhood of Naples*, London

Blackstone, W 1759. *The Great Charter and the Charter of the Forest, with other Authentic Instruments: to which is prefixed an introductory discourse, containing the history of the charters*, Oxford

Cannon-Brooks, P (ed) 1991. *The Painted Word: British history painting, 1750–1830*, Woodbridge

Carter, H B 1988. *Sir Joseph Banks*, London

Clark, P 2000. *British Clubs and Societies, 1580–1800: the origins of an associational world*, Oxford

Colvin, H (ed) 1973. *A History of the King's Works*, VI, London

Condon, M and Hallam, E 1984. 'Government printing of the public records in the eighteenth century', *J Soc Archivists*, **7**, 359–73

Crook, J M 1973. 'The surveyorship of James Wyatt', in Colvin (ed) 1973, 49–76

Crook, J M 1995. *John Carter and the Mind of the Gothic Revival*, Soc Antiq London Occas Pap 17, London

Evans, J 1956. *A History of the Society of Antiquaries*, London

Folkes, M 1736. *A Table of English Gold Coins from the 18th Year of King Edward III when Gold was first Coined in England*, London

Folkes, M 1745. *A Table of English Silver Coins from the Norman Conquest to the Present Time*, London

Folkes, M 1763. *Tables of English Silver and Gold Coins, First Published by Martin Folkes Esq, 1736–45, and Now Reprinted*, London

Ford, B 1974a. 'James Byres: principal antiquarian for the English visitors to Rome', *Apollo*, **99**, 446–61

Ford, B 1974b. 'Thomas Jenkins: banker, dealer and unofficial English agent', *Apollo*, **99**, 416–25

Garlick, K and Macintyre, A (eds) 1979. *The Diary of Joseph Farington*, 12 vols, New Haven and London

Gascoigne, J 1994. *Joseph Banks and the English Enlightenment: useful knowledge and polite culture*, Cambridge

Gough, R 1780. *British Topography*, 2 vols, London

Hamilton, Sir W 1777. 'An account of the discoveries at Pompeii', *Archaeologia*, **4**, 160–75

Harley, J B 1963–4. 'The Society of Arts and the surveys of English counties, 1759–1809', *J Soc Arts*, **112**, 43–6, 119–24, 269–75, 538–43

Hoock, H 2003. *The King's Artists: the Royal Academy of Arts and the politics of British culture, 1768–1840*, Oxford

Ingamells, J 1998. *A Dictionary of British and Irish Travellers in Italy, 1701–1800*, New Haven and London

Jessup, R 1975. *Man of Many Talents: an informal biography of James Douglas, 1753–1819*, London

King, E 1784. *A Speech Delivered by Edward King, Esq., President of the Society of Antiquaries of London*, London

Kippis, A 1784. *Observations on the Late Contests in the Royal Society*, London

Levine, P 1986. *The Amateur and the Professional: antiquaries, historians and archaeologists in Victorian England, 1838–1886*, Cambridge

Lyons, H 1944. *The Royal Society, 1660–1940*, Cambridge

Lyons, S 1797. *An Account of the Roman Antiquities Discovered at Woodchester*, London

Lysons, S and Lysons, D 1806. *Magna Britannia; being a concise topographical account of the several counties of Great Britain*, London

MacGregor, A (ed) 1994. *Sir Hans Sloane: collector, scientist, antiquary, founding father of the British Museum*, London

Martyn, T and Lettice, J 1757. *The Antiquities of Herculaneum: translated from the Italian*, London

Maty, P H 1784. *An Authentic Narrative of the Dissensions and Debates in the Royal Society*, London

Nichols, J (ed) 1780. *Bibliotheca Topographica Britannica*, I, London

Nichols, J (ed) 1814. *Literary Anecdotes of the Eighteenth Century*, VIII, London

Nichols, J (ed) 1822. *Illustrations of the Literary History of the Eighteenth Century*, IV, London

Nichols, J (ed) 1831. *Illustrations of the Literary History of the Eighteenth Century*, VI, London

Nichols, J (ed) 1848. *Illustrations of the Literary History of the Eighteenth Century*, VII, London

O'Raifeartaigh, T (ed) 1985. *The Royal Irish Academy*, Dublin

Pegge, S 1773. 'Observations on Dr Percy's account of minstrels among the Saxons', *Archaeologia*, **2**, 100–6

Pegge, S 1779. 'Examination of the mistaken opinion that Ireland and Thanet were void of serpents', *Archaeologia*, **5**, 160–5

Pierce, S R 1965. 'Thomas Jenkins in Rome', *Antiq J*, **45**, 200–29

Pinkerton, J 1788. 'Letters to the people of Great Britain on their cultivation of their national history', *Gent's Mag*, **58/2**, 1149–51

Scharf, G 1865. *A Catalogue of the Pictures Belonging to the Society of Antiquaries, Somerset House, London*, London

Sorrenson, R 1996. 'Towards a history of the Royal Society in the eighteenth century', *Notes Records Royal Soc London*, **50**, 29–46

Strong, R 1978. *And When Did You Last See Your Father? The Victorian painter and British history*, London

Sweet, R 2001. 'Antiquaries and antiquities in eighteenth-century England', *Eighteenth-Century Stud*, **34**, 181–206

Sweet, R 2004. *Antiquaries: the discovery of the past in eighteenth-century Britain*, London

Watson, J 1775. *The History and Antiquities of the Parish of Halifax*, London

Webb, P C 1756. *A Short Account of Some Particulars Concerning Domesday Book*, London

Whitaker, J 1773. *History of Manchester*, 2 vols, London

RICHARDVS II REX ANGLIE

Ex Tabula antiquissima In Choro D. Petri Westmonast. Pulvinari insidet aureo, induitur, interior reste viridi cui grandiusculi intexuntur flores aurei et Nominis sui elementum initiale coronatum, utroq; Pes eminet retro et crepula aurea relatus. Donum coronam sustinet Iecha cocinea Pellibus Armeniacis duplicata quae et aureo Collare subnectitur. Gapes inaurato varioq; Monilis et Crucibus protuberante quod reliquum in eo Tabulæ elucitur. SOCIETAS Londini Rei Antiquariæ Studiosa in Ære incidi Curavit A.D. MDCCXVIII.

SOCIETAS Londini Rei Antiquariæ Studiosa in Ære incidi Curavit A.D. MDCCXVIII.

CHAPTER FIVE

THE SOCIETY OF ANTIQUARIES AND THE GRAPHIC ARTS: GEORGE VERTUE AND HIS LEGACY

Martin Myrone

Writing to his friend, the antiquary William Cole, in September 1778, Horace Walpole, erstwhile antiquary and art historian, connoisseur, collector and disgruntled younger son of the late prime minister, famously gave vent to his deep loathing for the Society of Antiquaries:

> The antiquaries will be as ridiculous as they used to be; and since it is impossible to infuse taste into them, they will be as dry and dull as their predecessors. One may revive what perished, but it will perish again, if more life is not breathed into it than it enjoyed originally. Facts, dates and names will never please the multitude, unless there is some style and manner to recommend them, and unless some novelty is struck out from their appearance. The best merit of the Society lies in their prints; for their volumes, no mortal will ever touch them but an antiquary. Their Saxon and Danish discoveries are not worth more than monuments of the Hottentots; and for Roman remains in Britain, they are upon a foot with what ideas we should get of Inigo Jones, if somebody was to publish views of huts and houses that our officers run up at Senegal and Gorec. Bishop Lyttelton used to torment me with barrows and Roman camps, and I would as soon have attended to the turf graves in our churchyards. I have no curiosity to know how awkward and clumsy men have been in the dawn of arts or in their decay.

> I exempt you entirely from my general censure on antiquaries.[1]

This outburst expressed bitter sentiments that had been festering for over a decade against the Society, its members, its administration and its ideals. By his own account, 'sick of their ignorance and stupidity', Walpole attended hardly any meetings of the Society during the later 1760s.[2] Stung by criticisms of his antiquarian speculations on Richard III, and personally antagonistic to the new President, Jeremiah Milles, Walpole had broken with the body almost entirely by 1770 and could hardly mention them in his correspondence without some snide aside or scathing irony. Samuel Pegge's scholarly discussion of Dick Whittington and his cat late in 1771 brought things to a head, and the ripe lampooning of the Society by Samuel Foote in his play

Fig 28. 'Richard II': engraving by George Vertue; published as plate IV in *Vetusta Monumenta*, I (1747) (after Giuseppi Grisoni, 'Imago Antiquo Richardi II'). *Photograph*: Society of Antiquaries of London.

The Nabob (first staged in London on 29 June 1772) was the final straw: 'as I do not love to be answerable for any fooleries, but my own, I think I shall scratch my name out of their books'.[3]

Walpole's catty and provocative characterization of the Society of Antiquaries might be dismissed as a negligible bit of pique. Still, there are several points of interest to be taken from this passage. When Walpole makes the assertion that the Society of Antiquaries published volumes that no one would want to touch 'but an antiquary', he is suggesting that there are forms of antiquarianism that are acceptable and those which are not, and in excusing Cole from censure, indicates that this divide may be the foundation of personal as well as intellectual judgements. One form of antiquarianism is introverted and dull, bookish and irrelevant. This is what was lampooned by caricaturists and satirists, whose stereotypes have cast a long shadow over an appreciation of the achievements of the eighteenth-century antiquaries. The other is the antiquarianism that has 'taste' – that crucial, yet fuzzy, term which helped define a 'polite' modern culture. This is aligned – literally and metaphorically – with the experience of the visual, and which is thus more immediately (and enjoyably) absorbed. The 'prints' are to be valued as expressions of such a form of antiquarian activity, despite the utterly reprehensible character of the body that sponsored them, while their 'volumes' (meaning the text-heavy volumes of *Archaeologia*) could be dismissed. The Society, Cole himself, the Antiquaries' prints and their books are all to be termed antiquarian; yet there are, Walpole asserts, important distinctions to be drawn between them.

The relational – or oppositional – definition of the antiquarian was typical of the era, which followed in various permutations the old Baconian distinction between 'Perfect History' and 'Antiquities' to define and often enough derogate the antiquarian in general and the Antiquaries in particular.[4] What Walpole does, here, is introduce the issue of visuality into these defining oppositions. In his flippant and deeply prejudiced way, Walpole takes us to the heart of a set of questions that must guide our understanding of the role of prints in the Society's early activities. The relationship between 'prints' and 'volumes' – that is, between text and image – and the relative values attached to each was significant to the definition of the antiquarian project in the eighteenth century in ways that register much larger social and intellectual changes in the period. Managed and made visible by the exercise of 'taste', this relationship further opened up antiquarianism to the wider social and cultural realm. This was not just, as Walpole seems to suggest, because it projected the concerns of the Society to the public, but also because the production of prints necessarily involved the Society with the world of commercial publication and, less tangibly, exposed the practices of antiquarianism to schema of aesthetic judgement that had broader social currency. To ask questions of the Society's publication of prints in the eighteenth century is to ask also what role the visual had in the constitution of historical knowledge in an era when, it has been claimed, the graphic and sensory aspects of understanding were decisively marginalized – or at least segregated away from what were emerging as the dominant norms of the practice of history.[5]

In this chapter, I want to pose the question of how the shifting history of the Society of Antiquaries and of antiquarianism itself can (or cannot) be placed in relation to the technical and technological history of printmaking and publication, as well as the history of taste, changing patterns of professional approbation and career advancement and the commercial activity within which these technical questions obtain more generally relevant significance. The ground for this enquiry has been well prepared by reassessments of antiquarianism which, even where they have not focused on the graphic arts, allow us to think of 'the "antiquarian" attitude' as 'a specific, lived relationship to the past' which therefore involves issues of taste, experience and vision as much as more purely theoretical dimensions – supposedly pure and free from the taint of immediate social realities.[6] This has meant readdressing the general thesis, promulgated influentially by D C Douglas and Stuart Piggott, that the period 1660 to 1730 constituted a golden age or heroic era of antiquarian scholarship after which date the discipline, such as it was, went into rapid and terrible decline, 'from rational to romantic, from classical calm to barbarian excitement'. But it has also opened the way to seeing as something other than paradoxical the emergence of the Society, with all its energetic commitment to graphic productions, at the supposed point of degeneration for the discipline.[7] Crucially important here are questions of production and economy. Work on textual histories has interrogated the role of serialization and subscription as important means of changing the history communicated in particularized social contexts.[8] There are comparable questions to be asked of antiquarian print production. Consequently, in place of the succeeding eras of rationalism and irrationalism, of reasoned method and immethodicality, sometimes proposed in the past, we might review antiquarianism in association with a nuanced appreciation of shifting relations between public and private spheres, registering the possibility of antiquarianism opening up more subjective, private spaces of historical understanding.[9]

Quite aside from these arguments, we can assert confidently that the art of engraving had a central place in the activities and identity of the Society of Antiquaries in the eighteenth century. The revival of the Society in 1717 was in no small degree the creation of an organization for the production and dissemination of images of historical artefacts and architecture. As Maria Grazia Lolla has reminded us, while the Society's view of the art of engraving has too often in the past been seen as passive, even naively so, the Antiquaries had a finely calibrated appreciation of the aesthetic properties and representational capacities of various print media.[10] Even before the revived Society was put on a formal footing, a subscription was being raised for an engraving of the font of St James's Church in November 1717.[11] As early as February 1718, George Vertue was set to work on the impressive plate of the painting of Richard II, completed as a proof before the end of that year (fig 28).[12] At its inception, then, the Society was conceived of as an organization whose tangible outputs would encompass visual materials, not then only as a supplement to textual manifestations, but as products with their own vital life.

According to Vertue, it was John Talman who first proposed engravings as the primary output of the Society's activities.[13] But it was William Stukeley who introduced into the first Minute Book the strikingly direct statement: 'Without drawing and designing the Study of Antiquitys or any other Science is lame and imperfect'.[14] Stukeley elaborated on this view considerably in the 'Preface' to his *Itinerarium Curiosum* (1724):

> It is evident how proper engravings are to preserve the memory of things and how much better an idea they convey to the mind than written descriptions, which often not at all, and oftener not sufficiently, explain them: beside, they present us with the pleasure of observing the various changes in the face of nature, of countries, and the like, through the current of time and vicissitude of things. These embellishments are the chief *desiderata* of the excellent Mr Camden's *Britannia*, and other writers of this sort, whose pens were not so ready to deliver their sentiments in lines as letters: and how hard it is for common artificers to draw from mere description, or to express well what they understand not, is obvious from our engravings in all sciences. I am sensible enough, that large allowances must be made for my own performances of this kind, and some for the artificers parts therein, who, for want of more practice in such works, cannot equal others abroad. I know not whether it will be an excuse, or a fault, if I should plead the expedition I used in the drawing part; but I may urge, that a private person, and a moderate fortune, may want many useful assistants and conveniences for that purpose. It is enough for me to point them out; to show things that are fine in themselves, and want little art to render them more agreeable, or that deserve to be better done; or any way contribute toward retrieving the noble monuments of our ancestors; in which case only, we are behind the other learned nations in Europe. It is not that we have a less fund of curiosities than they, were the description of them attempted by an abler hand, and more adequate expence.[15]

As described here by Stukeley, the graphic arts served antiquarianism broadly in the terms offered by post-Lockean epistemology, which placed an emphasis on the primacy of vision in the acquisition of knowledge as all the more natural, spontaneous and efficacious by comparison with the repetitious exercises of bookish learning (a distinction echoed in Walpole's comments at the head of this essay). It also served a progressive purpose, marking the supremacy of the moderns over their forebears and in this, patriotically, allowing Britons equity in the field with continental peers.[16] But, importantly for Stukeley, the pursuit of graphic representations of antiquities brought with it considerable technical and material challenges. It was, quite simply, expensive, time-consuming and dependent on skills and technologies that might not yet be widely developed.

Stukeley is here writing in the capacity of a private individual introducing the fruits of his personal antiquarian project. His assumption of a defensive attitude around the technical execution of his illustrations serves both as an apology, and as a means of underscoring his genteel persona (which would necessarily mean denigrating the 'mechanick' dimension to realizing such a project). But the 'large allowances' that he expects the reader to make in that context might be taken to apply to the Society's activities as well, and as the century progressed would become a more aggravated issue.

The prints flowed readily from the outset, published usually at a rate of about two a year and in a regular folio format. It was soon imagined that these would be issued as a collection, as early title-pages indicated through their titles: *Res selectae ab Antiquariorum Societate Londini editae* and *Collectenea antiquitatum sumptibus Societatis Antiquariae Londinensis impressa. Ab Anno Domini MDCCXVII*. In 1747 the definitive title-page for what was the first volume of seventy plates was issued: *Vetusta Monumenta: quae ad rerum Britannicum memoriam conservandam Societas Antiquanorium Londini sumpto suo edenda curavit*. As Stephen Bann has noted, in the context of antiquarianism, *vetusta* does not just mean old, but imputes to the state of antiquity an element of decay, and therefore potential loss, making explicit the idea of engraving as a surrogate for, and means thereby of preserving, the physical artefact.[17]

It needs to be stressed that there was no programme of print publication or systematic approach. Viewed as a serial publication, the *Vetusta Monumenta* was, depending on one's point of view, enormously flexible and responsive, incorporating plans, views, detailed depictions of individual objects (fig 29), facsimiles and (latterly) more evocative 'picturesque' or 'romantic' images, or simply incoherent. Whichever

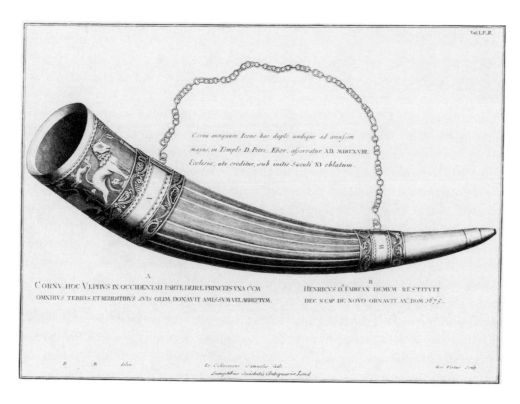

Fig 29. 'Ulphi Cornu': engraving by George Vertue, published as plate II in *Vetusta Monumenta*, I (1747). *Photograph*: Society of Antiquaries of London.

is the case, the financial viability of the project rested, still, on a form of patronage, even where this was mediated by the Society. As John Talman complained in the 1720s, 'I am pleasd to hear that such persons as Dukes, &c buy whole sets of our Prints; but at the same time am chagrined at the smallness of the numbers'.[18]

The early history of the *Vetusta* must inevitably be described in relation to the personal history of George Vertue (1684–1756). He was made 'official engraver' at the revival of the Society, when he was also made a Fellow, and retained the post until only months before his death when ill health and age forced him to withdraw from active participation. By the time of the revival, Vertue was already fairly well established as an independent printmaker and print publisher with a wide-ranging practice. During the period that he was official engraver he was responsible for engraving and publishing almost every print issued by the Society. He undertook the engraving of all the plates in the first volume of *Vetusta Monumenta*, except one (plate VI, of Walsingham Abbey), which was engraved by Michael Vandergucht, and the first seventeen of the fifty-five plates of the second volume. On average Vertue received around £20 worth of work each year, though this figure fluctuated considerably, depending on the scale and complexity of the project.[19] Further variations would come, depending on whether Vertue or the Society provided the copper plate or whether he did the printing and supplied the paper.

While Vertue's payments hardly constituted the foundation of a fortune – and we should remember that he could expect six to ten guineas for executing a single portrait plate for his private clients – it did provide, exceptionally for a professional engraver, a steady and reliable annual income.[20] Also, although the largest sums that were received by Vertue from the Society related to the production of new prints, he was involved in a range of other activities throughout his tenure. He was responsible also for republishing old prints, acted as an agent for the Society at sales, delivered papers at the Society, and performed more mundane tasks, such as creating storage for the growing collections.

Over this time, Vertue maintained a professional career as an engraver in the commercial realm, albeit in part by exploiting his association with the Society. He would often announce his membership of the Antiquaries on the lettering of the prints, lending a degree of prestige to what were basically commodities floating on an unregulated market, and he was frequently employed by individual members on their private projects. The projects that Vertue ventured as commercial enterprises could, even, coincide intimately with the Society's range of interests. Indeed, the first subject of Vertue's ambitious publication 'Nine Historical Portraits' (1742–51), of the 'Royal Family Piece' after Holbein (fig 30), had been suggested as a suitable subject for inclusion in the *Vetusta Monumenta* as early as 1719.[21]

If Vertue's association with the Society of Antiquaries benefited him in his capacity as a commercial engraver, the Society itself was more conscious of the commercial dimensions to its activities than might be expected. As early as 1719 it was determined by the Society that existing prints could be sold to trade.[22] Crucially, Vertue did not maintain ownership of the plates he executed for the Antiquaries, so the Society was able to republish the prints itself, and lend out plates for publication elsewhere.[23] The 'Royal Family Piece' was among the plates acquired and republished by the Society in the 1770s. For all the jokes and snide comments made in print and in private, antiquity had commercial currency in the eighteenth century, and a social reach which went beyond the old duffers imagined as typical antiquarians.[24] Even so, it was not clear that the Society was especially well equipped to deal with the commercial aspects of its prints; by 1735 a major review of the Society's publishing was undertaken, resulting in the appointment of Charles Frederick as Director and Vertue as Sub-Director, and William Bowyer as printer. The problem of distributing prints was not resolved until 1756, when John Boydell was made the Society's agent in the City, and a 'Mr Tovey' the same in Westminster.[25]

Vertue's close association with antiquarianism allowed the artist to negotiate

Fig 30. 'The Royal Family Piece': engraving by George Vertue after Hans Holbein; first published in 1742 and republished by the Society of Antiquaries in 1776. *Photograph*: Society of Antiquaries of London.

105

between contrasting marketing conditions, each of which provided alternative frame-works for the production and reception of a print. It is an indication of Vertue's dual role as an antiquarian and an entrepreneur that while after his death his independently executed antiquarian plates were acquired from his widow by the Society of Antiquaries and republished for their members, those plates that were included in the posthumous sale were purchased by leading commercial print-sellers, including, for instance, John Boydell.[26] Like his literary counterparts, Vertue inhabited a mixed economy of patronage in the process of shifting from the aristocratic and exclusive forms predominant in the seventeenth century to the commercial world of free enterprise characteristic of the later eighteenth, and encompassing the new sociable institutions of the metropolis.[27] Vertue's status and reputation as an antiquarian served him well in dealing with these shifts. His graphic renditions of antiquity linked rather than divided the worlds of polite taste and the antiquarian, which the satirists and wits claimed were opposed. It was this potential for transgression that even Walpole had to recognize in his comments on their prints in 1778.

While in a literal sense this double status of antiquarianism as commerce and as scholarship was secured through his official post and Fellowship at the Society of Antiquaries itself, Vertue's peculiar success as a graphic antiquarian rested upon distinctive characteristics of his graphic manner – indeed, the characteristics that later commentators down to the present day have found so hard to value. Vertue was, committedly, a line engraver, using intaglio methods involving the direct cutting of the copper plate almost to the exclusion of other techniques, meaning that his images rendered their effects entirely though the use of line, modulated in thickness, weight, direction and length. This was traditionally viewed as the purest and most noble form of printmaking, achieving, through the most disciplined means, the finest effects. One of the most prominent claims made for line engraving in art-critical discourse since the seventeenth century was that the medium had the greatest capacity to evoke surface qualities, the substance of forms, even colours, purely through the combination and juxtaposition of lines.[28]

In its descriptive potential, we might casually admit that engraving was peculiarly suited to the production of antiquarian imagery. More significant, however, are the kinds of authorial presence associated with the practice of engraving. The engraver worked with a repertoire of lines, dots and lozenges whose forms were dictated by the intractability of the copper plate and by the traditional nature of the tools used to work it – the burin or 'graveur'. The basic notational unit of the engraver, the slightly swelling cut line, was tiny compared to the surface necessarily filled with such marks to create tonal effects that did not intrude upon the representational functions of the print: it, quite simply, took a very long time to create even the most basic tonal effects. For the print to be apprehended as an image of a thing, rather than a raw mass of abstract marks, the dots and lines had to be organized densely, meaning that the labour of the engraver was all the more intense and prolonged.

The significance of these points in the context of antiquarianism can be clarified with reference to Vertue's own writings on the art of engraving, scattered through the extensive notebooks he prepared with a view to writing a history of British art (an important antiquarian project in its own right), but also in his important unpublished essay, 'On engraving history or portraiture: a simile'. Here, he drew an analogy between the reproductive engraver and the literary translator, claiming that the engraver 'translates from a modern language to a universal one'.[29] Vertue went on to stress the 'universal' character of engraving, as the act of reproducing an image could free it from 'particular dialects, manners &c', a claim which fits nicely with Stukeley's propositions about the value of engraving to the antiquarian. What Vertue developed out of such claims was a precise hierarchy of artistic value based on the notion of raw, direct labour. Drawing on a vocabulary developed by John Evelyn in his *Sculptura* (1662), Vertue distinguished line engraving from other forms of printmaking on the basis of the intensity of physical effort that was required. Engraving is the most elevated technique, because it 'is properly and naturally a plowing in brass or metal of any kind – like furrowing'.[30] This is opposed to etching – 'done with the point or needle on grounds and eaten in with Aquafortis . . . an invention for Expedition' – which takes only half the time of engraving, and mezzotint, a process of 'scraping on the copper' which takes 'one fourth of time – that the same work and dimension can be as well done by the Burinator'.[31] As the technique becomes more expeditious, so it becomes, in terms of Vertue's semiotics of artistic labour, more superficial, even literally, physically so – from 'plowing' or 'furrowing' through to just 'scraping'. The transformed physical matter of the copper plate itself is presented as the bearer of value, over and above the representational artefact that is derived from it. The plate is a form of sculpture, with all that that suggests about heroic physical labour, the need for personal hardiness, and, we might say, the manliness of the endeavour.

In practice, Vertue did often use elements of etching within his engravings, in particular to accent architectural forms and in the characterization of the staffage (human figures) in topographical views. The relatively fluid and flexible marks possible with the etching needle served well in producing such ornamental accents. Such a 'mixed method' was standard to engravers, even if they did not admit this expediency given the way etching was generally denigrated. Vertue's theory of art was, however, preoccupied with the purity of engraved line. While the connection between engraving and sculpture was of long standing – and by reference to Biblical precedent had considerable power as a means of establishing the high cultural value of printmaking – Vertue tied his comments to the marketplace in an explicit way. In the 'Notebooks', he explained the commercial logic of printmaking in more detail:

> the necessity of such works being printed on paper. a sheet being of small value – subsequent to be multiplyed. and consequently more in number so each of less value. and allways – appears less worthy of esteem on the paper than on the copper plate it-self.[32]

On the face of it this is a nonsensical statement to be made by a reproductive engraver whose job was, after all, to multiply a given image through the deployment of his skills. In fact, his complaint is not that engravings are, perforce, multiples, but that the act of multiplication exposes the engraver himself to the machinations of commercial print-sellers. As the mass production of prints meant the reduction in economic value of each unit, so more had to be produced and sold. Given the high levels of labour and time that had to be invested into the working of a plate, most engravers necessarily became dependent on publishers for support. These commercial middlemen are cast as the villains of the piece by Vertue, for they 'squeeze and screw. trick and abuse . . . to raise their own fortunes by devouring that of the Sculpture-Engravers'.[33] Furthermore, the general sale of prints on the free market meant that the engraver was divorced from personal relations with any individual patron: as the engraver's fate is 'every.bodys business so it is nobodys' – the open market that helped undermine the traditional structures of social distinction is thus damned for its cruel anonymity.[34]

Vertue's comments are locked into a self-defeating logic of anti-commercialism that was, latterly, to help define an idea of a national school of engraving.[35] Well into the nineteenth century, the claims for line engraving remained significant as a means of proclaiming prestige for the reproductive artist in the face of more expedient and commercial, and supposedly less skilful, graphic techniques. But in the case of Vertue, these claims were co-ordinated to the desires and expectations of the Society of Antiquaries. The distinguishing feature of the antiquary, as the producer of historical discourse, was his tendency to amass rather than order, his obsessive concern with, as Walpole put it, slightingly, 'minute accuracy about very indifferent points'.[36] Engraving, as an artistic practice, and certainly as it was imagined by Vertue, demanded such a myopic form of attention, and such a disregard for the judgements that would assert one thing was important, another 'indifferent'; each element of an image was accorded equal significance. It was precisely this, Vertue's robust refusal to make the way he laboured correspond to a hierarchy of subjects or aesthetic values, which helped secure his position as the pre-eminent antiquarian engraver of his age.

Vertue found in the culture of early eighteenth-century antiquarianism a means of professional support of an exceptional nature. The Society of Antiquaries offered him social prestige, financial support and access to a network of patrons. Just as importantly, it gave his work an exclusive stamp of authority that was of service in the larger market. His achievement was not to be repeated. After his death, the Society ruled that no subsequent official engraver could also be a Fellow. Rather, the commercial potential of the market for antiquarian prints was to be exploited to the full, using independent professional engravers and print-sellers.[37] The alignment of commercialism and Vertue's specifically graphic antiquarian practice had proved to be temporary.

The rise of new values around the appreciation of visual art, encompassed in the word 'taste', helped bring about this change. Where Vertue claims that labour in printmaking is to be valued for itself, the predominant claim that arose from the mid-century was that speed, personality and expressive beauty were of greater importance in the quality of a print. The key text here is the Revd William Gilpin's *Essay Upon Prints* (1768). In his catalogue of engravers' lives, which often tends to sharpness, the Reverend was briefly dismissive of Vertue. His criticism can be quoted in full:

> VERTUE was an excellent antiquarian, but no artist. He copied with painful exactness; in a dry, disagreeable manner, without force, or freedom. In his whole collection of heads, we can scarce pick out half a dozen, which are good.[38]

Thirteen years later, in the third edition of the *Essay*, Gilpin was even less favourable to the artist. Vertue was now only a 'good antiquarian' and a 'worthy man'; he remained 'no artist'.[39] John Nichols, more admiringly, had nonetheless to admit the specialized appeal of Vertue's techniques:

> Mr Vertue would have had more admirers as an engraver, if his style had been more spirited. But the Antiquary and the Historian, who prefer truth to elegance of design, and correctness to bold execution, have properly appreciated his works, and have placed that ingenious artist, in point of professional industry at least, next to his predecessor Hollar.[40]

Vertue would have been flattered by the comparison, as he admired Wenceslaus Hollar to excess, not just as an exemplary printmaker, but also as a model of what an artist could achieve if he had the kind of sustained private patronage the eighteenth-century engraver always hankered after. More usually, Hollar was to be appreciated with certain limitations within the graphic arts, which meant that his works were less the products of 'taste' than of dead scholarship, as Gilpin had stated:

> If we are satisfied with *exact representation*, we have it no where better, than in Hollar's works. But we are not to expect pictures . . . Hollar is most admired as an antiquarian. We consider his works as a repository of curiosities; and records of antiquated dresses, abolished ceremonies, and edifices now in ruins.[41]

Gilpin rather sneakily elides antiquated and obscure subject matter with the representational technique which are meant to share these qualities, which may hardly be justified or at least fully argued out. But what such statements suggest is that aesthetic value and antiquarian utility were to be seen as antithetical, matching antagonistic definitions of the 'historian' in opposition to the antiquary, and the satirical image of the antiquary in general.[42]

Vertue had informed the Society at the end of 1755 that he was too ill to work; on 12 March 1756 he had been forced to admit that he wouldn't even be able to super-intend another engraver. His retirement and death brought to an end not just a special relationship between a professional engraver and the Society, forged through a unique sympathy of artistic ambitions and historical comprehension, of graphic and historiographical methods, but also of an era in which antiquarianism could find graphic expression. Excluded from the membership of the Society, no future engraver could, then, participate in meetings, give papers or enjoy the social equity that Vertue appears to have enjoyed. Arguably, Vertue's practice of engraving was closely attuned to the notion of antiquarianism dominant within an elite class, whose members felt little compulsion to demonstrate their authority by displays of connoisseurial 'taste', and were, correspondingly, self-assured about their public duties as historians. The graphic arts were not, in this context, intended to be assessed as an expression of the inscrutable values of 'good taste', so much as a tool for the dissemination of historical knowledge, the beauty of which derived from its highly crafted functionality.

As the century progressed, both the discourse of antiquarianism and the discourse on graphic art were transformed, while the material conditions of the practice of both were increasingly subject to commercial pressures and redefined with reference to an expanding public of consumers. Further transformations in the practices of antiquarianism, in the form of local history, romantic antiquarianism and, eventually, the nascent modern discipline of history, brought the antiquary and his methods into growing disrepute. In corresponding developments within the field of artistic production, the reproductive engraver became a more suspect figure. New notions of authorial originality, exemplified in Gilpin's comments here, began to dictate the assessment of the graphic arts in theory and in commercial practice. Vertue's industriousness, his very lack of imagination or technical flair, may have qualified him for a place within an elite sector of society, when mediated by the dominant values of antiquarianism. But subsequent relations between the Society and its successive official engravers suggest that this was the result of a short-lived situation.

More practically, Vertue's retirement from the Society heralded a period of instability in the production of new plates. 'Wood the engraver' was briefly brought into employment, before James Green (brother of the better-known mezzotinter, Benjamin Green) was given the task. It was Green who engraved plate XIX (and probably plate XVIII, which is unsigned) of the second volume of the *Vetusta*, but his death in February 1759 left the post open again.

The next selection was to prove more enduring. James Basire (1730–1802) was appointed engraver to the Society on 8 March 1759. Basire was the son of an engraver, and was trained into the profession by apprenticeship. But while Vertue had been educated in the context of a London artistic culture barely emerging from artisanal origins, Basire came to maturity in a more confident, even stridently assertive, art community. He was associated with the reformed classical taste that was rising to dominate metropolitan cultural affairs in the 1760s, the decade that saw the birth of public art exhibitions, the foundation of a Royal Academy (from whose membership engravers were tellingly excluded) and a boom in levels of cultural consumption. Basire was well placed to take advantage of these changes. He had been taken to Italy by Richard Dalton in 1749–50, had studied drawings by Guercino and Raphael and was latterly employed to engrave plates for James Stuart and Nicholas Revett's seminal *The Antiquities of Athens, Measured and Delineated* (1762–1816), a cornerstone of the revised vision of the classical world which underpinned the ascent of 'taste' in these decades. Vertue may have worked in a range of commercial, private and public contexts, but he did so always essentially as a line engraver working in an antiquarian mode. Basire was, instead, a highly adaptable printmaker, who drew considerable esteem from his association with classical culture and the established masters of the past. The engraver to the Society of Antiquaries was also the engraver of a print reproducing Benjamin West's *Pylades and Orestes* (1766; Tate, London), one of the first classical history paintings to be seen in London's new art exhibitions, and one of the first of the publisher John Boydell's prints to be issued after a work of a contemporary artist working in Britain. This same engraver was also one of the innovators of soft-ground etchings for Charles Rogers's *Collection of Prints in Imitation of Drawings* (1778), where the novel technique was deployed to evoke completely, mimetically, the chalky textures of original drawings. The textural and tonal effects achieved by such prints and the physical process of etching itself would have been anathema to Vertue.

All the plates for the second volume of the *Vetusta Monumenta* from plate xx onwards were by James Basire, apart from plate xxvii (1784) by John Pye, and the mezzotint portrait of Charles Lyttelton (1770) by James Watson. These plates could approach a degree of elegance unknown to Vertue, as with the two views of an antique bronze in the collection of Thomas Hollis – two elegant, and fully realized, views of the sculpture by Basire engraved after the drawings by the famously gifted Italian academic draughtsman G B Cipriani (plates xxi and xxii) – which brought the Society into contact with the most self-consciously progressive proponents of classical aesthetics. Still, Basire arguably adapted his manner to the circumstances. It has been remarked that Basire's technique for his antiquarian plates was 'surprisingly bold, even at times crude by late-eighteenth century standards' (fig 31).[43] His plates for the Society are reckoned as 'among the last representatives of the old school, untouched by modern techniques', such as the 'ever more complex linear patterns and processes' favoured by the more fashionable engravers Robert Strange and William Woollett.[44]

Vertue's presence at the Society was revived in this new era. Twenty-two plates of his were given by his widow in 1775 and printed by the Society. After her death in 1776, the Society published a further group of plates, and in the next two years set about reissuing these prints. The republication of the plates obtained from Vertue's widow, while opportunistic, also helped plug a recognized gap that had appeared with the slowing down and then complete suspension through the 1770s of the *Vetusta Monumenta*. As early as 1768, Richard Gough had noted the many prints published by the Society over the previous half century and that 'This is still a part of their plan, though the public does not receive such frequent presents from them. Vertue himself, who thirsted after our antiquities, did many at his own expence.'[45] While the sheer economics of print production may be to blame, there was a more fundamental shift in the Society's priorities. From 1770, *Archaeologia* featured plates almost all identified as by Basire (and we can assume that those unsigned were by him or from his studio) that range hugely in their format – from vignettes to relatively large sheets – and in their content. With its retrospective and miscellaneous effects,

Fig 31. 'Brass trumpets and other instruments found in Ireland, and a shield found at Hendinas in Shropshire': engraving by James Basire, published 28 April 1763 and reproduced as plate XX in *Vetusta Monumenta*, II (1779). *Photograph*: Society of Antiquaries of London.

this seemed perfectly suited to the antiquarian project as it had developed over the previous decades, as Gough might have anticipated when he compared the piecemeal situation of scholarly publishing in England with that in France, with its Academy of Inscriptions and its sustained publishing projects:

> For want of an uniform method of communicating them to the world . . . the Philosophical Transactions and the Gentleman's Magazine have served as channels; out of which an useful miscellany of antiquarian fugitive pieces might be formed, with occasional comment. Many little essays have been published in the form of pamphlets. A considerable number of prints have been engraved. Several whole counties have been surveyed and described; and copious materials are come to light for doing the same service to others.[46]

Without a central literary academy to authorize an official version of history, the history of Britain had been, rather, in the words of J G A Pocock, 'one shaped by the productive activity of a London press industry never lastingly subjected to censorship and existing in the interplay between court, city and country'.[47] The miscellaneous, unsystematic, staggering progress of the Society's print publications arguably matches this situation closely, and would, with it, become swiftly outmoded in the eyes of those (like Walpole) self-consciously modish.

In place of progressing the *Vetusta Monumenta*, the Society determined to publish large single plates instead, starting with the impressive engraving by Basire of the paintings of the Field of the Cloth of Gold (*c* 1550–80) initiated in 1770.[48] The papermaker James Whatman was charged with creating a new size of sheet capable of carrying such a magnificent engraving as was planned by the Society, with the resulting format – still known as 'Antiquarian' – of 53 by 31 inches successfully produced for the first time in 1773.[49] This was a highly prestigious and innovative project and it took years to realize. The Society (with a personal contribution from Lord Hardwicke) paid Basire £200 and eventually, in June 1778, printed only 400 copies, some sold to the public for 2 guineas. This was the kind of exclusive, high-investment production that could not be – and was not – often repeated.

When the *Vetusta Monumenta* was finally resumed in 1780 it was rededicated to medieval subjects. The third volume consisted – by the time the title-page was issued in 1796 – of forty-four plates, only one of which was of a non-medieval subject. This development can be referred to the rise of forms of 'romantic antiquarianism', with its more emotional interest in the past, and the revaluation of the Gothic in a more general sense.[50] The hybrid character of the Society's response to these developments is encapsulated in the contrast between plates I and II of the third volume, which comprise atmospheric depictions of Magdalen Chapel near Winchester (fig 32), and plate III, which reverts to a more traditional presentation of plans, details and exterior views juxtaposed without regard to pictorial space (fig 33). The fissured relationship between what Sam Smiles has characterized as 'antiquarian exactitude and aesthetic pleasure' that emerges in the visualization of the Gothic is here given emphatic visual form and resolved by being distributed between physically proximate but visually distinct – separately framed – images.[51] All the plates of the third volume are signed by Basire, except the group of plates illustrating Thomas Astle's *An Account of the Seals of the Kings, Royal Boroughs and Magnates of Scotland* (1792) by Barak Longmate (plates XXVI to XXX).

By this date, the ascent of romantic antiquarianism and the stirrings of early conservationism were putting new and different pressures on the graphic representation of antiquities. In 1788 Richard Gough could lament that: 'The art of engraving, which helps to make ancient buildings known, and preserves their form to a certain degree, contributes, I fear, to their demolition. "Is such a thing engraved?" – "O, yes!" – "Then it is preserved to posterity".'[52] Introducing his own *Sepulchral Monuments* (1786), Gough was to reflect on the changing context of antiquarian printmaking in a telling fashion:

> The walk of fame for modern Artists is not sufficiently enlarged. Emulous of excelling in History, Portrait or Landscape, they overlook the unprofitable, though not less tastful, walk of Antiquity; or, in Grecian and Roman, forget Gothic and more domestic monuments. The unfrequency of the pursuit enhances the price. I must exempt from this reproach my friend Basire, whose praise it is to be faithful in his transcripts and modest in his prices; though it is almost a perversion of his burin, which shines so much on living portraits, to employ it on Gothic ones.[53]

The foundation of the Royal Academy in 1768 had raised the hopes of a generation of artists, combining with a booming international market for British reproductive prints and the massively increased public for art to prompt high-prestige print projects from purveyors of more complex engraving techniques such as William Woollett and Robert Strange, Bartolozzi and, on occasion, Basire himself. Their pursuit of what Gilpin had called, with reference to Hollar, 'pictures' – composed, elegant renderings of narrative subjects – garnered greater prestige (and perhaps material reward) than the emphatically non-narrative, fragmented depictions of antiquities traditionally demanded by antiquaries, and the bold, emphatic, even crude engraving techniques favoured by them. As Gough notes, such a pursuit might alienate the professional engraver from the wider practice of antiquarianism.

The major new project undertaken in the last decade of the eighteenth century was of a scale, and ambition, which was far beyond anything risked earlier in the century. This was the series of large-scale, elaborately executed and researched renderings of English cathedrals engraved by Basire after drawings specially prepared by John Carter (1748–1817).[54] Richard Gough may have referred to Carter as 'This industrious young man, into whom I thought the spirit of Vertue was passed by a metempsychosis not unfamiliar to Professors of Antiquity', but the contrast between the characteristic productions of these graphic artists was great.[55] Carter's huge, highly refined designs demanded attention and praise in terms of their size and elaboration, perhaps, rather than in terms of the sheer labour that Vertue had expected to meet with admiration and which might be expressed equally in a little plate of a coin or fragment as in

Fig 32. 'Inside view of Magdalen Chapel, near Winchester, from the west': etching and engraving by James Basire after Jacob Schnebbelie, published 23 April 1790, and reproduced as plate I in *Vetusta Monumenta*, III (1796). *Photograph*: Society of Antiquaries of London.

Fig 33. 'Magdalen Chapel near Winchester': etching and engraving by James Basire after Jacob Schnebbelie, published 23 April 1790, and reproduced as plate III in *Vetusta Monumenta*, III (1796). *Photograph*: Society of Antiquaries of London.

Fig 34. 'An antique statue of bronze, discovered in Suffolk': etching and engraving by James Basire after Richard Smirke, published 23 April 1807, and reproduced as plate XIV in *Vetusta Monumenta*, IV (1815). *Photograph*: Society of Antiquaries of London.

such a scheme as these. Four elaborate, and to some eyes extravagant, volumes of plates were published, of St Stephen's Chapel, Westminster (1795), Exeter Cathedral (1797), Bath Abbey (1798) and Durham Cathedral (1801). In 1798 Farington reported anxiously that 'Carter charges 15s a day while employed measuring a Cathedral, besides his expences, – and charges for drawings separately'.[56] Escalating costs meant that the series was abandoned, leaving the Society with a £5,000 printing bill which could not be met.[57] A fifth volume, depicting St Albans, was issued in 1810 only by virtue of Richard Gough's bequest.

From this date, the Society's sponsorship of engraved images rather staggered forward into the new century. James Basire the younger (1769–1822), trained by apprenticeship with his father, was appointed engraver to the Society on the death of Basire senior in 1802. Basire the younger was already in the employ of the Society, at least as a draughtsman, by 1799, when his drawings of the Roman helmet (published as plates I to IV of the fourth volume) (see fig 36, chapter 6) were preferred by the Society over those prepared by Thomas Richard Underwood.[58] The fourth volume of the *Vetusta Monumenta* was eventually given a title-page as late as 1815. All fifty-two plates are by the younger Basire, apart from the second of the three reproductions of the Rosetta Stone (plates V to VII; 1803) by J C Stadler. Noteworthy here are plates XIV and XV, depictions of antiquities executed in the 'linear style', given new currency by the massively popular commercial publication of John Flaxman's line illustrations to classic texts in England in 1805 (fig 34).[59]

The association of the Basire family with the Society of Antiquaries was carried over to a third generation when James Basire the younger's son, also James Basire (1796–1869), succeeded him as the preferred engraver in 1822. Although it has sometimes been suggested that by this time the younger Basire had been displaced in his role as engraver, his name appears on all the prints of the fifth volume of the *Vetusta Monumenta* (1816–35, comprising sixty-nine plates). A group of seventeen coloured plates illustrating the Bayeux Tapestry were engraved by Basire after drawings by Charles Stothard in 1821–3, and Basire remained in the Society's employment for the belated further plates issued in 1839 and 1842, along with G F Storm. The only exceptions are the group of lithographs of St Mary's Abbey, York (plates LI to LX), variously 'Drawn on stone' from drawings by R H Sharp and S Sharp, presumably by the publishers, C J Hullmandel, or Engelmann, Graf, Coindet & Co., or drawn directly on the lithographic stone by the draughtsman Frederick Nash (fig 35). Lithography was also introduced into *Archaeologia* in 1827. What would Vertue have made of such a method, which involved no permanent cutting or scoring of a metal plate and instead involved direct drawing on to a stone, and which did not thus require a trained engraver to intervene between the draughtsman and the published image, thus removing printmaking from the ennobling association with 'sculpture'?

The plates published in 1842 were the last to be issued by the Society for almost three decades. The death of John Gage (1786–1842), the latest Director of the Society to have been active in promoting graphic projects in the 1830s, helped ensure a prolonged lull.[60] The next numbers of the *Vetusta* were not published until 1868 and

1870. These were eventually joined by a further group in 1883, when a title-page was issued and the sixth volume belatedly completed. But these later illustrations belong to a quite different world. The use of lithography and wood engraving were the favoured graphic vehicles of the new discipline of archaeology, and make graphic the shifts of ambition and method that were taking place by this date.[61] The seventh volume of the *Vetusta Monumenta*, incorporating photographic reproductive techniques, takes us into a completely new era of archaeological illustration. By this point, the intimate bond between antiquarianism and the graphic artist had been irrevocably broken.

The period of Vertue's tenure was one of an exceptional degree of sympathy between the Society's membership of scholarly and leisured gentlemen and a professional artisan, who rather proudly defined himself in terms of his labour, on the grounds that hard work could be the basis of a claim to social distinction. This can be appreciated as a more than purely personal affinity. The print market of the first half of the eighteenth century was complex, and still unfolding. It gave sustenance to Vertue's self-definition in terms of his labour, an artistic self-image which corresponded to the Antiquaries' interests and ambitions closely enough to facilitate a uniquely intensive relationship. The cooler, and arguably increasingly detached,

Fig 35. 'A general plan of the ground occupied by the abbey of St Mary, York': lithograph, 'drawn on stone from a drawing R H Sharp' and printed by C J Hullmandel, published 23 April 1829, and reproduced as plate LI in *Vetusta Monumenta*, v (1835). *Photograph*: Society of Antiquaries of London.

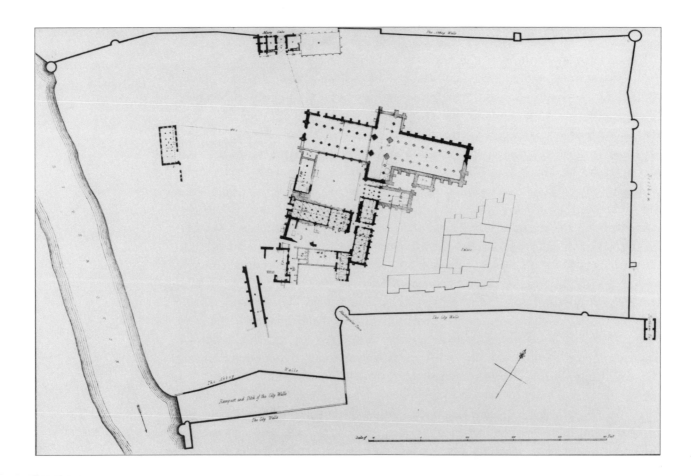

118

relationship with succeeding engravers marked a wider change in the cultural field and in the field of professional historical knowledge. Now, seemingly, less committed to sustaining a regularized programme of print publication, the role of the engraver in achieving the Society's aims might not be so clearly articulated as it was by Stukeley in the 1720s. For Gough and the 'romantic' generation, prints might be prestigious and beautiful, satisfying the requirements of 'taste'; but the real work of the anti-quarian was more properly in the field of preservation and observation. The act of surrogation earlier associated with the graphic representation of antiquities (where the engraving effectively takes the place of the object itself) could no longer satisfy the committed antiquarian, and new, apparently more direct, technologies of reproduction (namely, lithography and photography) displaced the professional engraver from the equation altogether.

The Society's promotion of engraved prints through the eighteenth century is important not just as a dimension of its own history, but also for what it shows about a very particular phase in the history of knowledge. An examination of the Society's print-publishing activities helps illuminate a specific kind of intellectual engagement with artistic labour that has been lost. The declining appreciation of Vertue as a printmaker, and of the antiquarian print as a means of conveying knowledge, helps mark the ascent of new modes of history, which were, paradoxically, apparently available to a wider social spectrum, but also more exclusive, excluding and mysteri-ous. As such, the antiquarian prints of the eighteenth century should merit greater attention than has, until recently, been paid to them. If, as the literary historian David Simpson has provocatively suggested, the fragmented – even crude – nature of antiquarian research might offer a salvational route beyond the impasse of post-modernity – with its scepticism about, and moral condemnation of, grand narrative – we might wonder what the possibilities are for rediscovering the curiously fragmented, incoherent and perhaps surprising images produced by Vertue and Basire for the Society of Antiquaries?[62]

NOTES

1. Horace Walpole to William Cole, 1 Sept 1778, in Lewis 1937–83, II, 116.
2. Horace Walpole to William Cole, 20 Dec 1770, in ibid, I, 206.
3. Horace Walpole to William Mason, 21 July 1772, in ibid, XXVIII, 40; also Walpole's 'Short Notes 1772', in ibid, XIII, 47. See Evans 1956, 166–8.
4. On antiquarianism and the genres of history, see Hicks 1996, 33–6; Groom 1999, 3–40; Phillips 2000, 22–4.
5. Stafford 1994 and 1996; but for a contrary argument see Smiles 2000, esp 2–3.
6. Bann 1990, 102.
7. Piggott 1976, 117–18; Sweet 2001.
8. Woolf 2000, 273–93.
9. Woolf 1997, 650–6; Phillips 1996.
10. See Lolla 2003, 18–25.
11. SAL, MS 268: cited in Evans 1956, 57.
12. Evans 1956, 62–3.
13. George Vertue to Andew Coltée Ducarel, 13 Feb 1754, in Nichols 1812–15, VI, 159–60.
14. Evans 1956, 57.
15. Stukeley 1969, I, i–ii. See Sweet 1997, 24–5.
16. For the patriotic dimension of the *Itinerarium* see Haycock 2002, 110–13.
17. Bann 1990, 111.
18. John Talman to Samuel Gale, 7 Mar 1725, in Nichols 1812–15, VI, 160.
19. See SAL archives, MS 'Treasurer's Account Book 1718–38' for a record of payment. All the plates are listed with their dates of publication in Fenn 1784, table II; also Nichols 1812–15, II, 247n.
20. See the prices quoted in George Vertue to Zachariah Grey, 19 July 1737, in Nichols 1812–15, II, 250.
21. Evans 1956, 70.
22. Ibid, 69.
23. Sweet 1997, 25–6.
24. For some stimulating and important comments on the commercial potential of antiquarianism in the context of music publishing, see Dugaw 1987. For some brief comments on the market for antiquarian prints, see Clayton 1997, 63–6.
25. Evans 1956, 117–18.
26. See Fenn 1784, 19. Vertue's plates were sold by Ford's,
16–19 and 21–22 March 1757, first day's sale, lots 17–41. An annotated copy of the catalogue is in the National Art Library, Victoria and Albert Museum, London, Box II 94.O.
27. See Korshin 1974 and Griffin 1996.
28. See Lambert 1987, 61–3.
29. BL, Add MS 23, 082, fols 7–7v.
30. Vertue 1930–55, III, 147. On the connection between engraving and sculpture, see Eaves 1992, 117–18.
31. Vertue 1930–55, III, 148.
32. Ibid, III, 146.
33. Ibid, III, 146.
34. Ibid, III, 79.
35. See Eaves 1992, 219–32.
36. Letter to the Revd William Cole, 15 Feb 1782, in Lewis 1937–83, II, 300.
37. See Evans 1956, 129.
38. Gilpin 1768, 126–7.
39. Gilpin 1781, 127.
40. Nichols 1812–15, II, 254.
41. Gilpin 1768, 154.
42. Levine 1977, 114–29.
43. Essick 1991, 2.
44. Essick 1980, 6.
45. Gough 1768, xxxix.
46. Ibid, xxxiii.
47. Pocock 1999, II, 165–6.
48. Evans 1956, 160–1.
49. Krill 2002, 84.
50. Badham 1987.
51. Smiles 2000, 60.
52. See Evans 1956, 191–2.
53. Gough 1786.
54. Evans 1956, 206–14; Crook 1995, 11, 23.
55. Quoted in Crook 1995, 69.
56. Farington 1978–84, III, 1025.
57. Evans 1956, 214.
58. See Farington 1978–84, IV, 1174.
59. The classic account of the ascent of this 'linear style' remains Rosenblum 1967.
60. Birrell 1996, 76.
61. Piggott 1978, 52.
62. See Simpson 1999.

BIBLIOGRAPHY

Arnold, D and Bending, S (eds) 2003. *Tracing Architecture: the aesthetics of antiquarianism*, Oxford

Badham, S 1987. 'Richard Gough and the flowering of romantic antiquarianism', *Church Monuments*, 2, 32–43

Bann, S 1990. 'Clio in part: on antiquarianism and the historical fragment', in Bann (ed) 1990, 100–21

Bann, S (ed) 1990. *The Invention of History: essays on the representation of the past*, Manchester and New York

Birrell, T A 1996. 'The circle of John Gage (1786–1842),

Director of the Society of Antiquaries, and the bibliography of medievalism', in *Antiquaries, Book Collectors and the Circles of Learning* (eds R Myers and M Harris), 71–82, Winchester

Clayton, T 1997. *The English Print 1688–1802*, New Haven, Conn, and London

Crook, J M 1995. *John Carter and the Mind of the Gothic Revival*, Soc Antiq London Occas Pap 17, London

Dugaw, D 1987. 'The popular marketing of "Old Ballads": the ballad revival and eighteenth-century antiquarianism reconsidered', *Eighteenth-Century Studies*, **21**, 71–90

Eaves, M 1992. *The Counter-Arts Conspiracy: art and industry in the age of Blake*, Ithaca, NY, and London

Essick, R N 1980. *William Blake, Printmaker*, Princeton, NJ

Essick, R N 1991. *William Blake's Commercial Book Illustrations: a catalogue and study of the plates engraved by Blake after designs by other artists*, Oxford

Evans, J 1956. *A History of the Society of Antiquaries*, Oxford

Farington, J 1978–84. *The Diary of Joseph Farington* (eds K Cave, K Garlick and A MacIntyre), 16 vols, New Haven, Conn

Fenn, J 1784. *Three Chronological Tables Exhibiting a State of the Society of Antiquaries of London*, London

Gilpin, W 1768. *An Essay Upon Prints*, 2nd edn, London

Gilpin, W 1781. *An Essay Upon Prints*, 3rd edn, London

Gough, R 1768. *Anecdotes of British Topography*, London

Gough, R 1786. *Sepulchral Monuments in Great Britain*, London

Griffin, D H 1996. *Literary Patronage in England, 1650–1800*, Cambridge

Groom, N 1999. *The Making of Percy's Reliques*, Oxford

Haycock, D B 2002. *William Stukeley: science, religion and archaeology in eighteenth-century England*, Woodbridge

Hicks, P S 1996. *Neoclassical History and English Culture: from Clarendon to Hume*, Basingstoke

Korshin, P J 1974. 'Types of eighteenth-century literary patronage', *Eighteenth-Century Studies*, **7**, 452–73

Krill, J 2002. *English Artists' Paper: Renaissance to Regency*, 2nd edn, Winterthur

Lambert, S 1987. *The Image Multiplied: five centuries of printed reproductions of paintings and drawings*, New York

Levine, J M 1977. *Dr Woodward's Shield: history, science and satire in Augustan England*, Berkeley, Los Angeles and London

Lewis, W S (ed) 1937–83. *The Yale Edition of Horace Walpole's Correspondence*, 48 vols, New Haven, Conn

Lolla, M G 2003. 'Monuments and texts: antiquarianism and the beauty of antiquity', in Arnold and Bending (eds) 2003, 11–29

Nichols, J 1812–15. *Literary Anecdotes of the Eighteenth Century*, 9 vols, London

Phillips, M S 1996. 'Reconsiderations on history and antiquarianism: Arnaldo Momigliano and the historiography of eighteenth-century Britain', *J Hist Ideas*, **57**, 297–316

Phillips, M S 2000. *Society and Sentiment: genres of historical writing in Britain, 1740–1820*, Princeton, NJ

Piggott, S 1976. *Ruins in a Landscape: essays in antiquarianism*, Edinburgh

Piggott, S 1978. *Antiquity Depicted: aspects of archaeological illustration*, London

Pocock, J G A 1999. *Barbarism and Religion*, Cambridge

Rosenblum, R 1967. *Transformations in Late Eighteenth-Century Art*, Princeton, NJ

Simpson, D 1999. 'Is literary history the history of everything? The case for "antiquarian" history', *SubStance: a review of theory and literary criticism*, **88**, 5–16

Smiles, S 2000. *Eye Witness: artists and visual documentation in Britain 1770–1830*, Aldershot

Stafford, B M 1994. *Artful Science: enlightenment entertainment and the eclipse of visual education*, Cambridge, Mass, and London

Stafford, B M 1996. *Good Looking: essays on the virtue of images*, Cambridge, Mass, and London

Stukeley, W 1969. *Itinerarium Curiosum: Or, an account of the antiquities, and remarkable curiosities in nature or art, observed in travels through Great Britain*, 2nd edn, 2 vols (facsimile of 1776 edn), Farnborough

Sweet, R 1997. *The Writing of Urban Histories in Eighteenth-Century England*, Oxford

Sweet, R 2001. 'Antiquaries and antiquities in eighteenth-century England', *Eighteenth-Century Studies*, **34**, 181–206

Vertue, G 1930–55. *Vertue Note Books*, 6 vols (The . . . annual volume of the Walpole Society, 18, 20, 22, 24, 26, 30), Oxford

Woolf, D R 1997. '"A Feminine Past?": gender, genre, and historical knowledge in England 1500–1800', *American Hist Rev*, **102**, 645–79

Woolf, D R 2000. *Reading History in Early Modern England*, Cambridge

Antique Helmet of Bronze, of the same Size, found at Ribchester, in the Possession of Charles Townley Esq.

Vetust. Mon. Vol. IV. pl. 1.

J. Basire delt.

CHAPTER SIX

ART AND ANTIQUITY IN THE
LONG NINETEENTH CENTURY

Sam Smiles

The Society of Antiquaries moved into Somerset House in the winter of 1780–1, holding the first meeting in its new quarters on 11 January.[1] The Society's business would now take place in rooms adjacent to those of the Royal Society and the Royal Academy, both of which were also housed in William Chambers's impressive building. These new arrangements not only confirmed the national significance of the Society of Antiquaries but also provided the opportunity for mutually beneficial intellectual exchanges. In his address to the members, the President, Jeremiah Milles (see fig 27, chapter 4), used the occasion of this first gathering in Somerset House to draw attention to the relations that should exist between the institutions. With respect to the visual arts, the subject of this present essay, Milles anticipated a fruitful dialogue:

> The relation which the Study of Antiquities bears to the [Royal] Academy . . . of arts . . . is no less certain . . . History, Science and Art may claim an equal share in the Attention and Labour of the Antiquary. In History, to ascertain particular facts of remote Antiquity, to collect Materials of the Lives, Habits and Reputation of various Artists and Men of Genius in successive Ages of past Time, will find its merit with those, whose systematic Line of Study, and of Practice in the Arts is founded upon, and supported by the Authority of Antiquity. But from the judicious Investigation of ancient Science, and Art, a more general and useful Field of Knowledge is opened to the modern Artist. The most valuable Hints for the Direction of his Studies are to be collected from the Works of Antiquaries; and the Repositories of Arts have been enriched with a Variety of necessary Information from the same Source.[2]

Taking Milles's address as its starting point, the purpose of this essay is to examine the ways in which artists and antiquaries approached the visualization of antiquity, from documentary records to historicist interpretations, and from empirical exactitude to imaginative exploration.

Looking over the course of the nineteenth century, it is clear that Milles's outline of the benefits the Society might confer on the visual arts was, in fact, rather too optimistic. With respect to the biographical and historiographical project indicated in his remarks, the Society made very little contribution. Horace Walpole, of course, had

Fig 36. James Basire the younger, *The Ribchester Helmet* (1799). Watercolour, 410 × 340mm. *Photograph*: John Hammond; © Society of Antiquaries of London.

123

profited from George Vertue's researches to produce *Anecdotes of Painting in England* in 1762, whose fifth edition would appear in the 1820s and whose achievement prompted at least one similar venture in the early 1800s.[3] This was, indeed, precisely the kind of study Milles had in mind when recommending the collection of 'Materials of the Lives, Habits and Reputation of various Artists and Men of Genius'. Yet in the nineteenth century the Society played little direct part in helping to develop the field of art history. Admittedly, the Society numbered the scholars and collectors Francis Douce, Samuel Rush Meyrick and the Revd Thomas Kerrich among its Fellows and published important documents in the 1860s and 1870s relating to Holbein and his contemporaries, but these are atypical instances of its association with art-historical research.[4] The fact is that few members of the Society made major contributions to the field and it is debatable whether historians of art, preoccupied as most of them were with the Italian Renaissance and successive eras, had their researches nourished by the Society's activities. It is notable that none of those who attempted new thinking about the history of art, from William Roscoe to John Ruskin, belonged to the Society of Antiquaries.[5]

It was the second area Milles identified – the potential of antiquarianism to enrich the visual arts – that would prove to be more fruitful, promoting a variety of exchanges between artist and antiquary; but, as we shall see, the terms of that relationship were not always as Milles had expected them to be. While there is some evidence of history painters making direct use of antiquarian knowledge, in just the way Milles imagined, for the most part the Society's influence on the higher genres of the visual arts was indirect, helping to foster the turn towards historicism that was so typical of Victorian art but only intermittently providing the actual research from which a painter might profit. Nevertheless, although the Society's direct impact on history painting was slight, in other areas of artistic production its influence was more long-lasting. Before turning to history painting, therefore, some review of these other activities is required.

The production of drawings and watercolours for engraving in publications or for collection in portfolios or cabinets is a notable feature of the period, ending roughly at the mid-century, when photography replaced drawing as the primary recording medium for objects of antiquarian interest. In the previous hundred years, the depiction of antiquities was sometimes undertaken by antiquaries themselves, of which William Stukeley's *Abury, A Temple of the British Druids* (1743) and James Douglas's *Nenia Britannica, or a sepulchral history of Great Britain* (1793) are notable examples. More typically, topographers and antiquarians recruited talented artists to do this work for them. Even when such publications had little or no direct connection with the Society of Antiquaries, it is not unreasonable to see the Society's promotion of antiquarian study as providing the impetus for many of these commissions.

At first sight it seems strange that the production of antiquarian illustration was not mentioned by Milles in his remarks of 1781, especially given the Society's own recognition, via Richard Gough, Charles Lyttleton and others, that a visual record of antiquity could provide accurate data for further research. Milles's silence about such activities was, perhaps, motivated by polite deference to his new neighbours in the

Royal Academy, whose status was closely bound up with the intellectual dignity of their calling and the independence of the arts from any servile employment. Indeed, as Gough noted a few years later, the major problem frustrating the visual recording of the material heritage was the reluctance of talented artists to be associated with such a lowly occupation as antiquarian illustration: 'The walk of fame for modern artists is not sufficiently enlarged. Emulous of succeeding in History, Portrait, or Landscape, they overlook the unprofitable, though not the less tasteful, walk of Antiquity, or, in Grecian and Roman forget Gothic and more domestic monuments.'[6]

Gough's anxieties were real, but the Society was fortunate in its early promotion of the visual record, with capable artists producing drawings that were in turn expertly engraved. John Carter (1748–1817) had been appointed in 1784 as the Society's first draughtsman but he was temperamental and refused to work for the Society from 1785 to 1790, with Jacob Schnebbelie (1760–92) appointed to cover for his absence. Carter's own position was altering, in any case, as he became an increasingly authoritative and, indeed, combative presence in the antiquarian world, publishing scholarly treatments of the medieval heritage and conducting a vigorous campaign against those who would damage it. He was elected FSA in 1795.[7] Thomas Richard Underwood (c 1772–1835) took over Carter's vacated position as draughtsman to the Society in 1792, but the Council resolved that his appointment would not preclude them from employing other artists as circumstances might require.[8] For engravers, the Society relied above all on James Basire the elder (1730–1802), who had succeeded George Vertue, and James Basire the younger (1769–1822). The drawings made c 1790–1840, now in the Society's possession, thus contain work from a variety of artists including Carter, Schnebbelie, Underwood, the Basires and others.

The wisdom of the Council's decision not to rely entirely on one draughtsman was borne out in the late 1790s when accurate drawings were required of the Ribchester helmet, owned by Charles Townley. Discovered in 1796 on the site of the Roman fort at Ribchester, Lancashire, this Roman cavalry parade helmet dates from about AD 100. It is a highly sophisticated piece of metalwork, decorated with relief figures, and today is one of the most notable examples of Roman armour in the British Museum's collection. The Council minutes of 23 January 1798 reveal that Underwood was originally charged with making drawings of the helmet under Townley's direction. Underwood, however, was essentially a landscape artist and declined the commission, 'human figures being out of the line of art to which he has applied'.[9] Townley therefore appointed William Skelton and Andrea Tendi to make drawings instead and the Society subsequently instructed James Basire the younger to make further drawings of the helmet (fig 36).[10] The meticulous rendering of the helmet, delineating its damaged elements with scrupulous integrity, demonstrates the extent to which Basire was capable of rising to this challenge. Indeed, whereas one might normally harbour suspicions that a minutely accurate drawing could never approach the creative and imaginative possibilities of 'true' art, Basire's image has an iconic power of its own precisely because he was so accurate in his representation.

The overall quality of the engravings reproduced in *Vetusta Monumenta* and other ventures supported by the Society demonstrate that Gough's worries about the walk of fame had been at least partially alleviated. Notwithstanding his identification of a genuine difficulty with respect to the recruitment of ambitious artists, his and others' pioneering efforts had helped give such work a respectable profile. And, as is well known, the antiquarian project embraced some artists whose reputations today are associated with much more imaginative productions. A number of important nineteenth-century painters made contributions to the visual illustration of antiquarian research, among them William Blake, Thomas Girtin, J M W Turner, John Sell Cotman, William Müller and Frederick Sandys. With respect to such nationally significant figures, it is notable that these contributions tended to be made at the beginning of the artist's career, at a time when he had had little opportunity to assert his creative independence and was prepared to subordinate his talent to his patron's demands. By the same token, such artists as Frederick Mackenzie (1788–1854), who made their professional living by providing illustrations for topographical and antiquarian publications, have dropped into relative obscurity, despite their evident technical virtuosity. As a result, the numerous exchanges taking place between artists and antiquaries in this period are still subject to critical neglect: professional illustrators are overlooked by dint of the lowly status associated with such work, while the antiquarian work of canonical figures suffers from accusations of its being uncharacteristic hack-work or mere juvenilia.

William Blake (1757–1827) is a case in point. In 1772, aged seventeen, he was apprenticed to James Basire the elder and, as part of his training, he was put to recording medieval monuments in Westminster Abbey. These depictions, forty-seven of which are listed in Martin Butlin's catalogue raisonné of Blake's paintings and drawings, were variously commissioned by the Society of Antiquaries and by Richard Gough.[11] Blake recorded the appearance of Edward i's coffin, exhumed by Sir Joseph Ayloffe, FSA, in Westminster Abbey on 2 May 1774, and also the discoveries made in the presbytery in the summer of 1775. The drawings typically bear inscriptions ascribing them to Basire, as do the prints derived from them.[12] It has long been recognized, however, that Basire's declared authorship is a customary device to cover the production of his workshop; as Basire's apprentice Blake's name would not have been recorded. Figure 37 shows Blake's drawing of the tomb effigy of Countess Aveline, the first wife of Edmund Crouchback, Earl of Lancaster, as seen from above, which was reproduced as an engraving in Ayloffe's *An Account of Some Ancient Monuments in Westminster Abbey* (1780) and in the second volume of *Vetusta Monumenta* (1789: pl xxx). As the earliest known works by Blake to survive, such drawings are of signal importance. Their style is unremarkable; necessarily, given Blake's youth and the need for documentary precision, they can betray nothing of the mature artist's creative abilities. Nevertheless, it is clear that Blake's engagement with these medieval monuments had a profound impact on his art, not merely in his 'Illustrations to English History' (c 1779 and c 1793), which included a number of episodes from the Middle Ages, but also in his abiding commitment to a type of image-making that was monumental, non-naturalistic and spiritual.

Fig 37. William Blake, *Tomb Effigy from
Westminster Abbey of Countess Aveline, First Wife
of Edmund Crouchback, Earl of Lancaster* (1775).
Watercolour, 257 × 78mm. *Photograph*: Society
of Antiquaries of London.

A generation later, both Thomas Girtin (1775–1802) and J M W Turner (1775–1851)
were persuaded to illustrate British antiquities at the outset of their careers. Girtin's
early reputation was established on the basis of his watercolour drawings of architecture. Working with a technical ability in watercolour unmatched by any artist save
Turner, he took the topographical and antiquarian tradition and infused it with a
more sophisticated sense of design. Girtin's contributions to the visualization of the
medieval architectural heritage constitute circumstantial evidence for the likelihood
of him making a purely illustrative watercolour of antiquities, now in the Society's
possession (fig 38). As a unique example, this drawing cannot be compared with
anything else in Girtin's oeuvre, but it has recently been authenticated and is
published here for the first time.[13] The drawing shows a flanged palstave and a
Roman bow brooch, and bears the inscription 'Thoˢ Girtin del' in Girtin's hand,
together with a short text by another writer describing the circumstances in which
the two objects were found: the celt in May 1792 on Stanley Moor, Derbyshire, and
the fibula when excavating the canal between Little Eaton and Derby. The drawing
was exhibited on 28 January 1796 by its owner, the Revd Homfray, FSA, so can
be firmly dated between early 1793 (when work on the canal began) and January
1796.[14] This period coincides with that point in Girtin's career when his six-year

Fig 38. Thomas Girtin,
*Flanged Palstave and
Roman Bow Brooch*
(*c* 1794). Watercolour,
198 × 247mm.
Photograph: John
Hammond; © Society
of Antiquaries of
London.

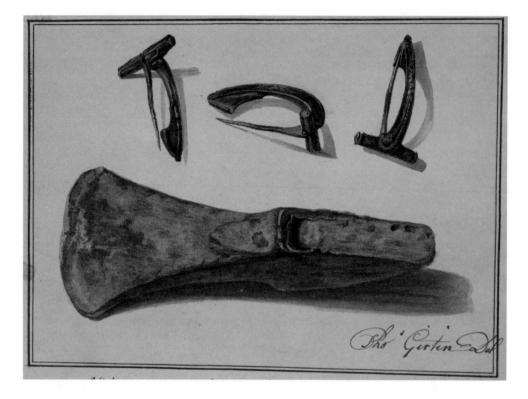

apprenticeship (1788–94) to the topographical draughtsman Edward Dayes came to
an end. He made his first sketching tour in 1794, travelling through the East Midlands
with the antiquarian scholar James Moore, FSA, producing a number of architectural
watercolours for Moore and other antiquaries.[15] No further details surrounding the
production of this drawing have emerged, but it is conceivable that Moore introduced
the young artist to Homfray in 1794 and that the latter commissioned this drawing
of his recent finds.

Turner's contribution to the recording of British antiquities was, like Girtin's,
primarily the product of his ability to deploy sophisticated and innovative technical
procedures in the watercolours he painted of medieval architecture. The work he
produced in the 1790s for the *Oxford Almanack*, together with numerous watercolours of medieval buildings in England and Wales, quickly developed his reputation
as an architectural topographer and he received commissions from important antiquaries. James Douglas, FSA, ordered a watercolour of Rochester Castle *c* 1793 and
by 1798–9 Sir Richard Colt Hoare, FSA, was alone responsible for twenty-seven of the
sixty commissioned watercolours Turner then had in hand. Besides these commissions – typical of what we might expect a landscape artist to contribute to the study
of British antiquities – Turner also produced two remarkable series of resolutely
antiquarian illustrations. The first of these was for the Revd Thomas Dunham
Whitaker, FSA, a Yorkshire antiquary who published a number of local historical
and topographical studies in the early nineteenth century.[16] Turner's first venture for
Whitaker was to provide watercolour drawings to appear as engravings by Basire in

Whitaker's *History of Whalley* (1800–1). While most of these are architectural in their focus, two of them show collections of objects and are depicted with exemplary accuracy. One is entitled 'Ancient Crosses at Whalley' and shows three Saxon cross-shafts, two monumental brasses and three misericords; the other, 'Seals of Whalley Abbey' (fig 39), shows seals of various churchmen associated with the abbey, as well as some seals of the de Lacy family.[17] Some fifteen years later (*c* 1815), Turner produced a series of watercolours for his great friend and patron, the Yorkshire landowner Walter Fawkes, constituting a private album, entitled *Fairfaxiana*, in which are depicted arms, armour, documents and relics associated with Fawkes's ancestors and the Civil War.[18] These instances of Turner's willingness to subordinate his art to a high degree of documentary minuteness are exceptional. The work of the earlier commission from Whitaker, as with Girtin's work for Moore, can readily be explained as a young artist's compliance with a patron's demands; equally, *Fairfaxiana* was a unique and highly unusual project, willingly produced for a man who was Turner's fastest friend and who had been his most loyal patron since the early 1800s.

Two further examples of patronage from antiquaries need to be mentioned in this connection, for between them they provided work for some of the most significant watercolour artists working in early nineteenth-century Britain. John Britton (1771–1857), FSA, was unquestionably one of the most prolific publishers of topographical and antiquarian collections.[19] *The Architectural Antiquities of Great Britain* (five volumes, 1807–26), *Cathedral Antiquities of England* (five volumes, 1836) and similar works provided employment for many artists, and the extent of Britton's patronage is best judged by examining the numerous plates illustrating his various publications.[20] For some of Britton's employees, such as Frederick Mackenzie, the mainstay of their working life was the production of topographical illustrations for his and others' various endeavours, but a number of artists passed briefly through Britton's hands for whom topography needed to be reconciled with wider professional ambitions – among them Samuel Prout, George Cattermole and John Sell Cotman.[21] Britton's patronage was inextricably bound up with his publishing activities, and he commissioned watercolours primarily for the good commercial reason that the public had come to expect numerous engraved plates in works of topography. Britton's desire to employ the most capable artists in the service of antiquarian and topographical illustration is epitomized by the eleven watercolours of prehistoric antiquities he installed on the outside of his so-called Celtic Cabinet, now in Devizes Museum (fig 40).[22] Whereas other collectors might have displayed work of this quality in portfolios, or framed them as individual pictures, Britton mounted them on the outside of a cabinet containing models of megalithic structures, providing them with a context that balanced any aesthetic response with a more scholarly and antiquarian appraisal. In miniature, this cabinet exemplifies Britton's *modus operandi*; from the 1800s until the 1840s his commissions continued, to some extent, what the Society of Antiquaries had promoted in its own publications, but his need to secure commercial sales inevitably compromised the strictest standards of antiquarian research, accommodating a much more picturesque approach to

Fig 39. J M W Turner, *Studies of Seals from Whalley Abbey* (1799–1800). Watercolour with pen and ink, 267 × 194mm. *Photograph:* reproduced by permission of the Syndics of the Fitzwilliam Museum, University of Cambridge. © Fitzwilliam Museum, University of Cambridge.

Fig 40. John Britton's 'Celtic Cabinet' (1820s). *Photograph:* © The Wiltshire Archaeological and Natural History Society.

British antiquity than the Society of Antiquaries would have encouraged.[23]

In like manner, the Revd James Bulwer (1793–1879) assembled a major series of antiquarian drawings, including examples by Cotman, Müller and Sandys. Bulwer's enthusiasm for antiquarian study saw him contribute eleven papers to the journal *Norfolk Archaeology* between 1847 and 1879 and also his election as Vice-President of the British Archaeological Association in 1857.[24] Bulwer began his association with John Sell Cotman (1782–1842) in the early 1800s, taking drawing lessons from him and building up an important collection of Cotman's antiquarian drawings from the years 1806 to 1818, when the artist was concentrating on such subject matter.[25] After his ordination in 1818 and several years work abroad, Bulwer became curate of St Mary Redcliffe, Bristol, and there, in the early 1830s, patronized the young landscape artist W J Müller (1812–45), primarily to provide drawings of prehistoric and medieval antiquities that were bound into extra-illustrated volumes of local topography.[26] Relocated to Norfolk in the 1840s, Bulwer's third episode of antiquarian patronage concerned Frederick Sandys (1829–1904), whom he met in 1846. Like Cotman and Müller before him, Sandys produced studies of architectural antiquities for Bulwer, but he also depicted numerous examples of prehistoric finds, medieval metalwork and painting and manuscript illumination (fig 41). Sandys was elected an associate member of the British Archaeological Association in 1853, presumably as a result of Bulwer's patronage and his recommendation. Bulwer possessed a discerning eye and was capable of spotting artistic talent in Müller and Sandys when they were still teenagers. It is no exaggeration to say that his collection of drawings (now dispersed) included some of the highest-quality drawings of British antiquities produced in the nineteenth century, but it was collected for his own pleasure and Bulwer

130

himself made no major contribution to antiquarian research. Moreover, none of the artists whose drawings he collected remained committed to the antiquarian cause: for all their production of work with antiquarian or archaeological interest, all three artists believed in their professional dignity as painters, not illustrators: Cotman and Müller sought success as landscape artists, Sandys as an engraver and figure painter.[27]

Nevertheless, towards the end of his tragically short life, Müller did venture two bodies of work that can be broadly described as antiquarian. The first of these comprises the twenty-six watercolour drawings reproduced as lithographs by Louis Haghe and published as *Müller's Sketches of the Age of Francis 1st* (1841).[28] The publication can be regarded as designed to compete with Joseph Nash's very successful *The Mansions of England in the Olden Time* (1839–41). Both publications offered a view of the later Middle Ages dwelling on its refinement of manners and cultural sophistication, as opposed to its political and military events. Elegantly costumed figures are positioned against architectural backgrounds, conjuring up a seductive image of the late medieval world. This type of publication, capitalizing on a popular fascination for the romance of the past, cannot be strictly designated antiquarian study, and is closer in spirit to R P Bonington's slightly earlier watercolours, depicting so-called 'troubadour' subjects.[29] Nevertheless, the very fact that such publications were an appropriate commercial speculation in the 1830s and 1840s demonstrates that antiquarianism can usefully be considered as part of a larger phenomenon; by mid-century the recuperation of the past ranged from rigorous scholarly works through topographical guides to costumed evocations of a world long vanished.

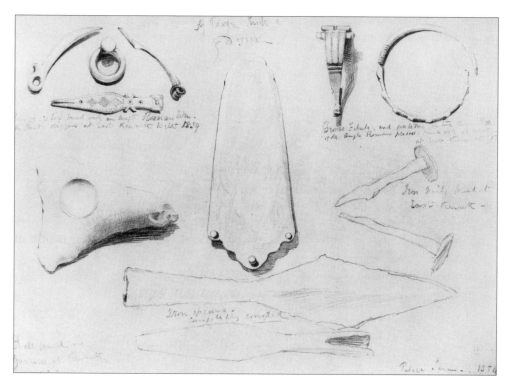

Fig 41. Frederick Sandys, *Antiquities Found at Kennett, Wiltshire* (1854). Pencil, 235 × 337mm. *Photograph:* © V & A Images/Victoria and Albert Museum.

Müller's antiquarian impulse also led him on to some of his most successful work: the watercolours produced in Lycia in the winter of 1843–4, during Charles Fellows's final season of excavations at Xanthus (fig 42).[30] The expedition's official artist was George Scharf (elected FSA in 1852) and Müller's images were therefore free of the need to provide accurate documentation, a process he described as akin to 'taking medicine'.[31] Such a pithy remark sums up the misgivings of ambitious painters, anxious to be seen as creative artists and suspicious of the restrictions surrounding antiquarian illustration. As an archaeologist, Fellows was interested in Xanthus as a repository of archaeological data and Scharf's official record tends to abstract Xanthus and other sites from the incidental contingencies of the Lycian coast in the 1840s. Müller's watercolours, in contrast, are marked by the quality of his response as an artist, whose lyrical representation of light and colour makes of the ruins picturesque, even elegiac, subjects. Müller's drawings are widely considered to constitute some of the finest work in the medium, but they achieve this at the price of systematic study and the provision of detail. What archaeological information one might glean from such records is clearly limited. Yet, notwithstanding the loss of precisely rendered data, the reluctance to make minutely detailed documentary records is not to abandon the idea of engagement with the past. What the creative credo of Müller and other artists proposes is that antiquity can be as usefully approached via more general understandings as it can by minute particularities. In Asia Minor, Müller not only caught the overall disposition of the ruins Fellows was investigating, he was also a diligent witness of the life and landscape surrounding them. In one sense, this insistence on context is sympathetic

Fig 42. William Müller, *Water Tomb, Telmessus* (1844). Watercolour and gouache, 365 × 533mm. *Photograph*: © copyright the Trustees of the British Museum.

to modern understandings, respectful of archaeological discoveries not merely as relics of antiquity but also as bound into contemporary cultural situations.

This brief and inevitably selective review shows clearly that capable artists were drawn into the antiquarian orbit as illustrators of antiquities, albeit briefly in many cases. Yet while individual antiquaries were commissioning painters of note for their own purposes, with respect to the Society's direct impact on artists the record is patchy. It is particularly noticeable in this regard that very few of the artists elected to membership of the Society made use of its discoveries in their own work. Indeed, as Joan Evans has pointed out, the suspicion arises that the majority of these artist members were attracted more by the engravings in *Vetusta Monumenta* than by any serious intention to contribute to or benefit from antiquarian research.[32] Sir Joshua Reynolds had been elected FSA in 1772 and in the 1790s other members of the Royal Academy followed his lead – among them Benjamin West, Joseph Farington, Richard Cosway, Thomas Lawrence, Osias Humphrey, William Beechey, Robert Smirke and George Stubbs.[33] Of these, only Benjamin West (discussed below) can be regarded as seriously concerned to effect some sort of union between antiquarian study and the practice of art. In the nineteenth century even this token allegiance faltered, with few of the most significant artists of the day joining the Society. Those who were elected in the nineteenth century included the painters William Alexander, Samuel Prout and Charles Lock Eastlake, the sculptors Richard Westmacott and Francis Chantrey and the illustrators and engravers Charles Alfred Stothard and Frederick William Fairholt.

With the exception of Benjamin West, only Stothard and Fairholt can be considered as fulfilling Milles's prospectus. Charles Alfred Stothard (1786–1821) received the Society's patronage in 1816 to make facsimile drawings of the Bayeux Tapestry (fig 43) and was elected FSA in 1819, when he made a notable series of drawings of the Painted Chamber at Westminster.[34] Despite working on these commissions, Stothard's relationship with the Society was not a menial one and should be distinguished from that enjoyed by the Basire family, Jacob Schnebbelie and Thomas Underwood. Like John Carter before him, Stothard was not merely the Society's employee. Although he worked for the Society to prepare the Bayeux Tapestry and Westminster drawings, in so far as he made his own distinctive contribution to antiquarian research he is better considered as an independent scholar as well as an artist and engraver. He had made his early career as a painter, specializing in romantic scenes from history, and approached the Society with his professional artistic identity already established. Moreover, he had a relish for antiquarian research and had begun publishing his *Monumental Effigies of Great Britain* in 1811. His untimely death, falling from a ladder while copying a window at Bere Ferrers, Devon, robbed the Society of one of the very few early nineteenth-century members whose artistic and antiquarian allegiances were held in balance.

Frederick William Fairholt (1813–66), FSA, may be said to have inherited Stothard's mantle in so far as he gravitated naturally from the artistic profession to antiquarian research. Trained as an engraver, and first earning a living as a

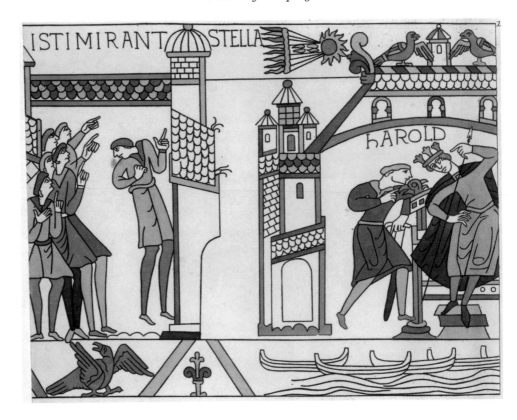

drawing-master and scene-painter, he was taken up in the 1830s by two authors and publishers – first Charles Knight and then Samuel Carter Hall, for whom Fairholt contributed a large number of articles on various subjects to the *Art Journal*. From the 1840s to the 1860s especially, he illustrated numerous antiquarian publications, as well as publishing a wide variety of illustrated antiquarian and topographical books and articles of his own.[35] His major contributions to antiquarian study lay in the field of historic costume, first publishing a series of articles in the *Art Journal*, and then issuing *Costume in England* in 1846.[36] This book, along with the slightly earlier publication of a *History of British Costume* (1834) by James Planché, FSA, brought to a close a succession of studies on costume originally initiated by Joseph Strutt and others in the late eighteenth century.[37] Fairholt insisted that anachronistic detail resulted in pictures that were 'painted lies' and demanded that 'no painter should falsify history by delineating the character on his canvas in habits not known until many years after their death, or holding implements that were not at the time invented'.[38] Fairholt's zeal is indicative of the high tide of historicism running at mid-century and it points to the impact of antiquarian scholarship on the visual arts. It was these kinds of researches, and allied investigations into architecture, furniture, arms and armour, that had been in Jeremiah Milles's mind when he made his remarks in 1781 about the 'Variety of necessary Information' antiquaries could provide fine artists and he would, no doubt, have been gratified by the volume of such studies appearing over the next sixty years.

The record of artists actually using such materials to produce a more authentic re-creation of the past is not as full as Milles might have hoped, but at the time he made his remarks he would have been aware that the painter Benjamin West (1738–1820), FSA, was already informing his paintings of British history with the fruits of antiquarian learning. By the late 1760s West had become one of the pre-eminent history painters in Britain; and, what is of particular significance, through his work for George III and other patrons, he produced more images of the national history than of Greek or Roman history and mythology.[39] At a time when history painting was identified above all else with classical subject matter, this was a remarkable achievement; it would not be until the middle of the nineteenth century that historicist interest in the northern medieval past challenged the lure of Mediterranean history and culture. Moreover, in doing this, West attempted to produce images whose details were authenticated by recourse to genuine medieval survivals: architecture, illuminated manuscripts, sculpture, vestments, arms and armour. This historicist zeal represents a very significant turning away from the Grand Manner in history painting advocated by Reynolds, whose fourth discourse of 1771, in particular, had explicitly counselled against historical accuracy.[40]

From 1779 to 1801 the bulk of West's activity concerned the refurbishment of the Upper Ward of Windsor Castle, supplying religious subjects for the Royal Chapel and historical compositions for the Audience Chamber in the State Apartments. The Audience Chamber paintings celebrate a moment in English history – the reign of Edward III – that was widely considered to represent the apogee of British medieval culture. The room was hung with eight paintings by West: six of them were subjects derived from Edward III's military campaigns in Scotland and France, one showed St George and the dragon and one the installation of the Order of the Garter (fig 44). These imposing canvases – the three largest of them were 2,870mm high by 4,483mm wide – were all produced between 1786 and 1789.[41] West's researches were extensive and he made use of the Tower of London armouries, the royal library and the royal heralds as well as published texts – among them Strutt's *The Regal and Ecclesiastical Antiquities of England* (1773) and his *Horda Angel-Cynnan, or a compleat view of the manners, customs, arms, habits &c of the inhabitants of England* (1775–6).[42] Given the prestige of the commission and the diligence West had shown in preparing to re-create the world of the Middle Ages, it is not surprising that Milles was disposed to imagine others would follow, placing the work of the Society of Antiquaries and the Royal Academy in a very healthy relationship.

What could not have been anticipated in the 1780s was that the Windsor commission would prove to be so exceptional. Although a small number of artists chose to imagine the world of the Middle Ages over the next forty years, very few of them grounded their interpretations in antiquarian scholarship. By the middle 1820s, however, a growing historicism is detectable. Planché records in his *Recollections and Reflections* (1872) a number of occasions on which he advised painters on historical detail and by the 1840s an attitude more generally comparable to West's is evident. As Sir Roy Strong, FSA, has demonstrated, the key painting evoking the spirit of

Fig 44. Benjamin West,
*The First Installation of
the Order of the Garter,
in St George's Chapel*
(1787). Oil on canvas,
2,870 × 4,483mm.
Photograph: The Royal
Collection © 2007,
Her Majesty Queen
Elizabeth II.

'Merry England' – William Powell Frith's oil painting *Coming of Age in the Olden Time*
(1849) – makes selective use of Fairholt and of Joseph Nash's *Mansions of England
in the Olden Time* (1839–41).[43] Frith and fellow artists benefited from a widespread
fascination for historical research; by the middle of the century, they were able to turn
to the collections in the South Kensington Museum and to a variety of published
sources to aid their evocations of the past. In addition to Joseph Strutt's work of
the late eighteenth century, the publication of Planché's *British Costume* (1834)
and Fairholt's *Costume in England* (1846) coincided with the extensive researches of
Henry Shaw (1800–73), FSA, into medieval manuscripts, furniture and decorative
items, many of them subsequently published by the firm of William Pickering,
the ablest establishment in London for high-quality colour reproduction. Shaw's
Specimens of Ancient Furniture Drawn from Existing Authorities (1836) contains an
introduction by Sir Samuel Rush Meyrick, FSA, which explicitly recommends the
book to painters as a means of avoiding anachronisms in historicist paintings.
Probably the most well-known example of a painter making use of these aids to
accuracy is Ford Madox Brown's *Chaucer at the Court of Edward III* (1847–51) (fig 45).
Roy Strong has suggested that the artist had already turned to Henry Shaw's
researches in a painting of *c* 1847 – *John Wycliffe Reading his Translation of the Bible
to John of Gaunt* (Bradford Art Galleries and Museum) – whose lectern and canopied
chair bear close similarities to those illustrated by Shaw.[44] With *Chaucer*, Brown's
attempts to provide an accurate *mise-en-scène* drew him to Strutt's *Regal and
Ecclesiastical Antiquities* for the women's head-dresses, Stothard's *Mounumental
Effigies* for Edward III and the Black Prince, and Camille Bonnard's *Costume
Historique* (1829–30) for other details.[45]

136

Fig 45. Ford Madox Brown, *Chaucer at the Court of Edward III* (1847–51). Oil on canvas, 3,720 × 2,960mm. *Photograph*: purchased 1876, Art Gallery of New South Wales; photograph: Ray Woodbury for Art Gallery of New South Wales (acc no. 703).

Yet, despite a number of painters benefiting from the medievalist research to be found in antiquarian publications, no closer links with the Society are detectable. Ford Madox Brown, for example, for all his resolute engagement with antiquarian study, never seems to have attempted a more formal liaison with the world of the antiquaries themselves. Probably the most significant Victorian painter to become a member of the Society of Antiquaries was, in fact, not a medievalist at all, but a classicist. In 1884, two years before his election to FSA, Sir Lawrence Alma-Tadema exhibited at the Royal Academy *Hadrian in England: Visiting a Romano-British Pottery*. Originally a substantial painting, measuring some 2,200mm by 1,670mm, the picture was dismembered at some time in the 1890s and the complete composition can only be seen in the wood engraving made after it (fig 46).[46] Its exemplary rigour in attempting to provide an archaeologically sound interpretation of this imagined scene is, however, attributable to Alma-Tadema's continental training rather than any impetus he may have received in Britain. His artistic studies in Antwerp in the 1850s had brought him into regular contact with Louis de Taeye, a minor painter and Professor of Archaeology at the Antwerp Academy. Taeye valued archaeological accuracy and encouraged a painter's recourse to antiquarian data to supply it, in just the way Milles had anticipated so optimistically for British artists in the 1780s. Alma-Tadema was also influenced by the Belgian history painter Baron Henri Leys, whose insistence on absolute accuracy in detail was equally uncompromising.[47] Having begun his exploration of history with pictures detailing Merovingian culture, Alma-Tadema experienced at first hand the archaeological riches of Italy in 1863, and this was to prove a decisive discovery. His attitude to classical antiquity was one of meticulous research, not only making measured drawings of ruins, but accumulating

Fig 46. After Sir Lawrence Alma-Tadema, *Hadrian in England: Visiting a Romano-British Pottery* (1884). Wood engraving. *Photograph*: private collection.

an extensive library and photographic archive.⁴⁸ Relocated to London in 1870, Alma-Tadema made his career as a painter of the classical world and this picture represents his only foray into British territory, imagining a visit of the Emperor Hadrian to a Romano-British pottery *c* AD 121.⁴⁹ In preparation for the picture, Alma-Tadema studied Romano-British pottery and employed J J Gaul to make drawings of examples in British collections.⁵⁰ The arm bracelet worn by the Briton on the stairs shows that the artist had also taken care to examine Iron Age material with his customary diligence, using this detail to assert the cultural separation of the British potter from the Roman dignitaries gathered above.

Although Alma-Tadema's painting can, perhaps, be seen as continuing that fascination with the Romano-British world evident in the depictions of the Ribchester helmet and other items, it also alerts us to one final observation about the interaction of artists and antiquarians in the long nineteenth century. While the Society of Antiquaries' orientation towards British antiquities was not total, its exploration of a broader archaeological prospect was limited. The Society did not commission extensive surveys of classical remains, such research being associated more typically with the Society of Dilettanti and the British Museum. Notwithstanding the interest of many artists in medievalist research, the Society's preoccupation with British remains had to compete with the sequence of major surveys and excavations in the Mediterranean and the Middle East, from James Stuart and Nicholas Revett's *Antiquities of Athens* (1762–1830) to Austen Henry Layard's *Monuments of Nineveh* (1849–53). The successive installation at the British Museum of the Townley collection of classical sculpture, the Elgin marbles, the Bassae reliefs, the new Egyptian displays and Layard's Assyrian sculpture provided an immediate and more productive stimulus to nineteenth-century artists than the world of British antiquities. As a result, even when the historicist current was running strongly in the nineteenth-century art world, the Society's concerns were effectively too narrow to capitalize on it.

The relationship between the arts and the study of antiquity merits further investigation. While we can see clearly that the needs of the antiquaries themselves were largely satisfied by the provision of high-quality visual records, it is more difficult to sum up or assess the impact of antiquarian scholarship on British nineteenth-century art as a whole. When considering the variety of activities outlined in this essay, the question remains whether they constitute evidence for what Milles had anticipated in the 1780s, the enrichment of the visual arts from the store of antiquarian knowledge. To answer this, we need first to consider the model Milles proposed for the relationship between antiquarianism and art. One thing that is immediately apparent is the direction of influence in his remarks. Milles assumed that knowledge derived from the study of antiquities could assist works of art. The antiquary is the more active partner, for it is his researches that will animate the artist's productions. Although Milles's generation valued the use of good-quality images as a means of promulgating antiquarian research, what does not appear to have been considered is the reciprocal benefit that the study of antiquities might receive from the visual arts. The model

Milles proposes is essentially that of the needy artist drawing nourishment from the study of antiquities; not the needy antiquary reappraising his understanding of antiquities thanks to an artist's interpretation. Thus whereas an artist can benefit from antiquarian scholarship it is not presumed that he can produce insights of his own; the sole contribution art can make to antiquarian study is the illustration of the material record.

However, from an artist's point of view what Milles recommended was contentious, for it seemed to leave little space for the exercise of the creative imagination. As an illustrator, all that was required of the artist was the production of accurate visual transcripts of material objects. But the incorporation of detail by history painters, in so far as it challenged the artist's freedom to invent, struck at the very centre of what painting stood for. In academic theory history painting stood at the top of the hierarchy that descended via portraiture, landscape and genre scenes to still life. The history painter thus occupied the role which best demonstrated the invention, imagination and creativity of the artist. But should a history painter have succumbed to Milles's recommendations, to the extent that he incorporated antiquarian research, he was in danger of ceding the imaginative interpretation of the past to a prescribed notion of authenticity. We have already noted Sir Joshua Reynolds's celebration of the Grand Manner as inimical to detailed representation and Richard Gough's recognition of the antipathy between working as an illustrator of antiquities and attempting to achieve respect within the artistic profession. Even though Reynolds's recommendations were displaced by new concerns in the nineteenth century, it is clear that the needs of the antiquary and the artist were rarely reconciled. We observed, too, that the most important nineteenth-century artists are infrequently associated with antiquarian illustration, an employment that emphasized manual dexterity and only rarely allowed an artist to demonstrate his mental capacities. When it comes to history painting the case is more complicated. It is manifestly true that in the decades either side of 1850 numerous artists had recourse to antiquarian publications to furnish them with appropriate details of dress, furniture and architecture. Yet, that said, it is equally true that the arts criticism of the day found occasion to comment disapprovingly on those artists who incorporated so much detail that the overall composition lost its unity. In truth, a picture that was merely a repository of antiquarian research was no picture at all.

The major difficulty frustrating Milles's predictions of improved relations between artist and antiquary was at bottom the status of art itself. Aesthetic theory, together with the study of the classical heritage and the Old Masters, was strongly committed to a view of art that stressed its intellectual dignity and its creativity. Like the Old Masters, the imagination of a gifted artist was too precious to be cribbed and cabined by minute description and an obsession with antiquarian detail. Thus, even at the height of that mid-century commitment to the truth of representation, as exemplified by the early work of the Pre-Raphaelites, the artist was still expected to produce work that conformed to critical expectations about the role and status of painting: historical detail on its own was not enough. What then of those who did supply the precision

140

Milles had called for? The historical painter Edward Armitage admitted that the Old Masters and the modern artist pursued different quarries:

> We may not be able to paint like Titian or Correggio, but we attempt an approximation to truth which they never did; and not only is a modern historical painter more truthful about the costume of his personages and the architecture of his backgrounds, but in the disposition and action of his figures he honestly endeavours to represent the scene as it actually may have occurred.[51]

Armitage was writing in the 1880s and, as we have seen, artists like Alma-Tadema were also active then; but already the concern for accuracy was waning. By the 1870s the balance between historical truth, vouchsafed by antiquarian knowledge, and pictorial effectiveness had swung decisively in favour of the latter. Frederic Leighton is a good example of this. His early painting *Cimabue's Celebrated Madonna is Carried in Procession through the Streets of Florence* (1853–5) (The National Gallery, on loan from HM Queen Elizabeth ii) bears a good deal of antiquarian precision in its costume and architecture. By the 1870s, however, he talked of how his

> growing love of form made me intolerant of the restraints and exigencies of costume and led me more and more, and finally, to a class of subjects, or more accurately to a state of conditions, in which supreme scope is left to pure artistic qualities, in which no form is imposed upon the artist by the tailor, but in which every form is made obedient to the conception of the design he has in hand.[52]

As Robyn Asleson has shown, Leighton did not abandon an interest in archaeology. He was intellectually informed through his associations with the Society of Dilettanti, the Hellenic Society and the British Museum and some of his pictures make knowing references to archaic art.[53] But his art cannot be said to have emphasized this knowledge, making a virtue instead of its aesthetic coherence. By the end of the nineteenth century, with the move among many artists to aestheticism and art for art's sake, the contrast between the exercise of the imagination and the seemingly documentary record of an artist like Alma-Tadema was even more extreme.[54] A century after Milles had made his optimistic remarks, the gap between antiquarian scholarship and artistic practice had become almost unbridgeable.

What artists could supply, however, was precisely what Milles had not envisaged, a poetic apprehension of antiquity. Certainly, from a rigorously antiquarian viewpoint, the more fanciful the interpretation of the past the more irrelevant it must seem to the serious prosecution of research. Yet there was also a case to be made for the creative recuperation of the past as a supplement to empirical enquiry. Medieval culture, creatively reimagined by Rossetti or Burne-Jones, say, was always bigger than the sum of its parts. For example, when composing the tapestry design of *The Attainment: The Vision of the Holy Grail to Sir Galahad, Sir Bors and Sir Perceval* (1895–6), Burne-Jones drew on researches he had made into medieval arts, selecting the eighth-century Tasilo Chalice for the Grail cup and the fourteenth-century

Westminster Psalter for one of the knights (fig 47). But although Burne-Jones was indeed availing himself of antiquarian research, very much in the way Milles had recommended, his wilful combination of details from different periods clearly indicates that this was no historicist endeavour. The anachronistic combination of items from different centuries helps remove the Arthurian story from any particular era. No matter that some details may have owed their origins to antiquarian knowledge, Burne-Jones's approach to the Arthur story attempted to convey not a particular time or place, but a narrative that transcended history.[55] Moreover, rather than attempting to open a window into the past, images like this suggest the suspension of time, such that the distance separating the nineteenth century from its historical antecedents is radically diminished. This mode of apprehension prompts thoughts about the limits of empirical evidence, the extent to which antiquity can be truly known or understood from a modern viewpoint. To approach the past as creatively as this is to reveal the extent to which the past is a product of modern enquiry: it is always and inevitably fashioned by the intellect, the emotions and the imagination.

Fig 47. After Edward Burne-Jones, *The Attainment: The Vision of the Holy Grail to Sir Galahad, Sir Bors and Sir Percival* (1895–6). Wool and silk tapestry, 2,450 × 6,930mm. *Photograph*: © Birmingham Museums & Art Gallery.

NOTES

1. The Society's new quarters can be seen in the line engraving by Henry Melville after Frederick William Fairholt, published in *London Interiors: a grand national exhibition of the religious, regal and civic solemnities, public amusements, scientific meetings, and commercial scenes of the British capital* (London: Joseph Mead, 1841–4). Fairholt was elected a Fellow of the Society in 1844, the year the print was published.

2. Jeremiah Milles, Presidential Address, 11 Jan 1781, quoted in Evans 1956, 176.

3. The fifth edition of Walpole's *Anecdotes*, edited and extended by James Dallaway, was published in 1827–8. Edward Edwards's *Anecdotes of Painters Who Have Resided or Been Born in England* (1808) was designed to function as a continuation of Walpole's publication.

4. For Holbein see Evans 1956, 290.

5. None of the authors of these significant art-historical publications, appearing between the 1790s and the 1850s, became a Fellow of the Society of Antiquaries: William Roscoe, *Lorenzo de' Medici* (1793) and *Leo X* (1805); the Revd Robert Bromley, *A Philosophical and Critical History of the Fine Arts* (1793–5); James Northcote, *Life of Titian* (1830); Henry Fuseli, *History of Art in the Schools of Italy* (1831); John Ruskin, *Modern Painters* (1843–60); Lord Lindsay, *Sketches of the History of Christian Art* (1847); Anna Jameson, *Sacred and Legendary Art* (1848).

6. Gough 1786, 9.

7. For Carter see Crook 1995.

8. Resolution reprinted in Evans 1956, 206.

9. SAL, Council Minutes, III (not paginated), 25 May 1798. Although Underwood was right to state his lack of expertise, he was a careful draughtsman and had recently illustrated geological specimens with exemplary accuracy for Philip Rashleigh's *Specimens of British Minerals* (1797). Moreover, by 1802 he was a member of the Sketching Society for 'Historic Landscape' which required some rudimentary ability in figure drawing.

10. William Skelton was an engraver, the pupil of James Basire and William Sharp. I have assumed that the reference in the minutes to 'Mr Tendi' refers to Andrea Tendi, known for the drawings of Renaissance paintings engraved in Marco Lastri's *L'Etruria Pittrice* (Florence, 1791–5). If so, it is likely that Townley first met him in Italy. Skelton made two drawings and Tendi one (a bird's-eye view), all three being shown at the meeting of 25 May 1798. Basire was instructed to engrave them, but Basire's own drawings of the helmet were selected at a meeting of 15 Mar 1799 as more appropriate for engraving. My thanks to Elizabeth Lewis, FSA, for showing me her transcripts of the minutes.

11. Joseph Ayloffe opened the tomb of Edward I in May 1774, publishing the results in *Archaeologia*, *3*, 1786, 376–413. He read a paper to the Society, on 12 Mar 1778, on three further monuments uncovered in 1775 and it was decided to publish this account at the Society's expense, with nine (later reduced to seven) engravings by Basire. Ayloffe's *An Account of Some Ancient Monuments in Westminster Abbey* was published in 1780 and reissued in *Vetusta Monumenta*, II (1789). All of Blake's drawings for Ayloffe's researches are in the Society's collection. Blake also prepared twenty-nine drawings for engraving in Richard Gough's *Sepulchral Monuments*. In addition, Gough owned seven replicas of Blake's drawings recording Ayloffe's work at Westminster, owned by the Society (see above). All of Gough's Blake drawings are now in the Bodleian Library, Oxford.

12. Butlin notes that the signatures or monograms of Basire are written in the same ink and hand as are the descriptive inscriptions referring to the plates in *Vetusta Monumenta*, published in 1789. In all likelihood, then, these inscriptions are later additions added to the drawings when Blake's apprenticeship to Basire had been over for some years: see Butlin 1981, 3.

13. I am grateful to Susan Morris, the Girtin authority, for authenticating this drawing on the basis of its signature and its style.

14. Presumably this was the Revd John Homfray, later of Sutton, Norfolk, who was elected FSA on 1 Dec 1794 (indexed as Homfrey) and who died on 25 Dec 1842.

15. Moore published *Monastic Remains and Ancient Castles in England and Wales* (1791), including aquatint engravings after his own designs by Jacob Schnebbelie, and *A List of the Principal Castles and Monasteries in Great Britain* (1798).

16. The most extensive account of Turner's work for Whitaker can be found in Warburton 1982.

17. Of the seals depicted in this watercolour, seven appear among the fifteen engraved in plate III (Seals of Whalley Abbey) and seven in plate X (Seals of the Lords of Blackburnshire) in the *History of Whalley*. The watercolour for the eight other seals shown in plate III is untraced.

18. The album comprised an elaborate frontispiece (a cupboard with opening doors) and sixteen watercolours. These are now in a private collection, but may be viewed online via Tate Britain's *Turner Online* website. Another frontispiece, a still life of armour and heraldic devices, separated from the album at an early date, is in the collection of the Ashmolean Museum and is entitled *At Farnley Hall (a frontispiece)*.

19. A number of Britton's commissioned drawings are now in Devizes Museum. Others were acquired by the American clergyman and scholar, the Revd Elias Lyman Magoon, and are now in the collection of Vassar College. For the latter see Consagra 1999.

20. Among other works with which Britton was associated either as author or editor are *The Beauties of Wiltshire* (1801, 2 vols, with a third added in 1825), *The Beauties of England and Wales* (1801–15), *Architectural Antiquities of Normandy* (1825–7), *Picturesque Antiquities of English Cities* (1830), *History of the Palace and Houses of Parliament at Westminster* (1834–6) and *Dictionary of the Architecture and Archaeology of the Middle Ages* (1838).

21. Cotman's brooding and atmospheric rendition of the Devil's Den cromlech near Marlborough, drawn in 1802, was used as the illustration on the title-page of the third volume of Britton's *Beauties of Wiltshire* (1825). This watercolour is now in the collection of the Francis Lehman Loeb Art Center, Vassar College: see Holcomb 1973.

22. See Chippindale 1985. Two of the watercolours are attributed to Cotman. Although the attribution has been questioned, the artist responsible, if not Cotman himself, was evidently capable of producing work of the highest quality. Without further evidence to the contrary it is not unreasonable to consider the attribution to Cotman sound.

23. For contemporary critical commentary on the compromised status of Britton's publications, see Smiles 2000, 64–76.

24. This, in itself, is noteworthy, for the Association had been founded in 1843, largely because of dissatisfaction with the complacency and lack of direction in the Society of Antiquaries. For information on Bulwer see Elzea 1991 and Gladstone 1945.

25. As seen in the production of his *Miscellaneous Etchings* (1811), *Architectural Antiquities of Norfolk* (1812–18), *Specimens of Norman and Gothic Architecture in the County of Norfolk* (1816–18) and *Architectural Antiquities of Normandy* (1822).

26. For example, the Revd John Collinson's *The History and Antiquities of the County of Somerset* (1791) and the Revd Samuel Seyer's *Memoirs Historical and Topographical of Bristol and its Neighbourhood* (1821–3).

27. Sandys's last antiquarian gesture is, perhaps, the inclusion of Pictish designs in Morgan le Fay's robe in his picture *Morgan Le Fay* (1862–3), now in Birmingham Museum and Art Gallery.

28. Müller made over forty sketches in total, from which a selection was made. Although not specified, it is assumed that Louis Haghe provided the figures in the lithographed plates: see Greenacre and Stoddard 1991, 133–41.

29. In the 1820s, Bonington studied Sir Samuel Rush Meyrick's collection of armour and also had recourse to the work of Joseph Strutt on occasion: see Strong 2004, 48 and 81.

30. A publication was announced for 1844, reproducing Müller's work in Xanthus in twenty-six lithographs, but his death in 1845 forestalled it: see Greenacre and Stoddard 1991, 142–63.

31. 'Whilst at Pinara or Tlos, Müller, after making many splendid pictorial and generalised sketches, said one day to his young companion, "Oh, Johnson! I feel I ought to work hard making careful pencil outline-drawings of the tombs and temples, with all their details." This Muller called "taking medicine". It was, without a doubt, very repugnant to him to lay aside his colours which he loved so much; but he did it, nevertheless, and he went in for some hours daily (for a time) at severe pencil-work of a most conscientious and accurate character.': see Solly 1875, 189.

32. Evans 1956, 237.

33. Stubbs was only elected ARA, rather than becoming a full Academician.

34. The Bayeux tapestry plates, engraved by Basire, were reproduced in *Vetusta Monumenta* in 1821–3. For information on and illustrations of Stothard's copies of wall paintings in the Painted Chamber at Westminster, see Binski 1986, 24–30.

35. For example, *A Dictionary of Terms in Art* (1854); *The Dramatic Works of John Lilly* (1858); *Gog and Magog: the giants in Guildhall; their real and legendary history. With an account of other civic giants at home and abroad* (1859); *Up the Nile and Home Again* (1862).

36. Fairholt 1846. Fairholt's collection of books on civic pageantry was bequeathed to the Society of Antiquaries; his collections relating to costume were bequeathed to the British Museum.

37. Strutt's *The Regal and Ecclesiastical Antiquities of England* was published in 1773, followed by his *Horda Angel-Cynnan, or a compleat view of the manners, customs, arms, habits, &c. of the inhabitants of England, from the arrival of the Saxons, till the reign of Henry the Eighth* (1776) and *A Complete View of the Dress and Habits of the People of England* (1796). In the 1780s publications included John Carter's *Specimens of the Ancient Sculpture and Painting now Remaining in this Kingdom* (1780), Francis Grose's *A Treatise on Ancient Armour and Weapons* (1786) and Joseph Cooper Walker's *The Dress of the Ancient and Modern Irish* (1788). In the 1810s appeared Samuel Rush Meyrick and Charles Hamilton Smith's *The Costume of the Original Inhabitants of the British Islands* (1815) and John Carter's *Specimens of English Ecclesiastical Costume, from the Earliest Period Down to the Sixteenth Century* (1817).

38. F W Fairholt, *Costume in England*, in the introduction to the 1860 edition, cited in Strong 1978, 55.

39. West was decidedly George III's favourite artist. His first mature history painting had been painted in Rome in 1763 for the King's Librarian, Richard Dalton, and George III began his own patronage of the painter in 1768. Between 1768 and 1801 West painted some sixty works for the king and was paid over £34,000 for them, in addition to an annual stipend of £1,000 paid annually from 1780. From 1772 he styled himself 'Historical Painter to the King' in the Royal Academy's exhibition catalogues.

40. Wark 1975, 57–73.

41. The subjects of the paintings were as follows: *The Surrender of Calais to Edward III; An Entertainment Given by Edward III, after defeating the French in their attempt upon Calais; The Passage of Edward III over the River Somme; The Interview between the King and his Victorious Son, the Black Prince, after the Battle of Cressy, in 1346; The History of St George; The Battle of Poitiers, where Edward the Black Prince took King John and his son Philip prisoners, whom he afterwards brought over into England; The Battle of Neville's Cross, where David, King of Scotland, was taken prisoner by Queen Philippa, while her royal consort, Edward III, was besieging Calais; The First Installation of the Order of the Garter, in St George's Chapel.*

42. See Greenhouse 1985.

43. See Strong 1978, 90–3.

44. Ibid, 65.

45. Ibid, 58.

46. The wood engraving is reproduced in Blackburn 1884, 20, who specifically notes 'great archaeological research on the part of the painter' (my thanks to Donato Esposito for this reference). The three fragments of the painting that survive are the upper portion of the design, *Hadrian in England: Visiting a Romano-British Pottery* (Van Gogh Museum, Amsterdam, on loan from the Stedelijk Museum, Amsterdam), the right-hand figure on the stairs, *A Romano-British Potter* (Musée d'Orsay, Paris) and the bottom left of the composition, *The Roman Potters in Britain* (HRH Princess Juliana of the Netherlands). They are all reproduced in Becker and Prettejohn 1996, 224–8.
47. See Julian Treuherz's 'Introduction to Alma-Tadema' in Becker and Prettejohn 1996, 13–16.
48. This material is now in the care of the University of Birmingham.
49. The picture was inspired by *The Emperor* (1881), a novel written by Alma-Tadema's friend, Georg Ebers, Professor of Egyptology at Leipzig, in which Hadrian is described as visiting a papyrus factory in Alexandria.
50. For information on this picture and its origins see the catalogue notes by Prettejohn in Becker and Prettejohn 1996, 224–8.
51. Edward Armitage, *Lectures on Painting* (1883), 237; cited in Prettejohn 1991, 42–3.
52. Cited in Staley 1978, 24.
53. See Asleson 1999.
54. In fact, Alma-Tadema's approach to the past is a good deal more complicated than this: see Prettejohn 2002.
55. I have discussed this more fully in Smiles 2004.

BIBLIOGRAPHY

Arnold, D (ed) 2004. *Cultural Identities and the Aesthetics of Britishness*, Manchester

Asleson, R 1999. 'On translating Homer: prehistory and the limits of classicism', in Barringer and Prettejohn (eds) 1999, 67–86

Barringer, T and Prettejohn, E (eds) 1999. *Frederic Leighton: antiquity, renaissance modernity*, London

Becker, E and Prettejohn, E 1996. *Sir Lawrence Alma-Tadema*, Zwolle

Binski, P 1986. *The Painted Chamber at Westminster*, London

Blackburn, H 1884. *Academy Notes*, London

Butlin, M 1981. *The Paintings and Drawings of William Blake*, London

Chippindale, C 1985. 'John Britton's "Celtic Cabinet" in Devizes Museum and its context', Antiq J, 45/1, 121–37

Consagra, F 1999. 'The "Ever Growing Elm": the formation of Elias Lyman Magoon's collection of British drawings, 1854–60', in Consagra, Lukacher and Smiles (eds) 1999, 85–131

Consagra, F, Lukacher, B and Smiles, S (eds) 1999. *Landscapes of Retrospection: the Magoon collection of British prints and drawings 1739–1860*, Poughkeepsie, NY

Crook, J 1995. *John Carter and the Mind of the Gothic Revival*, London

Elzea, B 1991. *Frederick Sandys 1829–1904: a catalogue raisonné*, Woodbridge

Evans, J 1956. *A History of the Society of Antiquaries*, Oxford

Fairholt, F W 1846. *Costume in England: a history of dress from the earliest period till the close of the eighteenth century*, London

Gladstone, H 1945. 'British birds named after persons', *Trans Dumfriesshire Galloway Natur Hist Antiq Soc*, **23**, 178–84, 189

Gough, R 1786. *Sepulchral Monuments in Great Britain, applied to illustrate the history of families, manners, habits, and arts, at the different periods from the Norman Conquest to the seventeenth century*, London

Greenacre, F and Stoddard, S 1991. *W J Müller*, Bristol

Greenhouse, W 1985. 'Benjamin West and Edward III: a neoclassical painter and medieval history', *Art History*, 8/2 (June), 178–91

Holcomb, A 1973. 'Devil's Den: an early drawing by John Sell Cotman', *Master Drawings*, **11**/4, 393–8

Prettejohn, E 1991. 'Images of the past in British painting 1855–71', unpublished PhD thesis, Courtauld Institute of Art, University of London

Prettejohn, E 2002. 'Lawrence Alma-Tadema and the modern city of ancient Rome', Art Bull, **84**/1, 115–29

Smiles, S 2000. *Eye Witness: artists and visual documentation in Britain, 1770–1830*, Aldershot

Smiles, S 2004. 'Albion's legacy – myth, history and "the matter of Britain"', in Arnold (ed) 2004, 164–81

Solly, N 1875. *Memoir of the Life of William James Müller*, London

Staley, A 1978. 'Post Pre-Raphaelitism', in *Victorian High Renaissance*, 21–31, Manchester City Art Gallery and Minneapolis Institute of Arts, Minneapolis, Minn

Strong, R 1978. *And When Did You Last See Your Father? The Victorian painter and British history*, London

Strong, R 2004. *Painting the Past: the Victorian painter and British history*, London

Warburton, S 1982. *Turner and Dr Whitaker*, Burnley

Wark, R (ed) 1975. *Sir Joshua Reynolds' 'Discourses on Art'*, London

C.H.S. del.   Aquatinted by R. Havell.

An Arch Druid in *His Judicial Habit.*

Published June 1, 1815, by R. Havell, 5 Chapel Street, London.

CHAPTER SEVEN

ANTIQUARIES AND THE INTERPRETATION OF ANCIENT OBJECTS, 1770–1820

Susan Pearce

In 1770 the Society of Antiquaries of London was well over fifty years old.[1] Between 1770 and 1820, to take broad dates, the number of Fellows rose remarkably, from around 290 at the beginning of the period to around 800 at the end. By 1820 the Society had accumulated a substantial library, a growing collection of prints and drawings and some objects. It had produced significant publications, it had a narrative of its own history in the shape of minutes of meetings running back to 1718[2] and it had a relatively secure financial position. In 1751 the Society received its Royal Charter, the recognition of its significance and acceptability in establishment circles, and in 1780 it was able to secure space in the newly built Somerset House, in parity (more or less) with the Royal Society and the Royal Academy. All this was a considerable achievement for an organization that had begun without royal or major aristocratic patronage, and a significant index of its impact was the level of caricature which it was beginning to attract.[3] Jeremiah Milles became President in 1769[4] and Richard Gough Director in 1771;[5] both were energetic men with wide-ranging antiquarian experience. By around 1770, past and present weaknesses notwithstanding, the Society had become a mature, self-confident institution, with an established place in the national life, and the recognized right to set significant frameworks for the understanding of the past. This chapter explores how that past was interpreted by the Society through the activities of its Fellows in the decades either side of 1800. It will concentrate upon their visions of the meanings of material culture, understood in its narrower sense of archaeological artefacts – rather than as monuments and buildings, or as objects of art and *vertue* and still less as manuscripts and books (although all these things will come into the story).

THE FELLOWSHIP

First, it is helpful to consider the character of the Fellowship. Roughly a third of the members were gentlemen with private means, and the number of landed squires, such as Sir Philip Rashleigh,[6] from Cornwall, or Robert Riddell,[7] of Glenriddell in the Scottish Lowlands, was growing, as was that of peers. About a quarter of the

Fig 48. Coloured aquatint by Robert Havell, published as plate x in Meyrick and Smith 1815, entitled 'An Arch Druid in his Judicial Habit'. The description explains that on his finger is 'Logh-Draoch', the chain-ring of divination; his hand rests on the Peithyuin or Elucidator, which is on the stone altar; on the altar lies a gold horn and vessel, and a sprig of mistletoe: most of this is derived from the writings of Iolo Morgannw. *Photograph*: Society of Antiquaries of London.

Fellows lived in London, and a considerable number were of the 'gentlemen' class, suggesting a substantial group of leisured men who drew their incomes from family money. Some – like Thomas Pennant[8] – also earned an income through their writing. Clergymen – overwhelmingly of the Church of England, of course[9] – made up perhaps 13 per cent, and they ranged in standing from Charles Lyttelton, Bishop of Carlisle, who had died in 1768, to parish incumbents. The Anglican clergy of the later eighteenth century was drawn from a surprisingly broad social mix but, again, many of the clerical Fellows had influential links. The other professions were sparsely represented, with a scattering of army officers and medical men and, rather surprisingly, few lawyers, although these few included such men as Daines Barrington.[10] A very few, such as Peter Muilman, were directly in trade.[11]

The group of 'professional antiquaries' was probably more important than their simple numbers suggest. John Ives was Suffolk Herald, with all the access this implies, and John Topham was at the State Paper Office: such men as these must have been glad to have a satisfactory outlet through which material could be made known and eventually published. The odd architect Fellow, for example, Henry Holland,[12] was helpful, as were the painters, such as Richard Cosway.[13] William Norris and John Brand, both Secretaries, were Fellows, and so – a social concession this – were John Carter, the Society's draughtsman, and the Society's publishers, the Nichols, father and son.[14] Thomas Jenkins was also a Fellow, and his regular letters giving news of material appearing in Rome were thinly disguised advertisements for his services as a dealer.[15]

Jenkins apart, the continental dimension to antiquities was not forgotten. Not too many of the Fellows seem to have been on the Grand Tour, either as young gentlemen or as 'bear-leaders' (tutors),[16] and classical material from outside Roman Britain does not make a great showing in the records.[17] However, significant links were maintained through the useful device of Honorary Fellowship, which led to connections with such men as Francesco Bayer, canon of the cathedral at Toledo.[18] Foreign guests, such as Wang At Jong and Captain Maimieux, also attended meetings.[19] The Society received contributions from Ireland,[20] Scotland[21] and Wales,[22] and had members in areas like Cornwall that were then considered remote.[23] By the later eighteenth century a number of women were seriously interested in British antiquities. Most came from the same backgrounds as the Fellows, and had links with them. They seem to have provided the kind of ancillary services that women have continued to provide for their scholastic menfolk, but public interventions by women were rare.[24] Although the social spread of the Society looked superficially limited, its scope should not be underestimated.

The Society's links included major collectors, such as Charles Townley[25] and Sir William Hamilton,[26] and many – perhaps most – of the Fellows were collectors in a minor way. Some were interested in earlier collectors, like the lengthy memoir of Thomas Martin contributed in 1780.[27] In contrast to its library and its holding of prints and drawings, the Society never took a formal decision to build up a museum, and although the project was discussed intermittently over a long period, it never came to fruition. This was because both space and sufficient material were lacking.[28] Space would have encouraged donations, and a determined spirit of acquisition would have gathered enough material for Fellows to press – perhaps successfully – for proper provision; this might have resulted in what England has never had – a national museum of archaeology – but the Society's accumulation was, in the event, largely haphazard, even though it included a number of archaeologically significant pieces (fig 49), such as Thomas Mantell's Anglo-Saxon material excavated from barrows in Kent.[29] About a third of the deliberate donations were of exotic material, and a quarter of medieval, with a small number of prehistoric, Romano-British, Anglo-Saxon and post-medieval gifts.[30] Formal donations comprise about three-quarters of the total holding; the rest seems to consist of objects simply left behind after they had been shown and discussed at a meeting, or even just left without being shown. Presumably they were felt to have little financial or aesthetic interest – that is, they were not of 'cabinet quality' – and they are often heavy or awkward, which explains why about a third are prehistoric (including five of the Hoxne hand-axes) and another third are Romano-British. The immediate importance of all this material was clearly its accessibility. Two large cupboards in the Meeting Room at Somerset House were shelved out to take the collection, and the Society seems to have been a place where Fellows could find ancient objects on tables and seats and handle and discuss them informally; they had the run of the material in the museum in the same way that they did of books in the library. This added a distinctive, perhaps crucial, element to the Society's character as the forum for developing an understanding of past material culture.

Antiquaries tended to be enthusiastic travellers and correspondents, maintaining contact and keeping each other well informed. They come across as warm-blooded

Fig 49. Late Bronze Age hammered bronze shield from Beith, Ayrshire, Scotland, found 'in a peat moss' about 1780 at Luggtonrigge (now Lugtonridge) and presented to the Society by Dr Ferris in 1791, the only one to have survived of several shields that were found together. It was probably a ceremonial offering, and the holes show how it was ritually 'killed' before deposition. The Society was one of a very few institutions at the time which would preserve such British objects. *Photograph*: John Hammond; © Society of Antiquaries of London.

souls, happy and excited (and so open to ridicule) by the prospect of the past opening up before those who were able to examine its remains accurately, honestly and generously. By no means all the Fellows were regular visitors to the Society's rooms, and some may well have appeared only once or twice. Naturally, those living in London came most often, both to read in the library and to attend the meetings. It is to these meetings that we now turn.

THE SOCIETY IN PRACTICE

At the heart of the Society's practice was the weekly meeting, held every Thursday, except during the brief Christmas break and the summer vacation, in the Society's own chambers – at Chancery Lane until 1780, and then in Somerset House. The chair was taken by the President or Vice-President, and the meetings were attended by the Director, the Secretary, Fellows – usually those living in or near London – and the guests they had invited. In Chancery Lane, most of those present seem to have sat around one large table. The new Meeting Room at Somerset House provided 'a very large Mahogany Table for the members and others for the President, Secretary and Treasurer'. These were arranged in a T-shape, with three ranks, each of three benches, on both of the long sides; all present were thus able to see material on exhibition, although increasing numbers may sometimes have made free discussion more difficult (especially on the relatively few occasions when large numbers attended).[31]

After routine business, and the procedures for electing new Fellows, each meeting turned to antiquarian affairs, sometimes interesting, sometimes lacklustre, depending upon who turned up and what communications had been sent in. Gifts, usually of books for the library, were received. A typical meeting was the one held on 4 March 1802,[32] when eight Fellows invited eight guests, although more Fellows were also present. A single book and a set of books were given. 'A curious head of stone' from the site of Merton Abbey was given by James Halfhide, but presented by Sir William Hamilton; neither was at the meeting but Hamilton sent a note from Halfhide with the head, saying that it had been found in 1797, and a letter from himself noting that he had seen the sculpture 'on a visit I made lately to Mr Halfhide at his calico manufactory within the ancient walls of Merton Abbey', and that he 'desired that it might remain in the possession of the Society'.

Next came the objects exhibited. These were an image of Buddha, sent by Thomas Coxe, and sketches of various antiquities, made by Mr Edwards around 1778 and presented by William Blizzard, all with substantial notes. According to custom, all the communications were read out – sometimes involving lengthy papers – and the material or sketches were passed around so that everybody could handle them and comment as they chose. Then, 'the evening being now pretty far advanced', the meeting ended.[33] The Secretary, as was customary, wrote up the minutes, transcribing the full texts of all that had been read; drawings were copied or pasted in, unless they were needed for publication.[34]

A number of lines of thought are suggested by this brief description. The Society had clearly become the recognized repository for detailed information relating to material from the past, and the meetings received considerable quantities of finds which would now be considered archaeological. Indeed, the minutes contain the fundamental accounts of many types of find – particularly of Bronze Age metalwork, Romano-British material and coins – that have set the agendas for all subsequent research work. This was achieved because key Fellows, such as Hamilton, were able and willing to encourage men across England to send in what they had found, with supporting information. Sometimes the find had been made several years before, and often it seems to have passed through several hands before it came to a meeting.[35]

We sense here the developing network by which means active Fellows kept in touch with each other and disseminated their interest to others, so that new finds had a chance of coming to attention. Beneath this, there was a penumbra of local people who appear briefly; people such as the 'plowman, who, in ridging the land pretty deep', found a pot of gold coins,[36] and those who learnt on the rural grapevine that money might be paid even for less obviously thrilling finds. Since many of those interested were parish clergymen, the network drew substance from the social structure, as when the Revd Malachy Hitchins, of St Hilary's, in Cornwall, happened to mention a find of bronzes at his Easter vestry meeting in 1802, and was immediately told of another.[37] This network was particularly effective at a time of increased rural activity brought about by the efforts of enclosing and improving landowners – like the 'ploughing of some new enclosed pasture ground' which produced a stone axe[38] – and with the enterprises concerned with canal digging and turnpike building, all of which involved the ploughing of new land, deeper digging and hence more finds.

ARCHAEOLOGIA AND ITS IMPLICATIONS

The increasing recognition of the quantity of important information held in the minutes encouraged the idea of publication, and the first volume of *Archaeologia* appeared in 1770.[39] The papers were chosen by Richard Gough from a trawl through the existing minutes, and he tried to combine quality with a broad mix that would appeal to the Fellowship. The second volume, for example, had papers originally read between 2 April 1727 and 9 June 1772 and volume 18 between 11 February 1813 (a paper by Samuel Lysons begun in 1808) and 13 March 1817. Naturally, the time-lag lessened as the years went on, and there begin to be marginal notes in the minutes, marking what publication decisions had been taken. So, towards the end of 1801, a transcript of exhibited mid-seventeenth-century manuscripts is glossed 'not to be printed', while in the following week a communication on some stone coffins found near Dunbar is marked 'to be printed in the appendix to 14th vol. of *Archaeologia*', and a paper on tombs at Tewkesbury, 'to be printed'.[40] Some volumes show a decision to concentrate on a particular topic, for example, the run of papers on horns in volume 111, and it was not long before they started to embody the spirit of debate and disagreement (often expressed in fairly strong language) without which no academic discipline can grow.[41]

By 1820 eighteen volumes of *Archaeologia* had been published (table 1) – an average of nearly one every two years – and they were substantial works, with twelve of the volumes having around 400 pages. The balance of papers is enlightening, even allowing for the fact that, as we have just seen, the written chronology of the papers could be quite different from the published chronology. The number of papers in each volume fluctuated, with low points in 1777 and 1794–6.[42] Ecclesiastical and state materials are the main foci, along with the physical remains of the past in the broad sense. Across the period, manuscripts and monuments both have a strong presence, with profiles that tend to balance each other, and both reflect the strong, steady interest firstly in medieval and (especially from 1796) post-medieval topics. Archaeological material makes a relatively strong showing overall. There is a steady interest in inscriptions and art objects, regardless of provenance, but a surprisingly small showing of coins. Around 30 per cent of the papers in each volume concerned material not from the British Isles. However, within the country, there is a wide geographical spread, with no great bias towards south-east England.

It was soon clear that the publication of papers did not exhaust the potential of the records, and so it was decided to form extracts from the minutes to be 'prefixed to each future Volume of the *Archaeologia*'.[43] The first appendix appeared in volume 7, for 1785, and it became a regular feature (table 2). As with the papers, the extracts were chosen by trawling through the past record, and gradually most items of significance seem to have been published, so that analysis of the appendices gives a good indication of what was exhibited at meetings,[44] although there could, of course, be a substantial delay between exhibition and publication, as when items recorded as shown in February 1764 did not appear in print until 1787.[45] Archaeological material from the broad past predominated, reflecting the genesis of the entries, and it seems to have been fairly proportionately divided between the time periods. Within the regions, East Anglia seems under-represented (particular circumstances may apply to Ireland). The extracts were more heavily edited than the papers; so, for example, the publication of the Merton stone head reported by Hamilton lacks the interesting detail about the calico works, which contributes to our understanding of Hamilton's network, and hence of that of antiquaries in general.[46]

In 1806, to take a single date, 169 of the prints making up *Vetusta Monumenta* had been bound and issued as three volumes, and these were advertised in that year's volume,[47] together with ten engravings produced towards a fourth volume.[48] The content of the first three volumes is overwhelmingly British, and roughly half is devoted to medieval monuments, with a good showing also of modern topics, all strongly royal and/or ecclesiastical in character. There is a sprinkling of Romano-British material, mostly mosaic pavements, and of coins; there is only one plate of prehistoric objects, which shows two brooches and two Late Bronze Age trumpets (all found in Ireland) and an object described as a shield.[49]

The subject-matter balance of the papers, together with that of the appendix items and the engravings, suggests a primary interest in medieval manuscripts and monuments, and in post-medieval manuscripts. The stress on post-1500 material is interesting, given that the image of the Fellows tended to emphasize their medievalism; it appeared also in the subjects chosen for the large prints. This was accompanied by a steady flow of Romano-British, Anglo-Saxon and prehistoric material.

The nature of the topics pursued across the Society's activities clearly arose from the interests of the Fellows, clarified by the choices made by such men as Gough, but it also reinforced them by providing an increasingly prestigious forum for record, discussion and argument. There was not, however, a complete match between the preoccupations of Fellows and the efforts of the Society, because a substantial proportion of members were concerned with county or local history, seen as focusing upon the medieval and later genealogies of prominent families, and the descent of landed property.[50] This underlines the sense that what interested most people most about the past was its personal connection to their family and their locality,[51] giving the past the quality of memorial, and its material the character of souvenir or relic. For the growing Society, the intellectual link it could provide between the local interests of family history and the broader scene was significant, channelling vitality in both directions and virtually ensuring steady recruitment, which, of course, enhanced the trend.

It was through all this activity that the discipline of interpreting the past – especially the British past and especially through its material culture – was advanced in the decades either side of 1800. Two of the most striking things about this period at the Society are how the members managed to set the agenda for much future work, and how they succeeded in developing the fundamental methods through which information could be offered for evaluation. The idea of the corpus of a particular group of archaeological objects begins to appear.[52] The detailed study of the fabric of ecclesiastical structures, of the hoard finds of prehistoric material and coins, of the pattern and topography of Roman military installations, of mosaic pavements and their significance, of early inscriptions: all these current interests can be traced back to the efforts of these Fellows. Even specific topics, such as Caesar's crossing of the Thames,[53] or the course of Roman roads,[54] are still returned to again and again.

A number of the papers and appendix pieces published were straightforward reportage, together with (usually) good drawings, in which a discovery was put on record.[55] The style of these is often admirably clear and unpretentious, and they remain the original, useful accounts of important finds that they were intended to be. Other contributions, however, show how an interlocking reference frame of previous reports and finds was being developed, which could be used to place a new find within an ancient sequence and a contemporary intellectual scheme. In 1771 Mr Barrington presented from Thomas Pennant a drawing of one of the gold torcs 'in possession of Sir Roger Mostyn Bart. of which an account is given by the famous Antiquary Mr Lloyd, in the Additions to Camden's Britannia' (fig 50);[56] presumably at least some of those present had digested the remarks Edward Lhuyd made in this connection (for which, see below). In his paper on stone hatchets, read in 1765 and published

TABLE 1: PAPERS PUBLISHED IN *ARCHAEOLOGIA*, 1770–1817

Volume	1	2	3	4	5	6	7	8	9	10	11	12	13	14	15	16	17	18
Year	1770	1773	1775	1777	1779	1782	1785	1787	1789	1792	1794	1796	1800	1803	1806	1812	1814	1817
Families	0	0	10	3	3	2	0	0	0	0	2	3	3	2	3	1	4	3
Civic	3	1	0	0	0	2	1	2	0	1	3	2	0	2	1	1	0	2
State	13	5	5	4	9	0	3	4	1	4	3	5	11	5	12	9	6	16
Church	8	6	3	4	8	2	2	4	4	13	8	5	7	5	8	2	5	5
Linguistics	1	0	1	0	3	0	3	0	1	0	0	0	2	1	0	0	7	2
Collections	3	0	0	0	0	0	0	3	0	0	0	0	1	0	0	0	0	1
Past	22	24	18	5	16	12	22	17	21	18	8	12	2	11	6	14	10	9
MSS	19	7	6	3	8	2	8	7	8	10	7	9	12	6	15	15	18	3
Coins	0	0	2	4	7	0	2	0	0	0	0	0	4	0	1	0	0	1
Archaeological artefact	7	10	19	4	12	5	9	12	10	10	8	6	3	12	7	8	8	4
Inscriptions	2	1	0	0	1	1	1	1	0	0	1	1	2	1	0	0	1	1
Art	4	2	2	0	0	1	0	4	1	2	0	0	1	1	0	0	1	4
Monuments	18	16	8	5	11	9	11	6	8	14	8	11	4	6	7	4	4	1
England	17	10	15	5	13	4	10	18	5	8	6	7	16	3	11	10	15	21
North	5	10	8	0	9	3	6	2	6	6	1	3	1	2	3	2	5	1
South	10	6	2	5	8	5	3	4	3	8	8	5	6	5	9	2	3	8
Midlands	9	3	3	2	4	2	4	6	8	8	3	7	1	4	1	5	2	5
South West	1	1	1	1	2	1	0	0	1	1	2	1	0	5	2	1	3	2
East Anglia	0	1	1	0	0	0	0	0	0	3	1	1	1	4	4	2	0	0
Wales	3	1	4	1	1	1	1	0	0	0	0	2	0	2	0	2	1	0
Scotland	2	1	1	0	2	2	0	0	3	2	3	1	1	0	0	0	1	0
Ireland	3	3	2	0	0	0	7	0	1	0	0	0	0	1	0	3	2	0
Prehistoric	3	7	5	1	4	3	9	2	3	4	2	1	2	2	3	7	1	1
Roman	12	12	11	2	7	5	8	11	10	9	3	1	7	7	1	2	4	4
Anglo-Saxon	6	4	1	1	6	2	1	1	3	5	0	1	3	3	0	0	7	1
Medieval	17	10	13	11	15	6	8	18	10	14	13	12	8	8	18	9	16	13
Post-medieval	12	3	7	1	7	2	5	8	1	4	6	11	6	6	8	9	4	18
No. papers	61	42	44	25	44	30	45	37	31	40	26	28	30	34	39	45	37	46
No. scored	50	36	37	16	39	18	31	30	27	36	24	27	26	26	30	27	32	37
Total pages	411	366	425	420	440	395	405	422	361	459	424	400	389	216	385	355	319	416

KEY TO DEFINITIONS OF CATEGORIES:

Families: family history, including heraldry
Civic: town/city history
State: central government and royalty
Church: all ecclesiastical
Linguistics: language
Collections: collecting and collectors
Past: everything not included in the above but largely archaeological monuments and finds

MSS: all documents
Coins: includes seals and medals
Archaeological artefact: past material culture
Inscriptions: writing on stone, metal, wood
Art: object, painting, sculpture, etc, considered at the time to have aesthetic rather than archaeological value
Monuments: past remains *in situ*
England: applying to whole of England

TABLE 2: APPENDICES PUBLISHED IN *ARCHAEOLOGIA*, 1785–1817

Volume	7	8	9	10	11	12	13	14	15	16	17	18
Year	1785	1787	1789	1792	1794	1796	1800	1803	1806	1812	1814	1817
Families	1	2	0	1	1	2	0	1	4	0	0	0
Civic	0	1	0	1	0	1	0	1	2	0	0	0
State	1	3	0	1	1	1	4	2	6	0	0	1
Church	0	3	5	4	1	1	5	5	2	0	3	8
Linguistics	0	0	0	0	0	0	0	0	0	0	0	0
Collections	0	0	0	0	0	0	0	0	0	0	0	0
Past	12	13	8	10	7	5	5	11	12	15	12	12
MSS	2	3	0	0	1	2	4	3	5	0	1	4
Coins	2	6	1	0	1	0	3	3	4	0	2	9
Archaeological artefact	8	7	7	8	8	8	3	9	10	10	6	3
Inscriptions	1	0	0	0	0	2	1	0	0	0	0	0
Art	0	1	1	2	0	0	1	1	3	0	0	1
Monuments	1	4	4	7	0	0	1	3	4	6	6	4
England	1	2	0	0	0	2	3	4	7	1	0	2
North	4	3	3	5	4	3	2	1	7	3	3	1
South	3	11	5	0	3	4	4	2	4	4	6	4
Midlands	3	1	4	2	1	0	2	4	6	3	3	7
South West	0	1	1	0	0	1	0	4	0	0	2	2
East Anglia	0	0	0	1	0	0	2	2	0	1	0	2
Wales	2	2	0	1	0	0	1	2	0	2	0	2
Scotland	1	1	0	8	0	0	0	1	0	2	0	0
Ireland	0	0	0	0	2	0	0	0	2	0	1	1
Prehistoric	5	3	2	5	3	2	1	2	2	11	4	4
Roman	6	3	5	1	2	1	2	5	6	2	7	6
Anglo-Saxon	1	2	0	1	0	0	0	0	1	1	1	0
Medieval	1	7	6	5	4	4	5	9	11	1	3	10
Post-medieval	1	6	0	5	1	3	6	4	6	1	0	1
No. appendices	14	25	14	19	12	11	15	21	30	16	15	23
No. scored	14	21	13	17	10	10	14	20	26	16	15	21
No. pages	16	25	17	18	11	15	18	30	44	5	16	28

Table 1. Number of papers published in *Archaeologia* in the period 1770–1817, scored by topic

Table 2. Appendices published in *Archaeologia* in the period 1785–1817, scored by topic

North: Yorkshire, Lancashire, Cumbria, Northumberland, Durham, Lincolnshire

South: Kent, Middlesex, Hertfordshire, Surrey, Sussex, Hampshire, Berkshire, Wiltshire

Midlands: Cheshire, Northamptonshire, Leicestershire, Rutland, Derbyshire, Warwickshire, Oxfordshire, Staffordshire, Bedfordshire, Buckinghamshire, Cambridgeshire, Huntingdonshire, Gloucestershire, Worcestershire, Herefordshire

South West: Cornwall, Devon, Dorset, Somerset
East Anglia: Norfolk, Suffolk, Essex
Wales, Scotland and Ireland: self-explanatory
Prehistoric: self-explanatory
Roman: Romano-British
Anglo-Saxon: c AD 400–1066
Medieval: 1066–1500
Post-medieval: after 1500

Fig 50. Drawing of a
Middle Bronze Age
gold torc added to
the Minute Book for
12 December 1771,
which Mr Barrington
presented from Thomas
Pennant. *Photograph*:
Society of Antiquaries
of London.

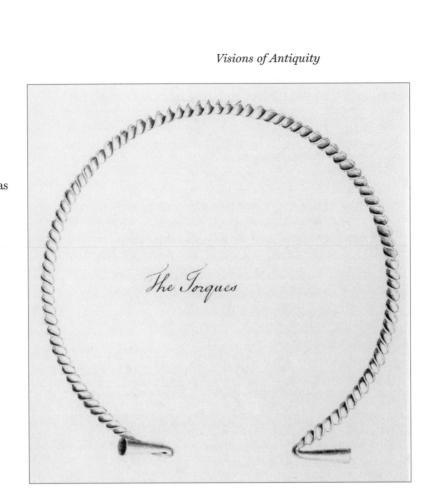

The Torques

in 1773, Bishop Lyttelton cites comparative material from the works of Sir Robert
Sibbald, from Dr Plot and his references to the Ashmolean collections, and from
his own research in the material in the British Museum. Similarly, Charles Harford,
looking for material to compare with coin moulds from Edington, Somerset, says
he followed up (unsuccessfully) a reference in Camden to Aubrey's manuscripts.[57]
Soon, *Archaeologia* itself was being quoted, and so Thomas Walford, in 1807, cites
volume 14, pages 71 and 275, in his letter about finds at Sturmere, Essex.[58]

Key questions are why all this activity was generated, and what imaginative
shapes it took. In relation to material culture, the critical issue is the nature of the
Society's interest in the country's ancient past, and in the unimpressive humps
and bits of pot, stone and metal through which mostly it seemed to be accessible.[59]
Such interest had begun, intermittently and tentatively, in the works of John Leland,
William Dugdale, Robert Plot, William Camden and Edward Lhuyd, and this
produced enough momentum to encourage interest in this past from the Society's
earliest days. It was maintained through the steady stream of prehistoric, Romano-
British, Anglo-Saxon and later material culture received and recorded in a way that
was new. The disgust of the famous connoisseurs and cartoonists apart, it is difficult
to tell how this tendency was viewed by the bulk of the Fellows, but it was never
allowed undue prominence and seems to have become endorsed across the network.

OBJECTS AS ILLUSTRATING HISTORY

We now turn to the shapes this intellectual value took. All educated men of the time were able, of course, to construct a mental history of France, the Mediterranean and the Middle East by putting together the narratives of classical historians and of the Bible. They could do the same for the British Isles by relying on a few standard works. To this, and specifically in relation to Britain, antiquaries were adding the essentially new dimension of administrative and social history, derived from manuscripts in state and local repositories. A significant part of their scholarly tradition emphasized the paramount requirement to argue from specific sources rather than conjecture, and they had begun the process of giving British history its concreteness of time and space, thickness of detail and reliance on demonstrable evidence. It was, therefore, inevitable that material culture should be seen as something which could be illuminated by being fitted on to the narrative scheme, rather than as a form of information in its own right. In his introduction to the first volume of *Archaeologia* in 1770, Gough suggested that the antiquary, through his collecting and editing, supplied the material for the writing of history, which he saw as 'the arrangement and proper use of fact'. Thomas Burgess, whose *Essay on the Study of Antiquities as a Commentary on Historical Learning* was published in 1782, floated the idea that the narrative produced by historians could be clarified and sustained by the efforts of antiquaries to discover evidence showing 'the great secret influence' that 'minuter actions (often dismissed by the historians as trifling)' had on important events. Similar points were made by Pownall in his book of 1782, *Antiquities as the Commentary to Historical Learning*.[60] Material which seemed to lack any intrinsic interest could be given importance by its capacity to underscore and endorse known history.

Britain had a recognized written history which ran back to the comments of classical authors on the pre-Roman inhabitants of the island in the last centuries BC and was continuous thereafter, and the scope which this offered was taken up with alacrity. That is why so much effort was expended by Fellows in the search for material remains in places believed to be the sites of recorded Roman place-names, and upon the search for the Roman roads recorded in the various itineraries. Coins, obviously, responded particularly well. It is also one of the main reasons why medieval monuments, especially those with inscriptions or heraldic symbols, attracted so much attention, for these, like the manuscripts being recorded by the same general group, could be bound into the broad rhetorical narrative: the narrative was the authoritative account of the past, while the material and the inscriptions played a supporting role.

This had a number of consequences. One was the mind-set which saw ancient societies in terms familiar from Gibbon or Clarendon, where consequence and change were presented as depending upon the actions of key individuals. Where knowledge of individuals was lacking, the gap was filled by treating recorded groups as persons, giving us 'the Celts' or 'the Saxons', notions which also worked with the growing nationalism. Another was the desire to reconcile the written narrative and the physical material, using the material in a subsidiary capacity as evidence for what was already known, not as its own kind of information, a process in which the material was cut and pasted to match the story.

But to contemporaries, the main consequences were manifested in relation to prehistory. There is no need to repeat in detail here how it gradually dawned upon antiquaries that the gold, bronze and stone objects that turned up frequently, together with the barrows and other sites from which they came, were pre-Roman, and represented evidence for a significant prehistoric past, which it was not easy to justify from Biblical texts.[61] Some key moments came with the 1722 publication of Lhuyd's additions to Camden's *Britannia* in Edmund Gibson's revised and enlarged edition of Camden's book, translated by Lhuyd,[62] with Banks's speculations about his find of a barbed-and-tanged arrowhead[63] and with Borlase's 1774 discussion of Cornish Bronze Age hoards.[64] The Biblical rhetoric had to be salvaged by bringing in Phoenician traders,[65] a good instance of material being bent to fit 'natural' history, but meanwhile doubts about the significance of the Deluge, with its compression of the time-scale, had been expressed by Lhuyd in 1695,[66] and were implicit in Frere's short, but profound, account of the stratigraphy at Hoxne.[67] The most acute minds among the Fellows realized that the interpretation of these pre-Roman finds needed a different vision, which must, in default of any other information, treat the material as able to express its own meaning.

OBJECTS AS APPEARANCE

A major contemporary way of creating value in objects was by applying standards of design and workmanship to the physical appearance of the piece. This achieved accepted varieties of aesthetic derived essentially from the surface of the object, rather than its provenance and biography, although these always had their significance. It led to the absorption of ancient material culture into the contemporary social production of taste, and consequently into its use as styling for interiors. In around 1790 Sir Richard Worsley, one example of many, physically incorporated his genuine classical marbles into his Dining Room, Colonnade Room and Bathroom at Appuldurcombe.[68] His approach exemplifies a view which valued surface structure, rather than content.

In the 1760s Johann Joachim Winckelmann[69] produced the idea that this vision of surfaces could be turned into a sequence by observing a number of key, but changing, characteristics of form across a group of broadly similar objects, and using these to construct a chronological scheme of growth, maturity and decay into which the pieces could be slotted. The resulting typology was material culture's answer to the taxonomy that was the basis of contemporary biology, and in 1762 Thomas Warton showed how similar typological sequences could be produced for medieval English architecture.[70] Lyttelton was exploring similar ideas,[71] and in 1796 William Wilkins declared: 'It is well known that the dates of ancient MSS may frequently be ascertained by the forms of the letters only . . . likewise, that the respective dates of architecture are distinguishable by peculiar characters also'.[72] Gough drew on typological sequencing for his *Sepulchral Monuments in Great Britain*, and developed an extended discussion in his introduction, telling us – in relation to cross forms, for example – that: 'The variety of crosses in stone or brass is so great that it has cost no small pains to reduce them into classes, in four plates' (fig 51).[73] This resulted in ten classes. The method appears again in his (somewhat breathless) study of 113 British fonts.[74] By sorting these through their visual characteristics into roughly four groups, and linking the groups, or members of them, to a wide range of dated documents, he was able to create a typology which represented the historical sequence of the material from Saxon to late medieval.

All these medieval topics both possessed a developing aesthetic appreciation, to which the works contributed, and belonged within a historical documentary framework to which they could contribute. But antiquaries also realized that here was a method of making sense of material that could be applied fruitfully to objects and structures lacking both artistic merit and parallel written narratives to which the sequence could be pegged. It seemed to marry the attributes of history and appearance to produce a material history in its own right, primary evidence from which a narrative of the past could be viewed, engraved and written. In 1793 James Douglas created a typology of barrows which allowed him to conclude that the small, conical burial mounds found in southern England were Saxon in date and character.[75] This method was followed by Richard Colt Hoare who, in 1817, classified prehistoric barrows into four main typological categories, and concluded that 'the two first [the long barrow and the bowl-shaped barrow], from the general simplicity of their structure, appear to be the most ancient'.[76] He went on to subdivide the long barrows into those with and without the use of large stones in their interior construction.[77]

The method had begun to be used, albeit tentatively, in relation to objects. In his 1773 paper on stone hatchets, Lyttelton looked at material across Britain, and compared it with pre-colonial material from Mexico and the West Indies, concluding that: 'There is not the least doubt of these stone instruments having been fabricated in the earliest times, and by barbarous people, before the use of iron or other metals was known' and that 'these stone axes are by far the most ancient remains existing at this day of our British ancestors, and probably co-eval with the first inhabitants of this island'.[78] In 1803 Charles Harford compared bronze axes with non-metal specimens recently brought from the South Seas,[79] and in 1814 Payne Knight showed that some stone axes were the precursors of similar bronzes.[80]

By focusing on comparative characteristics of surface design, the typological method created a value in ancient objects otherwise perceived as possessing curiosity value at best, and it seemed to offer a powerful key to the understanding of past sequences. Its inherent problem derived from the contemporary belief in the significance of forms and their normative behaviour: like the 'naturalistic' view of the ancient past as history, it assumed a 'natural' progression (by analogy with human life) in which 'primitive' is succeeded by 'more complex and mature', and ends in

Fig 51. Plate 1 from Richard Gough's *Sepulchral Monuments in Great Britain* (1, pt 1), showing examples of the types of crosses that he had defined. 'Plain Crosses': 1: Welbeck, Notts; 4: Winterborne, Berks; 6: Tankersley, Yorks; 9: Ernley, Yorks; 10: Kirklees, York; 11: Ramsey, Hunts; 'Less Plain': 2: Kirklees, York; 3: Kirkby in Ashfield, Notts; 5: Kirklees, York; 8: Buckland, Berks; 'Inscribed': 12: Long Sutton, Lincs (7 is unlisted here). On page cvii, Gough tells us that 6 and 9 resemble 'rude stone crosses of our western and northern counties'. *Photograph*: © University of Leicester Library Special Collections.

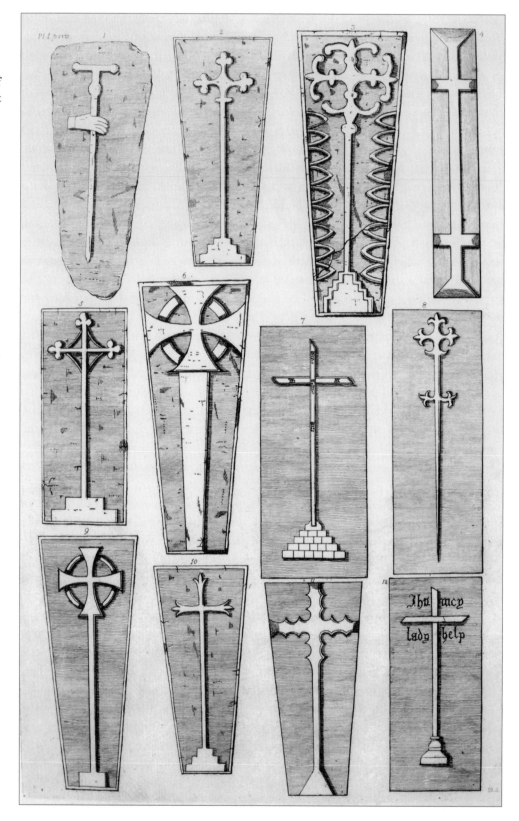

'decadent and late'. This works fairly well (although far from inevitably) in relation to material from communities such as those of Roman Britain or medieval England, where the known documentary sequence is helpfully at the back of the investigator's mind, and where the inhabitants shared something of the antiquaries' mind-set – but it is misleading in the very different circumstances of prehistoric communities, where 'common sense' is not a reliable guide.[81] A typology of objects, unlike an historical, associational view, is eminently suited to demonstration, whether by handing round examples at a meeting, bringing them together on the engraved page or displaying them in a museum case. Knowledge appears to be created through the observation of juxtapositions, but because this understanding is not linked to the context of the find, typology all too easily becomes a species of board game, detached from all except itself.

OBJECTS AS THE PAST IN THE PRESENT

Alongside the view of material culture as a (supportive) variety of historical rhetoric, and as a variety of aesthetic, both of which seemed to integrate antiquities into an understanding of the flow of the past through time, and which the Fellows embraced and used in their own studies, the late eighteenth and early nineteenth centuries produced a third view of the past. This offered earlier times as a variety of experience, as a past that could be visited by the proper contextual arrangement of objects in a slice across time. Through the intrinsic nature of objects as a real part of the past in which they had operated, past reality could be brought into the present. With this notion, the Antiquaries had a complicated relationship, which must be considered at greater length.

The discoveries at Pompeii became generally known to the interested world from around 1763. Here was an amazing site, where the remains of streets and houses could be cleared of volcanic ash reasonably easily, and the description of the eruption by Pliny the Younger gave unimpeachable documentary testimony. It is important to understand how vivid was the impact of a new site which could give the sense of actually walking the same pavements which the ancients had walked and seeing the things which they had handled more or less *in situ*. This was not a sequence through time, but a slice across time. John Moore, who was in Italy in 1772–7, put the feeling powerfully:

> It is to be wished that they would cover one of the best houses with a roof, as nearly resembling that which ordinarily is to it as they could imagine, with a complete assortment of the antique furniture of the kitchen and each particular room. Such a house fitted up with accuracy and judgement, with all of its utensils and ornaments properly arranged, would be an object of universal curiosity, and would swell the heart of the antiquarian with veneration and delight.[82]

The Antiquaries were fortunate in having a member who could give an authoritative, first-hand account of the remains, and Sir William Hamilton duly obliged, first with the exhibition of a series of drawings, and then with their publication in *Archaeologia*.[83] His plate XII showed the principal entrance to the city, and plate XIII the houses in the street just inside the gate, both with a wealth of urban detail.

The impressive site at Pompeii, and the careful exhibition of the finds in the Royal Museum at Portici, were an important strand in the development of works that aimed to depict historical events as they had happened. In London, William Gell and John Gandy produced a pair of engravings in 1817, one showing the entrance to Pompeii from the north east as a contemporary romantic ruin, and the other the same scene as it might have been on the day before Vesuvius erupted.[84] They were part of a major shift in aesthetic taste, in which the capacity of history to enlarge sentiment and feeling was an important part.

The Society's early response to this gathering trend was to cease the production of plates in the *Vetusta Monumenta* series,[85] which were often original records in their own right, and, much to Gough's chagrin,[86] turn to the reproduction of historical scenes instead. These were of well-known events – that was their point – and derived from well-known paintings, or well-recognized collections. The first, taken from a painting of the Field of the Cloth of Gold in the Royal Collection at Windsor Castle, was issued to the Fellowship in 1775. The second, depicting the attack of the French on Portsmouth at the end of Henry VIII's reign, was issued in 1778.[87] Of course, the start of *Archaeologia* in 1770 gave scope for the original publication of varied material, but the speed with which the Society issued the historical engravings shows the pressure for the new venture.

This contextualizing tendency was relatively brief within the Society itself, but re-emerged among some Fellows. The urge to produce grand historical compositions had been preceded, and then accompanied, by a desire for works which would show how the ancestors looked and, particularly, what they wore. A clutch of such works had been produced at the end of the sixteenth century by men such as de Heere, White and de Bry, and by Speed at the beginning of the seventeenth.[88] These hints were taken up in the 1772 publication of *The Habit of an Antient Briton*, and Strutt's book on dress,[89] but reached their fullest form in Meyrick and Smith's production of a volume of plates of persons in ancient costume in 1815.[90] Meyrick was a prominent Fellow,[91] and the Society's copy was presented by him. The twenty-four watercolour engravings are accompanied by a commentary explaining the sources of the material culture shown. Eleven of the plates cover the 'Ante-Roman Period', five the Roman, four the 'Post-Roman' (an interesting use of the term), and four the 'Inhabitants of the Baltic', presumed to be the ancestors of the Anglo-Saxon/Danish inhabitants of Britain. The detail shown in the prints, and the corresponding commentary, gets noticeably thinner as the book progresses.

'A Briton of the Interior' (plate I) shows a man dressed in a calf skin, holding a spear, the head of which draws on finds from Merioneth,[92] and a shield, said to be like one from Cardiganshire.[93] The small illustration below the main image shows the socketed axe with a bead through its ring from Tadcaster.[94] 'An Arch Druid in his Judicial Habit' (plate x) features an Irish Late Bronze Age gold gorget round the Druid's neck, said to be that 'from a turbary in Limerick',[95] and an Early Bronze Age gold lunula upside-down on his head (fig 48).[96] A Late Bronze Age gold arm-ring lies on the table.[97] Two bronze hemispheres appear in the space below the main engraving of 'Boadicea Queen of the Iceni' (plate xii), arranged side by side,[98] and the supposed tombstone of the saint[99] is shown below the image of 'Saint Iestin ab Geraint' (plate xx). The horn shown in plate ix ('An Irish Ollamh and an Heraldic Bard') probably derives from those published in *Vetusta Monumenta*.[100] This book is telling, because much of the archaeological material in the engravings is derived from the Society's publications, but the Society had no formal relationship to it.

Two of the plates show carefully realized scenes of daily life. 'British Fishing and Husbandry' (plate v) shows a country landscape with two men working coracles in the river, and a ploughman with his team in the middle distance. The other, plate xi, is more ambitious, featuring a 'Grand Conventional Festival of the Britons', and showing a crowd surrounding a restored Stonehenge, through which a druidical procession makes its way to the centre of the monument (fig 52). Many of those who appear in the large figure engravings are also recognizable in the crowd. These, like the historical paintings, were the two-dimensional equivalents of the Diorama, which Daguerre brought to London from Paris in 1825, and which showed such scenes as 'The Ruins of the Chapel of Holyrood', with lighting creating the illusion of reality.[101]

This desire to create the illusion of real presence by assembling objects that had truly participated in original action at the appropriate date in order to produce a contextual metaphor of past times and other places fascinated others who had links with the Society, just as the emotion of 'really being there' which the shows provoked enthralled the viewers. The natural history collection of Sir Ashton Lever, who had given books to the Society,[102] was put on show by William Bullock[103] in the Egyptian Hall from 1812. Perhaps in the same year, he opened an extension called the Pantherion,[104] where mounted animals 'are exhibited as ranging in their native wilds; whilst exact models . . . of . . . plants . . . give all the appearance of reality; the whole being assisted with a panoramic effect of distance and appropriate scenery . . . which makes the illusion so strong, that the surprised visitor finds himself suddenly transported from a crowded metropolis to the depth of an Indian forest'.[105] The show included the re-creation of a basaltic cavern, like 'Fingal's Cave in the Isle of Staffa',[106] and a wolf's den made of rocks.[107] In 1821, having been shunned by the British Museum but lionized by society hostesses, G B Belzoni created his reconstruction of the tomb of Pharaoh Seti i, which he had excavated, at the Egyptian Hall. Here the brightly painted walls, copied from the tomb itself, the judicious use of the (relatively few) real objects and the careful lighting 'deeply impressed' the visitor 'with the solemnity that surrounds him. The mind naturally reverts to . . . the "living manners" of a people of whom History has scarcely transmitted a vestige'.[108] Following the Seti exhibition, Bullock mounted a show of Lapp (now Saami) life (fig 53), which included a large range of Saami material culture, and a genuine Saami family accompanied by

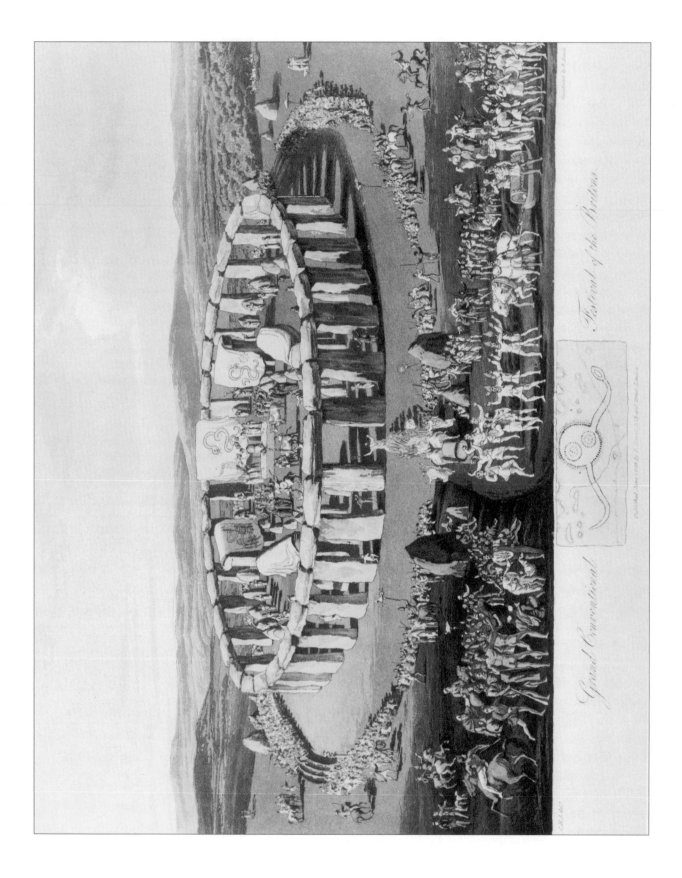

Grand Convention!   Festival of the Britons.

Published June 1 1815 by F. ... 33 ... Bond Street.

a small herd of reindeer.[109] Similar things were happening in Paris, where the stress was on the re-creation of the medieval past.[110]

Antiquaries lived in a world that valued the emotional enlargement of sentimental feeling. They were capable of expressing emotional excitement when they imagined their sites repeopled with the dead, and of gentle teasing about it too, as when Lord Dacre wrote to Philip Morant: 'I wish you joy of your tessellated pavement . . . as it raises . . . up in your imagination Proconsuls, Generals etc in all their glory'.[111] It is clear that a range of people who had links with the Society were very interested in the possibilities of the new re-creative *genre*. However, we do not find in the Society's publications any papers describing 'daily life in Elizabethan England' or endeavouring to put a Roman fort in context, apart from that about Pompeii already described, nor do such matters seem to have been discussed at meetings. There is no overt,

Fig 52. Coloured aquatint by Robert Havell published as plate xi in Meyrick and Smith 1815, entitled 'Grand Conventional Festival of the Britons'. It shows Stonehenge in its supposed original form, with the festival in progress. *Photograph*: Society of Antiquaries of London.

MᴿˢBULLOCK'S EXHIBITION OF LAPLANDERS.

Fig 53. Print engraved by Thomas Rowlandson (1822), showing the exhibition of Lapland life mounted at the Egyptian Hall in that year. The elaborate scenic backdrop shows snowy mountains and the Norwegian North Cape. Just visible are the two dwellings, a canvas and pole tent for summer and one partly of reindeer moss (providentially found on Bagshot Heath) for winter. To the left of the reindeer, which seems to be giving sledge rides, are the Lapp parents with their child, all in heavy fur clothes, and behind them is an enclosure with more reindeer, being petted by some of the visitors. Assorted Lapp artefacts line the walls. *Photograph*: reproduced by permission of the British Library (BL, Percival Collection, xiv, 213–19).

conceptual, reason why Fellows should not have directed their passion for evidence and detail, and their desire to integrate the documentary and the material past, into a turn towards the study of contextual, rather than chronological, assemblages, piecing together a segment of the past in its perceived full contemporary state, but the Society did not take this direction.

One reason, no doubt, was the continuing commercial nature of the books and the exhibitions.[112] Another may have been the desire to retain control over the process of generating antiquarian knowledge. Virtually all the Fellows identified with the governing classes (in spite of rumours of Jacobite sympathies earlier in the century), and were accustomed to manage the creation of understanding through the modes of history and typology which they were themselves developing, in ways which were compatible with their social loyalties. Although they loved ancient objects, the notion of surrendering their intellectual expertise in a Faustian bargain to gain the experience of becoming themselves the objects upon which the emotional power of assembled artefacts worked to present the past, did not appeal.

SOME FINAL THOUGHTS

Objects are now, of course, considered to sustain an infinite number of meanings, according to the embracing time, place, persons, material and action, with each contextual meaning as important and as true as any other: while acknowledging this, it is also clear that objects themselves help to create these meanings by carrying (some of) their accumulation of assigned meanings with them. What we see within the Society of Antiquaries in the decades either side of 1800 is the fostering of a historicizing approach linked with the gathering of evidential and typological detail, and the institutional rejection of a contextualizing tendency in the perceiving of meaning in objects. The imaginative power of this effort, in the minds and writings of very able men such as Gough and Milles, worked to enhance what they saw as the proper influence of the Society, and so to strengthen the particular impact of *Archaeologia* and the kind of papers it carried.

The work of the Antiquaries at this time, with its concentration on formal relationships between objects and their chronological sequencing, viewed from a controlling distance, contributed to the slowly emerging narrative of enlarged post-Biblical time-scales and dynamic Darwinian trajectories; all these depended upon the same ways of looking at the physical world. Their institutional self-distancing from efforts geared to representing past worlds, which, however flawed, offer another kind of emotional enlargement, left this field to showmen, artists, curators and novelists. The cleft was to grow deeper as the nineteenth century wore on.

NOTES

1. For the early years, see MacGregor this volume.
2. Evans 1956, 51–7.
3. This is already well covered: see Brown 1980.
4. Jeremiah Milles (1714–98), President, Dean of Exeter, Devon historian, 'improver' of Exeter Cathedral.
5. Richard Gough (1735–1809), Director, private means, Romano-British and medieval interests; his relationship with the Society was stormy.
6. Sir Philip Rashleigh (1729–1811): Cleevely 2002.
7. Robert Riddell (1755–94): see Royal Commission on Historical Manuscripts 2003, 174.
8. Eg Thomas Pennant (1726–98), who went on tour in Scotland 1774–6, when he saw Staffa and Fingal's Cave.
9. John Disney (1773–1845) became a Unitarian clergyman in 1782, but began as vicar of Swinderby, Lincs; some non-clergy were not Anglicans, such as the Catholic Sir Henry Englefield.
10. Daines Barrington (1727–1800), Cornish, Vice-President.
11. The experiment was not a success: Muilman was accused of using the Society to further commercial aims and, after a violent scene, was expelled from the Society: SAL, Minutes, XIV, 50–2, 9 Feb 1775; ibid, 82–4, 2 Mar 1775.
12. Henry Holland (1745–1806), admitted 10 Nov 1796: SAL, Minutes, XXVI, 123.
13. Richard Cosway (1742–1821): Evans 1956, 201.
14. See Julian Pooley at <jpooley@surreycc.gov.uk> for the Nichols archive.
15. Thomas Jenkins (1722–98) was a banker and antiquities dealer, based in Rome: see Pierce 1965.
16. Some, of course, had – like Thomas Pennant in 1776: see Sweet 2004, 93–4.
17. About forty-two papers on classical topics and about four appendix items (these are naturally few because the appendices featured material which had been exhibited) in the period 1770–1817. The number of classical papers became markedly fewer after 1779.
18. Bayer thanked the Society for election: SAL, Minutes, XIV, 3, 12 Jan 1775. A list of the then Honorary Fellows is given in *Archaeologia*, 15, 1806, after p 423 at p 14.
19. Wang was a guest on 16 Feb 1775 (SAL, Minutes, XIV, 57) and he may have been the 'Chinese gentleman' present on 12 Jan 1775 (ibid, 1). Maimieux, a Russian officer, was at the meeting on 4 May 1775 (ibid, 145).
20. Twenty-one papers on Irish topics and five appendix items for the years 1770–1817; see also O'Halloran 2004 for later 18th-century Irish antiquarian culture.
21. Twenty papers on Scottish topics and thirteen appendix items in 1770–1817.
22. Seventeen papers on Welsh topics and nine appendix items in 1770–1817.

23. Eg Vivian Jago and Malachy Hitchins.
24. Woolf 1997; see also Catalani and Pearce 2006.
25. Charles Townley (1737–1803) exhibited material from Praeneste (SAL, Minutes, XXII, 268, 13 Dec 1787), and donated three engravings of paterae in his collection: *Archaeologia*, 15, 1806, 412. His Ribchester helmet was published in Weston 1800.
26. Sir William Hamilton (1730–1802): see Jenkins and Sloan 1996.
27. SAL, Minutes, XVII, 171–81, 23 Nov 1780.
28. In his introduction to *Archaeologia*, 1, 1770, Gough mentions the museum aspirations of the Elizabethan group with apparent approval. In 1754, Henry Baker presented two urns 'to be lodged in some future museum of the Society', and Council was asked to find a suitable museum room, but nothing was done: Evans 1956, 116. In January 1828 an open letter from the Director, Markland, to the President, the Earl of Aberdeen, published in the *Gentleman's Magazine* (98/1, 61–4), noted that: 'It may be asked, how does it happen that, although more than half a century has elapsed since the Society was incorporated ... the nucleus of a collection should barely have been formed?' (p 63); urged that 'a Museum, or Repository of Antiquities, would be a most important and useful acquisition' (p 61); and asked 'should not some effort be made to collect in one spot specimens of the Antiquities of the kingdom, than which no collection could, with greater propriety, be styled a *national* one' (p 62); but this effort came to nothing. During this time, the Ashmolean and the British museums had been hostile or half-hearted towards the idea of collecting British material, and the Society was an obvious home. The history of society collections, national and provincial, suggests that, eventually, proper arrangements would have been made.
29. Sir Thomas Mantell (1749–1831), doctor and senior public official in Dover during the Napoleonic Wars.
30. The Society's collection catalogues are being computerized, and at the time of writing around half of the probable eventual inventory was available for consultation. The estimates given here are based on this, and on viewing the material itself; experience suggests that the estimates are unlikely to be too far astray.
31. Evans 1956, 177; her plate XXI reproduces the plan of the Antiquaries' rooms at Somerset House by Sir William Chambers, 1781 (wrongly dated to 1777 by Evans; now SAL, MS 760), which shows the layout of the Meeting Room.
32. SAL, Minutes, XXIX, 134–43, 4 Mar 1802.
33. Ibid, 143.

34. As the minutes go on, these grow fewer, reflecting how *Archaeologia* established itself, but in 1772, for example, there are impressive drawings of the 'Pictish' tower at Brechin Cathedral by Gough (SAL, Minutes, XII, drawing facing p 378, 2 Apr 1772), and a statue of Henry VII, by Tyson (ibid, drawing facing p 388, 9 Apr 1772).

35. Eg William Blizzard exhibited a silver spoon drawn by Mr Edwards, found after 1771 in a pier of the Old Bridge at Newcastle, in possession of Mr Bromwell in 1787.

36. SAL, Minutes, XII, 3, 8 Nov 1770; they were medieval, from near Biggleswade, Beds.

37. *Archaeologia*, 15, 1806, 118–21: 'As soon as I heard of this [the first] discovery I went to the spot' (p 119).

38. Lyttelton 1773, 118.

39. See Evans 1956, 137–47, for details of the production.

40. SAL, Minutes, XXIX, 6, 19 Nov 1801; ibid, 15, 26 Nov 1801. The underlining is in the original.

41. Eg Pegge to Gough: SAL, MS 447/1 (see Willetts 2000, 217).

42. In tables 1 and 2 the numbers in the columns do not add up to the number of papers per volume because papers have been scored according to the topics listed, and some did not qualify.

43. Resolved Council, 11 Dec 1776 (SAL, Council Minutes, II, not paginated), and stated before each appendix; it was later resolved that exhibits should be drawn on the spot for use in appendices: SAL, Minutes, XIX, 260, 11 Mar 1784.

44. The published list of presents, mostly books, began in volume 13 of *Archaeologia* (1800).

45. *Archaeologia*, 8, 1787, 429–30.

46. *Archaeologia*, 14, 1803, 282 n 25.

47. *Archaeologia*, 15, 1806, 417–26. The Society's publications were regularly advertised at the end of volumes of *Archaeologia*, and this list gradually lengthened as material was brought out.

48. A group by George Vertue (1684–1755), the Society's engraver, was acquired after 1755. These prints are mostly of Tudor subjects: Evans 1956, 162; Myrone 1999.

49. From Hendinas, Salop.

50. Eg the Revd Foote Gower presented his pamphlet on the history of Cheshire: SAL, Minutes, XII, 261, 12 Dec 1771; Samuel Howe was commended for election as 'conversant in the history and antiquities of this county' (Middlesex): SAL, Minutes, XXIX, 2, 19 Nov 1801.

51. The same is still true today, as Merriman's survey (1991, 119–30) showed; it is at the root of the popularity of information about the past in the media.

52. Lort 1779, 106–10, gives reference to a corpus of axes.

53. Eg Frere 1974, 34–6.

54. Eg Jones and Mattingly 1990, 23–42.

55. Eg Rashleigh 1789; Milles 1782.

56. Walters 1984, 69–70, suggesting the torcs, and the word, are pre-Roman British.

57. Lyttelton 1773, 118; Harford 1803b.

58. SAL, Minutes, XXXI, 353, 12 Nov 1807.

59. Ie, prehistoric, Romano-British, Anglo-Saxon, medieval and post-medieval artefacts and the (often unimpressive) sites which produced them; for the Gothic taste, and the quarrels over church preservation, not considered here, see Sweet 2004, 237–76.

60. Gough 1770, ii–iii; Burgess 1782, 6, 25; Pownall 1782 (see esp 2–3); O'Halloran 2004, 3, 187.

61. Piggott 1984.

62. Walters 1984, 10–11, 69–70, 78, 90; Lhuyd's additional material had been first published in the 1695 edition, but the 1722 edition in translation may have been more influential.

63. Megaw 2001.

64. Piggott 1984, 123.

65. As in Payne Knight 1814, 221.

66. Walters 1984, 90, figs 27–29: coal fossil plants suggest 'whoever would prove . . . an effect of the universal Deluge, will meet with . . . difficulties'.

67. Frere 1800.

68. Sir Richard Worsley (1751–1805); the document drawn up about his collection for probate gives details of the placing of some of the material: Worsley MSS Lincolnshire archives (Earl of Bradford archive); papers by Milles and John Brook on a seal in his collection appeared in *Archaeologia*, 4, 1777, 176–89.

69. Johann Joachim Winckelmann (1717–86) expressed his typological chronology of (as he believed) Greek art in his *Geschichte der Kunst des Alterthums* (1764); he was elected an Honorary Fellow in 1761.

70. Aubrey had put medieval windows in typological/chronological order in his 'Chronologia Architectona' *c* 1670: Piggott 1978, fig 24; this was partly published by Thompson (1766), and Aubrey's MSS were consulted: Harford 1803a, 90–1. Thomas Warton produced a chronological scheme in 1762, but it was 'brief, unillustrated, quirky – and buried in a commentary on Spenser's *Faerie Queen*': Piggott 1978, 38.

71. Lyttelton: see Sweet 2004, 431–2.

72. Wilkins 1796, 174.

73. Gough 1786–96, Introduction, I, pt 1, cvii. The ten types were plain, less plain, on ridged coffin lid, accompanied by sword, bow, or other thing, accompanied by coats of arms, ramified and emblematic of the vine branch, with inscriptions, with the Holy Lamb or some other figure, with figures of Christ, the Virgin or saints, and surmounted by the figure of the party buried below.

74. Gough 1792. This paper stands at the head of a stream of archaeological papers published from that time to

the present day, and which continues, that takes the form of 'an X from Y and its implications': it is a key framework which enables an archaeologist to engage with an unpublished find, new or old, and develop a review of its comparanda, and the chronology and social implications.

75. Douglas 1793.
76. Colt Hoare 1821, 43 (on p 48 he makes an interestingly early comment on the baleful effects of sugar on teeth).
77. Ibid, 44.
78. Lyttelton 1773, 118; read 5 Dec 1765.
79. Harford 1803a.
80. Payne Knight 1814, 220.
81. When Clarke (1968, 29–32) expounded these problems, the then accepted typology of megalithic tombs was one of his prime examples.
82. Moore 1781, 178–9. I am grateful to Rosemary Sweet for this reference. Moore (1729–1802) was a medical man and accompanied the young Duke of Hamilton on his Grand Tour, 1772–7. He was the father of Sir John Moore who died at Coruña in 1808.
83. Exhibited 26 Jan, 2 and 9 Feb 1775: SAL, Minutes, XIV, 26–31; 41–7; 52–6. Hamilton 1777.
84. See Vaughan 1998, especially 66–9 and figs 15 and 16.
85. The engravings which made up the *Vetusta Monumenta* collection were originally issued separately, and eventually bound into six volumes and part of a seventh, beginning in 1747; for a list of the engravings made to that date see, for example, *Archaeologia*, 15, 1806, 417–26.
86. For Gough's feelings, see Sweet 2004, 98.
87. Eventually seven historical prints were issued in the series, most relating to the early Tudors: listed *Archaeologia*, 15, 1806, 418.
88. See Piggott 1989, 73–5.
89. Strutt 1796.
90. Meyrick and Smith 1815.
91. Sir Samuel Meyrick (1783–1848), lawyer, collector of armour; for the antiquities of Cardiganshire, see Meyrick 1808.
92. Later Bronze Age rapiers, Cwm Moch, Maenwrog, Merioneth: *Archaeologia*, 16, 1812, 365, pl LXX; the plate also shows a spearhead from the find, which might have suggested the depiction of the rapier as a spearhead.
93. Rhyd-y-gorse, Aberystwyth, later Bronze Age shield, Cardiganshire, found c 1806: Meyrick 1831, 95, pl XIII, fig 1.
94. Tadcaster find: *Archaeologia*, 16, 1812, 326, pl LIV, no. 2.
95. Irish gorget finds are very confused: one from Shannongrove, Co Limerick, is now in the Victoria and Albert Museum: Eogan 1994, pl XIV; four others, now lost without record, came from the Bog of Cullen, Co Tipperary: Pownall 1775; Eogan 1983, 154–6.

96. See Pococke 1773. Pl XI shows a lunula, provenanced to Ireland. On p 36 Pococke quotes views in favour of the use of lunulae as headdresses, but comes down on the side of their function as breast plates (they are now considered to have been worn as neck-rings).
97. Pococke 1773 shows three objects similar to the arm-ring (pl CXI, figs 1–3), but other models were available: eg *Archaeologia*, 16, 1812, 363, pl LXVIII, the Beachy Head find.
98. These two pieces are described as a 'very curious ancient British female relic, being no less than a pair of bronze breast plates, discovered on ploughing a field near the top of Polden Hill, Somerset': Harford 1803a. Each plate has a diameter of 10¾ins (273mm). 'Curious' continued to be the normal, complimentary, word used by the Society well into the 19th century to thank men for their contributions. The earliest use of the word in its later sense of 'pornographic' is recorded in the *OED* as 1877: p 145. The changing use of 'curious' is interesting, and possibly the declining status of the antiquary was a factor.
99. For the supposed tombstone, see Barrington 1779. Justin's father is given as Gereint ap Erbin, described as 'of the Devonshire British', correctly, as according to the Welsh 'Bonedd y Sant': see Bartrum 1966, 58, 65; Pearce 1971.
100. See *Vetusta Monumenta*, II, 1789, pl XX, figs 3–5. Vallancey 1781–1804 was also a source (thirteen numbers presented to the Society by him: *Archaeologia*, 7, 1785, 432).
101. Bann 1984, 54–7.
102. *Archaeologia*, 7, 1785, appendix; they were MSS relating to Edward I and Edward II. John Frere refers to the Hoxne material as having been in the Lever Collection, and therefore 'probably now in Parkinson's Museum' (Parkinson owned the collection between Lever and Bullock): Frere 1800.
103. William Bullock (c 1780–c 1843): see Survey of London 1960, 266–70, pls 44 and 45. Bullock's family also had connections with the Society: on 5 May 1803 'William Bullock jun. of Liverpool' exhibited a seal impression (SAL, Minutes, XXIX, 484), and he also presented a plaster cast of a lamp from Herculaneum: *Archaeologia*, 15, 1806, 412.
104. For an engraving of the Pantherion exhibition, see Survey of London 1960, 267; for a plan of the museum and Pantherion, see The National Archives (drawing CREST 6/115).
105. Bullock 1812, iv.
106. Ibid, 2.
107. Ibid 1812, 19–20.
108. Pearce 2000; *Gent's Mag*, 1821, 91/1, 447–50.
109. The Saami were Jens and Karlina, together with their little son, and Bullock had met them in Stavanger: BL, Percival Collection, XIV, 213–19, CRACH 1 Tab 5b. For

the history of the reindeer, see Altick 1978, 273–5.

110. Bann 1984.

111. Sweet 2004, 33–4; she also comments on the rhetoric of childhood fascination with the past (p 32), still a common trope in archaeological autobiography.

112. The semi-commercial (or blatantly commercial) nature of some attractions which used the word 'museum' did not help. Even Cox's museum, for example, which had substantial exhibits elegantly presented, was visited chiefly for its ability to amaze rather than enlighten. It was opened by James Cox in Spring Gardens, Charing Cross, London, in 1772 and displayed jewellery and automata which his firm produced, with the stiff entrance fee of half a guinea: see Octavius Morgan's notebook (SAL, MS 913: Willetts 2000, 425–6). Folded into Morgan's notebook is an interesting small pamphlet dated 1807 by an additional note, advertising Weeks's Museum in Tichborne Street. This also displayed automata for sale, and showed two model, mechanical temples, both nearly seven feet high, embellished with moving elephants, etc, 'ordered by the Emperor of China'. The museum had a complicated, but again quite steep, pricing structure: half a crown to see the temples, and a guinea to see the whole show when it opened.

BIBLIOGRAPHY

Altick, R 1978. *The Shows of London*, Harvard and London

Anderson, A, Lilley, I and O'Connor S (eds) 2001. *Histories of Old Ages: essays in honour of Rhys Jones*, Canberra

Bann, S 1984. *The Clothing of Clio*, Cambridge

Barrington, D 1779. 'Observations on St. Justin's (or Justinian's) tomb', *Archaeologia*, 5, 143–6

Bartrum, P 1966. *Early Welsh Genealogical Tracts*, Cardiff

Brand, V (ed) 1998. *The Study of the Past in the Victorian Age*, Oxford

Brown, I 1980. *The Hobby-Horsical Antiquary: a Scottish character 1640–1830*, Edinburgh

Bullock, W 1812. *A Companion to Mr. Bullock's London Museum and Pantherium*, 12th edn, London

Burgess, T 1782. *An Essay on the Study of Antiquities*, 2nd edn, Oxford

Catalani, A and Pearce, S 2006. '"Particular Thanks and Obligations": the communications made by women to the Society of Antiquaries between 1776 and 1837, and their significance', *Antiq J*, 86, 254–78

Clarke, D L 1968. *Analytical Archaeology*, London

Cleevely, R 2002. 'Carew and Rashleigh – a Cornish link with the "Age of the Curiosity Collector"', *J Roy Inst Cornwall* [no vol no.], 9–29

Colt Hoare, R 1821. 'An account of a stone barrow in the parish of Wellow at Stoney Littleton in the county of Somerset', *Archaeologia*, 19, 43–8

Douglas, J 1793. *Nenia Britannica: or a sepulchral history of Great Britain*, London

Eogan, G 1983. *Hoards of the Irish Later Bronze Age*, Dublin

Eogan, G 1994. *The Accomplished Art*, Dublin

Evans, J 1956. *A History of the Society of Antiquaries*, Oxford

Frere, J 1800. 'An account of flint weapons discovered at Hoxne in Suffolk', *Archaeologia*, 13, 204–5

Frere, S 1974. *Britannia*, London

Gough, R 1770. 'Introduction: containing an historical account of the origin and establishment of the Society of Antiquaries', *Archaeologia*, 1 (2nd edn), i–xl

Gough, R 1786–96. *Sepulchral Monuments in Great Britain, applied to illustrate the families, manners, inhabitants and arts, at the different periods from the Norman Conquest to the seventeenth century*, 2 vols, London

Gough, R 1792. 'Description of the old font in the church of East Meon, Hampshire, 1789: with some observations on fonts', *Archaeologia*, 10, 183–209

Hamilton, W 1777. 'An account of the discoveries at Pompeii', *Archaeologia*, 4, 160–75

Harford, C 1803a. 'An account of antiquities found in Somersetshire', *Archaeologia*, 14, 90–3

Harford, C 1803b. 'An account of moulds for casting Roman coins, found at and near Edington, in the county of Somerset', *Archaeologia*, 14, 99–104

Hitchins, M 1806. 'An account of antiquities discovered in Cornwall', *Archaeologia*, 15, 118–21

Jenkins, I and Sloan, K 1996. *Vases and Volcanoes: Sir William Hamilton and his collection*, London

Jones, B and Mattingly, D 1990. *An Atlas of Roman Britain*, Oxford

Lort, M 1779. 'Observations on Celts', *Archaeologia*, 5, 106–18

Lyttelton, C 1773. 'Observations on stone hatchets', *Archaeologia*, 2, 118–23

Markland, J 1828. 'Letter', *Gent's Mag*, 98/1, 61–4

Megaw, J V S 2001. '"Your Obedient and Humble Servant": notes for an Antipodean antiquary', in Anderson, Lilley and O'Connor (eds) 2001, 95–110

Merriman, N 1991. *Beyond the Glass Case*, Leicester

Meyrick, S 1808. *The History and Antiquities of Cardigan*, London

Meyrick, S 1831. 'Description of two antient British shields, preserved in the armoury at Goodrich Court, Herefordshire', *Archaeologia*, 23, 92–7

Meyrick, S R and Smith, C H 1815. *The Costume of the Original Inhabitants of the British Islands from the Earliest Periods to the Sixth Century*, London

Miket, R and Burgess, C (eds) 1984. *Between and Beyond the Walls: essays in honour of George Jobey*, Edinburgh

Milles, J 1782. 'An account of some Roman antiquities discovered at Exeter', *Archaeologia*, 6, 1–5

Moore, J 1781. *A View of Society and Manners in Italy; with anecdotes relating to some eminent characters*, 2 vols, London

Myrone, M 1999. 'Graphic antiquarianism in eighteenth-century Britain: the career and reputation of George Vertue (1684–1756)', in Myrone and Peltz (eds) 1999, 35–66

Myrone, M and Peltz, L (eds) 1999. *Producing the Past: aspects of antiquarian culture and practice 1700–1850*, Aldershot

O'Halloran, C 2004. *Golden Ages and Barbarous Nations: antiquarian debate and cultural politics in Ireland, c 1750–1800*, Cork

Payne Knight, R 1814. 'Conjectures concerning instruments called celts', *Archaeologia*, 17, 220–3

Pearce, S M 1971. 'The royal king list of Dumnonia', *Trans Honourable Soc Cymmrodorion*, Session 1971, pt 1, 128–39

Pearce, S M 2000. 'Giovanni Battista Belzoni's exhibition of the reconstructed tomb of Pharaoh Seti I in 1821', *J Hist Collect*, 12, no. 1, 109–25

Pierce, S 1965. 'Thomas Jenkins in Rome', *Antiq J*, 45, 201–29

Piggott, S 1978. *Antiquity Depicted: aspects of archaeological illustration*, London

Piggott, S 1984. 'Bronze, Britons, and Romans', in Miket and Burgess (eds) 1984, 117–25

Piggott, S 1989. *Ancient Britons and the Antiquarian Imagination*, London

Pococke, R 1773. 'An account of some antiquities found in Ireland', *Archaeologia*, 2, 32–41

Pownall, T 1775. 'An account of some Irish antiquities', *Archaeologia*, 3, 355–70

Pownall, T 1782. *A Treatise on the Study of Antiquities as the Commentary to Historical Learning*, London

Rashleigh, P 1789. 'An account of antiquities discovered in Cornwall, 1774', *Archaeologia*, 9, 187–8

Royal Commission on Historical Manuscripts 2003. *Papers of British Antiquaries and Historians*, Guides to Sources for British History 12, London

Strutt, J 1796. *A Complete View of the Dress and Habits of the People of England, from the establishment of the Saxons in Britain to the present time, illustrated by engravings taken from the most authentic remains of antiquity*, 2 vols, London

Survey of London 1960. *Parish of St James, Westminster. Part I: South of Piccadilly*, xxix, London

Sweet, R 2004. *Antiquaries: the discovery of the past in eighteenth-century Britain*, London

Thompson, P (ed) 1766. *The Fashion of Windows in Civil and Ecclesiastical Buildings before the Conquest*, London

Vallancey, C (ed) 1781–1804. *Collectanea de rebus Hibernicis*, Dublin

Vaughan, W 1998. 'Picturing the past: art and architecture in Victorian England', in Brand (ed) 1998, 61–76

Walters, G (ed) 1984. *Camden's Wales . . . by Edward Lhuyd*, Carmarthen

Weston, S 1800. 'Observations on Mr. Townley's antique bronze helmet found at Ribchester in Lancashire', *Archaeologia*, 13, 223–6

Wilkins, W 1796. 'An essay towards a history of the Venta Icenorum of the Romans, and of Norwich Castle; with remarks on the architecture of the Anglo-Saxons and Normans', *Archaeologia*, 12, 132–80

Willetts, P 2000. *Catalogue of Manuscripts in the Society of Antiquaries of London*, Woodbridge

Woolf, D 1997. 'A Feminine Past? Gender, genre, and historical knowledge in England, 1500–1800', *American Hist Rev*, 102, 645–79

Behold, Antiquaries, ye
most illustrious reliques
of Antiquity.

THE ANTIQUARIAN SOCIETY.

CHAPTER EIGHT

THE SOCIETY, ITS COUNCIL, THE MEMBERSHIP AND PUBLICATIONS, 1820–50

Richard Hingley

This chapter provides an account of the Society that focuses on the issues of social class and ideas of antiquarian scholarship that developed in the period from 1820 to 1850.[1] This was an important period for the study of antiquity, when Biblical ideas of the Creation began to be challenged by new knowledge from geology and monuments of pre-Roman date and by the study of early human remains.[2] Antiquarian research and publication often paid little attention to these new ideas. Although history was perceived as a 'Providential Plan', changes in thought about the 'primeval' past were beginning to emerge.[3] Throughout the early nineteenth century, the main emphasis of the work of the Society lay in the study of medieval history and architecture,[4] though a review of the balance of papers in *Archaeologia* indicates that interest in the study of the classical and Roman past increased to a degree in the 1830s and 1840s.[5]

During the first half of the nineteenth century, the idea that high social standing provided an inherent justification for power and influence began to be challenged. New money, created by the involvement of some individuals in art, industry and engineering, enabled the existing principles of social distinction to be questioned.[6] The increasing institutionalization of historical research that occurred during the second half of the century would, in turn, further develop this trend.[7] The growing interest in antiquarian studies led to the establishment in 1843 of the British Archaeological Association (BAA), which held its first meeting in 1844.[8] Two authors – Albert Way and William Jerdan – writing in the first volume of the *Archaeological Journal*, in 1845, reflected upon archaeology as a developing subject that was attracting people from a wider social spectrum than was represented by the membership of the Society of Antiquaries. The Society did not react effectively to this changing situation.

The altering expectations of the Fellows caused problems for the Society's officials, and this chapter contains an extended study of the activities of the Council and its relationship with the members in this regard. For the majority of the period (1812–46), the Antiquaries were presided over by George Gordon, the Earl of Aberdeen (1784–1860).[9] Joan Evans has described Aberdeen's term in office as 'a period when the Society was not very distinguished in its work or very creditable in its state'.[10] At this time, Aberdeen became a senior politician, and by the early 1830s he appears to have lost much of his former interest in antiquarian studies. The

Fig 54. 'The Antiquarian Society' by George Cruikshank (coloured engraving, 1812). The scene is the Meeting Room, Somerset House. Lord Aberdeen presides; Carlisle and Lysons sit to his left. *Photograph*: © Society of Antiquaries of London.

Society's problems of the 1820s, 1830s and early 1840s, which are reviewed in outline by Evans,[11] appear to have constituted an almost permanent state of affairs. Only fragments of the story can be reconstructed, however, as the surviving records (particularly the correspondence) are heavily edited, presumably by the Society's officers.[12] Nevertheless, the surviving information provides glimpses of how the President, the elected officials and the paid officers were operating at this time.

CLASS AND GENDER IN THE ANTIQUARIES

Nicholas Harris Nicolas made some direct observations on class and the Society. He was an ex-Navy serviceman who had been called to the Bar and was elected to the Antiquaries in 1825.[13] He became a serious critic of the Society during the late 1820s and early 1830s (see below) and, while his comments display a particular personal grievance, they are also informative. In one of his public attacks, Nicolas reflected upon the system by which the Council was elected:

> The respect of the public is lessened by the disgraceful system of exclusion which has long marked the conduct of its chief officers, in selecting their own personal friends for the council, and passing over men whose talents are fully appreciated by the world.[14]

We shall see that Nicolas was excluded from the Council in 1827 and the tone of his comments is to be seen in this context. Elsewhere, he stated:

> At present the council is chosen by those gentlemen [the existing Council], and is normally approved by the president, the qualifications of the persons selected being rank, or a disposition to leave the order of things undisturbed. One peer, one bishop, and two or three baronets, or, if they can not be obtained, a knight or two, form the decorative part of the council, and as these persons rarely attend, the routine business is conducted by the officers and their friends. All the officers are members of the council, so that when the aristocratic part is added to the named officers, the number of members who are to be chosen for their *merits* is very small.[15]

An examination of the names of those who made up the Council, and of the individuals who attended Council meetings between 1815 and 1850, indicates that Nicolas's comments were well informed.

Social standing also influenced the election of Fellows. Philippa Levine has discussed the 'homogeneity' of those with an interest in history and antiquity at this time, arguing that intellectual consideration cannot be separated from a study of social position.[16] In a reflection on the Society's statutes, Nicolas observed that:

> the veriest dolt on earth, if a nobleman, is to be received into a literary society with a mark of respect which is denied to a man of the highest literary talents.

> My lord B- is admitted with sycophantic eagerness by a body formed for the purpose of advancing the knowledge of the history and antiquities of our country; whilst a Lingard, a Hallam, a Turner, a Southey, or a Scott, must undergo six weeks' probation.[17]

Nicolas's comments related to the part of the statutes of the Society that provided direct encouragement to those of 'high rank and dignity' to become Fellows. The charter, which was already seventy-six years old in 1827, determined that members of high rank and dignity were an advantage to any society.[18]

At this time antiquarianism was a pursuit of the wealthy classes, and men who needed to earn a living were not necessarily to be encouraged to join the Society.[19] The election of members was a rather incestuous affair; testimonials recommending membership repeatedly feature the same few names, the work of an active core of the membership who eased the passage of their friends into the Society.[20] It appears that deliberate exclusion was also practised. Charles Roach Smith, the leading authority of his time on Roman London, was proposed for Fellowship in 1836.[21] He recalls:

> My certificate was well signed, duly presented, and read in proper form . . . friends, Fellows of the Society, congratulated me on what seemed to them an inevitable and speedy result. But while the good men were sowing wheat, the enemy was sowing tares. There was an enemy; and he had written a letter which Sir Henry Ellis the acting secretary deemed worthy of consideration. The writer had stated, not that I was not a fit and proper person to be elected, but that I was in business![22]

Roach Smith was eventually elected after the intervention of his friends,[23] but others may well have been 'blackballed' on comparable grounds.[24]

The membership list for 1817 (table 3) indicates that around 17 per cent of Fellows were 'titled', with a broad range of nobility represented. The clergy, including thirteen bishops, made up around 15 per cent of the Fellowship, while 3 per cent were senior ex-Army and Navy men. The broad make-up of the membership lists from the period from 1816 to 1850 suggests a similar situation. Comparable information on the Royal Archaeological Institute (RAI) has been collected by Linda Ebbatson.[25] The institute grew out of the British Archaeological Association following a serious dispute and a division of the membership in 1845.[26] From its beginnings, the RAI had a much larger membership (1,500 in 1845) than the Antiquaries (592 in 1846). Ebbatson's figures suggest that titled people formed 6 per cent of the membership of the institute on its foundation,[27] far lower than the proportion of titled members in the Antiquaries. Titled members of the RAI rose gradually, to around 12.5 per cent in 1893, but the proportion was never as high as the figure in the Society of Antiquaries. By contrast, the number of clergy in the RAI appears to have been rather higher than in the Antiquaries. In 1845, 34.9 per cent of the membership of the institute was made up of clergy, compared with 15.5 per cent at the Antiquaries. By 1861, the proportion of clergy in the RAI had fallen dramatically, to 19.8 per cent.

Table 3. Analysis of the membership of the Society of Antiquaries of London in 1817 by social categories (information derived from the lists of Fellows kept by the Society)

TABLE 3: MEMBERSHIP OF THE SOCIETY OF ANTIQUARIES IN 1817

Category	Number	Percentage of total membership
Titled*	129	17
Duke	5	
Marquis	9	
Earl	31	
Viscount	7	
Lord	28	
Baron**	1	
Knight	48	
Clergy***	119	15.5
Bishop	13	1.5
Revd	106	13.5
Military and Navy	22	3
Admiral	1	
General	2	
Lieut-Gen	3	
Major-Gen	5	
Colonel	4	
Lieut-Col	6	
Major	1	

KEY:

* not including bishops who are styled 'Lord Bishop' or Honourables
** Baron of the Holy Roman Empire
*** including Lord Bishops

Two papers written by Albert Way and William Jerdan in the first volume of the *Archaeological Journal* (published by the Central Committee of the BAA) reflect upon the Antiquaries' membership by association. In an introduction to the volume, Way wrote:

> The British Archaeological Association has been devised, wholly independent of the [Society of Antiquaries] . . . yet wholly subsidiary to its efforts, and in extension thereof; the system of operation, of which the project is now submitted to the public, being such as has been deemed more generally available to all classes, as a ready means of obtaining any desired information on ancient arts and monuments, and of securing their preservation, through the medium of an extended correspondence with every part of the realm.[28]

Way wished to encourage a membership that was broad in both geographical and social terms. In a paper written and published as 'an introduction to the completion of the first year of our journal', William Jerdan, FSA, MRSL, made a powerful personal statement of the purpose of the institute.[29] He proposed the foundation of an Archaeological Club within the institute, and stated that:

> science and literature are the only true republics impervious to 'class', doubt or censure. The equality is a noble one, and such a Club as I have alluded to would need no canvassing for the admission of members, no ballot boxes to guard against the ingress of the unworthy. Being enrolled in the British Archaeological Association would be title enough; for the simple fact of being devoted to pursuits of this description ought to be admitted as proof of intellectual ability and respectability, which should make the candidate, lowest perhaps in the gifts of situation and fortune, an eligible associate, fully as far as such institutions require, for the most exalted in rank and the most powerful in wealth . . . In our Club, then, peers would have no dislike to meeting with the well-informed husbandman, nor the head of the Church with the unpresuming lay-brother. A cairn or barrow would make them companions.[30]

Jerdan evidently felt that these views might be regarded as rather extreme by some, since he wrote, in an afterword, that 'My purpose is only to request my fellow-members not to be too startled by any of my propositions.'[31] Ebbatson has stressed that membership of the institute was socially exclusive and intellectually elitist,[32] but the figures for the Antiquaries demonstrate a far greater degree of social exclusion.

A number of new clubs and learned societies were established during the first half of the nineteenth century, including the Society of Noviomagus (1828), the Numismatic Society (1838), the Yorkshire Philosophical Society (1822), the Oxford Architectural Society (1839), the Cambridge Antiquarian Society (1840) and the Somersetshire Archaeological and Natural History Society (1849).[33] These foundations show a growing interest in antiquarian researches around the country. The *Gentleman's Magazine* also performed an important role at this time, since it often contained reports of antiquarian researches, including detailed accounts of meetings of the Society. These accounts of objects and sites will have reached a wider audience than that represented by the Fellows and will have helped to create a widening interest in antiquity. The comments of Way and Jerdan about the aims of the BAA are to be seen in the light of the encouragement by local societies of the inclusion of working men in their membership, reflecting what Philippa Levine has called the Victorian dedication to 'self-improvement'.[34]

The motivation of some of the early founders of the BAA and RAI provides an insight into the changes that were occurring in English society as a result of the Industrial Revolution.[35] They demonstrate the continued value of an interest in, and knowledge of, the past to any man who was attempting to improve his situation in life.[36] Also reflected in the growth of antiquarian pursuits is the increase in archaeological discoveries that resulted from the construction of canals, railways and the digging of quarries. These societies did not often include female members,[37] and women, with the exception of Queen Victoria, are rarely mentioned in the records of the Antiquaries between 1820 and 1850. Just two papers were published by women at this time.[38] Another rare female appearance in the records of the Antiquaries is that of Mrs Elizabeth Anne Martin, who wrote to Sir Henry Ellis on 29 October 1849 to ask for financial help after the death of her husband, who had been employed by the Antiquaries;[39] her request was declined by the Council.[40] On its foundation, the BAA had only one woman member.[41] Female interest was, however, encouraged by this new association and 'many ladies' are mentioned at the meeting at Heppington in September 1844.[42] Women also joined the RAI, and the female membership of this society had risen to around 7 per cent by 1860.[43] The Antiquaries did not elect a female Fellow until after the period covered by this chapter.

The writings of Way and Jerdan suggest that the creation of the BAA and RAI represented a final reaction against the exclusiveness and lethargy of the Antiquaries;[44] but this is to over-simplify the situation. Attitudes to the past were changing as interests became broader,[45] a situation to which the Antiquaries could only react slowly. At least five of the founders of the BAA were also Fellows of the Society of Antiquaries, while Way was the Director of the Antiquaries and one of the two Secretaries of the BAA.[46] About 10 per cent of the initial members of the BAA were Fellows of the Antiquaries.[47]

LORD ABERDEEN

The changing expectations of the Fellows, combined with the presidency of the Earl of Aberdeen,[48] created a series of crises for the Antiquaries from the 1820s through to the early 1840s. The young Aberdeen was a classical scholar of considerable promise. His investigations into the archaeology of the eastern Mediterranean have been described as 'remarkably scientific for that period'.[49] He played an active role in the Society of Dilettanti and was an important member of the Council of the Royal Society, and a Trustee of both the British Museum and the National Gallery.[50] He was elected to the Antiquaries in June 1805; his contentious appointment as President in 1812 has already been addressed and will not be considered again here.[51] His busy political career drew him away from his presidency and included a period in 1828 as Wellington's Foreign Secretary. In 1852–5, after the end of his term as President, he became Prime Minister.

Initially, Aberdeen began his term in office with the best of intentions (fig 54). On 30 December 1811, he told his friend Hudson Gurney that, were he elected, he would 'try to do something with that Society'.[52] At the time of his election, it would have appeared that Aberdeen was the perfect choice for the presidency, being both a prominent nobleman and a distinguished antiquary.[53] Despite this early promise, the earl proved to be a very inattentive President. In the same letter of 30 December 1811, Aberdeen expressed the wish that Gurney might help him to run the Society, once he had relaxed from his 'weighty and profitable pursuits'. Gurney eventually became Vice-President in 1819. On 31 November 1822, Aberdeen wrote to Gurney to say:

I am happy to learn that you placed yourself in my chair at the Antiquaries, why that should not be your place as well as mine, I cannot imagine, and I believe that if the regular attendees of the Society were examined on that subject, I should have some chance of being deposed from my present dignified position.

Aberdeen left the running of the Council mainly to the Vice-Presidents and to the other officers and officials.[54] Consequently, serious problems occurred with both the finances and the administration of the Society and these were often ignored, only to re-emerge later on. Although he regularly attended the Thursday meetings between 1818 and 1824,[55] Aberdeen often failed to attend meetings of the Council.[56] Indeed, surviving fragments of the original correspondence allow us to see that, at times, his absences caused considerable concern and annoyance to officials, Council members and Fellows alike.[57] On 12 April 1826, Aberdeen wrote a letter to the Secretary, Nicholas Carlisle, excusing himself from a meeting of the Council to be held on the following day:

> Having received His Majesty's command to go to Windsor for the purpose of holding a meeting of the Commissioners for the improvement of Windsor Castle, it will not be in my power to attend at Somerset House tomorrow. I will thank you to explain the cause of my absence to the Council, and to lay before it the enclosed papers.[58]

Carlisle himself had written a note in pencil on this letter, stating 'Received at five o'clock on Thursday 13th April'!

His failings as President appear to have related to the demands of his very busy life, his gradual loss of interest in antiquarian pursuits and to the growing pressure placed on the officials of learned societies due to the increasing demands of the members.[59] During the 1830s, Aberdeen's interests began to shift away from antiquarian researches to botany and science in general. On 14 December 1833, he wrote to Gurney:

> Your account of the 'worshipful' [ie, the Antiquarian Society] may be considered good and prosperous. I see no drawback, except that you appear to be more strongly impressed with the moderate folly of their pursuits. In this respect I cannot help you, for there is nothing to be said. But their folly is innocent and we may rather be permitted to laugh than to scold.

On 21 December 1835, he set out his feelings about the Antiquaries in greater detail in a letter to Gurney:

> I am a little weary about the worshipful society. I feel that I neglect them unmercifully, and some of them must, no doubt, be disposed to resent it. If, in addition to this, they are neglected by my representatives, an open rebellion must speedily be the result . . . for some years, my interest in all matters of antiquity has considerably diminished. Ancient rubbish, whether Greek,

Roman, or English, has lost its charm, and I rather inverted the usual order of things, and have been a zealous antiquary only in my youth.

Aberdeen's reference to 'rubbish' in this context appears to be very damning to the whole idea of antiquarian research, but it was actually a term that he had been using in his correspondence with Gurney since the early days of their friendship, when he had been taunted for bringing home 'ancient rubbish' from expeditions abroad.[60] The tone of this letter suggests that Aberdeen was surprised that he still held the role of President. It is perhaps unfair to place the full blame on Aberdeen for his absences from the 1820s to the 1840s, since he had a growing number of diplomatic duties to attend to. Indeed, the membership of the Society as a whole seems to have been unsure whether it wanted to retain its extremely high-powered honorary figurehead or to elect a new President who could attend full time.[61]

NICHOLAS HARRIS NICOLAS

Under Aberdeen's presidency, the Society was very slow to reform. Nicholas Harris Nicolas wrote in 1829 that Aberdeen 'never evinced the slightest interest in the institution, and . . . his deportment was cold and apathetic . . . he, like the council and even the treasurer and director, is little else than a puppet in the hands of the secretaries'.[62] This suggests that both the elected officials and the President took too little interest in the running of the Society and left most of the administration to a series of paid officials, who were either ineffectual, or merely did not work with efficiency due to a lack of supervision.

From 1827 to 1829, Nicolas was the Antiquaries' most serious critic. Evans describes him as 'a man of litigious character and reforming zeal'.[63] He was also a very active historian, publishing numerous historical documents during the 1820s to 1840s,[64] including various papers in *Archaeologia*. Initially, he made friends in the Antiquaries. Francis Palgrave recalls how Carlisle, a Secretary of the Society, proposed that Nicolas should be appointed to the Council when a vacancy arose due to the death of Taylor Coombe.[65] Nicolas attended a Council meeting late in 1826 and made himself a nuisance.[66] Palgrave describes 'a degree of violence of deportment and gesticulation which gave offence'. The Anniversary Meeting was imminent and when the House List was prepared for the new Council, Nicolas's name was not included.[67] At the subsequent General Meeting, Nicolas burst into a 'paroxysm of anger, and gave vent to language indicating his feelings, and which excited much notice and surprise'.[68] Consequently, Nicolas 'declared a war of extermination' against the Antiquaries in general, but more particularly against Henry Ellis and Carlisle (fig 55).[69]

Nicolas wrote in 1827 that he (and *The Retrospective Review*, which was under his editorship) intended to become the 'Historians of the Society of Antiquaries', and between 1827 and 1830 he published a number of trenchant critiques of the running of the Society and its Council.[70] These attacks indicate that he had a particularly

180

Fig 55. 'A Point of Antiquity' (lithograph, 1833, signed O P, and published by Thos Maclean of 26 Haymarket). Nicholas Carlisle holds the leg-piece of a suit of armour, and Frederic Madden the helmet. The third figure is Sir Henry Ellis. *Photograph*: Society of Antiquaries of London.

personal grievance,[71] but Evans suggests that he also had a measure of support from other Fellows. Nicolas's main complaints against the Council related to the nature of its publications and to the running of its finances. He proposed that these should be reformed, but was opposed by the Council during 1826 and 1827.

Nicolas's letters to the Council of 13 August and 12 November 1827 appear not to have been kept, but we do know that they requested whether 'a Fellow of the Society is entitled to inspect extracts from the Minute Book, and the accounts of the Receipts of Expenditure, from its incorporation to the present time?'.[72] His concerns with these topics are evident from his comments in 1827 that:

> The entire management of the funds of the Society is intrusted to the council
> . . . Upon the president or vice-president taking the chair, the accounts in a
> bundle are placed before him, who, in holding them in his hand asks, 'Is it your
> pleasure, gentlemen, to confirm these accounts?' The balloting box is handed
> round, and they are instantly passed without a single individual having
> opened, much less examined them; an even without a single remark having
> been made.[73]

Nicolas's knowledge of the practices of the Antiquaries was informed by his experiences at the one Council meeting he attended. His apparently unacceptable behaviour on that occasion may well have been a reaction to the failings that he had observed in the Council's procedures. One immediate result of Nicolas's campaign was that the Council ordered the Clerk to call at the houses of all London members to collect their subscription arrears.[74] Proposed reforms to the statutes of the Society drafted by the Council were not well received by Nicolas,[75] since they were intended to give more power to the elected officials.

Nicolas took his campaign to the Fellows at a meeting on 27 March 1828, at which the auditors made a report and Nicolas gave notice of his intention to move for a Committee (selected from members not in the present Council) to investigate the expenses of the recent publications of the Society.[76] The situation escalated, and, on 16 April 1828, the Council Book mentions a discussion of legal problems over the statutes of the Society.[77] On 17 April 1828, a very full meeting of the Society greatly overran the usual hour in discussing Nicolas's motion that three or five Fellows, who were not members of the current Council, should be appointed to study the accounts. This was a result of the Society having learned from the auditors that a sum exceeding £800 had been spent on publications.[78] Nicolas apparently introduced the subject 'in a pointed and animated speech', but the Treasurer Thomas Amyot's answers to his questions led him to conclude that the object of his motion had been 'fully attained'.[79] Despite the auditor and the Council's rebuttal of Nicolas's request, the accounts for 1831 were published for the first time in *Archaeologia* in 1834 (pages 362–3), indicating that the justice of his motion had finally been accepted.

An application was also received around this time to increase the salary of what Nicolas called the 'second secretary' (Carlisle):

> who, it appeared to many, was already amply paid for doing little, except to help the senior secretary to do nothing, and the statutes having been violated by the usual notices not being given of the measure, it was opposed on the ballot, by a minority which shook the confidence of the council in the stability of their power.[80]

This proposal failed and Carlisle continued as Secretary until 4 May 1847, when he was given a pension of £150 a year and the continued use of the apartment supplied to him by the Antiquaries.[81] He was certainly not universally liked. The Revd C H Hartsthorne wrote a letter to Albert Way on 30 April 1839 about a meeting that he had just attended,[82] in which he stated: 'Carlisle I conceive to be a perfect incubus, a dead weight on the whole machine.' Evans suggests that the Secretary was not fitted for the responsibilities that fell on his shoulders as a result of Aberdeen's absences and that he was 'the Society's most gifted exponent of inactivity'.[83] He had one aim in life – to make money. He received a salary and lodgings from the Antiquaries, but his activities were mainly centred at the British Museum, where he held the position of a senior assistant.

On 23 April 1828, at the Anniversary Meeting held to elect the new Council, a second list, including Nicolas's name, was produced in opposition to the House List.[84] The official List was accepted by a vote of 103 to 22,[85] but this outcome indicates that there was support for Nicolas's intended reforms. He subsequently tendered his resignation from the Society, which was noted by the Council on 17 June 1828. The justice of his cause is suggested by the fact that a number of his proposed reforms were actually carried out during the following twenty years.[86] In his publications, Nicolas explains some of his concerns regarding the administration of the Antiquaries. Much of his writing focused on the poor quality of many of the papers presented at the meetings and those published in *Archaeologia* (see below), criticisms that reflected his personal bias towards historical literature, but which did not prevent him from continuing to publish papers in the journal after his resignation.

CONTINUING PROBLEMS

Nicolas's resignation had not led to an immediate cessation of hostilities within the Society. On 2 April 1829, Lord Balmanno sent a letter to Aberdeen, forwarding a communication, signed by twenty-six Fellows, asking for the establishment of a *Conversazione* after the meetings.[87] The Council Minute Book for 3 April 1829 indicates that this communication suggested that meetings were considered to be too short (one hour's duration, from 7 o'clock in the evening). It raised the concern that members are not able to 'discuss among themselves the merits and character of such curiosities – they are handed round in silence, while the Minutes, or papers relating to them are read, and removed without comment'.[88] The Council did make some concessions, but Balmanno felt it necessary to resign in 1829.[89] A letter of 7 July 1829, from Amyot to Carlisle, indicates that certain Fellows were intending to cause trouble at the meeting that evening.[90]

The records of the Society for the early and mid-1830s are rather incomplete, but we do know that problems emerged in 1837 and 1838, when Aberdeen was called upon to smooth over a serious quarrel between William Hamilton and Carlisle which threatened to cause the Antiquaries to split.[91] By the late 1830s and early 1840s, pressure was mounting to remove Aberdeen from the presidency, as his attendance diminished to 'almost vanishing point'.[92] In his letter to Albert Way referred to above, Hartsthorne discusses the election of Council members during 1839:

> I went to the Antiquaries for admission on Tuesday week, and came away not vastly impressed with the talents of the body assembled . . . All of these men, no not all, but the powers that be are vastly behind the times . . . On Tuesday came the election of officers – it seems the Council have always been in the habit of nominating their successors, but this year an effort was made to elect more active members among that body, chosen from the body of the Society. Your name [Way] was down as one of the new list. And conceive the feeling that actuates the body, when I tell you that <u>one</u> of the council objected to it, because you were a <u>young</u> member . . . I, not knowing the politics of the Society, voted as I was directed which was against the new list . . . I sat between Stapleton and Willement at the dinner the later [*sic*] of whom let me into the secrets of the society: and I suspect that next year many of the members intend to make a great struggle to put the thing on a better footing.[93]

At the Anniversary Meeting of 1840, five Fellows scratched out Aberdeen's name on the voting paper and substituted that of Hamilton.[94] After this meeting, on 26 April, Aberdeen wrote to Gurney to record that the elections had exhibited 'less formidable symptoms of hostility than you expected',[95] and the President survived.

Dr Lee presented a proposal to a meeting of the Society on 27 February 1845 in which he included four points, the first and fourth of which were:

> that the President be requested to attend the next Anniversary of the Society, and to deliver an Address on the state of the Society, and of the Science of Archaeology, as is now customary with the Presidents of the Royal, Geographical, Geological, Astronomical, and other Scientific Societies;

> that a general opinion having been expressed that the office of President should not always be filled by the same individual, however accomplished and erudite he may be, no person be allowed to hold the office of President in future beyond the term of four years.[96]

Council requested more time to consider the first point (perhaps because the President was not in attendance), but refused the suggestion that no President should serve for more than four years on the basis that it went against the charter of the Society.[97] Despite the increasing sense of crisis, meetings of the Council occurred less and less frequently at this time.[98]

Further problems occurred during the early part of 1846. Spencer Joshua Alwyne, the Marquis of Northampton, wrote to an unnamed individual in the Antiquaries on 20 March 1846. The letter is partly illegible, but it appears to report an argument at the Antiquaries on the previous night about the proposed House List.[99] Northampton tells his correspondent:

> But there will be a fight next week. Probably a Council first . . . Reflexion was made on Ld Aberdeen, and I did my best to defend him, by praising his good qualities and saying that I was sure that he regretted that official business kept him so much away.'[100]

It appears that certain influential members of the Society were no longer willing to put up with Aberdeen's absences, or with his failure to provide leadership. It also appeared likely that the membership might vote down the House List and that Carlisle's position as Secretary was finally under threat.[101]

Just four days later, on 24 March 1846, Aberdeen wrote to the Council to say:

> For a considerable time past my various associations [?] have prevented me from attending to the general business of the Society of Antiquaries and even from being present at the Weekly Meetings of the Society.

> I should feel unwilling to resign a situation which I have filled for so many years, did I not perceive that the present state of the Society requires from its President a degree of personal attention much greater than it would be possible for me to afford – but under these circumstances, I must express a hope

that at the approaching Elections on St George's day, a choice will be made of some person as President, who may be more capable than myself of promoting the welfare of the Society, by devoting more of his time to its interests.[102]

At this stage, Aberdeen had not attended a meeting of the Council since 1 March 1836, and he appears to have missed sixty-six consecutive Council meetings.

In reply, the Council wrote to Aberdeen of their wish:

to transmit to Your Lordship the unanimous vote of the Society at their Meeting on the 26 March, expressing its deep regret at your desire not to be nominated again as their President. And they wish to accompany this vote by an expression of their own entirely concurrent with the feelings of the Society – sensible of the loss, which the whole Body will sustain, and gratefully remembering the advantages they have derived from your Lordships distinguished character, and the urbanity with which you have presided over its meetings.[103]

We need have no doubt of the benefits that Aberdeen brought to the Society through his social and political contacts. The Council Minute Book, for example, itemizes various loyal addresses made to monarchs by the Society and the replies made to the Council. Aberdeen ensured that the Society maintained a high social standing.[104] Despite his useful social connections, the membership fell by at least 15 per cent during Aberdeen's presidency (table 4). In addition, a number of Fellows fell into serious arrears with their annual payments, a problem that was left to his successor to pursue.[105]

In 1829, Nicolas had concluded his review of the finances and running of the Antiquaries by stating that:

The end must be, either that the Society will be dissolved on the death of the present fellows, a circumstance extremely likely, from the very few who, since

TABLE 4: MEMBERSHIP OF THE SOCIETY OF ANTIQUARIES, 1812–52

Year	Number of Fellows	Percentage gain / (loss)
1812	788	
1817	777	(1.5)
1822	778	0
1827	805	2
1832	764	(5)
1837	703	(8)
1842	688	(2)
1847	571	(17)
1852	473	(17)
1812–52 cumulative		(40)

Table 4. Membership of the Society of Antiquaries of London, 1812–52 (information derived from the lists of Fellows kept by the Society)

the exposures which have been made relating to it, seek admission into the fraternity; or that it will drag out a disreputable existence, affording shelter and a pension to one or two dependants of great personages, but utterly profitless to literature or science.[106]

During the early 1840s it must have appeared to certain Fellows that Nicolas's prophesy was coming true, but at this time a new President was elected who made it his purpose to reform the finances and administration of the Antiquaries.

A NEW PRESIDENT

Following Aberdeen's resignation, the Council discussed who should fill the vacancy. Philip Henry Stanhope, Lord Mahon, could not attend the meeting on 7 April 1846. He wrote a letter to the Council in which he mentioned that several people felt that he was a suitable successor, but that he himself wished to nominate Henry Hallam. Hallam declined, so Mahon was proposed and seconded,[107] and the membership subsequently confirmed his presidency. Mahon, who had been Vice-President since 1842, already had considerable experience of the operations of the Council.[108]

The new President soon discovered the full extent of the Society's financial problems. In fact, the major fall in membership between 1842 and 1852 (34 per cent) was, at least in part, a result of the fact that the Council now took more direct control of the finances and expelled Fellows who were in serious arrears.[109] The Council Book entries for the following three years demonstrate that Mahon swiftly took control of both the finances and the administration.[110] In the process, the Council carried out many reforms, including a number that Nicolas had called for almost two decades earlier. On 7 May 1846, the Council determined that the auditors were to make their report at least one week before the relevant Council meeting.[111] On 19 May, Finance and Library Committees were set up to deal with the problems.[112] On 23 June, the Council discussed the 'long standing custom, which appears to be highly objectionable, of deferring the settlement of the tradesmen's accounts of each year, to the year following'. It was agreed, in due course, that these bills should be settled as swiftly as possible.[113] The Finance Committee reported to the same meeting that the Society had debts for the past year of around £330; it was agreed to sell £600 of stock.[114]

When the auditors reported back to the Council on 8 March 1847, it emerged that the debts were greater than had been previously reported.[115] The Auditors' Report referred to the new President's consideration of the conditions of the finances. It included a note to explain why the accounts showed receipt and expenditure far in excess of the usual levels and referred to the establishment of the Finance Committee. The report recorded sums of £812 and £1,200, which were liabilities that were not brought before the auditors in 1845 (including expenses of £812 related to the publication of Anglo-Saxon papers). It defined the future aims of the Council and auditors, to include all the bills and liabilities that had been received in future accounts and that outstanding demands should be confined 'strictly within the narrowest limits'. A new system of accounting was also featured, while measures were suggested to reduce the expenditure of the Antiquaries.

The Council Minute Book indicates that attempts to raise income were made. Back copies of the Antiquaries' publications and copper plates were sold to Mr Lumley, a bookseller, on 5 December 1848 and 20 February 1849. On 6 June 1848, the Council determined that the funds of the Society could, 'with strict propriety', not be used to subsidize Fellows to attend the Annual Dinner. As a result, it was agreed that, in conformity with the practice of the Royal and other societies, each Fellow present at the event should pay his full share.[116] This last measure rectified an abuse that Nicolas had written about in 1829.[117]

The Council now also turned serious attention to those Fellows who had not kept their subscription payments up to date.[118] The Collector's Book for this period shows the lengths to which even the wealthiest Fellows went to avoid paying.

> Monday April 19, 1847, Lord A Conyngham. Serv[an]t said Lord A was not at home. I saw LA leave the house directly after . . . Saturday July 10 Mr Thoms, 2nd call. not got his chekbook but going to pay but as he was going into the Country directly wd not said he should be short of money for it . . . Saturday Feb 12, 1848, Mr T Wright, 3 call. was thinking about it & not having it now would bring it.[119]

On 27 May 1847, the Council drafted a letter to the defaulters, stating that 'The Committee is satisfied that in many, if not in most cases, non-payment has arisen from neglect of the Clerk, which the present notice is intended to remedy.'[120] On 20 November 1849, the Council discussed new ways in which Fellows could pay their subscription that would avoid the expense of employing a collector.[121] These measures led to a reduction in the number of Fellows (see table 4), but also placed the Antiquaries on a more secure financial footing.[122]

THE BALANCE OF ANTIQUARIAN STUDIES

The regular publication of *Archaeologia* between 1820 and 1850 was one of the major achievements of the Society of Antiquaries, and one that enables an assessment to be made of the nature of the interests of the Fellows and Council. The early nineteenth century was a time when substantial changes in the study of antiquity were beginning to occur. Classical antiquities had interested many gentlemen in the second half of the eighteenth century but a growing fascination with medieval topics is evident during the early years of the nineteenth century.[123] Despite the classical interests of Aberdeen, the Antiquaries were mainly concerned with medieval history and architecture.[124] By 1850, however, there were signs of major changes taking place in the study of archaeology that would gain momentum during the second half of the nineteenth century.

The balance of papers in *Archaeologia* between 1820 and 1850 reflects an enthusiasm for English national history at a time when the intellectual elite was increasingly conscious of the greatness of national destiny.[125] The vast majority of papers published in *Archaeologia* covered topics drawn from British and Irish history (fig 56) of the early medieval, medieval and post-medieval periods (fig 57).[126] As Evans has argued, the old feelings of inferiority before the elegance of France and the cultural riches of Italy were being forgotten during the early nineteenth century with the growing emphasis upon the greatness of English national history, which focused on the early medieval and medieval origins of society.[127] In 1841, Thomas Arnold, in the publication of an inaugural lecture presented in Oxford, wrote:

> Our history clearly begins with the coming of the Saxons; the Britons and Romans had lived in our country, but they were not our fathers . . . We, this great English nation, whose race and language are now overrunning the earth from one end to the other – we were born when the white horse of the Saxons had established his domain from the Tweed to the Tamar.[128]

Such an approach suggested that ancient and Roman remains were those of the ancestors of others.[129]

The writings of certain Fellows demonstrate a strong bias towards written history. Reviewing the twenty-second volume of *Archaeologia*, Nicolas provided an ironic description of the 'stuffing' of the volume with:

> the promising description of 'suits of armour', 'pieces of bricks', 'stones presumed to be Druidical', 'monuments usually presumed to be Druidical', 'Mosaic pavements', 'Roman remains', 'Roman baths', marked with the impression of dog's toes, and therefore accurately engraved; 'Roman lime-kilns', 'bracelets', &c. &c. all and every one of which we commend to the perusal of those persons who may desire to form an accurate estimate of the talents or researches of the Society; or who having in vain swallowed as much opium as their physicians can with safety prescribe, may still wish for a powerful and irresistible soporific.[130]

Nicolas picked out 'Druidical' and 'Roman' artefacts and monuments for particular ridicule (fig 58). Although he mentioned suits of armour as items of scorn, he is not so critical of the numerous studies of medieval history and architecture that appeared in *Archaeologia*. Nicolas had a particular bias towards historical documents, which

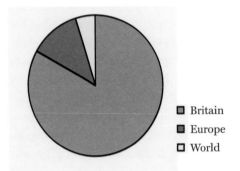

□ Britain
■ Europe
□ World

Fig 56. Papers published in *Archaeologia* from the 1820s to the 1840s that deal with various parts of the world (total = 699). *Drawing*: Christina Unwin.

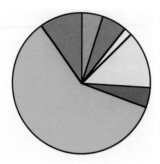

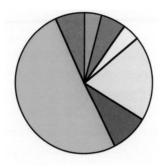

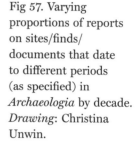

Fig 57. Varying proportions of reports on sites/finds/documents that date to different periods (as specified) in *Archaeologia* by decade. *Drawing*: Christina Unwin.

1820s: proportions of sites reported upon (total = 178)

1830s: proportions of sites reported upon (total = 197)

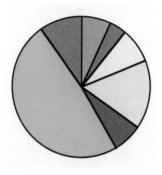

□ Neolithic/Bronze Age
■ Iron Age
□ Classical
□ Roman
■ Anglo-Saxon
□ Medieval
■ Post-medieval

1840s: proportions of sites reported upon (total = 309)

were, in his opinion, the only form of interest to be pursued, but he did not condemn serious medieval studies; by contrast, he saw little value in work on pre-Roman and Roman artefacts and sites.[131] Although he was more outspoken than most, Nicolas's bias towards the medieval was shared by many of his contemporaries.[132] Analysis of the papers published in *Archaeologia* demonstrates the fascination of the Fellows and Council with antiquarian studies at this time (figs 57 and 59), as do other volumes published by the Society in the early nineteenth century.[133]

In this context, *Archaeologia* contained a relatively limited number of contributions on classical and pre-Roman topics (see fig 57).[134] Nevertheless, some important papers did emerge. Despite Nicolas's critique, the twenty-second volume of *Archaeologia* contained a significant study of Cornish cliff castles and a short paper, by Alfred Kempe, on 'Celtic' megalithic monuments and hut circles on Dartmoor (fig 60). The major shift in attitudes on the ancient ('primeval') past that was to take place in the second half of the nineteenth century as the result of studies of geology and early human remains was, however, still to impact upon the Antiquaries. The idea of the antiquity of the human race gradually began to emerge during the first half of the nineteenth century in Belgium, France and England.[135] Developing knowledge of geology and the discovery of the skeletal material of early humans were slowly beginning to cast doubt upon Archbishop Ussher's Biblical chronology for the

Fig 58. 'Bricks and tiles found among the Roman remains at North Stoke' (from Turnor 1829, fig opposite p 32). The tile discussed by Nicolas in 1829 is in the top line, second from the left. *Photograph*: Society of Antiquaries of London.

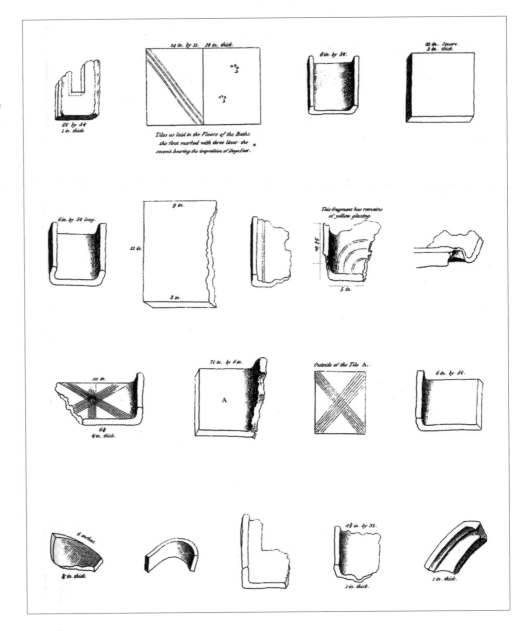

world,[136] but the importance of these events was not widely appreciated by antiquaries.[137] *Archaeologia* contains no significant papers on early human origins,[138] although papers on Neolithic and Bronze Age subjects are better represented. The excavation of barrows was increasing knowledge and understanding of these periods. Throughout the early nineteenth century, notable antiquaries, including William Cunnington, Sir Richard Colt Hoare and Dean Merewether, excavated and published pre-Roman monuments. Glyn Daniel writes of their reports as 'filling the pages of *Archaeologia*',[139] although by the 1820s such papers were heavily outnumbered by those on medieval subjects.

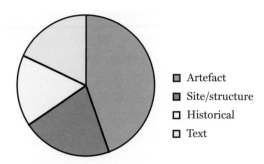

Fig 59. Proportions of different types of report published in *Archaeologia*, 1820s to 1840s. *Drawing*: Christina Unwin.

☐ Artefact

☐ Site/structure

☐ Historical

☐ Text

Artefact = reports on artefacts, rubbings of monastic seals, etc

Site/structure = reports on excavations, architectural surveys and burial monuments

Historical = broadly historical surveys of items and events

Text = publication of historical text (usually accompanied by a discussion)

The reports of this work on pre-Roman archaeology in *Archaeologia*, and other books that were published on early Britain at this time, served to emphasize the significance of pre-Roman populations.[140] Bronze Age and Iron Age artefacts and sites were described periodically and important papers were published, including J Y Akerman's inspirational suggestion of a 'Celtic' date for the Uffington White Horse, based on the similarity of this hill figure to images of horses on Iron Age coins (fig 61).[141] Despite significant work on monuments, understanding of the chronology of the pre-Roman period was sketchy at best. John Rickman proposed that the megalithic monuments at Avebury and Stonehenge were 'Celtic' in inspiration and that they had been completed after the Roman invasion.[142] In 1845 Way wrote:

> students of Antiquity [are] now no more compelled to have recourse to vague terms in describing objects, which present themselves, attributing to a Druidic, a Roman, or a Danish period, remains which formerly might have perplexed them by their antique aspect.[143]

Historical knowledge was evolving, but pre-Roman Britain still appeared, to Way at least, to represent a single and unproblematic phase of human development.[144] The pre-Roman monuments and artefacts addressed in *Archaeologia* are commonly called 'Celtic', and a clear knowledge of prehistoric sequence only emerged in the latter half of the century. The objects discovered at this time helped to raise questions in people's minds, but major advances in the understanding of pre-Roman metalwork did not come until the second half of the century.[145] The emergence of the idea of the Three Age System, an early nineteenth-century concept of Danish and Swedish prehistorians, proved to be a highly significant force for change (see chapter 10). Later in the century, this provided a framework within which the chronology of the developing subject of prehistory would be constructed,[146] but it had, at the most, only a limited impact on the publications of the Antiquaries during the first half of the nineteenth century.

The Roman Empire provided contrasts and comparisons with the foreign territories and the governance of the growing British empire,[147] while the common discovery of Roman villas and artefacts during the construction of canals, railways and buildings brought finds of this date to the attention of antiquaries. Samuel Lysons, who had conducted a significant campaign of villa excavations, died in 1819, but his

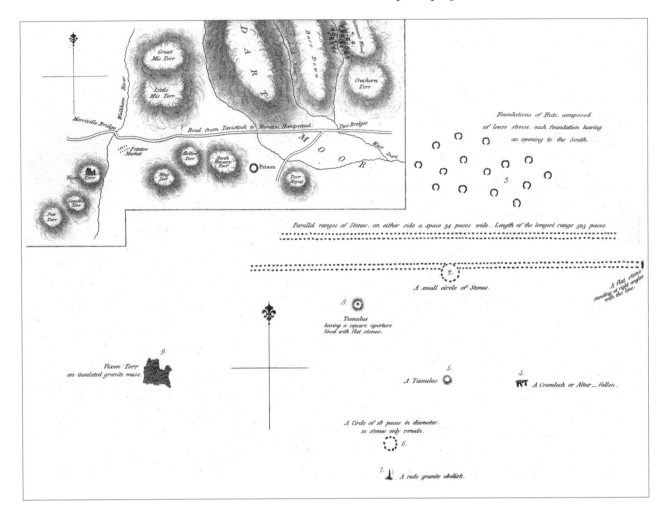

Fig 60. 'Vestiges supposedly Druidical, on Dartmoor near Tavistock, Devon' (from Kempe 1829b, fig opposite p 430). *Photograph*: Society of Antiquaries of London.

work was continued by such scholars as Roach Smith, who undertook research on Roman London, and by John Gage, who carried out important excavations on the Roman barrows at Bartlow Hills. References to topics derived from the classical cultures of the Mediterranean and Near East were rarely featured in *Archaeologia* during the 1820s and 1830s. State-funded expeditions to obtain objects and structures for the galleries of the British Museum commenced during the 1840s and are reflected in the increased number of papers on classical topics.[148]

Despite these occasional contributions to *Archaeologia*, papers drawn from medieval England dominated each volume. The emphasis upon the early medieval and medieval past privileged the history of Britain as a nation, but it also fitted with the dominant interpretation of the past as a 'Providential Plan'.[149] The balance of antiquarian interests was, however, gradually changing. Way's introduction to the first *Archaeological Journal* shows that the intention of the recently founded British Archaeological Association was to widen studies to include all aspects of antiquity and to involve people across the whole of Britain. The formation, within the new association, of distinct 'Sectional Committees' – 'Primeval', 'Medieval', 'Architectural'

192

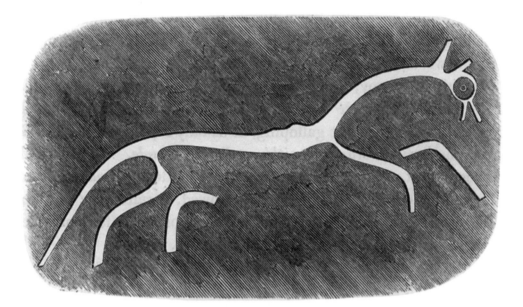

Fig 61. 'The White Horse at Uffington' (from Akerman 1846, fig opposite p 298). *Photograph*: Society of Antiquaries of London.

and 'Historical' – indicates the broadening of the agenda, as does the inauguration of regional meetings. A reaction against the particularist historical and architectural focus of the Antiquaries may have been one of the reasons for the dissatisfaction that led to the establishment of the British Archaeological Association.

The constitution of the Society of Antiquaries limited the speed at which it could react to changing circumstances. The papers published in *Archaeologia* during the 1830s and 1840s do, however, demonstrate an increasing interest in the pre-Roman and classical past and a broadening out of the focus of antiquarian interest. This formed part of a wider cultural trend within British society that became increasingly significant as the nineteenth century progressed, and through their meetings and publications the Antiquaries performed a significant role in the changing conceptions of the ancient and historic past of Britain during the early nineteenth century.

ACKNOWLEDGEMENTS

I am grateful to Susan Pearce for inviting me to write this chapter, to Bernard Nurse and all at the Society of Antiquaries for assisting with my research, and to the staff at the Norfolk Record Office. Pam Lowther and Martin Millett supplied a number of useful references, while Jennifer Price drew my attention to the issue of Roach Smith's election. Christina Unwin and Chris Evans provided advice and discussion. Finally, I am grateful to the anonymous referees for several very helpful comments and suggestions.

NOTES

1. See Levine 1986 for the broader context of Victorian antiquarian studies.
2. Bowler 1989; Levine 1986, 4; Morse 2005, 127–50.
3. Levine 1986, 56; but see Torrens 1998 for an alternative viewpoint.
4. Evans 1956, 232–7.
5. A review of the contribution of the *Gentleman's Magazine* to the development of antiquarian pursuits at this time would be a valuable addition to the published literature. Although such a review is not undertaken in this chapter, a number of specific papers in the journal are addressed below.
6. For the major changes that were occurring at this time, including the dramatic increase in the population and the results of industrialization upon society, see Brooks 1998, 3–4. Ebbatson (1994, 35–43) discusses the influence of those with 'new wealth' on the development of the Royal Archaeological Institute during the mid-part of the 19th century.
7. Levine (1986, 2, 87–100) discusses the institutionalization of archaeology and history from the 1850s on.
8. Brooks 1998, 16; Evans 1956, 227.
9. Evans 1956, 241–2.
10. Ibid, 251.
11. Ibid, 239–51.
12. Bernard Nurse, pers comm.
13. Lee 2004.
14. Nicolas 1827, 157.
15. Nicolas 1830, 23.
16. Levine 1986, 7. See Evans 1956, 238, for the nature of elections at this time.
17. Nicolas 1827, 160.
18. Ibid, 160.
19. Levine 1986, 22.
20. Ibid, 55. The anonymous reader of this chapter pointed out to me the significance of the Society of Noviomagus, a dining club made up of various Fellows many of whom worked for a living, including William Jerdan and Alfred Kempe. The society was established in 1828 and continued until at least 1851 (Evans 1956, 231), providing an alternative venue for certain Fellows to meet and talk.
21. For Roach Smith and the Antiquaries, see MacGregor 1998.
22. Smith 1883, I, 115–16. Levine 1986, 21, refers to these events.
23. Evans 1956, 263; Smith 1883, I, 116.
24. Levine 1986, 21–2.
25. Ebbatson 1994 and 1999.
26. Wetherall 1994.
27. Ebbatson 1994, fig 3, and 1999, 40, fig 3.
28. Way 1845, 3.

29. Jerdan 1845, 297.
30. Ibid, 298–9.
31. Ibid, 300.
32. Ebbatson 1994, 23.
33. Evans 1956, 227–8; Hudson 1981, 15; Levine 1986; Wetherall 1994, 9. For the Society of Noviomagus, see note 20 above.
34. Levine 1986, 57. Sweet (1997, Appendix 8) includes information about the occupations of English urban historians prior to 1825, which supports this observation.
35. Ebbatson 1994, 32.
36. For the value of the study of antiquity to English gentlemen in the 18th century, see Sweet 2004.
37. For the perceived place of women at this time, see Levine 1986, 9, 54.
38. A short note by Lady Mantell was published in the appendix to vol 25 of *Archaeologia* (p 604), and an interesting account by Frances Stackhouse Acton of the excavation of a Roman villa near Church Stretton, in Shropshire, was featured in vol 31 (pp 339–45).
39. Antiquaries Correspondence (MS collection in SAL library).
40. SAL, Council Minutes, VI, 54, 13 Nov 1849.
41. For the recruitment of female members to the BAA/RAI, see Ebbatson 1994, fig 2, and 1999, fig 5.
42. *Archaeological Journal* 1845, 275.
43. Ebbatson 1994, 34.
44. Evans 1956, 227.
45. Brooks 1998, 19.
46. Although SAL, Council Minutes, V, 377–9, shows that he resigned from this post on 17 Nov 1846.
47. Ebbatson 1994, table 3.
48. See Chamberlain 1984 for an account of Aberdeen's life and achievements.
49. Ibid, 5. For a detailed account of Aberdeen's scholarly activities, including works on Troy and classical Greek buildings, see ibid, 61–78.
50. Ibid, 75. Aberdeen was a member of the Council of the Royal Society in 1812–13, 1817–18 and 1821–2.
51. Nurse 2000. Chamberlain (1984, 73) also provides a brief account.
52. Letter from Aberdeen to Gurney (Norfolk Record Office, RQG 334). All references to letters from Aberdeen to Gurney quoted below are held in this collection in chronological order.
53. Chamberlain 1984, 73.
54. Evans 1956, 242.
55. Chamberlain 1984, 73, referring to the letters in the Norfolk Record Office (RQG 334).
56. Evans 1956, 241. Evans also refers (241, n 1) to a letter dating to 3 Nov 1813, which already drew attention to

Aberdeen's tendency to desert his post.

57. Ibid, 241.
58. Antiquaries Correspondence.
59. Wetherall 1998, 27.
60. Chamberlain 1984, 74.
61. Ibid, 73.
62. Nicolas 1829, 402.
63. Evans 1956, 247.
64. Lee 2004.
65. Palgrave 1831, 6–7.
66. Nicolas recalled (1830, 28) that he objected to some of the papers that the Council planned to publish and also raised an objection to another proposition, consideration of which was put off to the next meeting.
67. Nicolas 1830, 29; Palgrave 1831, 7.
68. Palgrave 1831, 7–8.
69. Ibid, 8.
70. For the suggestion of his desire to act as a historian see Nicolas 1827, 156. For attacks on the Antiquaries, see Nicolas 1827, 1829 and 1830.
71. A letter from Thomas Pettigrew to Carlisle in the Correspondence of the Society regarding certain charges levelled against Carlisle by Nicolas suggests that the name of the latter 'is however to be *condemned* [?] for being too sensibly alive to his own reputation & the opinion of the world'. The letter is recorded in the Antiquaries' collection as dating to 24 Nov 1837 but presumably it actually dates from 1827, a time at which we know that Nicolas was writing letters to the Council.
72. SAL, Council Minutes, IV, 456–7, 16 Jan 1828.
73. Nicolas 1827, 161.
74. SAL, Council Minutes, IV, 445, 13 June 1827. Evans (1956, 244) links this decision by the Council to criticism made by Nicolas in his 1827 article, but I can find no such observation.
75. Nicolas 1830, 32.
76. *Gent's Mag*, 1828, **98**/1, 255.
77. SAL, Council Minutes, IV, 468.
78. *Gent's Mag*, 1828, **98**/1, 350.
79. Ibid, 350.
80. Nicolas 1829, 402.
81. SAL, Council Minutes, V (not paginated). It is noted on 16 Nov 1847 (ibid) that Carlisle had died.
82. Antiquaries Correspondence, 30 Apr 1839. A typed copy of this letter was sent to Joan Evans by Claude Blair in 1966 and is in the correspondence filed under its original date. Way subsequently played a significant role in the Antiquaries and the foundation of the BAA: Levine 1986.
83. Evans 1956, 245.
84. The other list contained the names of N H Nicolas, the Revd James Dalloway, Isaac D'Israeli, Rich Duppa, Michael Jones and Edmund Lodge in place of certain of those included on the House List. They also

contained a number of names in common.

85. *Gent's Mag*, 1828, **98**/1, 350–1; Nicolas 1830, 30.
86. Nicolas 1829, 401–2. For a critical reply to some of Nicolas's observations on the Society, see the contribution by 'Antiquarius' to the *Gent's Mag*, 1829, **99**/2, 417–26. 'Antiquarius' was a pseudonym adopted by Kempe (see Kempe 1829a).
87. Antiquaries Correspondence.
88. SAL, Council Minutes, IV, 493, 3 Apr 1829.
89. Note in the card index for Antiquaries Correspondence, 2 Apr 1829.
90. Antiquaries Correspondence.
91. Chamberlain 1984, 74.
92. Ibid, 75.
93. See note 82.
94. Evans 1956, 241, quoting information in the Ellis Papers in the British Museum.
95. Correspondence in Norfolk Record Office (RQG 334).
96. These are listed in SAL, Council Minutes, V, 300–1, 5 Mar 1845, and are also published in an account of a meeting of the Society held on 27 Feb 1845 in *Gent's Mag*, 1845, **115**/1, 407.
97. SAL, Council Minutes, V, 302, 5 Mar 1845.
98. They met only five times during 1841–2, four times during 1842–3 and a total of five times during the two sessions of 1843–5: Evans 1956, 246.
99. Evans 1956, 253, quotes letters from Ellis to Way that record the same dispute.
100. Antiquaries Correspondence.
101. Evans 1956, 253.
102. Letter reproduced in SAL, Council Minutes, V, 340–1, 25 Mar 1846.
103. Text of a letter signed by Mahon, Vice-President, on behalf of the Council in SAL, Council Minutes, V, 343–4, 31 Mar 1846.
104. See Nicolas 1829, 413. Evans (1956, 238–9) discusses the tradition of royal patronage of the Society, which continued under Aberdeen.
105. Some serious efforts had been made to retrieve arrears from defaulting Fellows, particularly in 1843: Evans 1956, 244.
106. Nicolas 1829, 413.
107. SAL, Council Minutes, V, 346–7, 7 Apr 1846.
108. Evans 1956, 252.
109. Evans (ibid, 263) also notes a number of resignations as a result of dissension over Carlisle in 1847.
110. Evans (ibid, 258–62) discusses the finances in some detail.
111. SAL, Council Minutes, V, 349.
112. Ibid, 352 and 354 respectively.
113. Ibid, 366–9.
114. This continued the earlier policy of the Council to sell off stock to relieve deficits: Evans 1956, 243–4. The Council's serious attempts under Mahon to raise income and reduce expenditure demonstrate, however,

that the sale of stock was not considered a viable future option by the new President.

115. A copy of the auditors' report is pasted into SAL, Council Minutes, v, between pp 402 and 403.
116. SAL, Council Minutes, IV, 20.
117. Nicolas 1829, 407-8. Evans (1956, 244) discusses the cost of the Annual Dinner to the Society at this time.
118. Evans (1956, 243, 244) discusses the Council's often half-hearted attempts to deal with defaulters during Aberdeen's period of presidency.
119. Levine 1986, 58-9, quoting Collector's Book for 1847-9.
120. SAL, Council Minutes, v (not paginated).
121. SAL, Council Minutes, VI, 56.
122. Evans 1956, 261.
123. Daniel 1975, 29; Evans 1956, 225; Gerrard 2003, 30. Daniel (1975, 29) considers some of the classical studies that occurred in the first quarter of the 19th century and associates the decline of interest to the passing away of 'the great age of dilettantism'.
124. Evans 1956, 232; Way 1845, 1-2. In fact, perhaps, this is one reason for Aberdeen's growing disenchantment with antiquarian studies in general.
125. Levine 1986, 74, 86.
126. Figs 56, 57 and 59 derive from an analysis of the papers published in the main parts and the appendices of vols 19 (1821) to 32 (1847) of *Archaeologia*.
127. Evans 1956, 225, and Mandler 1997, 82-7. For nationalism and historical/antiquarian studies, see Levine 1986, 4, and Mandler 1997.
128. Arnold 1841, 32.
129. Hingley 2000, 20-1.
130. Nicolas 1829, 416. For comparable comments, see Nicolas 1830, 24.
131. For this bias toward the publication of historic documents, see Nicolas 1830, 41-3.
132. Evans 1956, 250. See, however, the comments of Kempe (1829a, 419) for a far more upbeat assessment of the significance of the publication of antiquarian reports about pre-Roman, Roman and Saxon remains. For one relevant example of such a publication in *Archaeologia*, see also Kempe 1829b.
133. The Council vetted papers for publication. See Evans 1956, 233-7, for the medieval volumes published at this time. Gerrard 2003, 30-5, provides a summary of the development of medieval studies at this time.
134. These papers were also more likely to be placed in the appendix to each volume than those that examined medieval topics.
135. Daniel 1975, 33.
136. Bowler 1989, 131.
137. Daniel 1975, 54-5, although see Torrens 1998, who concludes that geology was beginning to have a significant impact upon archaeology during the middle years of the century.
138. For John Frere's important paper of 1797, see Torrens 1998, 37.
139. Daniel 1975, 30.
140. Ibid, 30.
141. Akerman 1846, 297.
142. Rickman 1840.
143. Way 1845, 2.
144. For the context, see Levine 1986, 95-6.
145. Morse 2005, 127-41.
146. Daniel 1975, 28. For an early paper, see Rhind 1856.
147. Levine 1986, 82-3, 98; Hingley 2000, 21-2.
148. Cook 1998 discusses the collection of classical objects.
149. Levine 1986, 56.

BIBLIOGRAPHY

Akerman, J Y 1846. 'Observations on the White Horse of Uffington', *Archaeologia*, 31, 297-8

Archaeological Journal 1845. 'Wednesday Sept. 11, Medieval Section', *Archaeol J*, 1, 273-6

Arnold, T 1841. *An Inaugural Lecture in the Study of Modern History Delivered in the Sheldonian Theatre, Oxford, Dec 2, 1841*, Oxford

Bowler, P 1989. *The Invention of Progress: the Victorians and the past*, Oxford

Brand, V (ed) 1998. *The Study of the Past in the Victorian Age*, Oxford

Brockliss, L and Eastwood, D (eds) 1997. *A Union of Multiple Identities: the British Isles, c 1750-1850*, Manchester

Brooks, C 1998. 'Introduction: historicism and the nineteenth century', in Brand (ed) 1998, 1-20

Chamberlain, M E 1984. *Lord Aberdeen: a political biography*, London

Cook, B F 1998. 'British archaeologists in the Aegean', in Brand (ed) 1998, 139-54

Daniel, G E 1975. *A Hundred and Fifty Years of Archaeology*, 2nd edn, London

Ebbatson, L 1994. 'Context and discourse: Royal Archaeological Institute membership 1845-1942', in Vyner (ed) 1994, 22-74

Ebbatson, L 1999. 'Conditions of emergence and existence of archaeology in the nineteenth century: the Royal Archaeological Institute 1843-1914', unpublished PhD thesis, University of Durham

Evans, J 1956. *A History of the Society of Antiquaries*, Oxford

Gerrard, C 2003. *Medieval Archaeology: understanding traditions and contemporary approaches*, London

Hingley, R 2000. *Roman Officers and English Gentlemen: the imperial origins of Roman archaeology*, London

Hudson, K 1981. *A Social History of Archaeology*, Basingstoke

Jerdan, W 1845. 'Suggestions for the extension of the British Archaeological Association', *Archaeol J*, **1**, 297–300

Kempe, A J 1829a. 'The Society of Antiquaries', *Gent's Mag*, **99**/2, 417–26

Kempe, A J 1829b. 'Monuments conjectured to be British, still existing on Dartmoor', *Archaeologia*, **22**, 429–35

Lee, C 2004. 'Nicolas, Sir Nicholas Harris (1799–1848)', in *Oxford Dictionary of National Biography: Online Edition* (eds H C G Matthew and B Harrison), <http://www.oxforddnb.com/view/article/20169> (22 July 2006)

Levine, P 1986. *The Amateur and the Professional: antiquarians, historians and archaeology in Victorian England, 1835–1886*, Cambridge

MacGregor, A 1998. 'Antiquity inventoried: museums and national antiquities in the mid nineteenth century', in Brand (ed) 1998, 125–38

Mandler, P 1997. 'In olden times: Romantic history and English national identity', in Brockliss and Eastwood (eds) 1997, 78–92

Morse, M A 2005. *How the Celts Came to Britain: Druids, ancient skulls and the birth of archaeology*, Stroud

Nicolas, N H 1827. 'Society of Antiquaries', *Retrospective Review*, 2nd ser, **1**, 156–62

Nicolas, N H 1829. 'Art. VII – *Archaeologia*, Vol. XXII, Part II. *Vetusta Monumenta*, Vol. V. Plates, LI–LX', *Westminster Review*, 5/2 (October), 401–16

Nicolas, N H 1830. *Observations on the State of Historical Literature*, London

Nurse, B 2000. 'George Cruikshank's *The Antiquarian Society*, 1812, and Sir Henry Charles Englefield', *Antiq J*, **80**, 316–20

Palgrave, F 1831. *Remarks submitted to The Right Hon Viscount Melbourne in reply to a Pamphlet addressed to him by Nicholas Harris Nicolas, Esq and entitled 'Observations on the state of Historical Literature' & C*, London

Rhind, A H 1856. 'On the history of the systematic classification of primeval relics', *Archaeol J*, **13**, 209–14

Rickman, J 1840. 'On the antiquity of Abury and Stonehenge', *Archaeologia*, **28**, 399–419

Smith, C Roach 1883. *Retrospections, Social and Archaeological*, 3 vols, London

Sweet, R 1997. *The Writing of Urban History in Eighteenth-Century England*, Oxford

Sweet, R 2004. *Antiquaries: the discovery of the past in eighteenth-century Britain*, London

Torrens, H S 1998. 'Geology and the natural sciences: some contributions to archaeology in Britain', in Brand (ed) 1998, 35–60

Turnor, E 1829. 'Account of the remains of a Roman bath near Stoke in Lincolnshire', *Archaeologia*, **22**, 26–32

Vyner, B (ed) 1994. *Building on the Past: papers celebrating 150 years of the Royal Archaeological Institute*, London

Way, A 1845. 'Introduction', *Archaeol J*, **1**, 1–6

Wetherall, D 1994. 'From Canterbury to Winchester: the foundation of the Institute', in Vyner (ed) 1994, 8–21

Wetherall, D 1998. 'The growth of archaeological societies', in Brand (ed) 1998, 21–34

A Declaration for the certaine time of drawing the great standing Lottery.

Eiakintomino

Matahan

Once, in one *State*, as one *Stem*,
Meere *Strangers* from IERVSALEM,
As *Wee*, were *Yee* till *Others* Pittie
Sought, and brought You to *That Cittie*.

Deere *Britaines* now, be *Yee* as kinde;
Bring *Light*, and *Sight*, to V's yet blinde:
Leade V's, by *Doctrine* and *Behauiour*,
Into one *Sion*, to one SAVIOVR.

IT is apparent to the world, by how many former Publications we manifested our intents to haue drawne out the great standing Lotterie long before this day: which not falling out as our selues desired, and others expected, whose moneys are already aduentured therein. We thought good therefore for auoiding al vniust and sinister constructions, to resolue the doubts of al indifferent minded, in three special points for their better satisfaction.

The first is, for as much as the aduentures came in so slackly with such poore and barren receits of moneys at the Lottery house for this twelue moneth past, that without too much preiudice to our selues and the aduenturers in lessening the blankes & prizes, we found no meanes nor ability to proceed in any competent proportion, but of necessity are driuen to the honourable Lords by petition, who out of their Noble care and disposition to further that publike plantation of Virginia, haue recommended their letters to the Counties, Cities and good Townes in England, which we hope by sending in their voluntarie Aduentures, will sufficiently make that supply of helpe, which otherwise we should not in any reasonable time haue effected.

The second poynt for satisfaction to all honest and wel affected minds, is, that notwithstanding this our meanes of Lottery answered not our hopes, yet haue we not failed in that Christian care of the Colony in Virginia, to whom wee haue lately made two sundry supplies of men and prouisions, where wee doubt not but they are all in health, and in so good a way with corne and cattell to subsist of themselues, that were they now but a while supplied with more hands and materials, we should the sooner resolue vpon a diuision of the Countrey by lot, and so lessen the generall charge, by leauing each seuerall tribe or family to husband and manure his owne.

The third and last is our constant resolution, that seeing our credits are now so farre engaged to the Honourable Lords, & to the whole State for the drawing and accomplishment of this great standing Lotterie, which we intend shall be our last of all standing Lotteries for this plantation, that our time fixed and determined for accomplishing thereof, shall be if God permit, without longer delay, the 26. of June next being in Trinity tearme, desiring all such as haue vndertaken with bookes to solicite their friends, and all such as intend the prosperity of that worthie plantation, that they will not withhold their monies till the last weeke or moneth be expired, lest we be vnwillingly forced to proportion a lesse value and number of our blankes and prizes which hereafter follow.

And whosoeuer vnder one name or posie shall ad-

VVelcomes.

To him that first shall bee drawne out with a Blanke	100. Crownes.
To the second	50. Crownes.
To the third	25. Crownes.
To him that euery day during the drawing of this Lottery shall bee first drawne out with a Blanke	10. Crownes.

Prizes.

1. Great Prize of	4500 Crownes.
2. Great Prizes, each of	2000. Crownes.
4. Great Prizes, each of	1000. Crownes.
6. Great Prizes, each of	500. Crownes.
10. Prizes, each of	300. Crownes.
20. Prizes, each of	200. Crownes.
100. Prizes, each of	100. Crownes.
200. Prizes, each of	50. Crownes.
400. Prizes, each of	20. Crownes.
1000. Prizes, each of	10. Crownes.
1000. Prizes, each of	8. Crownes.
1000. Prizes, each of	6. Crownes.
4000. Prizes, each of	4. Crownes.
1000. Prizes, each of	3. Crownes.
1000. Prizes, each of	2. Crownes.

Rewards.

To him that shall bee last drawne out with a Blanke	25. Crownes.
To him that putteth in the greatest number of Lots vnder one name or Posie	400. Crownes.
To him that putteth in the second greatest number	300. Crownes.
To him that putteth in the third greatest number	200 Crownes.
To him that putteth in the fourth greatest number	100. Crownes.

If diuers bee of equall number, then these Rewards are to be diuided proportionably.

Addition of new Rewards.

The Blanke that shall bee drawne out next before the Greatest Prize, shall haue	25. Crownes.
The Blanke that shall bee drawne out next after the said Great Prize, shall haue	25. Crownes.
The Blankes that shall be drawne out immediately before the 2. next Greatest Prizes, shall haue each of them	20. Crownes.
The seuerall Blankes next after them shall haue also each of them	20. Crownes.
The seuerall blankes next before the foure Great Prizes, shall haue each of them	15. Crownes.
The seuerall Blankes next after them shall haue also each of them	15. Crownes.
The seuerall Blankes next before the six Great Prizes, shall haue each of them	10. Crownes.
The seuerall Blankes next after them shall haue also each of them	10. Crownes.

uenture twelue pounds ten shillings or vpward, if he please to leaue & remit his Prizes and Rewards, bee they more or lesse, the Lottery being drawne out, hee shall haue a bill of Aduenture to Virginia, for the like sum he aduentured, & shall be free of that Company, & haue his part in Lands, & all other profits hereafter arising thence, according to his aduenture of twelue pounds ten shillings or vpwards.

Whosoeuer is behinde with the payment of any sum of money, promised heretofore to be aduentured to Virginia, if hee aduenture in this Lotterie the double of that sum, & make payment thereof in ready money to Sir Thomas Smith Knight, Treasurer for Virginia, he shall be discharged of the foresaid summe so promised to haue been aduentured to Virginia, and of all actions and damages therefrom arising, and haue also the benefit of all Prizes and Rewards whatsoeuer in this Lottery, due by reason of the like sum which he shall bring in, and yet notwithstanding, if after the Lottery drawne, he list to remit al his said Prizes and Rewards, he shall haue a bill of aduenture to Virginia for the said entire summe according to the last preceding Article.

And if vpon too much delay of the Aduenturers to furnish this Lottery, we bee driuen to draw the same before it be full, the we purpose to shorten both blanks and Prizes in an equall proportion, according to that wherein wee shall come short, bee it more or lesse, that neither the Aduenturers may bee defrauded, nor our selues, as in the former, any way wronged.

The Prizes, Welcomes, & Rewards shall be paid in ready Money, Plate, or other goods reasonably rated. If any dislike of the said Plate or other goods, he shall haue ready money for the same, abating onely a tenth part: Except in small Prizes of tenne Crownes or vnder, wherein nothing shall be abated them.

The money for Aduentures is to be paid to Sir Thomas Smith Knight, Treasurer for Virginia, at his house in Philpot lane: or to such officers as shall be appointed to attend for that purpose at the Lottery house: or to such other as shall elsewhere, for the ease of the Countrey be authorised, vnder the Seale of the Company, for receipt thereof.

The Prizes, Welcomes & Rewards being drawne, they shall be paid by the Treasurer for Virginia, without delay, whensoeuer they shall be demanded.

And for the better expedition to make our sum compleat, as wel to hasten the drawing of our Lottery, as chiefly to inable vs the sooner to make good supplies to the Colonie in Virginia: Whosoeuer vnder one name or posie shall bring in ready money three pounds, either to the Lottery house, or to any Colletor, the same party receiuing their money, for euery three pounds so receiued, shall render them presently a siluer spoone of 6. shilings 8. pence price, or 6. shilings 8. pence in money.

Imprinted at London by *Felix Kyngston*, for *William Welby*, the 22. of Februarie. 1615.

CHAPTER NINE

THE DEVELOPMENT OF THE LIBRARY

Bernard Nurse

Libraries hold a central place in cultural history as storehouses of knowledge. The unique nature of the Society's library arises from the continuous support of the members over nearly 300 years. They have included the leading scholars in their field, whose writings have transformed our knowledge of the material past. The results of their research have been presented to the library, which has developed to reflect their interests and respond to their needs. Originally established as a private library for the use of members, access has gradually been opened up to others.

ORIGINS: 1717–53

One of the earliest decisions of the Society once formalized in 1718 was to order the Director 'to provide us a box to lay up the books in'. The first book purchased was Strype's 1720 edition of Stow's *Survey of London*.[1] The chief purpose of the Society was to encourage the study of British antiquities, and the articles of association mentioned a library only in passing. Article XI stated that 'when any Six of the Members shall subscribe to any Book to be printed, it may be done at the Society so that the advantage of a seventh copy may accrue to the library, and for that End all proposals shall lye upon the Table'. Collecting and publishing drawings and engravings was envisaged as a more important role at the start, with an Officer responsible elected by the members. Under Article VI, 'The Director shall Superintend and regulate all the Drawings, Prints, Plates and books of the Society and all their works of Printing, drawing or Engraving'.[2]

Prints and drawings continued to form the most distinctive element in the library for much of the eighteenth century. The first Secretary, William Stukeley, wrote in his personal copy of the minutes, some time after 1726: 'without drawing and designing the study of Antiquities or any other Science is lame and imperfect'.[3] He was particularly concerned that what was observed should be exactly recorded in the spirit of scientific inquiry promoted by the Royal Society. He was a member of the older society, as were all but one of the Directors of the Antiquaries between 1727 and 1867.

The original drawings published in the Society's *Vetusta Monumenta* were kept in

Fig 62. 'A Declaration for the certaine time of drawing the great standing Lottery' (1615), one of several unique printed broadsides relating to the Virginia Company donated in 1757 by Thomas Hollis (Lemon 1866, cat. no. 151). The lottery was later suppressed by James I. *Photograph*: John Freeman & Co; © Society of Antiquaries of London.

'portifolios' acquired in 1721, and the first substantial collection purchased, that of the Director, John Talman, after his death, included several illustrations of Italian churches and the oldest architectural drawing belonging to the Society.[4] Charles Frederick, the Director chosen in 1736, was also an accomplished draughtsman. Drawings of items exhibited at meetings were often added to the Minute Books, and Frederick drew as a group the notable Bronze Age spears and axe heads found on Arreton Down, Isle of Wight, which have since been dispersed.[5] A larger collection of British topographical prints, in eight albums, was purchased in 1742 from the sale of Edward Harley, Earl of Oxford; but this was not as extensive, especially for county views, as the collection of about 1,200 prints donated in 1754 by Lord Coleraine's mistress in accordance with the wishes he expressed before his death.[6]

By 1754, therefore, the Society possessed a small but varied collection of historical material. It comprised a good collection of topographical prints and drawings, in twenty albums or portfolios, and a few manuscripts, of which the most important were letters to Oliver Cromwell formerly in the care of John Milton and donated in 1746.[7] Three royal portraits had been purchased in 1718,[8] and one of Henry VII was given in 1753. Some antiquities had been presented, including the lamp used as the Society's emblem, then thought to be Roman but now believed to be medieval (see fig 22, chapter 3).[9] In 1722 a nest of drawers was made to receive the coins and other similar donations.[10] It is difficult to establish how many books the Society had at this time. The minutes occasionally record orders such as for Gibson's second edition of Camden's *Britannia*, published in 1722, or, in 1737, regulations to purchase a stamp to be impressed on the title-page and last leaf of all books. In 1735 a German visitor to London, C Kortholt, wrote that the Society had 'a diminutive library whose shelves abound with choice books'.[11] In 1736 loans were considered and it was decided that no member should 'take any book belonging to the Society home to his own house without leave first given by the Society'.[12]

Apart from a three-year period when the Society hired rooms in Gray's Inn and the Temple, the members met in the Mitre Tavern in Fleet Street until 1753. Although in 1752 the Society's books, prints and bookcases there were insured for £200, there was little room for possessions. By contrast, the Royal Society had freehold premises nearby in Crane Court and, by 1747, had 3,250 books as a result of gifts, exchanges and purchases. A library keeper and library committees had been appointed from time to time and a catalogue of books prepared in 1744.[13]

CHANCERY LANE: 1753-80

In order to develop its collections, the Society needed corporate status and fixed accommodation. William Stukeley recorded Richard Rawlinson's views given at a meeting in November 1749: 'Dr Rawlinson spoke, that it was high time to think of obtaining a charter, and of removing from a tavern, to a place where they could be secure of what they already had.'[14] The charter granted in 1751 gave the Society the power to receive bequests and enjoy in perpetuity any antiquities, manuscripts, goods and chattels. The field of interest was widened beyond British antiquities to encompass the study of the past in this and other countries, responding to the growth of interest in classical and other ancient civilizations.

The Society moved into the Robin's Coffee House in 1753. Although on a yearly lease, these were the first premises of which it had exclusive use and they were large enough to accommodate a resident Secretary, a meeting room and space for its possessions. The following year, Council addressed the issue of storage by putting the library with the publications and assigning 'the large room of this house up two pairs of stairs' which was fitted out with shelves and drawers to take the stock of the engraver, as well as books, pamphlets and papers.[15] Some notable gifts came in the following years. One unexpected donation was received in 1757 and formed the basis of the Society's major collection of printed broadsides and proclamations. It originated in the purchase of two volumes of early proclamations from the sale of the books of the late President, Martin Folkes. These had originally been part of a much larger set of broadsides and proclamations formed in the early seventeenth century by the notary public and book collector, Humphrey Dyson. When, soon afterwards, another twelve volumes came up for sale with the same provenance, they were bought by the wealthy collector, Thomas Hollis, who generously presented them to the Society. Some are unique: of the fifteen issued by the Virginia Company in the reign of James I, five are known only through the Society's copies (fig 62). With others donated over the next 150 years, the Society's collection has become one of the largest and most important in the country.[16]

Fellows gave their own publications and drawings of objects in their possession, and those abroad communicated discoveries. The Society's growing international interests were reflected, for example, in the communications of Thomas Jenkins and Sir William Hamilton. Between 1758 and 1772 Jenkins sent several drawings of antiquities from Rome and in 1767 also dispatched a large cork model of the Temple of the Sybils at Tivoli.[17] In 1775 Hamilton sent drawings for publication in *Archaeologia* that he had commissioned of new discoveries at Pompeii. A few years later, the Society acquired some of the earliest watercolours attributed to William Blake; he was apprenticed at the time to the Society's engraver, James Basire, and had recorded monuments in Westminster Abbey for *Vetusta Monumenta*.

Despite the hopes of those who promoted the charter, the first substantial legacy did not come until the death in 1768 of Charles Lyttelton, Bishop of Carlisle, who had been President from 1765. His bequest added another thirty manuscripts to the dozen or so already held and established the Society as a place of deposit for manuscripts on antiquarian and historical subjects. The gift included his own papers on Worcestershire history and those of Thomas Habington from the seventeenth century, the first of several important county collections. The sixteenth-century Illyrian Armorial was the first of many heraldic manuscripts. The early thirteenth-century Lindsey Psalter is one of the Society's greatest treasures. Lyttelton's pioneering work on identifying Romanesque churches (which he called Saxon) resulted in the album of *Drawings of Saxon Churches*, which he inscribed as 'the only collection of Saxon buildings that ever was made'.[18]

Lyttelton also gave about sixty books and Council decided a reorganization of the premises was needed, with regular opening hours for the first time. The library was to be open on Wednesday and Friday mornings from 9am to 12 noon 'for the use of such members as shall have occasion to resort thereto'. None of Lyttelton's books or manuscripts was allowed to be lent out for a year, after which the manuscripts were to be lent only to members if they gave a bond for £100 for safe return.[19] One scholar, Dr Treadway Nash, elected a Fellow in 1773, made considerable use of Lyttelton's material. Council gave him permission to use Habington's papers in his own *Collections for the History of Worcestershire* (1781–2), the first occasion on which a request to publish manuscripts from the Society's collections had been received.[20]

The books, prints and other possessions had increased considerably in value and were insured for £1,500 in 1770.[21] The core collection of books on British topography was in place and the first loan register was ordered in 1771. When Richard Gough, the Director, examined the library in 1773, he found that the county histories were almost complete but suggested to the President, Jeremiah Milles, Dean of Exeter, that the library might be kept in better order in some separate room, rather than in the ante-chamber to the apartment of Mr Norris, the Resident Secretary. Milles agreed and commented that 'I suppose Mr Norris no longer uses the library as a dressing room. It wanted cleaning, painting and embellishment.'[22]

SOMERSET HOUSE: 1781–1840

In around 1780, Richard Gough had complained in a letter to the President, Dean Milles, about provision for the Society's library in the new Somerset House: 'the S. of A. are on the point of removing to Apart[ments] magnific[ent] indeed and where their seats and tables may make a figure without Accommodation or . . . dignity and their library wch. is no small orn[ament] to them be hid if not in danger of being lost'.[23] The room provided was on the ground floor overlooking the Strand, with no room for expansion, poor natural light and noise from the busy road outside (fig 63).[24] It was, however, the first purpose-built library of the Society, measuring 28ft by 22ft 9ins (about half the size of the Meeting Room in Somerset House) and fitted with deal bookcases with enclosed cupboards beneath, painted stone colour with grained mahogany doors. Readers sat at mahogany tables by the windows. By April 1781 the books had been checked against the library catalogue, found in order, mended and set in presses 'in Proper Classes' with shelf marks. An alphabetical catalogue annotated with press marks was drawn up to be kept on the library table. Three years later the books were reshelved by size to make more room and the previous subject arrangement disregarded.[25]

Fig 63. Plan of the Society's library and museum on the ground floor of Somerset House, 1781 (SAL, MS 760). Some of the museum collections were also displayed in cases in the Meeting Room. *Photograph*: Society of Antiquaries of London.

202

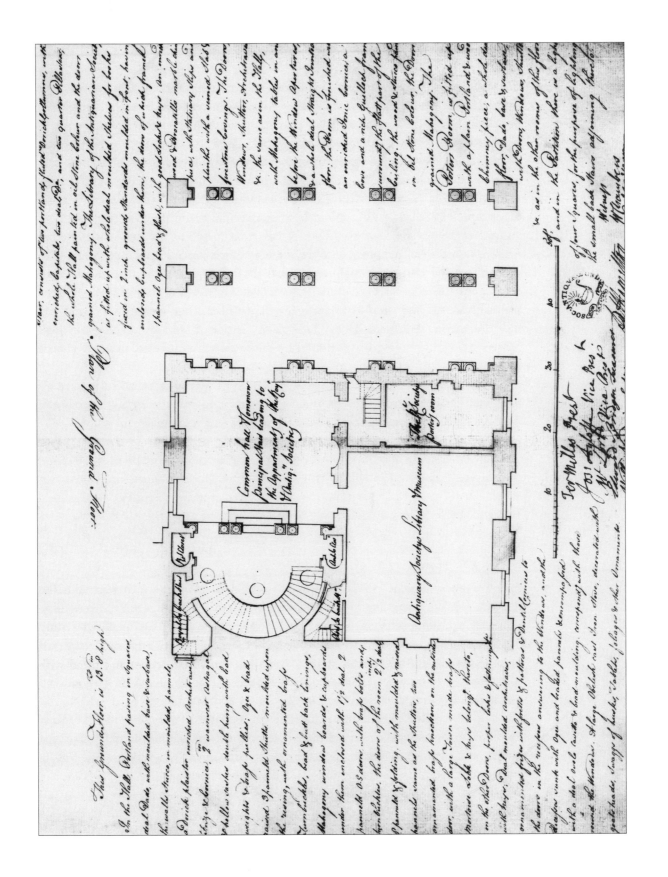

Manuscripts

The Society was acquiring many items of historic importance in this period as its status grew and proposals were made to publish inventories and household books. In particular, under the treasurership of John Topham (1787–1804), several manuscripts significant for British history were purchased. These included the twelfth-century Winton Domesday (MS 154) and part of the inventory of Henry VIII (MS 129). In 1785 Daines Barrington presented the wardrobe books of Edward I and Edward II (MSS 119–122), and in 1793 Robert Riddell gave an autograph copy of his 'Antiquities and topography of Nithsdale' (MS 117) with a poem by his friend, Robert Burns. In 1796 Joseph Jekyll gave some early heraldic manuscripts, including the Antiquaries Roll of *c* 1352–60 and a jousting cheque from the Field of the Cloth of Gold, 1520 (MSS 136/1, 2: fig 64). The most substantial bequest was that of John Thorpe (d 1792), who left his father's collections relating chiefly to Kent (MSS 155–202). By 1816 there were 216 manuscripts and 34 rolls and charters listed in the first printed catalogue and index, ably compiled by Sir Henry Ellis, then Keeper of Manuscripts at the British Museum. Not all manuscripts acquired by that date were included, and the Thorpe bequest accounted for about a quarter.[26]

Topham's interest in early household books and inventories reflected a constant theme in the Society's acquisitions, that of the source material for British history and the importance of documents as well as artefacts and monuments in studying the past. Inventories combined both interests. The wardrobe book of Edward I (MS 119) was published in 1787 and the household book of Edward IV (MS 211) in *A Collection of Ordinances and Regulations* in 1790. Others intended for publication had to wait longer. The Winton Domesday (MS 154) was published by the Record Commission in 1816 and the Inventory of Henry VIII (MS 129) not until 1998.

Drawings and paintings

Publication also provided the incentive to commission drawings which were added to the collections in increasing numbers between 1770 and 1840. In 1784 the President, Edward King, proposed that the most interesting items exhibited at meetings should be drawn on the spot, the drawings kept in a special portfolio and some engraved in an appendix to *Archaeologia*. John Carter was appointed, although most of this work appears to have been carried out by another artist, Thomas Underwood, who was appointed draughtsman-in-ordinary in 1792 and others who followed. Not all drawings were published and sometimes drawings of objects were sent in, rather than the objects themselves, or an artist was sent to record significant finds. Richard Smirke, one of the most accomplished, was probably the artist who drew the Viking gold bracelet from the hoard found at Hare Island in Ireland which appeared in a London goldsmith's shop in 1812 and was seen there by Francis Douce. The entire hoard was later melted down, leaving the drawings published in *Archaeologia* as the sole record.[27] The Society's role in recording antiquities discovered was well enough

Fig 64. Jousting cheque for a tournament held at the Field of the Cloth of Gold in 1520, showing the arms of those attending the meeting and the scores of the combatants (SAL, MS 136/2). *Photograph*: John Hammond; © Society of Antiquaries of London.

204

known to the outside world to be gently satirized by Charles Dickens in *Pickwick Papers*. Mr Pickwick's lecture on an ancient stone with an indecipherable inscription was followed up by 'a faithful delineation of the curiosity which was engraved on stone, and presented to the Royal Antiquarian Society and other learned bodies'.[28]

By 1828 the Society had accumulated such an extensive collection of illustrations that the Director, John Gage (later John Gage Rokewode), was asked to report on their preservation and cataloguing.[29] He commented that many loose prints and drawings were in open drawers, arranged and with a separate catalogue. There were also eight bundles of loose drawings engraved in *Archaeologia* but without a catalogue, and another twelve bundles of postponed papers, some with drawings. The rest of the collection had been bound into twenty-six volumes, including the Harley and Coleraine collections, some with an index in each volume and one portfolio.[30] No action to organize the collections was taken until 1840, however.

From its earliest days, the Society had possessed a small collection of historical portraits. After the first three were purchased in 1718, the remainder were received mostly by gift, and included several portraits of Fellows. The first subject painting, a 1616 diptych of St Paul's Cathedral, with its much reproduced view of the preaching cross, was purchased about 1781 and initially kept in the library.[31] The collection was then transformed by the bequest of the Revd Thomas Kerrich, received in 1828. He gave twenty-six fifteenth- and sixteenth-century paintings, including Hans Eworth's full-length portrait of Mary I, and two of the earliest portraits of Edward IV and Richard III, as well as a large panel painting of the legend of St Etheldreda (fig 65). Accepting such gifts created problems of display, as John Nichols complained the same year in a comment on the St Paul's diptych:

> Grieved I am to add that it is now consigned, with several other pictures and curiosities at various times presented to the Society, to a subterranean warehouse. It is to be hoped that space may soon be procured for displaying the many treasures the Society possesses. As it is, presents are totally discouraged from those that have been made being never exhibited.[32]

Such problems did not prevent the Society purchasing an even larger painting in 1829 – the portrait of William Stukeley which now dominates the main stairs in Burlington House.[33]

Printed books

The lack of room for the growing number of printed books had already been felt some years earlier. In 1797 extra storage was found by fitting bookshelves in the basement kitchen. Ten years later Robert Smirke was commissioned to add a gallery to the library. Later plans show a gallery of about 6ft high above the 10ft-high shelving on the main floor (fig 66).[34] An indication of the main sources of growth is given by the first printed catalogue of books published in 1816. By contrast with Sir Henry Ellis's well-organized catalogue of the Society's manuscripts, Nicholas

Carlisle's catalogue of the printed books is poor. Arranged as a dictionary catalogue in alphabetical order of author and subject entries, the headings, sometimes in Latin, are inconsistent and often duplicated.[35] It is difficult to establish the extent of the library from the catalogue but approximately 3,000 titles are listed; some titles, such as the journals of the Houses of Parliament, had many volumes. The main growth area would have been in periodicals, already numbering perhaps 400 volumes by 1816. Regular exchanges of publications had been agreed with the Royal Society, the Asiatic Society and the Royal Irish Academy, as well as with societies in Brussels, Paris and Göttingen.[36] Prompted by the foundation of the Royal Society of Northern Antiquaries in 1825, a sub-committee was appointed to consider the growing number of exchanges with foreign societies with similar interests.[37]

The 1816 catalogue reveals that the library was strongest in topography, heraldry,

Fig 65. *The Legend of St Etheldreda* (*c* 1455). Painted on panels found in a cottage in Ely that were being reused as cupboard doors, they were bequeathed to the Antiquaries by Thomas Kerrich in 1828. *Photograph*: John Hammond; © Society of Antiquaries of London.

Fig 66. The south elevation of the Society's library in Somerset House *c* 1847, showing the gallery added in 1807 and the location of journals on the shelves (SH2 at 196i). *Photograph*: Society of Antiquaries of London.

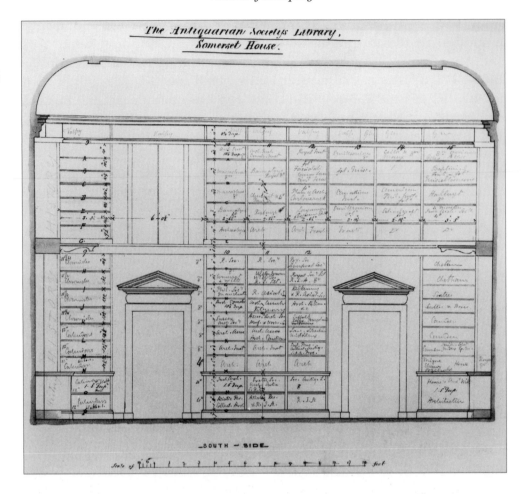

numismatics and record publications relating to British history. Funds for purchases were granted very occasionally: up to £200 was allocated in 1785 to a committee of three to buy books on English history and antiquities, and William Benson Earle left 200 guineas for the purchase of books in 1796. Most items, however, were presented, including major European works such as Sir William Hamilton's *Campi Phlegraei* (1776–9) and *Collection of Engravings from Ancient Vases* (1791–5), Montfaucon's *L'Antiquité expliquée* (1722 and 1757) and *Les Monumens de la monarchie françoise* (1729–33). A broad range of studies, which was a feature of the Enlightenment and the wide interests of Fellows at the time, is reflected in some of the subjects included. Sir Henry Englefield's researches on comets can be found with his works on the history of Southampton and of St Stephen's Chapel, Westminster. Items on medicine, poetry, natural history and horticulture are also to be found in the catalogue.

Relying mostly on gifts, there were several surprising omissions, with no copies of Stukeley's works on Stonehenge and Avebury and only one edition of Camden's *Britannia* before the edition of 1722. Some series were incomplete, such as Schnebbelie's *Antiquaries Museum*. The most active private collectors had larger

208

libraries. Sir Walter Scott had some 20,000 volumes on British history and topography in 1829. Sir Richard Colt Hoare's library at Stourhead was extensive and widely used; his catalogue published in 1840 lists more than 10,000 works on topography alone. Richard Heber had acquired about 150,000 books by the time of his death in 1833. In London, the library of the London Institution (founded in 1806) was noted for its topographical collections, and the British Museum Library (founded in 1753) was available to scholars.[38]

At Somerset House, the additional storage space provided in the basement and gallery was recognized as insufficient by the 1820s. Sir Nicholas Harris Nicolas complained in 1829 that 'the library room is too confined and incommodious for the number of valuable books which it contains, and for the members to resort to it generally as a place of study'. He said that one-sixth of the floor space was taken up by the cork model of the Temple at Tivoli, and the Society's publications also occupied much space. Council was aware of the problem and pointed out to the Lords Commissioners of the Treasury responsible for Somerset House that 'it is now impossible for them to receive any adaptations to their library or to arrange their present library of books in a proper manner, nor could they afford any space whatever for objects of Antiquity'.[39] At this time, the Treasury was not prepared to extend the Society's premises beyond the rooms provided in 1781; space was needed for government purposes and the Society remained constricted.

It is not possible to say how many members used the library in the nineteenth century, and other scholars were only rarely permitted access.[40] In 1796 Charles Clarke told Samuel Denne that he wanted to become a Fellow to gain access to the Society's collections for studying architecture.[41] The library was essentially for use by Fellows, but instead of developing as a subscription library popular in the late eighteenth and early nineteenth centuries, the regulations for the loan of books became increasingly restrictive. In 1786 Council ordered that no minute book, manuscript, drawing or print should be removed from the library without Council's express permission.[42] In 1798 a cumbersome procedure was adopted to authorize loans. Council decided 'that every Fellow desirous of borrowing a printed book shall make known such request to the Society during their meeting or to the Council during their sitting in writing'. During the vacation, the Resident Secretary could lend books on application in writing. No one could have more than three books on loan at any one time or keep them for more than a month.[43] Richard Gough objected in verse:

> But London's A.S.S.'s bray
> Like Country Asses tied from hay
> Beside Bethesda's Pool.
> Till Chairman or till Council come
> Not one poor pamphlet dare take home
> Though every shelf is full[44]

As a result the maximum number of books loaned in any one year between 1798 and 1808 was twenty-seven.[45] They included substantial volumes, such as Gough's

Sepulchral Monuments, Nash's *Worcestershire*, Nichols's *Leicestershire* and Dugdale's *Baronage*, *St Paul's* and *Warwickshire*. Borrowers included Craven Ord, James Dallaway, Francis Douce and Charles Townley, all Fellows who probably had extensive collections of their own but could not necessarily obtain the particular books they wanted. Other Fellows would have found some purchases too expensive. In 1815 Council restricted the library to reference only, ruling that no books should be lent. In this they were going further than the Royal Society, which permitted the borrowing of books that could be replaced and allowed those who were not Fellows to borrow books if they gave a bond for their safe return. To allow a longer time for reading on a day when more Fellows came to Somerset House, the library opening hours were extended in 1829 to 10pm after Thursday meetings.[46]

REFORM: 1840–75

The problems facing the library and collections – of lack of space, poor condition and organization and inadequate catalogues – were all addressed to some extent in the period 1840–75, culminating in the move to Burlington House. Necessary changes were driven by more energetic Resident Secretaries from 1848, new Directors – especially Albert Way and Wollaston Franks – and dedicated Fellows, such as Robert Lemon and Charles Perceval. The spirit of reform was also felt in the Royal Society, the Antiquaries' neighbours, until 1857.

Prints, drawings and collections

The prints and drawings were the first to benefit. The Director's report of 1828 was finally acted upon in 1840 when William Long was engaged for half a guinea a day to catalogue and arrange them in portfolios. Most were topographical but they included about 1,500 drawings of antiquities and archaeological finds which were extracted and bound into albums in the late 1860s. They were arranged by period, from *Primeval Antiquities* to *Early Medieval*, and by subject such as *Arms and Armour*, *Personal Ornament* and *Utensils and Furniture*. The earliest drawing in the albums is of the sword of state of the earldom of Chester (1743). Others depict some of the British Museum's greatest treasures, such as the Bronze Age cape from Mold and the Lewis chessmen, and outstanding objects whose present location is unknown, such as the late Saxon hanging-bowl found in the River Witham.[47]

The Society had by this time ceased to commission artists to record buildings and monuments, although fine colour facsimiles of illuminated manuscripts were published in occasional issues of *Vetusta Monumenta*, using outstanding women artists such as Margaret Stokes and Rosa Wallis. Additions to the collection came more from gifts and bequests, such as the several hundred early nineteenth-century drawings of Worcestershire bequeathed by Peter Prattinton in 1840. A few were purchased, including William Capon's watercolours of Westminster scenes drawn 1801–15 and acquired from his daughter in 1841.[48]

210

While William Long was arranging the drawings, Albert Way, the Society's Director from 1842, was cataloguing the museum collections, including the paintings. He carried out thorough research in the Society's archives to establish their provenance as far as he could, and arranged his catalogue, published in 1847, within primitive subject areas. Although not numbered until over a hundred years later, there were about 400 objects or groups of objects in the Society's possession by then. Nothing much had been done to display these items but some Fellows wished to see the collections develop. W D Haggard donated what he described as 'the first present made to the Society's museum' in 1840.[49] More notable gifts were two clocks given by B L Vulliamy in 1848 and 1850: the clock used by his great-grandfather to regulate the other clocks in his shop, and a rare globe clock of around 1690 driven by its own weight.[50] In 1851 G R Corner gave the fine fifteenth-century alabaster panel depicting the martyrdom of St Erasmus to join the three others that the Society already possessed. In 1860 Ludlow Roots gave his father's collection of finds from the Thames, including a remarkable series of bronze celts.

After the Society moved into the Royal Society's former meeting room in 1858, the opportunity was taken to rehang the Society's paintings in chronological order. George Scharf, the Director of the National Portrait Gallery, recognized that they deserved far fuller descriptions than those provided by Albert Way, and his catalogue was published in 1865. By then the Society had sixty-eight framed pictures, although some of these were watercolours.[51] The modest ambitions of the museum collection were emphasized by the President, Lord Stanhope, when he commented on the new arrangement in his 1863 Presidential Address:

> Our Meeting Room has . . . been enriched with two new cases in which the Society's collections have been arranged, with due regard to periods, to subjects, and to value, and with an absence of that overcrowding of objects which had hitherto not a little perplexed both our Fellows and our visitors. A museum in the proper sense of the word, we have neither the space, nor the inclination to keep up. We content ourselves with the humbler object of decorating our Meeting Room with a few typical specimens of antiquities, classical or medieval.[52]

Printed books and manuscripts

The problems of the library generally proved more intractable, but a start was made on addressing them in December 1845, when Council appointed the first Library Committee, whose members 'may examine the actual state of these collections generally and propose some measures for rendering them more readily accessible to the Fellows of the Society'.[53]

In practice the survey was carried out by Robert Lemon, who found many of the books double banked on the shelves and lying on the floor. He employed a carpenter to create more space by adjusting the height of the shelves and reshelving the books, calculating optimistically that 'sufficient space will remain for our accommodation for several years to come'. Many of the books were in a poor state, and the Society voted to spend £300 on binding and repairs to make the library 'more accessible and generally useful'.[54] As a result 1,034 volumes were bound or lettered. The opportunity was taken to brighten up the appearance with 'as bright and gay' bindings as price would allow. Lemon also removed the duplicates, which were offered for sale, and 'completed as many imperfect works' as he could (for example, series with missing volumes and volumes with missing sections).[55]

In 1846 the Library Committee proposed new rules setting out the opening hours as 10am to 4pm, Monday to Saturday, except during committee meetings (which were held in the library). In 1860 Saturday opening was restricted to 2pm. The library closed every September for cleaning. Fellows were once more allowed to borrow books in accordance with the practice of the Royal Society and the London Library. Except for those that were particularly scarce and valuable, up to four could be borrowed for three months on application to the Secretary or the attendant. For the first time those who were not Fellows were allowed to use the library, but 'strangers' were only admitted by the personal introduction of a Fellow, who had to remain with the visitor at all times. This rule was relaxed in 1860 to allow non-Fellows to study in the library for up to a week with a letter of introduction from a Fellow. The same year it was agreed that Fellows living in the country might borrow books if they applied in writing and the application was presented by an authorized agent.[56]

The campaign to improve the library had taken on renewed vigour when Franks was elected Director in 1859, Christopher Knight Watson was appointed Resident Secretary in 1860 and the President, Lord Stanhope, gave his strong support. Franks began by stating, at the meeting of 17 November 1859, that 'he considered the library one of the most important elements of the Society's progress, for the facilities which it affords to Fellows for the prosecution of their studies'. He urged on Fellows the necessity of increasing the collection of books.[57] Lord Stanhope took up the theme the following April in his Anniversary Address:

> The great value of a library, from which works can be borrowed, to all those who are engaged in antiquarian pursuits, need scarcely be insisted upon. It should contain all standard works of reference on the special subjects of our studies, namely Antiquities, History and Art. The space at our disposal being limited, it should be restricted to those or to cognate subjects. At present being the accumulation of accident rather than design, our library has the most glaring deficiencies, and, while it contains many works of great value, it wants others to which our Fellows have daily occasion to refer. The Council, being anxious to remedy in some slight measure these deficiencies have allotted £50 a year to be expended by the Library Committee, but it is only by the assistance of the Fellows that the Library can become as complete as it ought to be.[58]

£150 was also approved for completing the collection of county histories. Up until then, the Society had always been unwilling to spend an annual sum on purchases. The expenditure of twenty guineas had been authorized in 1853 for subscribing to forthcoming antiquarian publications. It was thought that by careful selection encouragement might be given to 'books of the fairest promise and of the highest class'. Donations were encouraged by the provision of a donations book and the practice of laying all gifts on the table at the next meeting after receipt where they could be seen by Fellows.[59]

Council did not want to increase the library by purchases until a printed catalogue had been issued and Fellows could be given the opportunity to fill gaps. Started in 1852, the catalogue was finally published in 1861. Franks noted in the preface that it had two purposes: Fellows would see the deficiencies and, it was hoped, remedy them from their own libraries, and those who lived at a distance could discover what was in the library. The Resident Secretary, John Yonge Akerman, had been given the task of compiling the catalogue, but had been unable to complete it by the time he resigned from ill health in 1860. John Williams, the former Assistant Secretary to the Royal Astronomical Society, was offered the job and given detailed instructions on the rules to follow. These were a much simplified version of those adopted by the British Museum; short-title entries and no subject headings further reduced the cost of printing. As a result, a far more concise and consistent catalogue was produced than that published in 1816. Other libraries with large collections, such as those of the British Museum and the Bodleian at Oxford, also found it impossible to produce a subject index to their holdings at the time.[60]

Soon after his arrival, the new Resident Secretary, Christopher Knight Watson, drew attention to the need for constant and unremitting care, and carried out his own report on the state of the library. He claimed that Lemon's report of 1846 'would admirably describe the wretched condition' found by him in 1860, and set out where he thought the strengths and weaknesses lay:

> Topography . . . is really . . . the only portion of our Library of which we may justly be proud. In History itself, though not in the materials of History, . . . and in other departments our Library might easily be surpassed by any average Gentleman's Library in the Kingdom; but in Topography in our collection of County Histories etc . . . we need not fear to invite comparison.[61]

In 1864, Watson set about reorganizing the shelves, substituting numbers for the letters which had previously marked the presses; such an arrangement is still used today. He placed all 10,000 volumes in a new order of his own, starting with biography and ending with the publications of foreign societies. Duplicates and works 'unsuited to our shelves' were set aside for disposal and the *Journals of the Houses of Parliament* were sold. The Library Committee commented that the library would no longer contain books 'which have been buried in dusty recesses, time out of mind, or which have been so imperfectly catalogued or referred to that they could be discovered only by accident. The library will now be properly bound, properly arranged, properly catalogued.'[62]

The appeal for donations proved extremely successful: J R D Tyssen, Lord Amherst, gave 400 volumes in 1857, the artist and engraver F W Fairholt donated about 200 finely illustrated books on pageantry in 1866[63] and Albert Way donated his collections of early dictionaries and seal impressions between 1869 and 1874. However, the largest bequest ever received came from the architect Arthur Ashpitel, who – impressed by the care and energy devoted to the library by Watson – bequeathed some 2,400 volumes in 1869. They included some of the earliest printed books in the Society's possession, some outstanding works by Piranesi and a collection of Greek vases. Interest in the broadsides and proclamations was revived when Robert Lemon arranged for their binding into volumes and published a catalogue of the broadsides in 1866; many more were donated subsequently.[64]

By the 1860s, exchanges of *Archaeologia* had been arranged with the journals of about sixty British and foreign societies, several of which would later be discontinued as not relevant to the Society's interests, such as those of the Institution of Civil Engineers and the British and Foreign Bible Society. American bodies were especially keen on exchanging publications from the middle of the nineteenth century, with the Smithsonian sending government publications on all subjects to numbers of other libraries.[65] Earlier in the century, the Society had published several medieval texts, such as Layamon's *Brut* (1847), but printing societies began to take on this role in more systematic and comprehensive programmes. It was cheaper to subscribe than to publish, and all the major series were taken, including those produced by the Chaucer, Percy, Chetham, Camden, Hakluyt, and Early English Text Societies, to be followed later by the county record societies. Subscribing from the first issues, the Society has comprehensive holdings of these series. As they gradually became more expensive, fewer works on early literature were acquired, and in 1862 the Library Committee decided it could not afford to subscribe to a series of facsimiles of Shakespeare's quartos.[66]

The increasing numbers of manuscripts donated to the Society placed a strain on its cataloguing resources. The most extensive bequest at the time was that of Peter Prattinton's papers, relating to Worcestershire history, which he wanted added to the other collections on Worcestershire given to the Society in the eighteenth century. Though received in 1841 when some of his papers were bound into parish volumes, most were not catalogued until 1931. After Knight Watson's report, Charles Perceval sorted and had bound 'not less than fifty parcels of manuscripts, which in their former state of confusion had been abandoned in sheer despair'. Many of these were part of the large Thorpe bequest on Kent received in 1793.[67]

Accommodation

Difficulties caused by the lack of space became more pressing until they were finally resolved by the move to Burlington House in 1874. The other societies that had occupied Somerset House since 1780 – the Royal Academy and the Royal Society – were similarly affected and had other reasons for wanting to move. The Royal Academy's highly successful summer exhibitions gave it greater financial resources and it moved out in 1837, initially to join the National Gallery in Trafalgar Square and later to Burlington House. The Royal Society moved out in 1857 to old Burlington House, with the intention of forming a group with other scientific societies. The Antiquaries had applied for more space in Somerset House in 1847,[68] and in 1851 plans were drawn up for the Antiquaries and the Royal Society to join the Royal Academy in Trafalgar Square. The drawings show a library twice the size of that in Somerset House and the same size as the new Meeting Room proposed for the building in Trafalgar Square.[69] The proposal came to nothing and more space was found for the library the following year when the library clerk gave up his rooms in the basement for an extra £16 a year on his salary.[70]

An opportunity for expansion arose in 1857 when the Royal Society moved out. However, the government was also faced with the growing demands of the Registrar General's office in Somerset House. The most the Antiquaries could achieve was the exchange of secretaries' apartments and meeting rooms – the Royal Society's being slightly larger. The library gained a little more space when three attic rooms were acquired in 1860, but by then the possibility of moving to new apartments in Burlington House was looking more likely.[71]

BURLINGTON HOUSE

The negotiations over the move to Burlington House were protracted but began in earnest in 1859 when the government proposed to build new wings between old Burlington House and Piccadilly to accommodate the learned societies still located in Somerset House as well as those in old Burlington House. From the government's perspective, this would free space in Somerset House for the growing civil service and in old Burlington House for the Royal Academy. The learned societies would gain more room for their activities as well as the advantages of 'juxtaposition'. As with Somerset House compromises had to be made, and the Antiquaries, having asked for a museum room and a Council room, had to accept plans without either. In 1875 the Vice-President who gave the first Anniversary Address in the new apartments summed up the considerable gains:

> The room in which our meetings are now held is not so light and cheerful as that which we have quitted, but it is larger; and as we assemble in the evening the loss of daylight is not felt. With respect to the library the gain is infinite. Instead of being obliged to place our books, not less than 20,000 in number, in several localities – some dark, others hardly accessible, on staircases and in cupboards – they are now brought together in one handsome and well-proportioned room, which allows of perfect classification, and affords ample space for additions.[72]

All the learned societies in Burlington House were provided with fine libraries, although the Royal Society's was the largest. The architects, Banks and Barry, made a particular feature of them in their innovative designs, which incorporated deep bays with shelving and seating areas, and two levels of receding galleries above. The Antiquaries' new library was 55ft long by 43ft, four times larger in lower-ground floor space than that at Somerset House and twice the size of the new Meeting Room in Burlington House (at 29ft by 43ft). The new library was made the most imposing room in the building, placed above the Meeting Room on the first floor to obtain the best natural light and approached directly by the main staircase. It was in a quieter position than at Somerset House, being at the end of the courtyard away from the busy traffic on Piccadilly. With two levels of gallery, some 3,500ft of shelving were available, providing perhaps 50 per cent more space for expansion without any need for further alterations (fig 67).[73] While the accommodation was provided rent-free, with generous space for the Resident Secretary, and the government paying for external repairs, the Society was responsible for maintaining the interior of the building. The library occupied a greater proportion of the Society's premises than in Somerset House and the Society also bore the costs of acquisitions, conservation, cataloguing and staff. The expense was considerable for a small membership, which did not exceed 900 until the 1950s.

Fig 67. The library in Burlington House looking south, 1921. *Photograph*: Society of Antiquaries of London.

Sufficient wall space was found in the Meeting Room and by the main staircase to hang the Society's pictures, but the museum collections were scattered. Two museum cases from Somerset House were refitted on either side of the Meeting Room fireplace; and another two were adapted for the library landing. A new case was made for the entrance hall and nine new cabinets were made to fit in the library galleries. Larger items that could not be accommodated were given away to Westminster Abbey, the British Museum and elsewhere.

Acquisitions

With the acquisitions of the previous 150 years, the reforms over the preceding 30 years and the move to Burlington House in 1874, the Society's library had finally fulfilled its potential to become the leading specialist library in Britain for research into the physical evidence of man's past. Its particular strengths in the fields of what would be described today as material culture and the historic environment were well established, covering archaeology, antiquities, historical sites and monuments, as well as the sources of British history. Increasing amounts of new research in these areas were published in journals issued by local societies. Over fifty of these societies were founded in England between 1844 and 1888,[74] and all their publications were taken. The Society was now in a position to respond to the tremendous rise in the number of publications by these bodies, and by foreign societies and specialist interest groups, from the middle of the nineteenth century. It was helped by the comparatively low price of archaeological journals compared with scientific ones, the cost savings of exchange agreements and the flexible space within the new apartments. To some extent, the building could be adapted to further increases in shelving as required. Basement areas, the Resident Secretary's living accommodation, rooms vacated by the Royal Society and the British Academy and the introduction of mobile shelving in the 1970s have all enabled the Society to accommodate its growing library collections. By the end of the twentieth century, about 16,500ft of shelving was available within the same building or elsewhere in Burlington House, some five times that available in 1875.

The Society's library has always been by far the largest of any archaeological society in Britain, although other societies have had more members. The Society of Antiquaries of Scotland modelled its library on that of its London counterpart, but its main interest was in collecting antiquities. County societies concentrated on collecting material relating to their own areas. The Antiquaries' library was international in scope, reflecting the outlook of its members, who were aware that the history, archaeology and topography of Britain could only be fully researched in a wider context.[75] The generous provision of space allowed the Society to accept some large donations of books and manuscripts. G E Cokayne, Clarenceux Herald, gave over 1,000 books on heraldry in 1895 and A W Franks gave his fine collection of heraldic books and manuscripts two years later, the two gifts laying the foundations for the Society's major holdings in this field. Important heraldic manuscripts – such as the seventeenth-century Hatton–Dugdale facsimiles of rolls of arms – were purchased from the bequest in 1926 of Lt-Col G B Croft Lyons.[76] Franks gave his collection of bookplates to the British Museum but an even larger one of about 45,000 armorial bookplates was acquired in 1964 from Hall Crouch after the Guildhall Library had rejected it.[77] Franks also gave his collection of brass rubbings, which he had amassed from various sources. In 1875 he considered he had rubbings of 80 per cent of English brasses made before 1700 and this huge collection of historic rubbings, including many from the early nineteenth century, was augmented later by Mill Stephenson's rubbings, to make it a complete collection of virtually all the pre-1700 brasses known in the British Isles. With later donations of rubbings of incised slabs and foreign brasses, the Society's collection of memorial rubbings is the largest in the country.

Acquisitions soon became more selective. About 350 items from the Royal Archaeological Institute were accepted in 1900 when its library was dispersed, but the libraries of the Society for the Promotion of Hellenic Studies and of the Anthropological Institute were refused in 1901 because of lack of space.[78]

The growth of the library had its effect on the museum. In 1901 Council asked that 'in view of the demand for more room for the Society's library the Executive Committee be requested to consider the desirability of transferring the Society's Museum to the Trustees of the British Museum'. Charles Hercules Read, the Society's Secretary and on the staff at the British Museum, recommended that the museum purchase everything for £450 except for the lamp, the mace and the seal impressions, but there were so many objections from Fellows that the proposal was abandoned. When the Resident Secretary left in 1910, his apartments were taken over for the use of the Society. The museum collections found a resting place in two former bedrooms on the top floor.[79]

The seal impressions had by then become the most numerous part of the museum. Originating in the Worcestershire seals bequeathed by Prattinton in 1840 and a few earlier gifts, Albert Way added a further 4,000, and by 1919 there were just under 10,000 examples, along with over 20 matrices and some detached original seals. Practically complete for the seals of bishops and royal seals, the value of the collection was enormously enhanced by being classified and arranged first by the former Treasurer, Charles Perceval, and later by the Assistant Secretary, Hugh Kingsford.[80]

CATALOGUES

The influx of new material enriched the collections but created the problem of having to catalogue so much material with limited resources. The publication of printed catalogues of books was abandoned in the twentieth century. A supplement to the 1861 catalogue was issued in 1868; a complete new catalogue came out in 1887 and a further supplement in 1899. The 1887 catalogue had a limited subject index of personal names and places but was only completed with outside help after Knight Watson, who had started it in 1883, had to retire on grounds of ill health.[81] The labour and expense had become too great, and the nineteenth-century aim of informing readers outside the library of its contents was not realized again until the online computer catalogue was completed in 2004. Instead an author and subject card catalogue was begun about 1911.[82] New accessions and the contents of journals were listed in the *Proceedings* and later in the *Antiquaries Journal*. In 1926 Ralph Griffin, Assistant Secretary, set out the problem in an appeal for funding to the Carnegie UK Trust:

> As the Society of Antiquaries exists for certain very special purposes, so is its library of a very special nature . . . the collection . . . now necessarily includes many old and rare works, unattainable elsewhere, and invaluable for the study of archaeology in all its branches . . . Interest in archaeology is becoming daily more widespread . . . The result of this has been a great increase in the number of works published on the subjects which fall within our field.

> This increase, even if we could cope with it, leads to another difficulty; for material, however valuable in itself, is but of little use unless it be made available to students by some form of catalogue based on the most modern principles.

> Our library then needs more books, needs better cataloguing, needs more attention to repairs. To these three wants we are only able to devote, having regard to the claims of our other interests, [a] proportion of the funds at our disposal. In 1925 we spent £196 on new books, £366 on cataloguing, £50 on binding and repairs.

He claimed that the Society should spend £600 on new books, £500 on binding and £600 for additional cataloguing staff. The Carnegie Trust offered a generous grant of £3,000, spread over three years; in return, the Society agreed to make its books available for loan through the National Central Library, and about fifty a month were lent in 1929.[83] The Society continued to employ additional cataloguing staff even after the Carnegie grant ceased. By 1988, when the subject card catalogue gave way to computer cataloguing, over 500,000 index cards had been compiled, two-thirds of them for periodical articles, and the author card catalogue contained about 100,000 entries and references (fig 68).

After the Second World War, Council became so concerned about the state of cataloguing of the non-printed material that a Catalogues sub-committee was set up 'to enquire into the possibility of compiling and publishing catalogues of the Society's manuscripts, pictures, prints and drawings and antiquities'. Dr Pamela Tudor-Craig was employed on this task between 1952 and 1954, but insufficient funds were available for her to carry on with the work. In those two years, however, she extracted much information on the collections from the Society's minutes, indexed many of the topographical prints and drawings and started work on the manuscripts and paintings. Except for research on the pictures, work then ceased for nearly thirty years. It was not until Irvine Gray's report for the National Register of Archives in 1985 and Pamela Willetts's appointment as manuscripts cataloguer in 1989 that any

Fig 68. The library in 1984 looking north west, showing the subject and author card indexes. By then, the long table had been brought up from the Meeting Room, the library had been redecorated, the columns marbled and new lighting installed. *Photograph*: reproduced by permission of English Heritage, NMR.

real progress was made. By the time Willetts's catalogue was published in 2000 the numbered manuscripts had grown from the 250 listed by Ellis in 1816 to 1,010, with some numbers incorporating many volumes.[84]

In the 1980s, Beatrice de Cardi, the Director, devoted much attention to the museum collection, which had grown to over 1,000 items from the 400 in Way's catalogue of 1847. She numbered the objects, photographed them and compiled an inventory and typescript indexes.[85] Basic information, with colour images, has since been added to a computer database. Support from the Getty Grant Program and other trusts has permitted cataloguing work to be carried out on those drawings not already indexed, and a programme to digitize the drawings was started in 2003 in co-operation with Lambeth Palace Library.

In the twenty-first century, the library has embraced new technology to reach out to a wider public. New methods have been used without departing in principle from previous policies. The Society has always been conscious of the obligations of its 1751 royal charter to encourage the study of the past, and has willingly lent manuscripts and paintings, published numerous catalogues of its collections in the nineteenth century and (since 1846) allowed those who are not Fellows to read in the library. However, personal use of the collections by others has only become significant since the 1920s.

Unfortunately, there are no statistics of use of the library by non-Fellows before 1925, and until 2002, the only years in which use by Fellows was recorded were between 1934 and 1939. An indication of the low level of use by non-Fellows in the early part of the twentieth century is shown by the numbers who visited the library on Friday evenings in 1903 when, as an experiment, it was opened until 10pm. Only four visitors (and fifty-four Fellows) attended in fifteen days, so the idea was dropped. In 1926 Council commented on the welcome increase in the number of students using the library, and numbers grew dramatically in the period before the Second World War. On most days of the week, the number of Fellows and visitors was about the same, but on Thursdays, when the Society held its meetings, there were often six times the number of Fellows present. Although women formed a small proportion of the membership of the Society in the 1930s, about half the visitors were female.[86] These figures reflect the growth of archaeology as an academic subject in the 1930s – culminating in the establishment of the Institute of Archaeology in London in 1937 – as well as the rise in the number of archaeological excavations and the lack of library facilities elsewhere specializing in the subject.

When visitors were first permitted, in 1846, they had to be accompanied by Fellows. In 1860 the regulations were relaxed to allow those with letters of introduction from Fellows to be admitted. However, it was not until 1946 that readers could be admitted at the discretion of the Assistant Secretary or Librarian, thereby allowing in members of the public and students who applied directly. Frequent users were encouraged to join the Royal Archaeological Institute, whose members were permitted to use the Society's library from 1900. Their membership then was low, at 320, but it reached 830 by 1956 when the Society's Fellowship had only increased from 713 to 915 in the same period. The Assistant Secretary suggested in 1958 that the main reason for the steadily growing membership of the institute was the privilege of using the Antiquaries' library; this particularly appealed to its professional members with related interests. For example, of the 850 visits made by non-Fellows in 1957, it was estimated that 720 were made by members of the Royal Archaeological Institute;[87] some of the most frequent users were people employed by the Ordnance Survey and the Ancient Monuments Inspectorate. The peak in numbers was reached in the mid-1970s. Students from the Courtauld Institute, where the study of medieval art and architecture was flourishing, and the Institute of Archaeology, which had developed dramatically, formed major groups of users, as did members of the Monumental Brass Society and investigators working for the Royal Commission on the Historical Monuments of England.

Personal visits by non-Fellows have declined since then, most noticeably in the 1980s. The number of Fellows increased to around 2,300 in 2004; and many of those earlier readers have now been elected as Fellows. University libraries have now developed strong collections in the fields covered by the Society, as has English Heritage; fewer students are thought to be studying material culture,[88] and heritage professionals are unable to devote as much time during the working week to carrying out research as they once did. Of course, many of those previously based in London have been dispersed to the National Monuments Record Centre in Swindon and to regional offices throughout the country. At the same time, public interest in archaeology, historic buildings, local history and genealogy has greatly increased. This is not so much reflected in greater use of the library by the wider public as more in the increasing use made by staff of publishers and broadcasting companies, abstractors for bibliographic services and exhibition organizers, all wanting to consult material held by the Society. External use has also grown dramatically with the development of online services and the use of e-mail.

THE LIBRARY TODAY

The Society's library has developed over nearly 300 years to reflect the interests and commitment of Fellows. During the second half of the nineteenth century, it became the leading specialist library in its field. The premises provided by the government in Burlington House in exchange for those in Somerset House gave it the space to expand in line with the huge growth in literature on archaeology and architectural history and in the published source material for British history. The Society's Fellows provided much of that material, as well as the funds to maintain the collections. They have allowed the Society's resources to be used for the public benefit and as a result grant-giving bodies have generously supported developments to the services.

The Society's library now possesses a unique collection of books, manuscripts, prints and drawings, pictures and museum objects. These materials – complemented by the catalogues, premises, staff and services – support research and provide written evidence for the past on which others can build. The holdings now encompass some 800 current journals and 100,000 printed book titles, which are all the more important given that half of these are not to be found in the British Library. The collection of journals is particularly strong because of the length of the runs and the breadth of international coverage built up by exchange agreements. All British county archaeological society journals and record series are taken; many of the printed books are presented by the authors. Research in the library's specialist areas continues to grow and is still largely published in traditional printed formats. However, catalogues are now computer-based and digitized copies of older sources and online or CD-based resources are assuming a greater importance. The library's task for the future is to respond to the demands of a rapidly changing information world and the expectations of users, while maintaining its existing strengths. Past experience over 300 years shows that the Society will rise to the challenge.

NOTES

1. SAL, Minutes, I, 17, 24 Dec 1718; ibid, 28, 16 Dec 1719.
2. Evans 1956, 58–60.
3. SAL, MS 268, fol 2; Evans 1956, 57.
4. The 1562 design for the new spire of St Paul's Cathedral by the Office of Works: see Pierce 1963; Evans 1956, 77. Talman died in 1726, and the Society spent £9 9s 6d at the auction of his collection the following year.
5. SAL, MS 265, fols 55v–56r: see Needham 1986.
6. Evans 1956, 116; Antiquaries Correspondence (MS collection in SAL library): 1754 report of Henry Baker.
7. SAL, MS 138; for other manuscripts received by then, esp MSS 48 and 67, see Willetts 2000, xi–xii.
8. Henry V (described as Henry VII), Edward IV (described as Edward III) and Elizabeth of York (now missing). Purchased at a cost of £2 13s 10d: see Evans 1956, 64, and SAL, Minutes, I, 11, 7 May 1718.
9. Emanuel 2000; Richmond 1950.
10. Evans 1956, 66–7.
11. Kortholt 1735, 10: *bibliothecam parvulam illam quidem, sed cuius plutei libris redundant, quos figurae aeneae exornant exquisitae* (translation in Bruce-Mitford 1951, 14).
12. Evans 1956, 86; SAL, Minutes, II, 160, 4 Mar 1736.
13. Hall 1992, 9.
14. Bodleian, Eng. Misc. e. 128, p 97: quoted by Evans 1956, 100–1. Rawlinson's original will left many of his possessions to the Society; he changed this in 1754, after failing to be elected to Council, and left all his collections to Oxford University instead: see Tashjian 1990.
15. SAL, Minutes, VII, 135, 20 June 1754.
16. SAL, Minutes, VIII, 21, 5 May 1757; Lemon 1866; Pantzer 1982.
17. Pierce 1965.
18. SAL, MSS 1, 5, 6, 51, 139–153: see Willetts 2000, xii.
19. SAL, Council Minutes, I (not paginated), 27 Apr 1769.
20. Evans 1956, 159, 178; SAL, Council Minutes, I (not paginated), 23 Apr 1774. The contents of MS 138 (letters to Oliver Cromwell) were mostly published before being presented in 1747.
21. SAL, Council Minutes, I (not paginated), 21 Feb 1770 and 20 Mar 1771; Evans 1956, 162–3.
22. Evans 1956, 162.
23. SAL, MS 447/1, fol 215, nd: quoted in Evans 1956, 180; see also Sweet 2004, 98.
24. Evans 1956, 177 and 317–18; SAL, MS 760. The room is currently used by the Courtauld Institute Galleries as a bookshop.
25. Evans 1956, 178.
26. Willetts 2000, xiii, xvi.
27. Campbell 1974. Douce wrote to the Secretary, urging that 'the Society should direct their draughtsman to make accurate drawings of these most precious relics, in order to preserve a faithful remembrance of them'.
28. Dickens 1837, ch XI. The inscription was later deciphered as 'BILL STUMPS HIS MARK'.
29. SAL, Council Minutes, IV, 473–4, 17 June 1828; ibid, IV, 483, 25 Nov 1828.
30. SAL, Antiquaries Papers: report of John Gage, 19 Apr 1831.
31. Tudor-Craig 2004.
32. Nichols 1828, IV, 597. For a description of the Kerrich collection, see Way 1847 and Scharf 1865.
33. Twenty years later, the Resident Secretary, J Y Akerman, wrote to see if it could be hung in the refreshment room of the University of London Senate: Antiquaries Correspondence, Akerman, 18 Jan 1849.
34. Evans 1956, 216; plans c 1847 in SAL, Plans SH2 at 196i.
35. Roe 1993, 216–21, compares the two catalogues in detail.
36. Carlisle 1816.
37. Evans 1956, 226.
38. Roe 1993, 79–81; for Colt Hoare's library, see Nichols 1840 and Woodbridge 1970.
39. Evans 1956, 245; SAL, Council Minutes, V, 134–5, 1 Mar 1836.
40. Peter Prattinton, for example, who was not a Fellow, was allowed to borrow MSS 143–148 on 7 June 1810: see Willetts 2000, 244 (MS 520).
41. Sweet 2004, 107, quoting Nichols 1817–58, VI, 662.
42. SAL, Council Minutes, III (not paginated), 20 Feb 1786: Evans 1956, 89.
43. SAL, Council Minutes, III (not paginated), 20 Feb 1798.
44. Bodleian, Eng. poet.c.5, fol 145: quoted in Evans 1956, 217.
45. SAL, Library Loans Register, 1798–1846.
46. Evans 1956, 240 and 245; SAL, Council Minutes, IV, 292, 12 May 1815; Hall 1992, 20.
47. SAL, Drawings Collection: *Personal Ornament* 18.1, *Utensils and Furniture* 45, 46, *Early Medieval Antiquities* 60. The Witham bowl was first published in Kendrick 1941, 161, and more recently in Campbell 2004. Drawings in these albums were digitized in 2004 and can be seen via the Society's website (<www.sal.org.uk>). For an overview, see Lewis forthcoming. For the Secretary, Christopher Knight Watson's, work in the 1860s, see *Proc Soc Antiq Lond*, 2nd ser, 4 (1867–70), 19 Nov 1868, 155.
48. Barnard 1931. Prattinton's drawings are now MS 520/I; LTS 1923–4: Capon's views are now MS 500. There was a revival in commissioning at the end of the nineteenth

century when G E Fox drew the mosaics and other finds from the Society's excavations at Silchester and C J Praetorius drew objects for illustration in *Archaeologia*. Both produced fine watercolours, which are in the Society's collections.

49. An early fifth-century BC Etruscan torch holder: Way 1847, 5, cat. no. 12; Evans 1956, 250.
50. Evans 1956, 257.
51. Ibid, 300; Scharf 1865.
52. *Proc Soc Antiq London*, 2nd ser, **2** (1861–4), 23 Apr 1863, 256–7.
53. SAL, Council Minutes, v, 322, 16 Dec 1845.
54. *Proc Soc Antiq London*, 1 (1843–9), 21 May 1846, 140–1.
55. SAL, Library Committee Minutes and Papers (for the years 1846–52; not paginated): report by Robert Lemon on the binding and arrangement of the library, 16 Nov 1846.
56. *Proc Soc Antiq London*, 1 (1843–9), 11 Nov 1847, 211–12; *Proc Soc Antiq London*, 2nd ser, 1 (1859–61), 20 Dec 1860, 283–4.
57. *Proc Soc Antiq London*, 2nd ser, 1 (1859–61), 17 Nov 1859, 8.
58. Ibid, 23 Apr 1860, 140.
59. SAL, Council Minutes, VI, 212, 3 May 1853; gifts of books are still tabled at meetings.
60. Roe 1993, 221–30.
61. Watson 1864.
62. *Proc Soc Antiq London*, 2nd ser, 3 (1864–7), 17 Nov 1864, 14.
63. Perceval 1867.
64. Lemon 1866; Bloomfield 1996.
65. Roe 1993, 251–5. By 2000 about 250 exchanges were in place, mostly for the *Antiquaries Journal*.
66. Roe 1993, 277; SAL, Library Committee Minutes (for the years 1853–1919; not paginated), 17 Feb 1862.
67. Willetts 2000, xvii–xix; Barnard 1931.
68. SAL, Council Minutes, v, 396–8, 5 Feb 1847.
69. SAL, Plans SH1 at 196i: P F Robinson, architect.
70. Evans 1956, 256.
71. Ibid, 300.

72. *Proc Soc Antiq London*, 2nd ser, 6 (1873–6), 23 Apr 1875, 358.
73. Evans 1956, 313–18; Stanhope commented on the library's 'tranquil situation' at the Society's first meeting in Burlington House.
74. Levine 1986, Appendix IV, 182–3.
75. Roe 1993, esp pp 256, 283 and 338–40.
76. Willetts 2000, xv–xvi.
77. Schofield 2006.
78. *Proc Soc Antiq London*, 2nd ser, 19 (1902–3), 23 Apr 1902, 114; Evans 1956, 362; Nurse 1996.
79. Evans 1956, 363.
80. *Proc Soc Antiq London*, 2nd ser, 31 (1918–19), 203–9; the gift by the late Dr Pierre Chaplais in 2000 of his collection of 358 examples of seals of different types and from different periods has further extended the Society's collection.
81. Roe 1993, 230–5.
82. *Proc Soc Antiq London*, 2nd ser, 24 (1911–12), 238.
83. *Antiq J*, 7, 371; Evans 1956, 395; SAL, Carnegie Trust file: memorandum of 21 Apr 1926; SAL, Library Delivery Book 1929–30.
84. Willetts 2000, xx–xxi; a new picture catalogue is in preparation (2007).
85. De Cardi 1988.
86. SAL, Visitors Book, 1934–9. There were 392 visits by non-Fellows in 1926, but 1,340 in 1930 and 2,128 in 1938/9. Between 1934 and 1939, the number of Fellows varied considerably: from 1,762 visits in 1934/5 to 3,166 in 1935/6 and 2,597 in 1938/9. In 1974, 2,461 visits by non-Fellows were recorded (343 first-time visitors and 2,118 repeat visitors).
87. SAL, Royal Archaeological Institute file: P Corder, Memorandum to the Executive Committee on the use of the library by the RAI, 11 Mar 1958.
88. For editorial comments in *Antiquity* on the decline in artefact studies in British universities, see Stoddart and Malone 2001, followed by Colin Burgess's remarks on p 663 of the same volume. In 2003–4, visits by 1,986 Fellows and 885 other readers were recorded.

BIBLIOGRAPHY

Barnard, E A 1931. *The Prattinton Collections of Worcestershire*, Evesham
Bloomfield, B (ed) 1996. *A Directory of Rare Books and Special Collections in the United Kingdom and the Republic of Ireland*, 2nd edn, London
Bruce-Mitford, R 1951. *The Society of Antiquaries of London: notes on its history and possessions. First issued on the occasion of the bicentenary of the Society's Royal Charter, 2 November 1951*, London
Campbell, J G 1974. 'A Viking hoard from Ireland', *Antiq J*, 54, 269–72

Campbell, J G 2004. 'On the Witham bowl', *Antiq J*, 84, 358–71
Carlisle, N 1816. *A Catalogue of the Printed Books in the Library of the Society of Antiquaries of London*, London
De Cardi, B 1988. 'Miscellaneous collections in the possession of the Society of Antiquaries of London', *Antiq J*, 68, 287–90
Dickens, C 1837. *The Posthumous Papers of the Pickwick Club*, London

Emanuel, R 2000. 'The Society of Antiquaries' Sabbath lamp', *Antiq J*, **80**, 308–15

Evans, J 1956. *A History of the Society of Antiquaries*, Oxford

Hall, M B 1992. *Library and Archives of the Royal Society 1660–1990*, London

Kendrick, T D 1941. 'A late Saxon hanging-bowl', *Antiq J*, **21**, 161–2

Kortholt, C 1735. *De societe antiquaria Londinensi*, Leipzig

Lemon, R 1866. *Catalogue of a Collection of Printed Broadsides in the Possession of the Society of Antiquaries of London*, London

Levine, P 1986. *The Amateur and the Professional: antiquarians, historians and archaeology in Victorian England*, Cambridge

Lewis, E forthcoming. 'Drawings of antiquities in the Society's albums c 1750–1860', *Antiq J*, **87**

LTS (London Topographical Society) 1923–4. *Views of Westminster . . . by William Capon*, London

Myers, R and Harris, M (eds) 1996. *Antiquaries, Book Collectors and the Circles of Learning*, Winchester

Needham, S P 1986. 'Towards a reconstitution of the Arreton Hoard: a case of faked provenances', *Antiq J*, **66**, 9–28

Nichols, J 1817–58. *Illustrations of the Literary History of the Eighteenth Century*, 8 vols, London

Nichols, J 1828. *The Progresses . . . of King James the First*, 4 vols, London

Nichols, J B 1840. *Catalogue of the Hoare Library at Stourhead, Co. Wilts*, London

Nurse, B 1996. 'The library of the Society of Antiquaries of London', in Myers and Harris (eds) 1996, 153–8

Pantzer, K F 1982. 'Ephemera in the STC Revision: a housekeeper's view', *Print Hist*, **4**, 36–8

Perceval, C S 1867. *Catalogue of the Collection of Works on Pageantry Bequeathed to the Society of Antiquaries by Frederick William Fairholt*, London

Pierce, S R 1963. 'Note on a drawing for a new spire for old St Paul's London', *Antiq J*, **43**, 128–31

Pierce, S R 1965. 'Thomas Jenkins in Rome', *Antiq J*, **65**, 200–29

Richmond, I A 1950. 'Stukeley's lamp, the badge of the Society of Antiquaries', *Antiq J*, **30**, 22–7

Roe, B J 1993. 'The libraries of archaeological institutions during the eighteenth and nineteenth centuries', unpublished MPhil thesis, University of Wales Aberystwyth

Scharf, G 1865. *A Catalogue of the Pictures Belonging to the Society of Antiquaries, Somerset House, London*, London

Schofield, B 2006. 'The Charles Hall Crouch legacy', *Bookplate Journal*, new ser, 4/1, 15–18

Stoddart, S and Malone, C 2001. 'Editorial', *Antiquity*, **75**, 4–5

Sweet, R 2004. *Antiquaries: the discovery of the past in eighteenth-century Britain*, London

Tashjian, G R 1990. *Richard Rawlinson: a tercentenary memorial*, Kalamazoo

Tudor-Craig, P 2004. *Old St Paul's: the Society of Antiquaries Diptych, 1616*, London

Watson, C K 1864. 'Report on the state of the library', *Proc Soc Antiq London*, 2nd ser, **3** (1864–7), 17 Nov 1864, 7

Way, A 1847. *Catalogue of Antiquities, Coins, Pictures and Miscellaneous Curiosities in the Possession of the Society of Antiquaries of London*, London

Willetts, P 2000. *Catalogue of Manuscripts in the Society of Antiquaries of London*, Woodbridge

Woodbridge, K 1970. *Landscape and Antiquity. Aspects of English culture at Stourhead, 1718–1838*, Oxford

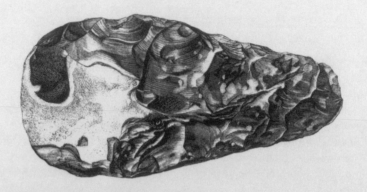

1.

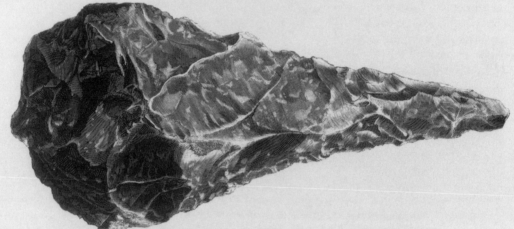

2.

3.

Plate XV.

FLINT IMPLEMENTS FROM THE VALLEY OF THE SOMME.

(*Full size.*)

CHAPTER TEN

PREHISTORY IN THE
NINETEENTH CENTURY

C Stephen Briggs

As currently accepted and understood, the identity of prehistory, fully equipped with a three-age chronology and the time-depth of human antiquity, remained conceptually immature until well after the appearance of Sir John Lubbock's *Prehistoric Times* in 1865, when words recognizing 'Palaeolithic' and 'Neolithic' were introduced. Although the eighteenth century had seen some advances in archaeological methodology, an overriding impression of its legacy today is of the antiquarianism dominated by Stukeley's obsessive Druidism and archaeo-astronomy.[1] By the mid-nineteenth century antiquaries had developed a better understanding of Roman and medieval archaeology, and thus became 'historical archaeologists'.[2] But to advance and broaden their agenda, and to define and accept a more distant human past with reliable chronologies would require input from several new disciplines as well as improved archaeological methodologies and credible supporting interpretations. Geology and comparative ethnography were vital, but little progress could be made without improvements in field survey and excavation techniques. Precise mensuration would enable better graphic – if not a three-dimensional – appreciation of monumental structures to set artefact associations within stratified cultural contexts.

Before there could be any measure of understanding about prehistory, two important conceptual hurdles had to be cleared. The more fundamental was to establish a geological time-depth for the antiquity of man. This would have to be complemented by an agreed chronology of successive cultural developments. The discussion which follows is meant to consider the Fellowship's involvement in these achievements, and how prehistory was conceived, born and grew into a challenging adolescent before the end of the century. It considers to what degree Fellows developed, absorbed, used or disseminated 'new' ideas, and how ideas came to be advanced, retarded, accepted or rejected. It also asks whether these ideas were affected by considerations of personal taste and standing or limited access to publication, and whether they became subject to national sensibilities.

Towards the end of the eighteenth century the empirical reasoning that had driven the first half-century of the Royal Society's activities after 1660 was being re-embraced. Having lain at least partially dormant for about seventy years, it began to facilitate a new phase of scientific interest and discovery. A more deductive

Fig 69. 'Flint implements from the valley of the Somme', drawn at full size (plate xv from Evans 1859). This plate, unaccompanied by a graphic stratigraphy, was engraved at Sir John Evans's own expense. *Photograph*: Society of Antiquaries of London.

discipline emerged, clearing the path from antiquarian speculation to archaeological method, and outmoding the primacy of classical learning, though leaving Druids omnipresent well into the nineteenth century. Initially, progress was slow, as antiquaries needed to take a deep breath to inhale and establish more facts at first hand.

At first, the Society had an important role to play in this resuscitation by acting as a forum for debate and, after 1770, by publishing its Fellows' contributions in *Archaeologia*.[3] But it was not alone. The new Society of Antiquaries of Scotland, founded in 1780,[4] and the establishment of the Royal Irish Academy in 1785[5] also invigorated that process. These were complemented by the founding of the Linnean Society[6] in 1788 and of the Geological Society[7] in 1807. From 1831 the British Association for the Advancement of Science held annual meetings which were to become the arenas for debating some of the most controversial geology-related issues of the day. Most famously they included evolution, but glaciation and cave stratigraphy had obvious relevance for archaeology.[8] Finally, the establishment of an Ethnological Society in 1843,[9] and an Anthropological Society in 1863,[10] combining to become the Anthropological Institute in 1872,[11] would contribute importantly, bringing greater eclecticism and coherence to European studies of prehistory.

This new spirit of enquiry emerged from the Enlightenment movements of both Old World and New.[12] Threatening the established order with popular ideas of democracy, they led first to the Revolutionary and then to the Napoleonic Wars on the Continent. In Britain it particularly invigorated the world of Scottish learning. For British gentry generally, the Napoleonic Wars effectively meant an end to the Grand Tour as they knew it.[13] But the Continent's loss brought greater progress at home, with opportunities for more thorough aesthetic, antiquarian and scientific explorations of the British Isles. Consequently, home-based picturesque tourism was being undertaken by the later 1780s to satisfy the curiosity of men (and women) drawn from an increasingly broader social spectrum than hitherto.[14] These travellers came from the clerical, professional and emergent industrial and merchant classes. Also among them was a small band of government surveyors and a sprinkling of university academics.

To judge from the bourgeoning tourist literature, from county and local histories and from analysis of *Archaeologia*'s contents, prevailing antiquarian interest in later eighteenth-century Britain was still focused on the Romans and their occupation.[15] As such importance was attached to the conquerors, the natives were still overlooked and pre-Roman monuments continued to be misattributed to the Romans or Danes in consequence. More positively, the Roman conquest offered a useful threshold of technological and social change against which to measure native achievement. For example, through descriptions of artefacts and waste products, Thomas Pennant believed it possible to distinguish between Roman and British approaches to metallurgy.[16] And whereas some important attributes of these Britons had been well defined by seventeenth- and eighteenth-century antiquaries, Stukeley still left confusion about such basic questions as who had built Stonehenge and when. So the prehistoric peoples of Britain would remain primeval and British throughout much of the period under discussion.

228

THE BARROW DIGGERS

If there was to be an understanding of the pre-Roman past, refined investigative methodology would be paramount. Here James Douglas, in 1793, published his contribution to a series of excavations on Anglo-Saxon barrow graves in Kent begun in 1730 by Charles Fagg and Cromwell Mortimer[17] and continued by Bryan Faussett.[18] Douglas's avowed adherence to deductive interpretational principles helped give a fillip to barrow investigation nationally.[19] His followers were curious to discover the contents, if not also the ages, of the many burial mounds which populated much of the still-uncultivated landscape. By 1800 sporadic forays were being made into these mounds the length and breadth of Britain, and by the middle of the nineteenth century up to a couple of thousand had been opened.[20]

Digging into ancient Wiltshire

The most important early nineteenth-century digging campaign on groups of largely pre-Roman mounds, or barrows, was begun on Salisbury Plain around 1800. It included Sir Richard Colt Hoare, a *nouveau riche* landowner;[21] William Cunnington,[22] a wool merchant and self-educated geologist;[23] Archdeacon William Coxe, cleric and historian,[24] and Philip Crocker, a surveyor in the government service.[25] They were usefully advised by the Revd Thomas Leman of Bath, a classicist.[26] Leman's interventions were not always welcomed and MacGregor describes his manner as 'stultifying'.[27] Excepting Crocker, all were Fellows of the Society. After Coxe had been eased from his lead role, they teamed up under Colt Hoare, who accepted financial responsibility for the digging. In return, he took the descriptive and illustrative material and even some of his colleagues' interpretational apparatus for his *Ancient Wiltshire* (1812–19) during an episode carefully analysed by Simpson in his introduction to the 1975 reprint.[28] Cunnington's part in the project is known from three manuscripts in his daughters' hands, not only describing the events as they unfolded, but also explaining his own interpretations of what they exhumed.[29]

Stukeley's legacy of classification to these new enthusiasts was clear. Round barrows were for Druids; being much larger, long barrows were therefore the graves of Arch-Druids. The process of questioning this wisdom was slow, though some of Stukeley's sites could be re-excavated. Dr J Thurnam later produced a useful correlation between Stukeley and Colt Hoare's barrows and their classifications.[30] Although a more developed view was that long barrows represented Saxon war cemeteries,[31] by 1803 William Cunnington believed 'that the earliest barrows were for inhumation and were accompanied by stone implements; cremation was introduced "long before the arrival of the Belgae"; but both customs prevailed at the same time, and at a very early period in this country'. Cremation must have lasted longest because (excluding secondary interments) the proportion of cremation to inhumation was eight to one. But cremations were never accompanied by articles which can be considered Roman and the practice must have been given up before the Roman conquest.[32] He also used the scarcity of iron in the barrows to strengthen his argument for their greater age, and his reading from recent observations of early Greek burial monuments reinforced their 'high antiquity'. Thus, by 1803 Cunnington was pronouncing Saxon mounds to be very rare and could confidently exclude the Danes and Phoenicians from authorship of any Wiltshire barrows.[33]

Some sites were believed to produce evidence for the slaying of Britons by Romans.[34] Four years on, he had no hesitation in stating that 'many of the tumuli on the Wilts and Dorset Downs contain urns with burnt bones and ashes of the Celtic Britons, which have been interred from five hundred to a thousand years before Caesar's invasions'.[35] Though prescient for its day, his introduction of this concept of distant time was alien to contemporary projections, then still inhibited by Ussher's Biblical date of 4004 BC for the world's origins.

As early as 1798, having dug around the larger stones of Stonehenge, Cunnington opined how 'our ancestors . . . were not so barbarous nor so ignorant of the arts as some suppose them when the Romans first invaded this isle'.[36] Later, after an examination of both the uprights and the stone chips found there and in nearby excavated barrow soils, he reached one of his more important deductions: Stonehenge must be pre-Roman. Initially, Colt Hoare was content to follow his proposal in *Ancient Wiltshire*,[37] though not everyone agreed, and Avebury and Stonehenge were being ascribed a date 'not earlier than the third century of the Christian era' as late as 1840.[38] Long later rehearsed a lengthy history of opinion on the subject.[39] But there were points of detail and even of interpretation where Colt Hoare was to publish his own, rather conservative, views, over Cunnington's more radical insights reached from mature on-site deduction. As is shown in the second volume of *Ancient Wiltshire*, his conservatism became more pronounced after Cunnington's death in 1810. Having made remarkable progress in archaeological interpretation through excavation, Cunnington died believing in the pre-Roman origins of barrow burials. Colt Hoare, however, almost turned the clock back on this intellectual achievement in the second volume of his *Ancient Wiltshire* in 1819, by firmly advancing barrow burials forward to the Dark Ages.[40]

Another important step in understanding came from Cunnington's basic classification of earthworks. He recognized hillforts as British (giving British origins for such earthworks as Knook Castle and Chiselbury in 1803 when his contemporaries still considered them Danish or Roman);[41] he proposed hut-groups as unfortified villages, and saw monuments with ditches inside their banks (henges) as civic or religious monuments.[42] One difficulty in establishing any lasting chronology in his day was that studies of stratification in an archaeological sense were then only in their infancy.[43] Regarding hillforts, Cunnington was keen to know how far the French earthworks compared to those he knew, so he asked Sir Joseph Banks, reasoning that if the foreign ones were similar, Saxon and Danish origins could be dispensed with in Wiltshire.[44] Although his approach to Banks proved in vain, Colt Hoare also appreciated the significance of this question, and – having compared the Welsh sites to Wiltshire's – supported Cunnington's thesis.[45]

In an intellectual sense Cunnington, not schooled in the classics, but with long experience and insight into practical landscape problems, sat uncomfortably among his peers. His own view of contemporary antiquarian learning is best summed up in a letter written to Thomas Leman in 1808:

> I must observe that I have ever had the highest respect for people who have had a liberal education like yourself, but I contend that the information to be gathered from the Roman & Greek historians will afford little information as data for illustrating Abury, Stonehenge, Marden &c &c, the works of an ancient people like the Celtic Britons.[46]

Although Colt Hoare has long been credited with advancing British prehistory through this Wiltshire barrow campaign,[47] it might be argued that his legacy to barrow studies was more managerial than scholarly. The practical and intellectual initiator, the critical mind central to these investigations and interpretations was William Cunnington. Stimulated and part-tutored by Leman, Cunnington, the practical geologist, emerged from the campaign as a new archaeologist or proto-prehistorian. As his biographer cogently remarked, 'Hoare never seems to have realized what Cunnington had done to free archaeology from the tyranny of books'.[48] Although constrained by the conventions of his own education, Colt Hoare initially, at least, paid lip service to Cunnington's unusual intellect, boldly introducing *Ancient Wiltshire* with the (now well-known) proclamation: 'We Speak From Facts, Not Theory'.[49] This he followed up with twenty-three pages combining an analysis of Cunnington's decade of field investigation with seemingly endless classical quotations which all but annulled the value of his pronouncement.[50] Apparently a tolerant individual, intellectually speaking, Cunnington cannot have found this very satisfactory. And he would certainly have been upset by some pronouncements in the later volume had he lived to read it. Because so few scholars could ever have afforded to publish so lavishly, once in print *Ancient Wiltshire* was, *de facto*, the instant authority and classic on its subject. If Colt Hoare had felt able to support Cunnington's open and critical, if not also radical, approach, it is possible that British prehistory might have developed more reliable recording techniques, chronologies and deductive methodologies sooner than it did.

Excavation methodologies and barrow analyses

MacGregor has noted the general absence of plans and sections from *Ancient Wiltshire*, cogently observing how when Cunnington published independently of Colt Hoare in 1802 and 1806, he, at least, 'was perfectly capable of intelligently observing and recording the stratigraphy of tumuli opened in Wiltshire'.[51] Unfortunately, Colt Hoare did not require section drawings. Furthermore, he reacted unfavourably to Cunnington's efforts at raising greater awareness of soil differences (*inter alia*) in their barrow excavations. Probably more interested in acquiring artefacts than in knowing

Fig 70. Before and after
records of a barrow
excavated by the Revd
Anthony Freston at
Duntisbourne Abbots,
Gloucestershire, in
1806: upper drawing
originally entitled 'No. 1
South East View of the
Barrow before it was
open'd'; the lower one
entitled 'No. 2 The
Hoar Stone – NB.
Below the dotted line is
under ground' (source:
SAL, *Primeval
Antiquities*, 54.2;
Freston 1812: plates
(engravings) dated
9 January 1806, sewn
in between pp 362–3,
pl LVII). *Photograph*:
Society of Antiquaries
of London.

Fig 71. Before and after
records of a barrow
excavated by the Revd
Anthony Freston at
Duntisbourne Abbots,
Gloucestershire, in
1806: originally entitled
'No. 3. The Kistvaen
before it was open'd'
and 'No. 4. The
Kistvaen after it was
open'd' (source: SAL,
Primeval Antiquities,
54.2, Freston 1812,
pl LVI). *Photograph*:
Society of Antiquaries
of London.

their exact contexts, Colt Hoare didn't encourage Crocker or Cunnington to provide what he saw as superfluous details from their sondages. He could hardly see the point of more expensively cutting down barrows to ground level (so as to interpret the sections better) or appreciate Cunnington's fastidiousness when insisting on the prompt labelling of finds or when submitting buried soils or stones to experts.[52]

A better appreciation of stratigraphy than Colt Hoare's was certainly required to achieve and progress the understanding of excavated structures and the contexts of finds. And outside Wessex, at least one barrow digger, the Revd Anthony Freston, produced a more appropriate visual record, with illustrations of an excavation at Duntisbourne Abbots (Glos) in 1806. It appeared in *Archaeologia* the same year as the first volume of Colt Hoare's *Ancient Wiltshire* (figs 70 and 71).[53]

John Yonge Akerman, FSA (a serial barrow digger who boasted to C J Thomsen in 1851 that he had opened more barrows in Kent than anyone else),[54] also showed little general inclination to the graphic record of excavated structures. In 1844, however, he at least promoted the practice by publishing a plan and three-dimensional barrow section, drawn by one Matthew Bell, presumably a local landowner (see figs 79c and d in chapter 11).[55]

The tragedy of Douglas and Colt Hoare's limited, though much-quoted, achievement was that the value of stratigraphy was rarely to be appreciated in excavation for most of the first half of the nineteenth century. There were odd exceptions. For example, as early as 1827 the Revd T Rankin, vicar of Huggate in East Yorkshire, drew and described in detail the cross-section of a local burial mound. But that remained unpublished in his day.[56] Similarly, although F C Lukis, FSA, drew meticulous sections of the tombs he excavated during the 1840s and 1850s, only one seems to have seen the light of day in print. In a paper sent to the new British Archaeological Association, Lukis begins with the internal stratigraphy of a megalith at L'Ancresse, Guernsey (fig 72).[57]

Whatever the methodological shortcomings of the early antiquaries, they inspired such curiosity that barrow digging had become a fashionable national pastime by the 1840s. Discoveries were regularly reported in the *Gentleman's Magazine*,[58] *The Times*[59] and in most regional newspapers, many of them repeated in the 'nationals'. This digging was often accompanied by a zest for antiquity collecting. In consequence, the exploration of English monuments to the dead would provide the greatest quantity of evidence for pre-Roman life until the third, if not the final, quarter of the century, by which time artefact typology and settlement studies were being taken far more seriously.

FIELD SURVEY AND THE INTERPRETATION OF SETTLEMENT SITES

A basic understanding of settlement-site morphology was, however, progressing slowly. And – Cunnington and Colt Hoare apart – few earthworks were published in detail until much later in the century.[60] In Ireland, the Ordnance Survey's Topographical Survey produced dozens of good-quality scale drawings and sections of

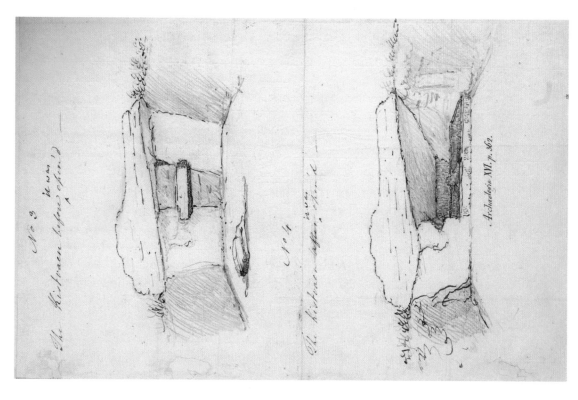

Nº 3

The Kistvaen before open'd

Nº 4

The Kistvaen after open'd

Archæologia XVI. p. 362.

Nº 1

South East View of the Barrow before open'd

situated in the parish of Daglestworth Stokets in Gloucestershire.

Archæologia XVI. p. 362.

Nº 2

The Hoar Stones —
B. Below the dotted lines is under ground.

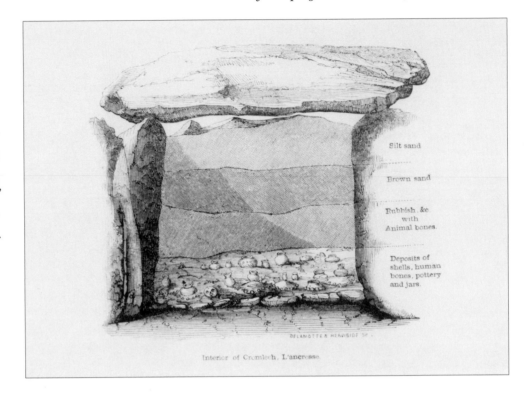

Interior of Cromlech. L'ancresse.

Silt sand

Brown sand

Rubbish, &c
with
Animal bones.

Deposits of
shells, human
bones, pottery
and jars.

Fig 72. Cross-section of a chamber of the megalithic tomb on L'Ancresse Common, Guernsey, prefacing F C Lukis's 'Observations on the primeval antiquities of the Channel Islands' in the first volume of the *Archaeological Journal*, 1845, p 142. *Photograph*: Society of Antiquaries of London.

Fig 73. Extract from a composite plate which illustrates probably the first published depiction of a co-axial field system from Britain, on Baildon Moor, Yorkshire (source: SAL, *Primeval Antiquities*, 38.3; originally published in *Archaeologia*, 31, 1846, by J M N Colls as pl VIII, between pp 306 and 307). *Photograph*: Society of Antiquaries of London.

monuments – prehistoric and later – during the 1830s,[61] but these remained unused and largely unpublished until after 1930. Measured and drawn up by disinterested surveyors, they are of remarkable quality for their day and often capable of useful reinterpretation.[62] In England, Wales and Scotland, surveys at a smaller scale were introduced by the Ordnance Survey in the 1850s, but even these better 25in. printed plans never achieved the graphic quality so frustratingly promised so early in Ireland.

As the century progressed, antiquaries throughout Britain increasingly described and planned features now known to be prehistoric. In 1846 *Archaeologia* published one of the earliest records of what was probably an Early Bronze Age co-axial field system on Baildon Moor in Yorkshire, by J M N Colls (fig 73).[63] This had been anticipated, though not in print, by a similarly accurate scale-drawing of Grimspound on Dartmoor of 1829 ('supposed to be An Ancient British Town'), surveyed as interest grew in non-sepulchral monuments. This is 'arguably the first adequate plan of a prehistoric site to be drawn in Britain'.[64] And by the time the geologist John Phillips had measured up the huts inside Ingleborough's 'great hill-fort of the Britons' in 1851,[65] similar (usually basic) records of hillforts had appeared in county histories[66] and were being published in the journals of national and county archaeological and natural history societies.

Notwithstanding this growing graphic testimony to 'British' settlements, when Thomas Wright, FSA,[67] wrote about 'British Villages' mid-century, he did so almost exclusively still in the context of Colt Hoare's *Ancient Wiltshire*, as if nothing had happened since. But, as will later be appreciated, Wright was to remain conservative

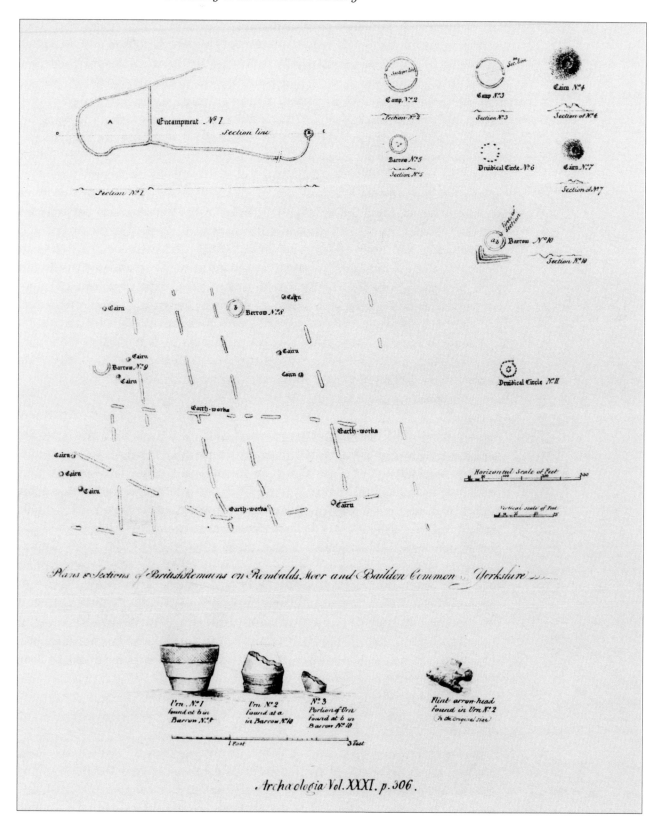

Plans & Sections of British Remains on Rombalds Moor and Baildon Common. Yorkshire

Archæologia Vol. XXXI. p. 306.

235

and exclusive in his citations of contemporaries' work to the degree that the Three Ages remained absent from his popular textbook, *The Celt, the Roman and the Saxon*, right up to its last edition in 1886.[68] By then, most continental scholars had already agreed their monuments' place within a clearly defined and subdivided prehistoric past. As early as 1846 J G Ramsauer, a mine surveyor, had begun his systematic survey of the now well-known Hallstatt cemetery and the adjoining salt mines in Austria. His appropriately scaled coloured plans and cross-sections are a remarkable three-dimensional graphic record[69] and it is difficult to appreciate why more British antiquaries should not have published work of similar quality. Some provincial anti-quaries did grasp the real value of graphic observation, however. The barrow digger Thomas Bateman, FSA,[70] set an important example, but unfortunately not everyone followed: Charles Warne, FSA, produced but one credible section in the monograph he devoted to barrows,[71] and the landmark *British Barrows* of 1877 by William Greenwell, FSA, is quite bereft of graphic testimony for structures. Llewellynn Jewitt, FSA, popularly promoted the sites and must have generated a climate more sympathetic to mensuration and graphic depiction, by illustrating a variety of barrow and cairn plans and their related sections in his publications of 1870[72] and 1877.[73]

Nowadays, General Pitt-Rivers[74] is generally thought of as the main exponent of section drawing in the archaeological community after about 1860.[75] But many of his 'sections' only gave height lines, without indicating stratigraphy. It seems his first proper barrow plan was made on Ganton Wold about 1866, and comes from one of Canon Greenwell's campaigns.[76] Joan Evans long ago noted[77] how little Pitt-Rivers published with the Antiquaries so, unsurprisingly, his landmark stratigraphies appear elsewhere – for example, in the journal of the Anthropological Institute, which printed one of the first attempts at a three-dimensional graphic depiction of a later prehistoric excavation, through his Cissbury cuttings of 1875 (see fig 82c in chapter 11).[78] It was not until Cranborne Chase in the 1880s that plans and stratigraphic sections really became the norm on his earthwork excavations.[79] So whereas plans and distribution maps had early been seen as basic components of the archaeologist's publishing apparatus, the visualization of two- and three-dimensional stratigraphies took much longer to accept. It says little for the national archaeological societies that initially they left it to regional barrow diggers to practise and promote better, if not sometimes then the best, survey and excavation recording techniques.

THE THREE AGES: CLASSICAL, ENGLISH OR DANISH INVENTION?

The Royal Society of Antiquaries of the North

While Colt Hoare was writing up Cunnington's investigations for *Ancient Wiltshire*, Denmark became a casualty of the Napoleonic Wars, when, through the Treaty of Kiel in 1816, she lost Norway to Sweden. A period of serious national insecurity of at least half a century followed, culminating in Denmark's loss of Schleswig in 1864 through invasion by Prussia.[80] Within a decade of this treaty, in 1825, a new historical society had been founded in Copenhagen – Det Kongelige Nordiske Oldskriftselskab, the Royal Society of Antiquaries of the North. Its activities would have a major impact on the development and understanding of European prehistory.[81]

The Northern Society's original intention was to re-examine Viking history through translating and publishing Denmark's extensive saga literature, but its founders also promoted archaeological research and excavation. Furthermore, it emphasized the country's need for a collection of national antiquities to illustrate its own past, and for provincial archaeological exhibitions to be made available as handmaids to public education. An ethnographic dimension also left Copenhagen with one of the most comprehensive collections documenting the material culture, *inter alia*, of the North American Indians. So the Society's objectives were truly international.

The achievements of Carl Christian Rafn (1795–1868), the society's founding secretary (1825–65) (and an Icelandic scholar with considerable business acumen) have not hitherto attracted great interest among historians of archaeology.[82] However, the society could not have prospered without him and, by the 1830s, it was producing both saga literature and archaeological journals in Danish, English and French. As a charitable publishing body it had few peers in the world of nineteenth-century learning. 'A Worldwide Danish Cultural Activity'[83] admirably describes Rafn's vision, since, by 1850, the society had a global and influential membership of about 2,000, a significant number admitted on life subscription so that almost perpetual publication was guaranteed from the invested capital.

C J Thomsen, national antiquities and the Three Age System

Nowadays, archaeologists abroad tend to remember C J Thomsen for his legacy to the organization of museums rather than for his role in the Northern Society. After beginning a national collection in 1807, he established a home for it in the Christiansborg Palace, Copenhagen, in 1832, having already devoted much time to popularizing museums and preserving monuments. As the keeper of this Royal, then National, Museum, he developed an empirical approach to organizing the artefacts and he proposed a 'Three Age Classification System' for the fledgling collection as early as 1815.[84] This particular classification first appeared in print when, in 1836, Rafn saw the opportunity to make known Thomsen's accumulated experience alongside that of other Danish scholars in a *Guide to Northern Archaeology* (in Danish), promoting the society's several interests.[85] Its availability, at the time in Danish and only later in translation, may have limited the degree to which it has been read and appreciated. Rafn's book sought to explain the Danish past through the society's activities, and particularly drew on its literary achievements in saga translation. So to call this a 'guide to the Copenhagen Museum' is misleading of the Danes' real intentions.[86]

Thomsen was not the most natural writer and those in Rafn's circle were hardly cast as popularizers, so their texts were not an easy read. Nonetheless, as this *Guide* circulated to subscribers worldwide, it afforded the 'Three Age System' (as it came to be known) critical scrutiny from a literary, if not also a scientific public. Sadly, being in Danish, few members abroad could read it, and anyway, outside Scandinavia, most were more interested in northern saga literature than in museum collections or the definition of a prehistoric past. Meantime, personal contact with Scotsmen had helped the full force of Thomsen's influence visibly to penetrate the Scottish antiquarian tradition.[87]

It is today hardly appreciated that Thomsen was made an Honorary Fellow of the London Antiquaries as early as 1829. His letter of acceptance mentions Sir Charles William Watkins Wynn, the eminent Welshman and politician,[88] who seems to have had a hand in the Dane's preferment. Wynn had seen the museum in Copenhagen (where he later became British ambassador), but it is unclear how far his enthusiasm for the 'Danish museum arrangement' or Thomsen's services to numismatics sparked off this recognition. Thomsen's letter to Wynn tantalizingly mentions the museum,[89] though unfortunately without any detailed insights.[90] It may be significant that only the year before, in 1828, Edward Hawkins, FSA, then the recently appointed Keeper of Antiquities at the British Museum, had already known something of the Danes' museum achievements. These he forthrightly pointed out in a memorandum to his trustees while campaigning – apparently with the backing of senior Fellows at the Antiquaries – for closer attention to be paid to developing a collection of (British) national antiquities.[91] Whereas the Society's wily secretary, Nicholas Carlisle, was importuning Rafn for personal 'recognition' through an award of the Royal Order of Danebrog around this time,[92] evidence for other British Antiquaries' contacts with contemporary Danish archaeologists before the 1840s is at present thin.

In fact, there was something of a lull in English antiquarian developments over the next fifteen years, and an uncritical view might suggest that it took J J A Worsaae's visit to awaken the nation to the need for a collection of British antiquities in the British Museum. An examination of the events of those years, however, suggests that the museum was not quite as bereft of displayed British antiquities as some contemporary and later critics have implied. It appears, for instance, that in 1839, alongside casts from the metopes of the Temple of Jupiter in Sicily, 'in the temporary building attached to the fifth room of the British Museum', were several glass cases containing scale models of the Trevethy Stones, the Chun and Lanyon Quoits, and the Plas Newydd and Dyffryn megalithic tombs.[93] They were overlooked by three oil paintings dramatizing Plas Newydd 'cromlech', the Great Tolmen of Constantine (Cornwall) and Stonehenge.[94] Both paintings and models had been donated by their artist and creator, Richard Tongue. Public curiosity was also attracted to a dug-out canoe from near Petworth, Sussex, exhibited out in the courtyard.[95]

A further little-known fact about C J Thomsen is that he visited the major museums and monuments of southern England in 1843. At the British Museum he was singularly unimpressed by 'the British antiquities everywhere covered in dust and not much esteemed', also largely without provenances.[96] This event probably went largely unnoticed by contemporaries because not being an evangelical tour, it contributed nothing to the growing debate on national antiquities.

Occasional notices of the Danes' proposed chronology were finding their way into English-language books around this time, however. The earliest came from the works of the physical anthropologist, James Cowles Prichard. First in 1841, then in editions of 1843 and 1845, he explained the Three Age System when writing on 'Arian Races, Europeans to Greeks'. This he ascribed not to Thomsen, but to the findings of 'Professor Eschricht . . . in a recent paper . . . published in . . . *Danske Folkblad*'.[97]

In the meantime, Hawkins continued to press his trustees on what he saw as the nation's requirements for a display of British antiquities in the capital's expanding institution.[98] Such actions clearly demonstrate a frustrated will among some contemporary antiquaries to advance the cause of British archaeology that has, so far, escaped the notice of its historians.

By this time, the German edition of the Royal Northern Society's *Guide* had reached England, where it was read in 1844 by Francis Egerton, the first Earl of Ellesmere.[99] A competent German scholar, he immediately suggested translating it, then, after experiencing some personal set-backs, paid to have it printed in Copenhagen in 1848.[100] This was eventually distributed *gratis* to learned bodies and to the society's members throughout the English-speaking world.[101] Unfortunately, Ellesmere's great benefaction and the impact of the book's original message were largely eclipsed by W J Thoms's translation of a similar work by Thomsen's junior, J J A Worsaae, which appeared the following year.[102]

J J A Worsaae

Jens Jacob Asmussen Worsaae was born in Vejle, Denmark, in 1821.[103] He developed a schoolboy interest in archaeology, and from 1838 worked voluntarily for C J Thomsen on the Royal Collections in Christiansborg. Thomsen and Worsaae, however, were not well matched, and the master seemed unable to find his talented pupil a salaried museum post.[104]

Undeterred by this initial lack of success, Worsaae published several controversial, if not also authoritative, articles. So in 1843, Rafn's society in Copenhagen commissioned him – with King Christian VIII's encouragement – to produce a second and new introduction to Danish archaeology. This appeared in Danish later that year,[105] and in English translation in 1849.[106] Its radical approach touched on runes, inscriptions, bog bodies and ethnography against the background of Thomsen's Three Ages. A lively work, it ventured well beyond the descriptive to employ archaeology and history in a transparently nationalistic call for Danes to use their past to help resist foreign domination (most obviously from Prussia). Less controversially, it aimed to raise a national consciousness for conservation, if not also preservation, and a greater curiosity for recognition and discovery. Readers abroad, sceptical of such blatant nationalist proselytizing through antiquarianism, might have found that aspect of the work offputting and its author's views irritating or even threatening, particularly given Denmark's place in the delicate balance of power in north-west Europe (incidentally, Rowley-Conwy has demonstrated that both Ellesmere and Thoms's translations on occasion departed significantly from their original, Danish, texts, largely to accommodate British archaeological taste).[107]

Worsaae's British and Irish tour of 1846–7

In common with its predecessor multi-authored volume, the initial circulation of Worsaae's book in Danish could not have attracted a wide readership abroad. However, Worsaae's credo was circulating Europe within a year in German translation. And meanwhile, as a rising star, he was able to travel abroad, mainly under royal patronage. In 1846–7 he toured Britain and Ireland,[108] going first to London, where Ellesmere wrote introductions and generally promoted his interests.[109] Worsaae's reputation had gone before him and there, to his surprise and delight, William Thoms was already translating *Dänemarks Vorzeit* into English and selecting appropriate text figures for local readers.

By his own account, the Dane was much sought after for lectures in the capital and indeed recalled that his maiden paper in English to the Society of Antiquaries won general applause.[110] It is, however, unclear quite which paper he was referring to, as none is recorded in the minutes.[111] Writing at such a remove, he may have confused some events of 1846–7 with a lecture he gave later, in 1852.[112] During this first visit he was certainly made the first twenty-five-year-old Honorary Fellow of the Society in May 1847.[113] He was also welcomed by the British Archaeological Association, where he made two interventions and was afforded honorary status in June 1846.[114]

In Edinburgh Worsaae met 'a much freer archaeological and historical atmosphere . . . than in England', where interest in the classical and exotic still prevailed, and where the Anglo-Saxons were afforded a cultural and historical importance disproportionate to other early cultures. The patriotic, formerly independent, Scots had tried to preserve a past that was 'quintessentially Scottish'.[115] He was admitted to the Society of Antiquaries of Scotland's museum, where he also made a presentation, though that was not published either.

R B K Stevenson at one time suggested that the Scottish Antiquaries' museum adopted 'the Copenhagen arrangement' as early as 1844, though on present evidence such an early date is difficult to sustain. He also drew attention to Worsaae's visit in relation to the Treasure Trove laws and to the consequent exchange of museum material with Denmark.[116] If the arrangement had existed prior to his arrival in Edinburgh, it would have been due to the influence of contacts with the Northern Society which brought artefacts into the Society's collection in 1815,[117] through David Laing's contacts made during a visit to Denmark in 1819,[118] or as a result of the Crown Prince of Denmark's artefact presentation made in 1844 during a royal visit to Edinburgh.[119] If the 'Copenhagen arrangement' was not in place before 1846, Worsaae not only had a profound and immediate effect upon its introduction to the museum, where it remained largely intact until the 1990s; he probably also influenced Daniel Wilson and his museum presentation by 1849,[120] and also in the way *The Prehistoric Annals of Scotland* of 1851 was structured,[121] as manifest in the organization of the work into four ages, the last being Christian. Curiously, Edinburgh was the only place in the British Isles where the Danes' Three Age System was so readily adopted.[122]

Worsaae was in Dublin over the winter of 1846–7, where in November he gave the first of two talks at the Royal Irish Academy.[123] An influential lecture, delivered impromptu, it interpreted the history and archaeology of early Hiberno-Norse relations and explained the organization of the Christiansborg museum. Although here he again explained Thomsen's Three Age System, his thrust was on the importance of forming collections of truly national antiquities.[124] This must have seemed a heaven-sent message, and the Irish Academicians seized upon it, hoping to lobby the (British) government for improved resources to promote scholarship and the Irish national collections.

In 1846–7 Worsaae had found in Dublin 'a finer and better arranged collection of antiquities than [was] to be seen in London or Edinburgh'.[125] Not long after his visit, in 1850–1, it was decided to catalogue this, the academy's museum (later to become the National Collection), and George Petrie was entrusted with making a 'more scientific arrangement' than then obtained.[126] There is evidence to suggest he had already arranged his private collection on Three Age lines.[127] But Petrie's progress was so slow that it was soon put in the hands of Dr (Surgeon) William Wilde to ensure completion.[128] Although Worsaae wined, dined and befriended ladies in Wilde's company while in Dublin,[129] at first sight the surgeon seems hardly to have been convinced by the Three Age System, for the Preface to his first part of the *Catalogue* asserted in 1857:

> The classification adopted in the arrangement of the Museum, and in this Catalogue, Is that according to MATERIAL and USE, irrespective of *Age*, for which latter we do not at present possess sufficiently authentic materials to enable us to adopt as a basis of arrangement the 'Period' theory of Scandinavian writers.[130]

And indeed, the academy's *Catalogue*, one of the most comprehensive publications of its time, seems relatively free of prehistoric periodization, with most early Irish peoples remaining unashamedly 'ancient', which seems odd, particularly as, in 1844, Wilde had produced a relative chronology of prehistory integrating traditional, Irish Annalistic references with the Scandinavian Three Age System.[131] Wilde, however, had probably been influenced by J M Kemble's attack on the Three Ages,[132] only a month before he was himself put forward to complete Petrie's catalogue, which he did on 16 March, to be in time for the British Association meeting in Dublin later in 1857.[133] Kemble (an FSA) had lectured on 9 February but died on 26 March. His bland entry in the *Dictionary of National Biography* hardly explains Kemble's contentious views or their significance.[134] The aberration on Wilde's part seems to have been temporary, however, since his integrated Three Age System was re-presented within the text of the fuller catalogue in 1861,[135] where it lies uncomfortably with his unchanged preface.

At this point, it may be useful to pause and speculate on what might have been the outcome had someone other than a Dane developed the Three Age System so early in the century. The system was, importantly, the culmination of a development of logical ideas, rather than a notion which could be exclusively attributable to Thomsen, as Alexander Rhind,[136] Sir John Evans[137] and Sir John Lubbock were all later to explain. Lubbock, indeed, introduced this into a defensive discussion on the Three Ages in the second edition of his *Prehistoric Times*.[138] All three authors pointed out how the classical writers had proposed relative materials-based ages within the ancient world, and that others, including British eighteenth-century scholars, had considered pre-Christian and pre-classical traditions as sources indicative of deductive thought on early chronology. In a comprehensive appraisal of the impact of the Three Ages in Britain, Rowley-Conwy has usefully distinguished between an earlier and more theoretical *tripartite system*, representing more traditional and classically based notions of a distant past, and the *Three Age System*, which was the Danes' practical way of classifying museum artefacts and placing them clearly within a chronology of stone, bronze and iron.[139]

It is well known that German writers proposed a system similar to that of the Scandinavians in the early nineteenth century.[140] Notwithstanding this long and complex history, the late Glyn Daniel was at pains to argue how 'Thomsen was the first to put forward the system on empirical grounds'.[141] To propose Thomsen as its sole progenitor, however, not only ignores these acknowledged contributions of contemporary scholarship abroad, but also overlooks the possibility of a significant input at home.

It has been noted how Cunnington argued by empirical deduction. So having examined the finds from several hundred Wiltshire barrows sites, his attraction to a tripartite system is unsurprising, though it was tempered by an appreciation that the artefacts of many barrows could be heavily mixed. The more visionary views of Cunnington's critic and friend, the bookish Thomas Leman,[142] were less loaded with caveat:

> I think we distinguish three great eras by the arms of offence found in our barrows, 1st those of bone and stone, certainly belonging to the primeval inhabitants in their savage state, and which may be safely attributed to the Celts, 2nd those of brass, probably imported into this island from the more polished nations of Africa in exchange for our tin, and which may be given to the Belgae, 3rd those of iron, introduced but a little while before the invasion of the Romans. The Britons on the coast from Essex to Lands-end at the time of Caesar's invasion were Belgae, a nation totally distinct from the Celts.[143]

Leman's brief analysis, obviously comparable to the Danes' simple Three Age System, has been accepted by recent writers, though there has been little speculation on its potential implications for antiquarian history.[144] His conclusions were based less on the artefacts, and more empirically on their circumstances of discovery, or contexts. According to one friend, Leman was 'a man of extraordinary talents, possessed of a natural bold genius, quick penetration, and almost unlimited knowledge'.[145] So there is irony in the late Richard Atkinson's remark that Leman's 'dogmatic opinions . . . would now, perhaps, repay further study as a formative influence in the history of British archaeology'.[146] The development of prehistoric studies in Britain would no doubt have benefited had Colt Hoare more strongly promoted this Leman–Cunnington concept in his *Ancient Wiltshire*.

In a later context, Lubbock's first defence of the Three Ages[147] suggests that 'Sir Richard Colt Hoare . . . expresse[d] the opinion that instruments of iron "denote a much later period" than those of bronze'. In later editions he added: 'Colt Hoare alludes to instruments of stone before the use of metals was known'.[148] Neither quotation is sourced, and no other critic seems to have referred to them. In fact he seems only to allude to a period 'before the use of metals',[149] and may have taken that from Cunnington.[150] That Colt Hoare was not prepared to promote and elaborate on Leman and Cunnington's interpretations only serves to underline his lack of commitment to a better-defined 'British' chronology. Blinded by conventional learning, he was ill equipped to take up that challenge, which, had it then been better championed, might have anticipated the Danes' publication by a quarter of a century.

BRITISH PREHISTORY IN ADOLESCENCE

If, before Worsaae's visit, British antiquaries had been unaware of Scandinavian proposals for a cultural and material-based chronology of the ancient past, or of the Danes' aspirations to universal education through museum displays, these became difficult to ignore thereafter. Timely reminders soon appeared in the form of Ellesmere and Thoms's translations. And with two new national British and one Welsh archaeological society formed in the 1840s, and many more local groups focused on counties and towns by the middle of the century,[151] the scene ought to have been set to apply commonsense principles to museum artefact displays throughout the land in the better interests of archaeological interpretation and public understanding.[152] But that would not easily be achieved.

Antiquarianism had been undergoing dramatic changes reflecting the processes of a society experiencing socio-economic revolution since the beginning of the century. By the late 1840s, it had shifted from a mainly gentleman's pursuit and was becoming a more socially inclusive affair. That is not to suggest that it was without social division. Far from it: Charles Roach Smith's letters to J J A Worsaae's of 1846–75[153] and the contemporary press[154] offer an explicit record of snobbery and prejudice.[155] Some 'traders' – amateurs whose income came direct from industry, shop-keeping or merchandizing, and whose pedigrees, social or educational backgrounds did not fit older conventions – were accepted, but with reluctance.[156] In retrospect, however, these class and educational distinctions were not as significant to contemporary intellectual developments as was the divergence that had for some time been growing between traditional classicists, medievalists and art or architectural historians (the historical archaeologists), and those scholars who, through archaeology, geology and the natural or even social sciences, were now progressing a more radical investigative agenda into the remote human past.

The two decades prior to Worsaae's visit had been difficult for the Society of Antiquaries, and its troubles were to continue for some time thereafter.[157] By 1840 the Fellowship was seriously dissatisfied with its own governance, though it had little idea what to do about it.[158] *Archaeologia* apart, there was no effective publication to promote its scholarly values. The *Proceedings*, begun as a gesture towards improvement only in 1843, were mainly abbreviated and bland records of meetings and administrative matters. The introduction of steel engravings in 1849 hardly added the sort of colour expected or needed. More disturbingly, during the 1840s and 1850s the *Literary Gazette*, the *Gentleman's Magazine* and *The Athenaeum* permitted greater insights into the Antiquaries' activities than were available through its own *Proceedings*. Some journalists (or moles from among the frustrated Fellowship) willingly exposed the Society's shortcomings, like the commentator of 1846 who wrote how the Antiquaries 'have yet much to do before they can elevate [the Society] to that rank among the scientific establishments of England which it ought to hold'.[159] A report in *The Times*,[160] openly accusing the Society's outgoing President, the Earl of Aberdeen, of apathy and inattention to duty, did little to improve its image.[161]

Through defection, the foundling rival societies, the British Archaeological Association and the Royal Archaeological Institute, also robbed the Antiquaries' Fellowship of some of its potential for effective officers, particularly between 1843 and 1846;[162] some simply abandoned the Society in frustration. Differences of approach and opinion expressed openly and unpleasantly during the 'great split' bringing the second new body into being[163] only served to confirm long-held public prejudices about how antiquaries traditionally behaved. This was sadly a climate that could only distract an increasingly curious public from absorbing those seminal new ideas that were now poised to alter for ever perceptions of Britain's, and the world's, distant human past.[164]

Revolutionary change: the antiquity of man

By numerical analysis of the papers on prehistoric topics published in major English archaeological journals, van Riper has demonstrated[165] how the 1850s were a low point in prehistoric studies.[166] Nonetheless, by 1850, fundamental investigations into the human past were proceeding apace in geological circles and would soon revolutionize an understanding of early man and prehistoric archaeology. The story of those investigations is told concisely by Oakley,[167] in greater detail by van Riper[168] and from a French viewpoint by Laming-Emperaire.[169]

The Antiquaries had themselves already enjoyed a fleeting glimpse of the Palaeolithic at the very end of the eighteenth century when, in 1797, John Frere, FSA, read his now well-known 'Account of flint weapons discovered at Hoxne in Suffolk' to the Society.[170] Frere's paper describes a brick-pit stratigraphy yielding 'weapons of war, fabricated and used by a people who had not the use of metals. They lay in great numbers at a depth of about 12 feet [*c* 3.8m], in a stratified soil'. One of these Acheulian ovates (for such they were) is illustrated here (fig 74). Frere felt: 'The situation in which these weapons were found may tempt us to refer them to a very remote period indeed, even beyond that of the present world . . . the manner in which they lie would lead to the persuasion that it was a place of their manufacture and not of their accidental deposit.' This paper apart, little is known of Frere's archaeological activities,[171] leaving it difficult to appreciate the intellectual development that led to his making one of the most visionary statements in the development of prehistory.[172] Whatever Frere's inspiration, it says much for the enlightened spirit of the London Antiquaries that they published his work at a time when nobody could make much sense of it and when its value as a key to the Palaeolithic could not be appreciated. Frere's would become an essential part of the supporting evidence when similar finds were made later, in Britain, France and elsewhere. Had the Geological Society already existed in 1797, this primacy of discovery might not have belonged to the Antiquaries.

Similar finds of flint ovates were made in stratified deposits during the half-century after Hoxne, but any claims of great antiquity were muted, largely because of religious prejudice. Cunnington's early appreciation of stratigraphical principle was to be shared by Dean William Buckland and William Pengelly in their later cave excavations. But even Buckland, probably the foremost geologist of his day, whose critical work introduced the notion of 'deep time',[173] found his religious convictions challenged after discovering a human skeleton at Goat's Hole, Paviland.[174] So although he produced a superb section of the cave's deposits as an exemplar for archaeologists to follow,[175] by later deterring McEnery from publishing his vital stratigraphy-based conclusions on the antiquity of man at Kent's Cavern, Torquay,[176] Buckland probably contributed to setting back stratigraphic archaeology in Britain by three decades.

Fig 74. Palaeolithic ovate hand-axe from Hoxne, found in 1797, first described by John Frere and illustrated by T R Underwood (source: SAL, *Primeval Antiquities*, 21.4; originally published in *Archaeologia*, 13, 1800, between pp 204 and 205, as pl xv). *Photograph*: Society of Antiquaries of London.

But field observation increasingly flew in the face of the Biblical story. And this began to support the potential for a relatively recent Ice Age. Complementarily, Darwin's work interrogating the potential for evolution in animal and plant life, also from first-hand field and laboratory observations, slowly came into the public domain from the late 1830s and made it easier to understand the physical potential for human evolution. Some of this science gradually enabled stratigraphic geology to marry physical and cultural archaeology and so to define the Palaeolithic as the earliest stage in human development.

Sir Arthur Keith's retrospective of this changing intellectual climate suggests how, between 1849 and 1860, it was 'a small company of Englishmen . . . [who] . . . gave Man a new history of himself and of his civilization'. He noted their gradual conversion from the Ussherian chronology, and explained how by 1860 'the small Darwinian advance-guard had torn [it] to tatters and carried man's history into an unlimited past'.[177]

Three independent prehistorians

Between 1850 and 1865, three signal contributions were to advance the course of prehistoric archaeology in all its forms. The first was Daniel Wilson's *Prehistoric Annals of Scotland* in 1851, a work introducing the very name of its new science.[178] A late infant of the Scottish Enlightenment, it was strongly influenced by the 'Scandinavian System' and set a valuable framework for prehistoric cultural studies, giving them a particular resonance in the British–Irish context.[179] Unfortunately, in England, some antiquaries probably saw it as an icon of nascent nationalism.

A second and even more momentous advance then introduced the concept of the more remote antiquity of man. This happened in 1859 and was inspired principally by geology. John Evans was a paper manufacturer whose main passion was numismatics.[180] He joined the Fellowship in 1852, unfettered by the baggage of conventional classical learning.[181] During the 1850s, with growing interests in archaeology and geology, he became fascinated by finds of the very earliest artefacts being made in British deposits and in the Somme gravels of northern France. At Amiens, Boucher de Perthes had inherited a project of stratigraphic exploration in the 1830s.[182] This apparently linked human artefacts with extinct faunal species (fig 75). Although extensively published,[183] probably as much on account of his vanity as due to conservatism within the scientific community, Boucher de Perthes had been unable to convince the French establishment that his artefactual discoveries were coeval with Pleistocene mammals.[184]

In 1858 Joseph Prestwich, who held the chair of geology at Oxford, and who was already working on the stratigraphy of Brixham Cave (Devon) and its archaeological implications,[185] was asked by his friend Hugh Falconer[186] if he would examine the French evidence.[187] Consequently, John Evans – a friend of Prestwich's – met him in Amiens in May 1859. Boucher de Perthes took them home, which (to quote from Evans's diary) was 'like a museum from top to bottom'.[188]

246

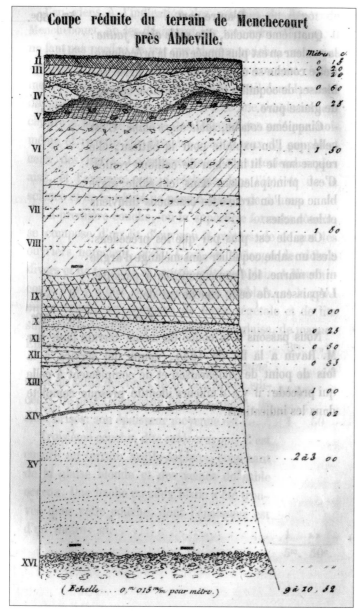

Compressed section of the deposit at Menchecourt near Abbeville
Explanation of the section:

Modern soils and alluvium
I   Surface soil of black organic humus
II   Lower organic soil, a mixture of humus and sand

Diluvial or water-washed deposits (of Brogniart's classification) to water-washed detrials
III   Brown sand, lower level
IV   Upper layer of rolled and flaked flints, interdigitated with lumps of white marl and pieces of rolled chalk
V   Compacted brown ferruginous clay

Loess sections
VI   Sandy marl dotted with shattered flint and white crust
VII   Gravelly clay (quarrymen's *'greasy' clay*)

Gravelly sand sections (VI–XIV waterborne loess of Brogniart's classification)
VIII   Fragments of pea-sized rolled chalk mixed with flinty gravels; these deposits pass through the marl-sand deposit (VI) at various levels
IX   White clay indurated with a vein of ochreous sand
X   Bed of white gravel (quarrymen's *sharp sand/gravel*), containing small fragments of rolled chalk and broken shell
XI   Gravelly grey clay
XII   Ochreous veined clay and gravel
XIII   Pure grey clay
XIV   Ochreous vein

Water-borne detrials
[Gravels]
XV   Alternating strata of oblique-bedded grey and white sands (the quarryman's sharp white sand); these are the sands which mainly produce the shells and early bones
[With Pebbles]
XVI   The lower deposit of rolled and flaked flint

The two heavy lines in layer XV indicate where flint axes were found.

The evidence they sought was visible and obvious in the gravel pits. Well-shaped artefacts could be pulled from Pleistocene bone-bearing strata. They returned hotfoot to London, where Prestwich addressed a receptive audience at the Royal Society,[189] and Evans spoke at the Antiquaries.[190] These presentations stamped joint geological and archaeological imprimaturs on the remote age of humans, vindicating and contextualizing John Frere's precocious vision, and, by implication, strengthening the credibility of Darwin's evolutionary thesis. Theirs was a ground-breaking revelation.

The Society then published John Evans's account of the Somme gravels in *Archaeologia*[191] and excitement at the discoveries spilled over into the *Proceedings*,

Fig 75. A section from the Somme gravels: Boucher de Perthes, *Antiquités celtiques et antédiluviennes*, 1849, 'Coupe réduite du terrain de Menchecourt près Abbeville', pp 234–5.
Photograph: author.

where an abbreviated account was printed to accommodate interest before his more definitive paper appeared.[192] It seems significant to an understanding of the contemporary publication process that this *Archaeologia* paper is illustrated by fine engravings of the artefacts, the costs of which were part-defrayed by the author (fig 69 demonstrates their quality). Unfortunately, Evans's account is accompanied neither by plan nor by any graphic stratigraphy indicating the artefacts' contextual positions. He went on to publish further discoveries from the drift in the next *Archaeologia*,[193] and on artefacts of Grand Pressigny flint in the one after that[194] – but these, too, were bereft of stratigraphic sections. The reason is hard to appreciate, unless Evans felt the historical archaeologists would have difficulty understanding them. Perhaps stratigraphy itself symbolized the growing difference between the old antiquarianism and new scientific prehistory?

Outside London, the thirst for news of these findings spread rapidly through effective press releases and, in August, Robert Chambers noted the Somme discoveries at a meeting of the Scottish Antiquaries.[195] Closer to home, John Kenrick, FSA, exhibited some of Sir John Evans's flint implements to the Yorkshire Philosophical Society in York, while pertinently reminding his audience that 'the historian must . . . enlarge his ideas of past duration beyond the narrow limits to which systematic chronology has hitherto confined us'.[196]

Lubbock's Prehistoric Times

The third and most influential work in this trilogy of investigative discovery came in 1865. To a degree it mirrored Sir Charles Lyell's new (geological) work on *The Antiquity of Man*, published in 1863: this was Sir John Lubbock's *Prehistoric Times*.[197] It first appeared in 1865, succinctly combining all the earlier new messages and eventually achieving seven editions by 1914. Its expanding text over that half-century became a veritable chronicle of the developing study, acting both as commentary and as leader in the reportage of British and European – if not also of world – prehistory and anthropology.

Elected to the Society only in 1864 (seven years after election to the Royal Society), though not actually admitted until 31 May 1866,[198] Lubbock was of a wealthy banking family,[199] schooled at Eton and mentored by Darwin. Sharing John Evans's independence of mind, and without religious prejudice, he, too was unaffected by an Oxbridge education or traditional classical learning. His intellectual convictions were the search for truth and promoting universal education. In these pursuits, his institutional loyalties were soon found to lie more with the Royal Society, the Royal Institution and the Ethnological Society than with the Antiquaries. Unable to accompany Evans and Prestwich to the Somme in 1859, he had followed a year after their initial exposé. Subsequently realizing that polished stone implements did not occur in gravels associated with extinct fauna, possibly as early as 1860 he soon determined on the terms Palaeolithic and Neolithic to define and distinguish between the Old and New Stone Ages.[200]

Over the next five years Lubbock published several popular studies in the *Natural History Review* on prehistory at home and abroad. 'About Danish shell-mounds', 'Swiss lake dwellings', 'Flint implements of the Drift', 'North American archaeology' and 'Cave-men', they formed the basis of the first edition of *Prehistoric Times* in 1865.[201] Authors' copies of all these works were donated to the Antiquaries' library, but his gift of *Prehistoric Times* does not appear to have survived there. Although carefully planned, in antiquarian circles the book's reception was mixed. But with texts explaining Danish, French, Swiss and American archaeology as well as ethnographic and anthropological components, it appealed to a new and curious public avid for facts on global human development. But while recognizing the radical and valuable contribution of its author, one of Lubbock's reviewers, in *The Times*, brought Church and religion into the reckoning. And indeed (as with the impact of *The Origin of Species*), established religion was to impede its general acceptance for several years. In this regard, both the first (1865) and the second editions (1869) were considered to have contributed to impeding Lubbock's early Parliamentary career.[202]

The 'campaign' for prehistory at the Antiquaries, 1860–80

Although in 1859 news of these Palaeolithic discoveries rippled across Europe and the world beyond, the English antiquarian community was slow to grasp its implications. Indeed, there seemed to be some danger that such dramatic news of remote human ancestry might even adversely affect any progress so far achieved in its appreciation of pre-Roman chronology. Converting antiquaries to archaeologists by stimulating their curiosities with early chipped stones was not easy. Indeed, it is possible to gain the impression that the old antiquarian guard believed prehistory should be discussed at societies which represented geologists, anthropologists and ethnologists: in fact anywhere but in their own rooms at Somerset House.

For the twenty years after Amiens and the Somme, Sir John Evans enjoyed a comfortable press among geologists as one of their own, and as one also knowledgeable about 'Man among mammoths'.[203] Conversely, at the Antiquaries, he was accepted as a scholarly numismatist[204] with a mystique of geological knowledge which they would have preferred had little to do with their interests. He did, nevertheless, contribute dozens of short notices, exhibitions and discourses on prehistoric subjects to the Society's *Proceedings*.[205] But if the rate at which the historical archaeologists took up prehistoric interests is anything to go by, he trod a difficult path among their antiquarian ways.

So sluggish was the uptake, so unenthusiastic the Fellowship in matters prehistoric, that seeing his friend John Lubbock already losing interest in the Society, Sir John Evans began his own 'educational' campaign in 1871. He organized an exhibition of Palaeolithic implements from 18 to 25 May at which he spoke, and where A W Franks gave an address on cave paintings. Over 500 people, Fellows and others, visited and saw the exhibits.[206] Encouraged by its success, six months later Sir John 'delivered an[other] address, in which he called attention to the general classification of Stone Implements of the Neolithic Period, as illustrated by [a further] collection exhibited on this occasion'.[207] Then, to accompany a final exhibition, this one of bronze implements and weapons on 6 to 13 January 1872,[208] Evans rounded off his trilogy by confessing to diffidence and speaking with humility about shortcomings in his own expertise on the 'Bronze Period'. This, he pondered a little unconfidently, 'may have extended over a period of several hundred years'.[209]

All things considered, Sir John Evans displayed remarkable stamina as the evangelist of prehistory at the Antiquaries. Besides the clutch of important papers on Stone Age matters that he published outside the Society,[210] his *Ancient Stone Implements* and *Ancient Bronze Implements* of 1872 and 1881 are memorable as visionary, near-encyclopaedic works. Fundamental to studies of the British and Irish past, they remain cornerstones of European prehistory and mark him as a giant among its founders. It is, however, possible that any absence of greater periodization in *Ancient Bronze Implements* is owed to his continuing apprehension of censure at a time when he was still anxious to win over acceptance of the basic tenets of a distant past by the Fellowship (this real and effective censure is discussed below).

Sir John Lubbock fared similarly in the antiquarian community, and after *Prehistoric Times* first appeared in 1865, he seemed to enjoy a brief honeymoon period among them. Accordingly, in 1866 the Royal Archaeological Institute established a 'Primeval Antiquities Section', enabling him to explain the importance of the new science. It met only once, in the Geological Museum, Museum of Economic Geology, Jermyn Street, on 18 July, with Lubbock as President.[211] That no further recorded meeting took place might reflect the reaction of the audience to his pronouncement that 'the antiquaries of the present day are no visionary enthusiasts'.[212]

By the 1870s, and even into the 1880s, the acceptance of prehistory as a study in its own right appeared stronger outside the Fellowship than within it. So whereas John Evans presided at the Antiquaries in 1885–92,[213] that accolade never came Lubbock's way, though, unsurprisingly, both served as Presidents of the Anthropological Institute (Lubbock 1871–2 and Evans 1877–8).[214] More significantly, Lubbock presided over the Third International Congress of Prehistoric Archaeology (established in Italy in 1865) at its Norwich Congress in 1868.[215] Through that congress, and privately, he promoted prehistory internationally for the rest of his life. These international prehistorians were, in fact, a confident community to which both Sir John Evans and General Pitt-Rivers also belonged. Its gatherings attracted enthusiasts from most European countries and some beyond. Thus in 1874 a general absence of the English when it met in Copenhagen[216] is noteworthy, and underlines the under-representation of prehistory in English antiquarianism.

When it came to rapid dissemination of the results, it cannot have been easy for any serious researcher that *Archaeologia* effectively remained the Antiquaries' only larger format publishing medium until the *Antiquaries Journal* was established in 1921. So it is understandable that during the third quarter of the century, some

Fellows strongly committed to prehistory would have been torn by their institutional loyalties. Along with several other Fellows, Evans, Lubbock and Pitt-Rivers presented some of their most important work to the Ethnological and Anthropological Societies. This practice continued well into the 1880s.

Respecting the question of institutional affiliation, contemporary sponsorship of Joseph Anderson's work on the horned cairns of Caithness in 1865 is of considerable interest.[217] Anderson, a keen prehistorian with an intellect much in Daniel Wilson's mould, was to become the Keeper of the National Museum of Scotland in 1869. In 1865 these Neolithic explorations were conducted under the banner of the Anthropological Society of London and not of the London (or Scottish) Antiquaries.[218] This rather confirms that in 1865 the investigation of prehistoric sites fell well outside the Antiquaries' perception of their remit.

RESISTANCE TO CHANGE

The most visible resistance to the Three Age System within the Society came from J M Kemble and Thomas Wright. No less hostile, Albert Way[219] was an effective but covert reactionary. Rowley-Conwy discusses these personalities and their views at some length.[220] Way and Wright were accomplished medievalists, the latter also with strong inclinations to Roman studies. Besides them, there was John Crawfurd, influential President of the Ethnological Society (1861–8), who was not an FSA. A man of exceptional intellect, he accepted the great antiquity of humans but was anti-Darwinian and reactionary against both artefact classification and some aspects of evolutionary racial theory.[221]

The appearance of the *Prehistoric Annals of Scotland* in 1851 forced resistance to the Three Age System into the open. Though recommended in the *Gentleman's Magazine* and *The Athenaeum* as a valuable reference work for the United Kingdom as well as for Scotland (one review was probably written by Roach Smith),[222] its unenthusiastic reception by antiquarian institutions south of the border only served to emphasize differences between English and Scottish approaches to the British, native and pre-Roman eras. In 1845 Albert Way seemed open to discussion about new artefact classification systems;[223] furthermore, two sub-parcels of drawings among the manuscripts deposited with the Society by Way's family in 1874 entitled 'Age of Flint [Stein=Zeitalter]' and 'Age of Bronze' are annotated respectively 'Worsaae Dänemarks Vorzeit Alterthümer aus dem Steinalter' and 'Alterthümer dem Bronzealter'. These appear to reflect his familiarity with Worsaae's *Dänemarks Vorzeit* of 1844.[224] Although his undated notes survive, his catalogue to the Society's museum in 1847 betrays no obvious new influence.

Also, encouragingly, the Revd A Hume, the Lancashire antiquary, had employed the term 'Stone Period' in 1851 within months of the appearance of Wilson's *Annals*.[225] (He was one of the few Fellows who belonged to the Scottish, London *and* Northern Societies of Antiquaries.) Furthermore, when editing notes on the Scottish society's anniversary meeting of 28 November for the *Archaeological Journal* the same year, and obviously referring to the Danish 'system', Way explained how '*by this desirable arrangement* [the Scots'] collection . . . had been deposited in the Royal Institution as the nucleus of a National Museum for Scotland'. Apparently still then sympathetic to this 'new' arrangement, he also mentioned Daniel Wilson's museum guide of 1849. But while quite enthusiastically reviewing the two Three Age translations recently made from the Danish, his *Archaeological Journal* avoided all mention of Wilson's landmark prehistory. Neither is there a record of the book's immediate acquisition for the London Antiquaries' library, which possessed only the second, two-volume work of 1868.[226]

In 1856 the Archaeological Institute's annual meeting and temporary museum were held in Edinburgh. Overseeing a particularly full annual exhibition on this occasion, Way might have graciously acknowledged Daniel Wilson's up-to-date museum arrangement. But he seems to have ignored it[227] and apparently avoided the Three Age classification by carefully 'passing over the early antiquities' (as did his reviewer in the *Gentleman's Magazine*).[228] Both concentrated instead on the exhibited medieval archaeology and works of art. Having emigrated to Canada the previous year, Wilson was not present to witness this bizarre event.

Neither Worsaae nor his book seems to have won over Way in his editorial role at the *Archaeological Journal*, except perhaps to replace the terms 'British' (and in some cases 'Celtic' and 'pre-Roman') with 'Primeval'.[229]

Like the others, the radical polymath J M Kemble was a strong medievalist, though he also dug Iron Age sites on German soil.[230] While attending the Archaeological Institute's Scottish meeting in 1856 he attacked the Scandinavian system by addressing 'the materials characterizing the Heathen period'.[231] This seems to have been a prelude to a further exposé in Dublin that was probably responsible for deterring Sir William Wilde from the courage of his earlier conviction of a Three Age System.[232]

Kemble was not as influential as Thomas Wright, whose conservative influence on the Three Age System has been thoroughly discussed by Rowley-Conwy.[233] Wright, a very prominent Fellow, was one of the most prolific of the 'historical archaeologists' with a remarkably high output of publications: some important, some simply hackwork.[234] He was another who had to some degree befriended or given help to Worsaae during his first visit.[235] His attitudes were particularly influential because of the various offices he held. His *Celts, Romans and Saxons*, first published in 1852, a book with remarkable staying power given its increasingly heretical messages, soldiered on beyond the end of the century. At first its text pointedly ignored the Three Ages; later editions contrived half a dozen or more reasons why, on the face of it, the system could not possibly work. Wright's view of native British Britain was impaired by an old short chronology inhabited by a couple of waves of invading tribesmen.

Throughout later life Wright restated and even strengthened these views. At first this confrontational stance served him well among the (mainly historical) Antiquaries. Scepticism was, after all, healthy, and initially he carried many with him. But he also went on to reject the great *Antiquity of Man*, a position which was not sustainable for long. So as time passed and objections to the Three Ages slowly fell beneath the accumulated wisdom of long-term research, his views became increasingly isolated as the value of Thomsen's edifice was vindicated. Wright's was a classic case of the ageing academic not being sufficiently well advised to know when the argument was over.

Rowley-Conwy has clearly shown how these views impacted on an acceptance of the Three Ages during the 1850s, particularly on a prolific, publishing barrow digger like Thomas Bateman, FSA. At first receptive to a prehistoric chronology, Bateman changed his tune in 1852, at a moment closely coincident with the first appearance of *The Celts, Romans and Saxons*. Given that Wright was at this time one of the most powerful officers of the new British Archaeological Association, that Way was editing the Archaeological Institute's *Archaeological Journal* and that both remained respected Fellows of the Society of Antiquaries, the generally poor turn-out in submissions and publication of papers on prehistoric subjects to or from the three main societies during the decade 1850–60, so carefully documented by van Riper,[236] hardly seems surprising.

Even so, it is difficult to understand why a group of such established 'historical archaeologists' as Wright and Way were so reluctant to examine the 'facts' which underpinned the 'Scandinavian classification', or why Wright found it so difficult to take in the concept of 'Palaeolithic'. Perhaps it is significant that both were mature scholars at the time of these new developments; younger antiquaries are usually quicker to embrace change while, axiomatically, the older guard can sometimes be too set in its ways to follow suit.

DISCUSSION AND SUMMARY

Whatever its contributions to London's social life, a close examination of the Society's intellectual contribution shows how during the early to mid-nineteenth century it never achieved status as a dynamic forum to debate the developing science of prehistory. That had to wait until the 1870s and 1880s. With perhaps the sole exception of the lecture bringing startling news of the antiquity of man from the Somme gravels in 1859, we have to look to the Anthropological, Ethnological, Geological and Royal Societies for firm evidence of regular empirical discussion advancing the formative development of prehistory between 1840 and 1870.

The most important adoption necessary for antiquaries pursuing their study of the remote past was that of stratigraphy. At the beginning of the century Sir Richard Colt Hoare, the most influential publishing antiquary of his generation, was made aware of it by the excavator William Cunnington, who was a geologist. But, blinded by his ambition for ostentatious publication, the baronet was unable to recognize, effectively apply and promote it.[237] Dean William Buckland's religious fears and conventions then became responsible for another thirty years of set-backs, particularly in the interpretation of cave deposits.

Whereas three-dimensional visualization of stratigraphy and the spatial awareness vital to understanding buried deposits gathered momentum in Roman and medieval excavations at home and abroad during this period, there was little enthusiasm for section drawings in the exploration of prehistoric sites for the first three-quarters of the century. Some of the Society's better-known Fellows continued to excavate barrows promiscuously without good visual record right into the twentieth century. To win over the 'historical archaeologists' and the wider public, the new prehistorians (or 'prehistoric movement') needed to adopt *their* graphic practices. Unfortunately, the prehistorians were slow to grasp this need, and three-dimensional graphics did not come until the 1870s and 1880s. Some perceptions of methodology were probably aided by developments in Victorian excavation abroad. There is, however, a strong possibility that news of professional excavation recording practices had reached England from Sweden, to be adopted by Lane Fox through Lubbock's acquaintance with Sven Nilsson during the 1860s.[238] But in spite of such example, it seems that for the purposes of British prehistory the regular application of stratigraphic principles and attendant graphics had to wait until after the founding of the Prehistoric Society of East Anglia in 1915.

Unfortunately, when attempts were made to introduce a Three Age System from Denmark, much of the Fellowship resisted it. This resistance is the more difficult to understand when the Society had embraced both Thomsen and Worsaae by making them Honorary Fellows early in their careers. In this regard, it is useful to be reminded that acceptance of intellectual progress usually depends on the standing of its author and the quality of evidence presented. Since, during their visits to Britain, both Danes were welcomed as personable guests, it seems possible that here neither the necessary evidence nor its authors were accepted for their scholarship, owing to deeply held prejudice. Given the rationality of the Scandinavian system, such prejudice is, at first sight, difficult to understand, but xenophobia cannot be ruled out as a contributory factor. It seems particularly odd that Victorian Britain, a wealthy industrial nation, well served with old and new learned societies and an expanding literate middle class, should have lagged so far behind the Danes in their adoption of such a simple classification system.[239]

It probably took Lubbock's landmark *Prehistoric Times* of 1865 and some of the public sympathy or guilt felt at the annexation of Schleswig-Holstein the previous year to shake off lingering fears of the Danes' nationalistic agenda, and to overcome most old prejudices against their Three Ages.[240]

Although hardly given adequate credit for their achievement today, the first Earl of Ellesmere and his brother, the Duke of Sutherland, were instrumental not only in facilitating the process which brought the Three Ages to Britain; they also helped fertilize the seeds of much archaeological curiosity, especially on the Vikings. But although he accepted Fellowship of the Antiquaries, Ellesmere's involvement with the Society was incidental to his literary interests and archaeology was peripheral to his responsibilities involving national governance. Curiously, the other Fellow involved in translating the Three Age message, as the editor of *Notes and Queries*, W J Thoms, was himself more committed to literary historical pursuits than to any new archaeology, or indeed, to the Society of Antiquaries.

The Fellowship can certainly claim for its own the two most influential personalities in the development of contemporary European prehistory – Sir John Evans and Sir John Lubbock. Unfortunately, their polymathic interests in geology, anthropology and ethnography, underpinning increasingly confident investigations into the antiquity of man, were not easily accommodated by a Fellowship curious mainly on historical topics. Lubbock even hesitated before joining, only being elected a Fellow after *Prehistoric Times* was already well advanced for the press. Close inspection of his relationship reveals that Lubbock flirted only fleetingly with the Society. Its (unstated) rebuttal of his ideas appears to have been akin to the reaction of a mature lady to the attentions of an infatuated youth. In reality, Lubbock's agenda encompassed a far wider study of mankind and nature than could ever have been accommodated by any one interest group, so the Society was fortunate to receive as much of his attention as it did. Then, sadly for him, after a first flush of enthusiasm for tools of the French (and English) Palaeolithic, the Fellowship's affection for Evans cooled or assumed an ambivalence for some years, as it became the reluctant pupil to his determined tutoring.

So while Evans and Lubbock were fêted (*inter alia*) as radical young prehistorians at the Geological and Ethnological Societies, the Antiquaries were too hidebound to seize upon and celebrate achievements that could potentially have reflected great institutional credit on them. Indeed, it is worrying to speculate how different things might have been had the pair not been such wealthy men, neither of them owing his livelihood to archaeology. Even in that apparently liberal intellectual climate, would Sir John Evans have produced such a prestigious paper on the Somme gravels had he not been able to afford the plates to illustrate it? One contemporary critic actually portrayed Lubbock as 'favourably circumstanced'.[241] Without private means, could either scholar have afforded to exercise his independence of mind by publishing dissident convictions, irrespective of their contemporaries', and of the older generation's, prejudices and conventions? Both men were extremely fortunate that for any subject matter the Antiquaries found discomfiting or unpalatable, they were usually able to find publication outlets in the journals of at least one of the other learned institutions that they patronized.

Not only did Lubbock produce what is probably the most important textbook establishing prehistory in late nineteenth-century Britain, he went on to pioneer a series of Ancient Monuments Acts from 1870. They ensured the endurance of that fundamental heritage resource – the very life-blood of any future Fellowship. His monument protection campaigns probably helped break down some of the remaining barriers that stood between historical and prehistoric archaeologists, uniting them in a common cause.

The growth of prehistory in Britain during the nineteenth century very much reflected the nation's state of science and scholarship generally. It was dominated by scholars of means whose 'amateur' contributions would attain a high, if not the very highest, professional quality.[242] Although several among the Fellowship were university academics, with another handful of scholars at the British Museum, only one Fellow noticeably crossed the divide from amateur to professional archaeologist: that was Pitt-Rivers who, by becoming the first Inspector of Ancient Monuments and thereby enhancing the value of Lord Avebury's Ancient Monuments Acts, was enabled to practise for the public good everything he had learned privately.[243]

A subject only briefly touched upon here is the degree to which the British Museum trustees, their staff and the commissions which examined the institution in the 1840s were concerned to exhibit and promote a remote British national past.[244] Matters certainly changed for the better in the 1850s, after the appointment of A W Franks, FSA.[245] His informed but unsung national collecting policies – and his pragmatic interventions at the Antiquaries, the Royal Archaeological Institute and the British Archaeological Association and elsewhere – certainly did more to raise an awareness of British prehistory than either his contemporaries or posterity have given him credit for.

Prehistory would penetrate the Society's ethos slowly after 1860, with the Fellowship remaining sanguine about the need for a better-defined pre-Roman past at least until the 1880s. By that time, greater certainties arising from prehistoric explorations abroad (such as Schliemann's at Troy) helped ease a more confident appreciation of Britain's remoter past. And by 1868, the public was probably forcing the pace of interest when one journalist wrote: 'Prehistoric archaeology [was] both more intelligible and more entertaining to the multitude than more established or developed sciences. Its . . . range [was] comparatively narrow, its objects . . . singularly interesting, and it involve[d] as much conjecture as to forbid anything like dogmatism.'[246] Unfortunately, the Antiquaries and the two new societies were not to lose their influential conservatives, Wright and Way, until the early 1870s.

While Levine muses[247] that 'the infant discipline of prehistory approached its radical findings with some hesitancy', expansion of that analogy for the Society might be discomfiting. Failing to recognize their own obvious part in prehistory's parentage, the Fellowship largely denied its precocious childhood and adolescence, abandoning them to foster parents in other disciplines.

In both the public eye and among some of the Fellowship, British and European prehistory at the Antiquaries never really achieved the same popularity as Mediterranean, Near- and Far-Eastern exploration in the later nineteenth century. Some, no doubt, still hankered after evidence of a Biblical or classical past, if not also for maritime adventure. But by 1880, British prehistory was refining its chronologies and enjoying the time-depth of an older antiquity of man (though still not without some religious objections). It was also starting to benefit from museums and government policies designed to protect the remains of the more distant past, many of them initiated by luminaries of the Society. Thereafter, a curiosity for what used to be 'British' and 'Druidical' antiquities would be informed by a growing range of textbooks and papers, many of them inspired by Society Fellows and their activities, if not actually written by the members themselves.

ACKNOWLEDGMENTS

In writing this chapter I have been afforded kindnesses by scholars too numerous to mention. Among those who have granted ready access to material in their care, offered constructive criticism to my developing interpretations of it, or who have generously shared the fruits of their own research are: Trevor Cowie, Å Gillberg, Richard Haworth, Cherry Lavell, Elizabeth Lewis, Barry Marsden, Arthur MacGregor, Jens Steen Jensen, O W Jensen, Timothy Murray, Bernard Nurse, Brendan O'Connor, Anne O'Connor, Kate Owen, Michael Rhodes and Heather Sebire. Anne O'Connor and Peter Rowley-Conwy have been particularly helpful. Both loaned the texts of their own forthcoming publications and offered provocative discussion; furthermore, Peter unstintingly provided translations of obscure Danish antiquarian texts whenever they were needed.

NOTES

1. Piggott 1985, 79–109; Sweet 2004, 129.
2. van Riper 1993, 15–43.
3. Evans 1956, 147.
4. Bell 1981.
5. Ó'Raífertaígh 1985.
6. Walker 1988.
7. Woodward 1907; Porter 1977.
8. Morrell and Thackray 1981.
9. Penniman 1952, 66.
10. Bloxam 1893, iv.
11. Ibid, viii.
12. Gay 1969; Porter 2000.
13. Black 1999; Dolan 2001.
14. Andrews 1989.
15. Sweet 2004, 155–87.
16. Pennant 1778, 50–67.
17. BL, Add MS 45663 (formerly Egerton MS 1041), of which the excavation account is one of four main components; see also Gough 1789–1805, 241.
18. Jessop 1975; the original account of Fagg's 1729 excavation campaign was eventually transcribed into Roach Smith's *Inventorium Sepulchrale* of 1856.
19. Ibid, esp 102–3: MacGregor 2003, 168.
20. Marsden 1974, 118, and 1999 *passim*, esp 154.
21. Woodbridge 1976; Hutchings 2006.
22. Haycock 2006; while it affords him some recognition as an important field archaeologist, this account does not clearly explain Cunnington's subservient relationship to Colt Hoare.
23. Cunnington 1975.
24. Knight 2006.
25. Woodbridge 1976, 206–7, 208–14.
26. Goodwin 2006.
27. MacGregor 2003, 169.
28. Simmons and Simpson 1975, 11–16.
29. Only the Society of Antiquaries' copy has been consulted here. It is unclear whether or not there was a definitive version (Cunnington 1975, 8), and there

may be minor differences between them. More detailed comparison is clearly desirable.
30. Thurnam 1869, 162–8.
31. Cunnington 1975, 14, 17.
32. Ibid, 56.
33. Ibid, 56–7.
34. Ibid, 19.
35. Ibid, 19.
36. Ibid, 10.
37. Simmons and Simpson 1975, 128–59.
38. Rickman 1840, 411.
39. Long 1876, 122–37.
40. Colt Hoare 1819, 111–12; Cunnington 1975, 133.
41. Cunnington 1975, 33.
42. Ibid, 79.
43. Ibid, 83.
44. Ibid, 29.
45. Simmons and Simpson 1975, 17.
46. SAL, MS 217/4: Willetts 2000; Cunnington 1975, 119.
47. Daniel 1975, 31.
48. Cunnington 1975, 134.
49. Simmons and Simpson 1975, 7; Cunnington 1975, 134.
50. Simmons and Simpson 1975, 7–30.
51. MacGregor 2003, 172 n 57; cf Lukis 1869, quoted in note 237 below.
52. Atkinson 1975, xv–xvi; cf Ashbee 1972, 56.
53. Freston 1812.
54. Copenhagen, National Museum of Denmark, MS 24/851, 6 May 1851 (letter in the Royal Coin Cabinet).
55. Akerman 1844.
56. Briggs 1981; cf Rankin 1846, a reference unknown to the writer in 1981.
57. Lukis 1845.
58. Gomme 1886, 81.
59. *The Times*, 2 Oct 1816: Portsdown Hill, Portsmouth; 11 Mar 1837: Hollin Stump, Westmorland; 14 Apr 1845: Aston, Berks; 19 Sept 1885: Upway [Upwey] Down, Dorset. A commentary on some sixty accounts

submitted by Canon Greenwell, FSA, to *The Times* in 1864–80, mainly about his work on northern barrows, is the subject of a forthcoming study by Dr Anne O'Connor and the present writer; cf Greenwell 1877.

60. Ashbee 1972, esp 55–60; MacGregor 2003.
61. Andrews 1975, 144–79; Ashbee 1972, 57.
62. Briggs 1985.
63. Colls 1846. In the Society's *Proceedings* (i, 81, Thurs 3 Apr 1845), Edward Hailstone titles him Samuel Colls, Esq [rather than J M N as in *Archaeologia*], and explains that the sites were noted 'during the progress of the Ordnance Survey'.
64. Fleming 1988, 12–14.
65. Phillips 1853, 28.
66. Coxe 1801, 376, 412: figs 13, and 15–16 respectively; Whitaker 1816, 160, 327.
67. Wright 1852, 86–90.
68. Rowley-Conwy 2004; Thompson 2006.
69. Eluère 1993, 24–7.
70. Bateman 1861.
71. Warne 1866.
72. Jewitt 1870, figs 2 to 22.
73. Jewitt 1877, figs 1 to 5.
74. Bowden 2006.
75. Bowden 1991 usefully scrutinizes all the General's techniques.
76. Kinnes 1977; Marsden 1999, fig 65.
77. Evans 1956, 341.
78. Lane Fox 1876; its importance is recognized in Bowden 1991, 80–1, fig 19.
79. Bowden 1991, 103–40; Thompson 1977.
80. Sandiford 1975.
81. Briggs 2005; Steen Jensen 1975.
82. Klindt-Jensen 1975, 57–8.
83. The title of Jensen and Steen Jensen's 1987 paper.
84. Graslund 1981; Rowley-Conwy 2004.
85. Rafn, Petersen and Thomsen 1836.
86. Writing in 1950, Glyn Daniel (1975, 41, 386) asserted that Thomsen's essay appeared in 'a guide-book to the National Museum' (cf Daniel 1962, 32: 'the first guide-book to the National Museum'). A number of scholars – including Evans (1956, 230), Wilson (2002, 91 n 240), Bahn and Renfrew (2005, 25) – have repeated it, assuming Thomsen's essay to have been the book's central purpose. Daniel (1975, 41) also states that 'parts of [Thomsen's] essay [were] elaborated by other members of the Archaeological Committee of the Royal Society of Antiquaries of the North'. This fails to acknowledge Rafn's true role as editor of a multi-authored work that was neither intended to be, nor to resemble, a museum guide. The English translation was certainly an excellent guide to the activities of Rafn's society.
87. Ash 1981, 87, 92, 101; Clarke 1981, 127. These early Scottish connections with Scandinavian scholars are more fully explored in Rowley-Conwy forthcoming.
88. For Watkins Wynn (1775–1850) see *DNB* Wales 1959, 1100; Evans 1956, footnote to 249.
89. Evans 1956, 230: Antiquaries Correspondence (MS collection in SAL library), 20 Nov 1829.
90. Rowley-Conwy 1984.
91. Wilson 2002, 89–91.
92. Copenhagen, Royal Library Archive, unpublished MSS.
93. *The Times*, 23 May 1839, 'British Museum', p 5.
94. *The Times*, 11 June 1839, 'Letters to the Editor': an explanatory letter from the artist.
95. *The Times*, 23 May 1839, 'British Museum', p 5. Christopher Evans (1994) has discussed the landscape and conservational aspects raised by Tongue's creativity as appreciated through these oil paintings and models depicting some of Britain's best-known prehistoric and certain other natural monuments, like the Tolmen.
96. Jensen (1992, 206–7) transcribes Thomsen's MSS travel notebooks (now in the First Department of the National Museum of Denmark, Copenhagen) and his correspondence with Hildebrand (in the Department of Coins). I am much indebted to Peter Rowley-Conwy for translations of these and other relevant Danish texts; Charles Roach Smith also recalled meeting Thomsen on this visit: Roach Smith 1886, 151.
97. Prichard 1841 (in the caption to a plate apparently added after the volume was typeset); Prichard 1843; the quotation is from Prichard 1845, 191–2. Peter Rowley-Conwy has kindly checked and provided the earlier two of these references, which were first noted by Morse (1999).
98. Wilson 2002, 90; Hawkins approached the Institute of British Architects in 1845, proposing that architects should regularly inform 'Rescue Archaeologists' who would record what was being found on building sites (*The Athenaeum*, no. 943, 1845, Nov, 1129; *The Builder*, iii, 1845, 22 Nov, 557) before conveying the same message to the directors of the new railway companies (*The Builder*, iii, 1845, 20 Dec, 609).
99. Boase 2006.
100. Egerton 1848; Rowley-Conwy (2004) suggests that Egerton's task also involved translating from the Danish. In his correspondence with Rafn (see note 101) there is evidence that he was making serious efforts to master the language.
101. Copenhagen, Royal Archive, Egerton–Rafn MSS correspondence.
102. Worsaae 1849.
103. Hermansen 1934 and 1938; Henry 1994; Klindt-Jensen 1975, 68–75.
104. Klindt-Jensen 1975, 55.
105 Worsaae 1843.
106 Worsaae 1849.
107. Rowley-Conwy 2004.
108. Henry 1994; Rodden 1981; Wilkins 1961.

109. Hermansen 1934, 140.

110. Ibid, 139–40.

111. See the printed *Proceedings* of the Society and manuscript Minute Books of meetings for 1846–7. The absence of a written record reflects the state of affairs obtaining during the closing months of Carlisle's chaotic, if not corrupt, forty years as General Secretary.

112. Worsaae 1852a and 1852b.

113. SAL, Minutes, XXXIX, 205, 11 Mar 1847, notes the proposal for his election. The ballot for election was announced for 6 May and it is recorded in the Register of Elections (SAL Archives) although the minutes for that date do not refer to it; cf 1848 given in Evans 1956, 280 n 3.

114. Worsaae was made a 'foreign member' at the meeting of the British Archaeological Association held on 10 June 1846 (*Literary Gazette*, no. 1534, 13 June 1846, 538). His attendance on 17 June was confusingly reported in *The Times* under the title 'British Archaeological Institution' on 19 June (p 7), where he is styled 'Mr Warsall', though properly titled in *The Builder*, IV, 1846, 27 June, 303. For the meeting of 27 Feb 1847, see *The Times*, 1 Mar 1847, 'British Archaeological Association 27th February', p 6. Worsaae's name is notably absent from the Archaeological Institute's published *Proceedings* for 1846–7, probably because he was discouraged from attending them by Roach Smith. It is difficult to sustain the view that any of Worsaae's lectures were 'popular', as is suggested by Chapman (1989, 28).

115. Hermansen 1934, 137–8; for Worsaae in Scotland see also Graham-Campbell 2004, 207–8.

116. Stevenson 1981a, 79; Ash 1981, 98.

117. Wilson 1849, 7.

118. Ash 1981, 93.

119. Wilson 1849, x, 7–8.

120. Ibid, 7; Trigger 1989, 82.

121. Wilson 1851, esp xi–xix.

122. Rowley-Conwy, pers comm.

123. Hermansen 1934, 332; Henry 1994.

124. Worsaae 1846.

125. Detail in a letter from P Chalmers of Auldbar to William Beattie at Montrose, 10 Dec 1846: MS letter at Montrose Museum; information kindly given by Mr N K Atkinson, District Curator, 18 Nov 1988.

126. Mitchell 1985, 114.

127. In the form of a manuscript catalogue of the Royal Irish Academy's collection by George Petrie, 1852: Dublin, Royal Irish Academy, MS 12 K 39, presented by Eleanor Knott in 1942. I am indebted to Richard Haworth for this reference.

128 Mitchell 1985, 114.

129. Author's unpublished research in Copenhagen and Dublin.

130. Wilde 1857, iv.

131. Morse 1999, 5.

132. Kemble 1857; Wilde 1863, v.

133. *Proc Roy Ir Acad, C*, **6** (1857), 493–4.

134. Haigh 2006.

135. Wilde 1861, 361. The catalogue was published in three parts, viz: stone, earthen and vegetable materials, 1857; articles of animal materials, and of copper and bronze, 1861; and articles of gold, 1862. These were bound and published as a single volume in 1863.

136. Rhind 1856. Rhind visited Worsaae in 1851, and in 1855 sought his counsel on how the Danes organized their antiquities and their monuments: letter now in the First Department of the National Museum of Denmark.

137. Evans 1872, 1–13.

138. Lubbock 1869, 4–6.

139. Rowley-Conwy, pers comm.

140. Graslund 1981; Daniel 1943.

141. Daniel 1943, 12.

142. Goodwin 2006.

143. Cunnington 1975, 76.

144. Ibid; Marsden 1999, 36–7; cf Rodden 1981, 65–6.

145. Cunnington 1975, 20.

146. Atkinson 1975, xvi.

147. Lubbock 1869, 4.

148. Lubbock 1900 and 1913, 6.

149. Colt Hoare 1812, 76; I am indebted to Peter Rowley-Conwy for this reference.

150. Cunnington 1806.

151. Ashbee 1972, 60; Piggott 1976, 171–95.

152. Cf Wilson 2002.

153. Housed in the First Department of the National Museum of Denmark.

154. *The Athenaeum*, no. 905, 1845, 1 Mar, 221.

155. Cf Levine 1986, 21.

156. Wetherall 1994, 14.

157. See ch 8, this volume; Levine 1986, 49.

158 Evans 1956, 239–51.

159. *Gent's Mag*, 1846, **16**/1, 21: letter to Mr Urban.

160. *The Times*, 21 Apr 1846, 'Society of Antiquaries', p 8; see Evans 1956, 240–53.

161. See ch 8, this volume.

162. Evans 1956, 227, 235. Way, who had been Director of the Society of Antiquaries, was one of the most senior antiquaries to 'defect' to the new society in 1844.

163. For example, in *The Times*, 13 Sept 1845, 'The British Archaeological Association', p 7. This comes from the present writer's unpublished survey of press reportage and opinion on the contemporary state of the Antiquaries, on the origins of the two new societies and 'the split'.

164. Cf Stocking 1987, 71.

165. van Riper 1993, 39.

166. Ibid, appendices 1–3.

167. Oakley 1964.

168. van Riper 1993.
169. Laming-Emperaire 1964, 123–205.
170. Frere 1800.
171. It is unclear from Frere's biography (Stoker 2006) how far he was familiar with geology and the British past. His understanding may have been informed by someone like T R Underwood, the Antiquaries' illustrator who drew the axes. An accomplished watercolourist, Underwood later achieved Fellowship of the Geological Society. Conversely, Underwood's early association with Frere might have been an important trigger to his own intellectual development. I am indebted to Elizabeth Lewis, FSA, for her insight into this question.
172. Evans 1956, 202–3.
173. Haile 2006.
174. Cf Daniel 1975, 33–8; Penniman 1952, 66–8.
175. Buckland 1824.
176. Clark 1961.
177. Keith 1924, 67.
178. Chippindale 1988.
179. Trigger 1992.
180. Evans 1943, esp 61–162; Foote 2006.
181. Evans 1943, 84.
182. van Riper 1993, 54–73.
183. Boucher de Perthes 1849 is the most relevant. Although a date of 1847 is often cited, publication was held over for two years owing to the author's difficulty in gaining support for the work.
184. Evans 1956, 281–4; Laming-Emperaire 1964, 158–75.
185. van Riper 1993, 76–100.
186. Moore 2006.
187. Prestwich 1899.
188. Evans 1943, 100–4; van Riper 1993, 104–5; White 2001.
189. Prestwich 1859.
190. Evans 1859.
191. Ibid.
192. Evans 1956, 285.
193. Evans 1861.
194. Evans 1865.
195. *Gent's Mag*, 1859, **129**/2, 150.
196. Ibid, 620.
197. Stocking 1987, 150–6.
198. *Proc Soc Antiq London*, 2nd ser, **3** (1864–7), ii, 418.
199. Alborn 2006.
200. Hutchinson 1914, 51.
201. Lubbock 1865.
202. Hutchinson 1914, 74.
203. *The Times*, 29 Sept 1859, 'Man Among Mammoths', p 8.
204. Gomme 1907, 229, lists over seventy contributions on coins.
205. See *Proc Soc Antiq London*, 2nd ser, *General Index* for **1–20** (1908), 140–1.
206. *Proc Soc Antiq London*, 2nd ser, **5** (1871), 165–9; Evans 1956, 306.
207. *Proc Soc Antiq London*, 2nd ser, **5** (1871), 229; Evans 1956, 306.
208. Evans 1956, 340.
209. *Proc Soc Antiq London*, 2nd ser, **5** (1871), 392–412.
210. Gomme 1907.
211. Lubbock 1866.
212. Ibid, 209; *Gent's Mag*, 1866, **136**/2, 341; cf van Riper 1993, 200–2.
213. Evans 1956, 326–45, and pl XXXVI.
214. Bloxam 1893, endpaper.
215. Norwich Congress 1869; Bloxam 1893, 111–12, 182–3 and 250–2.
216. *The Times*, 9 Sept 1874, 'An Archaeological Congress (from our Danish Correspondent)', p 5.
217. Bloxam 1893, 14–15. Chapman (1989) offers valuable insights on Pitt-Rivers in the 1860s, his institutional connections with the learned societies, and personal relationships with Lubbock and Franks.
218. Stevenson 1981b, 154.
219. Nurse 2006.
220. Rowley-Conwy forthcoming.
221. Turnbull 2006; *The Times*, 15 Apr 1863, s.v. 'The Ethnological Society'; Crawfurd 1864a and 1864b.
222. *Gent's Mag*, 1851, **121**/1, 500; *The Athenaeum*, no. 1221, 1851, 22 Mar, 326–7.
223. See ch 8, this volume.
224. These sub-parcels form part of SAL, MS 700/I, no.7. I am indebted to Elizabeth Lewis, FSA, for useful discussion of Way's manuscripts.
225. Hume 1851.
226. Anon 1870.
227. Way 1859.
228. Anon 1859, 323.
229. Cf Ebbatson 1999.
230. Haigh 2006.
231. Kemble 1856.
232. Kemble 1857.
233. The text of Rowley-Conwy forthcoming informs much of what follows in this section.
234. Thompson 2006, n 72.
235. In 1847 Wright wrote introductions to archaeologists in Paris for Worsaae (unpublished research by the writer).
236. van Riper 1993, tables 1–3.
237. Lukis (1869, 124–5) wrote uncompromisingly of *Ancient Wiltshire*: 'No volumes could contain less information in proportion to their bulk. We search through them almost in vain for intimations as to the materials of the barrows, the mode of their construction, and the position of the skeletons; and we are led to the conclusion that the principal, if not the sole object of the investigator was the possession of the articles which had been deposited with the human remains.'
238. This suggestion follows the presentation of a valuable

paper on 'Archaeological field practices in Sweden,
1870–1910', by O W Jensen and Å Gillberg, Dept of
Archaeology and Ancient History, Gothenburg
University, at the European Association of Archaeology
meeting in Cracow, 23 Sept 2006. The writer thanks
both authors and others attending the session for
valuable discussion.
239. Graslund 1981; Rodden 1981.
240. Briggs 2005.

241. Review of *Prehistoric Times* in *The Athenaeum*,
no. 1965, 1865, 24 June, 843–4.
242. Levine 1986; van Riper 1993.
243. Bowden 1991, esp 95–102.
244. Wilson 2002.
245. Caygill 1997; Cook 1997; Mack 1997.
246. *The Times*, 21 Aug 1868, leader/editorial: 'The
Meeting of the British Association at Norwich', p 6.
247. Levine 1986, 95.

BIBLIOGRAPHY

Akerman, J Y 1844. 'An account of the opening by Matthew
Bell, Esq, of an ancient British barrow, in Iffins Wood,
near Canterbury, in the month of January, 1842, in
a letter from John Yonge Akerman Esq, FSA, to
Sir Henry Ellis, KH, FRS Secretary', *Archaeologia*,
30, 57–61

Alborn, T L 2006. 'Lubbock, Sir John William, third
baronet (1803–1865)', in *Oxford Dictionary of
National Biography: Online Edition*
(eds H C G Matthew and B Harrison),
<http://www.oxforddnb.com./view/article/17119>
(24 July 2006)

Anderson, R G W, Caygill, M L, MacGregor, A G and Syson,
L (eds) 2003. *Enlightening the British: knowledge,
discovery and the museum in the eighteenth century*,
London

Andrews, J H 1975. *A Paper Landscape: the Ordnance
Survey in nineteenth-century Ireland*, Oxford

Andrews, M 1989. *The Search for the Picturesque*, Aldershot

Anon 1859. Review of the *Catalogue of Antiquities, Works
of Art and Historical Scottish Relics Exhibited in the
Museum of the Archaeological Institute of Great
Britain and Ireland during their Annual Meeting,
held in Edinburgh, July, 1856*, in *Gent's Mag*, 1859,
129/2, 321–30

Anon 1870. 'Supplement to the list of printed books in the
Society of Antiquaries of London, London' (MS in the
Society's Library)

Ash, M 1981. '"A fine, genial and hearty band": David Laing,
Daniel Wilson and Scottish archaeology', in Bell (ed)
1981, 86–113

Ashbee, P 1972. 'Field archaeology: its origins and
development', in Fowler (ed) 1972, 38–74

Atkinson, R J C 1975. 'Introduction', in Cunnington 1975,
ix–xviii

Bahn, P and Renfrew, C 2005. *Archaeology: theories,
methods and practice*, London

Bateman, T 1861. *Ten Years' Diggings on the Celtic and
Saxon Grave Hills in the Counties of Derby, Stafford
and York, from 1848 to 1858*, London

Bell, A S (ed) 1981. *The Scottish Antiquarian Tradition:*

*essays to mark the bicentenary of the Society of
Antiquaries of Scotland and its museum 1780–1980*,
Edinburgh

Black, J 1999. *The British Abroad: the Grand Tour in
the eighteenth century*, Stroud

Bloxam, G W 1893. *Index to the Publications of the
Anthropological Institute of Great Britain and Ireland
(1843–1891)*, London

Boase, G C 2006. 'Egerton, Francis, first Earl of Ellesmere
(1800–1857)', rev H C G Matthew, in *Oxford
Dictionary of National Biography: Online Edition*
(eds H C G Matthew and B Harrison),
<http://www.oxforddnb.com./view/article/8585>
(24 July 2006)

Boucher de Perthes, J 1849. *Antiquités celtiques et
antédiluviennes*, I, Paris

Bowden, M C B 1991. *Pitt Rivers: the life and archaeological
work of Lieutenant-General Augustus Henry Lane Fox
Pitt Rivers, DCL, FRS, FSA*, Cambridge

Bowden, M C B 2006. 'Rivers, Augustus Henry Lane
Fox Pitt (1827–1900)', in *Oxford Dictionary of
National Biography: Online Edition*
(eds H C G Matthew and B Harrison),
<http://www.oxforddnb.com./view/article/22341>
(24 July 2006)

Briggs, C S 1981. 'An early communication on a rusticated
beaker from Flamborough and a description of two
tumuli in Thixendale', *Yorkshire Archaeol J*, **53**, 1–6

Briggs, C S 1985. 'Some problems of survey and study in
prehistoric Ireland: highland and lowland distributions
in Central Ulster *c* 3,600–1,800 BC', in Burgess and
Spratt (eds) 1985, 351–63

Briggs, C S 2005. 'C C Rafn, J J A Worsaae, archaeology,
history and Danish national identity in the
Schleswig-Holstein question 1848–1864', *Bull Hist
Archaeol*, **15**/2, 4–25

Buckland, W 1824. *Reliquiae Diluvianae: or observations
on the organic remains contained in caves, fissures,
and diluvial gravel, and of other geological
phenomena, affecting the action of an universal
deluge*, 2nd edn, London

Burgess, C B and Spratt, D A (eds) 1985. *Upland Settlement in Britain: the second millennium BC and after*, BAR Brit Ser 143, Oxford

Caygill, M 1997. 'Franks and the British Museum – the cuckoo in the nest', in Caygill and Cherry (eds) 1997, 51–114

Caygill, M and Cherry, J (eds) 1997. *A W Franks: nineteenth-century collecting and the British Museum*, London

Chapman, W 1989. 'The organizational context in the history of archaeology: Pitt-Rivers and other British archaeologists in the 1860s', *Antiq J*, 69, 23–42

Chippindale, C 1988. 'The invention of words for the idea of "prehistory"', *Proc Prehist Soc*, 54, 303–14

Clark, L K 1961. *Pioneers of Prehistory in England*, London

Clarke, D V 1981. 'Scottish archaeology in the second half of the nineteenth century', in Bell (ed) 1981, 114–41

Colls, J M N 1846. 'Letter upon some early remains discovered in Yorkshire', *Archaeologia*, 31, 299–307

Colt Hoare, R 1812. *The Ancient History of Wiltshire*, I, London

Colt Hoare, R 1819. *The Ancient History of Wiltshire*, II, London

Cook, J 1997. 'A curator's curator: Franks and the Stone-Age collections', in Caygill and Cherry (eds) 1997, 115–29

Coxe, W 1801. *An Historical Tour in Monmouthshire*, London

Crawfurd, J 1864a. 'On the supposed stone, bronze and iron ages of society', *Ethnol Soc London*, new ser, 4, 1–12

Crawfurd, J 1864b. 'On the supposed stone, bronze and iron ages of society', *Brit Ass Rep 1864*, 143

Cunnington, R H 1975. *From Antiquary to Archaeologist* (ed J H Dyer), Princes Risborough

Cunnington, W 1806. 'Further account of tumuli opened in Wiltshire, in a letter from Mr William Cunnington, FAS, to Aylmer Burke Lambert Esq, FRS, FAS, and FLS communicated by Mr Lambert', *Archaeologia*, 15, 338–46

Daniel, G E 1943. *The Three Ages: an essay on archaeological method*, Cambridge

Daniel, G E 1962. *The Idea of Prehistory*, London

Daniel, G E 1975. *A Hundred and Fifty Years of Archaeology*, 2nd edn, London

Daniel, G E (ed) 1981. *Towards a History of Archaeology: being the papers read at the first Conference on the History of Archaeology in Aarhus, 29 August–2 September 1978*, London

DNB Wales 1959. *The Dictionary of Welsh Biography Down to 1940*, London

Dolan, B 2001. *Ladies of the Grand Tour*, London

Duff, U G (ed) 1924. *The Life-Work of Lord Avebury (Sir John Lubbock) 1834–1913*, London

Ebbatson, L 1999. 'Conditions of emergence and existence of archaeology in the 19th century: the Royal Archaeological Institute 1843–1914', unpublished PhD thesis, University of Durham

Egerton, F 1848. *Guide to Northern Archaeology by the Royal Society of Northern Antiquaries of Copenhagen*, London, James Rain, Haymarket; printed by Berling Brothers, Copenhagen

Eluère, C 1993. *The Celts: first masters of Europe*, London

Evans, C 1994. 'Natural wonders and national monuments: a meditation upon the fact of the Tolmen', *Antiquity*, 68, 200–8

Evans, John 1859. 'On the occurrence of flint implements in undisturbed beds of gravel, sand and clay', *Archaeologia*, 38, 280–307

Evans, John 1861. 'An account of some further discoveries of some flint implements in the drift on the Continent and in England', *Archaeologia*, 39, 57–84

Evans, John 1865. 'On the worked flints of Pressigny-le-Grand', *Archaeologia*, 40, 381–8

Evans, John 1871. 'The "Bronze Period"', *Proc Soc Antiq London*, 2nd ser, 5, 392–412

Evans, John 1872. *The Ancient Stone Implements, Weapons and Ornaments of Great Britain*, London

Evans, John 1881. *Ancient Bronze Implements*, London

Evans, Joan 1943. *Time and Chance: the story of Arthur Evans and his forebears*, London

Evans, Joan 1956. *A History of the Society of Antiquaries of London*, Oxford

Fleming, A 1988. *The Dartmoor Reaves: investigating prehistoric land divisions*, London

Foote, Y 2006. 'Evans, Sir John (1823–1908)', in *Oxford Dictionary of National Biography: Online Edition* (eds H C G Matthew and B Harrison), <http://www.oxforddnb.com./view/article/33040> (25 July 2006)

Fowler, P J (ed) 1972. *Archaeology and the Landscape: essays for L V Grinsell*, London

Frere, J 1800. 'An account of flint weapons discovered at Hoxne in Suffolk (letter read on 22 June 1797)', *Archaeologia*, 13, 204–5

Freston, A 1812. 'An account of a tumulus, opened on an estate of Matthew Baillie, MD, in the parish of Duntisbourne Abbots, in Gloucestershire, communicated to Samuel Lysons, Esq, Director, by the Revd Anthony Freston, Rector of Edgeworth, in the same county, 9 January 1806', *Archaeologia*, 16, 361–2

Gay, P 1969. *The Enlightenment: the science of freedom*, London

Gomme, G L 1886. *Archaeology: a classified collection of the chief contents of the* Gentleman's Magazine *from 1731 to 1868*, 2 vols, London

Gomme, G L 1907. *Index of Archaeological Papers 1665–1890*, London

Goodwin, G 2006. 'Leman, Thomas (1751–1826)', rev A E Brown, in *Oxford Dictionary of National Biography:*

Online Edition (eds H C G Matthew and B Harrison), <http://www.oxforddnb.com./view/article/16421> (25 July 2006)

Gough, R 1789–1805. *Britannia*, 3 vols, London

Graham-Campbell, J 2004. '"*Danes* . . . in this Country": discovering the Vikings in Scotland', *Proc Soc Antiq Scotl*, **134**, 201–39

Graslund, B 1981. 'The background to C J Thomsen's Three Age System', in Daniel (ed) 1981, 45–50

Greenwell, W 1877. *British Barrows*, Oxford

Haigh, J D 2006. 'Kemble, John Mitchell (1807–1857)', in *Oxford Dictionary of National Biography: Online Edition* (eds H C G Matthew and B Harrison), <http://www.oxforddnb.com./view/article/15321> (24 July 2006)

Haile, N 2006. 'Buckland, William (1784–1856)', in *Oxford Dictionary of National Biography: Online Edition* (eds H C G Matthew and B Harrison), <http://www.oxforddnb.com./view/article/3859> (25 July 2006)

Haycock, D B 2006. 'Cunnington, William (1754–1810)', in *Oxford Dictionary of National Biography: Online Edition* (eds H C G Matthew and B Harrison), <http://www.oxforddnb.com./view/article/6938> (24 July 2006)

Henry, D (ed) 1994. *Viking Ireland. Jens Worsaae's accounts of his visit to Ireland: 1846–7*, Balgavies

Hermansen, V 1934. *J J A Worsaae, En Oldgranskers Erindringer*, Copenhagen

Hermansen, V 1938. *J J A Worsaae: Af en Oldgranskers Breve 1848–1885*, Copenhagen

Hume, A 1851. 'Archaeological intelligence', *Archaeol J*, **8**, 434

Hutchings, V 2006. 'Hoare, Sir (Richard) Colt, second baronet (1758–1838)', in *Oxford Dictionary of National Biography: Online Edition* (eds H C G Matthew and B Harrison), <http://www.oxforddnb.com./view/article/13387> (24 July 2006)

Hutchinson, H G 1914. *The Life of Sir John Lubbock, Lord Avebury*, 2 vols, London

Jensen, I and Jensen, J Steen 1987. 'Det Kongelige Nordiske Oldskriftselskabs breve 1825–1864. Dansk Kulturformidling på verdensplan', *Aarbøger for Nord Oldk og Hist*, 211–74

Jensen, J 1992. *Thomsens Museum – Historien om Nationalmuseet*, Copenhagen

Jensen, J Steen 1975. 'Det Kongelige Nordiske Oldskrift-selskabs stiftelse 1825', *Aarbøger for Nord Oldk og Hist*, 5–19

Jessop, R F 1975. *Man of Many Talents: an informal biography of James Douglas 1753–1819*, London

Jewitt, L F W 1870. *Grave-Mounds and their Contents: a manual of archaeology*, London

Jewitt, L F W 1877. *Half-Hours Among Some English Antiquities*, London

Keith, A 1924. 'Anthropology', in Duff (ed) 1924, 67–105

Kemble, J M 1856. 'Heathen periods', *Archaeol J*, **13**, 388–9

Kemble, J M 1857. 'On the utility of antiquarian collections in relation to the pre-historic annals of the different countries of Europe, with especial reference to the museum of the Academy', *Proc Roy Ir Acad, C*, **6**, 462–80

Kinnes, I 1977. 'British barrows: a unique visual record?', *Antiquity*, **51**, 52–3

Klindt-Jensen, O 1975. *A History of Scandinavian Archaeology*, London

Knight, J K 2006. 'Coxe, William (1748–1828)', in *Oxford Dictionary of National Biography: Online Edition* (eds H C G Matthew and B Harrison), <http://www.oxforddnb.com./view/article/13387> (2 Oct 2006)

Laming-Emperaire, A 1964. *Origines de l'archéologie préhistorique en France*, Paris

Lane Fox, A H 1876. 'Excavations in Cissbury Camp, Sussex', *J Anthropol Inst*, **5**, 357–90

Levine, P 1986. *The Amateur and the Professional: antiquarians, historians and archaeologists in Victorian England, 1838–1886*, Cambridge

Long, W 1876. 'Stonehenge and its barrows', *Wiltshire Archaeol Natur Hist Mag*, **16**, 1–244

Lubbock, J 1865–1913. *Prehistoric Times* (1st edn 1865; 2nd edn 1869; 6th edn 1900; 7th edn 1913), London

Lubbock, J 1866. 'Primæval antiquities', *Archaeol J*, **23**, 190–211

Lukis, F C 1845. 'Observations on the primeval antiquities of the Channel Islands', *Archaeol J*, **1**, 142–51

Lukis, W C 1869. 'On the flint implements and tumuli of the neighbourhood of Wath', *J Yorkshire Archaeol Topog*, **1**, 116–26

Lyell, C 1863. *The Geological Evidences of the Antiquity of Man, with Remarks on Theories of the Origin of Species by Variation*, London

MacGregor, A G 2003. 'The antiquary *en plein air*: eighteenth-century progress from topographical survey to the threshold of field archaeology', in Anderson, Caygill, MacGregor and Syson (eds) 2003, 164–75

Mack, J 1997. 'Antiquities and the public: the expanding Museum, 1851–96', in Caygill and Cherry (eds) 1997, 34–50

Marsden, B 1974. *The Early Barrow Diggers*, Aylesbury

Marsden, B 1999. *The Early Barrow Diggers* (rev edn), Stroud

Milliken, S and Cook, J (eds) 2001. *A Very Remote Period Indeed: papers on the Palaeolithic presented to Derek Roe*, Oxford

Mitchell, G F 1985. 'Antiquities', in Ó'Raífertaígh (ed) 1985, 93–165

Moore, D T 2006. 'Falconer, Hugh (1808–1865)', in *Oxford Dictionary of National Biography: Online Edition* (eds H C G Matthew and B Harrison), <http://www.oxforddnb.com./view/article/9110> (25 July 2006)

Morrell, J and Thackray, A 1981. *Gentlemen of Science: the early years of the British Association for the Advancement of Science*, Oxford

Morse, M A 1999. 'Craniology and the adoption of the Three Age System in Britain', *Proc Prehist Soc*, **65**, 1–16

Norwich Congress 1869. *International Congress of Prehistoric Archaeology: transactions of the third session, 20–28 August, 1868*, London

Nurse, B 2006. 'Way, Albert (1805–1874)', in *Oxford Dictionary of National Biography: Online Edition* (eds H C G Matthew and B Harrison), <http://www.oxforddnb.com./view/article/28903> (25 July 2006)

Oakley, K P 1964. 'The problem of man's antiquity: an historical survey', *Bull Brit Mus Natur Hist*, **9/5**, 83–195

Ó'Raífertaígh, T (ed) 1985. *Royal Irish Academy: a bicentennial history 1785–1985*, Dublin

Pennant, T 1778. *A Tour in North Wales* MDCCLXXIII, London

Penniman, T K 1952. *A Hundred Years of Anthropology*, London

Phillips, J 1853. *The Rivers, Mountains and Sea-Coast of Yorkshire, with essays on the climate, scenery and ancient inhabitants of the county*, London

Piggott, S 1976. *Ruins in a Landscape*, Edinburgh

Piggott, S 1985. *William Stukeley: an eighteenth-century antiquary*, Oxford

Porter, R 1977. *The Making of Geology: earth science in Britain 1600–1815*, Cambridge

Porter, R 2000. *Enlightenment*, London

Prestwich, G A 1899. *Life and Letters of Sir Joseph Prestwich*, Edinburgh

Prestwich, J 1859. 'On the occurrence of flint-implements, associated with the remains of animals of extinct species in beds of a late geological period, in France at Amiens and Abbeville, and in England at Hoxne', *Proc Roy Soc London, B*, **10**, 50–9

Prichard, J C 1841. *Researches in the Physical History of Mankind*, 3rd edn, 3 vols, London

Prichard, J C 1843. *The Natural History of Man*, 1st edn, London

Prichard, J C 1845. *The Natural History of Man*, 2nd edn, London

Rafn, C C, Petersen, N M and Thomsen, C J 1836. *Ledetraad til Norsk Oldkyndighed*, Copenhagen: Køngelige Nordiske Oldskriftselskab

Rankin, T 1846. 'Notices of the ancient tumuli on the Yorkshire Wolds, particularly of the two twin barrows', *Trans Brit Archaeol Ass, 2nd Annual Congress,*

Winchester, August 1845, 218–20, London

Rhind, A H 1856. 'On the history of the systematic classification of primeval relics', *Archaeol J*, **13**, 200–14

Rickman, J 1840. 'On the antiquity of Abury and Stonehenge', *Archaeologia*, **28**, 399–419

Rodden, J 1981. 'The development of the Three Age System: archaeology's first paradigm', in Daniel (ed) 1981, 51–68

Rowley-Conwy, P 1984. 'C J Thomsen and the Three Age System: a contemporary document', *Antiquity*, **58**, 129–31

Rowley-Conwy, P 2004. 'The Three Age System in English: new translations of the founding documents', *Bull Hist Archaeol*, **14/1**, 4–15

Rowley-Conwy, P forthcoming. *From Genesis to Prehistory and the Adoption of the Three Age System*, Oxford

Sandiford, K A P 1975. *Great Britain and the Schleswig-Holstein Question 1848–1864: a study in diplomacy, politics and public opinion*, Toronto

Simmons, J and Simpson, D D A (eds) 1975. *The Ancient History of South Wiltshire* (by Sir Richard Colt Hoare: facsimile of the original 1812 and 1819 edns), EP Publishing, Wakefield, in collaboration with Wiltshire County Library

Smith, C Roach (ed) 1856. *Inventorium Sepulchrale: an account of some antiquities dug up at Gilton, Kingston, Sibertswold, Barfriston, Beakesbourne, Chartham, and Crundale, in the county of Kent, from AD 1757 to AD 1773, by the Rev. Bryan Faussett*, privately printed

Smith, C Roach 1886. *Retrospections Social and Archaeological*, 3 vols, London

Stevenson, R B K 1981a. 'The museum, its beginnings and its development to 1858', in Bell (ed) 1981, 31–85

Stevenson, R B K 1981b. 'The National Museum to 1954', in Bell (ed) 1981, 142–211

Stocking, G W 1987. *Victorian Anthropology*, New York

Stoker, D 2006. 'Frere, John (1740–1807)', in *Oxford Dictionary of National Biography: Online Edition* (eds H C G Matthew and B Harrison), <http://www.oxforddnb.com./view/article/10173> (25 July 2006)

Sweet, R 2004. *Antiquaries: the discovery of the past in eighteenth-century Britain*, London

Thompson, M W 1977. *General Pitt-Rivers: evolution and archaeology in the nineteenth century*, Bradford-on-Avon

Thompson, M W 2006. 'Wright, Thomas (1810–1877)', in *Oxford Dictionary of National Biography: Online Edition* (eds H C G Matthew and B Harrison), <http://www.oxforddnb.com./view/article/30063> (24 July 2006)

Thurnam, J 1869. 'Ancient British barrows, especially those of Wiltshire and the adjoining counties', *Archaeologia*, **42**, 161–244

Trigger, B G 1989. *A History of Archaeological Thought*, Cambridge

Trigger, B G 1992. 'Daniel Wilson and the Scottish Enlightenment', *Proc Soc Antiq Scotl*, **122**, 55–75

Turnbull, C M 2006. 'Crawfurd, John (1783–1868)', in *Oxford Dictionary of National Biography: Online Edition* (eds H C G Matthew and B Harrison), <http://www.oxforddnb.com./view/article/6651> (25 July 2006)

van Riper, A B 1993. *Men among the Mammoths: Victorian science and the discovery of human prehistory*, Chicago

Vyner, B (ed) 1994. *Building on the Past: papers celebrating 150 years of the Royal Archaeological Institute*, London

Walker, M 1988. *James Edward Smith MD, FRS, PLS (1759–1828): first President of the Linnean Society of London*, London

Warne, C 1866. *The Celtic Tumuli of Dorset*, London

Way, A 1859. *Catalogue of Antiquities, Works of Art and Historical Scottish Relics, exhibited in the museum of the Archaeological Institute of Great Britain and Ireland, during their Annual Meeting, held in Edinburgh, July 1856*, Edinburgh

Wetherall, D 1994. 'From Canterbury to Winchester: the foundation of the Institute', in Vyner (ed) 1994, 8–21

Whitaker, T D 1816. *Loidis and Elmete*, Leeds

White, M J 2001. 'Out of Abbeville: Sir John Evans, Palaeolithic patriarch and hand axe pioneer', in Milliken and Cook (eds) 2001, 242–8

Wilde, W R 1857. *A Descriptive Catalogue of the Antiquities of Stone, Earthen and Vegetable Materials, in the Museum of the Royal Irish Academy*, Dublin

Wilde, W R 1861. *A Descriptive Catalogue of the Antiquities of Animal Materials and Bronze in the Museum of the Royal Irish Academy*, Dublin

Wilde, W R 1862. *A Descriptive Catalogue of the Antiquities of Gold in the Museum of the Royal Irish Academy*, Dublin

Wilde, W R 1863. *A Descriptive Catalogue of the Antiquities in the Museum of the Royal Irish Academy. Vol. 1, Articles of stone, earthen, vegetable, and animal materials: and of copper and bronze*, Dublin

Wilkins, J 1961. 'Worsaae and British antiquities', *Antiquity*, **35**, 214–20

Willetts, P 2000. *Catalogue of Manuscripts in the Society of Antiquaries of London*, Woodbridge

Wilson, D 1849. *Synopsis of the Museum of the Society of Antiquaries of Scotland*, Edinburgh

Wilson, D 1851. *The Archaeology and Prehistoric Annals of Scotland*, Edinburgh

Wilson, D M 2002. *The British Museum: a history*, London

Woodbridge, K 1976. *Landscape and Antiquity*, Oxford

Woodward, H B 1907. *A History of the Geological Society of London*, London

Worsaae, J J A 1843. *Danmarks Oldtid oplyst ved Oldsager og Gravehøje*, Copenhagen

Worsaae, J J A 1844. *Dänemarks Vorzeit, durch Alterthümer und Grabhügel beleuchtet* (trans Bertelsen), Copenhagen

Worsaae, J J A 1846. 'An account of the formation of the Museum of Copenhagen, and general remarks on the classification of the antiquities found in the north and west of Europe', *Proc Roy Ir Acad, C*, **3**, 310–15

Worsaae, J J A 1849. *The Primeval Antiquities of Denmark . . . translated and applied to the illustration of similar remains in England by W J Thoms*, London

Worsaae, J J A 1852a. 'Worsaae's address to the meeting, April 2nd 1852', *Archaeol J*, **9**, 198–9

Worsaae, J J A 1852b. 'Worsaae's address to the meeting, May 7th 1852', *Archaeol J*, **9**, 285

Wright, T 1852. *The Celt, the Roman, and the Saxon: a history of the early inhabitants of Britain*, London

COMPARATIVE GEOLOGY.

Or a Familiar method of illustrating the Vertical and lateral Positions of Rocks.

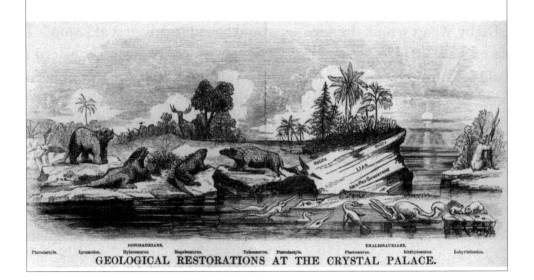

Pterodactyle.   Iguanodon.   Hylæosaurus.   Megalosaurus.   Teleosaurus.   Pterodactyle.   Plesiosaurus.   Ichthyosaurus.   Labyrinthodon.

DINOSAURIANS.   ENALIOSAURIANS.

GEOLOGICAL RESTORATIONS AT THE CRYSTAL PALACE.

CHAPTER ELEVEN

'Delineating Objects': Nineteenth-century Antiquarian Culture and the Project of Archaeology

Christopher Evans

In the first decades of the nineteenth century, antiquaries and 'antiquarianism' were the brunt of public lampooning. Often appearing rather pathetically self-obsessed, the obtuse musings of antiquaries exposed them to jest in the day's broadsheets, cartoons and novels.[1] Although the major intellectual and scientific debates of the century's middle decades were equally ridiculed in *Punch*, over the latter half of the century 'archaeology' came to be publicly esteemed. Its discoveries, both at home and abroad, commanded attention in the pages of the *Illustrated London News*. Its findings had, moreover, reconfigured the Christian-Creationist universe and were then enlisted to further the socio-evolutionary drive of empire. This itself is a well-rehearsed story. The key issue must be the inter-relationship of the *antiquarianism* of the first half of the century and the *archaeology* of its latter half. This chapter is less a contribution to society-specific history than a discursive study (though it draws upon the Society's materials as its prime source). Following initial scene-setting, it will explore three broad themes: the changing *performance*, *demonstration* and *content* of the past, and its adjudication or authority as they relate to the institutionalization of the subject.

INTELLECTUAL CIRCLES AND PATRIARCHS

Albeit invariably partial, the inclusion of the century's 'time-line' (table 5)[2] is essential on a number of counts, for any specialist history will always occur against a wider socio-historical background. It thereby throws into perspective the narrowness of our concerns and it is, for example, salient to realize that the landmark developments in archaeology during the 1840s were bookended by the Chartist Movement and the Irish Famine. Such framing is, moreover, necessary if the degree of change which British society then experienced is to be appreciated. After all, it spans the period from Blake and the Napoleonic Wars to Wells's *War of the Worlds*, the Boer War, the advent of the radio and telephone, and all that this implies of both technological change and social reform. Equally, there is the expansion and coalescence of the British Empire. Particularly relevant is the nation's continual exposure to, and amalgamation of, 'the

Fig 76. 'Before the Deluge'. *Top*: Penn's 1828 schematic method showing the 'vertical and lateral positions of rocks' with the Bible employed as its keystone (*Conversations in Geology*: in Freeman 2004, fig 46); *below*: card published by J Reynolds, showing the geological 'progress' (and respective strata) of amphibious life-forms to dinosaurs and mammals at the Crystal Palace (Natural History Museum, London: Secord 2004, fig 6.2; see note 5).

TABLE 5: A BRITISH 'ARCHAEOLOGICAL' AND SOCIO-HISTORICAL CHRONOLOGY

	Social/historical	*Archaeological*	*Cultural/scientific*
1800	Battle of Trafalgar (1805) Abolition of the Slave Trade Bill (1807)	Rosetta Stone ceded to England (1801)	Blake's *Jerusalem* (1804)
1810	Battle of Waterloo (1815) Gurkha War (1814–16)	Colt Hoare's *Ancient History of Wiltshire* (1812–19)	Byron's *Childe Harold's Pilgrimage* (1812–18)
1820	First Burma War (1824–6) Stephenson's *Rocket* (1829)		Constable's *The Hay Wain* (1821) Mantell's *Iguanadon* (1825)
1830	Victoria ascends the throne (1837) First Afghan and Chinese Opium Wars (1839–42) Chartist Riots (1839)		Lyell's *Principles of Geology* (1830) Dickens's *Nicholas Nickleby* (1838–9) Turner's *The Fighting Temeraire* (1838)
1840	Great Western Railway (1841) Franklin Expedition (1845) Madagascar Campaign (1845) Repeal of the Corn Laws (1846) Irish Famine (1846–50) Sikh Wars (1845–9)	British Archaeological Association (1843) Roach Smith's *Collectanea Antiqua* (1848–80) Thoms's translation of Worsaae's *Primeval Antiquities of Denmark* (1849)	Wordsworth, Poet Laureate (1843) Engel's *The Condition of the Working Class in England* (1845) C Bronte's *Jane Eyre* (1847) Ruskin, *Seven Lamps of Architecture* (1849)
1850	Great Exhibition (1851) Crimean War (1854–6) Palmerston's Governments (1855–8, 1859–68) Indian Mutiny (1857) Brunel's SS *Great Britain* (1859)	Mantell's 'On the remains of Man . . . imbedded in rocks and strata' (1850) Faussett's *Inventorium Sepulchrale* (ed Roach Smith 1856) Davis and Thurnam's *Crania Britannica* (1856–60)	Tennyson, Poet Laureate (1850) Landseer's *Monarch of the Glen* (1851) Hunt's *The Light of the World* (1851–3) Darwin's *The Origin of Species* (1859)
1860	London Underground, Metropolitan Line (1863) Abyssinian Campaign (1867–8) Gladstone's Governments (1868–74, 1880–5, 1886, 1892–4)	Dept of British and Medieval Antiquities and Ethnography, British Museum (1860) Bateman's *Ten Years Digging* (1861) Evans's *Coins of the Ancient Britons* (1864) Lubbock's *Pre-historic Times* (1865)	Lyell's *Antiquity of Man* (1863) Carroll's *Alice in Wonderland* (1866) Arnold's *Dover Beach* (1867) Gilbert Scott's *Albert Memorial* (1868)
1870	Death of Livingstone (1873) Second Afghan War (1878–80) Belize Campaign (1879) Zulu War (1879)	Evans's *Ancient Stone Implements* (1872) Greenwell's *British Barrows* (1877)	Darwin's *The Descent of Man* (1871) Hardy's *Far From the Madding Crowd* (1874) Natural History Museum, London (1873–80)
1880	National Telephone Company (1881) Siege of Khartoum (1884–5) Victoria's Golden Jubilee (1887)	Dawkin's *Early Man in Britain* (1880) Evans's *Ancient Bronze Implements* (1881) Ancient Monuments Act (1882) Lukis's *Prehistoric Stone Monuments of the British Isles* (1885) Pitt-Rivers's *Excavations in Cranborne Chase* (1887–98)	Stephenson's *Treasure Island* (1882) Burton's *Arabian Nights* (1885) Haggard's *King Solomon's Mines* (1886)
1890	Invention of Radio (1895) Boer War (1899–1902) Ashanti War (1900)		Wells's *War of the Worlds* (1898) Elgar's *Enigma Variations* (1899) Conrad's *An Outcast of the Islands* (1899)

Table 5. A British 'archaeological' and socio-historical chronology

foreign' and, in spite of the *Pax Britannica*, the incessant onslaught of its overseas wars during the century.[3] These conflicts with the 'colonial other', whether with the Maoris (1845–9) or the Andaman Islanders (1867), give context to the employment of the comparative/evolutionary ethnography that underpinned so much of the prehistoric archaeology of the latter half of the century. They provided an immediacy to Pitt-Rivers's study of 'Primitive Warfare' and situate the racist content that underlay much of the period's archaeology and ethnography.[4]

If such simplification is at all possible, the defining 'moment' of the century was surely the decade between 1850 and 1860. The publication of Darwin's *The Origin of Species* came at the end of the decade, in 1859, and the decade effectively commenced with the extravagant celebration of industrial and imperial Victorian Britain, the Great Exhibition of 1851. Aside from ethnographic material, when the exhibition was relocated to Sydenham (as the Crystal Palace) in 1854 it included dinosaur displays, whose 'antediluvian animals' mark the acceptance of geological time over the preceding quarter of the century (fig 76).[5] The Great Exhibition did not itself include any archaeology *per se* (even if relevant proposals had been discussed).[6] It tells, however, of the great advances made in the subject during the middle decades of the century and its impact on the nation's consciousness, that, had the exhibition occurred ten to twenty years later, such material would surely have featured.

The broader learned society background to this study has been thoroughly outlined in Evans's history of the Society and, more recently, variously reviewed by Levine, Stocking, van Riper and Sweet, thus requiring only brief discussion here.[7] In the first decades of the century the Society's meetings arguably served as an alternative for London's collectors to the fashionable salons of the Continent, and it included peers and royalty among its Fellows. In the century's later decades the Society could no longer be considered 'fashionable' and its membership was by then much more nationally representative, to the point that by 1890 the majority of its Fellows no longer gave a London address.[8] Though still heavily involved in collecting, the Society certainly included the bulk of the country's active/influential archaeologists and carried considerable authority.

Levine has declared that, by the later decades of the nineteenth century, antiquarianism was 'fast lapsing into obscurantism'.[9] Though even today any pronouncement of its complete demise would be misleading, it was certainly in some decline by the latter half of the century. This is primarily attributable to large-scale social dynamics (for example, the emergent middle class), institutionalization and also the rise of specialist-cum-professional 'domains'.[10] The latter can be charted through the advent of learned special-interest societies. Beginning with 'harder science', the Royal Geological Society and the British Association for the Advancement of Science were founded in 1807 and 1830 respectively; this impetus was furthered with the printing clubs of the 1830s and 1840s.[11] After the 1830s there was a blossoming of learned societies, including among many, the (now) Numismatic Society (1836), the Historical Society of Science (1840), the Royal Historical Society (1868), the Society for Biblical Archaeology (1870), the Society for the Protection of Ancient Buildings (1877) and the

Folklore Society (1878). For the purposes of this discussion, the most significant would have to be the formation of the British Archaeological Association (1843) and – subsequently engendered through factional split – the Archaeological Institute of Great Britain and Ireland (1846).[12] With its espoused 'activist'/populist ethos, as opposed to the perceived elitism and inertia of the Antiquaries of the day, the history of the latter has been much studied and need not be dwelt upon here.[13]

Membership of and attendance at the many learned societies of the time was by no means exclusive to their specializations. Take, for example, Thomas Crofton Croker. Active in the second quarter of the century, and a government clerk by profession, he was also a renowned folklorist with a private museum of Irish ethnography.[14] Aside from being a Fellow of the Society, he was a founding member of the Camden and Percy Societies and also the British Archaeological Association.[15] Equally, during the latter half of the century there was Sir John Evans. A successful paper manufacturer and eminent archaeologist, prior to his election as President of the Society in 1885 he had similarly held the same post for the Numismatic (1874) and Anthropological Societies (1878).[16]

This attests to multiple connections (and multi-faceted individuals) and overlapping intellectual networks, with the breadth of some being remarkable. In the middle/latter part of the century Pitt-Rivers's 'sphere', for example, encompassed (aside from his immediate archaeological colleagues) not only Spencer, Huxley, Tylor, Lubbock and even Darwin himself, but also the leading geologists, Boyd Dawkins and Prestwich, and the philologist Max Müller.[17] While perhaps lacking a comparable sense of interrelated intellectual purpose, earlier in the century such networks were, if anything, even more wide-ranging. Not only would this include the renowned Banks' Circle, but also that of John Britton, through whom connections can be traced from the architect Sir John Soane and the Colt Hoare family to Turner and the leading illustrators of the day.[18] Without any basis of formal training in excavation techniques, 'site-mentoring' fostered its own linkages. The dominant genealogy saw Pitt-Rivers tutored by Canon Greenwell (himself working with the other great barrow-diggers of the day, Thurnam and Lukis), and his own assistants. Foremost among the latter would be Harold St George Gray, who subsequently went on to have a significant impact on major sites of the earlier twentieth century, including Glastonbury.[19]

Accepting the 'bias' of what archaeological developments are considered of sufficient importance for inclusion in the century's time-line (for example, the 'great books' and landmark organizational/institutional foundations) then table 5 also well expresses the floruit of British archaeology from 1840 to 1890. Others, though, more concerned with mainstream intellectual developments (and prehistory alone), would see it beginning to lose its impetus by as early as the 1870s.[20] Whatever actual *terminus* is chosen, in the later decades of the century the project of British prehistory arguably stalled and it was not until the later 1920s and 1930s that it saw a significant resurgence. The key point here is that, when considering the drive towards 'archaeology' – which was arguably announced with the first publication of the *Archaeological Journal* in 1845 – we are, effectively, only dealing here with two

270

overlapping generations. The first, responsible for the Archaeological Association, coalesced around Way, Pettigrew and Roach Smith; the second, the Lubbock Circle, which aside from Lubbock himself included Pitt-Rivers, Evans and Franks (and otherwise an array of politicians and scientists).

Staring at us from their portraits, the bewhiskered patriarchs of the day – particularly Pitt-Rivers and Evans – stride across the history of the subject. Men of private means, and obviously rare talent, energy and intellect, their status was clearly furthered by high-ranking societal affiliations. Certainly this period of the subject's development has a quality of heroic individualism, but against this, a key, if somewhat contradictory, theme requiring exploration is the *group basis* of archaeology as a 'scientific' enterprise.

At this juncture we need not be overly concerned with any hard-and-fast definition of *antiquarianism* as opposed to *archaeology*, as in many respects the two were generally interchangeable.[21] The latter term came into greater use during the second half of the century and applied, in particular, to excavated remains, in contrast to the much wider breadth of antiquarian study, which also encompassed manuscripts, standing buildings, jewellery and much else. We need, however, to be wary of the implication that, based on the much-cited adoption of geological technique, archaeology was necessarily more scientific; in practice, much of its citation during the later nineteenth century was, if not rhetorical, then at least aspirational. In the early eighteenth century Stukeley, for example, could link antiquarianism and science: 'Without drawing or designing, the study of antiquities or any other science is lame and imperfect', just as Mantell in 1847 could directly compare geological and antiquarian procedures:

> In attempting to interpret the natural records of the earth's physical history, *the Geologist is often in the condition of the Antiquary who endeavours to decipher an ancient manuscript*, in which the original characters are obscured and partially obliterated by later superscriptions [emphasis added].[22]

COLLECTION, PERFORMANCE AND DISPLAY

Given the limits of transportation, much of the era's 'connections' were by letter. Accordingly, the majority of contributions to *Archaeologia* were *communications* – that is, letters sent to the Society. The head-line on many such letters sent throughout the century (though greatly decreasing over its second half) included the recipient's name at the Society (for example, 'a communication concerning [subject] sent to Sir Joseph Banks by [sender's name]').[23] Such reference suggests the influence of 'network patronage', with the recipient effectively supporting and vouching for the credibility of the correspondent.

At this time all contributions to *Archaeologia* were read out at Society meetings (with longer papers being presented over consecutive gatherings), even if distance prevented the attendance of their author. It was only in the middle decades of the

Fig 77. 'The sorting table'. Society meetings within Somerset House: (a) the Cruikshank print of 1812 with Aberdeen in the chair as President (with Carlisle and Lysons to his left: see Nurse 2000 on the political/societal satire of the image); (b) detail of the same, showing misattributed antiquities: (1) a pig sty labelled 'sarcophagus'; (2) a shaver bowl entitled 'a helmet'; (3) a coal scuttle tagged 'an ancient shield'; (4) a barrel hoop as the 'wedding ring of Hercules'; (5) preservative jars ('beans', 'cabbage' and 'gooseberry') presented as 'funerary urns'; (6) a boot-maker's leg masquerading as 'a fragment of Apollo'; (7) among the manuscripts scattered around the table are *The Antiquity of Rapes, Antiquity of the Black Joke* and *Essay on Royal Bastards*; (c) detail of the 1844 Fairholt print (see Evans 1956, pl xxxi for full original); note that the projector-like containers on the right side of both images are the Society's ballot boxes; (d) and (e) 'Learned Society room-plans' at Somerset House, with the central table arrangement of the Antiquaries in contrast to the 'lecture-layout' of the Royal Society (as detailed in Chambers's 1781 plan – wrongly dated to 1777 by Evans; now SAL, MS 760 – Evans 1956, pl xxi).

twentieth century that meeting presentation was no longer a prerequisite for publication. The public, or at least, meeting-based *performance of the past*, is, therefore, crucial to consider when evaluating antiquarian practices. Both it and the material technologies of the day directly situate the published accounts that otherwise only attest to their content today.

It was not until the 1890s that the Society acquired 'a magic lantern'.[24] Prior to that time, addresses could be illustrated by having figures pinned up on walls, held aloft by assistants or displayed afterwards. Pitt-Rivers, for example, is reported to have exhibited 'a series of diagrams, two models, and a large collection of flint implements and animal remains' in conjunction with his 1875 Cissbury lecture.[25] Equally, as depicted in the engraving of Schliemann's 1877 slide-less, audience-packed lecture concerning his work at Mycenae to the Society that appeared in the *Illustrated London News* of that year,[26] there seems little sense of polite lecturing distances and behaviour. Admittedly, that was a case of a special performance, but a similar sense of hubbub also effuses the Cruikshank print of 1812, rudely lampooning the tastes and misattribution of material by the Society's members (fig 77). This stands in marked contrast to the 1844 Fairholt print of a Society meeting which shows an altogether more sedate and dignified affair. The one, of course, suffers from exaggerated cartoon caricature, while the other is a formally staged portrait. Yet, commanding the centre of both is a grand table, with the President at its head and the Fellows arranged down its long sides. Things are on the table: in Fairholt's, books and rolled plans (and a ballot box); in Cruikshank's, manuscripts and a quixotic array of false antiquities. These were not front-focused lecturing spaces but rather more a parliamentary face-to-face forum, and it was these 'great tables' that structured the Society's meetings. Although the procedure was underlain by 'base' collectors' interests, in effect it was upon these tables that the past, or at least its artefacts, was sorted and judged. It reflects upon a division between the Society's collectors and archaeologists (and probably telling of an emergent emphasis upon printed pictorial representation) that a letter to the Executive Committee at the end of the century suggested that the exhibition of objects was taking up too much meeting time and rather these should only be displayed following the presentation of papers.[27]

The *conversazione* or 'temporary museum' displays of plans, artefacts and curios were also a feature of both local and other national society meetings, their primary purpose being the evaluation of findings.[28] Various staged events often accompanied these: among the most dramatic must surely have been that held on 10 September 1844 to mark the First Annual Meeting of the British Archaeological Association in Canterbury. Visiting members assembled in the morning at Breach Down to view the final opening of eight barrows that had previously been excavated to 'within a foot of the place of presumed deposit'. Later in the day they inspected two barrows dug in the grounds of the mansion of the Association's president, having previously viewed 'his lordship's interesting collection of antiquities'. It is necessary to recognize here just how central collecting was to antiquarian culture. It was what linked the great connoisseurs of the Society of Antiquaries and other London-based societies

A

B

C

D

E

with local enthusiasts. Though many individuals, indeed, held extensive personal museums, motivated by a spirit of local pride and edification, the massed material of a number of local groups provided the foundations for their respective town and county museums.[29]

Given the technological constraints upon the era's meetings, various display techniques were employed. Models were used to render buildings, monuments and sites, and they became part of the Society's collections.[30] This practice dated back to the later eighteenth century. In 1787 Field Marshall Conway presented a scale wooden model of a megalithic 'druidic temple' from Mont St Helier in Jersey. The monument had been found during military levelling operations and, presented to him by the island's assembly on his retirement as Governor, he had its stones re-erected in the grounds of his estate at Park Place, Henley-on-Thames.[31] Upon his bequest of the model to the Society, accompanied by a description of the site's discovery (1787; see also Molesworth in the same volume of *Archaeologia*), the Society remarked in its Minute Book upon this unusual gift.[32] This suggests that such model rendering was then rare, whereas in point of fact in 1767 they had received a cork model of the 'Temple of the Sibyl at Tivoli' (cat. no. 16). In 1830 Captain W Smyth similarly presented a model of the baths at Lipari (cat. no. 8).[33] These latter two pieces obviously reflect the impact of Grand Tours and can, therefore, be considered as mementoes to travel and testimonials to the appreciation of classical prototypes.

During the nineteenth century, model displays would seem to have featured in the Society's meetings. Stephen Stone's communication of the Standlake excavation, held to be among the first 'proper' open-area excavations in Britain (see fig 79a), was accompanied by a base-plan model.[34] Though Pitt-Rivers was obviously familiar with models through his military background, it would seem that Stone's rendering did indeed influence his application of this medium.[35] In turn, it was the display of his models at the Society that inspired the excavators of Silchester to explore such techniques.[36]

Among the other display techniques then used were paper-squeegee impressions to present cuneiform inscriptions,[37] and various types of casts and mouldings were also experimented with. Crucially, these attempts to duplicate artefacts attest to the educational aspirations behind such collections and tell of a sense of purpose beyond the rarefied value of objects alone. Although, of course, such practices also eroded the status of 'genuine' finds, given the trade in manufactured artefacts that then adorned many a collector's cabinet.[38]

The nineteenth century saw revolutionary changes in the technology of representation and published reproduction, primarily the advent of photography and lithography. Both had enormous repercussions for academic illustration. Invented in the 1830s, photography did not see any significant application in archaeology until the 1850s, when photographers accompanied Mediterranean and Egyptian expeditions.[39] As head of the Ordnance Survey, in 1867 Sir Henry James published a volume of zincographic photographs documenting Stonehenge and the stones of Callanish,[40] and an address by Pitt-Rivers to the Ethnological Society in 1869 was apparently accompanied by an exhibition of Thompson's photographs of the great henge and other megaliths.[41] *Notes and Queries* for 1852/3 carried correspondence on the use of photography in archaeology, with Dr Hugh Welch Diamond advocating that the Society consider this process largely for the purposes of recording materials exhibited at its meetings. Although the Society's response was positive, Diamond apparently did little to further this.[42]

The potential for photography to illustrate artefacts and also convey complex three-dimensional 'findings' (both architectural and stratigraphic) was obviously great, as it could significantly reduce the need for lengthy description. At first, however, photographs could not be printed directly but had to be stuck into texts and served rather as a means of converting images into lithographic or engraved formats.[43] Nevertheless, the Society seems to have been particularly conservative in the uptake of this medium (see, however, below concerning their status as 'proof').[44] In contrast, the *Journal of the Anthropological Institute* for 1875, for example, included photographs of Andaman Islanders,[45] and in 1868 the *Journal of the Ethnological Society of London* published a plate of a naked African male before a background grid in demonstration of a standard means of 'measuring the human form'.[46] Yet it was only in the century's last decade that excavation photographs for Silchester were included within *Archaeologia*,[47] and Greenwell's 'barrows' paper of 1890 was accompanied by photographic plates of carved chalk objects.

DEMONSTRATION, REPRESENTATION AND PRACTICE

Perusing the metres of shelf-space now occupied by *Archaeologia* conveys a sense of deep-rooted academic enterprise. First published in 1770, volume 2 of 1778 saw the inclusion of what can broadly be considered ten excavation reports (four of which related to barrow-digging, including Pownall's investigations at Newgrange). By its time depth, the journal provides a unique source by which to chart the development of archaeological reportage. Yet we must be wary of succumbing to its amassed weight and should, instead, attempt to situate its contents in the context of their day. The societal framing of these contributions is all important; within *Archaeologia* renowned fieldwork notices appeared cheek by jowl with studies of the 'Art of Watchmaking', 'Pirates' or the 'Resting place of the Ark', all telling of the eclectic breadth of antiquarianism and the 'miscellany of its tracts'.

In order to address the changing character of nineteenth-century fieldwork, a sample of twenty representative reports published within that journal has been analysed (table 6). Typical of the century's preoccupations, four-fifths relate to funerary sites and half consist of various forms of barrow-digging. In addition, the middle decades of the era saw a spate of Saxon (flat) cemetery excavations that are here attested by four sites (Barrow Furlong, Harnham, Long Wittenham and Frilford; fig 78). Equally representative is the fact that – Roman investigations aside (Caerhun, Holwood Hill and Silchester) – settlement sites hardly feature; the occupation remains encountered by Pitt-Rivers at Caburn were, if not incidental, at least of secondary concern in his investigations of the hillfort's earthworks.[48] In tracing developments within fieldwork reports, emphasis will be paid to their graphic provision. Not only does this relate to the establishment of subject-specific conventions, but also to the understanding that the subject's visual component itself relates to the realization of distinctly archaeological modes of knowledge and thought. In other words, understanding what it is to 'learn to see collectively' within a disciplinary framework and, by extension, to accept what came to constitute its proof of evidence and authority.[49]

Although Hodder's paper of 1989 concerning site reportage is less a historiographical study than a 'call to arms' for the writing of archaeology in the present, he is essentially correct in his appraisal that, during the earlier nineteenth century, archaeological reports were largely chronicles of discovery.[50] Their titles – variously 'an account of the opening of a . . . barrow' or 'the discovery of . . . remains' – accurately denote their content; few provide full inventories of what was found, but most detail the manner of 'the finding'. Drawing upon the pillars of the countryside, the clergy

Table 6. Nineteenth-century excavation reports published in *Archaeologia* (italicized entries indicate non-barrow/cemetery sites)

TABLE 6: NINETEENTH-CENTURY EXCAVATION REPORTS PUBLISHED IN *ARCHAEOLOGIA*

Site/publication date	Text (no. of pages)	Full-page plates	In-text figures	Map	Plan	Section (S)/ elevation (E)
Wiltshire tumuli (Cunnington 1806)	8	6	–	–	–	–
Derbyshire round barrow (Rooke 1809)	5	2	–	–	Y	–
Caerhun (Lysons 1812)	8	4	–	Y	Y	–
Stoney Littleton, Somerset (Colt Hoare 1821)	6	3	–	–	Y	E
Holwood Hill, Kent (Kempe 1829)	15	2	1	Y	Y	E
Barlow, Essex (Gage 1836)	18	5	–	–	Y	E
Breach Down, Kent (Conyngham 1844)	10	1	2	–	–	–
Iffins Wood, near Canterbury (Akerman 1844)	5	–	2	–	Y	E
Five Cambridgeshire barrows (Neville 1847)	5	–	1	–	–	–
Barrow Furlong, Northants (Dryden 1849)	9	3	–	–	Y	–
Harnham, near Salisbury (Akerman 1853a)	20	4	–	Y	Y	–
Long Wittenham, Berks (Akerman 1860)	16	3	10	–	–	–
West Kennet, Wilts (Thurnam 1860)	17	–	10	Y	Y	E
Frilford, Berks (Rolleston 1869)	69	3	–	–	–	–
Barrow near Dover, Kent (Woodruff 1880)	4	1	1	–	–	S
Caburn, Sussex (Pitt-Rivers 1881)	72	4	7	Y	Y	S
Yorkshire barrows (Greenwell 1890)	72	2	34	–	–	–
Youngsbury, Herts (J Evans 1890)	10	1	–	–	–	–
Aylesford, Kent (A Evans 1890)	70	6	17	–	–	S
Silchester (Fox and Hope 1901)	26	2	9	–	Y	–

and local gentry, the conditions of Lysons's work at Caerhun could be considered typical of much early practice:

> In the year 1800, Colonel Greville favoured me with an introduction to the Rev. Hugh Davies Griffith, the amiable and hospitable proprietor of Caerhun, from whom I received a pressing invitation to assist at the investigation of the Roman remains above-mentioned . . . In consequence of this invitation, I went into Caernarvonshire, in the latter end of July, 1801, and the morning after my arrival, Mr Griffth having got together as many labourers as could be spared from the hay-making, we proceeded to investigate these remains.[51]

The army itself was another occasional source of site labour and, through the patronage of Sir Joseph Banks, soldiers provided the equipment and manpower for Lysons's earlier investigations at Woodchester.[52]

There is an immediacy to these early letter-based accounts. Most were published in the year directly following the fieldwork and there is little indication of writing for any disciplinary 'eternity' (ie, they were not writing for 'us'). For example, the underlying structure of Akerman's 1853 report on the Anglo-Saxon cemetery at Harnham was essentially that of a diary, with the catalogue of its interments simply a register of graves dug each day (see fig 78). Equally, in these early fieldwork accounts there is a sense of the Society's collective participation. Some papers are accompanied by separately authored scene-setting contributions, usually by their better-established Society recipients; for example, Roach Smith's introduction to Dryden's Barrow Furlong report or Akerman's postscript to Conyngham's Breach Down account.[53] Akerman seems, in fact, to have written Bell's account of the Iffins Wood barrow investigations[54] and in his 1853 New Forest pottery kiln paper contributions by him bracket the Revd J Pemberton Bartlett's original letter-account of the fieldwork (fig 79e). Moreover, for correspondents within ready reach of London, the published presentation of artefacts might be kept to a minimum as the finds themselves could be displayed during Society meetings. This is the case with Kempe's account of his work at the Holwood Hill temple in 1828. Within the body of the paper there is scant mention or illustration of artefacts (see below), but a postscript outlines the subsequent display of materials, and it is to this that the only detailed finds drawing (painted stucco) is appended.

Surveying site reports within *Archaeologia* over the course of the century reveals basic trends and widespread discrepancies (see table 6). Certainly, those from its second half are generally substantially longer (thirty-eight text pages in average length, as opposed to nine prior to 1850), with the number of illustrations showing a comparable rise (from an average of four to eleven). Yet, the actual inclusion of what today is considered to be essential site data/representation – a location map and site plan – if anything, declines. With few exceptions, what the increased number of graphics attests is a greater emphasis upon chronology and finds classification, and the subsequent necessity to illustrate artefacts:

> The notion that a record of *facts* copiously illustrated but sparingly dilated with theory would be acceptable to the antiquary and to the historical inquirer, is

Fig 78. Saxon
cemeteries. *Top*:
Dryden's Marston St
Lawrence site of 1843
(note the indication of
compass-station points
for its surveying:
Dryden 1849);
below: Akerman's letter-
annotated Harnham
Hill plan (Akerman
1853a).

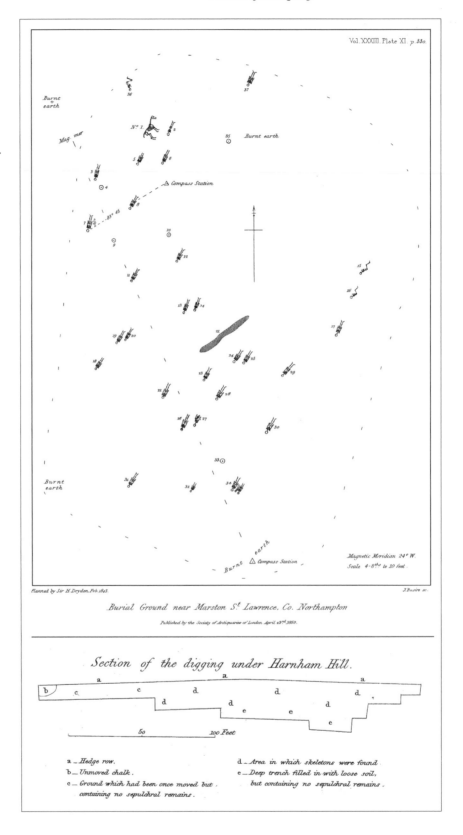

Vol.XXXIII. Plate XI. *p.380.*

Burnt + earth

Mag mer

No 1.

Burnt earth

△ *Compass Station*

Burnt earth

Burnt + earth

△ *Compass Station*

Magnetic Meridian 24° W.
Scale 4·8ths to 10 feet.

Planned by Sir H.Dryden.Feb.1843.   *J.Basire sc.*

Burial Ground near Marston St. Lawrence, Co. Northampton

Published by the Society of Antiquaries of London. April 28th 1850.

Section of the digging under Harnham Hill.

a   a   a
b   c   c   d   d   d   d
d   d   e   e   d
e

50   100 Feet

a _ *Hedge row.*
b_ *Unmoved chalk.*
c_ *Ground which had been once moved but*
containing no sepulchral remains.

d _ *Area in which skeletons were found.*
e_ *Deep trench filled in with loose soil,*
but containing no sepulchral remains.

278

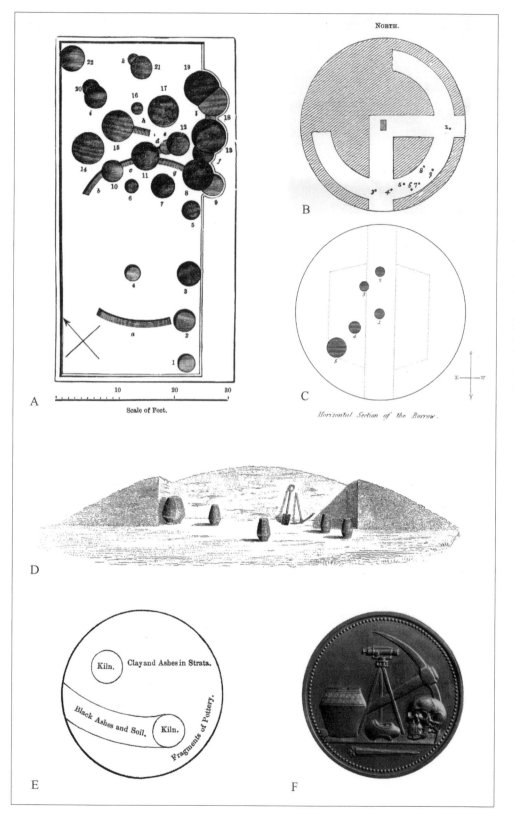

Fig 79. 'Perfect geometries'. Mid-century site graphics, whose stylization and paucity of convention reflects the difficulties of rendering soil-based plan data: (a) plan of Standlake (Stone 1857, 94); (b) plan of barrow at Collingbourn, Wilts (Thurnam 1871, fig 14); (c) and (d) plan ('horizontal section' with cremation urns indicated) and 'view' of the Iffins Wood barrow (Akerman 1844, 59, 60); (e) plan of the New Forest kiln excavations (Akerman 1853b); (f) Pitt-Rivers's excavation medallion (Bowden 1991, fig 59).

proved to have been well founded . . . *Many valuable essays and communica-*
tions are often obscure, if not rendered utterly unintelligible, from the absence
of <u>delineations of the objects</u> described and commented on, and nowhere is the
evil more conspicuous than in the proceedings of societies [emphasis added].[55]

The paucity of locational graphics within fieldwork reports is open to a number of
interpretations. On the one hand, it suggests a lack of surveying skills and map-
making abilities. While men of military and engineering survey background might
dominate the history of the subject (for example, Pitt-Rivers and Wheeler), such
skills were evidently not widespread nor maps readily available.[56] At least in terms of
mapping, their omission also seems to suggest a faith in a timeless countryside. The
entire concept of any potential widespread change within its fabric is probably only
a post-First World War phenomenon. Before that, announcing that an investigation
occurred within the corner of 'this or that's' squire's lands was evidently considered
sufficiently lasting reference. Equally, the paucity of excavation plans indicates just
how late any basis of site-specific comparison arose (ie, sites as 'types').

The quality and style of accompanying illustrations also varies enormously. Some
seemingly show the influence of distinct artistic traditions. The 'view' of Upton Great
Barrow in Cunnington's 1806 Wiltshire tumuli paper is entirely picturesque and
Conyngham's 1844 report on the marathon exploration of Saxon barrows at Breach
Down is introduced with a comparable landscape scene (fig 80a). Of the latter, with
the mounds set before a commanding windmill, gentlemen and their wives attend the
opening of one of the monuments as if at a picnic. A darker, almost 'Piranesi-esque'
romanticism suffuses a full-page-plate view of the remains of the Holwood Roman
temple (fig 80c).[57] The foreground is strewn with finds, such as sarcophagi and building tiles, and this is their sole illustration. In the Breach Down report, aside from an
engraving of shield bosses, the depiction of artefacts is restricted to a jumbled, *en
masse* 'still-life' setting (fig 81).[58] A comparable arrangement even accompanied John
Evans's 1890 report of a barrow at Ware, near Youngsbury, Hertfordshire. Its finds
were depicted on plinth-like boxes, which creates a more formal composition and, as
a single grave assemblage, has a contextual validity that the Breach Down figure lacks
(it also has a scale: see fig 81, top). Nevertheless, both show the material as *displayed*.
Artistic style may not, therefore, have been so much a crucial factor as rendering how
artefacts were actually presented at meeting venues.[59]

Relating to issues of analogy and 'everyday experience' (and the distance thereto),
it is clear in these early excavation reports that the character of the archaeology
encountered influenced its presentation. Roman-related accounts, such as those of
Caerhun or the Holwood temple, are greatly concerned with (stone) buildings and so
greater general competence is found and, accordingly, presentation of their remains
was more directly comparable to architectural modes. Certainly the most marked
variability is found in barrow reports. Just as stone circles were also reasonably
depicted (for example, fig 80b), of the latter as a *megalithic* tomb and therefore
involving more obviously 'architectural-type' components (ie, stone), Colt Hoare's 1821

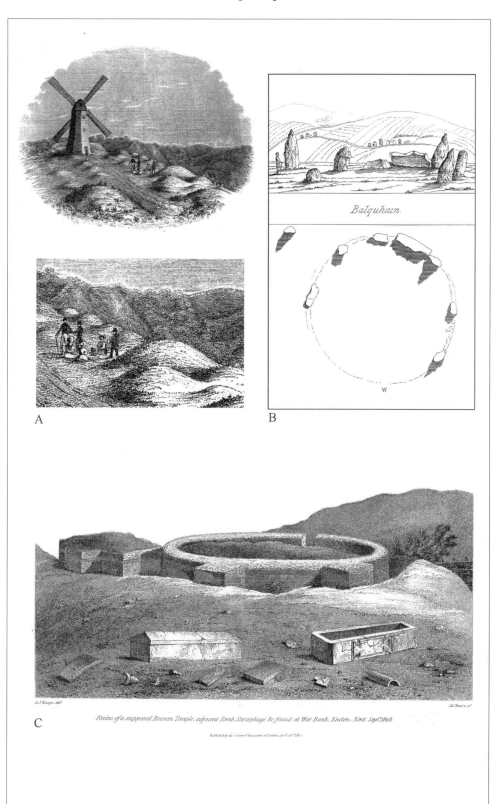

A

B

C

Ruins of a supposed Roman Temple, adjacent Tomb, Sarcophagi &c, found at War Bank, Keston, Kent. Sept.r 1828.

Fig 80. 'A picturesque pursuit'. (a) introductory view to Conyngham's Breach Down report of 1844 (*below*: detail of the opening of one of its Saxon barrows); (b) Logan's 1829 illustration of Balquhain stone circle (see Evans 2000 concerning such 'shaded plan' illustration styles); (c) Kempe's view of the Holwood Hill temple (1829; note the foreground littered with architectural and funerary fragments, and also the wall-chasing technique of its excavation).

Fig 81. 'Still-life' displays. *Top*: 'massed' finds group from Conyngham's barrow-digging 'marathon' at Breach Down in 1844; *below*: 'plinthed' grave-assemblage figure from the Youngsbury barrow (Evans 1890).

Antiquities found in the Breach Downs Tumuli.

VESSELS OF GLASS AND EARTHENWARE, ETC., FOUND IN A BARROW AT YOUNGSBURY, NEAR WARE.

Stoney Littleton report is well illustrated with a handsome plan and elevations. Yet, oddly enough given its author's renowned topographic interests, it lacks a map and there are no drawings of any finds. At the other end of the spectrum, there is Greenwell's 1890 publication, which outlines the excavation of no less than sixty-one barrows. At seventy-two pages, it includes thirty-four in-text figures and two plates, though all of the latter are of finds and there are no plans or sections whatsoever (a trait common to his other reports, such as Grimes Graves).

Between these extremes there was much diversity, something especially true of the representation of *earthen* barrows, where the problem was, of course, how to render (and excavate) 'soil'. Woodruff's 1880 report of a barrow near Dover, for example, is illustrated with a highly accomplished 'geological-style' section (extending down through the mound's deposits into the Collared Urn interments below), but it lacks any corresponding plan. Though in the Iffins Wood report there is an oddly schematic plan (termed a 'horizontal section') and a perspective outline drawing showing the location of urns within the sondage through its mound, no attempt has been made to render its soil sequence (figs 79b, c and d).[60]

Clearly some excavators simply had very little appreciation of 'graphic literacy' in their presentation of excavation results. Not only would this include Canon Greenwell but also John Evans, whose Youngsbury barrow – just as his earlier reports on the Box Moor villa site – has no plan or map representation.[61] Even Evans's renowned 1860 paper, 'On the occurrence of flint implements in undisturbed beds of gravel, sand and clay', is without adequate graphic documentation. Outlining observations concerning the occurrence of hand-axes in quarry deposits made when he and Prestwich toured France, this had a major impact in convincing Britain's learned communities of the deep antiquity of early mankind. Although describing the geological sequences, it is without any accompanying map or section figures whatsoever (the twenty-eight-page contribution having only two full-page illustrations of finds and a pair of in-text figures of the same).[62] As such, in the manner of its presentation and actual illustrative 'proof', this paper differs little from Frere's note on the Hoxne material from sixty years before.[63] Yet it was clearly stated in the 1859 *Proceedings* outlining the paper's reading that Prestwich presented the Society with the photographs of the findings *in situ*. Despite recent searches, this crucial – arguably 'world-turning' – record unfortunately cannot now be located.[64] Albeit without published verification (and Prestwich's 1860 paper arising from their inspection visit also lacked maps or sections), the 'proof' was evidently presented at the meeting of 2 June 1859 and, thereby, adjudicated by the body of the Society's membership.

The lack of graphic documentation in their papers seems, nevertheless, extraordinary and Darwin, writing to Charles Lyell on 4 May 1860, clearly appreciated the need for section-expressed information (fig 82a):

My dear Lyell
I had promised me an arrowhead found by Col. Erskine on his property in peat in Aberdeenshire; which I will send you; but the only point of interest about

the case, is that vast numbers were found at one place where there were many stones fitted for the manufacture. I daresay you know about it, but I may mention that John Lubbock tells me that the flint tools in France are found in such vast numbers, in Peat that M. Boucher de Perthes told him that he might take as many as he liked.

These facts, to my mind, remove one of the greatest difficulties of the case of the gravel-beds – celts – namely their surprising numbers. *I do hope that you will go to France again, & give us lots of Sections. I found that until J. Lubbock drew me a rough section I did not in the least understand their position*; & hardly anything seems known about the extension of the beds of gravel, clay & or their manner of formation. The case seems to me to deserve not day's but month's of work [emphasis added].[65]

A formal concept of *proof* only seems to have been introduced with Pitt-Rivers. In his recording of timber piles exposed in peat near London Wall in 1866 he actually named two 'witnesses' – Carter Blake and the Revd Heath – to vouch for the precision of his observations, and who publicly testified to such following the paper's delivery in 1866 (fig 82b).[66] (There is a certain irony in this as, led by Franks and obviously influenced by recent papers on the theme, he mistakenly interpreted these as the remains of a Late Iron Age lake village.) He went even further in this vein in his investigation of the earthworks at Caesar's Camp, Folkestone, in 1878. Trenching what he thought to be an Iron Age hillfort, he rather proved it to be a medieval castle. As a consequence of this revision, he stressed the veracity of his results in his report: 'In order that evidence obtained may be strictly reliable it should if possible, be of a character that might be *acceptable in a court of justice*' [emphasis added].[67]

It cannot be established with certainty where this emphasis upon proof within Pitt-Rivers's work originated. His legal experience may have contributed, and, from his background in military ordnance, he was obviously familiar with both formal test procedures and the generic modelling of operational principles and technical performance.[68] Equally, and as outlined below, the 'antiquity of mankind' debates of the 1850s had clearly thrust the evaluation of scientific evidence into the public lime-light (with Pitt-Rivers's own 1872 'flint in gravels' paper being thoroughly illustrated).

Yet, his more extreme declaration of the role of proof in the case of Caesar's Camp may well have related to an immediate impetus, that being the vexed interpretation arising from the first two seasons at Cissbury hillfort in 1867–8.[69] Having failed to understand the inter-relationship of the site's earlier flint mines and its later 'entrenchment' (nor establish the latter's Iron Age date), he saw both as relating to a 'Stone Age camp'. At this time Pitt-Rivers was primarily concerned with matters of artefact typology and, accordingly, the report only includes two pages of flint illustrations and is without feature-specific plans or sections.[70] Moreover, given his ideas concerning the long continuity of primitive forms, all of its flintwork was conflated into one assemblage encompassing both 'early' and 'late' types (ie, both Palaeolithic and Neolithic material).

284

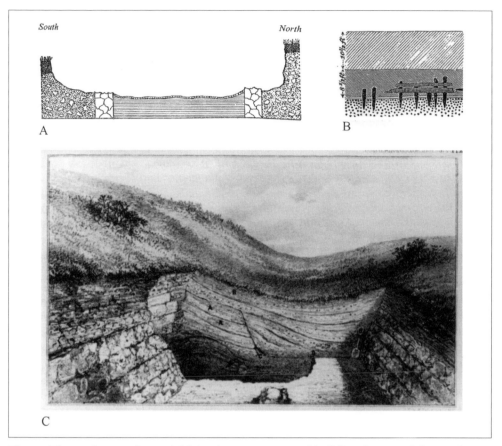

Fig 82. 'The testimony of strata'. (a) Section across a paved building floor at Silchester, from Darwin's *The Formation of Vegetable Mould, through the action of worms* (1881, fig 14); (b) one of Pitt-Rivers's 'piles near London Wall' sections (published full size: 1867b); (c) 'perspective section' across the ramparts of Cissbury hillfort, with flint mine shaft below (Pitt-Rivers 1875).

Darwin's Silchester section was rendered from sketches supplied by the Revd Joyce (Darwin's sons visited the site in 1877 as part of their father's worm/vegetation mould-generation researches). Joyce had directed the excavations since 1855 and it was probably he who produced the first 'proper' section in British archaeology. Otherwise unpublished and only occurring in his site journals (held by Reading Museum), it has been suggested that, after being displayed in the Society of Antiquaries, these sections may have inspired Pitt-Rivers's London Wall figures (Boon 1974, 24–6; Bowden 1991, 155).

The latter was obviously the source of some controversy, and in the years that followed the specific morphology of Neolithic flint mines was fully established by Greenwell's investigations at Grimes Graves and, through others, subsequently digging at Cissbury itself (Pitt-Rivers having failed to bottom its mine shafts and recognize their side galleries). In 1875 Pitt-Rivers duly returned to re-excavate Cissbury (raising the necessary funds by subscription through the Anthropological Institute) and, after much perseverance, demonstrated that its flint mines were indeed Neolithic and stratigraphically pre-dated the site's defences. The ensuing report set a high standard of documentation. It included a fine 'perspective section', with the eminent colleagues that accredited it being listed (fig 82c).[71] Telling of the stimulus of debate and 'mistakes' (and ensuing correction), this episode clearly propelled Pitt-Rivers's archaeology, with the result that his 1881 Caburn paper is the only one of those analysed in table 6 that fulfils all the expected 'modern' requirements of basic site reportage (it also includes his first site 'relics tables').

There is not the scope in this contribution to consider Pitt-Rivers's archaeology in detail, nor is there a need, given the extent of its study.[72] However, it is relevant to stress that, from the outset with his London Wall recording, it was with section-based recording that he associated scientific accuracy and, indeed, this was among the main facets of his work that led to his promotion as the 'father' of field archaeology.[73] This makes it all the more extraordinary that in the publication of his 'late period' Cranborne Chase site reports – for example, South Lodge and Wor Barrow – he actually dispensed with accurate section rendering, favouring instead their 'average' representation (though he still practised some degree of 'naturalistic' section recording in the field).[74] Their *raison d'être* was no longer the depiction of soil sequences as found, but rather the vertical stratigraphy of finds – and he variously projected all the artefacts (by period) recovered from the complete lengths of these sites' main ditches into one section.[75] Akin to the coloured pins used to depict the situation of period-attributed finds in the Wor Barrow models, he was, in effect, *modelling* the site's depositional processes in these figures.[76]

Pitt-Rivers's 'late period' site reports are idiosyncratic on other grounds. Possibly reflecting the need to produce display material for his Farnham museum, he was essentially creating a densely *visual archaeology*. Their reportage was led by graphic representation, of which the extensive use of photography (both on-site and for finds) was only one manifestation. Consider, for instance, the report for South Lodge from 1898.[77] Apart from its relics tables, it is forty-one pages long and has, in addition, ten full-page plates (and two small in-text figures). Yet the report proper only involves the first twelve pages of the text, with the remainder given over to plate captions. There are no separate finds reports *per se*, but these rather occur entirely as detailed caption descriptions (one being up to seven pages long). In effect, the site report has been transformed into a portfolio and, in being so dominated by illustrations, was unlike anything else published at the time (and even since).

Prior to the latter part of the nineteenth century, archaeology was essentially a personal pursuit, and excavation was a very personal project. This was not just determined by sponsorship and funding, but was also fundamental to its organization. Pitt-Rivers's Cranborne Chase campaigns are only the most extreme example of the (lone) director and his workmen labourers. Yes, he was accompanied by his trainee assistants, and eminent colleagues would visit to testify to the results, but the role of the site director was much more all-embracing than it became in the next century, and it was to him that the gamut of finds reportage fell. This in itself was a natural consequence of the infancy of the subject and reflects the paucity of specialist finds-based knowledge. While colleagues could pass learned opinion, there simply were not, for example, acknowledged prehistoric or Romano-British pottery specialists. This made for relatively seamless single-author reportage and obviously furthered the immediate, 'year-after' pace of publication.

Where specialist contribution first emerges is in the study of human skeletal remains. In Akerman's 1860 report of the investigations of the Long Wittenham Anglo-Saxon cemetery, Thurnam and Davis provided pertinent portions to the text.[78] Equally, Pitt-Rivers's 1872 Acton Terraces paper included a report on the animal bones by Busk, while his 1881 Caburn report cited soil analysed by Robb. Otherwise, the reportage of the site's finds was primarily the responsibility of its director.

This situation only began to change in the last decade of the century, with the Society's research excavations at the Romano-British town of Silchester. The Society had first started providing financial assistance to the excavations of its Fellows with the work at Harnham.[79] Other broadly comparable institutionally sponsored excavations had been proposed earlier, and some even implemented (though not by the Society). In the late 1860s there had been a British Association for the Advancement of Science (BAAS) initiative for Stonehenge; led by Pitt-Rivers, this was intended to involve both Lubbock and Evans.[80] Previously the Geological Society had sponsored the investigations at Brixham Cave (1858) while the BAAS also sponsored the excavations at Kent's Cavern (1865–80). Both these sites were of critical importance for stamping the antiquity of mankind, and their 'official' sponsorship lent greater credibility to their results.[81]

Nevertheless, the Society's funding for what would become the multi-specialist and interdisciplinary basis of archaeology at Silchester was of landmark significance.[82] The 1895 volume of *Archaeologia*, aside from including coin reports by Grueber and Haverfield, saw a contribution by Evans on ironwork from the 1890 season, and the 1900 report was followed by a separate paper by Gowland[83] on metallurgical industrial remains (with the report of the 1900 season including a section on plant remains by Reid). Yet there is still a haphazard quality to the inclusion of specialist contributions, and the Silchester reports cannot be considered particularly systematic. The site report 'formula' had yet to be achieved and, like the rise of widely acknowledged finds specialists, this only really arose in the early decades of the twentieth century. Nevertheless, the advent of archaeology as an institutionally orchestrated, group-based project at Silchester served to stamp the Society's authority on, and provide a model of, what was to become 'official' fieldwork practice.[84]

The haphazard, or almost incidental, quality of site reports over much of the nineteenth century suggests that there was little sense of prescription. Yet, as implied by the 1848 Roach Smith quotation above, 'programmatic' statements did begin to appear from its middle decades. In 1851 Akerman published his guide, *Directions for the Preservation of English Antiquities, especially those for the first three periods*, outlining the character of – and what finds might be expected from – the main site-types of prehistoric, Roman and Anglo-Saxon date.[85] In his role as the first Inspector of Ancient Monuments, Pitt-Rivers (in conjunction with the Anthropological Institute) led an initiative to improve the quality of barrow-digging,[86] and John Winter Jones's

1881 article in the *Edinburgh Review* equally tells of the growing divide between untrained amateur practitioners and 'career archaeologists':

> Meanwhile the rage for 'finding out something' by the spade and pickaxe requires anxious watching. Amateurs, however well meaning, cannot safely be left to their own devices. Some of them have already hidden more than they disclosed. There is a need to instruct and *discipline* the free lances of archaeology, and it is exactly here that an organization like that of the Society of Antiquaries may be best utilized in the interest of scientific discovery. Whatever may be thought of the advisability of subsidising a learned corporation by a grant from the Treasury, there can hardly be a doubt that the recognition of a society as a central board for controlling and systematising archaeological research would be a measure which could only produce excellent results [emphasis added].[87]

The cumulative weight of works published during the course of the century would surely itself have contributed to the development of archaeology as a longer term 'project'. Not only was this evident in the ever-growing amount of shelf-space occupied by *Archaeologia* (publishing the index of its first fifty volumes in 1889) and, eventually, the newer journals of its second half, but also in the number of 'great' books attesting to sustained campaigns of excavation – Roach Smith's *Collectanea Antiqua* (1848–80), Greenwell's *British Barrows* (1877), Bateman's *Ten Years Digging* (1861) or Pitt-Rivers's four *Cranborne Chase* volumes (1887–98) – as well as such major artefact studies as Evans's *Ancient Stone* (1872) and *Ancient Bronze Implements* (1881). In fact, the impetus variously towards massive and/or serial volumes by individual researchers suggests a desire for significant authority/impact through publication that verges on a 'personal institutionalization' of their work.[88] As the pages devoted to archaeology mounted, time would invariably contribute a sense of tradition to practice, and gone would be the immediacy of the succinct letter-accounts of the first half of the century.

In any review of developments in fieldwork during the century, this form of publication can only be considered crucial in the formation of archaeological practice. Certainly there were general improvements in the representation and intelligibility of reportage, and its interpretative framework greatly broadened, both in its geographical and in its temporal scope. This is not to say that near-equivalent quality reports were not produced in the early decades of the century, or that, on balance, its later years did not see work of a low standard. What is necessary is to try to distinguish whether there was any change in general consensus, as opposed to the groundbreaking initiatives of individuals and small-group factions (ie, 'genealogies').

On the one hand, the greater length and illustration of reports shows a distinctly 'textual' emphasis. Just as recovered artefacts did not require thorough illustration if they could themselves be viewed in Society meetings, the advent of more 'formal' report procedures reflects both a physical and a conceptual distancing of archaeological practice. Learning a 'language' of representation, one could be persuaded of results without personally knowing a site's director or having viewed its finds. In other words, this marks the onset of a distinction between *the reader* and the earlier *'listener'*/*'participant'*.

On the other hand, this was still very much a practice focused upon the reputation of the responsible individual(s); there was little sense of standardization and only highly diverse graphic documentation. Comparing, for example, the widely different quality of the excavation reports of John Evans and Pitt-Rivers (as opposed to their artefact studies), it becomes almost impossible to conceive of them as close colleagues. Add Greenwell to the canon of the time's leading archaeologists, then there is remarkably little baseline similarity in what they actually produced (all three being relatively eccentric).

Ultimately this raises the question of whether archaeology at the time should actually be considered *a formal discipline* as such. Despite Jones's pronouncement cited above, and the first steps towards issuing practical fieldwork guidelines, there seems to have been little sense of prescription generally. In short, there were no mechanisms to tell – and by public critique compel (the world still then being relatively 'gentlemanly') – other practitioners what to do. Reliant on acknowledged and/or institutionally endorsed standards of fieldwork – as marked by the accruing publication of the Society's Research Fund volumes and other excavation monographs (and also the proliferation of fieldwork manuals)[89] – any real sense of an accredited or persuasive disciplinary 'code' seems only to have arisen in the first half of the twentieth century.

Despite its widespread espousal, it is also essential to question just what kind of 'science' archaeology then actually practised. Section-recording and understanding of soil sequences/deposition was evidently not the norm, and typological artefact chronology was very much in its infancy (ie, it was as yet short of a formal classificatory science). What is obvious, however, is that – when decision-making mattered – there was *a group basis for arbitration*. The manner in which the Evans and Prestwich delegation travelled to France to decide formally upon the 'deep flints' issue is comparable to the *en masse* verification of Pitt-Rivers's section claims at Cissbury.

In this context another example is relevant: the 'cuneiform competition' hosted by the Royal Asiatic Society in London in 1857. Intended to quell doubts that the results of rival translators could be relied upon, three researchers (including Rawlinson) were each sent copies of an inscription from a recently discovered cylinder and then separately submitted their sealed translations to the adjudicating committee. It was the high level of correspondence between their accounts that provided the basis of verification, with 'truth' demonstrated in the concordance of independent research.[90] Occurring at a time when 'science' could not yet provide absolute results (as occurred later, for example, with radiocarbon dating), the recognition of this group-based adjudication of the past is essential to understanding the knowledge claims and procedures of the day. This must not be naive, nor ignore the existence of intellectual rivalry, the orchestration of results and the conscious mobilization of opinion. Nevertheless, *a basic collectivity* – a 'group seeing' – has been fundamental to the practice of archaeology.

SCIENCE AND THE CONTENT OF ANTIQUARIANISM

Van Riper has compared the contents of *Archaeologia*, the *Archaeological Journal* and the *Journal of the British Archaeological Association* between 1850 and 1875.[91] Dividing their contributions chronologically, the comparison shows a remarkable degree of consistency both between and, in each case, within the volume-by-volume contents of each (table 7). There was evidently little deviation within this 'mix' and it reflects a strong consensus of what a leading journal should then hold (generally twenty-two to twenty-eight papers in each). In all, medieval and later topics feature to the greatest extent by far and at more than three times the frequency of the next period – Roman studies. Prehistoric and Saxon contributions were roughly comparable (with *Archaeologia* having the highest representation of both) and, in all, non-European themes ranked lowest (again, though, being highest in *Archaeologia*).

Of course, this only provides limited insight into the content of 'antiquarian' production. To grasp its scope and potential changes throughout the century, different publication and intellectual contexts must be considered. The first of these issues is addressed in table 8, in which van Riper's criteria have been applied to contributions within *Archaeologia* throughout the nineteenth century. The basis of this analysis is not without difficulties: the assignment of a number of papers is ambiguous, as many concern multi-period themes that can only be categorized on the basis of their dominant topic; equally, such a breakdown provides little sense of relative 'weighting', so that minor contributions concerned, for example, with the carving on a church bench, are counted as equivalent to major excavation reports.

Again, the overall trend is one of remarkable consistency as regards their subject matter. The main difference that is readily discernible is a 10 per cent drop in the number of papers concerned with medieval and later themes after the first quarter of the century. This would seem largely attributable to the rise of printing clubs in the 1830s, as manuscript studies were among the main concern of many of the early entries of this type. Some of these were also very lengthy; for example, a translation of a French medieval manuscript in the 1824 volume ran to over 400 pages.[92] With this decline there was a corresponding rise in contributions concerned with Saxon, Roman and prehistoric material, with non-European subjects only increasing during

Table 7. Summary table of contents of *Archaeologia*, the *Archaeological Journal* and the *Journal of the British Archaeological Association* between 1850 and 1875 (based on van Riper 1993, Appendix 1)

TABLE 7: SUMMARY TABLE OF CONTENTS OF *ARCHAEOLOGIA*, ETC, 1850–75

Period	*Percentage of all papers*	*Average no. of papers per volume*
Medieval and later	60–69.7	15–17
Saxon	3.8–8.8	1–2
Roman	16.2–18.2	3–5
Prehistoric	4.7–7.4	1–2
Non-European	2.4–7.1	0.5–2

TABLE 8: SUMMARY TABLE OF CONTENTS OF *ARCHAEOLOGIA*, 1800–99

Table 8. Summary table of the contents of *Archaeologia*, 1800–99

	Medieval/later (%)	Saxon (%)	Roman (%)	Prehistoric (%)	Non-European (%)
1800–24	71.2 (23)	4.3 (1)	9.8 (3)	8.6 (3)	5.5 (2)
1825–46	61.2 (16)	9.1 (2)	13.7 (4)	10.3 (3)	5.6 (3)
1849–73	60 (17)	8.8 (2)	16.2 (5)	7.4 (2)	7.1 (2)
1875–99	60 (14)	5.4 (1)	17.1 (4)	10.9 (3)	6.9 (2)

the second half of the century. Throughout, the key factor is that, after the first quarter, medieval and later themes remain at a fairly constant 60 per cent of *Archaeologia*'s content. While there is no escaping its dominance, it is here that weighting becomes particularly relevant. Unlike the developments in fieldwork reportage charted above, for the most part the character of the journal's medieval and later contributions show little development over the course of the century (ie, they lack methodological refinement) and many were very brief. In addition, during the latter half of the nineteenth century there began to be published long synthetical studies on distinctly archaeological themes. For example, Thurnam's companion pieces on 'long' and 'round barrows' of 1869 and 1871 together run to 352 pages. Equally, this period saw the appearance of major international site summaries, ranging from the 'Swiss lake villages' (volume 38, 1860) to Schliemann's 'Troy' (volume 45, 1877) and even Gowland on Japanese dolmens (volume 55, 1897).

Thus far these analyses have demonstrated a strong homogeneity of antiquarian or archaeological content. What is necessary now is to extend the scope of these surveys to include both representative local and county journals and other academic publications. These are presented in table 9 for the period 1850–75. Despite the already rehearsed caveats (again using van Riper's categories), these also reflect the national trend, with medieval and later entries being in fact some 10–20 per cent higher, at around 80 per cent. Suggesting that the appellations 'antiquarian' and 'archaeological' were essentially interchangeable (see below), the publication profile of the Kent and Cambridge Societies is remarkably similar. Yet there are subtle differences. Cambridge had substantially fewer Saxon contributions than Kent's *Archaeologia Cantiana* (*Archaeol Cantiana*, established in 1858) and, whereas the latter was strictly limited to county coverage, the *Proceedings of the Cambridge Antiquarian Society* (*Proc Cambridge Antiq Soc*, established in 1840) included extra-county matters within Britain and also international and non-European papers. Cambridge's greater scope

Table 9. Summary of the contents of *Archaeologia*, local society and anthropology and ethnology journals, 1850–75 (entries in brackets indicate the average representation of papers per volume)

TABLE 9: SUMMARY TABLE OF CONTENTS OF *ARCHAEOLOGIA*, ETC, 1850–75

	Medieval/later (%)	Saxon (%)	Roman (%)	Prehistoric (%)		Non-European (%)		
Archaeologia	60 (17)	8.8 (2)	16.2 (5)	7.4 (2)		7.1 (2)		
Archaeol Cantiana	78.3 (9)	7.5 (1)	10.4 (1)	6.6 (1)		– –		
Proc Cambridge Antiq Soc	81.4 (31)	1.8 (1)	7.1 (3)	5.3 (2)		4.4 (2)		
J Anthropol Inst (I–IV; 1871–5)	9.1 (2)	7.6 (1)	1.5 (0.25)	34.8 (6)	+	47 (8)	=	81.8 %
Rep Brit Ass Advancement Sci	3.3 (0.2)	9 (1)	9 (1)	63.9 (4)	+	14.7 (1)	=	78.6 %

is surely attributable to the university affiliation of its prominent members, and the greater travel and overseas research interests that that afforded. However, these distinctions are essentially incidental and represent no more than minor variations within the established spectrum of 'antiquarianism'. Even from the Cambridge *Proceedings* you would not know that there had been a sea-change in the understanding of the (pre-)history of the world, there being little mention of 'early man' or 'geological' findings, nor for that matter any of Darwinism and 'science' whatsoever. As is apparent in table 9, their forums lay elsewhere.[93]

The contents of the *Reports of the British Association for the Advancement of Science* and the allied *Journal of the Anthropological Institute* attest to a markedly different agenda, and a comparable mixture is also common to the *Journal of the Ethnological Society* (1868–9). Approximately 80 per cent of their archaeological entries are either on prehistoric or non-European/international themes, with most of the latter concerned with prehistory. Again, the thematic attribution of a number of papers is problematic and must, invariably, be subjective – primarily, was their content in fact archaeological or anthropological? As variously advocated by Lubbock, Pitt-Rivers and others, this relates to the all-embracing character of the period's study of ethnology/anthropology. Certainly its emphasis was upon prehistory, which Levine has put forward as the driving force behind the formation of archaeology *per se* (ie, associating historicism with antiquarianism).[94]

This is not to say that these matters were ignored within *Archaeologia*. John Evans contributed papers to the journal on the 'geological' discovery of early flint implements[95] and Pitt-Rivers, in his 1869 Cissbury report, briefly outlined his precepts of 'evolutionary classification' that clearly showed the influence of Darwin:

many ancient forms are retained during subsequent ages, and still survive amongst others that have sprung from them, so *by a precisely similar process of natural selection*, if we may apply that term, and I think we may, to the earlier stages of human art, many ancient types of tools and forms of ornament are in like manner retained . . . long after they have been superseded by others of more modern origin [emphasis added].[96]

Drawing upon an organic metaphor (see below) he similarly expounded upon the inter-relationship of cultures in an 1871 address to a Society exhibition:

Assuming the general progression of humanity, or at least of human culture from a lower to a higher state, to be established, the question for sociologists to determine was, whether the lower phases of culture now found in the world are to be regarded as early branches from the same stem with the higher, or as independent growths; and if the former, then to what extent the existing foliage of the branches can be taken to represent the condition of the parent stem at the time they branched from it?[97]

The *Archaeological Journal* was only somewhat more adventurous in its contributions. 1850 saw Mantell's 'On the remains of Man, and works of art imbedded in rocks and strata', and Lubbock discussed Darwinism in his 1863 Presidential Address to the British Archaeological Association.[98] Generally, however, these matters were aired elsewhere. Both Evans and Prestwich contributed papers concerned with early man and flint implements to a number of other journals, including *The Athenaeum* (1859 and 1863), the *Philosophical Transactions of the Royal Society* (1860, 1864 and 1873), the *Proceedings of the Royal Institute* (1864) and the *Journal of the Geological Society* (1891); Pitt-Rivers's 'Thames flint tools' paper also appeared in the latter.[99]

Clearly neither the Society nor *Archaeologia* were considered the appropriate venue in which to venture the 'new' prehistory. Rather, the Ethnological Society was the focus of the 'geological archaeologists' of the Lubbock Circle.[100] All this surely reflects upon the broader interdisciplinary scientific context of such early man and 'evolutionary' researches, and also the broader public arena in which its debates unfolded.[101] It may also attest to the prevailing anti-theoretical character of the Antiquaries and related organizations, and more historically based 'archaeology' in general. As conveyed by the Roach Smith passage above (and thereafter echoed by Greenwell and others), their empiricist ethos of digging 'for facts and not theories' would not have entirely welcomed Lubbock's sweeping interpretative programme, underpinned as it was by comparative ethnography. Yet the then discredited 'theory' was not exactly as the term is understood today. It rather intended the over-ready application of historical/textual explanations from too meagre an artefactual basis; for example, postulating a migration of the Franks from the recovery of a single brooch alone. In other words, privileging the materialism and sustained recovery of artefacts over the immediate application of textual or other 'outside' sources. Lubbock's *Prehistoric Times* of 1865 was itself a prime exemplar of such suspect approaches. As argued by Murray, it effectively amounts to a denial of archaeology's prime achievement. Having created the challenge of the 'deep' antiquity of humanity, what Lubbock did was immediately to bridge this 'gulf of the time' with parallels drawn from present-day ethnography.[102]

The Lubbock Circle's distinctly prehistoric agenda was furthered by the International Congress on Prehistoric Archaeology, which held its meeting in Norwich in 1868 and by the advent of legislation for the protection of ancient monuments. The long and troubled passage of the latter (and earlier manifestations thereof) has been much studied.[103] It only needs to be discussed here, therefore, insofar as it directly related to the Society. Its contribution seems largely negative, which is generally attributed to rivalry between societies, the Society's more pressing concerns with matters of conservation abroad and also with building restoration within Britain. Of its limited participation in the process, two issues are particularly relevant. The first is the obvious dominance of the influence of Lubbock (*et al*) in the first schedule of monuments. Aside from one Roman earthwork, the Dorchester amphitheatre (and medieval Old Sarum), the thirty-eight sites listed for England and Wales were all of prehistoric attribution. Its definition of 'monument', moreover, specifically excluded 'any castle, fortress, abbey, religious house or ecclesiastical edifice'. The main grounds for the omission of such medieval sites were the incessant cost of their repairs, the issues of aesthetics that arose in their restoration and that their 'obvious' character itself promoted conservation (ie, their 'presence' and value being relatively self-evident).[104] Nevertheless, the list – comprising hillfort 'camps', megalithic rings and chamber tombs – was remarkably one-sided and, as Thompson remarked: 'It was indeed an extraordinary situation that in a Christian country only pagan monuments should be protected, on grounds of economy.'[105]

All this obviously flew in the face of the much broader interests of the Society of Antiquaries in the more recent historical past. In 1869 the First Commissioner of Works, Sir Austen Layard, appalled by the destruction of both archaeological and church-related monuments, had asked the Society to draw up a list of 'Regal and other Historical Tombs or Monuments' for government protection. Fellows across the country duly turned their hands to the task and, in 1871, presented a list of more than 600 entries. However, in 1869 the Ethnological Society – again reflecting the influence of Lubbock and Pitt-Rivers – had established a 'Prehistoric and Other Monuments Committee',[106] whose report was presented to the Anthropological Institute (the merged Anthropological and Ethnological Societies). In drawing up his bill for Parliament, Lubbock requested that the national antiquarian societies assemble lists of worthy monuments. While the Society of Antiquaries of Scotland and the Royal Irish Academy duly complied, the Society of Antiquaries of London failed to do so (despite having Pitt-Rivers as Vice-President). Although eventually endorsing the bill (after it had been referred to and appended by Franks), the Society also declined to participate in a joint committee for this purpose with the Anthropological Institute.[107]

The second point relates to the administration of the Act. In his 1873 bill Lubbock proposed that this be undertaken by the Inclosure Commissioners, along with the

Presidents of the three national antiquarian societies, the Master of the Rolls and the Keeper of British Antiquities of the British Museum. In 1874 this was altered to a series of named individuals (including Pitt-Rivers and John Evans), and was revised again in the 1880 bill to exclude all but the trustees of the British Museum. Among the reasons for this change (marking as it did the demotion of the role played by the national antiquarian societies) was the widely held belief that, due to self-interest and their own legacy of pillaging sites, antiquarians/archaeologists were inappropriate guardians of the nation's past:

> Some of the ancient barrows, though having been first rifled by antiquarians, have been carted away and levelled by farmers . . . *it was the antiquarians who had done the most mischief in England and if ancient monuments were to be placed in their hands they would do still more* [emphasis added] (Sir Edmund Antrobus, parliamentary speech, 15 April 1874).[108]

Alternatively, as President of the Society, Frederic Ouvry, in his Anniversary Meeting address of 1877 (when the Society could still be optimistic at the prospect of Lubbock's bill) characteristically considered the forthcoming legislation as a means to preserve monuments from over-zealous 'restoration':

> I should welcome the day when the Conservation of monuments, both prehistoric and historic, should be placed under the charge of this Society, duly subsidized by the government to carry out such measures as might be thought necessary for the ends in view . . . *I should like to see grants made for the Society of Antiquaries to preserve the records of the past, not so much from the ravage of time and decay, as from the far more noxious influences of 'restoring' committees, aided by injudicious architects* [emphasis added].[109]

Time, of course, showed that the Antiquaries were largely correct in their assessment of Lubbock's 1882 Ancient Monuments Act and its marked prehistoric bias. During the 1890s there were moves to extend its powers to the scheduling of Romano-British and medieval monuments, and its obvious shortcomings were, in effect, eventually rectified with the Ancient Monuments Consolidation and Amendment Act of 1913.[110]

'TREES OF KNOWLEDGE' – THE GROWTH OF DISCIPLINES

There is something compelling in the Lubbock Circle's formulation of archaeology/prehistory in the decades 1850–80. Eventually coalescing in the 1882 Ancient Monuments Act, it has the seductive appeal of a 'programmatic moment' when the course of the 'discipline' could be redirected. It has obvious parallels with what occurred during the resurgence of British prehistory in the 1920 and 1930s (for example, the work of Clark, Crawford and Hawkes); then it was the Society of Antiquaries itself that prompted reaction because of its near-monopoly of excavation funds and the dominance of its Late Iron Age/Romano-British agenda at that time.[111] There was, nevertheless, a comparable sense of manoeuvring by the 'Young Turks' of their respective days, and both episodes show how a small special-interest sector can come to dominate the field. It is reflected in the mutual promotion of their group's rise within the leading societies, the capturing of journals and the orchestration of their agenda by repeat-publication of 'mission-like' papers. Of course, where the effects of the 1920 to 1930s generation were essentially academic, the connections of the Lubbock Circle were much more socially (and scientifically) wide-ranging and, at least in Lubbock's case, led directly to the halls of state power.

Many of the main issues that dominated later nineteenth-century archaeology were common to the 1920 and 1930s, and, for that matter, are still prevalent today: the desire for state funding and for defining the role of the state in the co-ordination of the subject generally. The chief difference between the formulation of archaeology in the two centuries was, of course, the growth of universities and archaeology as a taught subject. With it came the question of what role the independent institutions – such as the Society of Antiquaries – should play betwixt state and university? Here it is crucial to recognize that, with few exceptions,[112] most histories of the subject essentially chart its intellectual development and pay little heed to its institutions *per se*. With its many special-interest bequests, wide-ranging membership (including the clergy: see note 5) and well-appointed offices, library and museum, the Society of Antiquaries has been rather more akin to an Oxbridge college or London club than, for example, a university department (splendid accommodation contributing to its institutional 'weight'). Thus endowed, and on the basis of its constitution, the Society could not readily have changed its broad remit for the sake of a 'special' cause.

Partially as a result of its relative longevity – even at that time – and partly because its membership included the leading practitioners of the day, the Society accrued significant institutional authority during the later nineteenth century. There is the behind-the-scenes role that it played in the 'early man' debates themselves. Having previously held Society displays on a number of medieval and later themes (for example, civic/company plate and seals, and early books and manuscripts), Franks, together with Pitt-Rivers, mounted successive, week-long exhibitions on Palaeolithic and Neolithic archaeology in 1871. More than 500 attended the first of these, and a similar exhibition was held for the Bronze Age in 1873 (fig 83).[113] In a comparable manner, in the letters exchanged within *The Athenaeum* in 1859 following Evans's and Prestwich's respective 'flint-in-gravels' papers, Evans's reply to Wright's accusation that the hand-axes were products of natural damage was reinforced when several examples were deposited in the Society's library so that readers could judge this issue for themselves.[114] Just as the presentation of the photographs to the Society from the visit of Prestwich and Evans to France constituted 'proof' of the antiquity of mankind (as well as reinforcing their reputation), the Society setting of these *demonstrations* of the 'new chronology' were surely not accidental. It provided credibility and authority to the otherwise radical agenda of the Lubbock Circle.

Equally, in the latter decades of the century there were other 'centralizing' initiatives by the Society that were intended to spur the direction of the discipline. Not only would this include its Research Fund excavations, but the decision was also

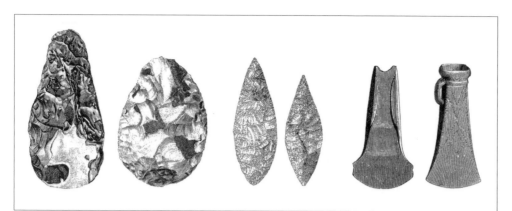

Fig 83. 'The new prehistory'. Palaeolithic, Neolithic and Bronze Age implements (respectively from Evans 1860, pl xv, and 1872, figs 273–275; Society of Antiquaries of London 1873, pl I; see note 113).

taken in 1888 to host an archaeological conference to co-ordinate research and the preservation of monuments, with the aims of promoting archaeological surveys and registers of monuments and finds.[115] With its delegates drawn from the other anti-quarian/archaeological societies ('Societies in Union'), this Congress of Archaeological Societies met annually thereafter and, at least under Charles Peers, was to have a major impact on the direction of research within Britain.[116]

The character of later nineteenth-century archaeology cannot be understood with-out acknowledging the lingering persuasion of antiquarianism. Of the fifty-five local and county societies established between 1834 and 1886, thirteen variously styled themselves 'antiquarian societies'.[117] Thirty-five rather used 'archaeological', while only the Cumberland and Westmorland Antiquarian *and* Archaeological Society of 1866 adopted both terms. If 1843 and the establishment of the Archaeological Association (and subsequently the *Archaeological Journal*) are taken as announcing the begin-ning of the archaeological 'project', then the fact that just two out of the twenty societies established between 1844 and 1860 used 'antiquarian' (as opposed to 'archaeo-logical') is only to be expected. The ensuing decade shows much the same trend, with two 'antiquarian' societies founded against eight 'archaeological'. However, between 1871 and 1886 seven out of fifteen established were variously entitled 'antiquarian'. Factors of marginality may be relevant in this context. Of those societies of antiquarian affiliation founded in the second half of the century, aside from that at Lewisham (established 1886), all fell well beyond the south-eastern county 'core': Huddersfield (1850), Cumberland/Westmorland (1866), Bath (1868), Dorset (1875), Bradford (1876), Lancashire/Cheshire (1883), Louth (1884), Clifton (1884) and Glastonbury (1886). Nevertheless, taking this pattern at face value, it could, if anything, actually suggest a resurgence of antiquarianism after *c* 1870, and this further confirms the consistency of the antiquarian content of most journals through-out the century.[118] Ultimately, what this reflects are the dual poles driving the study of the past during the second half of the nineteenth century. On the one hand, there is unquestionably a move towards greater academic *specialization* (ie, 'archaeology') and, on the other, its increasing *popularization* and which could be caricatured as a middle-class 'antiquarianism'.

In the last decade of the century a great 'totalizing' project was attempted, in the form of the Ethnographic Survey of the United Kingdom.[119] Suggested by A C Haddon (who had undertaken similarly comprehensive surveys in Ireland), representatives of the Folklore Society, the Anthropological Institute and the Society of Antiquaries met in London in 1892 to discuss its implementation. Thought necessary on account of 'the erosion of traditional society', it was to provide a *complete* ethnographic and historical account of the nation through the study of physical population type (ie, craniology), language dialects, beliefs and customs, monuments and other ancient remains. As instigated under the auspices of the British Association for the Advancement of Science, its amassed surveyors were to spread their way across the nation. Yet, after only limited canvassing, the project ground to a halt by the end of the century, with its failure being attributed to 'amateur' fieldworkers. (Agreement upon which social/population type constituted a representative regional sample was evidently also a source of much contention.)[120] In this instance, the dispute over amateur involvement reflects upon the increased specialization of the field, whereas the holistic breadth of this over-ambitious project can only be considered 'antiquarian'. While seemingly somewhat eccentric – and certainly more comprehensive than the Society's efforts toward an archaeological survey of the country – it is crucial to recognize that the notion of a *complete* country-based record of the nation's past did, of course, eventually have its realization with the establishment of the Royal Commission on Historical Monuments in 1908.[121]

Finally, in an attempt to provide an overview of the subject's development during the nineteenth century, it is appropriate to draw upon precepts that the Victorians themselves would have been aware of. Questions of the nature of social change – and particularly 'revolution' as opposed to gradual evolutionary processes – are of obvious relevance. Certainly Pitt-Rivers and other leading thinkers of the day were forceful advocates of the latter.[122] This also coincides with the attitude struck by most histories of the subject, which are suffused by an implicit belief that archaeology politely grew out of, and eventually superseded, antiquarian practice. Yet, far from dying out, many local societies even today essentially practise an antiquarian agenda. Reflective of the eclectic interests of their broad membership, and with their own wide-ranging socio-intellectual connections and different interest groups, within them medieval building or historic garden studies still feature alongside (and often prevail over) more strictly archaeological researches.

In this context a widespread metaphor of the era may be useful: that is, the prover-bial 'Tree of Knowledge', from whose many roots a dominant subject is formed – be it architecture or the human sciences in general – and whose branches represent its subspecialist offspring. The bifurcation this implies would, indeed, be appropriate to the development of the century's societies (and their journals), with many having their origins in the root-stock of the Society of Antiquaries. What, however, such organic analogies fail to account for (aside from portraying inter-factional splits as 'natural' subdivisions) are episodes of intentional coalescence. Here, rather, Kroeber's Tree – 'the tree of knowledge of good and evil . . . that is human culture' – may well prove a

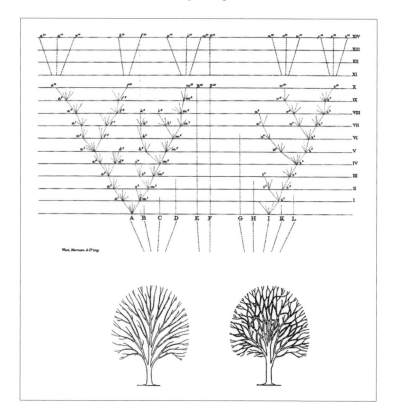

Fig 84. Networks and 'Trees of Knowledge'. *Top*: Darwin's 'Tree of Evolution', from *The Origin of Species* of 1859; *below*: Kroeber's 'Tree of Life' (left) and 'Tree of Knowledge' (right; from Ingold 2000, fig 8.1, after Kroeber 1948, 260).

more relevant metaphor (fig 84).[123] Instead of only regularly branching, its limbs can grow back to reconfigure themselves and their inter-relationship with other offshoots. What we see during the decades between 1850 and 1870–80 is just such a coalescence of *archaeology*: a moment when the subject itself was intentionally delineated in an awareness of its 'project'. From a foundation established by the Archaeological Association/Institute generation, and propelled by the Lubbock (*et al*) axis, the subject was configured by its adoption of the methodological principles of geology and an emphasis upon prehistory, with its interpretation driven by the 'new' socio-evolutionary anthropological framework of the day. Ultimately it was this – along with the Lubbock group's accompanying institutional orchestration and growing career professionalism and subject specialization generally – that eventually sidelined holistic antiquarian practice from the academic mainstream and into the 'dwindling branch' it has since healthily remained.

ACKNOWLEDGEMENTS

This chapter's broad and unwieldy themes have variously benefited from discussions with, and information generously supplied by, R Boast, R Bradley, M Edmonds, S Lucy, M Millett, T Murray, B Nurse and M L S Sørensen. The illustrations attest to the skills of Andrew Hall (Cambridge Archaeological Unit).

NOTES

1. Eg, Piggott 1976c.
2. Missing from this table are, of course, works relating to British-sponsored 'world' and Middle Eastern archaeology such as Layard's *Discoveries in the Ruins of Nineveh and Babylon* (1853), Rawlinson's translation of cuneiform (*c* 1846–57) and Schliemann's Troy (1871–90).
3. Eg, Hernon 2003.
4. Pitt-Rivers 1867a and 1868; see also, however, Cannadine 2001, who cautions against overemphasizing the impact of 'otherness' and argues that, with its widely tiered and hierarchical social structure, later 19th-century Britain could readily accommodate overseas sultans and warrior castes, just as it encompassed homeland gentry and labourers.
5. In the 1830s the London Coliseum apparently displayed scenes showing 'The Geological Revolutions of the Earth: Creation, the Age of the Iguanodon and Megalosaurus, the Garden of Eden and the Deluge', again mixing geological evidence and Biblical stories: Secord 2004, 143. During the later 19th century, the advent of Darwinian evolution, the great antiquity of mankind and a more scientific archaeology were evidently not changes of such magnitude as to alienate the Church from the pursuit of the past – with Canon Greenwell being only the most obvious case in point – while in 1900 clergymen still constituted over 12 per cent of the Society's Fellowship: Hudson 1981, 21. As a comparable local society exemplar, in the Bristol and Gloucestershire Archaeological Society (BGAS) the percentage of clergy stood at 20.3 in 1876 and 14.9 in 1900. By 1930 this figure had dropped to 3.8 per cent in the BGAS, and to 7 per cent in the Society. The decline of the participation of the clergy was not, however, due to a revolution of thought and the moral uncertainties of 'deep time', but rather the reorganization of parishes in the early 20th century that significantly impeded the leisure time of men of the cloth: Hudson 1981, 18–19. Moreover, as attested to by the formation of the Society for Biblical Archaeology in 1870, discoveries within Middle Eastern archaeology were actually then seen as authenticating Old Testament accounts: Levine 1986, 96–7.
6. Evans 1950, 3.
7. Evans 1956; Levine 1986; Stocking 1987; van Riper 1993; Sweet 2004.
8. Evans 1956, 323.
9. Levine 1986, 72.
10. Ibid, 124, concerning the decline of class patronage in public life.
11. Ibid, Appendix II, for full listing.
12. Eg, Wetherall 1994.
13. Eg, Ebbatson 1994; Wetherall 1998, 26–7.
14. Dorson 1968, 51, 62.
15. Levine 1986, 14.
16. Evans 1943; Sherratt 2002.
17. Bowden 1991, 3.
18. See papers in Banks *et al* 1994 for Banks's circle and Evans 2000 for that of Britton.
19. Kinnes and Longworth 1985, 10; Bowden 1991, 66–7, 104–7, 163–5.
20. Eg, Chapman 1989a, 34.
21. Sweet 2004, 345–50, identifies antiquarianism as a singularly 18th-century pursuit, whereas Ebbatson 1999, 138, remarks that 'antiquarian' was probably still used to describe the study of the past with greater frequency throughout the latter half of the 19th century; see also, for example, Hudson 1981, 2–4, and Schnapp 1996 and 2002.
22. Mantell 1847, 403.
23. See Evans 1950, 2.
24. Evans 1956, 364; see Harlan and Price 2003 for the use of magic lanterns in archaeology.
25. Pitt-Rivers 1875, 390.
26. In Bacon 1976, 55, fig 30.
27. Evans 1956, 352; it was only in 1929 that the central Meeting Room table was removed, being taken up to the library, and the venue reorganized into a standard lecture-setting arrangement: ibid, 363–4.
28. Chung 2002.
29. Ibid.
30. Evans 2004.
31. Hibbs 1985; Conway 1787.
32. Molesworth 1787; SAL, Minutes, xxi, 470 and insert between pp 470 and 471, 11 Jan 1787.
33. Way 1847, pp 5 and 4 respectively; Smyth 1830.
34. Stone 1857; Evans 2004, 119, fig 5.4.
35. Pitt-Rivers 1861 and 1887, 20; Evans 2004.
36. Pitt-Rivers 1892, 298; Evans 2004, 121, 124, fig 5.7.
37. Squeegee impressions were made by kneading balled, wet paper into carved inscriptions, letting it dry and then peeling it off as a thick, impressed paper sheet: Rawlinson 1852, 73; Adkins 2003, 218, 276.
38. See, for example, the legacy of Norfolk's 'Flint Jack': M Edmonds, pers comm; see Pitt-Rivers 1872b, 458, concerning the sale of lithic forgeries and J Winter Jones's article in the *Edinburgh Review* (1881) for the non-disclosure of finds among amateurs.
39. Cook 1998, 144, figs 31, 34, 37.
40. James 1867; see Chippindale 1983, 20.
41. Pitt-Rivers 1869b, 1.
42. Evans 1956, 290–1.
43. Ibid, 292.
44. C J Praetorius was the last artist employed by the Society to draw objects (*c* 1880–1913), using watercolours for this purpose to great effect: B Nurse, pers comm.

45. Dobson 1875, pls XXXI–XXXIII.
46. Lamprey 1868.
47. Fox and Hope 1895.
48. Stone's Standlake site (*Proc Soc Antiq London*, 1st ser, **4** (1857), 92–100), is credited with being the first excavation of a prehistoric settlement in Britain (see fig 79a); just as Leed's Sutton Courtney campaigns, featuring in *Archaeologia* 1923 (vol 73), 1926–7 (vol 76) and 1947 (vol 92), have a comparable status in Anglo-Saxon research.
49. Eg, Bradley 1997; Evans 2004.
50. Hodder 1989.
51. Lysons 1812, 129.
52. Lysons 1797; Sweet 2004, 104.
53. Dryden 1849; Conyngham 1844.
54. Akerman 1844.
55. Smith 1848–80; see also the Comte de Caylus's observations concerning the role of drawing in his *Recueil d'antiquités* of 1752: 'The ritual of a people can be recognized by the characteristic symbols of its divinities; the taste of a people is revealed in the manner by which it dresses its sculptures. *But all this knowledge would not be secure if drawing was not used, together with the practice of seeing and comparing. Drawing furnishes the principles, comparison gives the means to apply them . . .*' (emphasis added; in Schnapp 2002).
56. See also, for example, the Orkney study by Lieutenant Thomas, commanding HM Surveying Vessel, *Woodlark* (Thomas 1851).
57. Kempe 1829.
58. Conyngham 1844.
59. See Piggott 1978, 33, concerning the oeuvre of Guest of Salisbury who specialized in 'still life-like' paintings of grave-group assemblages.
60. Akerman 1844.
61. Evans 1853 and 1890. The same is true of Arthur Evans's celebrated excavation of the Late Iron Age cemetery at Aylesford, for which there is only the often-reproduced quasi-isometric rendering of its 'family cremation circle'; otherwise its 1890 report is without any formal site plan or map.
62. See van Riper's 1993 graphic 'translation' of their sequences (fig 6) and also Evans 1943, 100–4, concerning their trip generally.
63. Frere 1800.
64. See, though, Bahn 1996, 84.
65. Burkhardt and Smith 1985–, viii, 188; see also Rudwick 1976 and Freeman 2004 concerning the development of geology's visual language. Darwin, aside from having personal connections with Albert Way (a friend from his time at Cambridge: Desmond and Moore 1992, 58), Lubbock (his neighbour at Down House and among those who organized Darwin's funeral in Westminster Cathedral: ibid, 302, 664–9)

and Pitt-Rivers (Darwin sponsored his membership into the Royal Society), corresponded with other of the Society's Fellows. Listed in the Darwin Correspondence database are John Evans (see also Sherratt 2002), Hudson Gurney (the Society's Vice-President, 1822–46) and William H Dixon (editor of *The Athenaeum*, 1853–69); other archaeologists to whom Darwin also wrote include Charles Babington, Hodder Westropp and Jacques Boucher de Perthes, and there is also correspondence from 1877 with the Revd Joyce concerning the researches that Darwin and his sons undertook at Silchester for his *The Formation of Vegetable Mould* (Darwin 1881; see also fig 82a; Boon 1974, 26).

66. Pitt-Rivers 1867b, lxxiv, lxxx and lxxxi. We are told: 'Mr Carter Blake bore his testimony to the accuracy with which the investigations had been described, and to the care with which they had been made and in those respects he contrasted what had been done by Col. Lane Fox with the exaggerated representations by Troyon and others of lake habitations on the Continent, where some authors had exhibited what Mr Pike would term lamentable absence of "shame" in their accounts' (*Anthropol Rev*, **5** (1867), lxxxi).
67. Pitt-Rivers 1883, 436; see Bowden 1991, 86.
68. Eg, Pitt-Rivers 1861; while posted with the military in Ireland in 1862–6 he served as a legal prosecuting officer: Bowden 1991, 20–1, and R Bradley, pers comm.
69. Bowden 1991, 70–1, 77–81; Boast forthcoming.
70. Pitt-Rivers 1869a.
71. Among the eight listed were Evans, Busk, Rolleston and Godwin Austin, and the latter, together with Prestwich, appended letters of verification to the published report: Pitt-Rivers 1875, 374, 386–8.
72. Eg, Thompson 1977; Bowden 1991.
73. Wheeler 1954, 25–9; see also Thompson 1977, 117.
74. For example, those in the Wor Barrow site notebook or the watercolour section that contributed to Hawkes's study of Pitt-Rivers's Iwerne villa excavations (Hawkes 1947); both are held by the Dorset County Museum and I am grateful to R Bradley for drawing my attention to these.
75. See also, for example, Bowden 1991, fig 40.
76. See Evans 2004, 121–4, figs 5.5 and 5.6.
77. Pitt-Rivers 1898.
78. As Thurnam and Professor Owen had done earlier for his Harnham excavations: Akerman 1853a.
79. Akerman 1853a; Evans 1956, 274, 306.
80. Pitt-Rivers 1869b; see also Chapman 1989a, 39.
81. van Riper 1993, 212–14; Gruber 1965.
82. Fox and Hope 1895.
83. Gowland 1901.
84. Despite Wheeler's condemnation that Fox and Hope excavated the site as if 'digging for potatoes': Wheeler 1954, 127.
85. Evans 1956, 273.

86. Chippindale 1983, 14–16; Bowden 1991, 75–6.

87. Evans 1956, 345; see also Levine 1986, 171.

88. Designed by John Evans and intended to be deposited within his site-backfill, Pitt-Rivers's quasi-heraldic medallions are themselves an obvious manifestation of 'practising for eternity': fig 79f; Evans 1943, 154–5; Bowden 1991, figs 59 and 60; Evans 2005.

89. See Lucas 2001.

90. Adkins 2003, 337–41.

91. van Riper 1993, Appendix 1.

92. Webb 1824.

93. Reflecting upon the place of archaeology in the 'parliament of science', only after 1870 was it included alone under the banner of 'Anthropology' within the meetings and *Reports of the British Association for the Advancement of Science* (*Rep Brit Ass Advancement Sci*: see Stocking 1987, 245–8, concerning the rivalry and debates between the anthropology and ethnology factions). When archaeology previously appeared in the 'Geography and Ethnology' section, its contributions collectively resonated with 'empire', and respective papers variously vied with studies of comparative craniology and expedition reports (including Livingstone's from Africa; there are also a number of contributions on both archaeology and anthropology by Sir Richard Burton).

94. Levine 1986, 94–8; see also van Riper 1993, 39–43.

95. Evans 1860 and 1862.

96. Pitt-Rivers 1869a, 70.

97. Pitt-Rivers 1872a, 234.

98. Mantell 1850.

99. Pitt-Rivers 1872b; see van Riper 1993, Appendix 2, for a compendium of papers concerned with human antiquity during the period 1859–75.

100. van Riper 1893, 219–21; Chapman 1989a.

101. A meeting of the Ethnological Society concerned with the antiquity of 'flints in drift' was even reported in the *Illustrated London News* of 9 March 1861.

102. Murray 1993, 177.

103. Eg, Thompson 1977; Chippindale 1983; Murray 1989.

104. Chippindale 1983, 9–11.

105. Thompson 1977, 60.

106. Evans 1994, 200.

107. Chippindale 1983, 6–7; Evans 1956, 301, 331–3.

108. *Hansard* 1874, 588–9; see Chippindale 1983, 14–15, and Murray 1989, 61–3.

109. Evans 1956, 331.

110. Though, attesting to the 'landed' affinities of the Society's membership, in guarantee of the rights of private property they would not endorse compulsory purchase to this end: Evans 1956, 365–9; Chippindale 1983, 31–3.

111. Evans 1989.

112. Eg, Evans 1956; Hudson 1981; Chapman 1989b; Lucas 2001; Kaeser 2002.

113. Evans 1956, 306; Pitt-Rivers 1872a. The two published catalogues from the Society's 1870s prehistoric exhibitions list all those who lent material (Society of Antiquaries of London 1873 and 1874), which provides rare insights into the dynamics of contemporary collections. More than 1,140 flints were, for example, shown at the Neolithic exhibition. While the vast majority were of European origin (69.3 per cent), it tells of the breadth of the Society's prehistoric interests that material was also included from the Americas (16.5 per cent), the 'South Seas, etc' (7 per cent), Asia (4.9 per cent) and Africa (2.3 per cent). Equally, it must reflect upon the status of Danish prehistory and the impact of its 'Three Age System' (and also ensuing personal connections) that, after the 379 pieces shown from Britain, Denmark was the country next most represented (165 items, 20.8 per cent of European material); otherwise, for example, only 77 and 56 flints were respectively shown from Ireland and France (50 being of Mexican origin). In the list of those 27 individuals contributing material, not surprisingly John Evans and Pitt-Rivers rank foremost (225 pieces/19.7 per cent and 181/15.9 per cent respectively), and both had items from most of the 29 countries and territories represented. Twelve other Fellows, however, also exhibited material. Perhaps to be expected, the Society's main writers on the period were much in evidence: Greenwell (33 pieces, variously from Britain, Ireland, Spain and Portugal and North America), Lubbock (18, from Denmark, France and Greece), Franks (67) and Thurnam (21). Yet after Evans and Pitt-Rivers, the next most prolific exhibitors were the Revd W S Simpson, FSA, and the Revd J Beck (139 and 132 items respectively). Overall, of the 27 contributors, four were members of the clergy, three held military rank (including, obviously, Pitt-Rivers himself) and two were Fellows of the Geological Society (including Mr Flowers, lending 65 pieces); all were male and no women participated.

114. Evans 1859; see also van Riper 1993, 120–7.

115. The publication of archaeological maps was a theme of its first meeting, which led to the Archaeological Survey of England by county, with general standard surveys being published for Cumberland/Westmorland and Herefordshire in *Archaeologia* in the early 1890s.

116. Evans 1956, 329–30; Evans 1989.

117. Levine 1986, Appendix IV; see also Piggott 1976b.

118. The fortnightly journal, *The Antiquarian*, was founded as late as 1871; renamed *The Antiquary* in 1880, it continued to be published until 1915: see Hudson 1981, 99–100.

119. Urry 1984.

120. Ibid, 92–3; Evans 1994.

121. Evans 1956, 358–9, 367–8.

122. Eg, Bradley 1983; Bowden 1991.

123. Kroeber 1948, 26; Ingold 2000, 134.

BIBLIOGRAPHY

Adkins, L 2003. *Empires of the Plain: Henry Rawlinson and the lost languages of Babylon*, London

Akerman, J Y 1844. 'Account of the opening by Matthew Bell, Esq., of an ancient British barrow, in Iffins Wood, near Canterbury, in the month of January, 1843', *Archaeologia*, 30, 57–61

Akerman, J Y 1853a. 'An account of excavation in an Anglo-Saxon burial ground at Harnham Hill, near Salisbury', *Archaeologia*, 35, 259–78

Akerman, J Y 1853b. 'An account of the site of some ancient potteries in the western district of the New Forest', *Archaeologia*, 35, 91–9

Akerman, J Y 1860. 'Report on researches in an Anglo-Saxon cemetery at Long Wittenham, Berkshire, in 1859', *Archaeologia*, 38, 327–52

Bacon, E (ed) 1976. *The Great Archaeologists*, London

Bahn, P (ed) 1996. *The Cambridge Illustrated History of Archaeology*, Cambridge

Banks, R E R, Elliott, B, Hawkes, J G, King-Hele, D and Lucas, G L (eds) 1994. *Sir Joseph Banks: a global perspective*, London

Boast, R forthcoming. 'Continuity and evolution in late nineteenth-century archaeology: a close reading of Cissbury', in Cunliffe and Gosden (eds) forthcoming

Boon, G C 1974. *Silchester: the Roman town of Calleva*, Newton Abbot

Bowden, M C B 1991. *Pitt Rivers: the life and archaeological work of Lieutenant-General Augustus Henry Lane Fox Pitt Rivers, DCL, FRS, FSA*, Cambridge

Bradley, R 1983. 'Archaeology, evolution and the public good: the intellectual development of General Pitt-Rivers', *Archaeol J*, 140, 1–9

Bradley, R 1997. '"To see is to have seen": craft traditions in British field archaeology', in Molyneaux (ed) 1997, 62–72

Brand, V (ed) 1998. *The Study of the Past in the Victorian Age*, Oxbow Monogr 73, Oxford

Burkhardt, F and Smith, S (eds) 1985–. *The Correspondence of Charles Darwin*, 14 vols, Cambridge

Cannadine, D 2001. *Ornamentalism: how the British saw their empire*, London

Chadarevian, S de and Hopwood, N 2004. *Models: the third dimension of science*, Stanford, Calif

Chapman, W 1989a. 'The organizational context in the history of archaeology: Pitt-Rivers and other British archaeologists in the 1860s', *Antiq J*, 59, 23–42

Chapman, W 1989b. 'Towards an institutional history of archaeology: British archaeologists and allied interests in the 1860s', in Christenson (ed) 1989, 151–62

Chippindale, C 1983. 'The making of the first Ancient Monuments Act, 1882, and its administration under General Pitt-Rivers', *J Brit Archaeol Ass*, 136, 1–55

Christenson, A L (ed) 1989. *Tracing Archaeology's Past: the historiography of archaeology*, Carbondale, Ill

Chung, Y S S 2002. 'Prehistoric narratives in county archaeological society museums in mid-nineteenth-century England', *Stanford Journal of Archaeology*, 1, <http://archaeology.stanford.edu/journal/newdraft/chung/abstract.html> (9 Oct 2006)

Colt Hoare, R 1821. 'An account of a stone barrow, in the parish of Wellow, at Stoney Littleton in the county of Somerset', *Archaeologia*, 19, 43–8

Conway, H S 1787. 'Description of a Druidical monument in the island of Jersey', *Archaeologia*, 8, 386–8

Conyngham, A 1844. 'An account of the opening and examination of a considerable number of tumuli on Breach Down, in the county of Kent', *Archaeologia*, 30, 47–56

Cook, B F 1998. 'British archaeologists in the Aegean', in Brand (ed) 1998, 139–54

Cunliffe, B and Gosden, C (eds) forthcoming. 'A century of innovation, 1860–1960', *Encyclopaedia of Archaeology*, Oxford

Cunnington, W 1806. 'Account of tumuli opened in Wiltshire', *Archaeologia*, 15, 122–9

Darwin, C 1881. *The Formation of Vegetable Mould, through the action of worms, with observations on their habits*, London

Desmond, A and Moore, J 1992. *Darwin*, London

Dobson, G E 1875. 'On the Andamans and Andamanese', *J Anthropol Inst*, 4, 457–67

Dorson, R M 1968. *The British Folklorists: a history*, London

Dryden, H 1849. 'An account of a discovery of early Saxon remains at Barrow Furlong, on Hill Farm, in the parish of Marston St Lawrence, in the county of Northampton', *Archaeologia*, 33, 326–34

Ebbatson, L 1994. 'Context and discourse: Royal Archaeological Institute membership 1845–1942', in Vyner (ed) 1994, 22–74

Ebbatson, L 1999. 'Conditions of the emergence and existence of archaeology in the nineteenth century: the Royal Archaeological Institute', unpublished PhD thesis, University of Durham

Evans, A J 1890. 'On a late Celtic urn-field at Aylesford, Kent', *Archaeologia*, 52, 317–88

Evans, C 1989. 'Archaeology and modern times: Bersu's Woodbury 1938 and 1939', *Antiquity*, 63, 436–50

Evans, C 1994. 'Natural wonders and national monuments: a meditation upon the fate of "The Tolmen"', *Antiquity*, 68, 200–8

Evans, C 2000. 'Megalithic follies: Soane's "Druidic remains" and the display of monuments', *J Material Culture*, 5, 347–66

Evans, C 2004. 'Modelling monuments and excavations', in Chadarevian and Hopwood (eds), 2004, 109–37

Evans, C 2005. 'Captain Nemo, Lt-General Pitt-Rivers and Cleopatra's Needle: a story of flagships', *Bull Hist Archaeol*, 15, 37–44

Evans, J 1943. *Time and Chance: the story of Arthur Evans and his forebears*, London

Evans, J 1950. 'Archaeology in 1851', *Archaeol J*, **107**, 1–6

Evans, J 1956. *A History of the Society of Antiquaries*, Oxford

Evans, J 1853. 'Account of further excavation on the site of two Roman villas at Box Moor, Herts', *Archaeologia*, **35**, 56–9

Evans, J 1859. 'Flint implements in the drift', *The Athenaeum* (no vol no.), 1859, 25 June, 841

Evans, J 1860. 'On the occurrence of flint implements in undisturbed beds of gravel, sand and clay', *Archaeologia*, **38**, 280–307

Evans, J 1862. 'Account of some further discoveries of flint implements in the drift on the continent and in England', *Archaeologia*, **39**, 57–84

Evans, J 1872. *The Ancient Stone Implements, Weapons, and Ornaments of Great Britain*, London

Evans, J 1890. 'On the exploration of a barrow at Youngsbury, near Ware, Herts', *Archaeologia*, **52**, 287–96

Evans, J 1895. 'On some iron tools and other articles formed of iron found at Silchester in the year 1890', *Archaeologia*, **54**, 139–56

Fox, G E and Hope, W H St John 1895. 'Excavations on the site of the Roman city of Silchester, Hants, in 1893', *Archaeologia*, **54**, 199–238

Fox, G E and Hope, W H St John 1901. 'Excavations on the site of the Roman city of Silchester, Hants, in 1899', *Archaeologia*, **57/1**, 87–112

Freeman, M 2004. *Victorians and the Prehistoric*, London

Frere, J 1800. 'Account of flint weapons discovered at Hoxne, Suffolk', *Archaeologia*, **13**, 204–5

Gage, J 1836. 'A letter . . . communicating the recent discovery of Roman sepulchral relics in one of the greater barrows at Barlow, in the parish of Ashdon, in Essex', *Archaeologia*, **26**, 300–17

Gowland, W 1901. 'Remains of a Roman silver refinery at Silchester', *Archaeologia*, **57**, 113–24

Greenwell, W 1890. 'Recent researches in barrows in Yorkshire, Wiltshire, Berkshire, etc', *Archaeologia*, **52**, 1–72

Gruber, J W 1965. 'Brixham cave and the antiquity of man', in Spiro (ed) 1965, 373–402

Harlan, D and Price, M 2003. 'Henry Underhill: entomologist, grocer, antiquarian . . . and magic lantern artist', *The New Magic Lantern Journal*, **9**, 51–3

Hawkes, C F C 1947. 'Britons, Romans and Saxons round Salisbury and in Cranborne Chase', *Archaeol J*, **104**, 27–81

Hernon, I 2003. *Britain's Forgotten Wars*, Stroud

Hibbs, J 1985. 'Little Master Stonehenge: a study of the megalithic monument from Le Mont de la Ville, Saint Helier', *Soc Jersiaise Annu Bull*, **110**, 49–74

Hodder, I 1989. 'Writing archaeology: the site report in context', *Antiquity*, **63**, 268–74

Hudson, K 1981. *A Social History of Archaeology*, London

Ingold, T 2000. *The Perception of the Environment: essays in livelihood, dwelling and skill*, London

James, H 1867. *Plans and Photographs of Stonehenge*, London

Kaeser, M-A 2002. 'On the international roots of prehistory', *Antiquity*, **76**, 170–7

Kempe, A J 1829. 'An account of some recent discoveries at Holwood-hill in Kent', *Archaeologia*, **22**, 336–49

Kinnes, I A and Longworth, I H 1985. *Catalogue of the Excavated Prehistoric and Romano-British Material in the Greenwell Collection*, London

Kroeber, K L 1948. *Anthropology*, New York

Lamprey, J H 1868. 'On a method of measuring the human form', *J Ethnolog Soc London*, **1**, 84–5

Levine, P 1986. *The Amateur and the Professional: antiquarians, historians and archaeologists in Victorian England, 1838–1886*, Cambridge

Logan, J 1829. 'Observations on several circles of stones in Scotland, presumed to be Druidical', *Archaeologia*, **22**, 198–202

Lubbock, J 1865. *Prehistoric Times*, London

Lucas, G 2001. *Critical Approaches to Fieldwork: contemporary and historical archaeological practice*, London

Lysons, S 1797. *An Account of Roman Antiquities Discovered at Woodchester*, London

Lysons, S 1812. 'Some account of Roman antiquities discovered at Caerhun, in Caernarvonshire, and in other parts of the county', *Archaeologia*, **16**, 127–34

Mantell, G A 1847. *Geological Excursions Round the Isle of Wight*, London

Mantell, G A 1850. 'On the remains of Man, and works of art imbedded in rocks and strata', *Archaeol J*, **7**, 327–46

Molesworth, R 1787. 'Description of the Druid temple lately discovered on the top of the hill near St Hillary in Jersey', *Archaeologia*, **8**, 384–5

Molyneaux, B L (ed) 1997. *The Cultural Life of Images: visual representation in archaeology*, London

Murray, T 1989. 'The history, philosophy and sociology of archaeology: the case of the Ancient Monuments Protection Act (1882)', in Pinsky and Wylie (eds) 1989, 55–67

Murray, T 1993. 'Archaeology and the threat of the past: Sir Henry Rider Haggard and the acquisition of time', *World Archaeology*, **25**, 175–85

Neville, R C 1847. 'Examination of a group of barrows, five in number, in Cambridgshire', *Archaeologia*, **32**, 357–61

Nurse, B 2000. 'George Cruikshank's *The Antiquarian Society*, 1812, and Sir Henry Charles Englefield', *Antiq J*, **80**, 316–21

Penn, G 1828. *Conversations in Geology*, London

Piggott, S 1976a. *Ruins in a Landscape: essays in antiquarianism*, Edinburgh

Piggott, S 1976b. 'The origins of the English archaeological societies', in Piggott (ed) 1976a, 171–95

Piggott, S 1976c. 'The Roman camp and four authors', in Piggott (ed) 1976a, 161–70

Piggott, S 1978. *Antiquity Depicted*, London

Pinsky, V and Wylie, A (eds) 1989. *Critical Traditions in Contemporary Archaeology*, Cambridge

Pitt-Rivers, A H L F 1861. 'On a model illustrating the parabolic theory of projection in vacuo', *J Royal Unit Services Inst*, **5**, 497–501

Pitt-Rivers, A H L F 1867a. 'Primitive warfare, part I', *J Royal Unit Services Inst*, **11**, 612–45

Pitt-Rivers, A H L F 1867b. 'A description of certain piles found near London Wall and Southwark, possibly the remains of pile buildings', *Anthropol Rev*, **5**, lxxi–lxxxiii

Pitt-Rivers, A H L F 1868. 'Primitive warfare, part II', *J Royal Unit Services Inst*, **12**, 399–439

Pitt-Rivers, A H L F 1869a. 'Further remarks on the hill forts of Sussex: being an account of excavations in the forts of Cissbury and Highdown', *Archaeologia*, **42**, 53–76

Pitt-Rivers, A H L F 1869b. 'On the proposed exploration of Stonehenge by a committee of the British Association', *J Ethnolog Soc*, **2**, 1–5

Pitt-Rivers, A H L F 1872a. 'Address on the "Neolithic Exhibition"', *Proc Soc Antiq London*, 2nd ser, **5**, 232–5

Pitt-Rivers, A H L F 1872b. 'On the discovery of Palaeolithic implements in association with *Elephas Primigenius* in the gravels of the Thames Valley at Acton', *Proc Geol Soc London*, **28**, 449–66

Pitt-Rivers, A H L F 1875. 'Excavations of Cissbury Camp, Sussex', *J Anthropol Inst*, **5**, 357–90

Pitt-Rivers, A H L F 1881. 'Excavations at Mount Caburn camp, near Lewes, conducted in 1877 and 1878', *Archaeologia*, **46**, 423–95

Pitt-Rivers, A H L F 1883. 'Excavations at Caesar's Camp, near Folkestone, conducted in 1878', *Archaeologia*, **47**, 429–65

Pitt-Rivers, A H L F 1887. *Excavations in Cranborne Chase. Vol I*, privately printed

Pitt-Rivers, A H L F 1892. *Excavations in Cranborne Chase. Vol III*, privately printed

Pitt-Rivers, A H L F 1898. *Excavations in Cranborne Chase. Vol IV*, privately printed

Rawlinson, H 1852. 'Notes on some paper casts of cuneiform inscriptions', *Archaeologia*, **34**, 73–6

Rolleston, G 1869. 'Researches and excavation carried on in an ancient cemetery at Frilford, near Abingdon, Berks, in the years 1867–1868', *Archaeologia*, **42**, 417–85

Rooke, H 1809. 'Discoveries in a barrow in Derbyshire', *Archaeologia*, **12**, 327–33

Rudwick, M J S 1976. 'The emergence of a visual language for geological science, 1760–1840', *Hist Science*, **14**, 149–95

Schnapp, A 1996. *The Discovery of the Past*, London

Schnapp, A 2002. 'Between antiquarians and archaeologists: continuities and ruptures', *Antiquity*, **76**, 134–41

Secord, J A 2004. 'Monsters at the Crystal Palace', in Chadarevian and Hopwood (eds) 2004, 138–69

Sherratt, A 2002. 'Darwin among the archaeologists: the John Evans nexus and the Borneo caves', *Antiquity*, **67**, 151–7

Smith, C Roach 1848–80. *Collectanea Antiqua: etchings and notices of ancient remains, illustrations of the habits, customs and history of past ages*, 7 vols, London

Smyth, W H 1830. 'Account of an ancient bath in the island of Lipari', *Archaeologia*, **23**, 98–102

Society of Antiquaries of London 1873. *Exhibition of Bronze Age Implements and Weapons*, London

Society of Antiquaries of London 1874. *Exhibition of Palaeolithic and Neolithic Implements and Weapons*, London

Spiro, M E (ed) 1965. *Context and Meaning in Cultural Anthropology*, New York

Stocking, G W Jr (ed) 1984. *Functionalism Historicized: essays on British social anthropology*, History of Anthropology 2, Madison, Wisc

Stocking, G W Jr 1987. *Victorian Anthropology*, London

Stone, S 1857. 'Account of certain (supposed) British and Saxon remains', *Proc Soc Antiq London*, 1st ser, **4** (1856–9), 92–100

Sweet, R 2004. *Antiquaries: the discovery of the past in eighteenth-century Britain*, London

Thomas, F W L 1851. 'Account of some Celtic antiquities of Orkney', *Archaeologia*, **34**, 88–136

Thompson, M W 1977. *General Pitt-Rivers: evolution and archaeology in the nineteenth century*, Bradford-on-Avon

Thurnam, J 1860. 'On the examination of a chambered long-barrow at West Kennet, Wiltshire', *Archaeologia*, **38**, 405–21

Thurnam, J 1869. 'On ancient British barrows, especially those of Wiltshire and the adjoining counties (Part I: long barrows)', *Archaeologia*, **42**, 161–244

Thurnam, J 1871. 'On ancient British barrows, especially those of Wiltshire and the adjoining counties (Part II: round barrows)', *Archaeologia*, **43**, 285–552

Urry, J 1984. 'Englishmen, Celts and Iberians: the ethnographic survey of the United Kingdom 1892–1899', in Stocking (ed) 1984, 83–105

van Riper, A B 1993. *Men Amongst Mammoths: Victorian science and the discovery of human prehistory*, London

Vyner, B (ed) 1994. *Building on the Past: celebrating 150 years of the Royal Archaeological Institute*, London

Way, A 1847. *Catalogue of Antiquities, Coins, Pictures and Miscellaneous Curiosities in the Possession of the Society of Antiquaries of London*, London

Webb, T 1824. 'Translation of a French metrical history of the deposition of King Richard the Second', *Archaeologia*, **20**, 1–423

Wetherall, D 1994. 'From Canterbury to Winchester: the foundation of the Institute', in Vyner (ed) 1994, 8–21

Wetherall, D 1998. 'The growth of archaeological societies', in Brand (ed) 1998, 21–34

Wheeler, R E M 1954. *Archaeology from the Earth*, Oxford, Clarendon Press

Woodruff, C H 1880. 'An account of discoveries made in Celtic tumuli near Dover, Kent', *Archaeologia*, **45**, 53–6

Tintern Abbey
The West Front.

Roland W. Paul
delt. 1878

CHAPTER TWELVE

Fabric, Form and Function: the Society and 'the Restoration Question'

Rick Turner

Over the past 300 years, arguments have raged over 'the Restoration Question'. The debate can become polarized between two extremes, with the protagonists proposing minimal intervention at one end and wholesale re-creation at the other. For those topics that are of concern to the Society's Fellowship – ancient buildings, archaeological monuments and historic artefacts – the debate nearly always focuses on how far the original fabric is to be affected during a conservation or restoration programme.[1]

Bernard Feilden has attempted to identify the different levels of intervention in what is one of the most respected modern manuals on the conservation of historic buildings.[2] He describes seven such levels:

1. prevention of decay
2. preservation of the existing state
3. consolidation of the fabric
4. restoration
5. rehabilitation
6. reproduction
7. reconstruction

In this approach, the historic fabric is rightly regarded as of paramount importance. It always has the potential to tell us more about how and why any artefact was made, and how its appearance and use may have changed over time.

However, there are two other attributes of ancient buildings, monuments and artefacts that contribute to their value and influence our response to them. The first of these might be described as the form. This requires the consideration of the external appearance of a historic site or artefact and how it lies within its setting. Since the later eighteenth century, ruins in particular have evoked a very powerful emotional response. Sometimes their first depictions or descriptions can hold an extraordinary power over the viewer, and evoke reverie in the first-time visitor:

> The ascending over men's minds of the ruins of the stupendous past . . . is half-mystical in basis. The intoxication, at once so heady and so devout, is not the romantic melancholy engendered by broken towers and mouldered stones;

Fig 85. The west front of Tintern Abbey Church in 1899 (SAL, Roland Paul Collection). *Photograph*: © Society of Antiquaries of London.

it is the soaring of the imagination into the high empyrean where huge episodes are tangled with myths and dreams.[3]

Any conservation project will almost inevitably change the external form or appearance of a site and remodel its surroundings to some extent. For example, during the consolidation of the fabric of a ruinous building for the benefit of future generations, the ivy and other vegetation will have to be removed. If a building is re-rendered to help preserve its internal timberwork and finishes, its appearance is radically altered, even though no historic fabric is lost at all. Archaeological investigation can be more extreme. Though aimed at learning more about the history and development of a site, it often strips a site of its mystery and pulls back the veil of decay. Woodward, in his analysis of the artistic response to the ruins of the Coliseum following the excavations of the site in 1874, concluded that:

> The sewers and underground service corridors have remained exposed ever since, as bald as the foundations of a modern construction site. I cannot find a single writer or painter who has been inspired by the Colosseum [*sic*] since 1870.[4]

At the other extreme, the historic fabric may have been almost totally destroyed by some catastrophe, such as fire, earthquake or war. Here wholesale reproduction may be undertaken to restore a well-loved building, both physically and in the consciousness of the community that suffered.[5] There may be considerable periods between these two actions. In the case of the historic centre of Hildesheim, Germany, the bomb-damaged buildings were first reconstructed in a contemporary style in the 1950s. Subsequently, these were replaced in the 1980s by replicas of the historic buildings lost to wartime bombing.[6]

The second attribute of every ancient building, monument or artefact is that it was created to fulfil a function. Later in its history it will have taken on other functions. The value of things from the past is enhanced if we understand why they were made and how they came to be used. Our appreciation of their former function is most vivid if it can still be experienced to some extent today. Feilden's seven degrees of intervention can be applied to this aspect of a conservation or restoration project. New categories can be added. At one extreme, by allowing decay, the fabric can decay to such an extent that the function is lost. Things from the past can become institutionalized, for example, either by display out of context in a museum, or through the presentation of a country house frozen at the moment that it passed into the hands of, say, the National Trust. Most radical is the imposing of a new use, which may be at odds, or even be incompatible, with what has gone before. An example of this would be 'façadism' within a historic town, where the new building retained behind the façade bears no relation to the size, plan or use of the building which it replaced.

Nothing can resist the passing of time, the agents of decay or changes in circumstances. At intervals, interventions are inevitable, and they always pose 'the Restoration Question'. Conservation philosophy is as much subject to fashion and doctrine as any other discipline.[7] This chapter explores three aspects of the Society's long history to see how the three competing forces of the desire to preserve or restore fabric, form and function have been played out.

JOHN CARTER AND JAMES WYATT

Ruinous medieval buildings attracted both the admiration and the concern of antiquarians from the beginning of the seventeenth century. On the one hand, they admired the beauty and grandeur of noble ruins, while on the other they decried the dilapidated condition of those buildings that remained in use. For example, the architect John Vanburgh sought the preservation of the ruins of Woodstock Manor in the grounds of his new Blenheim Palace, while fifty years earlier, John Evelyn had recommended the demolition of Norwich Castle and its rebuilding on a new site.[8] During the eighteenth century, antiquarian concerns moved from recording and studying antiquities to making the case for the preservation of ancient monuments and buildings 'as the physical embodiment of the nation's history'.[9]

From early in its history, the Society employed draughtsmen and engravers – men such as George Vertue – to record and illustrate ancient objects brought to their attention. They also celebrated the work of other great draughtsmen and engravers of classical antiquities – such as Giambattista Piranesi (1720–78), who was elected an Honorary Fellow in 1757.[10] However from about 1770, a great interest developed in the 'Gothic Taste', which 'had begun as an admiration of romantic "gloomth" [and] was beginning to be as scholarly and creative as the Classical Taste that had preceded and still accompanied it'.[11] Fellows published a succession of descriptions and images of ancient churches and their contents. In 1776 the Society received a pamphlet signed 'D A' and ending with a poem that began:

> The GROANS Of the Abbays, Cathedrals, Palaces, and other antient buildings
> of North Britain. Illustrious Society, Can you tamely look on, and suffer our
> bodies, to be basely torn, barbarously mangled, and layed in ruins, by a selfish
> race of unfeeling Goths: Can you lamely look on, we say, and not punish
> these rude offenders. Many of us are entirely leveled! Some of us falling down
> with gothic irons! Some of us tumbling down with old age! Pity our forlorn
> situation, and procure us the necessary aid, by an Act of Parliament: Or soon!
> too soon alas! None of us will be left to Groan![12]

The benefits of recording were brought home after Sherwin was commissioned by the Society in 1778 to make drawings – later engraved by Basire – of the paintings in the Great Parlour at Cowdray House, Sussex, portraying the attack of the French on Portsmouth in Henry VIII's reign. These were to become the only pictorial record of this important historical event following the disastrous fire at Cowdray in 1793.[13]

Recording became more than a passive exercise following the appointment of John Carter (1748–1817), who had worked for the *Builder's Magazine*, as draughtsman to the Society in 1784 (see fig 24).[14] The Director, Richard Gough, began to see dangers in the recording and publishing of great buildings. In a letter written to the *Gentleman's Magazine* in 1788, he declared:

> The art of engraving, which helps to make ancient buildings known, and preserves their form to a certain degree, contributes, I fear, to their demolition. 'Is such a thing engraved?' – 'O, yes' – 'Then it is preserved to posterity.'[15]

Fears grew among the Fellowship as they heard of the fate of French abbeys and cathedrals following the Revolution.[16] This prompted the Society to pass a resolution on 30 March 1792:

> that it be desirable and useful for the Society to be in possession of Architectural drawings of the different Cathedrals and other religious Houses in the Kingdom and that the Council be authorized to employ such artists in making the same as they shall judge fitt & proper.[17]

A committee was set up under the chairmanship of Sir Henry Englefield and it granted Carter a string of commissions. He was working on St Stephen's Chapel, Westminster, in 1792 and 1793, and on Exeter and Wells Cathedrals and Glastonbury and Bath Abbeys in 1795 and 1796.[18] Also during the summer of 1795, Carter had produced measured drawings of Durham Cathedral as restoration work under the direction of the architect James Wyatt (1746–1813) was being undertaken.[19]

Wyatt's role at Durham was quite short-lived. He was first invited in 1794 by Bishop Barrington, who had been promoted from the see of Salisbury, where Wyatt had already undertaken a controversial restoration,[20] to make improvements at the bishops' residences at Bishop Auckland and Durham Castle. Later, in September 1795, Wyatt put forward his proposals for the repair and alteration to the cathedral. He had two main objectives: the first to improve the building architecturally and make it stylistically more coherent, and the second to make some functional improvements required by the bishop and the dean. Works of repair and redressing of the exterior had been underway since 1777, under the local architects John Wooler and George Nicholson, but Wyatt's proposals were much more radical – though, from 1798, he left them to another local architect, William Morpeth, to undertake.[21]

Carter, however, took great exception to the works carried out to Wyatt's designs. He lamented the destruction of the great statues from the east front of the Chapel of the Nine Altars, the reordering of the choir and the destruction of some of its ancient fittings (fig 86):

> Mr Carter concludes with observing that to regret the devastation continually making in our Cathedrals and other sumptuous buildings connected with them, will in itself be of no avail, unless some Efforts of laudable and animated Zeal be made for the preservation of the remaining ones . . .

and he hoped that George III, as patron of the Society, might:

Fig 86. One bay of the Chapel of the Nine Altars, Durham Cathedral, drawn by John Carter, 1795 (SAL, John Carter portfolio, fol VI). *Photograph*: © Society of Antiquaries of London.

prevent interested persons from effacing the still remaining unaltered Traits of our Ancient Magnificence which are but faintly to be imitated and perhaps never to be equalled.[22]

The Society did not act. Nor did the king for, in 1796, Wyatt, through his royal patron, became Surveyor of Somerset House, then home to the Society.[23] He wrote: 'whenever anything occurred in his Department as Surveyor of the Buildings by the Antiquarian Society, he should be honoured with their commands'. From that date the Society had to pay Wyatt ten guineas twice yearly for 'lighting, watching and other current expenses'.[24] He was put forward for a Fellowship in May of that year, was blackballed, but put forward again in July. Battle lines became drawn, with Gough and Carter ranged against Wyatt's influential supporters. In November, John Thomas Groves showed a sketch of the Galilee Porch at Durham as it still stood, while Carter presented a drawing demonstrating how Wyatt's plans to create a walk around the cathedral would lead to the porch's destruction (fig 87). Claims and counterclaims were made, but Wyatt was elected in December. Gough took this as a personal defeat and gave up the directorship, resigning his Fellowship a few days later. However, Carter continued to exhibit drawings documenting, in his view, the destruction of the site.[25] His support began to fall away, except for that of Sir Henry Englefield, Vice-President, who made a journey to Durham the following year and found that Carter's 'fidelity and accuracy' had been needlessly impeached.[26] Wyatt's work

Fig 87. The west front of Durham Cathedral, drawn by John Carter, 1795 (SAL, John Carter portfolio, fol III). *Photograph*: © Society of Antiquaries of London.

continued and, in 1801, the Society published Carter's drawings of Durham with descriptions intended not to cause any personal offence.[27]

Carter and Wyatt's feud spilled over to other sites – particularly the medieval palace of Westminster, where Wyatt was also the Surveyor.[28] He refused Carter access to St Stephen's Chapel, where important antiquarian discoveries were being made during its conversion to house the Irish MPs in 1800–1. Carter managed somehow to get in and produce his preliminary sketches 'under the extreme difficulty of access to the lower part of the Chapel, which he could only draw by lanthorn light and nearly lying at length under the benches'.[29]

This argument over the propriety of the restoration of a great building left a division in the Society, with Wyatt's supporters coming to the fore, so that John Buckler (1770–1851), the architectural draughtsman who took on Carter's mantle, was blackballed in 1808. Nevertheless, Carter's persistent campaigning in the cause of preservation, and his own contemporaneous publication of accurate drawings of cathedrals, abbeys and castles, 'made the connection between buildings and history as a form of public property and [was] to have pioneered the belief in the Gothic as a distinctively English architectural idiom'.[30]

RUSKIN, LUBBOCK AND THE MINISTRY STYLE

Fifty years were to pass before the Society became re-engaged in 'the Restoration Question'. John Ruskin (1819–1900) was inspired to write a pamphlet on the opening of the 'unrivalled mechanical ingenuity' of the Crystal Palace in 1854.[31] He reflected, before this great symbol of modernity, on the destruction and loss of great medieval buildings:

> Something may yet be done, if it were but possible thoroughly to awaken and alarm the men whose studies of archaeology have enabled them to form an accurate judgement of the importance of the crisis.

He volunteered the Society to oversee an association of local agents who could submit annual reports of monuments of interest in their neighbourhoods and any changes that were being proposed.[32] The Society would then act to buy threatened buildings or works of art or to assist their proprietors, both public and private, in the maintenance and so ensure their safety.[33] Ruskin concluded:

> The restorations have actually begun like cancers on every piece of Gothic architecture in Christendom; the question is only how much can be saved.

Later, Ruskin submitted this proposal to the Society's Executive Committee, with any fund established to be specifically aimed at medieval buildings. He made an offer of £25 for the purpose.[34] The Society moved cautiously, recognizing the scale of the task for which it was being volunteered, but agreed to create a 'Conservation Fund' separate from its other budgets to be applied to two objectives:

1. the formation of a list or catalogue of existing ancient buildings or other monuments;

2. the conservation of existing ancient buildings or other monuments in the sense of preservation from the further ravages of time, or negligence, without any attempt to add to, alter or restore.[35]

On 29 March 1855 the Council passed a resolution circulated to all Fellows, which ended with a paragraph on churches and the changing needs of divine service:

No restoration should ever be attempted, otherwise than as the word 'restoration' may be understood in the sense of preservation from further injuries by time or negligence . . . they contend that anything beyond this is untrue in art, unjustifiable in taste, destructive in practice, and wholly opposed to the judgement of the best Archaeologists.[36]

These statements – establishing the principle of 'minimal intervention' – were quite revolutionary.[37] Pugin's writings, the highly influential magazine *The Ecclesiologist* and Ruskin's earlier works set out the principles for the use of the Gothic style. They were concerned with applying the lessons learned from medieval buildings relating to structural form, honesty in the use of materials and the application of ornament, to the building of new churches.[38] Architects influenced by these ideals, when faced with the restoration of medieval churches, would be happy to rebuild, replace or even re-create parts of these buildings. For example, Sir George Gilbert Scott (1811–78) had an enormous practice, which dealt with over 800 buildings, including the design of many new churches and the restoration of many more.[39] However the mid-Victorian Gothic Revival was primarily concerned with stylistic accuracy, and not with conservation.[40]

The Society's objectives were laudable, but it had neither the money nor the power to carry them forward. Between 1856 and 1862 it made five grants totalling £35 before the committee and the fund ceased to act.[41] However, in Ruskin's ideas and the Society's actions, the basic structure for a state archaeological service was set out. By this date countries such as Prussia (1818), France (1830) and Greece (1834) had already established such services but another generation would pass before the idea was put forward in Britain.[42]

John Lubbock (1834–1913) made several attempts during the 1870s to pass legislation for the protection of ancient monuments through a series of private members' bills. These were consistently defeated, as many MPs and members of the House of Lords were concerned at what they considered to be an unjust interference with the rights of private property.[43] The Society put its weight behind Lubbock's bill and the Society's President, Lord Carnarvon, took charge of its passage through the House of Lords. It was not until 1882, when the Liberal government lent Lubbock its support, that the Ancient Monuments Protection Act was passed. It included a schedule of fifty ancient monuments, all of which had been offered into the guardianship of the state by their private owners. Nearly all of these were prehistoric tumuli, chambered tombs or stone circles. Pitt-Rivers was appointed as the first Inspector of Ancient Monuments and penalties were introduced against those who damaged any monuments on the schedule.[44]

Lord Carnarvon reported to the Society's Anniversary Meeting of 1883 that, though mutilated and crippled, it was still a bill.[45] However it did not help the Society in its principal aim, which was the conservation of medieval buildings. More significant in that respect was the foundation of the Society for the Protection of Ancient Buildings (SPAB) by William Morris in 1879. In his manifesto for the society,[46] he restated many of the principles put forward by the Society of Antiquaries in its statement on 'Restoration' in 1855. Under Morris's secretaryship, SPAB became an influential lobby against the unnecessary destruction of ancient buildings and a champion of the need for sympathetic, honest and reversible repairs.[47]

Just as significant as the work of SPAB in the protection, and ultimately the preservation by the state, of the country's great medieval buildings were the activities of two of the Society's longest-serving officers, William St John Hope (1854–1919) and Charles Peers (1868–1952). Hope was appointed as the Assistant Secretary in 1885, an office he held until 1910. In the last years of the nineteenth century he travelled all over England, reporting on buildings in danger.[48] He was equally vigorous in publishing articles on a wide range of topics concerning medieval buildings and artefacts, showing how an analytical or scientific archaeological approach could move understanding forward. As the new century dawned, much of his energy was devoted to running the Society's excavations, first at Silchester and later at sites such as Old Sarum and Windsor Castle. These excavations raised the issue of how to consolidate and present areas of low walling that had previously been buried from public view.

Charles Peers, an architect and architectural editor of the *Victoria County History*, was appointed as Secretary in 1908, so overlapping with Hope's term of office.[49] Two years later he was appointed as Chief Inspector of Ancient Monuments, a post he was to hold until 1933.[50] The work of the inspectorate had been in decline. Pitt-Rivers's initial inspection of the fifty sites on the schedule had led to only eighteen being taken into guardianship, of which four had seen conservation works and three had seen some form of enforcement.[51] A new Ancient Monuments Protection Bill had become law in 1900, empowering the Commissioner of Works to request the placing of any monument into guardianship whose preservation was in the public interest. However, it was not until 1913, when the Ancient Monuments Consolidation and Amendment Act was passed, that compulsory powers were made available to schedule ancient monuments.[52]

It was the analytical approach developed by Hope, and its application by Peers to the conservation of those great monuments that began to be taken into state care in the early twentieth century, which saw the development of the Ministry of Works' philosophy – summarized as 'Keep as Found'. Effectively, the ministry's style of presentation can also be traced to the same source.[53]

These ideas might be best explored by looking at one example – Tintern Abbey, in Monmouthshire – where Peers, and to a lesser extent Hope, played a prominent role. The abbey ruins were first presented to the public by Charles Somerset, fourth Duke of Beaufort, as early as the 1750s. He organized the clearance of the interior of the abbey church, the collection of the architectural fragments and the turfing of the ground for visitors to walk on. The Revd Barford wrote in 1758:

> The Building itself is the finest, and the most venerable Ruin, of the religious kind, one can meet with . . . and it is impossible not to feel a sort of melancholy Chill and horror occasioned by the Echo, the ruined Tombs, the disfigured statues of Saints, the clasping Ivy and the tottering Tower.[54]

Visitors came in increasing numbers during the eighteenth century, many inspired by William Gilpin's *Observations on the River Wye*, published in 1782, where Tintern was presented as the most beautiful scene on the river journey. He did, however, recommend that 'a mallet judiciously used (but who durst use it?) might be of service in fracturing some of them', referring to the well-preserved gable ends of the ruins.[55] Many artists, most notably Turner in 1792, came and painted the ivy-clad stonework. The abbey church stood largely in isolation, surrounded by what was described in 1839 as 'unpicturesque cottages and pigsties'. As interest in the Gothic Revival grew, a number of exact measured surveys of the abbey were undertaken, notably by Joseph Potter in 1847 and Edmund Sharpe in 1848.[56] Such was the importance and fragility of the abbey ruins (fig 85) that the Crown Estate bought the site from the ninth Duke of Beaufort in 1901 so that it was saved for the nation.[57] By this date, guardianship was an option but only if the site was being offered into care – and the Duke of Beaufort was at this time divesting himself of many of his estates in south Wales, along with the monuments that his family had acquired over the centuries.[58]

The restoration programme at Tintern Abbey was initiated by the Office of Woods and Forests on behalf of the Crown Estate. It appointed F W Waller, the Gloucester Cathedral architect, to supervise the works, which were commissioned through private contractors. As Waller's records[59] and the dates on the buildings show, he moved at considerable speed around the ruins. In doing so he clearly followed the principles of the Society of the Protection of Ancient Buildings. Where he reinstated lost masonry, he used smaller blocks of hammer-faced sandstone and did not restore dressed stonework even where its form could be confidently inferred (fig 88). Dressed stonework, where it needed to be replaced for structural reasons – such as the great east window – was replaced to its original profile. Repairs were regularly and conspicuously dated.

Hope had written to Waller about the work, and he visited the site with his disciple, Harold Brakspear, in April 1904.[60] In 1907 Harold Brakspear was commissioned to prepare a plan of the abbey, and did so following Hope's principles.[61] The survey led to the successive clearance of a number of vernacular buildings built over and partly out of the claustral ranges to expose the full plan of the abbey as it is seen today.

However, in 1908, concerns began to arise over some of the work Waller had supervised, particularly the enforced dismantling of the crossing arches. The contractors, Turners of Cardiff, did not reconstruct the arch to its former profile and left out the

Fig 88. Restoration of a buttress on the west front of Tintern Abbey Church by F W Waller in 1905. *Photograph*: Cadw, Crown Copyright.

toothing for the vaulting. Despite redoing some of the work, confidence was lost, and in 1913, responsibility for Tintern Abbey was handed over from the Office of Woods and Forests to the Office of Works. The works were now supervised by Charles Peers and his architect Frank Baines and undertaken by a direct labour force rather than contractors.[62] The conservation philosophy changed and became more conservative in some aspects and more interventionist in others. The replacement of dressed stone was much more limited, with repairs to laminations being carried out with copper strips and cement mortars. In some areas where Waller had reinstated lost string-courses, the new stones were removed.

The most significant piece of work was the repair of the south wall of the nave. This had undergone structural deformation – perhaps when the vaults had been brought down at the Suppression – and was in danger of collapse. Waller had inserted huge wooden shores in the church to prop the walls. Various schemes were considered, including dismantling and rebuilding and the use of new stone buttresses. Both of these would have been 'honest' repairs in SPAB terms. A much more ambitious approach was developed by Baines and Peers, however, and agreed by the Ancient Monuments Board. This began with the erection of a lattice steel truss bracing the south nave wall from the south aisle. Then a temporary arcade of brick arches to carry the clerestory was built, to allow the stonework of the nave piers to be dismantled. Steel stanchions were then erected on reinforced concrete pads to take the load of the wall above and the stonework of the piers cut out so they could be threaded back on to the stanchions. This enabled the wooden shoring to be removed and the abbey church to be reopened to public acclaim in 1928.[63] The Secretary of the SPAB, A R Powys, was less impressed, though, and wrote of Tintern Abbey:

> The building, analysed, weighed and measured, is no longer a thing of mystery; stripped of its foliage the deep shadows of the hidden recesses disappear. The observer, like the builder of old, can comprehend the whole. The painter no longer finds the contrast between stone walls and a delicate maze of leaves blended as though already in a picture. Though no stone be moved from its place, though arches still appear dangerously poised in mid-air, when once repair is complete, mystery is gone.[64]

So unlike Waller, Peers and Baines produced a scheme that kept the appearance of the external surface of the stonework of the church as found in 1901. It was done at a considerable loss to the historic stonework from the interior of the walls, and a great and unrecorded loss of the archaeological remains within the floor levels of the church. During this period the Ministry of Works continued to acquire the vernacular cottages to the north of the abbey. These were demolished and the ruins of the infirmary and abbot's lodgings were successively exposed, consolidated and laid out for public view (fig 89). The interiors of buildings were marked by Bredon gravel (except for the church, which had always been turfed) and the exteriors by well-managed lawns. The ruins were kept weed-free and contained by fences and railings. This approach and presentation is the epitome of the 'Ministry style'. Despite being based on a principle of 'Keep as Found', it can be highly interventionist and gives a strong sense of order and neatness.[65]

Fig 89. An aerial photograph of Tintern Abbey following the completion of the excavation and conservation work by the Ministry of Works. *Photograph*: Cadw, Crown Copyright.

KELMSCOTT MANOR

The Society's only opportunity to take responsibility for an important historic building came in 1962 with the acquisition of Kelmscott Manor. Though an interesting and well-preserved yeoman farmhouse, it was charged with special significance as William Morris's 'Earthly Paradise'. Many Fellows did not welcome their new responsibility, but skilful networking by the then President, Joan Evans, led to a generous donation, which provided funds for its restoration. This was managed with great enthusiasm by the Secretary, Dick Dufty, who later became resident in the manor as its honorary curator.

Modern visitors, like Morris before them, come to Kelmscott as pilgrims, seeking solace away from their busy lives. Kelmscott is now a rural conservation area, where the Society also maintains five of the cottages, their barns and grounds. Apart from the traffic cones and the occasional car parked along the grass verges, nothing jars. Visitors walk past pretty, characteristic cottages looking for the house just as Morris did in 1871 until they espy his 'heaven on earth' – 'close down on the river'.[66] More resolute visitors can still travel up the River Thames, as Morris and his family did in the 'Ark', or row down from Lechlade, to tie up at the meadows below the house. Here two concrete Second World War pillboxes were built, as if to defend the manor from the modern world.

In *News from Nowhere* the fictional Guest (William Morris) and Ellen (his wife, Jane) 'crossed the road, and again almost without my will raised the latch of a door in the wall and we stood presently on a stone path which led up to the stone house'.[67] This view became immortalized in C M Gere's engraving of the house, which formed the frontispiece of the Kelmscott Press edition of *News from Nowhere* (fig 90). This single image is so powerful that it guided the restoration of this part of the garden in the 1990s under Hal Moggeridge's supervision.[68] It also influenced the restoration of the long lead spouts that drain the roof. Unfortunately, the modern visitor is denied the thrill of raising the latch and passes through the former farmyard instead, where the visitor facilities and staff car park are now sited in amongst the limestone farm buildings. The requirements of any twenty-first-century historic house open to the public often intrude. Car parks, toilets, shops and cafés need to be accommodated where none were before. By siting them in the farmyard, an area not leased by Morris, they are separated from the house. The sights, sounds and smells of a working farmyard alongside Morris's idyll have evolved into their modern equivalents.

Tickets are timed, so entry into the house can be delayed, just as happened to Guest and Ellen, who took time to enjoy the garden, the birds and the 'fragrant sun-cured air':

> 'Come in', said Ellen. 'I hope nothing will spoil it inside; but I don't think it will'
> . . . We went in, and found no soul in any room as we wandered . . . from the rose-covered porch to the strange and quaint garrets amongst the great timbers of the roof.[69]

Fig 90. The frontispiece of *News from Nowhere* (Kelmscott Press, 1892), drawn by C M Gere, with a border designed by William Morris, and engraved by W H Hooper. *Photograph*: © Society of Antiquaries of London.

Fig 91. Condition survey of Kelmscott Manor in 1965, drawn by Ailwyn Best. *Photograph*: © Society of Antiquaries of London.

Today visitors are greeted by a succession of enthusiastic volunteer stewards, and will be lucky to wander alone. However, no ropes or barriers hinder the enjoyment of exploring the rooms, and you may even sit in the window seats and view the gardens and the open landscape beyond. Kelmscott's 'but little furniture' is not all from the house that William Morris knew and the walls are painted white so as not 'to re-ornament it' or detract from the rich patterns of the hangings and curtains.

The Society, it is clear, has gone to great efforts to re-create the experience described by Guest for their present guests. To preserve the house after a couple of generations of neglect, greater interventions into the fabric of the house were made than the architect, Peter Locke of Donald Insall and Associates, had hoped for (fig 91). He had been a Lethaby Scholar of the SPAB, and tried to adhere to Morris's principles of minimal intervention. As the work proceeded, from 1962 to 1966, the extent of the decay that was discovered as the building was opened up made this approach increasingly problematical.[70] Much of the success of the project rested on using the traditional skills of the local builders, Pethers of Burford. In the front garden, Hal Moggeridge specifically set out to re-create the form of the garden fixed in people's minds by Gere's engraving, even if photographs show that it may never have existed in this form.[71] Finally, great care has been taken (consciously and perhaps subconsciously) to allow the modern visitor to enjoy the experience of discovery and peace that so captivated William Morris and his family after they had found Kelmscott.

320

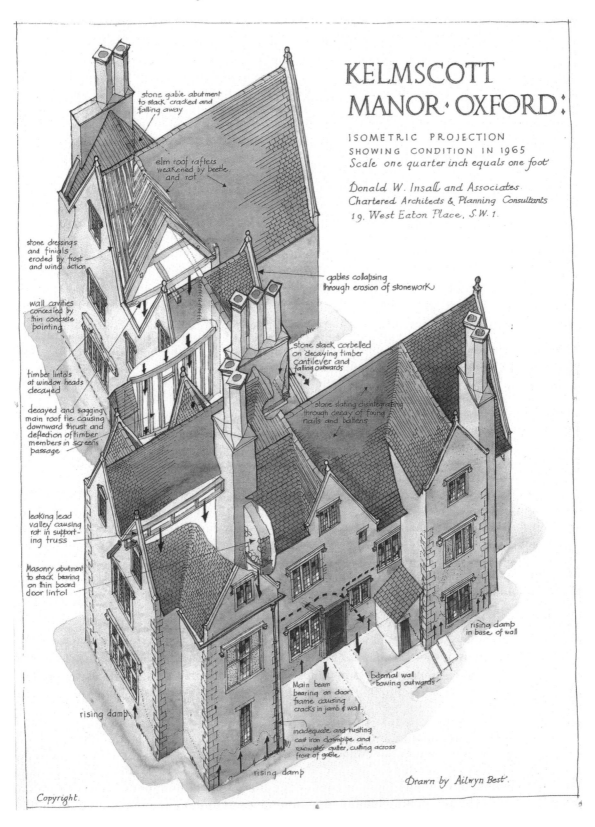

KELMSCOTT
MANOR · OXFORD:

ISOMETRIC PROJECTION
SHOWING CONDITION IN 1965
Scale one quarter inch equals one foot

Donald W. Insall and Associates
Chartered Architects & Planning Consultants
19, West Eaton Place, S.W. 1.

stone gable abutment
to stack cracked and
falling away

elm roof rafters
weakened by beetle
and rot

stone dressings
and finials
eroded by frost
and wind action

gables collapsing
through erosion of stonework

wall cavities
concealed by
thin concrete
pointing

stone stack corbelled
on decaying timber
cantilever and
falling outwards

timber lintols
at window heads
decayed

stone slating disintegrating
through decay of fixing
nails and battens

decayed and sagging
main roof tie causing
downward thrust and
deflection of timber
members in screens
passage

leaking lead
valley causing
rot in support-
ing truss

Masonry abutment
to stack bearing
on thin board
door lintol

rising damp
in base of wall

External wall
bowing outwards

rising damp

Main beam
bearing on door
frame causing
cracks in jamb & wall

inadequate and rusting
cast iron downpipe and
rainwater gutter, cutting across
front of gable

rising damp

Drawn by Ailwyn Best

CONCLUSIONS

It is time to review these three examples in the light of 'the Restoration Question' as framed in the introduction. Rather than imagine a single line depicting the stages between 'the prevention of decay' and 're-creation', a more complicated model is needed. This might consist of a three-dimensional graph with fabric, form and function forming the three axes. One end of each axis would be represented by no intervention and the other by a total change. The origin would be the point where these three attributes were at a point of balance. Any conservation or restoration project could be located in this three-dimensional space, depending on the philosophy that was adopted and the level of intervention that was applied in terms of the fabric, form and function.

At Durham Cathedral, John Carter was horrified by the wilful loss of the historic fabric and by James Wyatt's desire to impose new features with no apparent regard to the value of what he was intending to remove. Through his meticulous work, Carter established what should be the first principle of any conservation project. This is that any project must be informed by a detailed record and analysis of the fabric. There is no substitute for sitting, looking at, measuring, drawing and analysing what is there. In doing so Carter 'filled the first precepts of their institution (the Society), by disdaining any adventitious objects foisted on the work of antiquity'.[72] Through this work, Gomme credited Carter with changing the opinions of architects:

> as to the manner in which old buildings were to be treated . . . He did enormous good, and he did it unselfishly, and in response to a sense of duty which he felt absolutely placed upon him by his position and tastes.[73]

Carter, through his 380 articles in the *Gentleman's Magazine*, describing and campaigning for the preservation of examples of ancient architecture, was instrumental in developing the national consciousness towards the past and Gothic architecture in particular.[74] So, the row played out in the chambers and ballet boxes of the Society, at the very end of the eighteenth century, was to inform the more scholarly exponents of the Gothic Revival from the middle of the nineteenth.

At Tintern Abbey, the situation over the past 250 years has been more complicated and the three attributes of 'the Restoration Question' need to be considered separately. In relation to the fabric, Beaufort's first clearance of the site did not address the conservation of the standing fabric at all. It remained a heavy ivy-clad ruin until 1901, when Waller started work. Waller followed the principles of Morris and the Society for the Protection of Ancient Buildings in carrying out repairs in a visibly distinct manner and was happy to replace or restore components where they were in need of structural repair. Peers and Baines moved to the position where the preservation of the external surfaces of the stonework became the key objective, preserving both the appearance and the historically significant information that these show. Baines set out his personal philosophy in 1924: 'replicas of ancient work, however perfectly or accurately executed, can have no real historic or archaeological value whatever', and regretted the grievous and heavy losses 'partly, perhaps as a consequence and a result of the scholarship and knowledge of M Viollet-le-Duc'.[75] Peers was less dogmatic, writing in 1931 that 'it is better to risk a deception by inconspicuous additions than to proclaim them by conspicuous and unsympathetic materials'.[76]

Their joint philosophy resulted in the loss of considerable parts of the internal fabric of the abbey church in particular, and the loss of surface details, such as plasters, through comprehensive repointing. It also led to the clearance of a number of later (but still historic) structures from within and partly overlying the medieval ruins, sweeping away a period of history of the site fully equivalent in time to its monastic occupation.[77] The archaeological deposits within and beneath these buildings were removed without record. This was to reveal the footings of walls, showing the plan of the other abbey buildings. The work was aimed at showing the full extent of the abbey in its medieval heyday, but its result in some ways shows a palimpsest of different periods that would not have existed together and can be confusing to the general visitor.

Even today the form or appearance of the ruins and their setting within the steep wooded slopes of the Wye Valley is very beautiful. The extent of the upstanding masonry is little changed from the Buck brothers' view of 1732. However, the site of the ivy-clad church, rising through the cluster of vernacular buildings, has gone. In the eighteenth century, most visitors would have arrived by boat, some having spent over a day travelling down from Ross, their senses already heightened by the sublime qualities of the Wye Valley. Today, visitors mostly come by vehicle, and the abbey appears much more suddenly as you approach from east or west. The vegetation is gone and more modern facilities, such as the car park and shops, impinge upon the setting.[78] Much of the romance is lost, though Rose Macaulay could still say that:

> Tintern has, one supposes, given as much high poetic pleasure to ruin-gazers
> as even the finest English abbeys.[79]

Even so, artists who come to Tintern today still complain that the conservation works are 'ruining the abbey'.

It is hard to pin down the function of Tintern Abbey's church. It was only in use as a church for about 230 years before it was un-roofed at the Suppression. For a couple of centuries, the abbey was partly requisitioned for industrial purposes and partly abandoned.[80] Since 1750 it has been a visitor attraction. So it has been a ruin for twice as long as it was a building in use; and it was a church for about as long as it has been a tourist attraction. As guardianship by the state is 'in perpetuity', it will remain in its present condition, subject to selective and successful conservation, for ever. So Peers's and Hope's legacies at Tintern – and throughout the 'guardianship estate' – will be long-term and, in many ways, beneficial. Their influence, and the role of the Society, in acting as a forum for debate and providing a London base and library for generations of inspectors of ancient monuments (now dispersed into four home nations) represents another major contribution to the restoration debate.[81]

Kelmscott Manor provided the Society with an opportunity to put its own conservation philosophy into practice.[82] It has served many functions during its long history: manor house, farmhouse, country retreat, shrine, neglected lodging, museum and the embodiment of one man's philosophical outlook. Its external form is little changed since Morris's day even if, in the recent restoration of the front garden, artistic representation, rather than historical and archaeological records, provided the guide for the landscape architect.

There is no single answer to 'the Restoration Question'. When A R Powys gave his advice to those in charge of ancient buildings, he said:

> At the outset, however, it will be well to state that no fixed rule can be set up to be followed invariably. Each case must be considered on its merits.[83]

This remains true today. Every conservation project should begin with a comprehensive record and study, just as Carter pioneered at the end of the eighteenth century. Then a philosophy must be developed and applied throughout the project, addressing the fabric, the form and the function with equal care. Each action can then be tested against the philosophy to ensure consistent and valid decision-making. Finally, the project should be approached with love and enthusiasm, such as the Society has shown at Kelmscott Manor (fig 92), so as to leave something that:

> will belong to our descendants unless we play with them false. They are not . . . our property, to do as we like with. We are only trustees for those that come after us.[84]

Fig 92. A Fellows' Day at Kelmscott Manor. *Photograph*: © Society of Antiquaries of London.

NOTES

1. I would like to thank David Robinson and Helen Turner for reading and commenting on a draft of this chapter and Cem Oran for guidance on the philosophy of building conservation.
2. Feilden 2003, 8–12.
3. Beny 1977, 20.
4. Woodward 2001, 27.
5. See the chapter entitled 'Dust in the Air Suspended' in Woodward 2001, 208–26.
6. Jokilehto 1999, 285–7.
7. See Earl 2003, 50–64, for example.
8. See the section 'Better (Looking) Homes and Gardens' in Woolf 2003, 204–12.
9. Sweet 2004, 285.
10. Jokilehto 1999, 50.
11. Evans 1956, 154.
12. Ibid, 156; Sweet 2004, 300.
13. Evans 1956, 161.
14. For a full discussion of Carter's career, see Crook 1995, 17. The Society's accounts show that Carter only received work and payment intermittently until 1794, when his work on the cathedrals and abbeys began in earnest.
15. Evans 1956, 191.
16. For the reaction in England and France, see Sweet 2004, 305–6.
17. SAL, Council Minutes, III (not paginated), 30 Mar 1792.
18. SAL, Archives, Accounts Ledger 1782–1814. The Council Minutes Book (vol III, not paginated) gives some idea of how Carter worked. He was sent to the more distant cathedrals and abbeys for the summer recess, where he would hire lodgings and make his measured sketches. On his return to London he would draw up and wash the final drawings. In April 1794 he was paid 100 guineas for 152 days' work, including his expenses for producing the drawings of Exeter Cathedral. Work at Westminster could take place during the rest of the year.
19. Pevsner 1983, 166. He writes: 'Wyatt's designs for a number of devastating "improvements", including a Fonthill-like spire for the tower and the demolition of the Galilee (he got as far as removing the roof covering), for a carriage sweep, were successfully combated by the London Society of Antiquaries.'
20. The Society had received representations from another of its draughtsmen, Jacob Schnebbelie, about Wyatt's refusal to preserve the paintings in the choir during his restoration of Salisbury Cathedral: see Sweet 2004, 288.
21. This whole episode is analysed in depth in Jokilehto 1999, 102–9, and in Sweet 2004, 289–91.

22. Evans 1956, 207.
23. Wyatt's role at Somerset House formed part of his appointment as the Surveyor General for the Office of Works, following the death of Sir William Chambers. He owed this and other offices to the high regard in which he was held by George III. However, as the editors of the *King's Works* described it: 'Wyatt's arrival inaugurated a period of extravagance and confusion . . . As an administrator he was little less than disastrous. He was a bad correspondent and a born procrastinator': Crook and Port 1973, 49.
24. SAL, Council Minutes, III (not paginated), 31 Jan 1797, and the accounts for 1797 and the following years.
25. Carter wrote later in the *Gentleman's Magazine* in 1801–2: 'As I was engaged in this business nearly three months, I may be accredited in my several observations, which are not given from a hasty and indifferent decision of two or three days investigation, but from minute and deliberate memoranda and sketches of facts and existing objects.' This is almost the first manifesto for buildings archaeology: see Carter's seven pieces on Durham Cathedral reprinted in Gomme 1891, 167–86.
26. Evans 1956, 209–12.
27. Carter was more forthcoming in the *Gentleman's Magazine*: 'Two architects have each displayed their abilities in this way [alteration rather than repair]. One [Nicholson], who had got the start of the other [Wyatt], and who has since given place to his rival in the race for glorious change, has lain his new architectural dressings over the west and north fronts; and his successor was at it with professional fervour on the east front' (Gomme 1891, 176). The publication of the Durham volume was extraordinarily expensive for the Society. In 1801 the accounts record payments to Carter, to the engraver Basire, for the paper, and to the printers totalling £824.
28. Crook and Port 1973, 49–76.
29. Englefield 1811: quoted in Colvin 1966.
30. Sweet 2004, 293.
31. The Society's copy of this pamphlet is bound in as no. 3 in *101 Tracts Miscellanea*.
32. This is almost exactly what the present system of Field Monument Wardens now does for the government heritage agencies.
33. Ruskin 1854. The Scots should be credited with addressing this problem a generation earlier: see Fawcett 2002.
34. Evans 1956, 309–10.
35. Ibid, 310.
36. Ibid, 311.
37. Jean-Baptiste Lassus (1807–57) had published a

similar statement in the *Annales archéologiques* in 1845. He and Viollet-le-Duc were to put this practice of 'scientific archaeology' to use in their early years as inspectors of historic monuments in France, when restoring such buildings as La Madeleine, Vézelay. It was only later in his career that Viollet-le-Duc moved to the more full-scale restorations at such sites as Pierrefonds and Carcassonne: Jokilehto 1999, 138-48.

38. Dixon and Muthesius 1978, 182-204.
39. Cole 1980.
40. In Scott's defence he did publish *A Plea for the Faithful Restoration of our Ancient Churches* in 1850.
41. Evans 1956, 312.
42. Earl 2003, 42-4.
43. Chippindale 1983.
44. Ibid, 18-30.
45. Evans 1956, 333.
46. For the text of the manifesto and a commentary, see Earl 2003, 156-9.
47. For background and current information on the Society for the Protection of Ancient Buildings, visit its website at <www.spab.org.uk>.
48. Evans 1956, 336.
49. Peers remained the Secretary until 1921 when he was elected Director. He received the Society's Gold Medal in 1938.
50. Doggett 2004.
51. Chippindale 1983, table 1, 29.
52. Saunders 1983.
53. Keay 2004.
54. Cardiff Library Local Studies Collection, MS 2.727.
55. Gilpin 1782.
56. Robinson 2002, 21-3.
57. Robinson 1997.
58. For example, Chepstow Castle was put up for auction in 1899.
59. Now in the Gwent County Record Office, Cwmbran: ref nos GCRO D.902.1-2.
60. Robinson 1997, 52n20. Hope produced a remarkable annotated plan of the church, showing all the sockets visible in the masonry and speculating what wooden fittings they may have held.
61. This remarkable hand-coloured and phased drawing measures over 4.5m long and 1.2m wide and survives in Cadw's offices.
62. Peers and Baines were very active at this period in 'collecting' great medieval monuments for the Office of Works, and their personal philosophies were to determine the treatment of these buildings: see Keay 2004; Emerick 2003.
63. Robinson 1997, 47-9.
64. Jokilehto 1999, 180, quoting Powys's *Journal*. Oddly, Powys is highly complimentary of the detailed

structural analysis of the abbey church at Tintern undertaken by William Harvey for Sir Frank Baines in 1918: Powys 1929, 12-13.
65. For a recent critique of this approach, see Evans 2004.
66. William Morris to C J Faulkner 1871 in Society of Antiquaries 2004, 1.
67. Morris 1890, 173-4.
68. At Moggeridge's lecture to the Society (4 December 2003) on his restoration of the gardens at Kelmscott, there was considerable debate over the use of documentary sources only to guide the redesign, and the failure to carry out any archaeological excavation and recording before or during the works.
69. Morris 1890, 175.
70. These works involved the dismantling and rebuilding of the north wall and the use of concrete underpinning and grouting elsewhere in the building. There were radical repairs to a number of the roof trusses leading to the relaying of the roof covering. The chimney pots were changed and lead spouts added to match Gere's engraving. At the insistence of the local health board the well was capped. At Dufty's suggestion the north porch was added for the benefit of visitors, though it has never been used (Peter Locke, pers comm).
71. Society of Antiquaries 2004, 38.
72. Gomme 1891, 179.
73. Ibid, vi.
74. Sweet 2004, 293-7; Crook 1995, 11.
75. Baines 1923.
76. Peers 1931.
77. Courtney and Gray 1991.
78. Over the past few years, Cadw has tried to reverse some of the deleterious changes of the earlier twentieth century. This has involved the selective felling of trees and the laying of hedges to reopen the views of the abbey on the approach. The car park in front of the west end of the church has been grassed over and made an overflow only. For visitors inside the abbey something of the original solitude has been restored by allowing the hedge to the north to grow to the height of the lost precinct wall and reinstating the doors in the west end of the church to hide the modern world from view.
79. Beny 1977, 134.
80. Courtney and Gray 1991.
81. This chapter was written at the time when English Heritage was considering abandoning the title of Inspector of Ancient Monuments and Historic Buildings for something less confrontational.
82. Crossley, Hassall and Salway 2007, *passim*.
83. Powys 1929, 3
84. William Morris writing in 1889: quoted in Earl 2003, 2.

BIBLIOGRAPHY

Baines, F 1923. 'Preservation of ancient monuments and historic buildings', *J Roy Inst Brit Architect*, 31/4, 106

Beny, R 1977. *Roloff Beny Interprets in Photographs 'Pleasure of Ruins' by Rose Macaulay* (ed C Babington Smith), London

Chippindale, C 1983. 'The making of the first Ancient Monuments Act, 1882, and its administration under General Pitt-Rivers', *J Brit Archaeol Ass*, 136, 1–55

Cole, D 1980. *The Work of Sir Gilbert Scott*, London

Colvin, H (ed) 1966. 'Views of the Old Palace of Westminster', *Architect Hist*, 9, 24–5

Courtney, P and Gray, M 1991. 'Tintern Abbey after the Dissolution', *Bull Board Celtic Stud*, 38, 145–58

Crook, J M 1995. *John Carter and the Mind of the Gothic Revival*, Soc Antiq London Occas Pap 17, London

Crook, J M and Port, M H (eds) 1973. *The History of the King's Works. Volume VI: 1782–1851*, London

Crossley, A, Hassall, T and Salway, P (eds) 2007. *William Morris's Kelmscott: landscape and history*, Macclesfield

Dixon, R and Muthesius, H 1978. *Victorian Architecture*, London

Doggett, N 2004. 'Peers, Sir Charles Reed (1868–1952)', in *Oxford Dictionary of National Biography: Online Edition* (eds H C G Matthew and B Harrison), <http://www.oxforddnb.com./view/article/35454> (8 Aug 2006)

Earl, J 2003. *Building Conservation Philosophy*, 3rd edn, Reading

Emerick, K 2003. 'From frozen monuments to fluid landscapes: the presentation of ancient monuments from 1882 to the present', unpublished PhD thesis, University of York

Englefield, H 1811. *Description of the Additional Plates of St Stephen's Chapel*, London

Evans, D M 2004. 'Et in Arcadia? The problems with ruins', *Antiq J*, 84, 411–22

Evans, J 1956. *A History of the Society of Antiquaries*, Oxford

Fawcett, R 2002. 'Robert Reid and the early involvement of the state in the care of Scottish ecclesiastical buildings and sites', *Antiq J*, 82, 269–84

Feilden, B M 2003. *The Conservation of Historic Buildings*, 3rd edn, London

Gilpin, W 1782. *Observations on the River Wye and several parts of South Wales &c*, London

Gomme, G L (ed) 1891. *Sacred and Medieval Architecture: a classified collection of the chief contents of the Gentleman's Magazine from 1731–1868*, II, London

Jokilehto, J 1999. *A History of Architectural Conservation*, Oxford

Keay, A 2004. 'The presentation of guardianship sites', *Trans Ancient Monuments Soc*, 48, 7–20

Morris, W 1890. *News from Nowhere, or an epoch of rest* (ed J Redmond, 1970), London

Peers, C R 1931. 'The treatment of old buildings', *J Roy Inst Brit Architect*, 38/10, 311–25

Pevsner, N 1983. *The Buildings of England: County Durham* (revised E Williamson), London

Powys, A R 1929. *Repair of Ancient Buildings* (revised 1981), London

Robinson, D M 1997. 'The making of a monument: the Office of Woods and its successors at Tintern Abbey', *Monmouthshire Antiq*, 13, 43–56

Robinson, D M 2002. *Tintern Abbey*, rev edn, Cardiff

Ruskin, J 1854. *The Opening of the Crystal Palace, considered in some of its relations to the prospects of art*, London

Saunders, A D 1983. 'A century of ancient monuments legislation, 1882–1982', *Antiq J*, 63, 11–33

Scott, G G 1850. *A Plea for the Faithful Restoration of our Ancient Churches*, London

Society of Antiquaries 2004. *Kelmscott Manor: an illustrated guide*, London

Sweet, R 2004. *Antiquaries: the discovery of the past in eighteenth-century Britain*, London

Woodward, C 2001. *In Ruins*, London

Woolf, D 2003. *The Social Circulation of the Past: English historical culture 1500–1730*, Oxford

ENGLISH VILLAGES AND HAMLETS

HUMPHREY PAKINGTON

CHAPTER THIRTEEN

BREATHING THE FUTURE: THE ANTIQUARIES AND CONSERVATION OF THE LANDSCAPE, 1850–1950

Richard Morris

Like elephants, wrote the architect Clough Williams-Ellis (fig 94) in *England and the Octopus* (1928), archaeologists and antiquaries 'are generally useful but sometimes extremely dangerous'. Williams-Ellis – architect, conservationist, co-founder of the Council for the Preservation of Rural England, campaigner for national parks – was suspicious of antiquarian priorities that accorded more importance to prehistoric flints than to Georgian town halls or the twentieth century: 'Their gimlet eyes have a special and peculiar focus. They seem to have perverted standards of value, preferring what is merely rare to what is beautiful.'[1] When Williams-Ellis teased antiquaries for living out their 'blinkered lives' in surroundings 'that would give convulsions to a first-year architectural student', quite a lot of his tongue was in his cheek. This was, after all, the book that opened by asking if the English had been granted 'a special immunity against beauty'. But there again, *England and the Octopus* is the polemic that proclaims a 'gospel of beauty in the common setting of our daily life'.[2]

Were Williams-Ellis's antiquaries real? The caricature of the myopic scholar, so fixated by detail as to miss the big picture, was well known.[3] But if Williams-Ellis was just calling up a stereotype – why? In the 1920s why did antiquary and amenity campaigner not make common cause to counter crass development and social disintegration? If the improved planning system, national parks and nature reserves called for by conservation campaigners could protect the countryside from disfigurement and injury, surely they would do the same for archaeological assets in that landscape?

Lest we wonder if such questions are anachronistic, similar points were being made at the time. In 1926 Patrick Abercrombie described England's countryside as 'the greatest historical monument that we possess'.[4] We shall see how, in 1944, efforts were made to combine geological and archaeological conservation.[5] The Huxley Committee, set up in 1945 to consider the needs of nature conservancy in England and Wales, noted that the turf covering Neolithic pits at Maiden Castle:

> was probably established in the Bronze Age, and the charcoals found at different levels throw light on the vegetation of the neighbourhood at different times, so that both archaeological and botanical evidence, coupled with the evidence to be derived from the sub-fossil remains of snails and other animals, contribute to the elucidation of human, biological and climatic prehistory.[6]

Fig 93. Dust-jacket art between the wars: Batsford's *Face of Britain* series was part of a wider movement concerned with remembered landscape, the recording of rural crafts and traditions, and a return to local values and human scale in the face of automatism and industrialization. *Photograph*: Society of Antiquaries of London.

329

This was not an isolated case – the Huxley Committee was well aware of the relationship between archaeological and biological conservation.[7] The Committee's deputy chairman was Sir Arthur Tansley, a botanist and ecologist who, in 1930, had collaborated with O G S Crawford and E Cecil Curwen in drafting a memorandum to the inter-departmental committee that had been set up to consider the feasibility of establishing national parks in Great Britain. They proposed that the South Downs be designated as a national park to protect downland turf that also clothed fields and settlements in 'the condition they were in when abandoned by prehistoric man'.[8]

Such examples show that, at least from the early twentieth century, there were some who saw a correlation between antiquarian, scientific and social interests and called for combined action to achieve them. This chapter will explore aspects of the context in which those calls were made, and ask why, in the main, they went unheeded. Two aspects are given particular notice. The first concerns traditions of thought that shaped ideas about, and approaches to, rural conservation and land-scape down to the Second World War. The second is what happened during that war when, in the buzz of optimism surrounding hopes for post-war reconstruction, the Society did finally move by founding the Council for British Archaeology (CBA). The question here is why the Society acted so late, and why the council it then founded made so little headway. The Attlee government enacted legislation for National Parks, Sites of Special Scientific Interest, the Nature Conservancy, and planning. Listing aside, why was there no corresponding reform for the historic environment?

Before pursuing these questions, it is worth pausing to reflect that, until the 1940s, there was no compelling reason why the Society should have involved itself systematic-ically in such issues at all. The Society's main outdoor efforts were directed towards research, and ordinarily it was not a publicly campaigning body. It hardly needed to be: if change was afoot, it was normal for those considering it to turn at least to individual Fellows for advice. When HM Office of Works set up a committee in 1920 to consider amending the Ancient Monuments Act, five of its eight members were Fellows, including the Society's President, Secretary and a Vice-President. Initiating change was another matter: while the committee's report accurately noted that 'the Nation's interest in, and consequent duty towards, National monuments is far behind what is embodied in the legislation of other countries',[9] a decade was to pass before anything was done about it.

While the Society's aims implicitly embrace the land where many antiquities lie, the diversity of Fellows' interests meant that the cherishing of historic surroundings was but one of many topics, in many lands, with which they might be involved. Hence, where Fellows did engage with what we would now classify as conservation, it was usually as individuals – Fellowship was incidental. Corporate action was reserved for a small number of special causes – notably Stonehenge and its surroundings, and the preservation scheme that was prepared for Hadrian's Wall.[10] To leave the matter there, however, would be to miss the significance of the Society as a nexus for ideas – and gossip. Fellowship, for instance, enabled government servants and Inspectors from the Office of Works temporarily to step out of their official roles and cultivate ideas and proposals that would have been impossible to promote publicly.

Allied to this organic role was the Society's position as one of five learned societies ranged around Burlington House's courtyard. The shared concerns of the Linnean and Geological Societies with prehistory and human evolution drew on overlapping networks that embraced the living as well as the material world. Such networks, however, usually extended beyond Burlington House. To give one instance, Sir John Lubbock was elected to Fellowship of the Society of Antiquaries in 1864, the same year as Lane Fox. However, their key associations lay elsewhere. Darwin's mentoring of Lubbock (who had been a Fellow of the Royal Society since his mid-twenties) is well known, as is the friendship of both men with Alfred Russel Wallace. Lubbock was close to the zoologist Thomas Huxley, and during the later 1860s their intellectual friendship was exercised chiefly through the Ethnological Society of London, which also had interests in archaeology and the care of monuments, and of which Lane Fox was at the time secretary and co-editor. The Ethnological Society united with the Anthropological Society to form the Anthropological Institute in 1871, and it was from there that Lubbock launched his Ancient Monuments Bill, towards which, at the start, the Antiquaries were lukewarm.[11]

Another instance: in the 1930s, two profound developments in reconceptualizing landscape on a regional scale – Major G W G Allen's aerial reconnaissance of the upper Thames, and the ecological approach that emerged from the inter-disciplinary Fenland Research Committee – did not centre on the Society, although in each case Fellows were involved, and the Society helped to disseminate findings. Allen was an individual encouraged by friends; Fenland research grew up through a network based on the University of Cambridge, augmented by a variety of thematic kinships.[12] Other areas of outdoor scholarship – the trail blazed by John Saltmarsh, for instance, H L Gray's examination of field systems, or H E Salter's work on urban topography – seem to have impinged on the Antiquaries only lightly, if at all.[13]

VANISHING ENGLAND

Britain's landscape underwent more violent change between 1800 and 1950 than at any time in the previous 6,000 years. Industrial towns despoiled the countryside, and slaughtered their residents by polluting the air they breathed. Cyclical depression bred contradictions whereby millions of acres went out of production while places such as Whittlesey Mere and Hainault Forest were destroyed 'merely for a few more farms, some of which proved to be temporary'.[14] Crops were left to rot while labourers starved. Stricken by declining incomes and rising taxes after the Great War, some landowners broke up their estates, selling the pieces to farmers who had formerly rented them. However, lack of capital often led to further break-up, followed by piecemeal sell-off and development. To one onlooker in the 1930s, all England had become suburban 'except for the slums at one extreme and the Pennine moors at the other'.[15] Writing in 1937, E M Forster reflected: 'In the last fifteen years we have gashed it to pieces with arterial roads, trimmed the roads with trash, and ruined several selected areas systematically. We laugh at Ruskin, fretting and railing because a little dirt fell from a factory into a stream, but Ruskin knew what was ahead.'[16]

Antiquaries described what was happening to the land and buildings. At the end of the nineteenth century J R Mortimer's observations on the Yorkshire Wolds showed the extent to which intensified ploughing had been eradicating traces of ancient settlement that had survived well until a few decades before.[17] P H Ditchfield's *Vanishing England* (1910) was a threnody to the accelerating loss of meaning in ordinary surroundings. Five years before, in *London: vanished and vanishing*, Philip Norman reflected that down to *c* 1800, 'plain but well-proportioned' timber buildings had survived well. Now, there were virtually none. It was not only big changes that were damaging: much of the harm lay in the cumulative effect of myriad petty vandalisms: the quarrying of commons, dumping of junk, architectural dissonance, destruction of ancient bridges, 'pink asbestos bungalows'.[18] When the Council for the Preservation of Rural England (CPRE) came into being in 1926, its aim was not to halt change but to chase away meanness and restore beauty to everyday surroundings.

Britain and the Beast (1937) was the second of two polemical books engineered by Clough Williams-Ellis. *Beast* contained chapters by twenty-two different authors – among them such very well-known figures as J M Keynes and E M Forster – and a volley of goodwill messages from the likes of J B Priestley, Lloyd George and Lord Baden-Powell, but ne'er an antiquary in sight, save for a chapter on 'Our inheritance from the past' by the popular but academically eccentric Harold Massingham. Massingham's earnest lyricism was not the Antiquaries' style, and while he was an archaeological enthusiast, the Darwinian–Marxist theory of evolutionary progress had elicited from him a quirky counter-theory of regress, from a noble past to a degraded present. In 1926 he had published a book called *Downland Man* which was intuitive, rambling, unscientific to the point of being lunatic fringe, yet intermittently penetrating in ways that outflanked conventional thought:

> Modern archaeology is in bond to the fixed mechanical, evolutionary dogma that progress is an operative force among men by its own volition and that the sapling comes before the tree, the hut before the castle, the lower before the higher development, simply because it does.[19]

Massingham believed that Avebury had been a kind of holy city, 'Neolithic London and Jerusalem in one', the product of a sophisticated civilization that had been born at its high point and then declined. This challenged the notion of prehistoric people as savages. Instead, he argued, 'we are witness of an organised whole of civilised minds with definite aims'. In this idea was an allegory for the line he took in *Britain and the Beast*, wherein he traced England's soul to the village that had flourished down to 1750, and was now dead. Massingham's project was not to preserve – preservation, he said, is 'a losing game' – but rehabilitation.[20] This approach to conservation was not about turning landscape into exhibit, but community renewal.

Massingham was one of a number who worked within the genre of the 'country book' that had its floruit in the earlier twentieth century. Catherine Brace has gone as far as to suggest that certain publishers – notably Batsford through its *Face of Britain* series – were partially responsible for creating and popularizing 'a particular version of England and Englishness' (fig 93).[21] This may oversimplify England after the Great War – unmanned, stunned, remembering.

The ruralism of the 1930s took new turns, forming groups to champion the restoration of the independent, self-sufficient family farm, to be worked in balance with nature in a land of regional differentiation. One such group was 'A Kinship of Husbandry'.[22] Another was the 'Springhead Ring', founded in 1933 by Rolf Gardiner, a forester who aimed to renovate rural life in Wessex and reverse the effects of unimaginative landowners.[23] Organicists stood against automatism, unbridled markets, chemicals, industrialism, and global finance. Especially finance, for it was money power, said Massingham, that drove the cycle of despoliation:

> The moneylender bled the producer; cheap foreign food downed the good English stuff. Big business swallowed little craftsmanship. The town invaded the country, the machine conquered man. Debt declared war on security, economics on life, finance on God.[24]

Fig 94. Clough Williams-Ellis (1883–1978), architect, advocate for rural conservation and amenity planning, and campaigner for the environment: photographed in 1936 by Howard Coster. *Photograph*: The National Portrait Gallery, London.

This is familiar subsoil. Give or take some trace elements, it is also that of National Socialism, which is why, during the war, a number who were seminal to organic farming were detained under Defence Regulation 18b. Among them were Lord Lymington, much involved with the 'English Array', a freemasonry which was part gardening club and part a campaign for English racial purity,[25] and Captain George Henry Pitt-Rivers, the great-grandson of British archaeology's great mentor.

Racism was not, of course, necessary to organicism. For all the proximity of 'A Kinship of Husbandry' to neo-fascism, for instance, its muse, Massingham, flatly rejected the 'obsession with racial problems, culminating in the dangerous fallacies of the Nordic school, with its cant of racial superiority'.[26] Similarly, while Rolf Gardiner has sometimes been depicted as a Nazi sympathizer (locals 'excited themselves with the thought that, had Hitler invaded England, Gardiner would have stepped out of Springhead as the Gauleiter of Wessex'), his loyalties to the best of Germany 'placed him among the enemies of National Socialism'.[27]

For some, the Second World War came almost as a relief, for it brought land back into use and restored the self-esteem of those who farmed it. 'All those who have England on their hearts can be grateful for the new return to the land,' wrote Richard Harman in 1943. 'Fields that had fallen into disuse are again proudly displaying the even furrows of the plough. Farmsteads that were neglected are busy centres of man and beasts. England has become a well-kept land again.'[28]

To sum up so far: conservation originated in part in reaction to the moral and social degradation brought about by industrialization. This is what lay behind the campaigns to save Hainault and Epping Forests, and it is why conservation was historically anti-urban, its ultimate subject being the well-being of people rather than landscape itself. As Williams-Ellis put it in a 'Reconstruction Memorandum' in 1940: 'Agricultural land is *not* "undeveloped" land . . . Nor is "Amenity" land – whether accessible to the public for recreation or seclusion or as scenery to be enjoyed only visually. Planning must take full cognizance of these uses and rid itself of the too narrow purely Urban outlook.'[29]

CONSERVATION

Conservation during the earlier part of our period was driven by a few 'awakened people' who concentrated on specific places or types of land.[30] Thus the 1860s and 1870s saw the formation of societies for the preservation of commons, open spaces, footpaths and ancient buildings. The objective of the National Trust, founded in 1895, was the 'permanent preservation, for the benefit of the Nation, of lands and tenements . . . of beauty or historic interest'. The Ancient Monuments Act of 1882 tried to exempt special sites from everyday pressures. Both through law and voluntary action, then, the idea arose that conservation's task was to separate the special from the merely mundane. This idea was at odds with another, that of evidential significance in the landscape at large. Some saw this at the time. In 1929

O G S Crawford bemoaned the 'absurd spectacle' of two groups in neighbouring counties, 'the one trying unsuccessfully to collect the miserable sum required to excavate a threatened site before it is too late, the other raising a substantial sum to carry out a wholly unnecessary dig on a site of no urgent importance'. Such parochialism was everywhere, and a besetting sin: 'Money and labour are being frittered away on sites that can wait, while other sites are being destroyed a few miles away.'[31] For confirmation, he added, 'it would be enough to glance through the annual catalogue of destruction, most of it deliberate, recorded by the Earthworks Committee and published by the Society of Antiquaries'. Crawford continued:

> Conservation, not excavation, is the need of the day; conservation not only of purely archaeological features, but of the amenities that give them more than half their charm. Who cares for Oldbury and St George's Hill now that they are infested with villas? What is the use of preserving the walls of a village – such as were these earthen ramparts – if the site of the village they protected is to be built over? Combined effort and a little self-denial in the way of excavation, excursions, and even in publication, might have saved these and other sanctuaries for the Nation.[32]

Crawford's solution lay not with more stringent laws, but in the wholesale transfer of archaeologically sensitive land into beneficial management. For while in some cases 'intelligent application of the Town-Planning Act may suffice', in most instances 'nothing short of the purchase of the land is of the slightest use'. He continued:

> The need is really urgent; for with the approaching electrification of Southern England, the coniferous activities of the Woods and Forests Department and of private planters, the demands of the Services for aerodromes and manoeuvres, the spread of bungaloid eruptions, and the threat of arterial roads and ribbon-development – with all these terrors imminent, it is unlikely that any open country or downland will be left in Southern England in a hundred years' time.[33]

Crawford's plan to acquire large areas and keep them for posterity had been indirectly anticipated by Alfred Russel Wallace and the Land Nationalization Society half a century before. Adventurer, surveyor, bio-geographer, co-evolutionist, student of migrating birds, entomologist, social radical and more, Wallace had argued that the state should buy out existing landowners, and then lease land back to citizens on a basis that reflected both its inherent value and the worth that had been added to it. Wallace saw that value could inhere in aspects such as amenity and history as well as economic productivity, and accordingly suggested ways of applying land nationalization to public benefit that included ancient monuments, greenbelts, parks, and public access to open space.[34]

Wallace became a conduit for ideas that were crystallizing in the United States. In the later 1880s Wallace toured North America, where he was introduced to the concept of national parks and met John Muir, who, in 1892, was to found the Sierra Club – the first movement anywhere dedicated to 'preserving' the wild. The idea of 'protecting' nature by leaving it alone was carried to Britain, where it influenced Charles Rothschild's formation of the Society for the Promotion of Nature Reserves in 1912.

This has twofold relevance. Conservationists today often try to hybridize the two theories of conservation – one for people, the other for its own sake – or fail to discriminate between them. In looking back at how conservation took shape, these contrasting positions need to be kept clear. Second, alongside the Ancient Monuments Acts other streams of conservation thought were running through the Linnean and Geological Societies, some of whose Fellows were in turn helping to substantiate the case for nature conservation and national parks. Far from ignoring the past in the landscape, this biological case often embraced it. A case in point has been mentioned already: Sir Arthur Tansley, Sherardian Professor of Botany at Oxford and a Linnean Society gold medalist, whose publications on the vegetation of English chalk were known to O G S Crawford and E Cecil Curwen. Tansley was also known to Sir Cyril Fox, while Tansley's book – *Our Heritage of Wild Nature: a plea for organized nature conservation* – appeared in 1945 at the same time as Fox, the Antiquaries and the new CBA were engaged in making a cognate case for organized archaeology.

In 1864 the US Congress gave the Yosemite Valley to the State of California 'for public use, resort, and recreation'. Eight years later, the Yellowstone country in Montana and Wyoming was similarly set aside for public benefit. By 1930 parks in the United States had a combined area equivalent to nearly 5 per cent of Britain's land surface. One who studied the US example was Charles Bathurst, lawyer, landowner and agriculturalist, Conservative Member of Parliament for South Wiltshire from 1910 and Parliamentary Secretary at the Ministry of Food in 1916–17 (fig 95). In 1918 Bathurst became Lord Bledisloe, and from 1924 to 1928 he held office in the Ministry of Agriculture. In 1925 Bledisloe visited Yellowstone Park, and three years later wrote to Stanley Baldwin, proposing that the Forest of Dean should become Britain's first national park. Bledisloe stressed the area's beauty, its 'historical and archaeological interest, botanical and geological attractiveness and restful quietude'.[35]

Bledisloe's estate was nearby, at Lydney Park. His awareness of the area's archaeological significance was just then being reinforced by the presence of Mortimer and Tessa Wheeler. Bledisloe's great-grandfather had uncovered a Roman temple and other buildings in the deer park. By the 1920s the remains were overgrown, and Bledisloe asked the advice of the Society of Antiquaries on what to do with them. Charles Peers introduced Bledisloe to the Wheelers, and two seasons of re-excavation and fieldwork followed.[36] Bledisloe has been compared to Lubbock – a determined individual who single-mindedly pressed a case. Nothing immediately came of his Forest of Dean initiative, but, after the general election in 1929, the CPRE urged Ramsay MacDonald to revisit the arguments for national parks, and the following September an inquiry was opened through an inter-departmental committee chaired by Christopher Addison.[37] Addison had begun his career as a doctor. Like Octavia Hill (who had worked on social housing) and Lubbock (who had promoted education and public recreation), his interests in public welfare mapped across to conservation – another kind of social improvement.

336

Fig 95. Charles Bathurst, first Viscount Bledisloe (1867–1958), agriculturalist, advocate of national parks and owner of Lydney Park, photographed in 1928. *Photograph*: The National Portrait Gallery, London.

The Addison Committee reported in 1931. Implementation of its proposals was delayed – by monetary crisis, by external pressures and by the government's own decision to give priority to its new Town and Country Planning Bill. Not until the Second World War was there again an opportunity to shape a viable plan for national parks. Thinking, however, continued, and began to address the fundamental paradox that conservation and access may be at odds – a paradox still all too evident at Stonehenge.

Returning to 1928–9, it is interesting to see the extent to which archaeology featured in Bledisloe's proposal, and how certain names recur. Crawford's evidence to the Addison Committee has been noted. In 1929 Bledisloe said of the Forest of Dean that there was nowhere with more varied scenic attractions. 'I might without exaggeration have added that there is none of greater archaeological interest, if the term "archaeology" be given its fullest significance as regards both time and subject matter.'[38] At the same time, the newly formed Council for the Protection of Rural Wales (CPRW) was supporting the CPRE's call to Ramsay MacDonald for an inquiry into the case for national parks. The CPRW's Secretary was Wilfred Hemp, a former Inspector of Ancient Monuments in Wales, now Secretary of the Welsh Royal Commission, who managed to combine this and conservation campaigning without obvious ill effect. Hemp was a friend and holiday companion of Crawford.[39] Another

337

who gave evidence to the Addison Committee was Cyril Fox, who emphasized the importance of studying human settlement in relation to environment. Fox had recently been recruited by Wheeler as his successor at the National Museum of Wales.

Fox, Crawford and Wheeler were friends, and, given Wheeler's concurrent involvement at Lydney Park, it is difficult not to think that national parks were just then in the minds of all three. At any rate, Crawford's crusading editorial about conserving land appeared six months later, while, in 1944, when Fox was elected the first full-term President of the newly formed Council for British Archaeology, the strengthening of links with nature conservation was one of his aims.[40] In 1942, when the Minister of Works and Planning asked for a survey of potential national parks (the Lake District, Peak District, Dartmoor and Snowdonia), it was to Fox that the NRIC (the Nature Reserves Investigation Committee: see below) turned to arrange the necessary survey.

'Proponents of the establishment of a system of English and Welsh National Parks did not base their arguments on a theory of nature's rights. Rather, they argued from human needs': so argued Jonathan Bate, and he went on:

> The very word 'landscape' makes the point. A land-scape means land as shaped, as arranged by a viewer. The point of view is that of the human observer, not the land itself . . . Landscape was originally a technical term in painting; it denoted an artistic genre, not something in nature. Hence the term 'picturesque': a stretch of land that resembles a painting.[41]

While, for the reasons given, from the 1880s some Fellows of courtyard societies probably *were* thinking in terms of nature's rights, the wish to conserve landscape and ancient monuments remained anthropocentric, and, to a large extent, has remained so down to the present. What was venerable was believed to be instructive and antiquity was believed to induce a special mood of receptivity.

Alongside this dialogue can be traced another, caught in wartime memoranda. Observers from the Ministry of Town and Country Planning had attended a CBA conference, and were impressed by the potential of archaeological air photography as a tool for their own Land Utilization Surveys and other planning needs. One of them asked: 'Do you think Mr Dower would be interested? Of course, he is principally concerned with the question of Amenities, whereas we are interested in the scientific technique developed by the archaeologist, and its possible application to our specific problems.'[42] The perception of archaeology as academic and technical rather than as an extension of amenity – public interest – worked against the efforts of the Antiquaries and the CBA to push it higher up the agendas of government departments. 'Amenity' in the mind of John Dower had to do with recreation, seclusion, exercise, beauties for the eye or joy for the soul. Among key opinion-formers inside the new Ministry of Town and Country Planning, none of these sensations sprang to mind in relation to archaeology in 1944.

CONCEPTUALIZING LANDSCAPE

The Society's publishing during the period shows no sustained concern either for rural conservation or the conceptualization of landscape. Indeed, as far as one can tell, neither the Antiquaries nor any other pre-war archaeological grouping seems to have evolved a vocabulary with which to differentiate the historical dimension of landscape or to emphasize its extensive nature. One group that might have done so – the inter-disciplinary Fenland Research Committee – seems to have felt no need for new vocabulary at the time.

It may, of course, be objected that since landscape archaeology did not come of age until the 1970s, it is unnecessary to explain the failure of earlier strategic thinking to take account of it. But while there is truth in this, it oversimplifies. Three vivid books brought history and landscape together in the 1950s: O G S Crawford's *Archaeology in the Field* (1953) (fig 96), Maurice Beresford's *The Lost Villages of England* (1954) and W G Hoskins's *The Making of the English Landscape* (1955). While all three authors are remembered as pioneers, their influential books did not come out of a clear sky. If we look across antiquarian and archaeological literature, work on a landscape scale had been carried on at least since the later nineteenth century. J R Mortimer had approached East Yorkshire on such terms, and had noted the phenomenon of cropmarks.[43] E Cecil Curwen had published works on air photography and economic history. H J Randall declared that history was written not just in text, but 'in letters of earth and stone, of bank and ditch, of foliage and crop'.[44] Such scholars as Holleyman and the Orwins studied systems of fields across many miles.[45] In 1930, Wheeler reflected that the 'gravel banks of our English rivers teem with vestiges of prehistoric habitation',[46] while in 1940 E T Leeds noted in his obituary of Major G W G Allen that the late major had been finding archaeological *complexes* in the upper

Fig 96. O G S Crawford returning from a Mediterranean holiday, probably 1937. The aircraft, a de Havilland Puss Moth, belonged to a friend, Geoffrey Alington; the previous owner was Amy Johnson, who flew it across Siberia to Tokyo in 1931. *Photograph:* reproduced by permission of English Heritage, Crawford Collection, NMR.

Fig 97. Major G W G Allen (1891–1940) and his aircraft. Whereas most of the photographs for *Wessex from the Air* were taken in a few weeks on what Keiller described as an 'expedition', Allen pioneered recurrent reconnaissance. *Photograph*: reproduced by permission of the Ashmolean Museum, Oxford.

Thames valley.[47] 'Complex' is telling: by 1940 'site' no longer seemed adequate to describe what the film in Allen's camera had been registering.

Allen was an agricultural engineer with his own light aircraft, which, from 1931 to 1939, he used for archaeological reconnaissance (fig 97). Keiller had described his and Crawford's work in *Wessex from the Air* as an 'expedition'[48] – a word borrowed from the nineteenth century, implying a journey of fixed length into a new realm. Allen, by contrast, saw aerial archaeology as a process. Realizing that the things seen from above are co-varying and often fugitive, he understood that the timing of reconnaissance was critical. Beyond that, the presence and strength of marks in crops depended not only on weather or types of plant, but also upon climatic and agricultural influences in the past. Calculating that different things are visible at different times, Allen pioneered the idea of systematic reconnaissance, repeated from year to year, to enable the development of a composite picture, which he transcribed on to maps and published.[49]

The significance of this work lay not simply in the discovery of new kinds of monument or past settlement in unexpected places. Rather, the density and extensiveness of Allen's findings changed the very basis upon which prehistory had to be entertained, and with which conservation would sooner or later have to come to terms. Since Allen had shown that the landscape *at large* had historical meaning, it followed that selective preservation was inadequate. It also followed that future conservation would have to rely on planning – that is, the making of socially balanced choices about the use of land – rather than selective exemption. While over sixty years would pass before the implications of this entered general understanding, the revolutionary nature of Allen's work was recognized at the time. The Blue Paper that was put into circulation for him by Miss M V Taylor in late 1935 was signed by E T Leeds,

340

R G Collingwood, Crawford, Wheeler, Radford and St George Gray. Allen was duly elected a Fellow on 2 March 1936. Few Fellows had such support.

PLANNING FOR PEACE

Shortly after the bombing of Coventry in November 1940, Clough Williams-Ellis wrote to Sir John Reith pointing out that aerial bombardment might be a blessing in disguise: bombing cleared the way for urban renewal. Reith replied swiftly, saying how pleased he was to make Williams-Ellis's acquaintance and looking forward to an opportunity when he could come to stay. 'Meantime, I am enclosing a first draft of the document (or something like it) which I shall be putting up to Cabinet . . . I should like your views on it. Of course you will regard the matter as entirely private.'[50]

The spontaneity and rapport of this exchange stand out for several reasons. Foremost is the sense of exhilaration – despite the fact that the war was going badly, it was going to lead to a better world. Architects circulated proposals for new towns that would rise in place of shabby, grimy slums. Enlightened planning would bring about a fairer balance between different kinds of land use. The attainment of progressive policies that previously had only been struggled for now seemed assured. Behind all there lay a kind of subdued excitement, diagnosed by Dr F J E Raby in the Ministry of Works and Planning as 'a great ferment in the world of archaeology and architecture' over 'what is vaguely and conveniently called "Reconstruction".'[51] Reconstruction was a kind of atmosphere, and breathing it was like breathing anew. Williams-Ellis wrote an essay entitled 'New Towns for Old'. It began: 'The destruction caused by enemy bombs in Britain has not been wholly disastrous. The buildings most easily destroyed were the buildings that were most shoddily built. In many places the areas hardest hit have been precisely those which should have been cleared away many years ago.' It ended with calls for a great revival, a 'new renaissance'.[52]

One reason for this heady optimism was Churchill's decision in October 1940 to establish a new Ministry of Works and Buildings. Although this was primarily to co-ordinate different wartime building programmes, the appointment of Reith as Minister soon led to a review of land-use planning and management of the physical environment generally.[53] Reith's proposals were radical and controversial. To allay misgivings and promote inter-departmental liaison, Churchill put Arthur Greenwood, Minister without Portfolio, in overall charge of post-war reconstruction. Greenwood told the House of Commons that one of the aims of planning must be to preserve 'those beauties which, once gone, could never be restored'.[54] In July 1942, the statutory planning powers of the Ministry of Health were transferred to the Ministry of Works and Planning. Soon afterwards, however, in February 1943, the planning functions were abstracted to form an entirely new Ministry of Town and Country Planning.

This rapidly changing scene had consequences for voluntary bodies in general, and archaeology in particular. Reith's ministry contained a high-powered research group that included John Dower, W G Holford (Professor of Town Planning at the University of Liverpool) and, from 1942, George Pepler. Dower had been and remained at the heart of discussions about national parks, nature reserves and amenity. George Pepler was formerly Chief Town Planning Inspector in the Ministry of Health, and an ally of the CPRE. With others (there was also a consultative panel that included such figures as L P Abercrombie), they made a formidable team, and when it was transferred into the Ministry of Town and Country Planning in 1943 influence over future strategy moved with it. Voluntary bodies such as the Royal Society for the Protection of Birds and the Commons, Open Spaces and Footpaths Preservation Societies refocused their lobbying accordingly. For archaeology, however, the change caused a problem. While strategic thinking and influence had shifted to Town and Country Planning, archaeology and the Ancient Monuments Inspectorate remained in the Ministry of Works.

The split had further consequences. One was to divide the limited resources of the newly formed CBA, and so lessen the effect of its arguments. Another was to sharpen the contrast between the scope of inherited ancient monuments legislation and conservation possibilities inherent in the emerging Town and Country Planning Bill. A third was to provide officials in different ministries with limitless opportunity for buck-passing.

FOUNDING THE COUNCIL FOR BRITISH ARCHAEOLOGY

In the Society's own memory the CBA's beginning was in 1942, when members of the Hellenic and Roman Societies meeting in Oxford called upon the Society of Antiquaries to 'organize a representative body that should speak for archaeology to Government'. Significantly, nearly all the country's specialists on Romano-British archaeology were present.[55] A special meeting of societies was held in 1943, and out of it came agreement to form a 'Council for British Archaeology' that would promote British archaeology in all its aspects.

The new Council met in March 1944 under Alfred Clapham's presidency, and announced its formation to the public in a letter to *The Times* on 11 April. The Council defined its objectives as the 'safeguarding of all kinds of archaeological material and the strengthening of existing measures for the care of ancient and historic buildings, monuments, and antiquities'. Later that year Sir Cyril Fox took over as the CBA's President, an office he held in tandem with that of the Society's presidency. The Council set up excavation committees in a number of bombed towns, asked Government for information about reconstruction projects and encouraged its Regional Groups (so-called because they consisted of groups of county societies) to provide information about known sites. Education was a priority. While not explicitly concerned with 'landscape' as distinct from 'sites', the CBA did define archaeology in more extensive terms than some members of the Inspectorate and Antiquaries were accustomed to think. It also placed stress on the importance of aerial reconnaissance.

Before probing below the surface of these events, it is useful to ask what exemplars, if any, the CBA's founders might have had in mind. Most obvious was the CPRE itself, founded eighteen years before around a nucleus of existing bodies that included the Ancient Monuments Society and the Society for the Protection of Ancient Buildings as well as the Royal Institute of British Architects (RIBA), but not – apparently – the Antiquaries. While the CPRE's pre-war achievements had been limited, its effect on public opinion had been large, and the idea of a comprehensive planning system now seemed close to fulfilment. CPRE leaders enjoyed enviable access to ministers. Dower and Pepler were allies. Williams-Ellis was *persona gratissima* with almost anyone. When O G S Crawford was put forward as a Royal Commissioner in 1938, an official had to explain to Neville Chamberlain who he was,[56] but Williams-Ellis could write to a minister he had never met, and receive a draft Cabinet paper for comment by return.

Among the Antiquaries, one of the few who had this kind of easy rapport was Jacquetta Hawkes, who, by 1941, was working in the offices of the War Cabinet. Raby explained Clapham's entrée to the Reconstruction Secretariat 'because the way was made easy by Jacquetta Hawkes', adding 'whose husband C F C Hawkes, of the BM, has been actively behind the whole business, and is an ambitious young man'.[57] On another occasion, in 1941, we glimpse Hawkes escorting Reith to Impington Village College in Cambridgeshire. Impington was described by Williams-Ellis as the 'ideal type of organization for checking the disintegration of rural life that has been such an unfortunate tendency of the past century'. The idea of the village college was to provide facilities for adult education in a hub village that was accessible to villagers from other places round about. The scheme was being piloted in Cambridgeshire, where Impington's 'intense life' on the day of Hawkes's visit included dressmaking, air raid precautions, German language and Beethoven's 'Eroica' Symphony: the 'perfect instrument', enthused Williams-Ellis, 'for training the citizens of a free democracy'.[58]

There were other, more recent, prototypes. One was the Conference on Nature Preservation in Post-War Reconstruction, which met for the first time in June 1941 and had drafted a memorandum to Government on national parks, nature reserves and habitat. Given the CBA's initial make-up of county and local societies and museums, and its call to Government for a unified structure to oversee archaeology, it is interesting to see a leader in *The Times* describing 'how the various natural history societies and associations of local authorities had co-operated' to produce the memorandum 'which set out their collective views on nature preservation after the war'.[59]

In 1942 the Conference had formed the Nature Reserves Investigation Committee (NRIC), to identify endangered biota and to advise on the choice of nature reserves. To all intents and purposes the NRIC had taken over from the Conference. This, too, may have been a precedent. In 1945 the CBA's own records indicate no certainty that the Council would be needed permanently – it might be just one stage on the journey to something else. The Secretary of NRIC was Kenneth Oakley, who was elected to the CBA's Executive at the Council's first meeting, on 8 March 1944. Oakley had worked with Wheeler at Lydney, and combined geology (he worked at the British Museum (Natural History)) with the study of lithics. As we shall see, there were constructive discussions between the CBA and NRIC in 1944.[60]

A third model was the Council for the Promotion of Field Studies. Formed in 1943, and soon known as the Field Studies Council, its aim was to see the creation of a number of field centres after the war, each in an area outstanding 'for the richness and variety of its ecological features, geological and geographical interest, and archaeological and historical importance'.[61] From 1942 the Ministry of Education was considering suggestions for the post-war use of Ministry of Supply hostels and hutting on redundant aerodromes for educational purposes that involved fitness and outdoor activity, including archaeology[62] – a scheme with resemblances to the village colleges described above.

Records of the Ministry of Works, the Ministry of Town and Country Planning and of the Treasury illuminate the CBA's beginnings in ways that modify the received story. At the risk of substituting one over-simplification for another, the CBA's genesis lay less in the desire for a representative body for British archaeology than in a covert campaign mounted from within the Ministry of Works to ensure the post-war excavation of Roman and medieval London, followed by disillusionment when the CBA showed that it had a mind of its own. Such is the interest of the sources that only a précis can be given here, itself confined to just two aspects: influences upon the Council's creation, and the CBA's lack of political effect in 1945–8.

From the end of the London Blitz in May 1941, Raby and Brian O'Neil, Chief Inspector of Ancient Monuments in England, were contemplating an unprecedented archaeological opportunity. After a winter of bombing, an area roughly equal to that of Roman Silchester lay open west of the Walbrook. O'Neil reasoned that, since many of the lost buildings had been built without basements or deep foundations, the strata of Roman and medieval London would survive. The chance to study them on such a scale would never come again. The question was how to bring this about. Civil Service rules of discipline and hierarchy prevented O'Neil from campaigning publicly. Reasoning that if 'propaganda in various quarters' produced a climate of opinion in favour of excavation, official policy would be 'likely to tread the same path', he set about prompting others to bring such influence to bear.[63]

O'Neil worked discreetly on several fronts. From the autumn of 1941, he was in direct contact with F J Forty, City Engineer, to gather information on the practicalities of excavation.[64] He considered the whereabouts of small trial excavations, to be made before the war's end, to ascertain the depth and character of deposits, and did his best to ensure that W F Grimes should undertake them. He helped to arrange meetings with the Lord Mayor, partly to float the idea but also to take soundings on whether the Corporation of London might shoulder some of the cost. This was important – O'Neil knew there was little or no chance of ministry funds being committed to such a project, and without money nothing would happen. After the Baedeker raids he agreed that similar plans should be laid for other historic cities that had been visited by the Luftwaffe – notably Exeter and Canterbury – as well as others that had suffered in the Blitz of 1940–1. But his main objective was London. All the signs are that it was O'Neil who prompted some of those attending the Oxford conference in 1942 to encourage the Society to form a body that would have the independence and authority to call for such an excavation after the war's end.

The Antiquaries provided both a medium and an instrument for O'Neil's lobbying. In March 1943 Philip Corder, the Society's Acting Assistant Secretary, gave a BBC radio talk entitled 'Bombs and archaeology' in which he explained how 120 acres of Roman London awaited archaeological study. Interestingly, Corder also talked about 'invisible ancient monuments' in the countryside, obscured by agriculture, hidden under the plough or grass, but evidentially just as much a record of human past as structures or earthworks.[65]

Correspondence shows the extent to which O'Neil influenced this talk, and the constraints under which he worked. Early in March Corder had written to him, at his home address. 'I am very sorry that Civil Service etiquette has cut you off from a job for which you alone seem to me to be qualified.' In a PS: 'Can't you disguise yourself as me and do the job? I wish you could.'[66] After the broadcast, O'Neil was cock-a-hoop, telling Raby that the script was 'excellent' and that it said 'all on the topic we could desire'. Significantly, he put Corder's private letter into the Ministry file, with a note to say that he had not replied to it, because he 'was travelling and gathering strength to write what was required'.[67] Did O'Neil have a hand in Corder's script?

Just as the Conference on Nature Preservation in Post-War Reconstruction had kindled interest in the press, so newspapers began to carry stories and editorials about archaeology. In the summer of 1944 there were articles in the *Yorkshire Post* and *The Times*. A *Times* leader elicited supportive letters. Constructive Parliamentary Questions were asked in July, and in September the sense of gathering momentum was again documented in *The Times*.

The CBA saw its role as extending beyond arranging the excavation of smitten cities. While the Society's printed invitation to the establishing conference in May 1943 had acknowledged the 'immediate problem' of organizing archaeological work in historic towns, it continued: 'there is the far wider problem, concerning the future direction and supervision of ancient monuments in general, and of primary archaeological research in particular'.[68] The conference concluded that progress would require a new government department – something like a Department of National Antiquities – to incorporate all existing inspectorates and Royal Commissions. Other aims included better legislation, a co-ordinating body for museums, promotion of study of the past through schools and 'the encouragement of better use of leisure by the community, side by side with the study of nature and the appreciation and practice of the arts'.[69] With the transfer of planning responsibilities from the Ministry of Works to the new Ministry of Town and Country Planning, there were now two government departments for the CBA to talk to.

'This is a bit complicated', wrote George Pepler to Sir Stephen Tallents, public relations officer to the Ministry of Town and Country Planning, in April 1944. Clapham had recently met Tallents, who had correctly formed the impression that post-war archaeology would impinge inter-departmentally – on Health and Transport, as well as Planning. Pepler reminded Tallents of the role of the Ministry of Works, and suggested that they should refer the matter back to them.[70]

'Is it not curious that Clapham should not go to the Ministry of Works but to the Reconstruction Secretariat?', asked E de Norman of the Ministry of Works when news of the CBA's formation reached him. 'Have we ever been consulted about the set up of this Council and have we any representation on it?' Raby replied from Rhyl – the ministry was decentralized – pointing out that a preliminary memorandum on Post-war Administration of Ancient Monuments had been copied to him the previous February. O'Neil and Chettle had attended as observers, 'without committing ourselves on policy'. It was all part of the 'post-war planning ferment'.

Grumpiness soon broke surface. An official of the Ministry of Works repudiated Clapham's criticisms of the Ancient Monuments Acts on the unlikely ground that 'he has not thoroughly understood them'. O'Neil and his colleagues felt that they were being unjustly criticized, and that their 'unostentatious' work was being mistaken for inactivity. O'Neil noted in October 1944: 'There is a tendency in certain circles, chiefly female, to assume, because we do not blow our own trumpet, that we are inactive.'[71] 'Chiefly female' referred to Kathleen Kenyon (fig 98), the CBA's Secretary, whose directness of manner did not always win friends, and to Margot Eates. In May 1944 O'Neil reported that a meeting with George Hicks, MP, the Parliamentary Secretary, on guidance to local authorities had been made difficult because Kenyon was 'tactless' and attributed things to others that they had not actually said.[72] Kenyon's alleged tendency to misrepresent the CBA's real wishes was a recurrent problem. Recollecting the same meeting on the eve of D-Day, O'Neil said:

> It was unfortunate that Sir Cyril Fox, Chairman [*sic*] of the CBA, could not himself see the Secretary on the topic of Roman London, because Miss Kenyon, lacking experience as well as tact, may well have given, as well as she certainly received, a wrong impression at the meeting on April 27 . . . She then indulged in some very unwise, or at least very careless, publicity, for which she has been reprimanded.[73]

Kenyon saw that post-war urban excavation would require state funding, and often said so, without realizing the electrifying sensitivity of this subject inside Government. In meetings with officials of the Ministries of Works and of Town and Country Planning she repeatedly gave the impression not only that O'Neil concurred with her view but also that he had as good as promised that state funding would be forthcoming after the war. This put O'Neil in a difficult position. Such an undertaking would have been highly irregular – civil servants were not supposed to express personal views, let alone commit funds. 'I should like to be permitted to put it on record', he wrote, 'that I have never in any statement or writing, public or private, committed the Ministry to undertaking this task.'[74] Aside from his embarrassment and the risk of disciplinary action, O'Neil became frustrated by the fact that the CBA was seeming to undermine the very project for which he had helped to bring it into being. On another occasion he described a statement by Kenyon as 'at best tactless, at worst grossly insulting to all of us'.

The Ministry of Works was neurotic about funding. The year before, Sir Percival

Fig 98. Kathleen Kenyon (1906–78), who as the CBA's first Secretary became a source of upset in the Ministry of Works, is pictured in 1936 at work on the Jewry Wall excavations, Leicester, which she directed. *Photograph*: courtesy of City Museum Service, Leicester.

Robinson, the departmental secretary, had written tartly to Raby about proposed schemes of excavation in bombed towns like Exeter, Canterbury and London. 'I am afraid this is not quite what I wanted. Speaking frankly, I am very apprehensive lest you and your Inspectorate may, in their contacts with the Society of Antiquaries, local Archaeological Societies and Local Authorities, virtually commit the Ministry and Treasury to inevitable expense in these surveys before the question of principle has been considered by the Minister and the Treasury.'[75]

In September 1944 relations between the CBA and the Ministry of Works cooled further when Kenyon wrote to O'Neil about the discussions taking place with the NRIC on the conservation of large areas of landscape.[76] Potentially this was a large step, and Kenyon hoped that O'Neil would join the new Nature Reserves sub-committee that the CBA was setting up to see how it might be taken. An obvious question was how such large areas might relate to scheduling – and since the NRIC came under another ministry, how the Ancient Monuments Inspectorate would relate to it. The Ministry of Works dealt with the idea by declining to relate to it at all. O'Neil's participation was vetoed, and since the idea was 'probably controversial', Raby thought it best for the sub-committee to make up its own mind 'without being influenced by our advice'.[77]

Another progressive initiative was stifled a few weeks later. Earlier in the year, Kathleen Kenyon had met George Pepler, who, as we have seen, was a member of the research team in the Ministry of Town and Country Planning and a key figure in John Dower's circle, to gather information about the new Town and Country Planning Act. Their discussion had considered how a strengthened Act might help to regulate the management of land or remains that were not statutorily protected but might nonetheless have historic interest or evidential value. This was progressive talk, and Dower took soundings about it. In July 1944 he wrote a note to Holford:

> To cover us with the AM Section of the Ministry of Works I rang O'Neil and
> got a very firm reaction that he would wish us to keep clear of Miss Eates and

the other ladies (Miss Kenyon etc) who are nosing about ostensibly on behalf of the Council for British Archaeology but without that body's authority.[78]

However, while he thought that they had 'better hold off', Dower saw that the CBA had a point: 'It shouldn't be entirely neglected.' In November Dower met O'Neil and Raby to consider further, and two days before Christmas, at home in Kirkby Malham, Dower wrote a note on 'Sites and remains of archaeological interest: under the new Act and generally'. For the time being he recommended a gentle brush-off: the Ministry of Town and Country Planning should refer the CBA back to the Ministry of Works, 'while, of course, listening politely to their views and accepting gratefully any information they provide'. A fortnight later, Dower looked at the file again. 'I don't think any action is called for at the present: it seems best, and in view of their tendency to go off the rails, more comfortable – to leave it to them to reopen with us if and when they wish.' He told Raby: 'I am inclined to think that the Council will not bother you again.'[79]

The CBA did succeed in one respect: in 1946–8 there was a full-scale review of government responsibilities for archaeology. This was undertaken by the Treasury, which grasped the CBA's case for a unified approach to conservation almost better than the CBA had managed to put it itself – but then gently laid it to rest on the grounds that the government's hands were full, and that the public did not demand it. Whereas the case for national parks, amenity, access to land and nature conservation had been built up over many years, no comparable public consensus had been formed for archaeology. The Treasury entertained the idea of a Central Council for Archaeology (parallel to the Arts Council?), only to discard it on the now-familiar ground that it was not of sufficient priority. Intellectually, the Antiquaries and the CBA may have won their case; politically, they lost it.[80]

CONCLUSION

While the Society cared for buildings and excavation, its meetings and research show less feeling for landscape. However, at least from *c* 1900, some individual Fellows and groups of Fellows were keenly aware of the extensiveness of the past in everyday surroundings, and a few, such as Crawford, located themselves in relation to conservation's evolving theoretical framework. Kenyon and Fox saw the artificiality of trying to distinguish between areas of 'natural', 'geological' or 'archaeological' significance. Allen and the Fenland Research Committee showed the redundancy of the 'site'.

The legacy is something of a muddle. Whereas the idea of conserving historic landscapes comes from and belongs in an intellectual tradition concerned with public well-being, recent years have seen clumsy efforts to relate it to values associated with wilderness, 'leaving nature alone', and dark green ecology. This, along with the sometime need to choose, rather than compromise, between access and safeguarding, remains to be worked out.

NOTES

1. Williams-Ellis 1928, 131.
2. Ibid, 13.
3. Sweet 2001, 182.
4. Abercrombie 1926, 6.
5. Sheail 1976, 120.
6. Ibid, 119.
7. The National Archives (hereafter TNA), HLG 93/23.
8. Sheail 1976, 119; Godwin 1958.
9. HMSO 1921, 3.
10. Sheail 1981, 30–57; Evans 1956, 398.
11. Evans 1956, 300–1; Thompson 1977, 32–3. The Anthropological Society of London was formed in 1863 for 'Study of the human race in all its varieties, and in all the phases of its history and progress'. In 1871 the Society agreed to re-unite with the Ethnological Society. The Ethnological Society had rooms in St Martin's Place and rules modelled partly on those of the Society of Antiquaries. In 1870–1, Huxley, Lubbock and Lane Fox were editors of its journal. There was some cross-membership with the Antiquaries, including Canon Greenwell, Thomas Wright and T McK Hughes. See also Saunders 1983.
12. Smith 1997 and 2004; Phillips 1951.
13. For the historiography, see Roberts and Wrathmell 2000; also Roberts and Wrathmell 2002, 1–3; Gray 1915.
14. Rackham 1986, 26; Wallace 1878.
15. Taylor 1965, 167–8.
16. Forster 1937, 44–5.
17. Mortimer 1905.
18. Williams-Ellis 1928, 20.
19. Massingham 1926, 41.
20. Massingham 1937, 8–10.
21. Brace 1999 and 2001.
22. Moore-Colyer 2001a.
23. Wright 2001, 180–93; Moore-Colyer 2001b.
24. Massingham 1942, 40; cf Massingham 1945.
25. Wright 2001, 204–10; cf Griffiths 1980.
26. Massingham 1926, 313.
27. Wright 2001.
28. Harman 1943, 6.
29. TNA, HLG 86/13.
30. Sheail 1981, 18.
31. Crawford 1929, 2.
32. Ibid, 3.
33. Ibid, 4.
34. Wallace 1882, 129–30; cf Williams-Ellis, 'National Parks: arguments in favour of outright purchase of land as against control only, failing or pending Land Nationalization', Sept 1945: TNA, HLG 71/862. See also Hyder 1913; Wallace 1897.
35. Mair and Delafons 2001, 294.
36. Hawkes 1982, 145–7; Wheeler 1932.
37. One of the eight members of the Addison Committee was a Fellow: Dr Frederick J E Raby, Assistant Secretary in the Office of Works. Raby was best known for his work on secular and Christian Latin poetry. As we shall see, he played a part in shaping conservation developments in the 1940s.
38. Bledisloe 1929, 55.
39. Hemp (1882–1962) was one of Crawford's proposers for Fellowship in 1921.
40. CBA contact with Dr Herbert Smith, Nature Reserves Investigation Committee, 20 Sept 1944: TNA, WORK 14/2343. For Fox's life and career, see Scott-Fox 2002.
41. Bate 2000, 132; cf George Perkins Marsh, *Man and Nature* (1847).
42. Memoranda by R E M McCaughan, 2 Dec 1943, 18 Feb 1944: TNA, HLG 103/2.
43. Mortimer 1905, 369. For more of Crawford's context see Bowden 2001; more generally, Chandler 2000.
44. Randall 1934.
45. Holleyman 1935; Orwin and Orwin 1938.
46. Wheeler 1930.
47. Leeds 1940.
48. Crawford and Keiller 1928, vi.
49. Allen 1984.
50. Reith to Williams-Ellis, 23 Nov 1940: TNA, HLG 86/13.
51. Memorandum, 12 Dec 1942: TNA, WORK 14/2343. For Raby, see note 37.
52. TNA, HLG 71/862.
53. Sheail 1976, 90; Larkham 2003.
54. Sheail 1976, 93.
55. Evans 1956, 427.
56. TNA, PREM 5/163.
57. TNA, WORK 14/2343.
58. Williams-Ellis to Reith, 19 Feb 1941; Henry Morris to Williams-Ellis, 15 Feb 1941; Jacquetta Hawkes to Mr Root, 12 Mar 1941: TNA, HLG 51/869.
59. Sheail 1976, 96.
60. CBA archive, Council Minutes, 3 Oct 1944, 37 (iv).
61. Sheail 1976, 120–1.
62. TNA, ED 10/274.
63. Memorandum, 9 Sept 1941: TNA, WORK 14/2343. John Shepherd's account of the genesis of the post-war excavations and the Roman and Medieval London Excavation Council picks up the story from 1944: Shepherd 1998, xii, 2–5.
64. 16 Oct 1941: TNA, WORK 14/2343.
65. Manuscript, 'Bombs and archaeology', 24 July 1943: TNA, WORK 14/2343.
66. 5 Mar 1943: TNA, WORK 14/2343.
67. 17 Mar 1943: TNA, WORK 14/2343.

68. CBA archive, letter from Society of Antiquaries to archaeological societies, March 1943.
69. CBA archive, Minute, 4 May 1943.
70. 13 Apr 1944: TNA, HLG 103/2.
71. O'Neil to Raby, 7 Oct 1944: TNA, WORK 14/2343.
72. 26 May 1944: TNA, WORK 14/2343.
73. 5 June 1944: TNA, WORK 14/2343.
74. 24 May 1944: TNA, WORK 14/2343.
75. 26 July 1943: TNA, WORK 14/2343.
76. 20 Sept 1944: TNA, WORK 14/2343.
77. 10 Oct 1944: TNA, WORK 14/2343.
78. 10 July 1944: TNA, HLG 103/2.
79. 23 Dec 1944; 5 Jan 1945: TNA, HLG 103/2.
80. TNA, T 222/151. Over the same period, the Society of Antiquaries and the CBA demanded a voice in the stewardship of the large areas that were assigned to military training. In 1947, Fox wrote to Attlee about this. The reply, of 19 June 1947, skilfully referred the matter back to individual ministries.

BIBLIOGRAPHY

Abercrombie, P 1926. 'The preservation of rural England', *Town Plann Rev*, **12**, 5–56

Allen, G W G 1984. 'Discovery from the air', *Aerial Archaeol*, **10**, 37–90

Bate, J 2000. *The Song of the Earth*, London

Beresford, M W 1954. *The Lost Villages of England*, London

Bledisloe, C B 1929. 'Lydney, Gloucestershire. Presidential Address', *Trans Bristol Gloucestershire Archaeol Soc*, **51**, 55–78

Bowden, M 2001. 'Mapping the past: O G S Crawford and the development of landscape studies', *Landscapes*, **2/2**, 29–45

Brace, C 1999. 'Finding England everywhere: regional identity and the construction of national identity, 1890–1940', *Ecumene*, **6**, 90–109

Brace, C 2001. 'Publishing and publishers: towards an historical geography of countryside writing, *c* 1930–1950', *Area*, **33**, 287–96

Carpenter, E (ed) 1897. *Forecasts of the Coming Century. By a Decade of Writers*, London and Manchester

Chandler, J 2000. 'The discovery of landscape', in Hooke (ed) 2000, 133–41

Crawford, O G S 1929. 'Editorial notes', *Antiquity*, **3/9**, 1–4

Crawford, O G S and Keiller, A 1928. *Wessex from the Air*, Oxford

Crawford, O G S 1953. *Archaeology in the Field*, London

Evans, J 1956. *A History of the Society of Antiquaries*, London

Forster, E M 1937. 'Havoc', in Williams-Ellis (ed) 1937, 44–7

Godwin, H 1958. 'Sir Arthur George Tansley, FRS, 1871–1955', *J Hist Ecology*, **46**, 1–8

Gray, H L 1915. *English Field Systems*, Cambridge, Mass

Griffiths, R 1980. *Fellow Travellers of the Right: British enthusiasts for Nazi Germany: 1933–1939*, London

Grimes, W F (ed) 1951. *Aspects of Archaeology in Britain and Beyond. Essays presented to O G S Crawford*, London

Harman, R (ed) 1943. *Countryside Mood*, Blandford

Hawkes, J 1982. *Mortimer Wheeler*, London

HMSO 1921. *Report of the Ancient Monuments Advisory Committee*, Part 1

Holleyman, G A 1935. 'The Celtic field-system in south Britain: a survey of the Brighton district', *Antiquity*, **9/33**, 443–54

Hooke, D (ed) 2000. *Landscape: the richest historical record*, Soc Landscape Stud suppl ser 1, Amesbury

Hoskins, W G 1955. *The Making of the English Landscape*, London

Hyder, J 1913. *The Case for Land Nationalization* (with an introduction by A R Wallace), London

Larkham, P J 2003. 'The place of urban conservation in the UK reconstruction plans of 1942–1952', *Planning Perspectives*, **18/3**, 295–324

Leeds, E T 1940. 'The late Major G W G Allen, MC, FSA', *Oxoniensia*, **5**, 172–3

Mair, J and Delafons, J 2001. 'The policy origins of Britain's National Parks: the Addison Committee 1929–1931', *Planning Perspectives*, **16**, 293–309

Massingham, H J 1926. *Downland Man*, London

Massingham, H J 1937. 'Our inheritance from the past', in Williams-Ellis (ed) 1937, 8–31

Massingham, H J 1942. *Remembrance: an autobiography*, London

Massingham, H J 1945. *The Wisdom of the Fields*, London

Moore-Colyer, R J 2001a. 'Back to basics: Rolf Gardiner, H J Massingham, and "A Kinship of Husbandry"', *Rural Hist*, **12**, 85–108

Moore-Colyer, R J 2001b. 'Rolf Gardiner: English patriot and the Council for the Church and Countryside', *Agri Hist Rev*, **49**, 187–209

Mortimer, J R 1905. *Forty Years' Researches in British and Saxon Burial Mounds of East Yorkshire*, London

Orwin, C S and Orwin, C S 1938. *The Open Fields*, Oxford

Phillips, C W 1951. 'The Fenland Research Committee, its past achievements and future prospects', in Grimes (ed) 1951, 258–73

Rackham, O 1986. *The History of the Countryside*, London

Randall, H J 1934. 'History in the open air', *Antiquity*, 8/29, 5–23

Roberts, B K and Wrathmell, S 2000. *An Atlas of Rural Settlement in England*, London

Roberts, B K and Wrathmell, S 2002. *Region and Place*, London

Saunders, A D 1983. 'A century of ancient monuments legislation', *Antiq J*, **63**, 11–33

Scott-Fox, C 2002. *Cyril Fox: archaeologist extraordinary*, Oxford

Sheail, J 1976. *Nature in Trust: the history of nature conservation in Britain*, Glasgow

Sheail, J 1981. *Rural Conservation in Inter-War Britain*, Oxford

Shepherd, J D 1998. *The Temple of Mithras, London. Excavations by W F Grimes and A Williams at the Walbrook*, Engl Heritage Archaeol Rep 12, London

Smith, P J 1997. 'Grahame Clark's new archaeology: the Fenland Research Committee and Cambridge prehistory in the 1930s', *Antiquity*, **71**/271, 11–30

Smith, P J 2004. 'A splendid idiosyncrasy: prehistory at Cambridge, 1915–50', unpublished PhD thesis, University of Cambridge

Sweet, R 2001. 'Antiquaries and antiquities in eighteenth-century England', *Eighteenth-century Stud*, **34**/2, 181–206

Taylor, A J P 1965. *English History 1914–1945*, Oxford

Thompson, M W 1977. *General Pitt-Rivers: evolution and archaeology in the nineteenth century*, Bradford-on-Avon

Wallace, A R 1878. 'Epping Forest', *Fortnightly Review*, 11 Nov 1878, 628–38

Wallace, A R 1882. *Land Nationalization: its necessity and its aims: being a comparison of the system of landlord and tenant with that of occupying ownership in their influence on the well-being of the people*, London

Wallace, A R 1897. 'Re-occupation of the land', in Carpenter (ed) 1897, 9–26

Wheeler, R E M 1930. 'Mr Collingwood and Mr Randall: a note', *Antiquity*, 4/13, 91–5

Wheeler, R E M and Wheeler, T V 1932. *Report on the Excavation of the Prehistoric, Roman, and Post-Roman Site in Lydney Park, Gloucestershire*, Rep Res Comm Soc Antiq London 9, Oxford

Williams-Ellis, C 1928. *England and the Octopus*, London

Williams-Ellis, C (ed) 1937. *Britain and the Beast*, London

Wright, P 2001. *The Village that Died for England*, rev edn, London

CHAPTER FOURTEEN

THE GRAND EXCAVATION PROJECTS
OF THE TWENTIETH CENTURY

Michael Fulford

The opening and closing years of the twentieth century saw the Society engaged in two of its 'grandest' archaeological projects. 1900 saw the Society sponsoring the eleventh successive year of excavations at the Roman town of Silchester, Hampshire, while in the 1980s and 1990s the Society, in collaboration with the British Museum, was involved in the excavation of the site of the celebrated Anglo-Saxon royal cemetery at Sutton Hoo, near Woodbridge, in Suffolk. We shall return to these projects below. Over the course of the twentieth century the Society contributed grants towards dozens of different archaeological projects. With very few exceptions these were field projects – mostly excavations – and they were concentrated in the United Kingdom, and particularly in England, until the last quarter of the century (fig 100). To a few projects the Society made a very significant financial contribution in terms of its own resources, and these may be regarded as the Society's 'grand' excavation projects of the period. Even with the latter the Society was not the sole source of grants or help in kind. Right from the start of its first 'grand' project, the Silchester Excavation Fund was supported by public subscription.[1] Later, however, in the last two decades of the twentieth century, the Society contributed very large grants to a handful of projects (of which Sutton Hoo was one), but even in these cases the projects were still dependent on other sources of funding, such as from the British Academy, to be viable. Of course, it does not necessarily follow that the impact of a project was closely correlated with the amount of money expended on it. Where the size of the grant was not necessarily large, the Society often also contributed in kind, through publication in *Archaeologia* or the *Proceedings*, later the *Antiquaries Journal* (from 1921) or as a Report of the Society's Research Committee (from 1913). In fact, publication by the Society alone represented a major investment. The Society, of course, also published archaeological projects in which it had made no other financial contribution.

The origins of the Society's patronage can be traced back to the generous, pump-priming gift of £500 from the then President, Sir John Evans, towards the establishment by the Council of a specific fund for research in 1889. Twenty years later, in 1909, the Research Committee was established. The first big research project was the 'complete and systematic excavation of the site of Silchester'.[2] This was aided by a grant of £50 from the Society, of which £25 was from the newly created Research

Fig 99. Stonehenge: restoring a lintel to the sarsen circle, probably in 1919. *Photograph*: Society of Antiquaries of London.

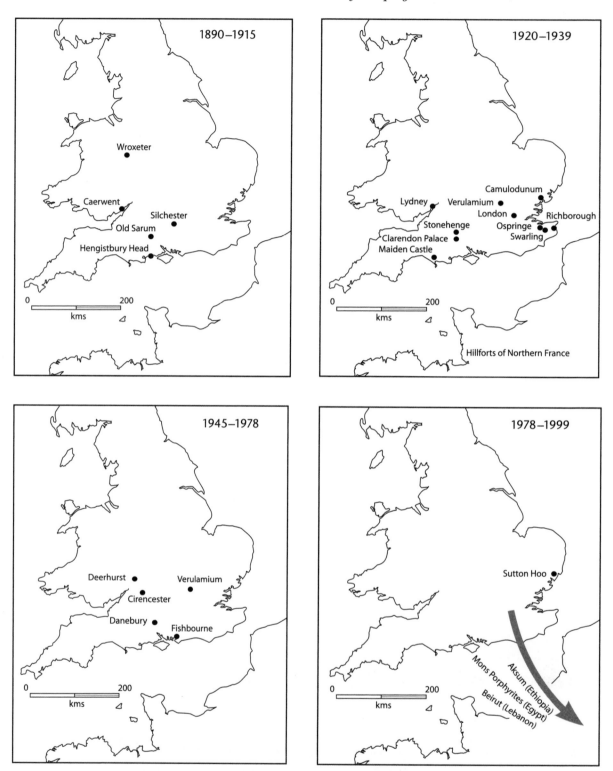

Fig 100. The location of the Society's 'Grand Excavation Projects', 1890–1999. *Drawing*: Margaret Mathews.

Fund. With the permission of the landowner, the Duke of Wellington, and with annual grants ranging between £20 and £50, this project continued for twenty years, achieving for the first time in the Roman world what was understood at the time to be the complete excavation of a Roman town within its walled area. The excavation was directed by William St John Hope, Assistant Secretary of the Society since 1885, George Fox and, increasingly, from the late 1890s, Mill Stephenson (fig 101). The last season, in 1909, saw some excavation on the pre-Roman earthworks and the Roman town defences, but the cemeteries and extra-mural suburbs remained undiscovered and undisturbed for future generations. Permission to explore the amphitheatre, just outside and to the east of the walled area and the property of a different landowner, was refused.

The town was explored insula by insula and the results of each season's work were promptly published in *Archaeologia* (volumes 52 to 62). These were largely confined to systematic descriptions of the individual buildings and their internal features – such as the floorings, including mosaics – but the trenching, which preceded the exposure of individual buildings, identified a large number of deep pits and wells rich in finds. Full treatment of the latter was limited at the time to a study of the pottery by Thomas May, which was published by the County Borough of Reading in 1916.[3] There were, however, many innovations in the research on site, including the first reporting of animal bones by Herbert Jones from 1891 onwards[4] and waterlogged seeds and plant remains by Clement Reid from 1899 onwards.[5] While the Society's

Fig 101. The directors of the Silchester Excavation Fund at Silchester in 1900, in insula XXIII, House 1. Left to right: Mill Stephenson, F Haverfield, W Gowland, G E Fox and W H St John Hope. *Photograph*: © courtesy Museum of Reading.

annual grant never accounted for more than about 10 per cent of the annual expenditure of the excavation fund,[6] we should not underestimate the Society's other contributions, the salary paid to the Assistant Secretary and the cost of publication. In 1892, for example, Council approved the payment of £28 1s 0d for the publication of site plans, a sum representing more than half the value of the annual grant to the excavation fund.

Despite reservations about this breathtaking programme of work, most notably the lack of a chronological framework, the contribution to knowledge was enormous. If the plan that we have is probably representative of the town in the late Roman period, it remains the most complete of any in the western Roman Empire.[7] As Wheeler later observed: 'I am not, for example, of those who scorn the horizontal excavation of the Roman town of Silchester. True it was dug like potatoes, without a shadow of the scientific nicety of the contemporary excavations in Cranborne Chase; and the resultant plan is the uncritical synthesis of a varying urban development through more than three centuries. But it gave at once, and with rough accuracy, the general impression of a Romano-British town such as fifty years of subsequent and often more careful work have failed to equal.'[8] As 2009 approaches we are almost in a position to substitute 'one hundred' for 'fifty' years. Remote sensing through aerial photographic survey and geophysical survey has enhanced our understanding of town and suburbs, but has proved no substitute for what was revealed by the early excavations.[9] As we shall see below, Wheeler's stratigraphic approach to excavation attempted to demonstrate the chronological development of another Romano-British town at Verulamium in the 1930s. Urban archaeology remains difficult and complex. If, since 1909, we have improved immeasurably our ability to excavate and record the stratigraphic sequence, we have still some way to go to resolve issues around the publication of urban excavations, many of which from the 1960s and 1970s remain unpublished.

As an indicator of their significance, several of the sites with which the Society was associated before the outbreak of the Second World War, including Silchester, have attracted further research. Following Wheeler at Verulamium, Molly Cotton's work on the Silchester defences and earthworks began to provide the basis of a chronological framework for the site from the Late Iron Age onwards.[10] This was further developed, particularly in relation to the Late Iron Age, by George Boon in the 1950s.[11] The author's own work in the 1980s, generously supported by the Society, revealed for the first time part of the plan of the Late Iron Age settlement as well as an important sequence of first-century AD Roman timber buildings underlying the masonry forum basilica of the second century.[12] Continuing excavations ('The Silchester Town Life Project') within the walls have confirmed the relatively superficial nature of the early excavations and the remarkable preservation of archaeological deposits.[13] This project aims to recover the fullest possible picture of changing urban life from late Iron Age origins through to the post-Roman abandonment of the city.[14]

With the interruption of the work of the Research Committee by two world wars, it is convenient to review the Society's large projects in three or four time periods. The first comprises the other major excavations undertaken between 1890 and 1915.

Although one or two small grants were made in the intervening years, the first significant research after the First World War was only undertaken in 1921 when the Stonehenge project was launched. The second group is accounted for by the projects of the inter-war years, up to and including 1939. A distinctive feature of the research undertaken before 1915 is that, with one exception, it was dedicated to sites that were not threatened by development or other forms of destruction. This was still largely the case in the inter-war period, but concern over damage to the archaeological record arising from redevelopment in the City of London prompted major investment there by the Society from 1928 onwards. It is a reflection of the significance of the sites selected for investigation that almost all – except for those projects responding to threats of destruction – have seen further work carried out on them, often with the support of the Society, in the period since the Second World War.

As in the course of the First World War, one or two small grants were made between 1940 and 1944, but the first of a series of small grants to help work in war-damaged towns and cities was made in 1945. The third group of Society-sponsored projects includes all the research supported from 1945 to the end of the century. However, the availability of increased levels of resources from the later 1970s, particularly from 1978 onwards, makes it appropriate to subdivide this group. In fact, as we shall see, there were no major projects for ten years after the Second World War, and between 1955 and 1978 only two sites – Verulamium and Corinium – received significant funding. Here resources were dedicated towards assisting with excavation in advance of major developments which threatened these two Roman cities. After 1978 the resources allowed for a greater proportion of funds to be spent on overseas projects and the Society was once more involved in supporting research – notably at Sutton Hoo – which was not driven by the threat of destruction by development.

1890–1915

The first group of research projects was dominated by research on Romano-British towns. Indeed, over the rest of the century the lion's share of the Society's research funds continued to be devoted to Romano-British or Late Iron Age and Romano-British archaeology. Hard on the heels of the undoubted success of the Silchester excavation came the decision in 1899 to excavate the Roman town at Caerwent (Venta Silurum) in south-east Wales. This was a locally led project, with Lord Tredegar, a local beneficiary, presiding over the Caerwent Exploration Fund, to which the Society's annual contribution (ranging between £5 and £25) was usually less than half that granted to Silchester. Supervision of the excavation was in the hands of Alfred Hudd and Thomas Ashby, later Director of the British School at Rome. Unlike Silchester, where the only standing buildings within the Roman town walls were the parish church and the adjacent farm and its outbuildings, the walled area of Caerwent is occupied by a village, ranged along the east–west route through the former Roman town. This limited the space available for excavation. By the time the excavations ended in 1913, almost two-thirds of the town had been explored, with very extensive work in the south-west and north-east quarters of the walled area. As with Silchester, the emphasis was on the recovery of the plan of each building and its associated structural features. Although there was an awareness of a complex, deep stratigraphy, the excavators did not attempt to grapple with the earlier timber buildings and the resulting plan is, essentially, that of the late Roman town.[15] Like Silchester, the results were published annually in *Archaeologia* (volumes 57 to 64).

Only with the third Romano-British town project, this time on the 'greenfield' site at Wroxeter (Viroconium), Shropshire, were the results published separately. This work was on a relatively limited scale, focusing on a series of buildings – shops-cum-workshops, a temple, a town house – fronting the main north–south street of the city, south of the forum. Limited work was also done on a small walled enclosure of uncertain function to the rear of the main street. The first ever report of the Research Committee published the results of the 1912 season of work,[16] while the results of the next two seasons were also published separately in the new series.[17] These publications represented a significant departure from the reports of the work at Silchester and Caerwent in that there was serious treatment of the finds – 'small objects', samian, coins and some of the coarse pottery. The approach of J P Bushe-Fox also showed a greater understanding of stratigraphy and the role that coins and samian could play in developing a chronology of individual buildings. At Site VI, for example, he demonstrated four phases of building – a late first-century phase of timber building; the construction of three narrow-fronted shop-cum-workshops early in the second century; their incorporation into one masonry building before the mid-second century; and a final, poorly dated, 'town-house' phase involving substantial alteration of its predecessor.[18] Further work at Wroxeter was then curtailed by the outbreak of war.

Three other sites were awarded significant resources in the period before the outbreak of war in 1914, of which the medieval project – the first of any size to be undertaken by the Society – at Old Sarum, Wiltshire, attracted the most (approximately £650, second only to Silchester). Indeed, in the context of all the research projects funded before the start of the rescue excavations initiated at Verulamium in 1955, this was the fifth largest in terms of resources allocated by the Society. Here the ambition was the excavation of the relatively short-lived (eleventh- to fourteenth-century) complex of inner bailey (castle) and outer bailey (cathedral, cloisters and associated buildings) located within the ramparts of the Iron Age hillfort. The work was undertaken under the direction of William St John Hope, Assistant Secretary of the Society until he resigned in 1910 to concentrate on Old Sarum. It was carried on over seven seasons (1909–15) in association with the Office of Works. Regrettably, the work was never published beyond the annual reports to the Society by Hope and Hawley that appeared in the *Proceedings*.[19]

Mostly concentrated into one year – 1912 – Bushe-Fox also undertook excavations at the largely prehistoric promontory fort at Hengistbury Head, Dorset (then in Hampshire) (1911–12).[20] This work was occasioned by the threat of development, the first 'rescue' excavation sponsored by the Society. It revealed evidence of a long chronology, but was particularly important for the finds associated with the first half of the first century BC, evidencing cross-Channel trade. In addition to the presence of Gaulish coins from Brittany and elsewhere in France, there was abundant ceramic evidence (pottery Class B, etc) for Breton contacts. Other finds (pottery Class D) suggested links with the Glastonbury lake-village, while Gowland's analysis of metal finds[21] pointed to links to West Country ore deposits. The significance of this site for our understanding of the nature of both the long-distance trade with Brittany and beyond and trade and exchange within the south west of Britain in the Late Iron Age has been subsequently developed by Barry Cunliffe's excavation and associated research from 1979. Also with generous support from the Society, this represents another example of a 'classic' type-site being revisited, again with spectacular results. Extensive evidence was recovered of the plan of the settlement and its buildings from the Early Iron Age through to the Roman period and new insights were gained into the relations of the site both with its Wessex hinterland and northern France. A significant component of the Late Iron Age pottery assemblage was represented by Dressel 1 wine amphorae of Republican Italian origin, which affirmed links with the Mediterranean. Important new insights were gained into glass and metalworking.[22]

The five projects described above do not, of course, represent the totality of the Society's investment in archaeological projects between 1890 and 1915, but they do represent the most significant. The Society made more modest contributions to a number of other sites in England as well as overseas, most notably, perhaps, to Sir Arthur Evans's work at Knossos, Crete, in the early 1900s. Over the five years from 1915 to 1919 the accounts of the Research Committee show how the Society invested heavily in the war effort through the purchase of war loans, war stock and war bonds, the total exceeding the amount spent on any pre-war project with the exception of Silchester, where the sums almost corresponded (at about £1,000).

1920–1939

Among the large number of projects to attract the Society's support in the inter-war period, often at a level of annual grant of £5 or £10, it becomes increasingly difficult to make a correlation between the impact of the project and the amount expended on it. In fact no more than ten projects received grants totalling in excess of £200. Among these, only three really significant grants were made in terms of the size of the award (of £950 or more): to Roman London, Richborough and Stonehenge. These can certainly be regarded as the Society's projects, but they were very different in kind and, indeed, in quality. The President of the Society, Lord Crawford, with the support of Mortimer Wheeler, as Director of the London Museum, was a prime mover of the Roman London project. Wheeler, however, is more celebrated for his direction of four of the second group of seven projects supported by the Society with grants of between £200 and £950: Lydney, Verulamium, Maiden Castle and Brittany (to be discussed further below). The Society also contributed £80 towards Wheeler's first post-war excavation – at the Roman fort of Segontium, at Caernarfon, in north Wales (1920–2) – where he made, with prompt publication, his first important methodological contribution to stratigraphic archaeology,[23] and £50 towards the total excavation of the amphitheatre of the Roman legionary fortress at Caerleon in southeast Wales (1926–7), which the Society also published.[24] Wheeler's work, and the Society's sponsorship of it, dominates the inter-war period, particularly the 1930s.

Roman London attracted a total of £1,802 over the ten years between 1928 and 1937 and was different in character from field projects that ran yearly on the traditional, seasonal basis. The allocated sum, initially of about £250, was used to pay the annual salary of an investigator – first Eric Birley, then Gerald Dunning and, from 1934, Frank Cottrill. The aim was to keep watch on developments in the City and to record what was observed. Although there was no brief to privilege one period rather than another, and though important medieval finds were made and published,[25] the discoveries that attracted most attention were Roman. There are three major achievements associated with the work of the three investigators. First, there was the recovery of further, crucial fragments of one of the most important tomb monuments from Roman Britain, that of the Gaulish procurator, Classicianus, appointed by Nero in the aftermath of the Boudiccan rebellion (fig 102).[26] Second, there was the recognition of the two fire horizons, one associated with the Boudiccan rebellion, the other dated to the Hadrianic period.[27] The latter have become benchmarks, not only for establishing a chronology of the material culture of the town, but also for

Fig 102. London: part of the inscription commemorating the procurator of Britain, Gaius Julius Alpinus Classicianus, discovered in 1935 built into Bastion 2 of the Roman city wall in Trinity Place, Trinity Square. *Photograph*: © Tower Hill Improvement.

assisting in understanding the spatial development of the settlement over time.[28] Finally, there is the contribution that both Dunning and Cottrill made to our understanding of the London forum basilica. In particular, Dunning's reconstructed plan of the basilica of 1931 has stood the test of time.[29]

The second most important project in terms of allocated resources (£1,632) was the excavation of the Roman fort at Richborough, in north-east Kent, under the direction of J P Bushe-Fox – in association with the Office of Works over the eleven years between 1922 and 1932, then under the Office of Works, but without grant-aid from the Society, until 1938. While the first three reports were promptly published in the style set by his work at Wroxeter,[30] the fourth was delayed by the serious accident incurred by Bushe-Fox in the course of his work.[31] After the deaths of Bushe-Fox in 1954 and then of his principal supervisor, B W E Pearce, in 1959, the final publication of the period between 1931 and 1938 was undertaken after an interval of thirty years by Barry Cunliffe.[32] The report also provided the opportunity for Cunliffe to review the results of the whole programme of work (in 'The Development of Richborough') and to consider some of their implications (in 'The British Fleet').

This huge excavation was the first extensive investigation of one of the late Roman walled fortifications around the coast of south-east England identified in the *Notitia Dignitatum* as forts of the 'Saxon Shore'. The site proved complex – with more than just a late Roman history – and a major contribution was the unravelling of the complex sequence from pre- to post-Roman. Work focused on the area within the late Roman walls, although it was appreciated that the settlement extended some distance beyond (fig 103). Major discoveries flowed, including the reasonable identification of the site as a major invasion base of the Roman army of AD 43. Alongside the development of London, the site continued to serve as a major port and the excavation produced important remains – for example, of later first-century timber granaries (fig 104). A major discovery was the interpretation of a massive foundation as the remains of an enormous, Carrara marble-clad monument. This in turn is interpreted as commemorating – later in the first century – the earlier Claudian invasion. Prior to the construction of the Roman walled fort in the late third century, the excavation found evidence of a triple-ditched defensive enclosure dug around the remains of the monument at some time in the mid-third century. The significance of the discoveries continues to emerge. Relatively recently, for example, a strong case was made for interpreting the late Roman masonry structure found in the first season of excavation in 1922 in the north west of the enclosed area as the base of a Christian baptistery.[33] Despite significant post-Second World War excavations at other coastal sites, including Saxon Shore forts, the work at Richborough remains pivotal to our understanding of the history of Britannia, late Roman (coastal) fortifications and cross-Channel traffic.[34] Methodologically, too, the excavation was important as, by the late 1920s, Bushe-Fox was clearly experimenting with open-area excavation.[35]

Although some work had been undertaken at Stonehenge in the early 1900s, a much larger project was launched in late 1919 as one of the first big post-war research projects and, like Richborough, in collaboration with the Office of Works (fig 99).

Fig 103. Richborough, Kent: view in 1924 of the late Roman bath-building (Site III), occupying the north-east corner of the fort (Bushe-Fox 1928, 24–5, pl XLII). *Photograph*: Society of Antiquaries of London.

Fig 104. Richborough, Kent: view in 1932 of Claudian/pre-Flavian granaries and super-imposed pre- or early Flavian timber buildings (Area XVII) (Cunliffe 1968, figs 2–4). *Photograph*: Society of Antiquaries of London.

Indeed this was the first substantial investigation by the Society of a major prehistoric site. Almost a thousand pounds (£950) were devoted to excavation under the direction of Lieutenant-Colonel W Hawley at Stonehenge between 1921 and 1926, but the results, which were regularly reported between 1921 and 1928, were regarded at the time as disappointing.[36] His final report concludes with a brief summary of his findings.[37] About half of the monument, including the henge ditch, had been explored and he was confident that the enclosure ditch and bank pre-dated the erection of the stones. He had located and excavated for the first time a number of pits which he associated with the observations of the seventeenth-century antiquarian John Aubrey, concluding that they were originally dug to hold posts, though they later contained cremation burials. Another significant discovery was that of the concentric 'Y' and 'Z' holes, contemporary with the stone phase of the monument. In the detailed description of their fills there is a clear interest in the lithology of the stone fragments.[38] This built on the work of Herbert H Thomas, petrographer of HM Geological Survey, who studied the stones and identified the Preseli Mountains as the source of the 'foreign stones'.[39]

It is worth quoting Joan Evans's comment on these excavations *in extenso*: 'They were not very fruitful, in the older antiquarian sense, and in June 1922 the President (Sir Hercules Read) made the revealing statement . . . that the finds so far reported represented a poor return on the labour and expenditure involved, but such was the case with most megalithic monuments.' The fourth report was not well received; the Society found a catalogue of unelucidated facts unpalatable. In 1924 the report stated that there were still few results: 'The more one digs the more the mystery deepens. Not a single object has yet been found that would suggest a date or a period, and it is useless to formulate theories when there is little to support them.'[40] No comprehensive report of the work was published and twenty years later Stuart Piggott drew attention to the inadequacy of the published reports and called for new work.[41]

Hawley's reputation has recovered very appreciably from the severe criticism visited on him, particularly (and very unfortunately, given the history of his own, inglorious involvement in the monument) by Richard Atkinson.[42] Despite his terse conclusion that 'The Hawley years, 1919 to 1926, were a disaster', Chippindale as well as Cleal (and her co-authors) were more sympathetic, showing an understanding of the physical and financial context in which Hawley worked in the 1920s.[43] Indeed, the latter noted that Hawley's records of the Aubrey Holes, for example, are of a quality to sustain and develop his interpretation, that they were probably post-holes secondarily used for cremation burials.[44]

Two other projects of the 1920s deserve comment. In 1921 – and in advance of gravel extraction – a small excavation was carried out at Swarling, Kent, by Leonard Woolley and Thomas May, with a grant of £270 from the Society. This was prompted by earlier discoveries of pottery vessels and it revealed the remains of some nineteen cremation burial groups dating to the second half of the first century BC. The close continental parallels of the Swarling pottery taken alongside earlier discoveries of similar material, notably those by Sir Arthur Evans at nearby Aylesford in the mid-nineteenth century, led Bushe-Fox to describe it as the Aylesford–Swarling type of pottery and associate it with the Belgae of Gaul.[45] Although opinion has varied about the extent to which the appearance of a new material culture can be equated with population movement, Aylesward–Swarling – and the definition of a larger Aylesward–Swarling culture – has dominated the literature of the latest Iron Age of south-east Britain and the emergence of the coin-using, proto-urban societies and dynasties of the Catuvellauni and the Atrebates.[46]

Like the work at Swarling, the publication of the Romano-British cemetery at Ospringe, Kent, where excavation had taken place intermittently since 1920, was published as a Report of the Research Committee.[47] The report concentrates on the burials excavated by Hawley in 1924–5, but Thomas May described the pottery groups from the earlier work as well. Altogether some 685 pottery vessels were catalogued. There is no other evidence of the Society's support of this project which represented the first systematic excavation and publication of part of a Romano-British cemetery, largely of cremations and, for the most part, of later first- to mid-third-century date. The settlement is located on Watling Street, some ten miles west of Canterbury, and there is no doubt about the lasting significance of the publication.

The closing years of the 1920s saw the first of four successive projects directed by Mortimer and Tessa Wheeler which were significantly sponsored by the Society. The total expended on all four was some £1,622 – close to the total amount spent on Richborough. At the invitation of the owner, Lord Bledisloe, the Romano-British temple at Lydney, Gloucestershire, and its environs were re-excavated in 1928–9, with the Society contributing £457 from its research funds.[48] As with their previous excavations, and those that followed in the 1930s, establishing the chronology of the site was a principal objective. The site occupies a promontory in the Forest of Dean overlooking the Severn and was defended by an earthwork. The strategy was to combine excavation of the previously untouched earthwork – to recover evidence of its character and chronology – with area excavation of the Roman buildings, which had previously been explored in the eighteenth and nineteenth centuries and published by W H Bathurst.[49] The rampart was demonstrated to be of late Iron Age origin. This phase was followed by early Roman occupation, with evidence of timber buildings ('huts') and the excavation of a Roman iron mine. The principal, and best known, phase of activity – the construction of the temple to Nodens and the associated 'guesthouse', 'long building' (or 'abaton') and the 'baths' – was dated to the late fourth century. Evidence for the heightening of the rampart after the AD 360s suggested a further, post-Roman, phase of occupation to the excavators. A subsequent excavation in 1980–1 by John Casey challenged the late chronology for the main Roman phase of the temple and the associated buildings. He argued instead for an initial phase of construction and occupation from the second half of the third century, followed by rebuilding in the fourth century.[50] The post-Roman phase was found to fall within the Roman period. Whether the Roman-period site was wholly religious in function, as the Wheelers believed, or had a significant military (naval) association remains to be further investigated.[51]

The second Wheeler project undertaken between 1930 and 1933 concerned the Roman city of Verulamium, on the outskirts of St Albans, Hertfordshire. This project was prompted by the acquisition by the St Albans Corporation of the southern part of the walled area as a town park in 1929. The Society was approached by the corporation and a Verulamium Excavation Committee was established, to which the Society contributed a total of £350. Although the bulk of the excavation was devoted to the exploration of the southern part of the walled area, the Wheelers 'kept one objective in view – the recovery of the historical framework of Belgic and Roman Verulamium'. This is reflected in the title of their final publication: *Verulamium: a Belgic and two Roman cities.*[52] A key aim – as developed later at Maiden Castle, Dorset, and the hillfort excavations in Brittany and Normandy, and later still at Stanwick, Yorkshire (see below) – was to knit the archaeology with the written and numismatic record. A particular focus, paralleled by Christopher Hawkes's work at Camulodunum (see below), was to attempt to understand the period between Caesar's and Claudius's invasions of Britain, and to find out more about the Belgae, the tribe mentioned by Caesar as having settled in south-east Britain from Gaul.

In order to achieve their framework for the origin and development of the Roman city – and building on the success of the Lydney project – effort was focused on the earthworks, which were believed to offer the best chance of encapsulating the site's chronology. Thus, several trenches were economically excavated through relevant earthworks 'across six miles of countryside' from Wheathampstead to Verulamium and to the associated earthworks at Prae Wood, to the south of the Roman city. This – along with Hawkes's contemporaneous approach to the earthworks (dykes) around Camulodunum – can surely be regarded as an early form of landscape archaeology. In addition to excavation on the defences and gates (fig 105), there was also extensive area excavation within the walls, but this was limited to the southern part of the city which had been acquired by the St Albans Corporation. Here several town houses and the 'triangular temple' where Watling Street meets the rectilinear street grid were examined (fig 106).

Excavation at the outset of the defended enclosure ('oppidum') of Wheathampstead, six miles to the north east of the Roman town, suggested that it was the predecessor of the Late Iron Age (Belgic) oppidum centred at Prae Wood to the west of the Roman city. The latter was founded lower down the slope in the valley of the River Ver soon after the Roman conquest of AD 43. This, the first Roman city, was destroyed by Boudicca in AD 60. The Wheelers identified the earthwork known as 'The Fosse', whose course was cut by the later city wall, as the defence of the first Roman city which was thus centred in the northern half of what later became the walled city. Subsequent work by Sheppard Frere (see below) demonstrated that this formed part of the larger, late second-century defence of the city,[53] whose area was reduced by the construction of the masonry city wall. The Wheelers' second city of the second century AD comprised the public buildings, including the forum and theatre, town houses and temples that formed the main focus of the excavations within the walled area. This city 'decayed into ruin' in the third century and 'had largely to be

Fig 105. Verulamium: view of the south-east 'London' gate from the north east. The men are standing on the two main roadways within the gate (Wheeler and Wheeler 1936, pls xxII and LXXXVI). *Photograph*: Society of Antiquaries of London.

Fig 106. Verulamium: the 'triangular temple', view from the north (Wheeler and Wheeler 1936, pl xxxIV). *Photograph*: Society of Antiquaries of London.

366

rebuilt' in the early fourth century. Then 'All material evidence ceases at Verulamium by the end of the fourth century.'[54] This interpretation of the development of the city was subsequently shown to be too simplistic as a result of further excavations undertaken by Sheppard Frere with sponsorship from the Society from 1955.[55] The prompt publication of the Wheelers' work was applauded, but it involved (deliberately) only a very selective publication of the finds. This decision was not well received by his reviewers.[56]

The third Wheeler project, conducted over three years in 1934–6, was the excavation of the prehistoric, defended, hilltop settlement at Maiden Castle in Dorset (fig 107). This was undertaken with relatively modest funding from the Research Committee (£565),[57] but with spectacular results.[58] Unusually, the introduction of the final report contained a short section on 'Finance', where the Society's grants can be seen in the context of the total expenditure on the excavation (£5,363) as representing about 15 per cent of the total.[59] In terms of objectives, the establishment of a chronological framework was once again paramount. As Wheeler described, he intended 'to investigate the structural history of the great fortifications which are now the distinctive feature of the site'. Secondly, he intended 'to identify and correlate the associated cultures'. This aim can be seen as an opportunity to test the recently developed cultural framework for the Iron Age of Britain, the threefold division known as the ABC system.[60] His third aim was 'to explore the possibility of recovering some part of the town plan'.[61] While he believed he had achieved his first two objectives, the third lay 'beyond our reach'.[62] However, he not only succeeded in unravelling the sequence of Iron Age occupation and defence of the hilltop, he also added

Fig 107. Maiden Castle, Dorset: southern portal of the eastern entrance of the Iron Age hillfort (Wheeler 1943, pl xcvi). *Photograph*: Society of Antiquaries of London.

a Neolithic phase with the excavation of the Bank Barrow (the 'long mound') and associated enclosure. Dramatic evidence of burials (the 'war cemetery') at the eastern entrance associated with evidence of wound trauma – including the famous 'ballista bolt' embedded in the spine of one individual – was interpreted by Wheeler as evidence of the siege of the hillfort by Vespasian's Legio II, in AD 44–5 (fig 108).[63] Important, too – in the revelation of an extended chronology from Neolithic to Roman – was the discovery of the late Roman temple on the hilltop, an indication of continuing paganism alongside the emergence of Christianity in Britain. The results were brought together under difficult conditions, but with admirable speed, and published by the Society in the middle of the Second World War in 1943.

As with other projects sponsored by the Antiquaries at what were perceived to be key sites, Maiden Castle was revisited some fifty years after Wheeler's investigations. Excavations and field survey led by Niall Sharples, on behalf of English Heritage, in 1985–6 focused on understanding the setting of the monument and a detailed geophysical and ground survey of the earthworks and interior, which set Wheeler's trenches in context. Selective excavation then developed Wheeler's chronology and conclusions with the study of the environmental evidence and material culture, adding significantly to our understanding of the monument and its social context.[64] The most significant advance in knowledge and understanding of the new project was in relation to the Neolithic settlement of the hilltop, the early, fourth-millennium BC causewayed enclosure and the later Bank Barrow. Wheeler had not anticipated this phase of occupation and his account of it is brief.[65]

Fig 108. Maiden Castle, Dorset: the 'war cemetery' at the eastern entrance of the Iron Age hillfort. General view from the south (Wheeler 1943, pl LII). *Photograph*: Society of Antiquaries of London.

The fourth, and last, of the Wheeler projects of the 1930s saw the export of his excavation methodology in the wake of Maiden Castle to tackle a group of hillforts in north-western France: 'it had become increasingly clear to us that, whatever the insular contribution, we could not place the results of our work in a sizeable context without some examination of the material – structural and other – across the Channel'.[66] This project was undertaken over two seasons in 1938 and 1939 with modest funding from the Society (£250) until the outbreak of war curtailed further work: 'On a Friday morning in mid-August 1939 I suddenly handed over to Miss Richardson, and on the following day was engaged upon an alien task in London.'[67] Five defended Iron Age sites were examined from Finistère to Normandy to ascertain the character of their defences, their date and the nature of their occupation, whether long- or short-lived. A significant premise of the project was that these hillforts might be linked to the Caesarian narrative and context of the Gallic Wars of the mid-first century BC, just as the latest phase of defence of Maiden Castle and the 'war' cemetery could be related to the later, Claudian invasion of Britain. This indeed proved to be the case with the cliff-castles of the west of Brittany linked with the Veneti, and the Normandy sites and their Fécamp-style of defence with the resistance of the Belgic tribes to Caesar and Roman methods of siege warfare. The writing of major monuments into the history of the Roman conquest of Britain and Gaul was a theme that re-emerged with the limited, post-war excavations at Stanwick, North Yorkshire, which coincided with the Festival of Britain.[68] Here the development of the massive series of enclosures was correlated with the fortunes of the Brigantes and the Roman conquest of the north as seen through the eyes of the Roman historian Tacitus. Though published as a Report of the Research Committee the excavation was not funded by the Society.

Throughout the duration of the Wheeler projects of the 1930s, the Society was also supporting Christopher Hawkes and Rex Hull at Colchester, where the proposal to build a bypass around the north of the town threatened considerable areas of extra-mural occupation of the Roman *colonia*. The investment of £580 on the part of the Society over eight years was comparable with its contribution to Maiden Castle over three. This project made an enormous contribution to knowledge of the Roman and Gaulish (Gallo-Belgic) material culture associated both with the Augustan and the Tiberian oppidum of the Trinovantian kings, and then the early Roman fortress and *colonia* up to the mid-60s of the first century AD.[69] The publication remains a pivotal work for understanding the nature of Late Iron Age tribal society, including its cross-Channel relations with the Roman world of Gaul and the Mediterranean. Its pottery typology, particularly of Gallo-Belgic wares, continues to exert its influence over the study of the ceramics of the late first century BC and early first century AD. Associated work that helped to unravel the complex sequence of earthworks (dykes) which defended the Late Iron Age oppidum was finally published much later, as *Camulodunum II*.[70]

In the years from the inception of the Research Fund in 1889 and the start of the Silchester project in 1890 up to the outbreak of the First World War, the 'grand projects' of the Society had been dominated by research on Roman Britain, particularly its towns. This emphasis on Romano-British archaeology continued to dominate the inter-war years of the 1920s and 1930s, most notably at London and Richborough. However, with the projects and publication of the work at Swarling, Camulodunum and Verulamium, there was a significant emphasis on the archaeology of the period of the Iron Age dynasties of south-east Britain between Caesar and Claudius and of making sense in material terms of what was understood by Caesar's reference to the settlement of the Belgae. With Hawkes and Wheeler the archaeological evidence was interpreted through the eyes of the ancient historians – especially Caesar, Dio Cassius and Tacitus – and was used by them to embellish and develop those written sources and to write the history of the Roman conquest of Gaul and Britain. As we have seen, only two prehistoric projects received significant support – Stonehenge and Maiden Castle – and the medieval period was largely ignored. Ranking tenth in the level of support provided by the Society, the excavation of the medieval royal palace of Clarendon, near Salisbury, Wiltshire, by Tancred Borenius was the only project to receive modest assistance. It was funded over the four years of 1931–4 to a total of £205, but the work was not finally written up and published (by the Society) until much later.[71] Just as in the early years of the Research Fund, support in the inter-war years was not solely limited to those excavations discussed here. Small grants of a very few pounds were given to support other prehistoric, Roman and prehistoric fieldwork projects in Britain, of which only a very few took place outside of England, and fewer still outside the British Isles. Indeed, only Wheeler's hillfort project in northern France attracted a significant grant.

1945–1977

As during the First World War, almost no grants were made in the period between 1940 and 1944.[72] Furthermore, as we have observed above, the ten years from 1945 were particularly lean in terms of grants for fieldwork by the Society. In the immediate aftermath of the war the Society's limited resources were used to help the archaeology of bomb-damaged cities, and between 1945 and 1948 almost £650 was spent on Canterbury, Dover, Exeter and London – the latter taking almost two-thirds of the total. Although small in absolute terms, a consistent attempt was made between 1948 and 1951 to support overseas projects in the British mandated territory of Libya (at Cyrenaica and Sabratha) and in Italy (the Apulia project). Nevertheless, whereas the majority of the research supported by the Society before 1939 had been dedicated to sites not threatened by development or other forms of destruction, between 1944 and the late 1970s, when a much more significant level of research funding became available, the majority of the Society's limited research funds were devoted to supporting rescue archaeology. Taking account of post-war inflation, the real value of the grants awarded between 1945 and the late 1970s was more or less maintained. While the paper value of the total grants awarded in any one year rose to about

£1,000 in the 1970s, with the value of £1 in 1960 about a half of what it was in 1940, the real value remained what it was in the 1930s.

The two 'grand projects' of the late 1950s and 1960s were the support of the rescue excavations in advance of road-widening at Verulamium and a variety of development-anticipated or development-led excavations in Cirencester, very largely concerned with the exploration of the Roman city. Between 1955 and 1961 Sheppard Frere's excavations at Verulamium attracted £2,200 from the Society, while John Wacher's work at Cirencester was granted £2,480 over a ten-year period between 1959 and 1968. Frere's work revealed – across a range of insulae which were affected by the road-widening – just how complex it was to explore a full Roman urban sequence from origins to abandonment, and time did not always allow for a full investigation of threatened buildings. Frere's achievements are best exemplified by insula XIV where, for the first time in the archaeology of the Roman Empire, a sequence of development alongside one of the principal streets of the town (Watling Street) was revealed and understood. Initially, and from the Claudian period, consisting of two periods of narrow-fronted timber buildings, of which the latter could be subdivided into four sub-phases, the properties were subsequently redeveloped in masonry in the late third century. Meticulous attention was paid to the complex stratigraphy and a tight chronology was developed using coins and sigillata with two clear, fire horizons – the Boudiccan destruction and the 'Antonine' fire – respectively separating Periods 1 from 2 and 2 from 3.[73] Important chronologies for the associated domestic pottery and other material culture emerged in association with this tightly dated sequence. The history of other properties across insulae XVII to XXII and XXVII and XXVIII was similarly explored, with the revelation of comparable early phases in timber in the first and second century. Equally, a major contribution was made towards understanding the history of the city after AD 400 with the discovery of a long sequence of activity in insula XXVII, probably extending into the sixth or seventh century.[74] Wheeler's simple model for the development and decline of Verulamium crumbled in the face of these well-executed and impeccably reported excavations.[75] Methodologically, with the appropriate abandonment of 'Wheeler' grid-squares in order to gain a better understanding of plan, the excavations saw the development on complex urban stratigraphy of an open-area approach to excavation, which was subsequently deployed with great effect by Martin Biddle at Winchester.

With the winding down of the Verulamium excavations, the Society agreed to the formation of the Cirencester Excavation Committee in 1958 and awarded its first grant of £100 in 1959. The Society continued to support the committee with annual grants, usually of £300 or £350, until 1968, with John Wacher as its director of excavations. As with other UK towns and cities, though not with the same intensity, open and built-up areas of Cirencester were threatened by development. This provided opportunities to investigate a major city of Roman Britain, second only in size to London in terms of its walled area, which also served as a provincial capital in the fourth century. Excavations were carried out on a number of sites, providing important new information on a variety of themes, including the origins of the town, the street grid, the defences and gates, the public buildings – notably the forum basilica and the amphitheatre – the shops and other urban buildings. In addition, excavation was carried out by David Brown on the site of Cirencester Abbey and on the remains of the possible Saxon church found beneath it in 1964–6.[76] Although, collectively, the work added significantly to our knowledge of the town, no one aspect of the work had the same impact as Frere's urban sequences at Verulamium. The results were initially published as interim reports in the *Antiquaries Journal*, followed by full publication between 1982 and 1998. A particularly significant development, which contributed to our understanding of urban origins in Roman Britain, was the discovery of part of the remains of a Roman fort of mid- to late first-century AD date underlying the centre of the town.[77] The remaining Roman sites were published later under Neil Holbrook's editorship.[78]

More significant for the 1960s, perhaps, was the discovery and excavation by Barry Cunliffe between 1961 and 1969 of the palatial Romano-British villa site at Fishbourne, just outside Chichester, West Sussex.[79] Through the Chichester Civic Society, the Antiquaries supported the excavations with grants totalling £680 – between a third and a quarter of the sum granted to the Cirencester and Verulamium projects. What is significant about Fishbourne is not only the scale and decoration of the building of the Flavian period, which has produced the best-preserved and earliest mosaic floors from Britain and a range of imported white and coloured decorative marbles, but the scale and décor of its Neronian predecessor, the 'proto-palace'. In addition, there is a Conquest-period phase of timber building which might be associated with a military supply base. The subsequent sequence of masonry building provides rare insight into luxury in early Roman Britain. Spectacular though this excavation was, and even allowing for the support evidenced by the two-volume publication,[80] it is debatable whether this counts as one of the Society's own 'grand projects'.

Despite the lean resources of the early 1970s, efforts were made to focus them on well-conceived projects. In December 1972 the Society launched two new thematic projects on 'The Archaeology of the English Church' and 'The Evolution of the English Landscape'.[81] These were economically funded over some five years with annual grants ranging between £250 for 'Churches' and £350 to £850 for 'Landscape', the two projects between them accounting for about one-third of the archaeology grants (a further substantial grant was also being made annually at this time for the revision of Papworth[82]). Excavation and a pioneering structural analysis of the Anglo-Saxon (and later) church at Deerhurst, Gloucestershire, was the focus of the 'Churches' project.[83] A survey of the incidence and use of sarsen across Wessex was one major theme of the 'Landscape' project,[84] a second being the aerial photographic survey under the auspices of the Royal Commission on the Historical Monuments (England) of the landscape around the Iron Age hillfort at Danebury on the chalk of north Hampshire (Palmer 1984).[85] More or less concurrently with Deerhurst, research was also being undertaken by Martin Biddle and Harold Taylor on the Anglo-Saxon church at Repton, Derbyshire, and by the Rodwells on the church at Rivenhall, Essex,[86] both with support from the Society.

1978–1999

An approach to the Society to resume excavations at Sutton Hoo in late 1978 (by Robert Pretty, owner of the estate which included the Anglo-Saxon cemetery) coincided not only with the end of five years of funding of the 'Churches' and 'Landscape' projects, but also with a marked increase in the resources that the Society could make available for research.[87] Part of this was tied by the terms of Hugh Phillips's bequest which 'shall aim to increase our knowledge of the life and customs in the British isles at any period prior to 1800 AD'. The Society was keen to develop a Sutton Hoo project, but it took some years before a final agreement was arrived at with those involved, including the principal partner, the British Museum. Professor Martin Carver, of the University of York, was selected as the director late in 1982 and the project began in earnest five years after the first approach from Pretty. The research programme received funding from the Society annually for ten years until 1992 at a level indexed to the first year's grant of £13,000 (£27,000 by 1992). This was a major departure for the Society, with other grants awarded over this period not exceeding the range of £1,000 to £1,400. In real terms the grant to Sutton Hoo was substantially more than the total sum allocated to Silchester over a twenty-year period around the start of the century.

The aims of the project were to contextualize the spectacular seventh-century AD ship burial discovered at the outbreak of war in 1939 and further investigated between 1965 and 1975.[88] Following three years of evaluation and survey at the cemetery – which overlooks the River Deben, in Suffolk – excavation was undertaken of an area of about one hectare – largely to the north of Mound 1, which had contained the celebrated ship burial (fig 109). This included several burial mounds and contiguous areas. All but one of the mounds had been robbed and seriously disturbed, but nevertheless provided important evidence of associated cremation burials. Beneath Mound 17 were found two separate inhumations, side by side: one of an adult male accompanied by sword, bucket, cauldron and horse harness and the other of a horse. Novel techniques were developed to excavate the mounds, to understand their environmental context and to recover evidence of the burials (sand bodies) whose remains had largely been destroyed by the acidic, sandy soil. Following the relatively brief late sixth-/early seventh-century phase of rich burials, there was a further episode of unfurnished burials of eighth- to tenth-century date. These were interpreted as the remains of execution victims. The project succeeded richly in fulfilling its aims, adding very substantially to the knowledge and understanding gained by the 1938–9 and the 1965–75 excavations.[89]

Looking back over the twentieth century it is startlingly clear how much late Iron Age and Romano-British archaeology was privileged over earlier prehistory and the medieval and early modern periods. Apart from St John Hope's unpublished excavations at Old Sarum before the First World War, Sutton Hoo and the two thematic projects of 'Churches' and '(Prehistoric) Landscapes' were the only major post-Roman projects to have been supported with substantial resources by the Society. Prehistoric

Fig 109. Sutton Hoo, Suffolk: the excavations on their completion in 1991, looking west. Mound 1, the site of the ship burial discovered in 1939, lies in front of the trees of Top Hat Wood and next to a spoil heap. The cruciform area, proposed in the research design of 1986, contains (north to south) Mounds 2, 5, 6 and 7, and (east to west) Mounds 14, 17 and 18. Outside the excavated area are Mounds 1, 3 and 4, and 8 to 12. The linear earthworks beside the campsite and offices are anti-glider ditches dug in the Second World War. *Photograph*: Justin Garner-Lahire; © Sutton Hoo Research Trust.

archaeology was correspondingly neglected, with Stonehenge – which failed to arouse the enthusiasm of the Society – and Maiden Castle the only two projects of significance to receive substantial support. Although projects were supported across the United Kingdom, the Society focused its efforts in England.

The only overseas projects to receive substantial support came towards the end of the twentieth century: Aksum (Ethiopia) and Mons Porphyrites (Egypt) shared the diminished pot available at the conclusion of Sutton Hoo. The former received £35,000 over four years (1993–6), and involved the exploration and survey of the Ethiopian centre.[90] Following the conclusion of these projects, the Society funded post-Civil War rescue excavation in Beirut, Lebanon.

The aim of the Aksum project was 'to illuminate aspects of Aksumite society which had not been emphasized in previous investigations: the domestic economy as well as long-distance trade, the living conditions and burial customs of commoners in addition to the tombs and palaces of the elite, local crafts and industries in comparison with imported luxuries'.[91] The project made a very significant contribution to knowledge and understanding of pre-Aksumite and late Aksumite society between the early first millennium BC and the late first millennium AD. The research showed that 'the subsistence economy and aspects of its technology were both firmly rooted in indigenous practices which may be traced back for many centuries, if not millennia'. This was a local, African civilization borne as a result of its location in the heart of the fertile Ethiopian highlands. Equally, it was shown that Aksum was 'directly ancestral to recent cultural phenomena in the northern Ethiopian highlands'.[92]

The project at Mons Porphyrites – directed by David Peacock and Valerie Maxfield

374

– involved the survey and limited excavation of the Roman quarries spread over an area of some 6sq km in the inhospitable Red Sea Mountains between the Nile and the Red Sea, where the nearest settlement today is Hurghada, some 70km distant on the coast (fig 110). In this harsh environment, summer temperatures reach up to 114°F (45.6°C). These mountains were the source of imperial porphyry, a dark purple gem-like rock, much sought after in the Roman and Byzantine worlds; it was used at Rome by successive emperors in a variety of structural and decorative ways from the first century AD as well as later, in the Byzantine period, at Constantinople. Using both conventional ground survey and satellite imagery, the quarries and associated settlements and fort were planned and the technology of extraction studied in detail. Quarrying seems to have been continuous from the first to the late fourth or fifth century AD.[93] The Society contributed £20,000 to this project over the same four-year period as Aksum.

The last of the Society's 'grand' projects of the twentieth century was its support of the rescue excavations in Beirut, Lebanon, in the aftermath of the Civil War. Between 1997 and 1999 the Society contributed £25,000 to this project. Large areas of the city (the Souks development) were explored and important discoveries were made which were associated with different phases of the city throughout its life from between the pre-Hellenistic Iron Age and the recent, Ottoman period.[94] The first final report – on the coins – was published in 2003.[95]

With seriously diminished resources available to the Society for research at the close of the twentieth century, the three overseas projects of the 1990s were the last major grants to be awarded up to the time of writing. With Sutton Hoo, these were the largest grants (in real terms) ever to have been made by the Society.

How do we assess the impact of the Society's projects? At one level, as a record of an unrepeatable experiment, each may be considered to have an enduring value, but some of the projects have clearly made a greater impact than others. Collectively they have undoubtedly made an unparalleled contribution to our understanding of Roman Britain and the Late Iron Age of south-east Britain. Even though, for example, we know now that the Silchester excavations of 1890–1909 have only revealed a fraction of the story, leaving the greater part of the town undisturbed, the Society's project to excavate and record the Roman town within its late third-century walled circuit, which is very much the town of the later third and fourth century, remains pretty much unparalleled across the Roman world for its 'completeness'. Collectively, the excavations sponsored in varying degrees by the Society at Silchester, Caerwent and Wroxeter transformed knowledge and understanding of the town in Roman Britain at the beginning of the century, with the Wheelers' work in the 1930s at Verulamium furnishing a chronological dimension. Frere's work at Verulamium from 1955 added a further very significant strand to this aspect of the Society's research with its unravelling of the complex biographies of individual buildings across the town, as well as the history of the development of the city at large. To this record we may add, in particular, the massive contribution of the research at Hengistbury, Swarling, Camulodunum, Verulamium and Maiden Castle to our understanding of society in

Fig 110. Mons Porphyrites, Egypt: view of the Lykabettus quarry village, with paths to the fort and the north-west quarries; the Red Sea coastal plain can be seen in the distance. *Photograph*: © Valerie Maxfield and David Peacock.

south and south-east Britain in the first century BC and the early first century AD and its developing relations with the Gallic and Roman worlds. As we noted above, these sites have remained pivotal to our understanding of the period, their significance underlined by subsequent research, often with the Society's support.

Of lasting value, too, is the work undertaken at Richborough, which has contributed in a number of directions to our knowledge and understanding of Roman Britain. Beside Bushe-Fox's methodological innovations – with his pioneering of open-area excavation – we note the insights it has provided into the Claudian invasion and imperial perceptions of Britannia in the form of 'The Monument', on the one hand, and the operations of the *Classis Britannica*, the development of the forts of the 'Saxon Shore' and the origins of Christianity on the other. As part of the infra-structure of knowledge which underpins the study of Roman Britain, the publication of quantities of the associated finds in successive volumes has massively advanced our understanding of Roman material culture in Britain. Very recently the Society published the remarkable research by Bayley and Butcher on the technology and typology of the brooches from the excavations.[96] As for the site itself, the results of recent aerial and geophysical survey point to the further potential of the area beyond the third-century fortifications, which has yet to be realized by a new programme of research.[97] Finally, in this litany of classic sites of Roman Britain, we must include Lydney. Although much more is now known about Romano-British temple complexes and their associated cults and cult activities, Lydney remains in many respects *sui generis*, a site which cannot be ignored in any discussion of Romano-British religion or of Roman society on the westernmost periphery of the 'Romanized' world.

Although Late Iron Age and Romano-British archaeology dominated the Society's research agenda in the twentieth century, it cannot in any way diminish the lasting

376

significance of the Stonehenge and Maiden Castle projects for their contributions to our knowledge and understanding of later prehistoric society and its monuments in southern Britain. Likewise, the Society's Sutton Hoo project, arguably the only major medieval field investigation to be undertaken and published by the Society in this period, cannot safely be ignored in any consideration of the emergence of the Anglo-Saxon kingdoms at the turn of the sixth and seventh centuries. In this context a priority for the future should surely be to reassess the results of the excavations at Old Sarum and develop a new programme of research on this fascinating prehistoric and medieval site.

Until the brief period when significant resources were available to the Society in the 1980s and 1990s and it was possible to support research which would not otherwise easily attract funding, the Society's research in the shape of 'grand' projects in the period after the Second World War did not, overall, have the same impact as in the period up to 1939, partly as a result of the domination of at first state-sponsored, then developer-funded rescue archaeology. There was also caution in the commitment the Society felt able to give to projects in the second half of the century, even in the brief years of plenty. Before 1939 projects were often conceived and executed over ten-year periods. Indeed, before the First World War we find Silchester and Caerwent supported over, respectively, twenty and thirteen years. Between the wars we find a willingness to support ten-year-long campaigns as with Richborough, London and, potentially, Stonehenge, or projects with a duration of between five and ten years as at Colchester (Camulodunum) or, at a lesser level of grant, at sites such as Meare, Somerset, or Clarendon Palace, Wiltshire. Wheeler was unusual in only normally seeking support for up to three years (exceptionally four at Segontium and Verulamium). In the second half of the twentieth century we find that Cirencester and Sutton Hoo were the only projects to attract significant funding from the Society over a ten-year period. Projects aided with lesser grants were regularly supported for five-year periods, sometimes between five and ten as with Barry Cunliffe's Roman to post-medieval research at Portchester Castle, Hampshire, in the 1960s and 1970s and subsequently published as five Research Report volumes between 1975 and 1988.

With rising costs – both in undertaking fieldwork and completing reports for publication – and with reduced resources – whether from heritage agencies, universities, national museums or the Society – research archaeology at the beginning of the twenty-first century – whether sponsored by the Society or not – is at a low ebb. As it celebrates its tercentenary the Society needs urgently to consider how it can recover the undisputed pre-eminence it enjoyed in archaeological research in the years between 1890 and 1939.

ACKNOWLEDGEMENTS

I am very grateful to the Society's Librarian, Bernard Nurse, for his help with the research for this chapter and to Sheppard Frere and Martin Millett for their helpful suggestions to improve the contents. My thanks, too, to Katy Whitaker who was extremely helpful in the selection of illustrations from the National Monuments Record and to Martin Carver, Valerie Maxfield and Brendan Carr, at the Museum of Reading, for the illustrations that they very willingly supplied. Margaret Mathews, of the University of Reading, drew the location map.

NOTES

1. Boon 1974, 28–9, fig 2.
2. Fox and Hope 1891, 92–3.
3. May 1916.
4. Jones 1892.
5. Reid 1901; Boon 1974, 27–32; Fulford and Clarke 2002.
6. Boon 1974, 28.
7. Ibid, 27–32.
8. Wheeler 1954a, 127.
9. Bewley and Fulford 1996.
10. Cotton 1947.
11. Boon 1969.
12. Fulford and Timby 2000.
13. Fulford and Clarke 2002.
14. Clarke and Fulford 2002; Fulford *et al* 2006.
15. Brewer 1997.
16. Bushe-Fox 1913.
17. Bushe-Fox 1914 and 1916.
18. Bushe-Fox 1914.
19. *Proc Soc Antiq London*, 2nd ser, **23** (1909–11), 190–201, 501–18; **24** (1911–12), 52–65; **25** (1912–13), 93–104; **26** (1913–14), 100–19; **27** (1914–15), 230–8; **28** (1915–16), 174–84.
20. Bushe-Fox 1915.
21. Ibid, 72–83.
22. Cunliffe 1987.
23. Wheeler 1924.
24. Wheeler and Wheeler 1928.
25. Eg Dunning 1937.
26. Cottrill 1936.
27. Dunning 1945.
28. Eg Perring 1991, figs 3, 5, 15, 31.
29. Marsden 1987, 8–10, 82–5, fig 4.
30. Bushe-Fox 1926, 1928 and 1932.
31. Bushe-Fox 1949.
32. Cunliffe 1968.
33. Brown 1971.
34. White 1961; Johnson 1976; Johnston 1977; Pearson 2002.
35. Bushe-Fox 1949; see pls VI–IX.
36. Hawley 1921, 1922, 1923, 1924, 1925, 1926 and 1928.
37. Hawley 1928, 173–6.
38. Hawley 1925.
39. Thomas 1923.
40. Evans 1956, 398.
41. Research Committee Minutes, 32/1/48.
42. Atkinson 1979, 196.
43. Chippindale 2004, 179–83; Cleal *et al* 1995, 12–15, 17–19.
44. Cleal *et al* 1995, 102–7.
45. Bushe-Fox 1925, particularly 27–39.
46. Eg Hawkes and Dunning 1931; Birchall 1965; Rodwell 1976; Cunliffe 2005, 149–77.
47. Whiting *et al* 1931.
48. Wheeler and Wheeler 1932.
49. Bathurst and King 1879.
50. Casey and Hoffmann 1999.
51. Fulford 2002, 99–100.
52. Wheeler and Wheeler 1936, 4.
53. Frere 1983.
54. Wheeler and Wheeler 1936, 2–3.
55. Frere 1972, 1983 and 1984; see also Niblett and Thompson 2005.
56. Myres 1938; and Wheeler's reply (1938); Taylor 1938.
57. The figure given by Wheeler for the Society's contribution is actually £790. The difference between this and the Research Committee figures may be accounted for by additional allocations authorized directly by the Council.
58. Wheeler 1943.
59. Ibid, 2–3.
60. Hawkes 1931.
61. Wheeler 1943, 3–4.
62. Ibid, 4.
63. Cf Sharples 1991, 100–1.
64. Ibid.
65. Wheeler 1943, 18–24.
66. Wheeler and Richardson 1957, xiii.

67. Ibid, xv–xvi.
68. Wheeler 1954b.
69. Hawkes and Hull 1947.
70. Hawkes and Crummy 1995.
71. James and Robinson 1988.
72. See also p 397 in this volume.
73. Frere 1972.
74. Frere 1983 and 1984.
75. Cf Frere 1983, 1–25; see also Niblett and Thompson 2005.
76. Wilkinson and McWhirr 1998.
77. Wacher and McWhirr 1982.
78. Holbrook 1998.
79. Cunliffe 1971.
80. Ibid.
81. Bowen and Cunliffe 1973; Taylor 1973.
82. Papworth 1874. The Society received a bequest in 1926 to prepare a new edition and the result is the *Dictionary of British Arms: medieval ordinary* which the Society is publishing in four volumes, with volumes I (1992) and II (1996) being published so far. An ordinary, in this context, is a collection of arms arranged alphabetically according to their designs, as opposed to an armory which is arranged alphabetically by surname.
83. Rahtz 1976; Rahtz and Watts 1997.
84. Bowen and Smith 1977.
85. Palmer 1984.
86. Rodwell and Rodwell 1985.
87. As note 72.
88. Bruce-Mitford 1975–83.
89. Carver 1998 and 2005.
90. Phillipson 2000.
91. Ibid, i.
92. Ibid, 486–7.
93. Maxfield and Peacock 2001.
94. Perring 1999 and 2003.
95. Butcher 2003.
96. Bayley and Butcher 2004.
97. Millett and Wilmott 2003.

BIBLIOGRAPHY

Atkinson, R J C 1979. *Stonehenge*, 3rd edn, London

Bathurst, W H and King, C W 1879. *Roman Antiquities at Lydney Park, Gloucestershire*, London

Bayley, J and Butcher, S 2004. *Roman Brooches in Britain: a technological and typological study based on the Richborough collection*, Rep Res Comm Soc Antiq London 68, London

Bewley, R and Fulford, M 1996. 'Aerial photography and the plan of Silchester (*Calleva Atrebatum*)', *Britannia*, **27**, 387–8

Birchall, A 1965. 'The Aylesford–Swarling culture: the problem of the Belgae reconsidered', *Proc Prehist Soc*, **31**, 241–367

Boon, G C 1969. 'Belgic and Roman Silchester: the excavations of 1954–8, with an excursus on the early history of Calleva', *Archaeologia*, **102**, 1–82

Boon, G C 1974. *Silchester: the Roman town of Calleva*, Newton Abbot

Bowen, H C and Cunliffe, B 1973. 'The Society's research projects: 1. the evolution of the landscape', *Antiq J*, **53**, 9–13

Bowen, H C and Smith, I F 1977. 'Sarsen stones in Wessex: the Society's first investigations in the evolution of the landscape project', *Antiq J*, **57**, 185–96

Brewer, R J 1997. *Caerwent Roman Town*, 2nd edn, Cardiff

Brewer, R J (ed) 2002. *Birthday of the Eagle: the Second Augustan Legion and the Roman military machine*, Cardiff

Brown, P D C 1971. 'The church at Richborough', *Britannia*, **2**, 225–31

Bruce-Mitford, R 1975–83. *The Sutton Hoo Ship Burial*, 3 vols, London

Bushe-Fox, J P 1913. *Excavations on the Site of the Roman Town at Wroxeter, Shropshire, in 1912*, Rep Res Comm Soc Antiq London 1, Oxford

Bushe-Fox, J P 1914. *Second Report on the Excavations on the Site of the Roman Town at Wroxeter, Shropshire, 1913*, Rep Res Comm Soc Antiq London 2, Oxford

Bushe-Fox, J P 1915. *Excavations at Hengistbury Head, Hampshire, in 1911–12*, Rep Res Comm Soc Antiq London 3, Oxford

Bushe-Fox, J P 1916. *Third Report on the Excavations on the Site of the Roman Town at Wroxeter, Shropshire, 1914*, Rep Res Comm Soc Antiq London 4, Oxford

Bushe-Fox, J P 1925. *Excavation of the Late-Celtic Urn-field at Swarling, Kent*, Rep Res Comm Soc Antiq London 5, Oxford

Bushe-Fox, J P 1926. *First Report on the Excavation of the Roman Fort at Richborough, Kent*, Rep Res Comm Soc Antiq London 6, Oxford

Bushe-Fox, J P 1928. *Second Report on the Excavation of the Roman Fort at Richborough, Kent*, Rep Res Comm Soc Antiq London 7, Oxford

Bushe-Fox, J P 1932. *Third Report on the Excavations of the Roman Fort at Richborough, Kent*, Rep Res Comm Soc Antiq London 10, Oxford

Bushe-Fox, J P 1949. *Fourth Report on the Excavations of the Roman Fort at Richborough, Kent*, Rep Res Comm Soc Antiq London 16, Oxford

Butcher, K 2003. *Archaeology of the Beirut Souks: Aub and Acre excavations in Beirut, 1994–1996. 1: Small Change in Ancient Beirut: the coin finds from Bey 006 and Bey 045: Persian, Hellenistic, Roman, and Byzantine periods*, Berytus Archaeological Studies 45 and 46, Beirut

Carver, M O H 1998. *Sutton Hoo: burial ground of kings?*, London

Carver, M O H 2005. *Sutton Hoo: a seventh-century princely burial ground and its context*, Rep Res Comm Soc Antiq London 69, London

Casey, P J and Hoffmann, B 1999. 'Excavations at the Roman temple in Lydney Park, Gloucestershire, in 1980 and 1981', *Antiq J*, **79**, 81–143

Chippindale, C 2004. *Stonehenge Complete*, 2nd edn, London

Clarke, A and Fulford, M 2002. 'The excavation of insula IX, Silchester: the first five years of the "Town Life" project, 1997–2001', *Britannia*, **33**, 129–66

Cleal, R M J, Walker, K E and Montague, R 1995. *Stonehenge in its Landscape: twentieth-century excavations*, Engl Heritage Archaeol Rep 10, London

Cotton, M A 1947. 'Excavations at Silchester', *Archaeologia*, **92**, 121–68

Cottrill, F 1936. 'A bastion of the town wall of London, and the sepulchral monument of the procurator, Julius Classicianus', *Antiq J*, **16**, 1–7

Cunliffe, B (ed) 1968. *Fifth Report on the Excavations of the Roman Fort at Richborough, Kent*, Rep Res Comm Soc Antiq London 23, Oxford

Cunliffe, B 1971. *Excavations at Fishbourne 1961–1969. 1: The Site; 2: The Finds*, Rep Res Comm Soc Antiq London 26, Leeds

Cunliffe, B 1987. *Hengistbury Head Dorset. 1: The Prehistoric and Roman Settlement, 3500 BC–AD 500*, Oxford Univ Comm Archaeol Monogr 13, Oxford

Cunliffe, B 2005. *Iron Age Communities in Britain*, 4th edn, London and New York

Cunliffe, B and Rowley, T 1976. *Oppida: the beginnings of urbanism in barbarian Europe*, BAR Int Ser 11, Oxford

Dunning, G C 1937. 'A fourteenth-century well at the Bank of England', *Antiq J*, **17**, 414–18

Dunning, G C 1945. 'Two fires of Roman London', *Antiq J*, **25**, 48–77

Evans, J 1956. *A History of the Society of Antiquaries*, Oxford

Fox, G E 1892. 'Excavations on the site of the Roman city at Silchester, Hants, in 1891', *Archaeologia*, **53**/2, 263–88

Fox, G E and Hope, W H St John 1891. 'Communication of 27th February 1890', *Proc Soc Antiq London*, 2nd ser, **13**, 85–97

Fox, G E and Hope, W H St John 1901. 'Excavations on the site of the Roman city at Silchester, Hants, in 1900', *Archaeologia*, **57**/2, 229–56

Frere, S 1972. *Verulamium Excavations. Vol 1*, Rep Res Comm Soc Antiq London 28, Oxford

Frere, S 1983. *Verulamium Excavations. Vol 2*, Rep Res Comm Soc Antiq London 41, London

Frere, S 1984. *Verulamium Excavations. Vol 3*, Oxford Univ Comm Archaeol Monogr 1, Oxford

Fulford, M G 2002. 'The Second Augustan Legion in the west of Britain', in Brewer (ed) 2002, 83–102

Fulford, M G and Clarke, A 2002. 'Victorian excavation methodology: the Society of Antiquaries at Silchester in 1893', *Antiq J*, **82**, 285–306

Fulford, M G, Clarke, A and Eckardt, H 2006. *Life and Labour in Late Roman Silchester: excavations on insula IX from 1997. Vol 1*, Britannia Monogr Ser 22, London

Fulford, M G and Timby, J 2000. *Late Iron Age and Roman Silchester: excavations on the site of the forum basilica 1977, 1980–86*, Britannia Monogr Ser 15, London

Hawkes, C F C 1931. 'Hill forts', *Antiquity*, **5**, 60–97

Hawkes, C F C and Crummy, P 1995. *Camulodunum 2*, Colchester Archaeol Rep 11, Colchester

Hawkes, C F C and Dunning, G C 1931. 'The Belgae of Gaul and Britain', *Archaeol J*, **87**, 150–335

Hawkes, C F C and Hull, M R 1947. *Camulodunum: first report on the excavations at Colchester 1930–1939*, Rep Res Comm Soc Antiq London 14, Oxford

Hawley, W 1921. 'The excavations at Stonehenge', *Antiq J*, **1**, 19–41

Hawley, W 1922. 'Second report on the excavations at Stonehenge', *Antiq J*, **2**, 36–52

Hawley, W 1923. 'Third report on the excavations at Stonehenge', *Antiq J*, **3**, 13–20

Hawley, W 1924. 'Fourth report on the excavations at Stonehenge', *Antiq J*, **4**, 30–9

Hawley, W 1925. 'Report on the excavations at Stonehenge during the season of 1923', *Antiq J*, **5**, 21–50

Hawley, W 1926. 'Report on the excavations at Stonehenge during the season of 1924', *Antiq J*, **6**, 1–25

Hawley, W 1928. 'Report on the excavations at Stonehenge during 1925 and 1926', *Antiq J*, **8**, 149–76

Holbrook, N 1998. *Cirencester: the Roman town defences, public buildings and shops*, Cirencester Excavations 5, Cirencester

James, T B and Robinson, A M 1988. *Clarendon Palace: the history and archaeology of a medieval palace and hunting lodge near Salisbury, Wiltshire*, Rep Res

Comm Soc Antiq London 45, London

Johnson, S 1976. *The Roman Forts of the Saxon Shore*, London

Johnston, D E 1977. *The Saxon Shore*, CBA Res Rep 18, London

Jones, H 1892. 'Note on the animal remains found during excavations at Silchester, 1891', in Fox 1892, 285–8

Marsden, P 1987. *The Roman Forum Site in London: discoveries before 1985*, London

May, T 1916. *The Pottery Found at Silchester*, Reading

Maxfield, V and Peacock, D 2001. *The Roman Imperial Quarries Survey and Excavation at Mons Porphyrites, 1994–1998. 1: Topography and Quarries*, Excavation Memoir 67, London

Millett, M and Wilmott, T 2003. 'Rethinking Richborough', in Wilson (ed) 2003, 184–94

Myres, J N L 1938. 'Verulamium', *Antiquity*, 12, 16–25

Niblett, R and Thompson, I 2005. *Alban's Buried Towns: an assessment of St Albans' archaeology up to AD 1600*, Oxford

Palmer, R 1984. *Danebury: an Iron Age hillfort in Hampshire. An aerial photographic interpretation of its environs*, Roy Comm Hist Monuments Engl Suppl Ser 6, London

Papworth, J W (ed A W W Morant) 1874. *An Alphabetical Dictionary of Coats of Arms Belonging to Families in Great Britain and Ireland; forming an extensive ordinary of British armorials*, London

Pearson, A 2002. *The Roman Shore Forts: coastal defences of southern Britain*, Stroud

Perring, D 1991. *Roman London*, London

Perring, D 1999. 'Excavations in the souks of Beirut: an introduction to the work of the Anglo-Lebanese team and summary report', *Berytus*, 43, 9–34

Perring, D 2003. 'The archaeology of Beirut: a report on work in the insula of the House of the Fountains', *Antiq J*, 83, 195–229

Phillipson, D W 2000. *Archaeology at Aksum, Ethiopia, 1993–7*, 2 vols, Rep Res Comm Soc Antiq London 65, London

Rahtz, P 1976. *Excavations at St Mary's Church, Deerhurst, 1971–73*, CBA Res Rep 15, London

Rahtz, P and Watts, L 1997. *St Mary's Church, Deerhurst, Gloucestershire: fieldwork, excavations and structural analysis, 1971–1984*, Rep Res Comm Soc Antiq London 55, Woodbridge

Reid, C 1901. 'Notes on the plant remains of Roman Silchester', in Fox and Hope 1901, 252–6

Rodwell, W J 1976. 'Coinage, oppida and the rise of Belgic power in south-eastern Britain', in Cunliffe and Rowley 1976, 181–367

Rodwell, W J and Rodwell, K A 1985. *Rivenhall: investigations of a villa, church, and village*, CBA Res Rep 55, London

Sharples, N M 1991. *Maiden Castle: excavations and field survey 1985–6*, Engl Heritage Archaeol Rep 19, London

Taylor, H M 1973. 'The Society's research projects: 2. archaeological investigation of churches in Great Britain', *Antiq J*, 53, 13–15

Taylor, M V 1938. 'Review of R E M Wheeler and T V Wheeler, *Verulamium: A Belgic and Two Roman Cities*, Rep Res Comm Soc Antiq London 11, Oxford, 1936', *J Roman Stud* 28, 107–8

Thomas, H H 1923. 'The source of the stones of Stonehenge', *Antiq J*, 3, 239–60

Wacher, J S and McWhirr, A D 1982. *Early Roman Occupation at Cirencester*, Cirencester Excavations 1, Cirencester

Wheeler, R E M 1924. *Segontium and the Roman Occupation of Wales*, London

Wheeler, R E M 1938. 'Mr Myres on Verulamium', *Antiquity*, 12, 210–17

Wheeler, R E M 1943. *Maiden Castle, Dorset*, Rep Res Comm Soc Antiq London 12, Oxford

Wheeler, R E M 1954a. *Archaeology from the Earth*, Oxford

Wheeler, R E M 1954b. *The Stanwick Fortifications*, Rep Res Comm Soc Antiq London 17, Oxford

Wheeler, R E M and Richardson, K M 1957. *Hill-Forts of Northern France*, Rep Res Comm Soc Antiq London 19, Oxford

Wheeler, R E M and Wheeler, T V 1928. 'The Roman amphitheatre at Caerleon', *Archaeologia*, 78, 111–218

Wheeler, R E M and Wheeler, T V 1932. *Report on the Excavation of the Prehistoric, Roman, and Post-Roman Site in Lydney Park, Gloucestershire*, Rep Res Comm Soc Antiq London 9, Oxford

Wheeler, R E M and Wheeler, T V 1936. *Verulamium: a Belgic and two Roman cities*, Rep Res Comm Soc Antiq London 11, Oxford

White, D A 1961. *Litus Saxonicum: the British Saxon Shore in scholarship and history*, Madison, Wisc

Whiting, W, Hawley, W and May, T 1931. *Report on the Excavation of the Roman Cemetery at Ospringe, Kent*, Rep Res Comm Soc Antiq London 8, Oxford

Wilkinson, D and McWhirr, A D 1998. *Cirencester Anglo-Saxon Church and Medieval Abbey*, Cirencester Excavations 4, Cirencester

Wilson, P (ed) 2003. *The Archaeology of Roman Towns: studies in honour of John S Wacher*, Oxford

CHAPTER FIFTEEN

CHANGING ROLES AND AGENDAS: THE SOCIETY OF ANTIQUARIES AND THE PROFESSIONALIZATION OF ARCHAEOLOGY, 1950–2000

Graeme Barker

In the first half of the twentieth century very few people in Britain earned their livelihood as professional archaeologists; those who did were mostly to be found in the old universities, the great museums and such public bodies as the Royal Commissions and the Ancient Monuments Inspectorate of HM Office of Works. J N L Myres estimated that there were probably no more than twenty-five to thirty such professionals when he was an undergraduate in the early 1920s;[1] and, according to Sir Mortimer Wheeler, 'when your President first attained to Fellowship [in 1922], there may have been scarcely more than a couple of dozen professional archaeologists in our active ranks. The British Museum supplied three or four, the Office of Works one or two, the Royal Commission and the Victoria County History perhaps half a dozen between them. A small – very small – scattering could be added from the universities'.[2] Archaeology was a subject pursued largely by people of independent means, or by people using their leisure time in an amateur capacity, people who still dominated the Society's Fellowship of *c* 900 in 1950.

In a recent survey, by contrast, the Institute of Field Archaeology estimated that more than 5,000 people in Britain earned their living as archaeologists,[3] mostly in developer-funded field archaeology, alongside unpaid volunteers and independent archaeologists. There are now over 500 permanent lecturing staff in British universities teaching and researching in the subject, and the Council for British Archaeology has over 600 entries in its 'institutional membership' category. Before the radio quiz programme *Animal, Vegetable, or Mineral?* brought archaeology to a wide audience in the 1950s, making Mortimer Wheeler (fig 111) and Glyn Daniel household names, the popular dissemination of archaeology was restricted largely to occasional articles in such magazines as the *Illustrated London News* and to public lectures arranged by museums and organizations such as the Workers Educational Association. Today, archaeological or archaeology-derived programmes on radio and television achieve mass audiences.

A transformation of prime importance in the practice of archaeology has been the expansion of university archaeology and – in parallel – of funding opportunities from government research councils, charities and learned societies in support of the research work of university-based archaeologists. Another has been the growth

Fig 111. Mortimer Wheeler, President of the Society of Antiquaries of London, 1954–9. *Photograph*: Society of Antiquaries of London.

of national and local government infrastructures: English Heritage, Cadw, Historic Scotland and the Department of the Environment in Northern Ireland (DOENI), and historic environment services within planning departments in local government and national parks. One of the most profound alterations to the landscape has been the establishment of developer-funded commercial 'units' attached to local government or universities, or operating as independent trusts and charities, as well as of independent consultants. Another has been the development of 'rival' national organizations such as the Council for British Archaeology (established in 1944) and the Institute of Field Archaeologists (1982), and of a large number of specialist learned societies with period interests, such as the Association of Industrial Archaeology and the Society for Post-Medieval Archaeology, or with methodological interests such as the Association for Environmental Archaeology, the Society for Landscape Studies, and so on. Yet another has been the establishment after the Second World War of new British Schools and Institutes abroad with a significant commitment to archaeological research.

So while the landscape within and directly outside Burlington House may not have changed much since 1950, the wider British archaeological landscape has certainly undergone tumultuous change. The purpose of this chapter is to offer some reflections on how the Society has fared amidst this process of enlargement and fragmentation that has so greatly affected the practice and understanding of archaeology in Britain during the second half of the twentieth century. To explore these questions, the chapter will concentrate on four topics: the key themes and issues of the day, and particular achievements of the Society, as identified by successive Presidents in their Anniversary Addresses; the constituency of the Fellowship; the use made of research funds awarded for archaeology; and the track record of the Society in publishing archaeological materials and findings of national and international significance.

'ITEMS OF CURRENT CONCERN': THE ANNIVERSARY ADDRESS, 1950–2000

For the last fifty years of the twentieth century, the President of the Society (table 10) has delivered an Anniversary Address on the Thursday closest to St George's Day. Until 1990 this was subsequently published in the *Antiquaries Journal* for that year, while between 1990 and 1999 it formed part of a separate Annual Report. The traditional format of the Anniversary Address includes a mixture of reflections on issues of the day of concern to the Society together with comments on the general health of the Society, on notable Fellows who had died in the preceding year and on particular activities of the Society since the preceding Address – major events, publications, meetings, gold medal-winners (table 11) and so on.

In the early 1950s, in the aftermath of the Second World War, a principal issue of concern was the state of many of the nation's major buildings, both ecclesiastical and secular, as a result of bomb damage, disrepair and neglect, and the threat to many

TABLE 10: PRESIDENTS OF THE SOCIETY BETWEEN 1950 AND 2000

President	Period of office	President	Period of office
James Mann	1949–54	Richard Dufty	1978–81
Mortimer Wheeler	1954–9	Christopher Brooke	1981–4
Joan Evans	1959–64	John Davies Evans	1984–7
Ian Richmond	1964	Michael Robbins	1987–91
Francis Wormald	1965–70	Barry Cunliffe	1991–5
J N L Myres	1970–5	Simon Jervis	1995–2001
Arnold Taylor	1975–8		

Table 10. The Presidents of the Society between 1950 and 2000

TABLE 11: GOLD MEDALLISTS OF THE SOCIETY, 1950–2000

1950	Albert van Giffen	Dutch prehistory
1952	Sir Cyril Fox	British prehistory
1954	Johannes Brønsted	Early medieval archaeology
1956	Gordon Childe	European prehistory
1958	Claude Schaeffer	Near Eastern prehistory
1960	Leonard Woolley	Mesopotamian archaeology
1962	Gerhard Bersu	European prehistory
1964	Harold Plenderleith	Museum conservation
1966	Carl Blegen	Aegean prehistory
1968	Dorothy Garrod	Palaeolithic archaeology
1970	Sirarpie Der Nersessian	Armenian art
1972	Ralegh Radford	British archaeology
1973	Joan Evans	Medieval studies
1976	J N L Myres	British archaeology
1977	Donald Harden	Medieval archaeology
1978	Grahame Clark	World prehistory
1981	Christopher Hawkes	European prehistory
1983	Stuart Piggott	European prehistory
1985	Desmond Clark	African prehistory
1986	George Zarnecki	Romanesque art
1988	Arnold Taylor	Conservation, British archaeology
1989	Sheppard Frere	Romano-British archaeology
1990	Thurston Shaw	African archaeology
1995	David Wilson	Medieval archaeology
1997	Philip Grierson	Numismatics
1998	Claude Blair	Armoury
2000	Gordon Willey	American archaeology

Table 11. Gold Medallists of the Society, 1950–2000, and their principal fields of expertise

that remained from uncontrolled post-war reconstruction. As Sir James Mann (fig 112) commented in his 1950 Address: 'the future of empty country houses and redundant churches is cause for the greatest anxiety. It is not generally realized, not even in this room, that more fine buildings have been demolished by the house-breaker since the war than were destroyed by enemy action, or for that matter wrecked by the military.'[4] He reported how, at the request of Council, he had put together an informal committee to lobby the government's Gowers Commission, set up to review the state of, and threats to, the architectural heritage. Lobbying of this kind eventually led to the passing of the Historic Buildings and Ancient Monuments Act in 1953 and the establishment of the Historic Buildings Council to advise Government on the allocation of grants towards the repair and upkeep of buildings of outstanding interest. In 1952 he was also able to report that four Fellows had been invited to join a special commission set up by the Archbishop of Canterbury to report on the state of the Church of England's estate; and in 1954 that the Society could take pride in its role in persuading the archbishop to establish the Historic Churches Preservation Trust and the Ministry of Works, following the Gowers Report, to establish the Historic Buildings Council.[5]

The second issue of national concern identified by Sir James was the need for improved legislation to control the export of works of art and antiquities. Several Fellows of the Society gave evidence to the government's Anderson Commission

Fig 112. James Mann, President of the Society of Antiquaries of London, 1949–54. *Photograph*: Society of Antiquaries of London.

addressing this problem, and the resulting legislation, exempting the chattels of houses handed over to the National Trust from death duties, was seen as a useful development to help reduce the flow of antiquities abroad, though the problem was clearly more widespread.[6]

As the decade advanced, the threats to the archaeological, as well as architectural, heritage were also being emphasized, though one silver lining in the cloud of destruction noted by Sir James in 1950 was the opportunity presented by post-war reconstruction for archaeologists to explore ancient towns such as London, Canterbury and Southampton. In 1954 he highlighted the increasing rate of destruction to the archaeological heritage in the countryside from mechanized farming and the ploughing up of grassland as well as urban expansion,[7] a point reiterated by Sir Mortimer Wheeler in 1955. In his final Address, though, Wheeler concentrated on the role of British archaeology abroad. He praised the importance of the current archaeological research of the British Schools abroad, and in announcing the setting up of the British Institute in East Africa, he called for the establishment of further schools of archaeology: 'vital regions such as trans-Saharan Africa, Iran, the Indo-Pakistan subcontinent and Ceylon, [and] the Far East are at present unprovided with these ambassadorial instruments of research'.[8] He made no apologies for this 'catholic and international note': in a world driven by nationalist partisanship, he said, archaeology constituted 'a humane link of the best possible kind between nations',[9] it was a force for good on political as well as academic grounds, and the Society needed 'to nurture an international perspective as never before'.[10]

When Joan Evans took office as the Society's first woman President in 252 years, she focused most of her first (1960) Address on fulsome praise of her predecessor, and of Sir Leonard Woolley, to whom the Society had awarded its Gold Medal, but who had died before he could receive it. One intellectual development she lamented was the focus of the new generation of medieval archaeologists 'on a few plans of cow-sheds and . . . rims of cooking pots' rather than on fine architecture, painting, and iconography,[11] thus giving us an inkling of the contemporary perception that the New Archaeology of the 1960s was a threat to traditional culture history. In 1962 Evans's principal theme was the appalling destruction of the built environment that was proceeding apace in the name of progress in most of Britain's historic towns and cities.[12] In those with the most philistine Planning Officers, she lamented, any building more than a hundred years old was fair game for destruction to make way for a ring road, a municipal car park, or 'modern buildings in the biscuit-box style' (most of which, thankfully, are now coming down). The priority for British research funds surely had to be the archaeology of Britain: 'I find it perfectly ridiculous that England should even consider spending millions on paying an Italian firm to lift a second-rate temple at Abu Simbel when we are told every month that she cannot afford thousands for the investigation, maintenance, and preservation of the monuments of England.'[13] So much for Wheeler's internationalist agenda!

Organizational reforms in what are now the British Museum, the Natural History Museum and the Science Museum dominated her 1963 and 1964 Addresses (she was a trustee of the British Museum), though her enthusiasm for these reforms contrasted with an other-worldly regret at the gathering pace of expansion in state education: 'I confess to a certain fear that our admittedly difficult and advanced disciplines may tend to be swamped in primary and secondary education and in the development of new Universities and Technical Colleges. The Treasury was – and is – often mean, but at least its officers tend to have acquired firsts at Oxford or Cambridge in Classics or History.'[14] This now seems somewhat beside the point in the face of the accelerating challenge posed to archaeological sites by development work throughout the 1960s.

By 1974 – a year of major restructuring in local government – public funding for rescue archaeology had been greatly increased and the British archaeological landscape was changing dramatically with the rapid and somewhat chaotic development of organizations responding to the new needs and opportunities – a situation described to the Fellowship by the President, J N L Myres (fig 113), as 'unfamiliar, and sometimes ill-defined, concepts such as "archaeological units", "regional committees", "co-ordinated support facilities", and the like'.[15] There was great uncertainty about the respective obligations of central and local government in the financing of the rescue work, and it was clear that a variety of different types of organizations and collaborations was going to have to develop in response to local circumstances. The key lessons for the Society, in Myres's view, were to welcome the new developments for the greatly increased investment in archaeological research they represented, to continue to promote the contribution of the non-professional sector, to resist any trend for a state monopoly in the control and financing of field archaeology and to be confident

Fig 113. J N L Myres, President of the Society of Antiquaries of London, 1970–5. *Photograph*: Society of Antiquaries of London.

in the continued importance of the Society's support for the latter. He also advocated the need for an accreditation service for the increasing numbers of professional field archaeologists working in rescue archaeology, a need that was to lead to the establishment of the Institute of Field Archaeologists in 1982.

The first Anniversary Address of the 1980s, the decade that was to close with the ending of the Cold War and the collapse of the Berlin Wall, began with some grim comments from the President on the new barbarism of international terrorism, on the one hand, and the need for the West 'to remain on the alert, mindful of the great Russian bear and his enveloping hug which shuts out the light'[16] on the other. Closer to home, though, the principal barbarian at the gate, at least in terms of the threat to the nation's heritage, appeared to be the government of Margaret Thatcher, and in the following years Richard Dufty reported on the substantial dismantling of the heritage conservation structures of the 1970s: the stricter application of project funding for archaeological units, the dissolution of Area Advisory Committees, the elimination of 'quangos' such as the Hadrian's Wall Committee, the closure of several Historic Monuments, the postponement of state aid for church maintenance and the withdrawal of Britain's subscription to the International Centre for the Study of the Preservation and Restoration of Cultural Property (ICCROM). Museum purchasing funds went unspent because regional museums had to match purchase grants from government pound for pound – but were unable to do so because of cuts to their running budgets, which promptly led the government to reduce the grant by a third – 'a glimpse into the Alice-in-Wonderland world we live in . . . our heritage is under threat, make no mistake'.[17] In 1982 it was the turn of the universities to take major cuts in government funding, which the Society protested about.[18]

But the main issue of the day was the government's consultation paper regarding the setting up of new independent heritage agencies in England, Scotland, Wales and Northern Ireland that was to lead to the eventual formation of English Heritage and its equivalents in Scotland, Wales and Northern Ireland in 1984. The Society was divided in opinion about the proposed reform, though some Fellows saw it as the opportunity to create, at last, 'a state archaeological service covering effectively the whole area of archaeology and conservation'[19] – but they were united in pointing to the shortcomings of the consultation document: 'It is superficial, since it treats briefly and cursorily of complex issues on which deeper, more expert advice could readily be found [ie within the Society!]; and immature, since it suggests that such a superficial examination may be the basis for legislation.'[20] By a curious coincidence the new Heritage Bill was read in Parliament on the same day (11 November 1982) that the Society received a visitation from its two recently elected Royal Fellows, the Prince of Wales and the Duke of Gloucester. They were greeted by a small demonstration of Department of Environment staff, though the Secretary of State, Michael Heseltine, cannily arrived after the protestors had dispersed.[21] A main concern of the Society was that the new organization 'sees clearly from the start that among its first and highest aims must be to sustain and enhance the dedicated scholarly standards – academic in the good sense of the term – for which the Department has been celebrated, if not for the whole of its hundred years, for at least two generations of them'.[22]

The new Historic Buildings and Monuments Commission for England (branded 'English Heritage') came into existence on 1 April 1984. Though the Society took comfort from the fact that several senior staff – including the Chief Inspector, the Deputy Chief Inspector and its own new Director (Geoffrey Wainwright) – were all Fellows, Christopher Brooke, President at the time, observed that: 'It has yet to prove that enhanced showmanship and commercialism are compatible with the care and skill and scholarship which have been so great a tradition in the former Inspectorate.'[23] The commercialism of the emergent 'heritage industry' was the main theme of John Evans's Address in 1987 – both the activities of English Heritage in encouraging heritage tourism and also the development of private tourist centres along the lines of the Jorvik Viking Centre. Whatever its innate misgivings about the treatment of heritage as a tourist commodity, the Society responded positively enough to a request from Chester City Council for advice concerning a proposed development, particularly on the importance of monument conservation as well as presentation. The tension between the needs of scholarship and of conservation on the one hand, and the demands of commercialism on the other, returned in Michael Robbins's Anniversary Address in 1989. He probably summed up much opinion when he said: 'Our duty . . . as Fellows of this Society must therefore, as I see it, be in general to welcome the broadening of the base of public interest and support so long as we do not succumb to the temptation to give way at any point touching the fundamental issue of the integrity of knowledge and the way it is presented.'[24]

In his first Address, in 1992, Barry Cunliffe (fig 114) celebrated the burgeoning interest in the study and conservation of the heritage between the 1950s and the 1980s, the numbers of organizations involved and their growing professionalism, but he chided the Society for how it had sometimes responded through those years: 'the Society did, I think, begin to lose its way. It showed a tendency to become withdrawn and, on occasions, not a little tetchy'.[25] A sign of the Society taking the lead on issues of current debate was the seminar organized with the Museums Association in 1991 to address the increasing storage crisis in Britain's museums, and the publication backlog caused by the deluge of excavated material. This led to the widely circulated report *Archaeological Publication, Archives, and Collections: towards a national policy*, recommending, among other things, that field report publications should consist of a printed summary accompanied by a curated site archive, that regional repositories of finds needed to be established and that rigorous selection needed to be conducted on materials proposed for permanent retention.

Another was the lobbying of Government on Treasure Trove legislation, the possible detrimental effects of local government reorganization on Sites and Monuments Records, Museum Services and Archive Services and the case for investing a percentage of the proceeds of the new National Lottery in research. Full support was given to the Treasure Bill being prepared by the Society's Fellows Lord Perth and Sir Patrick Cormack, though the Society would have preferred a more fundamental review of portable antiquities legislation. In collaboration with the Council for British

Fig 114. Barry Cunliffe, President of the Society of Antiquaries of London, 1991–5. *Photograph*: reproduced by permission of Tony Knight: <www.peopleandplacespics.com>.

Archaeology and the Museums Association, the Society prepared a set of guiding principles for such legislation, and commended them to the Secretary of State for National Heritage: that all objects of antiquarian interest found in the ground should in the first instance be regarded as Crown property and reported for recording; that those designated of national importance should be retained and the finder/landowner fully compensated; and that the remainder should be returned to the finder/landowner. To the Society's immense frustration the bill foundered in 1995, but was finally passed in 1996.

The day after the President's 1993 Address, the Department of the Environment arrived in the Society's rooms to hold the first of a series of consultative meetings to consider alternative routes for the A303 past Stonehenge: 'It is a noble vision to think of Stonehenge on the last day of the twentieth century freed at last from its strangling and disfiguring clutter of roads.'[26] The Society was involved over the next decade in the continued lobbying by the archaeological community for a planning solution that would do justice to the preservation and presentation needs of the World Heritage Site.[27]

By the middle of the decade, the mix of benefits and distortions in Britain's heritage industry represented by the Lottery Fund was becoming ever clearer. The *modus operandi* worked out over previous decades by the complex mix of governmental, quasi-governmental, charitable and quasi-private bodies was being completely destabilized by the 'emergence of a new and potentially dominant set of institutions, the Lottery distributors'.[28] The application-led process was obviously not conducive to the development of strategy, the requirement for matching funding had the potential to distort priorities, and it was already apparent that several projects were likely to founder from lack of revenue. The government's policy of free admission to the great public museums, though, was warmly supported by the Society.[29] On the other hand, the demise of the Royal Commission on the Historical Monuments of England in 1999, with its incorporation into English Heritage, was greeted with wariness, though not hostility: 'amalgamation and centralization invariably look good on paper . . . but there is a danger that the skills that the Commission has built up over the years may be diluted or diverted within a larger organization. We trust not.'[30]

THE FELLOWSHIP

In 1950 the Society's membership stood at about 900; it reached 1,000 by 1960, 1,500 in 1980 and over 2,000 in 2000. To gain insights into whether or not the character of the Society's membership altered significantly through this period, alongside its more than doubling in size, the information contained in the summary *curriculum vitae* paragraphs (a dozen lines of text, mostly handwritten) of a sample of Election Certificates has been reviewed. The sample consisted of the 898 certificates balloted upon in the years 1951–5, 1971–5 and 1991–5. In the first of these quinquennia, the smallest number of candidates elected in a year was thirty-two (in 1953), the largest (sixty-eight) in 1951, the average being forty-four. The corresponding figures were sixty-five, eighty-six and seventy-one in the 1970s quinquennium, and sixty, eighty-four and sixty-five in the 1990s quinquennium.

The information on the certificates was grouped under four headings. The first set consisted of the sex of the applicant, the category of the application (for Ordinary or Honorary Fellowship) and the result. Most applications and elections were for Ordinary membership, with a single *honoris causa* candidate being included under the Honorary category. The second set of information referred to the place of residence. The third category was the field of study that could be construed from the biographical text and cited publications. The final set of information was the nature of the applicant's employment.

Following the 1919 Sex Disqualification (Removal) Act of Parliament ('a person shall not be disqualified by sex or marriage from the exercise of any public office'), women were first elected to the Fellowship in 1921. The numbers remained very small, but through our period of review, elections of female members have at least climbed from 12 per cent in the 1950s to 18 per cent in the 1990s, and are continuing to rise (table 12), though the total female membership only increased from 15 per cent (195 individuals) in 1976 to nearly 17 per cent (329 individuals) in 1990. In 2004 women made up nearly 27.5 per cent of the Fellowship (475 women and 1,731 men). Female representation in the Fellowship in recent decades compares reasonably favourably with the British Academy, the premier learned society in the UK for researchers in the humanities and social sciences: in 1993 only 7.4 per cent of its total membership (Ordinary Fellows and Senior Fellows aggregated) was female, though the figure has since risen to 12.8 per cent. The 18 per cent figure for new female elections to the Society in the 1990s, and the overall membership of 17 per cent, compared even more

TABLE 12: ELECTIONS TO THE FELLOWSHIP, 1951–95						
	1951–5 (no.)	*1951–5 (%)*	*1971–5 (no.)*	*1971–5 (%)*	*1991–5 (no.)*	*1991–5 (%)*
Male (Ordinary), successful	174	86.1	258	78.2	255	79.7
Female (Ordinary), successful	25	12.4	46	13.9	59	18.4
Male (Honorary), successful	3	1.5	25	7.6	6	1.9
Female (Honorary), successful	–	–	1	0.3	–	–
Male, unsuccessful	15	7.8	19	6.3	6	2.3
Female, unsuccessful	2	7.4	4	8.0	–	–
Total	219		353		326	

Table 12. Successful and unsuccessful elections to the Fellowship, 1951–5, 1971–5 and 1991–5

favourably with the 4.6 per cent female membership of the Royal Society, the premier British learned society for scientists (though the number of women Fellows elected to the Royal Society since 1999 has climbed to 11 per cent).

It can be argued that Fellowship of the Society of Antiquaries is commonly obtained by candidates from mid-career onwards, whereas that of the British Academy and Royal Society is generally of scholars at a more senior stage of career, so in part the sets of figures reflect the triangular nature of female participation in British academe, with many women leaving the higher education sector in mid-career and still too few women breaking through the glass ceiling to senior positions. Data from the universities show that in 2004 the proportion of female senior academics in the UK system as a whole was about 18 per cent, a figure that has risen by almost a third compared with the same figure in 1998. Overall, therefore, the male to female ratio in the Society's Fellowship probably remains representative of the rapidly increasing but still overly restricted participation of British female scholars in antiquities studies.

There was continued abuse of 'blackballing' in the Fellowship elections of the late nineteenth and early twentieth centuries, with about 20 per cent of candidates being rejected every year.[31] In those decades successive Presidents warned the Society of the dangers of the capricious use of the veto on what Augustus Franks in his 1893 Anniversary Address termed 'dog-in-the-manger principles'. By the 1930s and 1940s voting behaviours had improved and the percentage of rejected candidates averaged about 6 per cent. The same was the case in the 1950s, despite 'that mysterious misanthropist who, ballot after ballot so long as I can remember, has crept into this room on ballot-nights to record his indiscriminately adverse vote with vindictive and (I have no doubt) senile glee'.[32] Table 12 shows that the trend has continued: rejections of both male and female candidates remained low, and steadily fell, throughout the period of review.

The addresses of candidates for election were coded within one of five categories: (1) the London postal area and the south east; (2) the rest of England; (3) Wales, Scotland and Ireland (the Republic and Northern Ireland combined); (4) Europe; and

(5) the rest of the world. Several candidates (such as Members of Parliament) would have had residences both in London and elsewhere in Britain, but for the purpose of this exercise it was assumed that the address given on the form was the primary residence. In the 'blackballing decades' of the late nineteenth and early twentieth centuries the candidate from the 'Golden Triangle' of London and Oxbridge had a far better chance of making it through the ballot successfully than the 'country candidate' – Welsh parsons and country doctors were notoriously favourite targets for exclusion.[33] A review of voting patterns in the 1930s and 1940s, though, indicated that 'contrary to the assumptions of many of us, country candidates had a better chance of election than persons in the London region or from Oxford or Cambridge'.[34] At first glance the residence information in our sample (table 13) indicates that the trend was then reversed in the second half of the twentieth century to the detriment of the 'country candidates', with the percentage of new Fellows from England outside London falling from sixty-five in the 1950s to fifty-three in the 1990s. In fact, the percentage of London-based candidates only grew marginally and the main growth was outside England, in Wales, Scotland, Ireland, Europe and beyond. To its credit, therefore, the Society developed a markedly broader base through the period of review in terms of the geographical spread of its membership.

The third category of information, the field of study, was coded as follows: (1) archaeology; (2) art and architectural history; (3) history; (4) science; (5) archive studies and palaeography; (6) librarianship; and (7) other. The first of these was used whenever the word 'archaeology' appeared in the *curriculum vitae* text unless there was contradictory evidence. The second group consisted of art historians and architectural historians, the 'history' category being used for scholars working on literary and document-based history. The 'other' category was used when the *curriculum vitae* referred to a general non-specialist interest in antiquity: examples included artists, authors, publishers, editors and chairs of influential committees involved in antiquities work.

A recurrent theme in the annual Anniversary Addresses of successive Presidents throughout the first half of the twentieth century concerned the balance of the

Table 13. Places of residence of candidates elected to the Fellowship, 1951–5, 1971–5 and 1991–5

TABLE 13: PLACES OF RESIDENCE OF CANDIDATES, 1951–95					
	1951–5 (no.)	*1951–5 (%)*	*1971–5 (no.)*	*1971–5 (%)*	*1991–5 (no.)*	*1991–5 (%)*
London and the south east	37	18.3	63	19.1	67	20.9
Rest of England	132	65.4	183	55.4	171	53.4
Wales, Scotland, Ireland	14	6.9	30	9.1	33	10.3
Rest of Europe	9	4.5	33	10	21	6.6
Rest of the world	10	4.9	21	6.4	28	8.8
Total	202		330		320	

Fellowship, especially the size and nature of the archaeological constituency in relation to other disciplines. Through the period of review, archaeology has remained the dominant discipline of the new Fellows, though the overall proportion has declined somewhat (table 14). The principal growth has been in art historians and architectural historians, from 19.3 per cent in the 1950s to almost 30 per cent in the 1990s, almost level-pegging with archaeologists. In the 1970s the growth in art historians and architectural historians was at first largely at the expense of document-based historians, with their numbers increasing slightly in the 1990s. Overall, though, these three disciplines continued to dominate the Fellowship, comprising 79.7 per cent of the new Fellows in the 1950s, 81.9 per cent in the 1970s, and 82.9 per cent in the 1990s.

The nature of the employment of the new Fellows in our sample (table 15) was coded as follows: (1) university or school; (2) museum; (3) central government; (4) local government; (5) archaeological field unit; (6) Church; (7) other profession; (8) other; and (9) independent. The first category in this list referred almost entirely to university staff, though it also included a handful of schoolteachers. 'Other professions' included lawyers involved in antiquities work, and examples of 'other' areas of employment included the BBC, a variety of charities, learned societies, the National Trust, journalism, town planning, banking, engineering and architecture. English Heritage, and its equivalents in Scotland, Wales and Northern Ireland, were coded under 'central government' to give continuity of coding for scholars working in the national heritage services from the time when the equivalent employers were the Department of the Environment and, before that, the Ministry of Works.

In 1957 Sir Mortimer Wheeler estimated that the number of professional Fellows (that is, Fellows employed broadly within the heritage sector) was probably seven times the figure a generation previously,[35] though non-professional Fellows with the traditional qualification of 'a general attachment to the study of antiquity' still constituted something like 80 per cent of the Fellowship. Unsurprisingly, the trend

TABLE 14: FIELDS OF STUDY OF CANDIDATES, 1951–95					
	1951–5 (no.)	1951–5 (%)	1971–5 (no.)	1971–5 (%)	1991–5 (no.)	1991–5 (%)
Archaeology	77	38.1	123	37.3	111	34.7
Art and architectural history	39	19.3	96	29.1	95	29.7
History	45	22.3	51	15.5	59	18.5
Science	6	3	13	3.9	17	5.3
Archive studies and palaeography	16	7.9	26	7.9	11	3.4
Librarianship	9	4.4	10	3	11	3.4
Other	10	5	11	3.3	16	5
Total	202		330		320	

Table 14. Fields of study of candidates elected to the Fellowship, 1951–5, 1971–5 and 1991–5

Table 15. Employment
of candidates elected to
the Fellowship, 1951–5,
1971–5 and 1991–5

TABLE 15: EMPLOYMENT OF CANDIDATES, 1951–95

	1951–5 (no.)	1951–5 (%)	1971–5 (no.)	1971–5 (%)	1991–5 (no.)	1991–5 (%)
University (and school)	49	24.2	141	42.7	134	41.9
Museum	26	12.9	53	16.1	41	12.8
Central government	26	12.9	24	7.3	40	12.5
Local government	8	4	7	2.1	12	3.8
Archaeological field unit	–	–	6	1.8	13	4.1
Church	7	3.5	14	4.3	5	1.6
Other profession	37	18.3	37	11.2	20	6.2
Other	1	0.5	4	1.2	10	3.1
Independent	48	23.7	44	13.3	45	14
Total	202		330		320	

to professionalism has continued inexorably (see table 15). The proportion of university-based new Fellows has increased dramatically, from 24.2 per cent in the 1950s to 41.9 per cent in the 1990s. The museum sector expanded slightly in the 1970s, but returned to 1950s levels (in proportional terms) in the 1990s, to 12.8 per cent. The proportion of new Fellows working for 'central government' (latterly for bodies such as English Heritage) has remained much as for the museum sector.

The rapid increase in posts in commercial archaeology led to a consideration in the 1970s of the advisability of creating a junior category of membership in the context of 'a genuine unease over the possible alienation of young professionals'.[36] The idea was rejected, but the number of new Fellows working in the commercial sector steadily increased from a low base in the 1970s to 4.1 per cent in the 1990s, overtaking the proportion of new Fellows employed in local government (3.8 per cent). The notable declines have been in the proportion of new Fellows working in 'other professions', from 18.3 per cent in the early 1950s to 6.2 per cent in the 1990s, and in new Fellows working as 'independents', from 23.7 per cent in the 1950s to 14.1 per cent in the 1990s. The combined decline of new Fellows working outside the professional heritage sector, from 42 per cent in the 1950s to just 20.3 per cent in the 1990s, is very striking. The Society has travelled a long way from 1893, when Augustus Franks reminded the Society 'that our pursuits are rarely of a remunerative character, and . . . we must largely look to amateurs. Good archaeologists, not a very numerous body, have a first claim on us, but collectors and patrons of art, men of rank, country gentlemen, and clergymen of good position may be very useful to us.'[37] On the other hand, the fact that in the transformed economic milieu of the late twentieth century the Society was still able to recruit a fifth of its membership from non-professional backgrounds remains a striking comment on the continued vitality and broad social base of British antiquarian studies.

RESEARCH

This section reviews the Society's changing policies towards research funding between 1950 and 2000, and the ways in which the money was used. A gift in 1889 by Sir John Evans of £500 of Preference Shares enabled the Society to establish its Research Fund, which remained one of the very few sources of funding in Britain for archaeological fieldwork until the outbreak of the Second World War. Wheeler's list of projects supported by the Research Fund through those decades, given in his 1955 Address, is a roll-call of most of the important Iron Age, Roman and medieval excavations in Britain up to that time: 'Silchester, Old Sarum, Caerwent, Wroxeter, Richborough, Stonehenge, Swarling, Ospringe, Lydney, Verulamium, Glastonbury, Clarendon, Maiden Castle'.[38] In the decade between the end of hostilities and his presidency, by contrast, the Society had undertaken no major enterprise in the field: 'the cloak has fallen from us', he stormed, 'we are no longer in the lead, or anywhere near it'. That year the Society had awarded fieldwork grants totalling just £495, for example, its two largest grants being for excavations at Colchester and for John Bradford's work on Neolithic sites discovered in Apulia in southern Italy from wartime air photographs (table 16). This was about the same amount as in the 1930s, but worth far less in real terms, whereas the British Academy had provided four times as much. Professor Grahame Clark's outstanding excavations at the Mesolithic site of Star Carr had been supported by the Prehistoric Society. The Council for British Archaeology, whose inception during the Second World War owed much to the Society (see page 342), was coming into its own as another potential funder of archaeological research. The British Schools[39] were further 'rivals' for the Society in funding archaeological research abroad. At home, by far the largest player now was the Ministry of Works, through its Ancient Monuments Department, which in 1955 had conducted excavations at some fifty sites, including a flagship project at Stanwick 'on something like our old scale'.[40] In short, most field archaeology was now being funded by the taxpayer through the ministry, the British Academy and museums and universities.

Moreover, Wheeler continued, the fact that most public money was going into the investigation of sites threatened by development meant that there was no overarching research strategy: 'An archaeological excavation financed from public funds must normally be justified in some simple objective fashion; and unhappily the most readily intelligible excuse for it is that of approaching destruction. Unparalleled building, agricultural and industrial operations . . . have yielded an embarrassing number of these excuses. The combined result has been a general acceptance of a great number of "rescue excavations" which have to be tackled more or less adequately in a great many places simultaneously, with no reference whatsoever to any balanced scheme of research.' Worse still, many of these excavations were having to be undertaken with a poorly trained workforce, and had poor prospects of publication. Despite the heroic efforts of a few individuals – such as Grahame Clark, Ian Richmond and Stuart Piggott – in his view 'a melancholy corollary emerges: field-research in this country has lost direction; it is unplanned, inconsequential, opportunist, scrappy'.[41]

TABLE 16: THE SOCIETY'S RESEARCH FUND ALLOCATIONS, 1950–2000

Year	Total funds allocated (£)	Number of grants awarded	Largest grant(s) awarded (£)	Project(s) receiving largest grant
1950	365	7	100 × 2	Apulia, Colchester
1951	511	10	100 × 2	Colchester, Tripolitania
1952	305	10	50 × 4	Euhesperides, Harran, Kouklia, Northolt
1953	522	12	200	Lullingstone
1954	460	9	200	Normandy and Brittany
1955	495	6	400	Apulia, Verulamium
1956	570	5	450	Verulamium
1957	730	7	545	Verulamium
1958	852	7	687	Verulamium
1959	902	9	487	Verulamium
1960	1,066	12	300	Cirencester
1961	1,283	16	415	Cirencester
1962	1,009	16	300	Cirencester
1963	885	16	350	Cirencester
1964	1,114	16	350	Cirencester
1965	1,006	14	350	Cirencester
1966	875	16	200	Cirencester
1967	1,400	22	200 × 2	Southampton, Stamford
1968	865	25	80 × 3	Cirencester, Longthorpe, Portchester
1969	1,200	23	210	Winchester
1970	800	17	100 × 3	Camelot, Portchester, Winchester
1971	800	17	100 × 2	Castle Hill (Bakewell), Winchester
1972	800	17	100	Portchester
1973	650	10	250	Deerhurst
1974	1,680	15	500	Evolution of the Landscape
1975	1,750	12	350	Evolution of the Landscape
1976	3,950	22	400	Repton

Table 16. The Society's Research Fund allocations for archaeological research, 1950–2000 (actual spending differed from allocations in some cases)

Wheeler ended this tirade with an appeal to the Fellowship for £10,000 to add to the £2,000 just received from an anonymous donor to help rebuild the Research Fund to a capital sum of £12,000. The fund grew modestly, having £600 to spend a year later. He then used his 1957 Anniversary Address to berate the Society's Research Committee for what he saw as its lack of strategic thinking: 'in plain language, it is high time that our Research Committee initiated a little research'.[42] He pointed out that the Research Committee had identified a series of desirable objectives in 1945, and that most of these had been met – but that was because, for the most part, they came down to the specific research interests of the members of the committee! They were 'a prophetic record of miscellaneous individual attention, not in any valid sense an over-controlling policy'.[43] The committee needed to seek a middle way between giving out small grants to all and sundry on the one hand, and making grandiose unrealizable plans ('castles in the stratosphere') on the other. Also, it needed to be

TABLE 16 (*continued*)

Year	Total funds allocated (£)	Number of grants awarded	Largest grant(s) awarded (£)	Project(s) receiving largest grant
1977	7,146	16	2,216	Deerhurst
1978	6,677	32	400 × 6	Brixworth, Dartmoor Reaves, Repton, Solway Firth
1979	10,620	29	1,000 × 2	Hengistbury Head, Silchester
1980	22,445	27	5,000	Winchester post-excavation
1981	26,080	40	1,500	Hengistbury Head
1982	27,550	44	1,500 × 3	Beidha, Hengistbury Head, Klithi
1983	46,925	61	13,285	Sutton Hoo
1984	39,980	54	13,975	Sutton Hoo
1985	40,725	57	14,668	Sutton Hoo
1986	45,579	52	15,479	Sutton Hoo
1987	48,153	56	16,083	Sutton Hoo
1988	58,796	64	20,000	Sutton Hoo
1989	65,050	53	32,400	Sutton Hoo
1990	69,950	50	23,000	Sutton Hoo
1991	74,800	51	25,500	Sutton Hoo
1992	85,900	54	27,000	Sutton Hoo
1993	101,282	58	15,000	Sutton Hoo
1994	48,950	31	10,000	Aksum
1995	51,250	32	10,000	Aksum
1996	45,408	39	5,000 × 2	Aksum, Imperial Porphyry Quarries, Egypt
1997	51,010	31	10,000	Beirut
1998	55,393	32	10,000	Beirut
1999	34,680	19	5,000	Beirut
2000	30,350	20	2,000 × 4	Als Survey (Denmark), Körös Culture Project, Roman Mosaics of Britain, Scotland's First Settlers

more imaginative, and fund not just excavations but also other important work such as surveys and artefact studies: 'It may usefully be reminded that it has a brain as well as a pocket; and we may hope that the former is appreciably larger than the latter.'[44]

Despite Wheeler's scorn, it can be seen in retrospect that, through the 1950s, the Research Committee had managed to support a reasonably varied programme of projects in terms of geography and site type, though Roman work dominated. In 1951, for example, the projects supported included work on Roman Bath and Colchester, the Roman villa of Whittington Court, Roman rural settlement in Libya (pioneering fieldwork by Richard Goodchild and John Ward-Perkins in Tripolitania), at Paphos in Cyprus, and on an Anglo-Saxon cemetery near Salisbury. Whereas Wheeler had advocated research over rescue projects, and the funding of work overseas as well as at home, Joan Evans urged the Research Committee instead to prioritize British archaeology, given the growing rescue threats. The result was that almost all the committee's funds in the years of her presidency were allocated to British projects, though research projects were just as likely to be funded as rescue projects, and the list includes an impressive range of classic sites of all periods from the Neolithic to medieval periods, and from all parts of the British Isles.[45]

By this time, though, it was becoming all too apparent that, with rising numbers of field projects and the rising costs of the excavation process, the Society's role as a significant funding force in British archaeology was steadily diminishing. In 1966 Francis Wormald noted the impact on the size of grant applications of the increasing use of mechanical diggers to strip topsoil. The result was that the amounts being given by the Research Fund to individual projects were becoming, in his view, little more than 'tokens of goodwill and symbols of our support'.[46] The following year the Society managed almost to double the total expended (from £875 in 1966 to £1,400 in 1967) and to increase the number of projects supported from sixteen to twenty-two, with the two largest grants going to new work at Southampton and Stamford. In 1968 he told the Fellowship that the goal should be a Research Fund of at least £3,000, even though one large-scale excavation, such as Winchester, cost much more than that.[47]

In 1971 J N L Myres reminded the Fellowship again of the new reality of fieldwork funding in Britain. Given the rising costs of excavation, and the numbers of archaeologists now in post in universities who in earlier days might have been glad to work for the Society, 'it may well be doubted whether the resources and energy of a Society such as ours can any longer be best employed in attempting major excavations on its own account. That kind of leadership may well have passed, and perhaps rightly passed, to hands better fitted in present conditions to provide it most effectively.'[48] Perhaps the main role of the Society henceforth should be 'in the spheres of initiation, direction, organization, consultation, and perhaps in the provision of various background facilities, than in the realm of pure finance',[49] though the Society needed to support rescue projects to the best of its ability and the value of small grants to individual projects, as part of 'mosaic funding', should not be under-estimated. Also, he suggested two years later, the Society should take comfort from the fact that its Fellows were heavily involved in the burgeoning rescue work: 'Many of the ablest of our younger Fellows . . . are to be found in key positions everywhere, whether it be in the urban archaeology of historic cities such as Winchester, York, Oxford, Lincoln, or Southampton, in the countryside of Kent, Somerset, or Salisbury Plain, on new-town projects such as that which will soon surround and transform Peterborough, on the lines of projected motorways; and also, one may add, in those all-important corridors of beneficent power now happily concentrated in the Department of the Environment in Fortress House.'[50]

The Research Committee responded robustly to Myres's comment that the Society might increasingly have to take a backseat in the national archaeological research agenda by initiating two flagship research projects, one on the Evolution of the English Landscape and the other on the Archaeology of the English Church. The key lesson it had learned, though, was the need to work in partnership with other organizations. The first project, headed by Collin Bowen and Barry Cunliffe, involved close collaboration with the Royal Commission on Historic Monuments, the role of the Society being envisaged as providing background facilities, co-ordinating the activities of fieldworkers and publishing the results. The second project, in collaboration with the Council for British Archaeology, was envisaged as a study of church evolution by combining the detailed investigation of standing buildings with excavations, the primary focus to be the important Anglo-Saxon church of Deerhurst in Gloucestershire, led by Harold Taylor and Philip Rahtz. The decision to launch these projects was encouraged by news of a recent bequest from a late Fellow, Hugh Phillips, 'for research and publication on British subjects before 1800'. At the same time, however, both projects were also attractive because only modest funds were needed to launch them at a time when the value of the Research Fund's meagre annual investment income of £650 was being greatly eroded by rampant inflation. In the years when these projects were supported (1973–8), the sums awarded – a total of £1,500 to the Landscape project and £3,398 to the Deerhurst work – amounted to just under a quarter of the total funds disbursed.

In 1978 the Director (John Evans) and Secretary (Ian Longworth) reviewed the Research Committee guidelines. It was agreed that the committee should adopt a policy of 'assisting well-defined research projects, whether small-scale or long-term' and prioritize the provision of start-up funding for new projects that would then be expected to seek funds elsewhere for their continuation.[51] The principal outcome was the decision to commit major funds to one flagship project, Sutton Hoo (directed by Martin Carver), though fieldwork only finally commenced in 1985 after lengthy and complex negotiations to set up collaborations with the British Museum, the National Maritime Museum and Suffolk County Council. Between 1983 and 1995 the project was awarded about £250,000 – just under a third of the committee's total budget through that period. At the same time, the Society was able to enlarge its Research Fund, allowing the committee to expand the number of projects it could support with minor grants, the latter generally representing contributions to 'mosaic funding' being assembled by the project directors. In 1985 John Evans (fig 115) reported that the committee had received seventy-nine applications and had decided to fund fifty-six – about half of the total on prehistoric topics and about half for research in the historical periods, and about half for work in Britain and half for work abroad.[52] About 70 per cent of the projects funded were also the subject of applications to the British Academy. The total amount awarded by the Research Committee in 1985 (including just under £15,000 for Sutton Hoo) was £40,000, while the British Academy expended £180,000 that year on archaeological projects through its main research grant scheme. As Evans noted, there was still much the same disparity between Society and Academy funding for archaeological research as when Wheeler had lamented the state of affairs in 1955.[53]

By 1992 the Society was disbursing £81,000, the British Museum £250,000, and the British Academy over £350,000 – all these sums being dwarfed by English Heritage's expenditure that year of £9 million. The Society's allocation to archaeological research topped £100,000 in 1993, but in the face of financial stringency the

Fig 115. John Evans,
President of the
Society of Antiquaries
of London, 1984–7.
Photograph: Society of
Antiquaries
of London.

Research Fund had to be steadily reduced through the rest of the decade to about £30,000 in 2000. Despite the pressures on its budget and rising demand (in 1999, for example, just nineteen out of sixty applications were successful), the Research Committee decided to commit significant funds to three major projects through the mid- and later 1990s: David Phillipson's excavations at Aksum in Ethiopia, David Peacock's work on Roman stone quarries at Mons Claudianus in Egypt and Dominic Perring's excavations in post-Civil War Beirut. The total expenditure on the three projects was £25,000 each, representing about a quarter of the available funds of the committee during the major years of support from 1994 to 1999 (Mons Claudianus had received a series of smaller grants from 1989). For the remainder of successful applications, the committee was aware that its grants were often little more than token contributions to a project's total costs, but at least in many instances the Society's support represented seed-corn funds that persuaded other funders to back a project. A typical example was the air photographic survey of Jordanian archaeological sites by Bob Bewley and David Kennedy, for which a grant of £1,000 from the Society helped them solicit thirty-three hours of flying time from the Royal Jordanian Air Force, which would have cost about £20,000 at full commercial prices.[54]

PUBLICATION

In 1952, to celebrate the bicentenary of the Royal Charter, the Society launched an appeal for the establishment of a special fund of £25,000 to aid the publication of monographs, the cost of *Archaeologia* and the *Antiquaries Journal* still to be met from the General Fund. In his 1952 Address, Sir James Mann was delighted to announce that generous gifts each of £3,000 had been received from two Fellows to kick-start the appeal, but a year later the sum collected had grown only a little, with seventy-seven (mostly small) contributions from a membership of 900.[55] The appeal to the Fellowship was relaunched – the fund would reach its target if every Fellow guaranteed to give £1 a year for seven years[56] – but a year later only 176 Fellows had contributed. Moreover, most of these were Fellows rarely seen at London meetings, who therefore received few benefits from membership of the Society apart from its publications, whereas, Sir James said pointedly in his final Address: 'there are Fellows who make full use of the facilities of the Society, finding here a rostrum to speak from and publications in which to express themselves, who have not come forward. This is a very delicate subject, and I hope I am not going too far if I say that in some cases this almost amounts to a debt of honour.'[57] The following year Sir Mortimer Wheeler 'earnestly invited renewed attention' to the fund,[58] the next year he appealed 'with a renewed sense of urgency' for every Fellow to contribute a guinea a year under a seven-year covenant,[59] and a year later, in a tone of increasing desperation, he asked once more for 'even the smallest contributions' from individual Fellows.[60] The outcome was that, through the 1950s and 1960s, the *Journal* was financed from general income, the Research Reports from the Bicentenary Publication Fund and *Archaeologia* sat somewhat uneasily in between. In 1970 the various publication programmes were brought together so that the income and expenditure of the various titles could be measured more easily, and a Publications sub-committee was established.[61] In 2000 the Society committed just over £145,000 to its publication programme, a sum that represented some 16 per cent of total expenditure that year.

Though financial restrictions dogged the Society's publication aspirations, the output for the period remains impressive: fifty volumes of the annual *Antiquaries Journal*; sixteen volumes (from volume 95 in 1953 to volume 110 in 1992) of *Archaeologia*, the larger-format journal with the charming subtitle *Miscellaneous Tracts Relating to Antiquity* (traditionally reserved for papers considered too long for the *Journal* and/or benefiting from larger-format illustrations), forty-eight Research Reports (from Number 17 in 1954 to Numbers 61 to 64 in 2000) and twenty volumes of Occasional Papers, mostly used in recent decades for publishing one-day meetings. This amounts to a publication record of over 120 monographs, most of them substantial. To characterize the scope of this publication programme, and to see how it had developed between 1950 and 2000 in terms of its coverage and priorities, it is useful to compare what the Society was publishing with the coverage of some of the 'competitor' publications (table 17). In this respect, the *Proceedings of the Prehistoric Society* (*PPS*) has been publishing prehistoric archaeology throughout the review period, *Medieval Archaeology* began in 1957, *Post-Medieval Archaeology* in 1967, *Britannia* entered the British publishing landscape as a major vehicle for Roman archaeology in 1970 and the Council for British Archaeology (CBA) began its Research Reports series in 1955.

To take the *Antiquaries Journal* first, the papers are divided by their coverage of wholly or primarily British or overseas subjects, and then into their broad period coverage: early prehistoric (Palaeolithic and Mesolithic), later prehistoric (Neolithic, Bronze Age and Iron Age), Greek and Roman, and medieval and post-medieval. The proportion of papers on British material is always high: 89 per cent in 1951–5 and 1971–5, and 79 per cent in 1991–5. The *Journal* has traditionally published a mix of papers on field archaeology, artefact studies, architectural studies of major monuments, studies of art-historical material (paintings, illustrated manuscripts and the like) and historical papers based on documentary studies. Separating the historical papers was relatively straightforward, and excluded papers dealing with paintings but included papers in architectural history which had clearly involved fieldwork and the recording and analysis of standing buildings. This calculation resulted in a dominance of papers dealing with the post-Roman centuries: 52 per cent in 1951–5, 35 per cent in 1971–5 and 61 per cent in 1991–5. Later prehistoric papers were the next major category in the 1950s (27 per cent), with papers dealing with classical archaeology comprising 16 per cent. There was an even balance between these two categories in the 1970s, but the positions were reversed in the 1990s (later prehistoric: 14 per cent; classical: 21 per cent). Only three papers were published on early prehistory, two in the 1950s and one in the 1990s. Overall, it would appear that over the review period the mix of archaeological papers published in the *Journal* has stayed more or less consistent in terms of its period mix and balance of British and non-British work.

Table 17. The distribution of archaeological papers in the *Antiquaries Journal*, 1951–5, 1971–5 and 1991–5

TABLE 17: DISTRIBUTION OF ARCHAEOLOGICAL PAPERS IN THE *ANTIQUARIES JOURNAL*

Volume	Year	British	Non-British	Early prehistoric	Later prehistoric	Greek/Roman	Medieval/post-medieval	Multi-period
31	1951	8	2	0	5	2	3	0
32	1952	7	1	0	4	1	3	0
33	1953	6	0	0	2	0	4	0
34	1954	12	0	2	1	2	7	0
35	1955	6	2	0	0	2	6	0
51	1971	9	3	0	5	4	3	0
52	1972	11	0	0	4	1	3	3
53	1973	9	1	0	1	2	5	2
54	1974	6	1	0	0	2	4	1
55	1975	11	1	0	2	4	3	3
71	1991	5	2	0	1	2	4	0
72	1992	5	0	1	2	1	1	0
73	1993	2	1	0	0	0	3	0
74	1994	6	1	0	0	2	5	0
75	1995	4	2	0	1	1	4	6

The 1950s were characterized by an acceleration in the reporting of fieldwork in the *Antiquaries Journal*, especially of small-scale interventions undertaken in the years immediately following the Second World War. The 1951–5 volumes of *PPS* (16–21) published sixty-eight papers. The first thing that stands out is the wider geographical spread of the papers compared with those of the 1951–5 *Journal*, with roughly half on British topics and half on non-British, the latter mostly but not exclusively papers with a European focus. Secondly, and unsurprisingly, given its specialist remit, *PPS* contrasts with the *Journal* in having papers reporting archaeological fieldwork across all periods of prehistory. Thirdly, excluding the several papers publishing individual artefacts, the *PPS* volumes contrast with those of the *Journal* in having numerous synthetic papers discussing sets of material culture and their cultural and/or chronological implications, from Palaeolithic spear-throwers (1955) to Iron Age pottery decoration (1952). There was also a series of papers presenting work broadly within archaeological science, including palynology (1954), petrological analysis (1951), plant remains (1952, 1954, 1955) and soil science (1953, 1955). The most striking contrast, though, is in the number of major thematic or review papers in *PPS*, such as Gordon Childe on wagons and carts (1951), or Christopher Hawkes on 'British prehistory half-way through the century' (1951). *Medieval Archaeology* also emulated *PPS* in embracing a broad mix of papers across its discipline, the three 1950s volumes including fieldwork reports, studies of standing structures and articles of review or synthesis such as Rosemary Cramp on 'Beowulf and archaeology'. By contrast, only one paper in the entire set of 1950s volumes of the *Antiquaries Journal* was in the latter category, Graham Webster's review of the use of coal in Roman Britain.[62]

In contrast with the rather narrow focus of many of the 1950s papers in the *Journal*, the four volumes of *Archaeologia* published in the decade presented some major studies spanning settlement archaeology, urban survey and typological/art-historical approaches, some of them representing milestone contributions to scholarship: these included, for example, D J Cathcart-King on the defences of the citadel of Damascus (1951) and J Ward-Perkins and R Goodchild's surveys of the archaeology of Roman Tripolitania in north-west Libya.[63] All four Research Reports published in the 1950s (table 18) were also classic field reports that have remained seminal publications in their respective fields. The four CBA volumes of the 1950s were all thematic studies rather than field reports, addressing Romano-British villas (1955), standing buildings (1955), post-medieval buildings (1955) and Anglo-Saxon pottery (1959).

The 1960s were characterized by the steady growth in learned societies and 'rival' publishing organizations, but in 1965 Sir Ian Richmond urged the Fellowship to welcome this development and be confident in the worth of its own publishing portfolio: 'the duality of our regular periodicals facilitated a measure of selection as between shorter and longer contributions and types of illustration', with the Research Reports remaining an ideal vehicle for specialist heavyweight archaeological studies, particularly excavation reports.[64] Furthermore, he commented, the Society should take pride in 'how much work is now done by our Fellows in other fields and published in other books and journals'.[65] The archaeological content of the 1960s volumes of the *Journal* consisted almost entirely of interim reports of field projects, many of them stemming from the burgeoning amount of 'rescue archaeology' of the period.[66] Only three significant review papers were published in the *Journal*, and all of those only at the end of the decade, on British Bronze Age chronology,[67] early pre-Roman Iron Age communities[68] and trade systems reconstructed from the petrological analysis of Glastonbury Ware.[69] The five Research Reports published in the decade (see table 18), though, were all significant excavation reports, on Colchester (21), Skorba, in Malta (22), Richborough (23), Bath (24) and Brough-on-Humber (25). In contrast, the four CBA monographs retained the CBA's focus on reviews, standards and methodologies.

At the end of the decade J N L Myres congratulated the Society on the quality of its publication record. Its publications had 'set over the years a standard of quality both in content and in presentation of which we are right to be proud, not least in their effect in stimulating a general improvement in the quality of archaeological publication in this country as a whole . . . Notably perhaps in Romano-British studies, they have played a leading part in making available in print the basic evidence from major excavations from which the growth of knowledge has so largely depended'.[70] He also commented that 'in an age of increasing specialization, the continuance of *Archaeologia* . . . may provoke a supercilious sneer from those whose vision is bounded by the blinkers of their own speciality', but 'its spacious format and our sensible practice of offprinting every *Archaeologia* article in substantial quantity for separate sale, have made it almost the ideal vehicle for small-scale monographs requiring generous illustration'. Certainly two of the five volumes of *Archaeologia* published in the 1960s consisted of major excavation reports of considerable significance and impact, on the Fussell's Lodge long barrow[71] and the Welwyn Garden City La Tène burial.[72]

Through the 1970s, the *Journal* retained its primary focus, in its archaeological coverage, on publishing interim reports on British field archaeology. The 1971–5 reports of this kind included a series of sites that have become household names in British later prehistoric, Roman and medieval archaeology, such as Cirencester, Danebury, Gloucester, Lincoln, Marden, Mucking, Portchester, the Somerset Levels, South Cadbury and Winchester. Significant papers were also published stemming from the Society's flagship projects on the Evolution of the English Landscape (Chalton) and on the Archaeology of the English Church (Rivenhall and Deerhurst). A welcome development was the inclusion of thematic or review papers in most volumes, such as on Bronze Age stock-rearing[73] and Roman trade.[74] In the Research Reports series there was a string of seminal excavation reports (see table 18). Further significant fieldwork was published in *Archaeologia* – for example, in 1973 on the Dyffryn Ardudwy chambered tomb.[75]

While Myres's claim about the standard-setting role of the Society in archaeological fieldwork publishing was justified, his other claim at the time – that the Society could still be regarded as 'the principal publication centre in this country for archaeological and antiquarian studies of all kinds'[76] – was surely questionable in view of what was being published in competitor journals and as monographs. In prehistoric studies, for example, a significant series of interim excavation reports was published in *PPS*. Interspersed with these in the 1971–5 volumes are important review papers on every major period of prehistory and from all parts of the world, including Australia, India, Mesopotamia and pre-Dynastic Egypt. There are significant papers with an explicit methodological focus, and others addressing a wide range of themes, including agriculture, archery, horse-riding, metallurgy, ideologies and trade. The 1971–5 volumes of *Britannia*, *Medieval Archaeology* and *Post-Medieval Archaeology* represented a comparable range of scholarly enquiry, with fieldwork reports, artefact studies and review articles. The CBA monographs of the period included *Aerial Reconnaissance for Archaeology*[77] and *The Effect of Man on the Landscape: the Highland zone*,[78] both significant studies of long-lasting impact. In short, by the 1970s the Society's publications certainly represented an important part of the archaeological landscape, but it could no longer claim to hold the centre ground except in the quality of its flagship excavation reports.

In 1989 a working party reviewed the publication policy.[79] It recommended that research and publication policies be linked more explicitly; that the *Antiquaries Journal* be published as a single volume each year; that *Archaeologia* be reserved as an occasional large-format series; and that the Occasional Papers, the new series of which had started in 1980 with a primary purpose of publishing one-day seminars (table 19), should continue unchanged. Though the range and focus of the *Journal* were not addressed explicitly, it is noteworthy that the 1991–5 volumes had a far greater proportion of thematic and review papers, and fewer interim excavation reports, than the 1951–5 and 1971–5 volumes. The trend to diversification in the *Journal*'s coverage has continued ever since, with an increasing number of more theoretical studies in recent years alongside the range of fieldwork reports, artefact studies and topic-based reviews. A similar diversity characterizes the Research Reports and Occasional Papers published in this period, spanning prehistory to classical antiquity and beyond, and archaeological science to art-historical approaches.

CONCLUSION

The second half of the twentieth century witnessed profound transformations in the archaeological landscape of Britain, characterized in particular by a dramatic increase in numbers of professional archaeologists in universities, museums, central and local government and, especially, in a private sector that did not exist in 1950. There has been a burgeoning in the sources of finance available for funding archaeology, and huge increases in real terms in the amount of money available for archaeological research, including rescue archaeology. There has been an inexorable trend towards subject specialization, one aspect of which has been the emergence of numerous

TABLE 18: RESEARCH REPORTS PUBLISHED BY THE SOCIETY, 1950–2000

17	1954	M Wheeler	*The Stanwick Fortifications*
18	1955	L Woolley	*Alalakh*
19	1958	M Wheeler and K M Richardson	*Hill Forts of Northern France*
20	1958	M R Hull	*Roman Colchester*
21	1963	M R Hull	*The Roman Potters' Kilns of Colchester*
22	1966	D H Trump	*Skorba*
23	1968	B W Cunliffe	*Excavations at Richborough V*
24	1969	B W Cunliffe	*Roman Bath*
25	1969	J S Wacher	*Excavations at Brough-on-Humber*
26	1971	B W Cunliffe	*Excavations at Fishbourne 1961–8. I: the site*
27	1971	B W Cunliffe	*Excavations at Fishbourne 1961–8. II: the finds*
28	1972	S Frere	*Verulamium Excavations I*
29	1971	G J Wainwright and I H Longworth	*Durrington Walls: Excavations 1966–8*
30	1973	J N L Myres and B Green	*The Anglo-Saxon Cemeteries of Caistor-by-Norwich and Barkshall, Norfolk*
31	1974	D S Neal	*The Excavation of the Roman Villa in Gadebridge Park, Hemel Hempstead*
32	1975	B W Cunliffe	*Excavations at Portchester Castle. I: Roman*
33	1976	B W Cunliffe	*Excavations at Portchester Castle. II: Saxon*
34	1977	B W Cunliffe	*Excavations at Portchester Castle. III: Medieval, the outer bailey and its defences*
35	1978	M Guido	*The Glass Beads of the Prehistoric and Roman Periods in Britain and Ireland*
36	1978	R W Lightbown	*Secular Goldsmiths' Work in Medieval France*
37	1979	G J Wainwright	*Mount Pleasant, Dorset: excavations 1970–1*
38	1979	A C Renfrew	*Investigations in Orkney*
39	1980	H Kilbride-Jones	*Zoomorphic Penannular Brooches*
40	1982	W J Wedlake	*The Excavation of the Shrine of Apollo at Nettleton, Wiltshire, 1956–71*
44	1987	G D B Jones	*Apulia I: Neolithic settlement in the Tavoliere*
45	1988	T B James and A M Robinson	*Clarendon Palace*

Table 18. Research Reports published by the Society, 1950–2000

'competitor' learned societies and professional associations, many of which include archaeological publication amongst their activities. How has the Society fared amidst these convulsions?

In terms of the composition of the Fellowship, as this review has shown, it has doubled in size, made its membership more representative geographically, and done rather better than some other academic organizations in shifting the gender balance. Perhaps most strikingly, amidst all the pressures of an increasingly money-rich/time-poor society, it has managed to maintain the professional/non-professional mix that has always been celebrated as its greatest strength, though the non-professional constituency continues to be squeezed. President after President in the review period has reiterated that one of the Society's main purposes in an age of increasing special-ization is to build scholarly bridges, bringing together scholars from the full span of research on antiquities. As Mortimer Wheeler put it: 'the study of antiquity is an

TABLE 18 (*continued*)

46	1990	J V Megaw and M R Megaw	*The Basse-Yutz Find. Masterpieces of Celtic art*
47	1990	C Higham and R Bannanurag	*The Excavation of Khok Phanom Di: a prehistoric site in central Thailand. I: the excavation, chronology and human burials*
48	1991	C Higham and R Bannanurag	*The Excavation of Khok Phanom Di. II: the biological remains (Part I)*
49	1994	J Stratford	*The Bedford Inventories: the worldly goods of John, Duke of Bedford, Regent of France*
50	1994	C Higham and R Thosarat	*Excavations at Khok Phanom Di. III: the material culture (Part I)*
51	1997	J Hines	*A New Corpus of Anglo-Saxon Great Square-Headed Brooches*
52	1995	B W Cunliffe	*Portchester V*
53	1996	G Thompson	*The Excavation of Khok Phanom Di. IV: the botanical evidence: the biological evidence (Part II)*
54	1996	J Chapman and R Shiel	*The Changing Face of Dalmatia*
55	1997	P Rahtz and L Watts	*St Mary's Church, Deerhurst, Gloucestershire*
56	1999	D Starkey	*The Inventory of King Henry VIII: the transcript*
57	1999	A G Poulter	*Nicopolis ad Istrum. A Roman to early Byzantine city: the pottery and glass*
58	1999	M Guido	*The Glass Beads of Anglo-Saxon England*
59	1999	J Geddes	*Medieval Decorative Ironwork in England*
60	1999	S Badham and M Norris	*Early Incised Slabs and Brasses from the London Marblers*
61	2000	N Tyles	*Excavations at Khok Phanom Di. V: the people*
62	2000	G Herrmann	*The Monuments of Merv*
63	2000	H G Slade	*Glamis Castle*
64	2000	P Fowler	*Landscape Plotted and Pieced*

integral study, whether the subject of it be hand-axes or handsom-cabs. The fact that some of our evidence is above ground, some of it subterranean, some of it even submarine, makes no matter'.[80] Three decades later, John Evans reminded the Fellowship that the Society was 'a bulwark against the increasing fragmentation of studies of the past through increasing specialization'.[81] And as Christopher Brooke reflected, in such an age of scholarly fragmentation 'there are strange and powerful forces of compensation, which reminds us ever and anon that we are members one of another . . . we are all amateurs, and in some of our work, unless shored up and protected by our colleagues in other fields, hopelessly amateurish'.[82]

Fifty years ago the research funds of the Society were the primary source of funding for archaeological research by British-based archaeologists. Today, they represent a small piece of the mosaic of total funding available, in many respects paling into insignificance in comparison with the sums flowing into the subject by one route or

TABLE 19: OCCASIONAL PAPERS PUBLISHED BY THE SOCIETY, 1980–2000

1980	1	F H Thompson	*Archaeology and Coastal Change*
1981	2	R P Wilcox	*Timber and Iron Reinforcement in Early Buildings*
1983	3	F H Thompson	*Studies in Medieval Sculpture*
1984	4	S Macready and F H Thompson	*Cross-Channel Trade between Gaul and Britain in the Pre-Roman Iron Age*
1984	5	H Wayment	*Stained Glass of the Church of St Mary, Fairford, Gloucestershire*
1985	6	S Macready and F H Thompson	*Archaeological Field Survey in Britain and Abroad*
1985	7	S Macready and F H Thompson	*Influences in Victorian Art and Architecture*
1986	8	S Macready and F H Thompson	*Art and Patronage in the English Romanesque*
1986	9	P Binski	*Painted Chamber at Westminster*
1987	10	S Macready and F H Thompson	*Roman Architecture in the Greek World*
1988	11	M Gibson and S M Wright	*Joseph Mayer of Liverpool, 1803–86*
1989	12	S M Wright	*Decorative Arts in the Victorian Period*
1991	13	M Newby and K Painter	*Roman Glass – Two Centuries of Art and Invention*
1992	14	M Fulford and E Nichols	*Developing Landscapes of Lowland Britain: the archaeology of the British gravels – a review*
1994	15	G Meirion-Jones and M Jones	*Manorial Domestic Buildings in England and Northern France*
1994	16	K Painter	*Churches Built in Ancient Times: recent studies in Early Christian architecture*
1995	17	J M Crook	*John Carter and the Mind of the Gothic Revival*
1996	18	L Parry	*William Morris: art and Kelmscott*
1996	19	D Morgan Evans, P Salway and D Thackray	*The Remains of Distant Times: archaeology and the National Trust*
2000	20	R Brewer	*Roman Fortresses and their Legions: papers in honour of George Boon*

Table 19. Occasional Papers (new series) published by the Society, 1980–2000

another from central government (including into the universities), local government, the research councils, developers, the Heritage Lottery Fund and so on. Yet, despite Wheeler's tirade in 1957 that the Research Committee did not do much and what little it did was largely in pursuit of its own interests, the roll-call of projects funded through the second half of the twentieth century is one of which the Society can be justly proud. In many cases (probably most projects in recent decades) individual archaeologists have put together a package of 'mosaic funding' for a field project, often getting the extra funding precisely because of the confidence expressed by the Society in its award; and when the Society has led the way and assembled a consortium of funding bodies for a flagship project, as in the case of the work at Sutton Hoo, the results have been outstanding.

Perhaps the most convincing, undeniable evidence of the effectiveness of any learned society is what is left on the shelf for future generations to read as a result of its activities. Through the review period successive Presidents complained about the overly conservative content of the *Antiquaries Journal* and *Archaeologia*, arguing that the *Journal* in particular would benefit from more synthetic, theoretical, or speculative papers alongside its traditional fare of 'papers of record'. It is certainly true that the increase of thematic papers alongside field reports in recent decades makes for a much more varied volume, which personally I have always welcomed. Nevertheless, given the ongoing crisis in the publication of archaeological fieldwork in recent decades with the withdrawal of commercial publishers because of the high costs and comparatively low returns of such publishing, and the archaeological community's attempts to deal with the storage and publication of the primary data that is the lifeblood of the subject (through microfiche, compact discs, internet publication, archived grey literature and so on), the continued commitment of the Society to the high-quality publication of archaeological fieldwork has to be one of its most vital and enduring contributions to scholarship. Certainly the contribution to scholarly knowledge of the Research Reports listed in table 18 is inestimable. They remain the gold standard for others to seek to emulate.

The final contribution of the Society is the most difficult to gauge: its influence on public archaeology, on how the subject is practised, organized and valued by contemporary society. The Anniversary Addresses show that the Society has certainly identified the major issues of the day as regards the British context: for example, threats to the built environment in the 1950s from post-war neglect; threats to buried (that is, hidden) archaeology from 1960s and 1970s development; the case for reforming state structures for conserving and managing the archaeological heritage in the 1980s, and the crisis in publication from developer-funded work in the same decade; and the need for research strategies in which to embed both research-based and development-driven work in the 1990s. How effective has the Society been at defining, shaping and changing such agendas? In the first year of the new millennium, in the new-style, anonymous *Annual Report*, Council reiterated a point made by many previous Presidents: 'Council does not see the Society behaving as a public pressure group, preferring to act through contacts provided by the Fellowship', adding somewhat opaquely: 'it continues to review the role it plays in public affairs'.[83] Nevertheless, while the Society has of course been just one voice amongst many (a steadily growing chorus, in fact), it has clearly been well placed in terms of its position as archaeology's senior learned society, the broad base of its membership, and its geographical location in the heart of the capital, to have a better chance than most of the archaeological community to reach the ear of decision-makers. It is difficult to measure indirect influence in policy making, but we can at least observe that the structures or solutions that eventually came about, whatever their inadequacies, have chimed more or less with what the Society was lobbying for. Wheeler was using his characteristic exaggeration when he wrote: 'that little room in which our successive Assistant Secretaries have been enshrined is still the veritable focus of the archaeological world',[84] but British archaeology, and the wider community, have much to thank the Society for the wisdom and commitment it applied to the advancement of both scholarship and heritage protection structures in the second half of the twentieth century.

ACKNOWLEDGEMENTS

I would like to express my particular gratitude to Derek Renn for his painstaking work on the compilation and interpretation of the Election Certificates for 1951–5, 1971–5 and 1991–5, without which the section on Fellowship trends would have been impossible to write, and for his detailed comments on the text. I am very grateful to Bernard Nurse for providing the comparative figures of male and female Fellows before 2004. I am also very grateful to Sue Pearce for the comparative figures for 2004 and for her skilful editorial leadership.

NOTES

1. Myres 1975, 5.
2. Wheeler 1957, 122.
3. Aitchison and Edwards 2003.
4. Mann 1950, 131.
5. Mann 1954, 151.
6. Mann 1953, 155.
7. Mann 1954, 150.
8. Wheeler 1959, 167.
9. Ibid, 167.
10. Ibid, 169.
11. Evans 1961, 152.
12. Evans 1962, 143.
13. Ibid, 144.
14. Evans 1964, 118.
15. Myres 1974, 5.
16. Dufty 1980, 1.
17. Dufty 1981, 2.
18. Brooke 1982, 3.
19. Ibid, 3.
20. Ibid, 3.
21. Ibid, 2.
22. Ibid, 3.
23. Brooke 1984, 4.
24. Robbins 1989, 9.
25. Cunliffe 1992, 7.
26. Cunliffe 1995, 12.
27. At the time of writing (in autumn 2006) the outcome of the planning inquiry held in summer 2004 on the relative costs and benefits of a shorter or longer tunnel is still eagerly awaited.
28. Jervis 1997, 11.
29. Jervis 1999, 13.
30. Jervis 2000, 10.
31. Evans 1956, 348.
32. Wheeler 1958, 169.
33. Evans 1956, 348.
34. Fox 1949, 137.
35. Wheeler 1957, 122.
36. Evans 1985, 3.
37. Evans 1956, 348.
38. Wheeler 1955, 156.
39. The British School at Athens was founded in 1886, the British School at Rome in 1901, the British School of Archaeology in Jerusalem in 1919, the British School of Archaeology in Iraq in 1932, the British Institute of Archaeology at Ankara in 1947, the British Institute in Eastern Africa in 1960, the British Institute of Persian Studies in 1961, the Society for Libyan Studies in 1969, the Society for South Asian (formerly Afghan) Studies in 1972 and the British Institute in South East Asia in 1978 (re-formed as the British Academy's Committee for South East Asian Studies in 1986).
40. Wheeler 1955, 158.
41. Ibid, 158–9.
42. Wheeler 1957, 126.
43. Ibid, 127.
44. Ibid, 129.
45. For example: Bath, Dorchester, Dragonby, Fifield Down, Fishbourne, Gadebridge Park, Hen Domen, Meare, Northton, Overton Down experimental earthwork, Portchester, Silchester, Wharram Percy and Winchester.
46. Wormald 1966, 175.
47. Wormald 1968, 158.
48. Myres 1971, 173.
49. Myres 1972, 4.
50. Myres 1973, 4. I am tempted to ask readers to fill in the names of the various Fellows he was thinking of!
51. Taylor 1978, 6.
52. Evans 1985, 6.
53. Ibid, 7.
54. Jervis 2000, 11; Kennedy and Bewley 2004.
55. Mann 1953, 156.
56. Mann 1954, 152.
57. Ibid, 152–3.
58. Wheeler 1955, 156.
59. Wheeler 1956, 170.
60. Wheeler 1957, 126.
61. Myres 1971, 171.
62. Webster 1955.
63. Ward-Perkins and Goodchild 1953.
64. Richmond 1965, 168.
65. Ibid, 168.
66. Including Breedon on the Hill, Caistor, Cirencester,

Dolaucothi, Durrington Walls, Fishbourne, Owslebury, Portchester, South Cadbury, Upton, Verulamium, Winchester and Winterton.
67. Burgess 1969.
68. Cunliffe 1968.
69. Peacock 1969.
70. Myres 1971, 169–70.
71. Ashbee 1966.
72. Stead 1967.
73. Bradley 1971.
74. Peacock 1974.

75. Powell 1973.
76. Myres 1971, 168–9.
77. Wilson 1975.
78. Evans *et al* 1975.
79. Robbins 1990, 3.
80. Wheeler 1955, 159.
81. Evans 1986, 3.
82. Brooke 1982, 6–7.
83. Society of Antiquaries 2000, 26.
84. Wheeler 1957, 125.

BIBLIOGRAPHY

Aitchison, K and Edwards, R 2003. *Archaeology Labour Market Intelligence: profiling the profession 2002/03*, Bradford

Ashbee, P 1966. 'The Fussell's Lodge long barrow excavations 1957', *Archaeologia*, **100**, 1–80

Bradley, R 1971. 'Stock raising and the origins of the hillfort on the South Downs', *Antiq J*, **51**, 8–29

Brooke, C N L 1982. 'Anniversary Address', *Antiq J*, **62**, 1–12

Brooke, C N L 1984. 'Anniversary Address', *Antiq J*, **64**, 1–10

Burgess, C B 1969. 'Chronology and terminology in the British Bronze Age', *Antiq J*, **49**, 22–9

Cunliffe, B W 1968. 'Early pre-Roman Iron Age communities in eastern England', *Antiq J*, **48**, 175–91

Cunliffe, B W 1992. 'Anniversary Address', *Annual Report and Proceedings 1991-2*, 1–10, London

Cunliffe, B W 1995. 'Anniversary Address', *Annual Report and Proceedings 1993-4*, 5–12, London

Dufty, A R 1980. 'Anniversary Address', *Antiq J*, **60**, 1–7

Dufty, A R 1981. 'Anniversary Address', *Antiq J*, **61**, 1–8

Evans, J 1956. *A History of the Society of Antiquaries*, London

Evans, J 1961. 'Anniversary Address', *Antiq J*, **41**, 149–53

Evans, J 1962. 'Anniversary Address', *Antiq J*, **42**, 141–7

Evans, J 1963. 'Anniversary Address', *Antiq J*, **43**, 185–9

Evans, J 1964. 'Anniversary Address', *Antiq J*, **44**, 117–21

Evans, J D 1985. 'Anniversary Address', *Antiq J*, **65**, 1–10

Evans, J D 1986. 'Anniversary Address', *Antiq J*, **66**, 1–8

Evans, J G, Limbrey, S and Cleere, H (eds) 1975. *The Effect of Man on the Landscape: the Highland zone*, London

Fox, C 1949. 'Anniversary Address', *Antiq J*, **29**, 137–44

Jervis, S J 1997. 'Anniversary Address', *Annual Report and Proceedings 1996*, 5–14

Jervis, S J 1999. 'Anniversary Address', *Annual Report and Proceedings 1998*, 5–16

Jervis, S J 2000. 'Anniversary Address', *Annual Report and Proceedings 1999*, 5–17

Kennedy, D and Bewley, 2004. *Ancient Jordan from the Air*, London

Mann, J 1950. 'Anniversary Address', *Antiq J*, **30**, 129–34

Mann, J 1953. 'Anniversary Address', *Antiq J*, **33**, 153–8

Mann, J 1954. 'Anniversary Address', *Antiq J*, **34**, 149–54

Myres, J N L 1971. 'Anniversary Address', *Antiq J*, **51**, 167–76

Myres, J N L 1972. 'Anniversary Address', *Antiq J*, **52**, 1–7

Myres, J N L 1973. 'Anniversary Address', *Antiq J*, **53**, 1–8

Myres, J N L 1974. 'Anniversary Address', *Antiq J*, **54**, 1–7

Myres, J N L 1975. 'Anniversary Address', *Antiq J*, **55**, 1–9

Peacock, D P S 1969. 'A contribution to the study of Glastonbury Ware from south-western England', *Antiq J*, **49**, 41–61

Peacock, D P S 1974. 'Amphorae and the Baetican fish industry', *Antiq J*, **54**, 232–43

Powell, T G E 1973. 'Excavation of the megalithic chambered cairn at Dyffrey Ardudwy, Merioneth, Wales', *Archaeologia*, **104**, 1–49

Richmond, I 1965. 'Anniversary Address', *Antiq J*, **45**, 167–72

Robbins, R M 1989. 'Anniversary Address', *Antiq J*, **69**, 1–9

Robbins, R M 1990. 'Anniversary Address', *Antiq J*, **70**, 1–11

Society of Antiquaries 2000. *Annual Report and Proceedings 2000*, London

Stead, I 1967. 'A La Tène III burial at Welwyn Garden City', *Archaeologia*, **101**, 1–62

Taylor, A J 1978. 'Anniversary Address', *Antiq J*, **58**, 1–7

Ward-Perkins, J B and Goodchild, R G 1953. 'The Christian antiquities of Tripolitania', *Archaeologia*, **95**, 1–84

Webster, G 1955. 'A note on the use of coal in Roman Britain', *Antiq J*, **35**, 199–216

Wheeler, R E M 1955. 'Anniversary Address', *Antiq J*, **35**, 153–61

Wheeler, R E M 1956. 'Anniversary Address', *Antiq J*, **36**, 165–71

Wheeler, R E M 1957. 'Anniversary Address', *Antiq J*, **37**, 121–30

Wheeler, R E M 1958. 'Anniversary Address', *Antiq J*, **38**, 165–73

Wheeler, R E M 1959. 'Anniversary Address', *Antiq J*, **39**, 163–9

Wilson, D R 1975. *Aerial Reconnaissance for Archaeology*, London

Wormald, F 1966. 'Anniversary Address', *Antiq J*, **46**, 173–7

Wormald, F 1968. 'Anniversary Address', *Antiq J*, **48**, 157–61

'A Tree with Many Branches': the Fellowship at the Start of the Twenty-first Century

David Gaimster

A 'tree with many branches' is how Sir Mortimer Wheeler characterized the Fellowship of the Society of Antiquaries of London in his Anniversary Address of 1957.[1] Fifty years ago, at a time when traditional antiquarian studies were beginning to come under pressure from professionalization, scientific and conceptual advances, new investigative technologies and the growth of new sub-disciplines in archaeology and related fields, Wheeler compared the Society to a general assembly of the United Nations in which the increasingly diverse enquiry of the material past was brought together and examined with rigour and with a common perspective.[2] He described the Fellowship in terms of 'a currency of educated minds in chosen contact',[3] its collective intellectual authority making a telling contribution to the study of the past and influencing the manner in which it was appreciated and protected.

Wheeler's 1957 Anniversary Address is notable for its opening interrogation of the Society's relevance as a learned body in the immediate post-war years: 'Are we, as a Society, keeping pace with changing need and circumstance? Times change; do we change in close enough harmony with them? To put it shortly and bluntly, is the Society doing its job?' Half a century on, the Society's Tercentenary affords a further opportunity to review the activities, profile and influence of the Fellowship, both among the cultural heritage community and in the wider public domain. Such a review must scrutinize the role and position of the Society in an increasingly competitive environment of devolved central government agencies, museums, libraries and archives, university departments, professional institutes and conservation bodies that make up the cultural heritage sector, both public and voluntary. At a time when knowledge-based organizations are being caricatured as 'narrow, elitist and self-interested', it is clearly important for the Society to reinforce its distinctive value as a learned society of academicians and the insight its broad interest base can bring to scholarship, conservation and to the public understanding of the past.

The relevance of the Society today and its work has been brought into focus through the national debate on British identity. Speeches by government ministers, among others, have sparked a widespread interest in how an understanding of 'Britishness' in all its diversity has been created.[4] It is not without significance that the Society was founded as a national body during the same year as the Act of Union

Fig 116. President Eric Fernie admitting new Fellow Melanie Hall on the occasion of the Society's Ordinary Meeting held on 2 November 2006 at the Houghton Library, Harvard University, Cambridge, Mass. Melanie is Director of Museum Studies at Boston University, and a scholar of the British heritage movement (1840–1920) in its international context. *Photograph*: © Society of Antiquaries of London.

in 1707. It is arguable that the Society's contribution to the forging of that island story is as relevant today as it was three hundred years ago.

This chapter is offered as an afterword to the review by Graeme Barker of the changing profile of the Society's Fellowship over the course of the second half of the twentieth century. Drawing on an analysis of citations for new Fellows admitted between 1999 and 2004 and on a questionnaire circulated to Fellows in 2005, it provides a snapshot of the Fellowship today: its age profile, gender mix, geographical distribution, professional background, research interests, institutional affiliations and spheres of influence. The exercise has been motivated by the desire to learn more about the extent to which the Fellowship is helping to shape its sector today, and what strategies the Society's Council might employ to ensure it is able to maintain its influence. The results of this review of the Fellowship will also be discussed in the light of the strategic objectives of the Society, which were revised in 2005.[5]

AGE, EMPLOYMENT AND GENDER

As of April 2006 the Society's Fellowship stands at around 2,335 Fellows, with new Fellows being elected at a rate of 175 per annum through seven ballots held over a twelve-month period (fig 116). The annual loss through death, resignation and amoval averages at fifty-five. Thus, at the current net gain rate of 120 Fellows a year, the Society should reach its agreed target of 3,000 Fellows by 2012 (the target figure of 3,000 was recommended by the Review undertaken in the year 2000 and endorsed by Council in 2005).[6] The policy of expanding the Fellowship reflects not a short-term financial imperative but a medium- to longer-term strategy to ensure that the size of the Fellowship corresponds proportionately to the cultural heritage sector as a whole and that the Fellowship reflects the size and ever-widening diversity of the sector. By way of a comparative benchmark, it is worth noting that in 2003 the number of paid employees within the archaeological profession was around 5,700.[7] Data on other professions represented among the Fellowship is not readily available.

One objective of the questionnaire was to capture information on the age profile of the Fellowship in order to gauge how well it reflects its constituency in terms of career progression and post-employment profile. Since age is not a barrier – nor a criterion, for that matter – to election, the Society has never before requested such information. Table 20 shows a breakdown of the Fellowship by age based on the 30 per cent sample generated by the questionnaire. The analysis confirms a predicted imbalance in the age profile of the Fellowship. Firstly, if we take 65 as the average retirement age, we see that 46.35 per cent of the respondents are of post-employment status. If we add those aged 60–65 (the second largest group at 15.15 per cent of the total), that figure rises to 61.5 per cent. The next highest peak belongs to the 50–60 age group, with a combined 27.6 per cent of the Fellowship, leaving the under-50s with just over 10.8 per cent. Less than 5 per cent of the Fellowship is aged below 45. The figures reflect an increasingly maturing Fellowship profile, with three-quarters of the Fellowship in the over-55 age group and less than a quarter of the Fellowship in mid-career (say, the 35 to 55 bracket). Perhaps the principle of peer election militates against the introduction of younger blood into the Fellowship, if existing Fellows mainly nominate new Fellows from their own age circle.

By way of contrast, the figures may be compared with the age profile of the archaeological profession taken in 2003.[8] In this case 87 per cent of working archaeologists were recorded as being between 20 and 50 years of age. Meanwhile, a British Academy survey of 2001 found that over 50 per cent of archaeological academic staff were under 40, and only 20 per cent were aged 51 or over.[9] This represents the youngest age profile of any area of full-time academic staff in the arts, humanities and social sciences reported by the Academy in its 1998–9 report. Although it is likely to be in keeping with the age profile of the cultural heritage sector as a whole, particularly if the voluntary element is included, the Fellowship of the Society of Antiquaries is clearly not reflective of those employed in this sector. As such, its influence may be weak among key decision-makers in senior positions. Fifty years ago, Sir Mortimer Wheeler noted the threat to the Society's vitality and its perception posed by electing new Fellows after they had retired. Quoting Disraeli's dictum that almost everything that is great has been done by youth, he said: 'I should like to see the bulk of our Fellowship admitted under the age of forty.'[10] In responding to the Society's post-millennium recruitment drive, Fellows have recognized the need to look for potential candidates within their networks who exhibit the desired quality of output and contribution at the mid-career stage. The drive to modulate the imbalance in the age profile of the Society is motivated by the acknowledgement that the Society's purpose is compromised if it is not able to demonstrate that it is reflective of its constituency.

Despite the skewed age profile of the existing Fellowship, it is striking that in recent years the proportion of new Fellows in full-time employment is rising. Only 8.4 per

TABLE 20: AGE PROFILE, 2005

Age	Responses	%
30–35	1	0.14
36–40	9	1.28
41–45	15	2.14
46–50	51	7.29
51–55	85	12.16
56–60	108	15.45
61–65	106	15.16
66–70	92	13.16
71–75	93	13.30
76–80	65	9.29
81+	74	10.58
Total	699	99.95

699 responses in total, representing 30.39 per cent of the Fellowship

Table 20. Age profile as captured in the 2005 questionnaire

cent of those elected during the period 1999 to 2004 were retired at the time of admission (table 21b). The questionnaire revealed that those Fellows aged 60 to 65 were mostly still in post, making a ratio of 27:23 of working to retired Fellows.

Of new Fellows elected during the most recent five-year period, by far the most (34.1 per cent) are employed by universities, while the almost 14 per cent engaged in museums represent the next largest group of new Fellows (see table 21b). The predominance of university and museum posts among new Fellows reflects the continuation of an existing trend among the existing Fellowship, as indicated by the 2005 questionnaire (40.4 and 13.9 per cent respectively: table 21a). The relatively high number working in higher education reflects the growth in recent years of student numbers in the arts, humanities and social-science disciplines and the consequent expansion in teaching posts in history, archaeology and related subjects.[11] The remainder of the new Fellows are employed across a wide range of professional contexts, among the largest groups being national government (including English Heritage, Cadw, Historic Scotland and other governmental agencies) and local government planning departments (6.9 and 4.8 per cent respectively according to the questionnaire). The development of private practice in the cultural heritage sector in the UK is reflected in the increase in Fellows who work in commercial archaeological and conservation practices and in cultural-resource consultancy (5.5 and 8 per cent respectively among new Fellows). It is noteworthy that the Society's current representation in libraries and archives and in public-sector conservation is relatively

Table 21a. Employment profile as captured by the 2005 questionnaire

Table 21b. Employment profile as captured by the 1999–2004 data

TABLE 21A: EMPLOYMENT PROFILE, 2005

Field	No.	%
Retired	326	46
Working	373	54
University	151	40.4
Museum	52	13.9
Library	3	0.8
Archive	8	2.1
Central government	26	6.9
Local government	18	4.8
Commercial heritage	9	2.4
Conservation	14	3.7
Heritage NGO	20	5.3
Consultancy	20	5.3
Other*	52	13.9
Total	699	99.5

* incl freelance researchers, authors, architects, barristers, journalists, military, clergy, etc
699 responses in total, representing 30.39 per cent of the Fellowship

TABLE 21B: EMPLOYMENT PROFILE, 1999–2004

Field	No.	%
University	145	34.1
Museum	59	13.9
Library	6	1.4
Archives	4	0.9
Central government	33	7.7
Local government	23	5.4
Commercial	22	5.1
Heritage conservation	2	0.4
Heritage NGO	14	3.3
Consultancy	34	8.0
Other	46	10.8
Retired	36	8.4
Total	424	99.4

424 records

low in both sets of figures and may reflect a significant decline in these sectors.

An examination of the 424 new Fellows elected between 1999 and 2004 reveals a 71 to 29 per cent split in the ratio of males to females. The questionnaire results showed only a marginal difference across the wider group of Fellows, with the gender percentage being 76 to 24 in favour of males. The figures compare relatively poorly to those issued by the National Museum Directors' Conference in 2003,[12] which revealed that this sector has a 50:50 balance (though it does not include separate data on the ratio of females to males in senior positions). In the archaeological profession as a whole, the percentage split is 64 to 36 in favour of males.[13] However, when compared to the UK demographic split of 51:49 and the working population split of 55:45, it is clear that women are under-represented in the Fellowship overall.

Despite the disparity, it is evident that female representation in the Fellowship is on the rise. Graeme Barker reports that in 1990 only 17 per cent of new Fellows were women (see p 392), compared to 29 per cent in the most recent five-year intake. In fact, the Society's current gender balance looks to be roughly in line with that of the British academic community overall. The British Academy's most recently published data on females in full-time work at British universities stands at 34 per cent. Those in senior positions (professorships and senior lectureships) in the arts, humanities and social sciences represent 38 per cent of the total.

LOCATION, LOCATION ...

The Society of Antiquaries of London was founded in the early eighteenth century as a national body with broad geographical interests. It was charged by its Royal Charter of 1751 with the 'encouragement, advancement and furtherance of the study and knowledge of the antiquities and history of this and other countries'. Any assessment of the Fellowship and its capacity to pursue that enlightened mission must take into account the residential distribution of its members, both domestically and overseas.

Of all the information held by the Society on the Fellowship, that of geographical location is the easiest to retrieve and is available for all Fellows. Table 22a shows the relative distribution of the Fellowship at April 2006 both in the United Kingdom and overseas. Predictably, the greatest concentration of Fellows is in London and the south east of England (16.6 and 22.7 per cent respectively), where the number of posts in higher education and national and regional cultural organizations is greatest. Although there is a fairly even spread of Fellows around the remainder of English regions, there is a distinct tail-off in numbers towards the Midlands and the north of England beyond Yorkshire. Wales, Scotland and Yorkshire each host around 5 per cent of the Fellowship. Although the number of Northern Irish Fellows has virtually doubled in the past year, the province is under-represented, with only sixteen Fellows; by contrast, the Republic of Ireland has thirty-three.

Table 22b contains a more detailed breakdown of the 118 Fellows (5.07 per cent) who are resident on the continent of Europe. Despite the good geographical spread in over twenty countries, the overall numbers are relatively low for a learned society that aspires to an international profile. Recent European enlargement and greater engagement internationally by Fellows from the UK offer opportunities to extend the Society's representation across the Continent. Given the clear international dimension of the Society's mission, recruitment of new Fellows here must fall within the Society's strategic priorities in the short to medium term.

As in Europe, the North American higher education community and network of major cultural institutions both offer further opportunities to grow the Society's international influence. The Society's Council will be looking to the existing North American Fellowship of over one hundred to recruit more actively in the future. A similar aspiration for growth can be made for the rest of the Anglophone world, particularly Australasia, where the higher education community is growing with deregulation and where, for example, a wide range of archaeological sub-disciplines is taught to PhD level in every Australian state.

The information contained in the citations for new Fellows elected between 1999 and 2004 reveals current trends in national and international recruitment patterns. In this survey the dominance of London as the base for a significant number of Fellows appears to be on the rise (22 per cent), possibly at the expense of the south-east region outside London (12 per cent). Overall, the combined London/south-east

Table 22a. Domicile of the Fellowship as at April 2006

TABLE 22A: DOMICILE OF THE FELLOWSHIP IN 2006

Residence	No.	%
London	388	16.66
South-east England	529	22.71
South-west England	232	9.96
East of England	192	8.24
East Midlands	100	4.29
West Midlands	85	3.65
North-west England	67	2.88
Yorkshire and the Humber	137	5.88
North-east England	52	2.23
Scotland	110	4.72
Wales	109	4.68
Isle of Man	8	0.34
Channel Islands	7	0.30
Northern Ireland	16	0.69
Republic of Ireland	33	1.42
Europe	118	5.07
North America and Caribbean	108	4.64
Australasia	29	1.25
Rest of the world	9	0.39
Total	2,329	100

TABLE 22B: OVERSEAS FELLOWS IN 2006			Table 22b. Overseas Fellows as at April 2006
Residence	*No.*	*%*	

Residence	No.	%
EUROPE		
Austria	3	2.54
Belgium	3	2.54
Bulgaria	1	0.85
Cyprus	9	7.63
Czech Republic	3	2.54
Denmark	4	3.38
Finland	1	0.85
France	29	24.58
Germany	17	14.41
Greece	9	7.63
Hungary	1	0.85
Iceland	1	0.85
Italy	11	9.32
Malta	2	1.69
Norway	2	1.69
Poland	1	0.85
Russia	3	2.54
Spain	3	2.54
Sweden	1	0.85
Switzerland	4	3.39
The Netherlands	10	8.48
Total	118	100
NORTH AMERICA AND THE CARIBBEAN		
Barbados	1	0.93
Bermuda	1	0.93
Canada	16	14.81
USA	90	83.33
Total	108	100
AUSTRALASIA		
Australia	24	82.76
New Zealand	5	17.24
Total	29	100
REST OF WORLD		
Israel	3	33.33
Japan	1	11.11
Kenya	1	11.11
Lebanon	1	11.11
Tunisia	1	11.11
Turkey	2	22.22
Total	9	99.99

figures for the period (34 per cent) are considerably up on those for 1991 to 1995 (20.9 per cent: see table 13, page 394). Moreover, the proportion of new Fellows based in the rest of England appears to be in decline (45 per cent; down from 53.4 per cent in 1991–5). From the figures it appears that the Society's Fellowship is becoming more London-centric than at any time in its recent history. In the 1950s only around 18 per cent of new Fellows originated in London and the south east of England (see table 13, page 394). Nevertheless, over the next few years a significant proportion of the metropolitan Fellowship may be redistributed as heritage bodies move staff from central London to new locations outside the capital.

A further disparity between the existing Fellowship profile and that for newly elected Fellows can be observed in the rest of Britain and Ireland, where the combined figures for new Fellows in Scotland, Wales, Northern Ireland, the Irish Republic, the Isle of Man and the Channel Islands appear to be on a slow but steady increase (10 per cent in the early 1990s, rising to around 12 per cent over the past five years). By contrast, having stressed the strategic importance of the Society's profile on the continent of Europe, it appears that the number of European Fellows outside Britain and Ireland is in decline. While in the 1970s 10 per cent of new Fellows were based in Europe, this figure dropped to 6.6 per cent during the early 1990s, and over the past five years, only 3 per cent of newly elected Fellows have come from the Continent.

EDUCATION, EDUCATION ...

Table 23a.
Qualifications of
Fellows as captured by
the 2005 questionnaire

Table 23b.
Qualifications of
Fellows as captured by
the 1999–2004 data

Tables 23a and b show the educational profile of the Fellowship today. Over 50 per cent of new Fellows and respondents to the questionnaire hold doctoral degrees and around 20 per cent hold Masters qualifications, while a further 20 per cent are educated to first degree level. In line with the highly professionalized nature of today's cultural heritage sector, it follows that relatively few Fellows lack higher education qualifications. Nevertheless, the fact that 6 per cent of new Fellows elected in the past five years have no degree is a clear illustration that the Society continues to recognize

TABLE 23A: QUALIFICATIONS, 2005		
Qualifications	*No.*	*%*
PhD	368	52.6
MA	145	20.7
BA	145	20.7
Professional accreditation	26	3.7
No qualification	15	2.1
Total	699	99.8

699 responses in total, representing 30.39 per cent of the Fellowship

TABLE 23B: QUALIFICATIONS, 1999–2004		
Qualifications	*No.*	*%*
PhD	218	51.4
MA	82	19.3
BA	90	21.2
Professional accreditation	8	2.0
No qualification	26	6.1
Total	424	100

424 records

contributions and achievements irrespective of the more traditional educational pathways.

Overall, the Fellowship's qualification profile reflects its status as a college of academicians; its postgraduate degree quota of 70-plus per cent is consistent with what might be expected of the membership of any senior international learned society. By way of comparison, it is notable that among the professional archaeological community in the UK only 10 per cent of accredited practitioners hold a doctorate, although 21 per cent have a Masters degree as their highest level of academic qualification.[14]

RESEARCH ACTIVITY AND INTERESTS

A clear-cut statistical breakdown of research interests and activities has been more difficult to achieve. Most Fellows have several areas of interest and many indicated active research in more than one field of study (699 individuals generated 1,156 responses: see table 24a). By way of calibration, the data collected from the citation notes for new Fellows elected between 1999 and 2004 helps in interpreting these figures (table 24b). Archaeology, the largest single field of study recorded, accounts for 22.8 per cent of new Fellows and 26.7 per cent of questionnaire responses. These latest figures are lower than those collected by Graeme Barker where 34.7 per cent of new Fellows elected between 1991 and 1995 listed archaeology as their main

Table 24a. Main fields of research interest as captured by the 2005 questionnaire

Table 24b. Main fields of research interest as captured by the 1999–2004 data

TABLE 24A: RESEARCH INTERESTS, 2005		
Field of study	*No.*	*%*
Antiquarian history	62	6.0
Archaeology	272	26.7
Archaeological science	26	2.5
Architecture	115	11.2
Archive studies	31	3.0
Artefact studies	63	6.1
Art history	88	8.6
Conservation studies	23	2.2
Heraldry/seals	18	1.7
Heritage management	38	3.7
History	167	16.4
Historical bibliography/library	15	1.4
Landscape studies	59	5.7
Manuscripts	41	4.0
Total	1,018	99.2
multiple responses		

TABLE 24B: RESEARCH INTERESTS, 1999–2004		
Field of study	*No.*	*%*
Antiquarian history	11	2.59
Archaeology	97	22.80
Archaeological science	18	4.20
Architecture	28	6.60
Archive studies	14	3.30
Artefact studies	68	16.00
Art history	50	11.70
Conservation studies	17	4.00
Heraldry/seals	1	0.20
Heritage management	9	2.10
History	47	11.00
Historical bibliography/library	15	3.50
Landscape studies	14	3.30
Manuscripts	11	2.50
Museology	10	2.30
Other	14	3.30
Total	424	99.39
424 records		

discipline (see table 14, page 395). However, when archaeology is combined with the sub-disciplines of archaeological science, artefact studies, cultural resource management, landscape studies and maritime archaeology, the collective figure for archaeology increases to 48.4 per cent of newly elected Fellows and 44.7 per cent of questionnaire returns. If architectural history (including, we assume, buildings archaeology), museology and numismatics were to be added to these totals, the aggregate return for those with archaeological interests would rise by another 12.2 per cent of new Fellows and 11.2 per cent of questionnaire respondents. How far those respondents indicating that their main field of study is art history or antiquarian history (11.7 and 2.6 per cent of new Fellows respectively) are engaged in archaeological activity is impossible to gauge, but it could be significant.

Whatever the precise disciplinary signature, what comes across very clearly in this survey is the plurality and vitality of antiquarian activity across the Society's Fellowship today. In addition to archaeology and architectural and art history, the study of heraldry, manuscripts and historical bibliography were also listed as main disciplinary fields. This overall diversity reflects the extent of sub-disciplinary specialization in the study of the material past that derives from continuous innovation in method and theory. Thus any snapshot of the research interests of Fellows may be examined as a barometer of current trends in an organic process of natural selection within the *ur*-disciplines of history, art history and antiquarian studies. As former President Simon Jervis has noted in referring to that first gathering of the Fellowship at a tavern on Fleet Street in 1707, 'a considerable degree of variety and change was genetically inevitable'.[15]

The plurality of antiquarian research engaged in by the modern Fellowship is also reflected in the data collected on period and geographical interests. The figures

Table 25a. Main period interest as captured by the 2005 questionnaire

Table 25b. Main period interest as captured by the 1999–2004 data

TABLE 25A: PERIODS OF INTEREST, 2005			TABLE 25B: PERIODS OF INTEREST, 1999–2004		
Main period	*No.*	%	*Main period*	*No.*	%
Early prehistory	10	1.4	Early prehistory	9	2.10
Later prehistory	47	6.7	Later prehistory	19	4.40
Classical	30	4.2	Classical	20	4.70
Romano-British	27	3.8	Romano-British	24	5.60
Early medieval	55	7.8	Early medieval	32	7.50
Later medieval	73	10.4	Later medieval	44	10.30
Post-medieval	93	13.3	Post-medieval	47	11.08
19th and 20th century	26	3.7	19th and 20th century	33	7.70
Multi-period	310	44.3	Multi-period	196	46.20
Other	23	3.2			
None	5	0.7			
Total	699	99.4	*Total*	424	100

699 responses in total, representing 30.39 per cent of the Fellowship

424 records

collected by the 2005 questionnaire and by the latest five-year survey (tables 25a and b) are broadly consistent in indicating that a majority of Fellows have multi-period interests (44.3 and 46.2 per cent respectively). Most of those represented in this category were engaged in the study of continuities and contrasts between early and late prehistory, between classical and Romano-British culture, between early and late medieval and between the post-medieval and the modern epochs. Those for whom an overriding period of interest can be determined were fairly evenly divided across prehistory, the classical world, Roman Britain, the Middle Ages and the early modern period (sixteenth to eighteenth centuries), the latter period accounting for the greater number of Fellows (some 13 per cent of questionnaire respondents). Other trends were discernible in the detail, notably the dominance of those concerned with later prehistory over early prehistory and the not insignificant growth in Fellows involved in nineteenth- and twentieth-century studies as their primary concern, particularly among the newly elected group (7.7 per cent).

In the case of prioritizing geographical areas of interest (table 26), a majority of respondents to the 2005 questionnaire indicated that they were primarily concerned with England (25.8 per cent) and Britain as a whole (18.5 per cent), while only a minority specified precise regions of Britain or Ireland. The questionnaire revealed that a significant proportion of Fellows conducted their research beyond the confines of Britain: western Europe accounted for 16 per cent of the returns, while 10 per cent of Fellows indicated they were engaged in the study of the antiquity and history of the Mediterranean. Relatively fewer respondents were active in the Middle East

TABLE 26: GEOGRAPHICAL RESEARCH INTEREST, 2005

Geographical research interest	No.	%
London	33	3.6
England	238	25.8
Scotland	31	3.3
Wales	31	3.3
Ireland	18	2.0
United Kingdom	171	18.5
Western Europe	147	15.9
Eastern Europe	21	2.2
Northern Europe	48	5.2
Mediterranean World	92	10.0
Middle East	31	3.3
Asia	10	1.1
Americas	18	1.9
Australasia	9	1.0
Other	24	2.6
Total	922	100
multiple responses		

Table 26. Geographical research interest as captured by the 2005 questionnaire

(3.3 per cent) and other regions of the globe (6.6 per cent).

Overall, the combined figures for international activity of the mainly UK-based Fellowship of the Society are encouraging. According to the 2005 questionnaire alone, around 43 per cent of the 699 respondents were actively engaged or primarily interested in the heritage overseas. Although predominantly resident in Britain and Ireland, this snapshot suggests a roughly equal balance of interest in the heritage and material history of Britain and Ireland and that of other countries.

INFLUENCE

One of the Society's principal strategic objectives is to influence policy making in the national and international heritage. It is well placed as an independent non-governmental organization to encourage and facilitate public debate on the management, conservation, presentation and public understanding of the cultural heritage. The depth and breadth of knowledge and expertise among the Society's 2,300-strong Fellowship gives it the ability to speak with authority on key issues of policy and delivery 'to those who have the power to influence events'.[16]

In addition to making statutory appointments to the boards of public and charitable cultural institutions (including the British Museum, Sir John Soane's Museum and the National Trust), the Council of the Society works to ensure it is represented through its Fellows at a senior level in organizations across the national and international cultural heritage and historic environment network. In an effort to establish the extent of the Society's current representation and influence in its sector, the 2005 questionnaire asked Fellows to list their principal voluntary managerial and advisory responsibilities in relation to a number of spheres. These were, namely, government departments, national heritage agencies, museums, libraries and archives councils, higher education research panels and more specialist research groups, and national and local voluntary sector conservation or heritage research bodies.

Out of a total of 699 respondents a relatively high number of 571 Fellows (81.7 per cent) indicated that they are active in some capacity or another (table 27). Over 12 per cent of these Fellows are involved in advising government departments and agencies on the historic environment and on policy for museums, libraries and archives. Although the questionnaire was not sophisticated enough to separate national from international activity, the return suggests a very respectable level of public policy engagement by individual Fellows whose expertise and insight are respected and in demand.

Over 11 per cent are active as trustees of national heritage charities and a further 5.8 per cent are involved in advising leading commercial archaeological practices. While relatively few Fellows are involved in a managerial or peer-review role with higher education research councils, such as the Arts and Humanities Research Council (under 2 per cent), a far greater number of respondents (11 per cent) are active in running research groups in their own spheres of interest. Bodies listed by

Fellows in the questionnaire ranged from the Nautical Archaeological Society to the Medieval Pottery Research Group. Among the most popular form of external activity were the national and county archaeological and historical societies. Over a quarter of respondents indicated that they were engaged at a senior level with these local bodies. One could say that the Fellowship remains, as it always has, the glue that binds much of the voluntary sector in the historical environment together. Finally, among the sizeable 'other' category of responses, the survey revealed that a significant proportion of Fellows are active in ecclesiastical conservation, notably as cathedral archaeologists, or as members of redundant churches or historic chapels trusts, or as members of diocesan advisory panels. It is from this expert group that the Council of the Society appoints its Morris Committee for the award of grants for the conservation of historic churches.

Drilling down further, perhaps a more qualitative index of Society influence in the UK cultural heritage sector can be found in the leadership positions held by Fellows in public and voluntary organizations. While Fellows have long been active as directors of national museums and galleries, together with university and local authority museum services, a quick glance at the spectrum of organizations listed by Fellows in the 2005 questionnaire reveals that representation is also healthy among the chairmanships, chief executive or board member positions of the national heritage agencies of the UK and the key voluntary sector bodies, including the Council for British Archaeology, the Institute of Field Archaeologists, the Association of Local Government Archaeological Officers, the Society of Antiquaries of Scotland, the Cambrian Archaeological Association, ICOMOS-UK and the Culture Committee of the UK National Commission for UNESCO. There is a strong representation of Fellows among the executives of organizations that make up The Archaeology Forum (TAF),

TABLE 27: INFLUENCE OF FELLOWS, 2005

Sector	No.	%
Government heritage agency	30	5.2
Government advisory group	21	3.6
Government museum/library/archive	22	3.8
University research council	11	1.9
Heritage NGO/charity	66	11.5
Research body	63	11.0
County or local society	150	26.2
Archaeological unit	33	5.8
Other	175	30.6
Total responses	571	100
No responses	128	
Total	699	

Table 27. Influence captured by the 2005 questionnaire as represented by Fellows sitting on boards of management or acting in advisory capacity

which published a public statement on the contribution of archaeology to national life in 2005.[17] Other Fellows act as expert advisers to the All-Party Parliamentary Arts and Heritage, World Heritage and Archaeology Groups. With a few notable exceptions, however, Fellows appear to be less prominent in the leadership of professional bodies concerned with conservation, art and architectural history, or in professional institutes for museums, libraries and archives. These gaps in representation and influence indicate where the Society might look to be more active in the future recruitment of new Fellows.

CONCLUSION

This chapter has taken the form of a snapshot of the Society's Fellowship as it faces its fourth century of endeavour.[18] The investigation has revealed a great deal about the current profile of the Fellowship and the future prospects for developing its individual and collective ability to shape future agendas for the historic environment and cultural heritage both for the regions and countries of the UK and also internationally.

Now, as in the past, among the Fellowship's great strengths is its plurality. It continues to grow organically in line with the expanding contours and growing diversity of its sector. There is neither a discipline nor special research interest in the historic environment or cultural heritage in which Fellows are not represented. The Society acts as a central point of reference and provides a coherent identity for an increasingly heterogeneous community. Election to the Fellowship continues to be a reminder to any individual, whatever his or her specialization, that they are also an antiquary and belong to that 'tree' of enquiry referred to by Wheeler that binds the Fellowship together as a collective force of knowledge and insight.

Among other performance indicators, the Fellowship, in keeping with its purpose as a leading learned society, retains a membership demonstrating the very highest levels of educational achievement, with over 50 per cent of Fellows possessing doctoral degrees. Its gender profile is also in line with best performance in the higher educational sector, and in an environment of near total professionalization, the peer-election process helps to maintain diversity in the sector through its support for amateur enquiry. The representation of a very significant number of Fellows in leadership roles among national agencies and a wide range of voluntary organizations enables the Society to contribute its knowledge and insight to the debate of public policy and the shaping of new agendas.

The weaknesses and threats to the Society revealed through this profiling exercise indicate opportunities for the future strategic development of the organization. The imbalanced age profile of the Fellowship and its relatively weak regional British and international representation provide clear signposts for where recruitment according to age and geography might be prioritized.

The Society's Executive is unable to recruit new Fellows to suit its objectives for strategic growth; only the Fellowship can do that. The introduction of electronic nomination and balloting procedures in 2005 is already helping to encourage more Fellows to participate in the peer-election process. Let us hope that the information collected and discussed here will act as a further incentive for Fellows to think about the future profile of the elected college and the importance of recruiting a balanced ratio of working and retired Fellows and achieving a wider geographical representation. In a globalized world in which the national heritage is increasingly seen from an international perspective (as in the case of Britain's World Heritage Sites), it is critical that the Fellowship retains, enhances and demonstrates its contribution and authority both domestically and overseas. This will be a constant refrain for the twenty-first century.

NOTES

1. Wheeler 1957, 130.
2. Ibid, 125.
3. Ibid, 130.
4. Brown 2004.
5. Society of Antiquaries 2005, 48–9.
6. Fernie 2005, 6.
7. Aitchison and Edwards 2003, 20–1.
8. Ibid, 22–3.
9. British Academy 2001, 42.
10. Wheeler 1957, 125.
11. British Academy 2001.
12. NMDC 2003.
13. Aitchison and Edwards 2003, 21.
14. Ibid, 36.
15. Jervis 2001, 4.
16. Cramp 2003, 4.
17. The Archaeology Forum 2005.
18. I would like to thank Derek Renn, FSA, for collating the 1999–2004 admissions data.

BIBLIOGRAPHY

Aitchison, K and Edwards, R 2003. *Archaeology and Labour Market Intelligence: profiling the profession 2002/3*, Bradford (Cultural Heritage Training Organisation) and Reading (Institute of Field Archaeologists)

The Archaeology Forum 2005. *Archaeology Enriches Us All*, York

British Academy 2001. *Review of Graduate Studies in the Humanities and Social Sciences: main report September 2001*, London

Brown, G 2004. Speech by the Chancellor of the Exchequer, Gordon Brown, at the British Council Annual Lecture, 7 July 2004, <http://www.hm-treasury.gov.uk/ newsroom_and_speeches/press/2004/press_63_04.cfm> (13 Sept 2006)

Cramp, R 2003. 'Anniversary Address', *Antiq J*, **83**, 1–8

Fernie, E 2005. 'Anniversary Address', *Society of Antiquaries Annual Report 2005*, London, 4–12

Jervis, S 2001. 'Anniversary Address', *Antiq J*, **81**, 1–14

NMDC 2003. *National Museum Directors' Conference HR Forum Benchmarking 2003*, <http://www.nationalmuseums.org.uk/news/ 1070496000.html> (13 Sept 2006)

Society of Antiquaries 2005. *Society of Antiquaries Annual Report 2005*, London

Wheeler, R E M 1957. 'Anniversary Address', *Antiq J*, **37**, 121–30

'Society of Antiquaries?'

Eric Fernie

The foregoing essays give the distinct impression that the Society has been subject to criticism throughout its history, from within as well as without. This may be no bad thing, but it is still remarkable, so this closing chapter is intended to examine primarily the effects of the Society's name, but also its public role and its politics, on the Antiquaries' reputation since 1707. I apologize to the contributors to this volume for shamelessly plundering their texts, and hope I have not distorted their meaning too much in search of brevity. I would also like to thank Thomas Cocke and Arthur MacGregor for their very helpful comments on my draft.

The current image of the antiquary is for most people that of a narrow self-absorbed scholar, interested in the trivial rather than the larger context, whose intellectual life is comfortable and self-indulgent. This looks like an instance of a word which has fallen in status, like knave or villain, but in fact the image of the antiquary for the century or so preceding the founding of the Society was as much a source of ridicule as it is now. Thus, from various dates between 1592 and 1707 the antiquary was described as having a musty vocation, living in the past, collecting rags and fragments, loving mouldy, worm-eaten things, dressing in old-fashioned clothes, being pretentious and easily fooled, and doting on ruins (see Woolf (chapter 2)).

Why then did our founders choose such a name? The answer appears to be because it accurately represented the principles they wished to espouse. They saw in a positive light ideals that others ridiculed. Their most important principle was to start with the concrete object, however insignificant, and work empirically from it, thereby rejecting the concept of 'Perfect History', the grand sweep of the national story intended to have a moral as well as a historical purpose. Nothing was excluded. 'Antiquarius', for instance, in the eighteenth century noted that all objects, however imperfect, were legitimate subjects for investigation, provided the antiquary endeavoured 'to weigh in equal scales the force of conflicting evidence, to reconcile discrepancies, and to draw strong conclusions out of minute facts which have escaped the general eye' (Pearce (1); Woolf (2); Myrone (5); Sweet (4)). William Stukeley, in an account of his travels of 1710–23, says that in examining objects he 'avoided prejudice, never carrying any author along with me', while Dr Johnson, in 1755, defines an antiquary as 'a man studious of antiquity; a collector of ancient things'. The Society tends therefore to have been criticized, not for falling short of its ideals, but for adhering to them. This in turn raises the question of the extent to which the Society has maintained these ideals since its founding. I have selected two periods to examine for answers: the second half of the eighteenth century, when there was a confrontation with high art, and the first half of the nineteenth, which saw the rise of archaeology.

During the eighteenth century the Society of Antiquaries was affected, along with scholarly society in general, by a decline in the application of the empirical method. It nevertheless took a number of positive steps in the spirit of its founding principles. The charter of 1751, for example, expanded the Society's area of interest from the 'antiquities and history of Great Britain' to those of 'this and other nations'. Next, 1770 saw the founding of *Archaeologia*. In the introduction to the first issue Richard Gough, who was to become Director in 1771, restated the Society's principles as being 'to separate falsehood from truth, and tradition from evidence, to establish what had probability for its basis' (MacGregor (3); Pearce (1); Woolf (2); Sweet (4)). The most influential policy, which lasted through the century, was the wide-ranging programme of prints, to the extent that the Society was described as an organization primarily for publishing images of artefacts and architecture. High standards of accuracy were maintained through the appointment in 1784 of John Carter as the Society's draughtsman, a man described as one of the best recorders of the age and as meeting 'the first precepts' of the Society (Myrone (5); Woolf (2); Sweet (4); Turner (12)).

By the second half of the century, however, the Society found itself being criticized not for its minute study of history but for the lack of aesthetic quality of its prints and its resistance to the artistic restoration of buildings. In 1768, for example, the prints of George Vertue, who worked extensively for the Society, were criticized for their lack of aesthetic value, and for copying 'with painful exactness', while for Horace Walpole, in a bitter tirade of 1778, 'it is impossible to infuse taste into them' (Myrone (5)). Both these quotations are examples of the sort of criticism in which the Society ought to have rejoiced, but on the whole it did not. In the 1770s, possibly as a response to the criticisms, a series of prints was produced of historical scenes taken from paintings, which, though popular and in keeping with the omnivorous aspect of antiquarian ideals, were at odds with the Society's primary scholarly ethos (Pearce (7); Sweet (4)). The same attitude is evident in the Anniversary Address for 1781, the year in which the Antiquaries, the Royal Academy and the Royal Society moved into Somerset House. In his text the President, Jeremiah Milles, made no mention of the Society's tradition of antiquarian illustration, almost certainly because he wanted to court the Royal Academy, from which engravers had been excluded at its founding in 1768 (Smiles (6)).

The other principled initiative which the Society took in the eighteenth century was the preservation of the integrity of ancient buildings. This was initiated by Gough and supported by Carter, most prominently in their resistance to James Wyatt, whose work pursued the contrary, but nonetheless idealistic, aim of re-creating the supposed sublime qualities of the buildings in question. The Society again executed a retreat, as Gough and Carter were no more able to protect Durham Cathedral from Wyatt's restoration than they were to prevent his election as a Fellow in 1797. As a result, Gough resigned, Carter lost commissions and Carter's protégé, Buckler, was black-balled in 1807 (Sweet (4); Turner (12)).

The first half of the nineteenth century saw another assault on antiquarianism, but this time from exactly the opposite quarter, that of scholarship itself, in the form of the development of archaeology. This constitutes one of the greatest adventures in the history of our understanding of the world and in intellectual culture in general, paralleling the contemporary emergence of disciplines such as geology, chemistry and philology, yet the Society for the most part resisted it. In order to assess the impact of archaeology on the Society and the antiquarian tradition, I have divided the discussion into three parts, beginning with a thumbnail sketch of some of the main developments, moving to how it has been presented in terms of antiquarianism and archaeology, and ending with an alternative interpretation of that juxtaposition.

First, to select a few of the many milestones, in 1793 James Douglas used deductive interpretational principles in the study of Anglo-Saxon graves, and in 1797, in an early indication of the central position of prehistory in the development, John Frere delivered his paper on the flints of Hoxne. In the first decade of the nineteenth century William Cunnington dated a number of barrows to pre-Roman times, and was also one of the earliest, along with C J Thomsen of Denmark, to propose the Three Age model of prehistory. Archaeologists found common cause with geologists in extending the age of the Earth, and adopted their stratigraphic techniques in conducting excavations. The Society's failure to respond adequately to these changes was one of the causes of the founding of new societies for related subjects in the 1830s and 1840s, including the Numismatic Society, the Camden Society and the British Archaeological Association, the last specifically citing the Antiquaries' narrowness as a reason for its initiative. Archaeological principles came to underlie the work of the Ordnance Survey, especially in Ireland, and by the 1870s Pitt-Rivers had established clear stratigraphic principles which were accepted by the archaeological community (Briggs (10); Hingley (8); Sweet (4); Evans (11)).

As to the presentation, archaeology was seen at the time, as it has been since, as a rejection of antiquarianism, and there is plenty of evidence to support this contention. Thus, while it is true that Frere's work was presented in the form of a paper delivered to the Antiquaries, and that other methodologically advanced papers appeared in *Archaeologia*, the Society was not as involved in the debate as some other societies, and the idea of prehistory was more widely accepted outside the Society than inside it. According to the *Gentleman's Magazine* of 1846, the Antiquaries 'have yet much to do before they can elevate [the Society] to that rank among the scientific establishments of England which it ought to hold', and there was more correspondence on the subject in *The Times* and *The Athenaeum* than in the Society's *Proceedings*. Archaeological developments helped to free investigators from the tyranny of books, the Ordnance Survey helped them work without antiquarian preconceptions, and both enabled researchers to move beyond antiquarian speculation to archaeological method. Only a few Fellows were involved in the development of archaeology, while the opposition was led by those most involved with texts, the classicists, medievalists and historians of art and architecture. Converting the Fellows from antiquarianism to archaeology has been described as an uphill battle (Briggs (10); Evans (11); Hingley (8)).

This confrontation can, however, bear another interpretation, namely that the Society did maintain its founding principles through this period, and it was the archaeologists among the Fellowship who did so. The juxtaposition of archaeology and antiquarianism is certainly justified, as the Fellows who were in opposition were not labelled antiquarians by archaeologists, but identified themselves as such. Yet it is fair to ask if they were justified in doing so, as those who called themselves archaeologists seem to have followed the founding aims of the Society, while those opposed can only be said to have departed from these aims.

What is new and archaeological turns out, on investigation, to be quintessentially antiquarian, as the following four examples suggest. First, freeing archaeology from the tyranny of books was arguably exactly what the antiquaries of the eighteenth century thought they were doing in rejecting 'Perfect History' for the evidence of the full spectrum of the material remains. Second, the stubborn resistance of the conservative strand of the Fellowship to empirical deductive analysis sounds like the sort of thing that Gough would have roundly condemned. Third, the Ordnance Survey drawings have rightly been described as lacking antiquarian preconception, but that is contemporary, nineteenth-century antiquarianism, rather than the open-minded antiquarianism of Gough or 1707. Finally, the antiquarian speculation contrasted with archaeological method was the kind of theorizing that lacked a basis in evidence, whereas speculation of some kind has always been essential to research. In fact, this is perhaps the one point on which the archaeologists departed from sound antiquarian principle, that is, in the claim that 'we speak from facts, not theory', made in the introduction to Cunnington's book (Briggs (10); Evans (11)). This can be seen as a new dogmatism, as there is no such thing as 'innocent' fact-gathering. If one applied the facts-not-theory principle rigorously, then rescue archaeology would represent the ideal approach to excavation.

Archaeology has ever since played its part in maintaining antiquarian principles, principles which have, in more recent years, protected the study of the past from the more outlandish aspects of post-modernism, though it has been pointed out that the eighteenth-century characterization of the antiquary as wayward and individualistic translates well into post-modern terminology as 'many-stranded, diverse and imbued with healthy cultural obstinacy' (Pearce (1); Myrone (5)).

The standing of the Society has also been affected by the public policies it has adopted and the ways in which it has chosen to implement them. From its inception the Society considered it a duty to contribute to the public good, and, after 1751, according to the *Gentleman's Magazine*, the Society was 'determined to demonstrate the public utility of the newly incorporated body' (MacGregor (3); Sweet (4)). The policy with the most practical outcome for the public good was arguably the Society's initiation of the conservation of ancient monuments. Begun by Gough and Carter, this movement was continued by Ruskin, who, in 1854, persuaded the Society to act as a conservation body for medieval buildings and to establish relevant principles. These principles were in turn used by William Morris when he founded the Society for the Protection of Ancient Buildings in 1879. By the 1860s the Society had set out the basis for a state archaeological service, supporting attempts by John Lubbock to pass legislation in the 1870s, which succeeded with the passing of the Ancient Monuments Protection Act in 1882, and, since the 1960s, the Society has been involved in practical conservation through its ownership of Kelmscott Manor. Finally, the excavation projects supported by the Antiquaries in the twentieth century must be considered akin to conservation in the extent of their contribution to the public good, from those at Silchester, Verulamium and Camulodunum to the most recent at Sutton Hoo (Turner (12); Fulford (14)).

In addition to pursuing its ideals in the form of such public policies, the Society also, of course, had pragmatic reasons for contributing to the public good, what might be called the external politics of the organization, intended to protect its existence and reputation. These policies are difficult to pin down, but appear to be closely reflected in the composition of the Fellowship. While this started at a relatively middling social level, already before 1717 there was an attempt to involve the aristocracy, unavoidably so in the pursuit of a royal charter. Yet the professions remained more important than the nobility, and Martin Folkes, President when the charter was received, was a commoner (Pearce (1); MacGregor (3)). The aristocracy became prominent only in the late eighteenth century, when there was a move to increase the Society's influence coupled with a drive for 'taste'. Already in 1803 the *Gentleman's Magazine* accused the Society of having become too fashionable to fulfil its original designs and of giving wealth and rank precedence in the admission of Fellows over ability in the study of antiquities. This trend culminated in the election of the Earls of Leicester and Aberdeen as successive Presidents whose terms of office covered almost the whole of the first half of the nineteenth century. Both were largely absentee officers, the assumption presumably being that this drawback was outweighed by the direct protection of a powerful aristocratic patron. This arrangement may in part explain the inadequacy of the Society's response to archaeology, also suggested by the request by Council in 1845 that Lord Aberdeen discuss the subject in his Anniversary Address. In the twentieth century, the intersection of academic research and politics in the interests of public amenity is most clearly pointed up by the conservation of the landscape (MacGregor (3); Pearce (1); Sweet (4); Hingley (8); Evans (11); Morris (13); Barker (15)).

To sum up, and starting with politics, the Society of Antiquaries has not had a high political profile, probably for two very good reasons. First, politics can be dangerous: many clubs of the eighteenth century avoided involvement in what Arthur MacGregor calls 'the road to ruination'. Second, political activism and concerted action do not seem to suit the character of the Fellowship. This is evident in the Society's opposition to Grand History, a kind of history which was thought to provide a guide to the affairs of the world. It is also there in the experience of the 1750s, when the Society determined to demonstrate its public utility in part by mounting projects intended to establish 'a comprehensive survey of the nation's antiquities' and a chronological register of improvements. These were based on questionnaires sent to Fellows, but they failed because, as Daniel Woolf recounts, Fellows did not respond well to being directed. Council acknowledged this characteristic in its *Annual Report* for 2000, saying that it preferred to act, not as a pressure group, but through contacts provided by Fellows. Yet the Society has been successful on what might be called an intermediate level between high politics and individual contacts in identifying the major issues of the day and seeking results which were often achieved, whether or not the Society set the agendas for action (MacGregor (3); Woolf (2); Barker (15)).

As to its public role, the Society has always felt it necessary, for both idealistic and practical reasons, to contribute to the public good, as much in earlier times as today under the eye of the Charity Commissioners. By far the most obvious positive contribution the Society can make in this respect is, it seems to me, to act as an umbrella and a focus for the multiplicity of bodies involved with material culture. While there are strong arguments for unity – as with the Royal Society of Edinburgh which includes the humanities and the sciences – there are also advantages in having smaller, dedicated bodies, such as those which came into existence in the 1830s and 1840s, but which make the need for an umbrella all the greater. As Rosemary Sweet puts it, diversity is a strength, but it can also cause a lack of focus. Multiple societies related via an umbrella body may therefore be the optimum arrangement. Specialist committees were considered by the Society in the 1830s, but rejected. That however was in an atmosphere of incipient disruption, and it may be time to reconsider the idea. In saying all of this I find myself in good company. In Graeme Barker's words: 'President after President [over the last half-century] has reiterated that one of the Society's main purposes in an age of increasing specialization is to build scholarly bridges, bringing together scholars from the full span of research on antiquities.' In constructing these bridges the diversity of the current Fellowship, as indicated in David Gaimster's essay, is one of our most powerful advantages (MacGregor (3); Sweet (4); Nurse (9); Evans (11); Barker (15); Gaimster (16)).

Finally, on the name, one of the chief lessons of this book is that the ideals of the Society today are fundamentally those of our founders, however much has changed in the shape of the past and in the techniques we use to understand it. The ideals in particular of the primacy of the material evidence, the empirical method, the weighing of evidence, and a resistance to abstract concepts still hold firm. Therefore, to the question 'Is the Society of Antiquaries capable of providing an umbrella for the societies, associations and activities connected with the study of material culture?' the answer, at least from the Society's point of view, is clearly 'yes'. The Society's name is not a barrier to this role, but rather a badge of honour.

CONTRIBUTORS

GRAEME BARKER is Disney Professor of Archaeology and Director of the McDonald Institute for Archaeological Research at the University of Cambridge. His principal research interests are in the origins of agriculture and the interactions between people and landscape over the long term. He has written widely on the development of Mediterranean landscape history, and the archaeology of desertification, based especially on fieldwork in Italy, Libya and Jordan. In recent years his interests have shifted to tropical rainforest landscape history, the focus of his current fieldwork in the Niah Caves in Sarawak. His most recent book is *The Agricultural Revolution in Prehistory: why did foragers become farmers?* (Oxford University Press, 2006). He was elected a Fellow of the Society of Antiquaries in 1979, a Fellow of the British Academy in 1999, and was awarded the Dan David Prize in 2005.
Address: McDonald Institute for Archaeological Research, University of Cambridge, Downing Street, Cambridge CB2 3ER, UK. <gb314@cam.ac.uk>

C STEPHEN BRIGGS worked at the Royal Commission on the Ancient and Historical Monuments of Wales as a Senior Investigator and sometime Head of Archaeology until his retirement in 2006. Trained as a prehistorian, his published research and fieldwork interests encompass geological, industrial and landscape aspects of archaeology, with a recent focus on historic gardens. His long-term antiquarian researches range from Edward Lhuyd through Danish nationalism to contemporary biography and institutional histories. These researches have informed the investigation and publication of several extended site and artefactual studies. He was elected a Fellow of the Society of Antiquaries in 1981.
Address: Llwyn Deiniol, Llanddeiniol, Llanrhystud, near Aberystwyth, Ceredigion SY23 5DT, Wales, UK. <cstephenbriggs@hotmail.com>

CHRISTOPHER EVANS is the Executive Director of the Cambridge Archaeological Unit of the University of Cambridge, which he co-founded together with Ian Hodder in 1990. He has directed major fieldwork projects abroad (in Nepal, China and Cape Verde) and in the UK, most recently publishing the results of the Haddenham Project in Cambridgeshire. His major papers on the history of archaeology have examined Gerhard Bersu and the impact of 'modernism', Grahame Clark and the advent of internationalism, Christopher Hawkes and 'informed' historicism and David Clarke and the 'new' methodology. He is also an expert on the discipline's model-making traditions and on other modes of illustrative representation. He was elected a Fellow of the Society of Antiquaries in 2001.
Address: Cambridge Archaeological Unit, Department of Archaeology, University of Cambridge, Downing Street, Cambridge CB2 3DZ, UK. <cje30@cam.ac.uk>

ERIC FERNIE retired as Director of the Courtauld Institute in 2003. He was elected to the Society in 1973, served as a Vice-President in the early 1990s and was elected President in 2004. His area of interest is the architecture of western Europe from the sixth century to the thirteenth, on which he has published four books and several articles. He has also written about the history of art history. He is a Fellow of the British Academy, the Royal Society of Edinburgh and the Society of Antiquaries of Scotland.
Address: 82 Bradmore Way, Coulsdon CR5 1PB, UK. <eric.fernie@courtauld.ac.uk>

MICHAEL FULFORD has been Professor of Archaeology at the University of Reading since 1988. Specializing in Roman archaeology, a major focus of his research has been the Iron Age and Roman town at Silchester, Hampshire, where he has conducted excavations on a number of sites since 1974. A major excavation of insula IX, begun in 1997, is continuing. The 'total' excavation of the Roman town at Silchester was the Society's first major research project (1890–1909). Elected to the Fellowship in 1977, he has served on the Society of Antiquaries' Executive and Research Committees as well as Council. He was elected a Fellow of the British Academy in 1994.
Address: Department of Archaeology, University of Reading, Whiteknights, PO Box 227, Reading RG6 6AB, UK. <m.g.fulford@reading.ac.uk>

DAVID GAIMSTER was appointed General Secretary of the Society of Antiquaries in 2004. Prior to that he was Assistant Keeper in the Department for Medieval and Later Antiquities at the British Museum (1986–2001) and Senior Policy Adviser in the Cultural Property Unit, Department for Culture, Media and Sport (2001–4). Elected a Fellow in 1996, he has published widely on medieval to early modern European archaeology and material culture, and on international cultural property policy issues. He is an Honorary Research Fellow of the Institute of Archaeology, University College London, and is Visiting Professor in Historical Archaeology at the Department of Cultural Studies, University of Turku, Finland. He was awarded the Order of Merit by the Society for Historical Archaeology in 2005.
Address: Society of Antiquaries of London, Burlington House, Piccadilly, London W1J 0BE, UK. <dgaimster@sal.org.uk>

RICHARD HINGLEY is a Reader in Archaeology at the University of Durham and has published extensively on Iron Age and Roman topics. His works include two volumes on the history of archaeology. *Roman Officers and English Gentlemen* (Routledge, 2000) examined the role that Roman Britain was made to play in the discourse of British imperialism during the late nineteenth and twentieth centuries. *Images of Rome* (Journal of Roman Archaeology Supplementary Series, 2001) is an edited book that examines the role of the Roman Empire as a myth of origin in a number of European countries and in the USA. A book on the rediscovery of Roman Britain from the late sixteenth century to the end of the nineteenth is currently in production. Richard Hingley was elected a Fellow of the Society of Antiquaries in 2006.
Address: Department of Archaeology, University of Durham, South Road, Durham DH1 3LE, UK. <Richard.Hingley@durham.ac.uk>

ARTHUR MacGREGOR was elected a Fellow of the Society of Antiquaries in 1980 and served as Director of the Society from 1996 to 2001. He has spent most of his career at the Ashmolean Museum in Oxford, where his responsibilities span antiquities from the end of the Roman Empire to the nineteenth century. He has published extensively on antiquities, museum history and the interface between man and animals. A past Director of the British Archaeological Association, he is currently a Vice-President of the Royal Archaeological Institute and is a Fellow of the Linnean Society. He is co-general editor of *The Paper Museum of Cassiano dal Pozzo* and editor of the *Journal of the History of Collections*. *Address*: Department of Antiquities, Ashmolean Museum, Oxford OX1 2PH, UK. <Arthur.MacGregor@ashmus.ox.ac.uk>

RICHARD MORRIS's work on the archaeology and topography of the Christian Church was recognized by his election to the Fellowship of the Society in 1983, and by the award of the Frend Medal nine years later. The present essay develops a theme from his forthcoming book, *The Triumph of Time*, which deals with the recent as well as distant past, and the social contextualization of archaeology and conservation. *Address*: 13 Hollins Road, Harrogate HG1 2JF, UK. <R.K.Morris@dsl.pipex.com>

MARTIN MYRONE is a curator at Tate Britain, specializing in eighteenth- and nineteenth-century British art. He was the co-editor, with Lucy Peltz, of the essay collection *Producing the Past: aspects of antiquarian culture and practice 1700–1850* (1999) and contributed the biography of George Vertue to the *Oxford Dictionary of National Biography* (2004). *Address*: Tate Britain, Millbank, London SW1P 4RG, UK. <martin.myrone@tate.org.uk>

BERNARD NURSE has been the Librarian of the Society of Antiquaries of London since 1986. Elected a Fellow in 1995, he has written articles relating to the history of the Society for the *Antiquaries Journal* and several other publications. As a Research Associate for the *Oxford Dictionary of National Biography*, he contributed numerous entries on antiquaries for the new edition published in 2004. *Address*: Society of Antiquaries of London, Burlington House, Piccadilly, London W1J 0BE, UK. <bernardnurse@btinternet.com>

SUSAN PEARCE has published a number of books on the nature of material culture and the collecting process, including *On Collecting: an investigation into collecting in the European tradition* (1995). She is particularly interested in the changing ways in which objects were viewed around 1800, and has published papers on Belzoni, the early contributions of women to the Society of Antiquaries, William Bullock and Charles Tatham (with Frank Salmon). She is now working on the letters of C R Cockerell. She is Emerita Professor of Museum Studies at the University of Leicester and a Senior Research Fellow of Somerville College, Oxford. She was elected a Fellow in 1979 and served as a Vice-President of the Society from 2002 to 2004. *Address*: Department of Museum Studies, University of Leicester, 105 Princess Road East, Leicester LE1 7LG, UK. <smp14@le.ac.uk>

SAM SMILES is Professor of Art History at the University of Plymouth. He has written widely on the contribution of the visual arts *c* 1750–1950 to the exploration of British antiquity and was one of the curators for the travelling exhibition of antiquarian drawings *Landscapes of Retrospection . . . 1739–1860* (Vassar College, 1999). His books include *The Image of Antiquity: ancient Britain and the Romantic imagination* (Yale University Press, 1994) and *Eye Witness: artists and visual documentation in Britain 1770–1830* (Ashgate Press, 2000). He recently co-edited *Envisioning the Past: archaeology and the image* (Blackwell, 2005). *Address*: Faculty of Arts, University of Plymouth, Earl Richards Road North, Exeter EX2 6AS, UK. <ssmiles@plymouth.ac.uk>

ROSEMARY SWEET is Professor of Urban History and Director of the Centre for Urban History at the University of Leicester. In addition to her work on urban history, she has also published on local history and antiquarianism in the long eighteenth century. Her most recent book, *Antiquaries: the discovery of the past in eighteenth-century Britain*, was published by Hambledon and London in 2004. She was elected a Fellow of the Society of Antiquaries in 2003. She is currently working on British travellers and antiquarianism on the Grand Tour in Italy during the eighteenth century. *Address*: Centre for Urban History, School of Historical Studies, University of Leicester, Leicester LE1 7RH, UK. <rhs4@le.ac.uk>

RICK TURNER is an Inspector of Ancient Monuments with Cadw. He studied archaeology at Cambridge University and has worked for Lancaster University, British Gas and Cheshire County Council. He was elected a Fellow of the Society of Antiquaries in 1992, and has published three papers in the Society's journal on a Roman bog body from Lincolnshire, St Davids Bishop's Palace and the Great Tower of Chepstow Castle. His interest in conservation philosophy arose from a study of the recent history of the Pentre Ifan burial chamber, and has developed through his responsibilities for the conservation of some of the great buildings of Wales. *Address*: Cadw, Plas Carew, Cefn Coed, Nantgarw, Cardiff CF15 7QQ, Wales, UK. <Richard.Turner@wales.gsi.gov.uk>

DANIEL WOOLF is Professor of History at the University of Alberta in Edmonton, Canada. He is the author of several books and many essays on the history of historical writing and has written in particular on the early history of antiquarianism in *The Idea of History in Early Stuart England* (Toronto, 1990) and *The Social Circulation of the Past: English historical culture 1500–1730* (Oxford, 2003). He is currently at work on a history of historical writing. He was elected a Fellow of the Society of Antiquaries in 2005, and is a Fellow of the Royal Historical Society and of the Royal Society of Canada. *Address*: Faculty of Arts, 6–33 Humanities Centre, University of Alberta, Edmonton T6G 2E5, Canada. <dwoolf@ualberta.ca>

INDEX

Compiled by Susan Vaughan

Page numbers in *italics* denote that the reference is, or includes, an illustration: *illus* – illustrated; 'n' – note.

Abercrombie, L Patrick 329, 342
Aberdeen, Lord *see* Gordon, George
Abu Simbel (Egypt) 387
Acton, Frances Stackhouse 194n38
Addison Committee (chaired by Christopher
  Addison) 336–7, 338
Addison, Joseph 18, 23, 67n2
Aelfric 14
aerial photography 338, 339–40, 342, 372,
  402
Agarde, Arthur 17, 25
Akerman, J Y
  Centenary Dinner arranged by 2
  *Directions for the Preservation of
    English Antiquities . . .* 287
  fieldwork and reports 232, 276, 277,
    278, 279, 287
  library catalogue 213
  on Stukeley portrait 223n33
  on Uffington White Horse 191, *193*
Aksum (Ethiopia), excavations 374, 399,
  402
Aldrovandi, Ulisse 21
Alexander, William 133
Algarotti, Francesco 51
Alington, Geoffrey 339
All-Party Parliamentary Groups 428
Allen, Major G W G 331, 339, *340*, 341,
  348
Alma-Tadema, Sir Lawrence 138–9, 141
  engraving after *138*
Als Survey (Denmark) 399
Alwyne, Spencer Joshua, Marquis of
  Northampton 184
Ames, Joseph 76
Amyot, Thomas 182, 183
Ancaster (Lincs), discourse on 53
Ancient Monuments Acts
  19th-century 255, 294–5, 314–15, 331,
    334, 434
  20th-century 315, 330, 346, 386
Ancient Monuments Inspectorate
  1883–1940 256, 287, 315, 317
  1940s 342, 344, 347
Ancient Monuments Society 343
Anderson, Joseph 251
Anderson Commission 386–7
Ankara (Turkey), British Institute 412n39
Anne, Queen of Denmark 18
Anne, Queen of England 47, 48
Anstis, John 61
Anthropological Institute
  Ethnographic Survey 298
  fieldwork funded by 285
  formation 228, 331
  initiative to improve barrow-digging
    287

library 218
Prehistoric and Other Monuments
  Committee 294
presidents 250
*see also Journal of the Anthropological
  Institute*
Anthropological Society 228, 251, 253, 270,
  294, 331
antiquarianism
  antiquarian culture, 19th-century 267,
    432–3
      background 267–71
      collection, performance and
        display 271–5
      demonstration, representation and
        practice 275–89
      growth of disciplines 295–9
      science 290–5
  antiquaries, image of 11–13
      Tudor 13–18
      17th-century: development of
        18–20; public face 24–34;
        virtuosi 20–4
      18th-century 34–6
      social class 91–2, 147–8, 173,
        174–8, 243, 434
  graphic expression, 18th–19th century
    99–119
  material culture, interpretation of,
    1770–1820 150–1, 166
      appearance 158–61
      historical significance 157–8
      as the past in the present 161–6
      publication 151–6
  visual art, relationship with 123–42
Antiquaries Journal
  content 403–7, 410–11
  establishment 250
  funding 402–3
  library accessions listed in 219
'Antiquarius' 6, 9n52, 195n86, 430
The Antiquary 302n118
antiquities, sale of 386–7
Antrobus, Sir Edward 295
Appuldurcombe (Isle of Wight), marbles
  158
Apulia project (Italy) 370, 397, 398
Archaeologia
  establishment and early years 82–4,
    93, 111–13, 201, 204, 228, 275
  1770–1820, interpreting material
    culture, role in 151–6, 157, 162
  19th century
      content (*illus*) 187–93, 275–93
      contributions read at meetings
        271–2
      exchange schemes 214

lithography 117
photography 275
20th century 402–3, 405, 406, 407,
  410
Archaeologia Cantiana 291, 292
Archaeological Institute 252, 253, 270
Archaeological Journal
  content 253, 290, 293
  establishment 270, 297
  Way's editorship 173, 176–7, 178, 192,
    252, 253
archaeology, professionalization 383–411;
  see also excavation reports
'The Archaeology of the English Church'
  372, 373, 400–1, 406
The Archaeology Forum 427–8
Archdall, Mervyn 95n55
arm-ring *146*, 163
Armitage, Edward 141
Arnold, Thomas 188
Arreton Down (Isle of Wight), hoard 59,
  61, 200
art
  association with antiquarianism
    123–42
  graphic arts and Society 99–119
Arundel marbles 21, 22, 94n10
Ashby, Thomas 357
Ashmole, Elias *32*
Ashpitel, Arthur 214
Asiatic Society 207
Association for Environmental Archaeology
  384
Association of Industrial Archaeology 384
Association of Local Government
  Archaeological Officers 427
Astell, Mary 23
Astle, Thomas 89, 90, 114
Aston (Berks), barrow 257n59
The Athenaeum 244, 251, 293, 296, 301n65,
  432
Athens (Greece), British School 412n39
Atkinson, Richard 242–3, 363
Attlee, Sir Clement 350n80
Aubrey, John 24, 26, 29–31, 156, 168n70,
  363
Aurelian Society 69n43
Austin, Godwin 301n71
Avebury (Wilts) 36, 68n18, 191, 230, 332
Aveline, Countess, tomb effigy 126, *127*
axes
  bronze 59, 159, 163, 200, 211, *297*
  stone 153–6, 159
  see also hand-axes
Aylesford (Kent), excavations 276, 301n61,
  363–4
Ayloffe, Joseph 95n44, 126, 143n11

Babington, Charles 301n65
Bacon, Francis 16–17, 63
Baden-Powell, Lord 332
Bagford, John 2, 46, 50, 91
Baildon Moor (Yorks), field system 234, *235*
Baines, Sir Frank 317, 318, 322–3, 326n64
Baker, Henry 59, 77–8, 167n28
Bakewell (Derbys), Castle Hill 398
Baldwin, Stanley 336
Bale, John 13, 14, 24
Balmanno, Lord 183
Balquhain stone circle (Aberdeens) *281*
Banks, Sir Joseph
    Dilettanti, membership of 54
    hillforts, asked to comment 230
    intellectual circle 270
    Lysons defers to 93
    prehistory, speculates on 158
    Royal Society, presidency of 68n21, 89–90
    Woodchester, supplies labour 277
Banks and Barry 215–16
Barford, Revd 316
Barlow (Essex), excavations 276
Barrington, Daines 37n12, 148, 153, 204
Barrington, Shute, Bishop of Durham 310
Barrow Furlong (Northants), excavations 275, 276, 277
barrows
    digging
        18th-century 59, 229, 275
        19th-century 229; Bartlow Hills 192; exhibition 272; failings 295; methodologies and analyses 231–2, *233*, 236; Pitt-Rivers leads initiative to improve 287; publication (*illus*) 190, 275, 276, 277, 279–83, 286; Wiltshire 229–31, 242
        20th-century 254
    typology 159
Bartlett, Revd J Pemberton 277
Bartlow Hills (Cambs), barrows 192
Bartolozzi, F 114
Basire family 133
    James
        engravings: Bayeux Tapestry 144n34; cathedrals 91; historical prints 84, 113, 309; Magdalen Chapel 113, *115*; metalwork *112, 116*
        as official engraver of Society 110–17, 125
        pupils of 126, 143n10, 201
    James the younger 117, 125
        watercolour by *122*
    James the younger II 117
Bassae reliefs 139
Bate, Jonathan 338
Bateman, Thomas 236, 253, 288
Bath (B & NES)
    Abbey 96n66, 117, 310

antiquarian society 297
    excavations 399, 406, 412n45
    Leman of 229
Bathurst, Charles (Lord Bledisloe) 336, *337*, 364
Bathurst, W H 364
Baudouin, F 12
Bayer, Francesco 148
Bayeux Tapestry 117, 133, *134*
Bayley, J 376
Beattie, William 259n125
Beauford, William 95n55
Beck, Revd J 302n113
Bede 14
Beechey, William 133
Beidha (Jordan), fieldwork 399
Beirut (Lebanon), excavations 374, 375, 399, 402
Beith (Ayrs), shield *149*
Belgae 364, 365, 370
Bell, Matthew 232, 277
Belzoni, G B 163
Bentley, Richard 24
Bere Ferrers (Devon) 133
Beresford, Maurice 339
Bersu, Gerhard 385
Bewley, Bob 402
Biddle, Martin 371, 372
Biggleswade (Beds), hoard 151, 168n36
Biondo, Flavio 12
Birley, Eric 360
Birmingham, Lunar Society 71n75
Bishop Auckland (Co Durham), palace 310
Black, Mary, copy of portrait by *82*
Blackstone, William 94n19
Blair, Claude 385
Blake, Carter 284
Blake, William, drawings by 126, *127*, 201
Blegen, Carl 385
Blenheim Palace (Oxon) 309
Blizzard, William 150, 168n35
Blundell, William 20, 39n83
Boece, Hector 35
Bog of Cullen (Co Tipperary), gorgets 169n95
Bolton, Edmund 22, 28
bone reports 287, 355
Bonington, R P 131
Bonnard, Camille 136
Boon, George 356
Borenius, Tancred 370
Borlase, William 94n11, 158
Borough, John 17
Borsselaer, Peter 39n79
Boston (Lincs), club 53
Botanical Society 69n43
Boucher de Perthes, J 246, 284, 301n65
Boudicca (Boadicea) 163, 360, 365, 371
Bowen, Collin 400
Bowyer, William 105
Box Moor villa (Herts), excavations 283
Boyd Dawkins, William 270
Boydell, John 105, 106, 111
Brabrook, Sir Edward 3, 5

bracelet, Viking 204
Bradford (Yorks), antiquarian society 297
Bradford, John 397
Brakspear, Harold 316
Brand, John 148
Brand, Thomas 94n10
Brander, Gustavus 94n10
brass rubbings 218
Brathwait, Richard 21
Breach Down (Kent), excavations 272, 276, 277, 280, *281–2*
breastplates 163
Brechin Cathedral (Angus) 168n34
Breedon on the Hill (Leics), excavation report 412n66
Brigantes 33
Bristol, St Mary Redcliffe 130; see also Clifton
Bristol and Gloucestershire Archaeological Society 300n5
British Academy
    Committee for South East Asian Studies 412n39
    fieldwork funded by 353, 397, 401
    membership 392, 393
    survey of archaeological profession 417, 419
British Archaeological Association
    Canterbury meeting 272
    dispute, 1845 175
    fieldwork funded by 287
    foundation and intentions 173, 176–7, 192–3, 270, 271, 297, 432
    membership 130, 176, 178, 240, 244
    officers 130, 253, 256
    paper on L'Ancresse 232
    Presidential address 1863 293
    see also Journal of the British Archaeological Association
British Association for the Advancement of Science 228, 269, 287, 292, 298, 302n93
British and Foreign Bible Society 214
British Institute in Eastern Africa 387, 412n39
British Institute of Persian Studies 412n39
British Institute in South East Asia 412n39
British Museum
    art and antiquity 139, 141, 210
    British antiquities 167n28, 238–9, 256, 295
    fieldwork and expeditions 139, 192, 373, 401
    library 65, 209, 213
    organizational reforms 387–8
    premises 76, 77
    Society of Antiquaries archives 5
    Society of Antiquaries collections 217, 218
    staff 63, 182, 204, 218, 238, 295, 426
    trustees 76, 79, 178, 256, 295, 388
British Schools 384, 387, 397
Britannia 403, 407
Brittany (France), fieldwork 365, 369, 370, 398

Britton, John 129–30, 270
    Celtic Cabinet 129, *130*
Brixham Cave (Devon), excavations 246,
    287
Brixworth (Northants), fieldwork 399
broadsides and proclamations *198*, 201, 214
Bromley, Revd Robert 142n5
Bromwell, Mr 168n35
Brønsted, Johannes 385
brooches 127, *128*, *131*, 152, 376
Brook, John 168n68
Brooke, Christopher 385, 390, 409
Brooke, Ralph 17
Brough-on-Humber (E Yorks), excavations
    406
Brown, David 372
Brown, Ford Madox 136–8
    painting by *137*
Brown, Revd Littleton 68n35
Brown, Lyde 79
Browne, Sir Thomas 22, 26
Bruce-Mitford, Rupert 3
Brussels (Belgium), Belles-Lettres, Royal
    Academy of 95n30
de Bry, T 162
Buchanan, George 35
Buck brothers 323
Buckland (Berks), cross *160*
Buckland, Dean William 245, 253
Buckler, John 313, 431
Budé, G 12
Builder's Magazine 309
building conservation 307–9, 433–4
    18th-century (Carter and Wyatt)
        309–13, 322
    19th–20th centuries (Ruskin, Lubbock
        and Ministry style) 313–18, 322–3
    20th-century (Kelmscott Manor) 319,
        320–1, 323, *324*
Bullock, William 163
Bulwer, Revd James 130–1
Burgess, Thomas 157
Burlington, Earl of 49, 52
Burne-Jones, Edward 141–2
    tapestry after *142*
Burns, Robert 204
Burton, Sir Richard 302n93
Burton, William 16, 29, *30*
Bushe-Fox, J P 358, 361, 364, 376
Busk, G 287, 301n71
Butcher, S 376
Byrne, Thomas 92

cabinets of curiosities 18, 22–3
Caburn (Sussex), excavations 276, 286, 287
Cadw 41, 384, 389
Caerhun (Conwy), excavations 275, 276,
    277, 280
Caerleon (Newport), excavations 360
Caernarfon (Gwynedd), Segontium 360,
    377
Caerwent (Venta Silurum) (Mon),
    excavations 357–8, 375, 377, 397
Caerwent Exploration Fund 357

Caistor (Lincs), excavation report 412n66
Caius, John 24, 26
Callanish (Lewis), photographs 274
Cambrian Archaeological Association 427
Cambridge (Cambs)
    Cambridge Antiquarian Society 177,
        291–2
    University 331
Camden, William
    Annales 17
    Britannia 15, 17, 24–5, 35, 102, 158,
        208
    antiquarianism 16, 17, 35, 37n5, 156
    at Oxford 17
    portraits 26, *27–8*
    Society of Antiquaries (Elizabethan),
        founds 14–15
Camden Society 214, 270, 432
Camelot Research Committee 398
canoe 238
Canterbury (Kent)
    BAA meeting 272
    excavation programme 344, 347, 370,
        387
Capon, William 210
Carcassonne (France) 326n37
Cardi, Beatrice de 220
Carew, Richard 15, 16, 25
Carlisle, Nicholas
    campaigns for Royal Order of
        Danebrog 238
    caricature of *172*, *273*
    library catalogue by 206–7
    lithograph of *181*
    secretaryship 93, 179, 180, 182, 183,
        184
Carnarvon, Lord 314, 315
Carnegie UK Trust 219
Carte, Samuel 9n26
Carter, John
    appointment as Society's draughtsman
        125, 204, 431
    drawings 91, 114–17, 144n37, 310,
        311–12, 313
    fellowship 148
    sketch portrait *74*
    Wyatt, opposition to 89–90, 310–13,
        322, 431–2
Carver, Martin 373, 401
Casaubon, Isaac 12
Casaubon, Meric 18–19
Casey, John 364
Cathcart-King, D J 405
Cathedral Antiquities 90–1, 114–17, 310
Cattermole, George 129
Caylus, Comte de 301n55
Cecill, Thomas, engraving by 26, *27*
Celsius, Anders 51, 76
Chalmers, P 259n125
Chalton (Hants), fieldwork 406
Chamberlain, John 22
Chamberlain, Neville 343
Chambers, Robert 248
Chambers, Sir William 123, 167n31, 325n23

Chantrey, Francis 133
Chaplais, Dr Pierre 224n80
Charles I 21, 22
Charles II 66
Charles, Prince of Wales 389
Chatterton, Thomas 95n29
Chaucer Society 214
Cheere, Sir Henry 94n10
Chepstow Castle (Mon) 326n58
Cheshire, antiquarian society 297
Chester (Ches), city council 390
Chetham Society 214
Chettle, G H 346
Chichester (W Sussex), mosaic 71n86
Chichester Civic Society 372
Childe, V Gordon 385, 405
Childrey, Joshua 38n25
Chiselbury (Wilts) 230
chorography 15–16, 24, 35, 36
Christian VIII, King of Denmark 239
chronologies, prehistoric *see* prehistoric
    studies
Chun Quoit (Cornwall) 238
Church of England, estate 386
Church Stretton (Shrops), villa 194n38
churches 314, 372, 373, 400–1
Churchill, Sir Winston 341
Cicero 16
Cipriani, G B 111
Cirencester (Glos), excavations 371–2, 377,
    398, 406, 412n66
Cirencester Excavation Committee 371
Cissbury (W Sussex), hillfort 236, 272, 284,
    285, 286, 289, 292–3
Clapham, Alfred 342, 343, 345–6
Clarendon, Earl of 27
Clarendon Palace (Wilts), excavations 370,
    377, 397
Clark, Desmond 385
Clark, Grahame 385, 396, 397
Clarke, Charles 209
Classicianus, Gaius Julius Alpinus,
    inscription *360*
Clerk, Sir John 56
Clerk, Thomas 69n42
cliff castles, Cornwall 189
Clifton (Bristol), antiquarian society 297
clocks 211
clubs and societies
    18th-century
        London 45–6, 49, 50, 51–3,
            54–6, 57
        provinces 52–4
    19th-century 177, 217, 243, 269–70,
        290, 297
coin moulds 156
coins 62–3, 78, 152, 200, 208
Cokayne, G E 217
Colchester (Camulodunum) (Essex)
    excavations 369, 370, 375, 377, 397,
        398, 399
    report 406
Cole, William 83–4, 99, 100
Colebrook, Josiah 76

Coleraine, Lord *see* Hare, Henry, Baron Coleraine
collecting 22–3, 272–4
College of Arms 33
Collingbourn (Wilts), barrow *279*
Collingwood, R G 341
Collinson, Revd John 144n26
Collinson, Peter 71n87
Colls, J M N 234
Colt Hoare, Sir Richard
    barrow digging 229, 231–2, 253, 276, 280–3
    barrow typology 159
    on chronology 230, 231, 243
    intellectual network 270
    library 209
    watercolours commissioned by 128
Conference on Nature Preservation in Post-War Reconstruction 343, 345
Congress of Archaeological Societies 297
conservation *see* building conservation; landscape conservation
Conway, Field Marshall, 274
Conyngham, Lord Albert 187, 276, 277, 280, 281, 282
Conyngham, William Burton 95n55
Cooke, Benjamin 71n87
Coombe, Taylor 180
Copenhagen (Denmark)
    congress 250
    museum 237, 238, 239
Corder, Philip 345
Cormack, Sir Patrick 390
Corner, G R 211
costume studies 134, 136, *146*, 162–3
Cosway, Richard 92, 133, 148
Cotman, John Sell 126, 129, 130, 131, 143n22
Cotterstock (Northants), mosaic 71n86
Cotton, Molly 356
Cotton, Sir Robert 15, 17, 20, 27, 28
Cottrill, Frank 360, 361
Council for British Archaeology
    church project 401
    conference on aerial photography 338
    conservation campaigning 336, 338
    foundation 330, 338, 342–8, 384, 397
    membership 383
    publications 403, 405, 406, 407
    Treasure Trove legislation 390–1
Council for the Preservation of Rural England 329, 332, 336, 337, 342–3
Council for the Promotion of Field Studies (Field Studies Council) 344
Council for the Protection of Rural Wales 337
county histories 15–16, 24, 202, 212
county record societies 214
Courtauld Institute 221
Coventry (W Mids), bomb damage 341
Cowdray House (Sussex), print 84, 85, 162, 309
Cox, James 170n112
Coxe, Thomas 150

Coxe, Archdeacon William 229
Cramp, Rosemary 405
Cranborne Chase (Dorset), fieldwork 236, 286, 356
Crawford, Lord 359
Crawford, O G S
    air photography *339*, 340, 341
    Archaeology in the Field 339
    landscape conservation 330, 335, 336, 337, 338, 343, 348
Crawfurd, John 251
cremations 229, 230
Crocker, Philip 229, 232
Croft Lyons, Lt-Col G B 218
Croker, Thomas Crofton 270
Cromwell, Oliver 200, 223n20
crosses, typology 159, *160*, 169
Cruikshank, George, print by *172*, 272, *273*
Cumberland, Duke of 91
Cumberland and Westmorland Antiquarian and Archaeological Society 297
Cunliffe, Barry
    excavations 359, 372, 377
    landscape project 400
    presidency 385, 390, *391*
    publication of Richborough 361
Cunnington, William
    classification of hillforts 230
    excavations
        barrows 229–32, 242–3, 253, 276, 280, 432
        Stonehenge 230
Curwen, E Cecil 330, 336, 339
Cwm Moch (Merioneth), rapiers 169n92
Cyrenaica (Libya), excavations 370

Dacre, Lord 165
daggers 59, *61*, *131*
Dallaway, Revd James 142n3, 195n84, 210
Dalton, Richard 110, 144n39
Dance, Nathaniel, portrait by *82*
Danebury (Hants), fieldwork 372, 406
Daniel, Glyn 242, 383
Dartmoor (Devon)
    hut circles 189, *192*, 234
    Reave Project 399
Darwin, Charles
    intellectual network 248, 270, 301n65, 331
    letter to Lyell 283–4
    The Origin of Species 246, 249, 269, 292–3
    Silchester research *285*, 301n65
Darwin, Erasmus 69n43
Davis, J B 287
Dayes, Edward 128
Dee, John 22
Deerhurst church (Glos), excavations 372, 398, 399, 401, 406
Delaram, Francis, engraving by 29, *30*
Denne, Samuel 96n69, 209
Department of the Environment 389, 391, 400

Department of the Environment in Northern Ireland 384, 389
Der Nersessian, Sirarpie 385
Dering, Sir Edward 17
Det Kongelige Nordiske Oldskriftselskab *see* Royal Society of Antiquaries of the North
Devil's Den cromlech (Wilts) 143n21
Devizes Museum (Wilts) 129, *130*, 143n19
Diamond, Dr Hugh Welch 275
Dibdin, Thomas Frognall 93
Dickens, Charles 206
Digby, Sir Kenelm 23
Dio Cassius 370
Disney, John 167n9
D'Israeli, Isaac 195n84
Ditchfield, P H 332
Dixon, William H 301n65
Dodderidge, John 15, *25*, 26
Dolaucothi (Carmarths), excavation report 413n66
Domesday Book 78, 81, 204
Donald Insall and Associates 320
Doncaster (Yorks), club 53
Donne, John 18, 22
Dorchester (Dorset)
    amphitheatre 294
    excavations 412n45
Dorset, antiquarian society 297
Douce, Francis 92, 124, 204, 210
Douglas, D C 101
Douglas, James 91, 124, 128, 159, 229, 232, 432
Dover (Kent), excavations 276, 283, 370
Dower, John 338, 341–2, 343, 347–8
Dragonby (Lincs), fieldwork 412n45
Drake, Francis 55, 61
Drake, Judith 23
Drayton, Michael 35
Druidism
    depictions of *146*, 163, *164*
    persistence 228
    ridiculed by Nicolas 188
    Stukeley 36, 227, 229
Dryden, Henry 276, 277, 278
Dublin (Ireland)
    Kemble delivers paper 252
    philosophical society 69n43
    Worsaae visits 241
Ducarel, Andrew 5, 59, 67n17, 72n108, 95n34
Dufty, Richard (Dick) 319, 385, 389
Dugdale, Sir William 28, *31*, 32, 35, 156, 210
Dunbar (E Lothian), coffins 151
Dunning, Gerald 360, 361
Duntisbourne Abbots (Glos), excavations 232, *233*
Duppa, Rich 195n84
Durham (Co Durham)
    castle 310
    cathedral
        engravings 91, 117, 310, *311–12*, 313
        restoration 90, 92, 310–13, 322, 431–2

Durrington Walls (Wilts), excavation report 413n66

Dyffryn Ardudwy (Merioneth), tomb 238, 406

Dyson, Humphrey 201

Earle, John 19–20, 21, 26, 36

Earle, William Benson 208

Early English Text Society 214

Eastlake, Charles Lock 133

Eates, Margot 346, 347

Ebers, George 145n49

The Ecclesiologist 314

Edinburgh
 Archaeological Institute meeting 252
 National Museum of Scotland 251, 252
 Worsaae visits 240–1

Edington (Som), coin moulds 156

Edward I 126, 143n11, 169n102, 204

Edward II 169n102, 204

Edward IV 204, 206, 223n8

Edwards, Mr 150, 168n35

Egerton, Francis, Earl of Ellesmere 239–40, 243, 254

Egerton, George Granville, Duke of Sutherland 254

Egyptian Society 55, 57

Elgin marbles 139

Eliot, George 11–12

Elizabeth of York 223n8

Ellis, Sir Henry
 library catalogue 204, 206, 220
 lithograph *181*
 secretaryship 175, 178, 180
 Society history 4

Elmham (Norfolk), urn 60

Elton (Hunts), parochial survey 94n8

Englefield, Sir Henry
 Carter commissioned by 310
 Catholicism 167n9
 research by 208
 Wyatt opposed by 89, 90, 92, 312

Englemann, Graf, Coindet & Co 117

English Heritage
 Fellows 395, 418
 formation of 384, 389–90
 funding by 401
 library 222
 Royal Commission incorporated into 392

Epping Forest (Essex) 334

Erasmus, St, panel depicting 211

Erdeswicke, Sampson 15–16, 25

Ernley (Yorks), cross *160*

Erskine, Col 283

Eschricht, Prof 239

Etheldreda, St, legend of 206, *207*

ethnography 227, 269, 293, 294

Ethnographic Survey of the United Kingdom 298

Ethnological Society
 founding of 228
 merges with Anthropological Society 228, 294, 331

Pitt-Rivers addresses 274–5
 prehistoric studies, contribution to 248, 251, 253, 255, 293, 294
 see also Journal of the Ethnological Society

Euhesperides (Libya), fieldwork 398

Eutychius 31

Evans, Sir Arthur
 excavations 6, 276, 301n61, 359, 363–4
 family relationships 6
 Presidential Address 2–3, 6

Evans, Joan
 on excavations at Stonehenge 363
 gold medal 385
 history of the Society of Antiquaries 3, 4, 6, 45
 presidency 319, 385, 387–8, 399–400

Evans, Sir John
 family relationships 6
 intellectual network 270, 271, 301n65, 301n71
 monument protection 295
 prehistoric studies 242, 246–7, 249–51, 255, 302n113
 publications and excavation reports 249–50, 288, 289, 292, 293
  Box Moor 283
  Silchester 287
  Somme *226*
  Youngsbury 276, 280, *282*, 283
 research fund 353, 397

Evans, John Davies 385, 390, 401, *402*, 409

Evelyn, John 23, 26, 107, 309

'The Evolution of the English Landscape' 372, 373, 398, 400–1, 406

d'Ewes, Sir Simonds 17

Eworth, Hans 206

excavation reports
 18th-century 275
 19th-century (*illus*) 275–90

Exeter (Devon)
 cathedral 96n66, 117, 310
 excavations 344, 347, 370

exhibitions 163, *165*, 166

Face of Britain, dust-jacket *328*, 333

Fagg, Charles 229

Fairholt, Frederick William 133–4, 136, 142n1, 144n36, 213–14
 print by 272, *273*

Faithorne, William, portrait by *33*

Falconer, Hugh 246

Falde (Staffs), William Burton 29

Farington, Joseph 90, 92, 117, 133

Farnham Museum (Dorset) 286

Faussett, Bryan 229

Fawkes, Walter 129

Fell, John, Bishop of Oxford 40n88

Fellows, Charles 132

Fenland Research Committee 331, 339, 348

Fernie, Eric *414*

Ferrers, Lord de (later Earl of Leicester) 88, 90, 92, 434

Ferris, Dr 149

Field of the Cloth of Gold
 engraving 84, 113, 162
 jousting cheque 204, *205*

field systems 234, *235*, 339

Fifield Down (Wilts), fieldwork 412n45

Fingal's Cave (Staffa), re-creation 163

Fishbourne Palace (W Sussex), excavations 372, 412n45, 413n66

Flaxman, John 117

Flint Jack 300n38

flint mines 284, *285*, 286

Flowers, Mr 302n113

Folkes, Martin 55, 62–3, 65, 66, 70n63, 201, 434

Folkestone (Kent), Caesar's Camp 284

Folklore Society 270, 298

fonts, typology 159

Foote, Samuel 37n12, 38n58, 99–100

Forest of Dean 336, 337

forgeries 274

Forster, E M 331, 332

Forty, F J 344

Foster, William 5

Fox, Sir Cyril 336, 338, 342, 346, 348, 350n80, 385

Fox, George E 224n48, 301n84, *355*

Franks, A Wollaston
 addresses 249, 393, 396
 Ancient Monuments bill referred to 294
 at British Museum 256
 exhibitions mounted by 296
 intellectual network 271
 library, donations to 217–18
 on London Wall 284
 reforms under 210, 212, 213

Frederick, Charles
 appointment 105
 drawings by 59, *61*, 200

freemasonry 55

Frere, John 158, 169n102, 244–5, 283, 432

Frere, Sheppard 365, 367, 371, 372, 375, 385

Freston, Revd Anthony 232

Frilford (Berks), excavations 275, 276

Frith, William Powell 136

Fuseli, Henry 142n5

Fussell's Lodge long barrow (Wilts) 406

Gadebridge Park (Herts), excavations 412n45

Gage, John (later Gage Rokewode) 117, 192, 206, 276

Gale, Roger 34, 54, 68n18, 75

Gale, Samuel *10*, 34, 49, 54, 60, 68n18

Gale, Thomas 34

Gandy, John 162

Ganton Wold (N Yorks), barrow 236

Gardiner, Rolf 333, 334

Garrod, Dorothy 385

Gaul, J J 139

Gay, John 23
Geerarts, Marc 27
Gell, William 162
Gentleman's Magazine
  antiquarian pieces 113, 177, 232, 244,
    251, 252
  Carter writes for 90, 322, 325n25,
    325n27
  letters
      18th-century 1, 87, 90, 91, 93,
        310, 433
      19th-century 195n86, 432, 434
  proposals for parochial surveys 77
Geoffrey of Monmouth 13
Geological Society
  conservation 336
  fieldwork funded by 287
  founding of 228
  prehistoric studies, contribution to
    253, 255, 293, 331
  *see also Journal of the Geological
    Society*
geology
  Geological Museum 250
  knowledge of, 19th-century 189–90,
    244
  prehistoric studies, influence on 227,
    244–8, 249, 271
  see also Geological Society; Royal
    Geological Society
George II 65, 66
George III 135, 310–12
George, Prince of Wales 91
Gere, C M, drawing by 319, *320*
Gereint ap Erbin 169n99
Getty Grant Program 220
Gibbons, Grinling 32
Gibson, Edmund 15, 36, 50–1, 158, 200
Giffen, Albert van 385
Gifford, Andrew 63
Gilpin, Revd William 109, 110, 114, 316
Girtin, Thomas, illustrations by 126, 127, *128*
Glastonbury (Som)
  Abbey 310
  antiquarian society 297
  lake villages 270, 359, 397
Gloucester (Glos)
  cathedral 96n66, 316
  fieldwork 406
Gloucester, Duke of 91
Gomme, G L 322
Goodchild, Richard 399, 405
Gordon, Alexander 58–9, 63, 70n63
Gordon, George, Earl of Aberdeen
  caricature *172*, *273*
  open letter to 167n28
  political career 8, 173, 178
  presidency 92–3, 178–86, 244, 434
gorget *146*, 163
Gothic Revival 314, 316, 322
Göttingen (Germany), university 95n30,
  207
Gough, Richard
  antiquary, use of term by 37n12

Archaeologia launched by 82, 83–4,
  151, 157, 431
bequest 117
Britannia, final revision 15
directorship 80–1
history of Society of Antiquaries by
  1–2, 5, 167n28
poem by 209
prints and engravings 111–13, 114,
  124–5, 126, 162, 310
  Cathedral Antiquities 90–1
  historical prints 84–5
sketch of *81*
Somerset House, move to under 85–6,
  202
typology of sepulchral monuments 159,
  160, 209–10
Wyatt, opposition to 89, 312, 431–2
Gould, Arthur 4
Gower, Revd Foote 80, 168n50
Gowers Commission 386
Gowland, W 287, 291, *355*, 359
Grafton, Richard 16, 37n12
Grand Tour 54, 79–80, 110, 148, 169n82,
  228, 274
Gray, H L 331
Gray, Irvine 219
Great Exhibition 269
Great Tolmen of Constantine (Cornwall)
  238
Green, Benjamin 110
Green, James 110
Green, Valentine 92
Greenwell, Canon William
  excavations
      barrows 236, 258n59, 275, 276,
        283, 288, 289
      Grimes Graves 285
  exhibition, contributes to 302n113
  intellectual network 270
Greenwood, Arthur 341
Greetham (Rutland), club 53
Greville, Col 277
Grew, Nehemiah 39n62
Grierson, Philip 385
Griffin, Ralph 219
Griffinrath (Co Kildare), trumpet 60
Griffith, Revd Hugh Davies 277
Grignion, J 25
Grimes, W F 344
Grimes Graves (Norfolk), excavations 283,
  285
Grimspound (Devon), settlement site 234
Grocyn, William 37n5
Grose, Francis 144n37
Groves, John Thomas 312
Grueber, H A 287
Guercino 110
Guest, Thomas 301n59
Gurney, Hudson 178–80, 184, 301n65

Habington, Thomas 201, 202
Hackendon (Kent), charnel pit 59
Haddon, A C 298

Hadrian's Wall 5, 330, 389
Haggard, W D 211
Haghe, Louis 131
Hainault Forest (Essex) 331, 334
Hakluyt Society 214
Halfhide, James 150
Hall, Melanie *414*
Hall, Samuel Carter 134
Hall Crouch, Charles 218
Hallam, Henry 175, 186
Hallstatt (Austria), fieldwork 236
Hamilton, Duke of 169n82
Hamilton, Sir William
  collecting activities 148
  finds submitted by 150, 151, 152
  publications 208
  quarrel with Carlisle 183, 184
  reports from Italy 80, 162, 201
hand-axes
  France *226*, 248, 283
  Hoxne 149, 244, *245*
  typology 296, *297*
Hanoverian Club 55
Harden, Donald 385
Harding, Sylvester, portrait by *74*
Hardwicke, Lord 85, 95n44, 113
Hare, Henry, Baron Coleraine 49, 55, 65,
  67n5, 200, 206
Hare Island (Co Westmeath), hoard 204
Harford, Charles 156, 159
Harley, Edward, Earl of Oxford 33, 68n25,
  200, 206
Harley, Robert, Earl of Oxford 33, 47, 48,
  49, 68n25
Harman, Richard 334
Harnham (Wilts), excavations 275, 276,
  277, *278*, 287
Harran (Turkey), fieldwork 398
Harrison, William 15
Hartshorne, Revd C H 182, 183
Harvey, William 326n64
Harwood (Yorks), finger-ring 71n91
Hasted, Edward 95n34
Hatcher, Thomas 25
Havell, Robert, aquatints by *146*, *164*
Haverfield, F 287, *355*
Hawkes, Christopher 343, 365, 369, 370,
  385, 405
Hawkes, Jacquetta 343
Hawkins, Edward 238, 239
Hawley, W 358, 363, 364
Haycock, David Boyd 6
Hearne, Thomas 13, 15, *31*, 40n89,
  68n26
Heath, Revd 284
Heber, Richard 209
de Heere, L 162
Hellenic Society 141, 342
Hemp, Wilfred 337
Hen Domen (Montgomery), fieldwork
  412n45
Hendinas (Shrops), shield *112*
Heneage, Michael 25
henges 230

Hengistbury Head (Dorset), excavations 358–9, 375, 399
Henley-on-Thames (Oxon), Park Place 274
Henry v 223n8
Henry VII 16, 17, 168n34, 200
Henry VIII 13, 84, 204
Henry, Prince of Wales 22
Heppington (Kent), meeting of BAA 178
heraldry 204, 207, 217–19, 372
Herculaneum (Italy) 80, 94n25, 169n103
Hereford (Herefs), cathedral 89
Heritage Bill 389
Heritage Lottery Fund 390, 391, 410
Hertford, Duchess of 70n61
Hertford, Lord (later Duke of Somerset) 49, 50, 56
Heseltine, Michael 389
Hesse Cassell Society of Antiquaries 95n30
Hibernian Society of Antiquaries 95n55
Hickes, George 12, 24, 40n88, 40n89
Hicks, George 346
Hildesheim (Germany), building reconstruction 308
Hill, Octavia 336
Hill, Thomas, portrait by 33, *34*
hillforts 230, 234
Historic Buildings and Ancient Monuments Acts 386
Historic Buildings Council 386
Historic Buildings and Monuments Commission 390
Historic Churches Preservation Trust 386
Historic Scotland 384, 389, 418
historical prints 84–5, 113, 162–3, 431
Historical Society of Science 269
Hitchens, Revd Malachy 151, 167n23
hoards 59, *61*, 151, 158, 200, 204
Holbein, Hans 104, 105, 124
Holbrook, Neil 372
Holford, W G 341, 347
Holinshed, R 15, 16
Holland, Henry 148
Holland, Philemon 15, 37n12
Hollar, Wenceslaus, illustrations by *31, 32,* 109, 114
Holleyman, G A 339
Hollin Stump (Westmorland) 257n59
Hollis, Thomas 79, 94n10, 111, 199, 201
Holwood Hill (Kent), excavations 275, 276, 277, 280, *281*
Homfray, Revd John 127, 128
Hooper, W H, engraving by *320*
Hope, William St John 301n84, 315–16, 323, *355*, 358, 373
Hopton (Norfolk), parochial survey 94n8
horned cairns, Caithness 251
horns *103*, 151, 163
Horsley, J 83
Horsley, Samuel 89
Hoskins, W G 339
Howard, Thomas, Earl of Arundel 21, 22
Howard, William, Lord Howard of Naworth 15
Howe, Samuel 168n50

Hoxne (Suffolk), hand-axes 149, 158, 169n02, 244, *245*, 283
Hudd, Alfred 357
Huddersfield (Yorks), antiquarian society 297
Huggate (E Yorks), burial 232
Hull, Rex 369
Hullmandel, C J 117, 118
Humble, George 39n75
Hume, Revd A 251
Humphrey, Osias 133
Huxley, Thomas 270, 331
Huxley Committee 329–30

ICOMOS-UK 427
Iffins Wood (Kent), excavations 276, 277, *279*, 283
Illustrated London News 267, 272, 383
Illyrian Armorial 201
Impington Village College (Cambs) 343
Ingleborough (N Yorks), hillfort 234
inscriptions 274, 289
Institute of British Architects 258n98
Institute of Field Archaeologists 383, 384, 389, 427
Institution of Civil Engineers 214
International Centre for the Study of the Preservation and Restoration of Cultural Property 389
Iraq, British School 412n39
Ives, John 148
Iwerne villa (Dorset), excavations 301n74
Izacke, R 39n82

Jacobsen, Theodore 76
Jago, Vivian 167n23
James I 17, 18
James, Sir Henry 274
Jameson, Anna 142n5
Jekyll, Joseph 204
Jenkins, Thomas 79, 148, 201
Jerdan, William 173, 176, 177, 178, 194n20
Jerusalem (Israel), British School 412n39
Jervis, Simon 385, 424
Jewitt, Llewellynn 236
Johnson, Amy 339
Johnson, Cornelius, engraving by 76, 77
Johnson, Maurice 5, 48, 53, 54, 56, 69n47
Johnson, Samuel 13, 20, 430
Jones, Herbert 355
Jones, Inigo 36, 99
Jones, John Winter 287–8
Jones, Michael 195n84
Jordan, air photography survey 402
Journal of the Anthropological Institute 236, 275, 292
Journal of the British Archaeological Association 290
Journal of the Ethnological Society 275, 292
Journal of the Geological Society 293
Joyce, Revd J G 285, 301n65
Julius Caesar, G 370
Justin, St 163

Keiller, A 340
Keith, Sir Arthur 246
Kelmscott Manor (Oxon) 319, *320–1*, 323, *324*, 434
Kemble, J M 241, 251, 252
Kempe, Alfred 189, 194n20, 195n86, 276, 277
    drawing by *281*
Kendrick, T D 5
Kennedy, David 402
Kennett (Wilts), finds from *131*
Kenrick, John 248
Kent
    archaeological society 291, 292
    barrows 229, 232
    manuscripts 204, 214
Kent, William 68n19
Kent's Cavern (Devon) 245, 287
Kenyon, Kathleen 346, *347*, 348
Kerrich, Revd Thomas 124, 206
Keynes, J M 332
King, Edward 86–7, 88, 204
Kingsford, Hugh 218
'A Kinship of Husbandry' 333, 334
Kirkby in Ashfield (Notts), cross *160*
Kirklees (Yorks), crosses *160*
Kit-Kat Club 55
Klithi (Greece), fieldwork 399
Knight, Charles 134
Knight, Payne 159
Knook Castle (Wilts) 230
Knossos (Crete) 6, 359
Körös Culture Project (Hungary) 399
Kortholt, C 200
Kouklia (Cyprus), fieldwork 398

Lacy family 129
Laing, David 240
Lambarde, William 15, 25
lamp 63, *64*, 200, 218
Lancashire, antiquarian society 297
L'Ancresse (Guernsey), megalith 232, *234*
Land Nationalization Society 335
landscape conservation 329–31
    beginnings 331–4
    conservation 334–8
    landscape, conceptualizing 339–41
    planning for peace 341–2
Lane Fox, Col 254, 301n66, 331
Lanyon Quoit (Cornwall) 238
Lassus, Jean-Baptiste 325n37
Lastri, Marco 143n10
Lawrence, Thomas 133
Layamon 214
Layard, Sir Austen Henry 139, 294
Ledwich, Edward 95n55
Lee, Dr 184
Leeds, E T 301n48, 339, 340
Leicester (Leics), Jewry Wall *347*
Leicester, Earl of *see* Ferrers, Lord de
Leicestershire, history of 210
Leigh, Dr Charles *33*
Leighton, Frederic 141
Leland, John 13–14, 24, 25, 156

Lely, Peter 29
Leman, Revd Thomas 229, 231, 242–3
Lemon, Robert 210, 211–12, 213, 214
Lennox, Charles, Duke of Richmond 50, 55, 65–6, 70n63
Lethieullier, William 70n63
Lever, Sir Ashton 163
Levine, Joseph 6
Levine, Philippa 6
Lewis chessmen 210
Lewisham (G London), antiquarian society 297
Lewisham, Lord 90
Leys, Baron Henri 138
Lhuyd, Edward 12, 24, 35–6, 153, 156, 158
Libya, fieldwork projects 370, 398, 399, 405, 412n39
Lichfield (Staffs)
    botanical society 69n43
    cathedral 89
Lincoln (Lincs)
    club 53
    fieldwork 406
Lindsay, Lord 142n5
Lindsey Psalter 201
Lingard, John 175
Linnean Society 228, 331, 337
Lipari (Italy), baths 274
Literary Gazette 244
lithography 117–18, 119, 274, 275
Livy 16
Lloyd George, David 332
Locke, Peter 320
Lodge, Edmund 195n84
Logan, James, illustration by *281*
London
    Acton Terraces 287
    Bear Tavern 2, 3, 34, 46
    British Museum *see* British Museum
    Buckingham Street, water gate 94n10
    Bull's Head 67n5
    Burlington House 215, *216*, 217–19, *220*, 221–2
    Chancery Lane 76, 85, 200–2
    Chandos Street, Lebeck's Head Tavern 55
    Charing Cross, Cox's Museum 170n112
    Chelsea College 17
    Coliseum 300n5
    Crystal Palace *266*, 269, 313
    Egyptian Hall 163, *165*
    excavations and fieldwork
        19th-century 192, 284, *285*, 286, 287
        1920–39 359, *360*, 361, 370, 377
        post-war 344–7, 370, 387
    Fleet Street
        Crane Court 57, 200
        Mitre Tavern 49, 56–7, 200
        Whitefriars' chapel 57
        Young Devil Tavern 8n5, 34, 46, 47
    Geological Museum 250
    Gray's Inn 56, 200

Great Queen Street, Virtuosi 69n40, 69n44
Gresham College 57
Guildhall Library 218
Imperial College 95n30
Institute of Archaeology 221
Lambeth Palace Library 220
London Institution 209
London Library 212
London Museum 359
London Wall 284, *285*, 286
Montagu House 76
National Gallery 178, 214, 215
National Portrait Gallery 211
Natural History Museum 343, 387
Pantherion 163
St Andrew Undershaft 25
St James, font 63, 101
St Martin-in-the-Fields, inscriptions 59
St Martin's Place 349n11
St Paul's Cathedral 25, 206, 223n4
Sir John Soane's Museum 426
Somerset House
    Antiquaries move to 85–7, 89, 123
    Meeting Room 149, 150, *172*, 211, 215, *273*
    library 202, *203*, 204–7, *208*, 209–10
    space, lack of 214–15
    surveyor 90, 312
Temple
    coffee houses 46, 48, 69n43
    King's Bench Walk 56, 200
Tichborne Street, Weeks's Museum 170n112
Westminster Abbey
    Blake records monuments 126, *127*, 201
    objects donated by Society 217
    Richard II, image of 63
    tombs 17, 24–5, 126, 143n11
Westminster Palace
    Painted Chamber 133
    St Stephen's Chapel 90, 117, 208, 310, 313
    surveyor 313
    watercolour scenes 210
Whitehall 47
Long, William 210–11
Long Sutton (Lincs), cross *160*
Long Wittenham (Berks), excavations 275, 276, 287
Longmate, Barak 114
Longthorpe (Cambs), fieldwork 398
Longworth, Ian 401
Lort, Michael 87–8, 95n44, 95n54
Louth (Lincs), antiquarian society 297
Lubbock, Sir John
    Ancient Monuments legislation 255, 294–5, 314
    intellectual network 254, 270, 271, 284, 296, 301n65, 331
    prehistoric studies
        campaign for 249, 250–1, 255, 293

material exhibited by 302n113
Prehistoric Times 227, 242, 248–9, 254, 293–4
on Three Age System 242, 243
Stonehenge initiative 287
Lukis, F C 232, 260n237, 270
Lullingstone (Kent), excavations 398
Lumley, Mr (bookseller) 187
Lumley, John, Lord Lumley 22
lunula *146*, 163
Lycia, expedition 132
Lydney Park (Glos), excavations 336, 338, 343, 364, 376, 397
Lyell, Sir Charles 248, 283–4
Lymington, Lord 334
Lysons, Samuel
    caricature *172*, *273*
    directorship 90, 93
    History of the Berkeley Family 92
    fieldwork 191–2, 276, 277
    paper by 151
Lyttelton, Charles, Bishop of Carlisle
    Banks sponsored by 96n59
    bequest 201–2
    paper on stone hatchets 153–6, 158, 159
    portrait 111
    social class 148
    visual records, on value of 124
    Walpole criticizes 99

Macauley, Rose 323
Macclesfield, Earl of 94n10
MacDonald, Ramsay 336, 337
mace 218
McEnery, Revd J 245
Mackenzie, Frederick 126, 129
Macky, John 46
Maclean, Thomas 181
Madden, Frederic *181*
Madox, Thomas 24, 40n89
Maffei, Marchese Scipione 51
Magoon, Revd Elias Lyman 143n19
Mahon, Lord *see* Stanhope, Philip Henry
Maiden Castle (Dorset)
    excavations 365, *367–8*, 370, 374, 375, 377, 397
    Huxley Committee on 329
Maimieux, Capt 148
Mann, Sir James 3, 4, 6, 385, *386*, 387, 403
Mannheim (Germany), society 95n30
Manningham, John 39n67
Manningham, Sir Richard 55
Mantell, Lady 194n38
Mantell, Thomas 149, 271, 293
manuscripts
    acquired by Society 153, 200, 201, 202, 204, 214, 217–18
    catalogue 219–20
    loans of 221
Marden (Kent), fieldwork 406
Market Overton (Rutland), club 53
Markland, J 167n28
Marmion, Shakerley 18, 23, 34, 38n50

Marston St Lawrence (Oxon), cemetery *278*
Martin, Elizabeth Anne 178
Martin, Thomas 148
Mary I 206
Massingham, Harold 332-3, 334
Master of the Rolls 295
Maxfield, Valerie 374
May, Thomas 355, 363, 364
Mead, Richard 67n18
Meare (Som), excavations 377, 412n45
Medieval Archaeology 403, 405, 407
Medieval Pottery Research Group 427
Melville, Henry 142n1
Mendes da Costa, Emanuel 56
Merewether, Dean 190
Merton Abbey (Surrey) 150, 152
Meyrick, Sir Samuel Rush 124, 136,
    144nn29 and 37, 147, 162
Milles, Dr Jeremiah
    depictions of *xii, 82*
    Egyptian Society, member of 70n63
    paper on seal 168n68
    presidency 82-3, 84, 85, 86, 123, 202
    visual arts, stresses importance of
        123-5, 134, 139-41
    Walpole antagonistic to 99
Milton, John 200
Ministry of Town and Country Planning
    338, 341-2, 344, 345, 346, 347-8
Ministry/Office of Works
    Commissioner 294, 315
    conservation and fieldwork 315, 330-1,
        397
        Old Sarum 358
        Richborough 361
        Stanwick 397
        Tintern Abbey 317, 318
    Council for British Archaeology,
        relationship with 344, 345-7, 348
    Historic Buildings Council 386
    national parks survey 338
    organization 341, 342, 345
Mitchell, Andrew 70n63
models 201, 209, 238, 272, 274, 286
Moggeridge, Hal 319, 320
Mold (Flints), cape 210
Monmouthshire, survey 94n8
Mons Claudianus (Egypt), excavations 402
Mons Porphyrites (Egypt), excavations
    374-5, *376*, 399
Mont St Helier (Jersey), model 274
Montagu, Duke of 49, 55
Montfaucon, B 85, 208
Monumental Brass Society 221
Moore, James 128
Moore, Sir John 161, 169n82
Morant, Philip 165
Morgan, Sylvanus 28, 31
Morgannw, Iolo 147
Morpeth, William 310
Morris, William 315, 319-20, 322, 324, 434
Morris Committee 427
Mortimer, Cromwell 60, 63, 72n108, 229
Mortimer, J R 332, 338

Morton, Charles 94n10, 96n59
mosaics 59, *60*, 71n86, 152, 399
Mostyn, Sir Roger 153
Mucking (Essex), fieldwork 406
Muilman, Peter 148
Muir, John 335
Müller, Max 270
Müller, William J, illustrations by 126, 130,
    131, *132*, 133
Museums Association 390, 391
Mycenae (Greece) 272
Myres, J N L 383, 385, *388*, 389, 400,
    406-7

Nash, Frederick 117
Nash, Joseph 131, 136
Nash, Dr Treadway 202, 210
Nashe, Thomas 18
National Central Library 219
National Maritime Museum 401
National Museum of Wales 338
National Parks 330, 335-6, 337-8, 343,
    348, 384
National Register of Archives 219
National Trust 308, 334, 387, 395, 426
Natural History Review 249
Nature Conservancy 330
Nature Reserves Investigation Committee
    338, 343, 347
Nautical Archaeological Society 427
Neve, Peter le 49, 55, 60, 67n5
Neve, Revd Dr Timothy 53, 68n35
Neville, R C 276
New Forest kiln excavations 277, *279*
Newcastle (Tyne and Wear), old bridge
    168n35
Newgrange (Co Meath), excavations 275
News from Nowhere 319, *320*
Newton, Sir Isaac 52, 67n18
Nichols (publisher) 148
Nichols, John 109, 206, 210
Nicholson, George 310, 325n27
Nicolas, Sir Nicholas Harris
    criticism of Society 5, 174-5, 180-3,
        185-6, 187, 188-9, 209
    papers by 180, 183
Nicolson, William, archdeacon of Carlisle
    50-1
Nilsson, Sven 254
Noble, Mark 4
Norden, Frederik 70n63
Norden, John 15
Norfolk Archaeology 130
Norman, E de 346
Norman, Philip 332
Normandy (France), fieldwork 365, 369,
    370, 398
Norris, William 148, 202
North, George 5, 9n29, 72n108, 75, 94n17
North Stoke (Lincs), tiles *190*
Northcote, James 142n5
Northolt (G London), fieldwork 398
Northton (Harris), fieldwork 412n45
Norwich (Norfolk)

castle 309
    International Congress 250, 294
Nowell, Laurence 25
Numismatic Society 177, 269, 270, 432

Oakley, Kenneth 343
Occasional Papers 403, 407, 410
O'Connor, Charles 95n55
Office of Woods and Forests 316, 317, 335
Office of Works *see* Ministry/Office of Works
Old Sarum (Wilts)
    excavations 315, 358, 373, 377, 397
    scheduling 294
O'Neil, Brian 344-5, *346*-8
Ord, Craven 210
Order of the Garter, installation of 135, *136*
Ordnance Survey 221, 232-4, 274, 432, 433
Ortelius, Abraham 15
Orwin, C S and C S 339
Ospringe (Kent), excavations 364, 397
Ouvry, Frederick 295
Overton Down experimental earthwork
    (Wilts) 412n45
Owen, Professor 301n78
Owslebury (Hants), excavation report
    413n66
Oxford (Oxon)
    Ashmolean Museum 5, 24, 32, 35, 156,
        167n28
    Bodleian Library 5, 27, 31, 68n25, 213
    Oxford Architectural Society 177
    philosophical society 69n43
    University 17

Paderni, Camillo 94n24, 94n25
Palgrave, Francis 180
palstave 127, *128*
paper-squeezes 274
Paphos (Cyprus), excavations 399
Papworth, J W 372
Paris (France), Académie des Inscriptions et
    Belles-lettres 76, 94n4
Parker, Matthew, Archbishop of Canterbury
    14, 25, 26, 37n5
Parkinson's Museum 169n102
Parry, Graham 6
Pattison, Mark 12
Paviland (Swansea), Goat's Hole 245
Payne, John 27
Peacham, Henry 21-2, 23
Peacock, David 374, 402
Pearce, B W E 361
Peers, Charles 297, 315-16, 317, 318, 322,
    323, 336
Pegge, Samuel 83, 88, 99
Peiresc, Nicolas Fabri de 27, 38n53
Pembroke, Earl of 54
Pengelly, William 245
Penn, G, drawing by *266*
Pennant, Thomas 37n12, 148, 153, 167n16,
    228
Pepler, George 341-2, 343, 345, 347
Perceval, Charles 210, 214, 218
Percy, Thomas, bishop of Drogher 83, 87-8

Percy Society 214, 270
Perring, Dominic 402
Perry, Charles 70n63
Perth, Lord 390
Peterborough (Cambs)
    Book Society 54
    Gentlemen's Society
        correspondence 68n35, 69n38, 72n101
        foundation and aims 53–4
        library 65
        meetings 57, 71n75
        membership 68n36, 70n61
        premises 70n70
Pethers of Burford 320
Petrie, George 241
Pettigrew, T G 8n9, 195n71, 271
Petworth (Sussex), canoe 238
Philistor 1, 87
Phillips, Hugh 373, 401
Phillips, John 234
Phillipson, David 402
Philosophical Transactions of the Royal Society 78, 113, 293
Phoenician traders 158, 230
photography 118, 119, 124, 274–5, 283, 286
Pickering, William 136
Pierrefonds (France) 326n37
Piggott, Stuart 6, 36, 101, 363, 385, 397
Pike, Mr 301n66
Pinkerton, John 8n1, 87
Piranesi, Giambattista 79, 214, 309
Pitt-Rivers, General A
    excavation medallion *279*, 302n88
    excavations 236, 276, 280, 284–7, 288, 289, 292–3
    as Inspector of Ancient Monuments 256, 287, 295, 315
    intellectual network 270, 271, 301n65
    lectures 272, 274–5
    prehistoric studies, contribution to 250, 251, 269, 296, 302n113
Pitt-Rivers, Capt George Henry 334
Planché, James 134, 135, 136
plant remains, reports on 287, 355
Plas Newydd (Anglesey) 238
Plenderleith, Harold 385
Pliny 161
Plot, Robert 35, 156
Pococke, Richard 55, 70n63
Polden Hills (Som), breastplates 163, 169n98
Poliziano, A 12
Polybius 16
Polydore Vergil 13
Pompeii (Italy) 80, 161–2, 165, 201
Pope, A 23
Pope's Head Club 70n57
Port Mahon (Menorca), vessels 60
Portchester Castle (Hants), excavations 377, 398, 406, 412n45, 413n66
Portsmouth (Hants), Portsdown Hill, barrow 257n59
Post-Medieval Archaeology 403, 407

Potter, Joseph 316
pottery, Anglian 60, *62*
Pownall, Thomas 83, 157, 275
Powys, A R 318, 324
Prae Wood (Herts), excavations 365
Praeneste (Italy), material from 167n25
Praetorius, C J 224n48, 300n44
Prattinton, Peter 210, 214, 218, 223n40
Prehistoric Society 397; *see also Proceedings of the Prehistoric Society*
Prehistoric Society of East Anglia 254
prehistoric studies 227–8
    British
        barrow diggers 229–32, *233*
        field survey and settlement site interpretation 232–6
        later 19th-century 243–51
        resistance to change 251–3
        summary and discussion 253–6
    Denmark
        Royal Society of Antiquaries of the North 236–7
        Thomsen 237–9
        Worsaae 239–43
Prestwich, Joseph 246–7, 270, 283, 289, 293, 301n71
Pretty, Robert 373
Prichard, James Cowles 239
Priestley, J B 332
Proceedings of the Cambridge Antiquarian Society 291, 292
Proceedings of the Prehistoric Society 403, 405, 407
Proceedings of the Royal Institute 293
Proceedings of the Society of Antiquaries 219, 244, 247–8, 249, 432
Prout, Samuel 129, 133
Prynne, William 17
Pugin, A C 90
Pugin, A W N 314
Punch 267
Pye, John 111

Raby, Dr F J E 341, 343, 344, 345, 346, 347–8, 349n37
Radford, C A Ralegh 341, 385
Rafn, Carl Christian 237, 238, 239
Rahtz, Philip 401
Ramsauer, J G 236
Ramsay, Allan 94n24
Ramsey (Hunts), cross *160*
Randall, H J 339
Rankin, Revd T 232
Raphael 110
Rashleigh, Sir Philip 143n9, 147
Rawlinson, Richard 81, 200, 289
Read, Sir Charles Hercules 8n10, 218, 363
Reid, Clement, 287, 355
Reith, Sir John 341, 343
Repton (Derbys), excavations 372, 398, 399
Research Committee Reports 358, 403, 405, 406, 407, 408–9, 411
The Retrospective Review 180
Revett, Nicholas 110, 139

Reynolds, J, card published by *266*
Reynolds, Sir Joshua 133, 135, 140
Rhind, Alexander Henry 242
Rhyd-y-gorse (Cardigan), shield 169n93
Ribchester (Lancs), helmet 117, *122*, 125
Richard II, engraving 63, *98*, 101
Richard III 99, 206
Richard, Duke of Gloucester 389
Richardson, Miss 369
Richborough (Kent)
    excavations 359, 361, *362*, 370, 376, 377, 397
    publication 406
Richmond, Ian 385, 397, 405–6
Rickman, John 191
Riddell, Robert 147, 204
Riley, John, portrait by *32*
Rivenhall church (Essex), excavations 372, 406
Robb, D R 287
Robbins, Michael 385, 390
Robinson, Sir Percival 346–7
Rochester Castle (Kent) 128
Rodwell, W and K 372
Rogers, Charles 111
Rogers, Daniel 25
Rolleston, George 276, 301n71
Roman Club 54
Roman Society 342
Rome (Italy)
    British School 357, 412n39
    Coliseum 308
    mosaic 71n86
Rooke, Hayman 88, 276
Roots, Ludlow 211
Roscoe, William 124
Rosetta Stone 117
Rossetti, D G 141
Rothschild, Charles 336
Rowlandson, Thomas, illustrations by *xii*, *165*
Royal Academy
    foundation 110, 114, 431
    history painting 84, 125, 138
    interaction with Antiquaries 91–2, 125, 431
    premises 76, 86, 90, 123, 214–15
Royal Academy of Sciences 95n30
Royal Archaeological Institute
    development in 19th-century 194n6
    library 218, 221
    membership 175–7, 178, 244
    prehistoric studies 250, 256
Royal Asiatic Society 289
Royal Astronomical Society 184, 213
Royal Commission on the Historical Monuments of England 221, 298, 372, 392, 401
Royal Commission on the Ancient and Historical Monuments of Wales 337
'Royal Family Piece' 104, *105*
Royal Geographical Society 184
Royal Geological Society 184, 269
Royal Historical Society 269

Royal Institute of British Architects 343
Royal Institution 248, 252
Royal Irish Academy 95n55, 207, 228, 241, 294
Royal Society
    Antiquaries, relationship with 65, 75, 88–90, 92
    charter and patronage 47–8, 65, 66
    collections 39n62
    finances 91
    library 200, 210, 212, 215
    meetings 57–8, 247
    membership 23, 51, 76, 91, 178, 393
    prehistoric studies 247, 248, 253
    premises 57, 76, 86, 89, 90, 123, 214–15
    provincial satellite 53
    publications 9n26, 71n94, 78, 207, 293
    role of 52, 78, 86, 199, 227–8
    split by Banks 68n21
    see also Philosophical Transactions of the Royal Society
Royal Society of Antiquaries of the North 207, 236–7, 239, 240, 251
Royal Society of Northern Antiquaries *see* Royal Society of Antiquaries of the North
Royston Cave (Herts), fieldwork *58*, *59*
Ruskin, John 124, 313–14, 332, 434
Rymer, Thomas 24, 40n89

Saami life, exhibition of 163, *165*
Sabratha (Libya), excavations 370
St Albans (Herts), cathedral 117
St Davids Cathedral (Pembs), engraving 90
St George Gray, Harold 270, 341
St Petersburg (Russia), society 95n30
Salisbury (Wilts)
    Anglo-Saxon cemetery, excavations 399
    cathedral 89, 310
Salter, H E 331
Saltmarsh, John 331
Sammes, Aylett 36
Sandon (Staffs), church 25
Sandwich, Earl of 55
Sandys, Frederick, illustrations by 126, 130, *131*
Savery, Salomon, engraving by 28, *29*
Savile, Sir Henry 12
Scaliger, J J 12
Schaeffer, Claude 385
Scharf, George 132, 211
Schliemann, H 256, 272, 291
Schnebblie, Jacob 115, 125, 133, 143n15, 208, 325n20
Scotland, research project 399
Scott, Sir George Gilbert 314
Scott, Sir Walter 12, 36, 37n12, 175, 209
seals 60–1, 114, 129, *130*, 214, 218
Selden, John 12, 17, 22, 35, 37n5
    portraits 29, *30*, 31
Seti I 163
settlement sites, interpretation of 232–6
Seyer, Revd Samuel 144n26

Shadwell, Thomas 23
Shakespeare, W 214
Shannongrove (Co Limerick), gorget 169n95
Sharp, R H 117, 118
Sharp, S 117
Sharp, William 143n10
Sharpe, Edmund 316
Sharples, Niall 368
Shaw, Henry 136
Shaw, Thurston 385
Sherborne (Dorset), parochial survey 94n8
Sherwin, J K 309
shields *112*, *149*, 152, 162
Shipley, William 69n41
Sibbald, Sir Robert 33, 156
Sidney, Sir Philip 16, 17, 20
Sierra Club 335
Silchester (Hants)
    excavations
        finds drawings 224n48
        Hope directs 315, 355
        models 274
        photography 275, *355*
        publication 275, 276, 287, 356
        Society supports 287, 353–6, 359, 377, 399, 412n45
        research by Darwin 285, 301n65
Silchester Excavation Fund 353, 355, 356
Simpson, Revd W S 302n113
Sites and Monuments Records 390
Sites of Special Scientific Interest 330
Skelton, William 125
Sketching Society for 'Historic Landscape' 143n9
Skorba (Malta), excavations 406
Sloane, Sir Hans 33, 51, 60, 63, 65, 72n101, 76
Smirke, Richard 90, 116, 204
Smirke, Robert 133, 206
Smith, Charles Hamilton 144n37, 147, 162
Smith, Charles Roach 175, 192, 243, 251, 271, 277, 288
Smith, Dr Herbert 349n40
Smith, Thomas 28
Smithsonian 214
Smyth, Revd Robert 70n54
Smyth, Capt W 274
Soane, Sir John 270, 426
Society of Antiquaries
    administration and finances
        18th-century 58–9, 90–1, 92–3, 208
        19th-century 178–87
        see also Research Committee
    archives 5, *44*
    collections (art and artefacts)
        early 18th-century 63, 65
        late 18th-century 86, 148–9, 150, 200–2, 204, 206, 274
        early 19th-century 204–6, 210–11, 274
        late 19th-century 214, 217
        20th-century 218, 219, 220, 221

        see also library
    conservation
        18th-century 59; Carter and Wyatt 309–13, 431–2; Ruskin, Lubbock and Ministry style 309–13
        20th-century: Kelmscott Manor 319, *320–1*, 323, *324*; landscape 330–1, 332, 336, 339, 342, 345, 348
    Fellowship 4
        early 18th-century 49–50, 51, 58
        late 18th-century 76, 80, 81, 88, 90–2, 147–50
        19th-century 174–8, 185, 187
        early 20th-century 216, 221, 383
        late 20th-century 221–2, 392–6, 408
        21st-century 415–29
    fieldwork
        18th-century 59
        19th–20th centuries 353–7; 1890–1915 *354*, *355*, 357–9; 1920–39 (*illus*) *354*, 359–70; 1945–77 *354*, 370–2; 1978–99 (*illus*) *354*, 373–7
        see also Research Committee
    gold medallists 385
    graphic arts (*illus*) 99–119, 123–5, 126, 129–30, 133, 139
    histories of 1–8
    history 430–5
        Elizabethan society 1–2, 14–15, 17
        1701–17 46–9
        1717–51: characteristics and contemporaries 49–56; engravings and paintings 101–9; meetings, premises and administration 56–65; royal charter 65–6
        1751–*c* 1800 75–6; directorship of Gough 80–1; divisions 88–90; engravings and paintings 99–100, 105, 109–17, 118–19, 124–8; foreign relations 79–80; historical prints 84–5; loss of direction 92–3; public reputation 87–8; publications 77–9, 82–4; social exclusivity 90–2; Somerset House, move to 85–7
        early 19th-century 173–4; class and gender 174–8; presidency of Aberdeen 178–86, 244; presidency of Stanhope 186–7
        late 19th-century: Ancient Monuments Acts, participation in 294–5; prehistoric studies, reaction to 249–51, 296; resistance to change 251, 252–3, 254–6, 293–4; role of 295–7, 298
        late 20th-century 383–4, 407–11; Anniversary Addresses, items of

current concern 384–92;
Fellowship 392–6; publication
402–7; research 397–402
library
1707–51 63–5, 199–200
Chancery Lane 86, 200–2
Somerset House: 1781–1840 202,
203, 204–7, *208*, 209–10;
1840–75 210–15
Burlington House 215, *216*,
217–19, *220*, 221–2
meetings
early 18th-century 56, 57–60
late 18th-century 79, 80–1, 83,
92, 150–1, 274
19th-century 183, 269, 271–2,
273, 274, 277
premises
1707–51 46, 47, 48, 49, 56–7, 200
Chancery Lane 76, 200–2
Somerset House 85–7, 89, 90,
123, *273*
Burlington House 215–17
see also library
publications
early 18th-century 61–3
late 18th-century 77–9, 82–5, 88
early 19th-century 182, 186,
187–93
20th-century 353, 402–7, 408–10
see also Antiquaries Journal;
Cathedral Antiquities; historical
prints; Occasional Papers;
*Proceedings of the Society of
Antiquaries*; Research
Committee Reports; *Vetusta
Monumenta*
Research Committee 353–7
1890–1915 357–9
1920–39 359–70
1945–99 370–7, 397–402, 409–10
royal charter 2, 47–8, 65–6
symbol 63, *64*
Society of Antiquaries of Scotland 217, 228,
240–1, 248, 251–2, 294
Society for Biblical Archaeology 269, 300n5
Society of Dilettanti 54, 94n21, 139, 141,
178
Society for the Encouragement of Arts,
Manufactures and Commerce 69n41, 87,
94n10
Society for Landscape Studies 384
Society for Libyan Studies 412n39
Society of Noviomagus 177, 194n20
Society for Post-Medieval Archaeology 384
Society for the Promotion of Christian
Knowledge 52, 68n25, 68n36
Society for the Promotion of Hellenic
Studies 218
Society for the Promotion of Nature
Reserves 336
Society for the Protection of Ancient
Buildings
foundation 269, 315, 434

Lethaby Scholar 320
principles 315, 316, 322, 343
Tintern Abbey conservation, opinion of
318
Society of Roman Knights 54–5, 68n32
Society for South Asian Studies 412n39
Solway Firth, fieldwork 399
Somerset Archaeological and Natural
History Society 177
Somerset family, Dukes of Beaufort 316, 322
Somerset Levels 406
Somme gravels (France), prehistoric finds
226, 246, *247*, 248
Somner, William 33
South Cadbury (Som), excavations 398,
406, 413n66
South Lodge (Dorset), excavations 286
Southampton (Hants)
excavations 387, 398, 400
history of 208
Southey, Robert 175
Spalding (Lincs), Gentlemen's Society 52–3,
56, 57, 65, 69n38, 70nn69 and 73,
72n103
Sparks, Jos 54
spearheads 59, *61*, *131*, 162, 200
Speed, John 28, *29*, 162
Spelman, Sir Henry 18, 26
Spencer, H 270
Sprat, Thomas 39n62
Springhead Ring 333, 334
Stadler, J C 117
Stamford (Lincs)
Brazenose Society 53
fieldwork 398, 400
Standlake (Oxon), excavations 274, *279*,
301n48
Stanhope, Philip Henry, Lord Mahon
letter to Aberdeen 195n103
presidency 2, 4, 186–7, 211, 212,
224n73
Stanley Moor (Derbys), palstave 127, *128*
Stanwick (N Yorks), excavations 365, 369,
397
Stapleton, Thomas 183
Star Carr (Yorks), excavations 397
statue, Roman *116*
Stephenson, Mill 218, *355*
Stevenage (Herts), barrow opening 59
Stokes, Margaret 210
Stone, Stephen 274, 301n48
Stonehenge (Wilts)
conservation 330, 337
dating 191, 230
excavations
1798 230
19th-century 287
20th-century 359, 361–3, 370,
374, 377, 397
illustrations 163, *164*, 238
photographs 274, 275
restoration *352*
road proposals 391
Stukeley on 36, 59, 68n18, 228

Stonesfield (Oxon), mosiac 59, *60*
Stoney Littleton (Som), excavations 276,
283
Storm, G F 117
Stothard, Charles, illustrations by 117, 133,
134, 136
Stourhead (Wilts), library 209
Stow, John 15, 16, 20–1, 25, 37n12, 199
Strange, Robert 111, 114
stratigraphy, recording 254, 432
barrow sites 231–2, 236, 283, 286
cave sites 245–6
Cissbury 284, *285*, 286
Hoxne 244
L'Ancresse 232, *234*
London Wall *285*, 286
Silchester *285*
Somme gravels *247*, 248
Strutt, Joseph 134, 135, 136, 144n29, 162
Strype, John 199
Stuart, James 79, 94n10, 110, 139
Stubbs, George 133
Stukeley, William
account of early Society by 3, 5, 49
on antiquarianism 430
barrow classification 229
biography 6
brother-in-law 34
Druidism 36, 227
engravings and drawings
donated by 63
on importance of 102–3, 107, 119,
199, 271
portrait 206
by Stukeley *frontispiece*, 124
societies, membership of 51, 53, 54–5
Society of Antiquaries, role in 49, 56,
57, 65, 76, 81
on Stonehenge 36, 59, 68n18, 228
Sturmere (Essex), finds 156
Sutton Courtney (Oxon), excavations
301n48
Sutton Hoo (Suffolk), excavations 373, *374*,
377, 399, 401
Swarling (Kent), excavations 363–4, 370,
375, 397
Sweet, Rosemary 6
Swindon (Wilts), National Monuments
Record Centre 222
Swiss lake villages 291

Tacitus 16, 370
Tadcaster (Yorks), axe 163
Taeye, Louis de 138
Talbot, Robert 25
Tallents, Sir Stephen 345
Talman, John
Catholicism 48
engraving by *64*
foundation of Society of Antiquaries
2, 46, 49
prints and drawings 63, 71n97, 101–2,
104, 200
social standing 50

Talman, William 68n19
Tankersley (Yorks), cross *160*
Tanner, Thomas, Bishop of St Asaph 56, 67n5
Tansley, Sir Arthur 330, 336
Tate, Francis 15, 25
Taylor, Arnold 385
Taylor, Harold 372, 401
Taylor, M V 340
Telmessus (Turkey), tomb *132*
Tendi, Andrea 125
Tewkesbury (Glos), tombs 151
Theobald, James 72n108, 77, 78, 94n13
Theobald, Lewis 39n59
Thomas, Lieutenant 301n56
Thomas, Herbert H 363
Thompson, Edward Maunde 27
Thompson, S 275
Thoms, Mr 187
Thoms, W J 239–40, 243, 254–5
Thomsen, C J 232, 237–9, 242, 254, 432
Thoresby, Ralph 51
Thorpe, John 204, 214
Thucydides 16
Thurnam, Dr J 229, 270, 276, 279, 287, 291, 302n113
Thynne, Francis 25
tiles, Roman *190*
The Times 232, 244, 345, 432
Tintern Abbey (Mon) *306*, 315–16, *317–18*, 322–3
Tivoli (Italy), temple 201, 209, 274
Tongue, Richard 238
Topham, John 90, 148, 204
torc 153, *156*
torch holder, Etruscan 224n49
Tovey, Mr 105
Town and Country Planning Bill 337
Townley, Charles 125, 139, 148, 210
Treasure Trove legislation 390–1
Tredegar, Lord 357
Trevethy Stones (Cornwall) 238
Troy (Turkey) 256, 291
Troyon, C 301n66
trumpets 59, 60, *112*, 152
Tudor-Craig, Dr Pamela 219
Turner, J M W 126, 127, 128–9, 175, 270, 316
watercolour by *130*
Turners of Cardiff 316–17
Twyne, Brian 17
Tylor, Alfred 270
typology 158–9, *160*, 161, 289, 293
Tyson, Michael 83, 168n34
Tyssen, J R D, Lord Amherst 213

Uffington White Horse (Oxon) 191, *193*
Ulph's Horn *103*
Underwood, Thomas Richard 117, 125, 133, 204, 245, 260n171
UNESCO, Culture Committee 427
Uppsala (Sweden), Antiquities College 68n29

Upton (Oxon), excavation report 413n66
Upton Great Barrow (Wilts), excavations 280
Upwey Down (Dorset), barrow 257n59
Ussher, James, Archbishop of Armagh 189–90, 230

Valetta, Francesco 94n25
Valla, L 12
Vallancey, Charles 95n55
Vanburgh, John 309
Vandergucht, Michael 104
Varro, M T 16
Verelius, Olof 68n29
Vertue, George
attends auction 63
as engraver of Society 81, 104–11, 118–19, 124, 431
portraits 25, *31*
Richard II 63, *98*, 101
'Royal Family Piece' 104, *105*
St James's font 63
seals 61
Stonesfield mosaic 59, *60*
Tudor subjects 168n48
'Ulphi Cornu' *103*
history of the Society by 5
opposes merger with Royal Society 72n108
pupil at Virtuosi academy 69n44
widow 111
Verulamium (Herts), excavations
pre-war 365, *366*, 367, 370, 375, 377
post-war 371, 372, 375, 398, 413n66
Verulamium Excavation Committee 365
Vetusta Monumenta
1747–51 63, *64*, 103–4, 199–200
1751–c 1800 85, 110–11, 113–14, 125–6, 133, 162, 163
1800 onwards 117, *118*, 144n34, 152, 210
see also Cathedral Antiquities; historical prints
Vézelay (France), La Madeleine 326n37
Victoria, Queen 177
Victoria County History 315, 383
Vincent, Augustine 17
Viollet-le-Duc, E E 323, 326n37
Virginia Company, broadside relating to *198*, 201
virtuosi 20–4, 36, 89
Virtuosi of St Luke 69n40, 69n44
Vulliamy, B L 211

Wacher, John 371
Wainwright, Geoffrey 390
Walford, Thomas 156
Walker, Sir Edward 28
Walker, Joseph Cooper 144n37
Wallace, Alfred Russel 331, 335
Waller, F W 316–17, 318, 322
Wallis, Rosa 210
Walpole, Horace

Anecdotes 123–4
criticism of antiquaries 63, 99–100, 102, 106, 108, 431
Walsingham Abbey (Norfolk), engraving 104
Waltham Cross (Herts) 59
Wang At Jong 148
Wanley, Humfrey
classical scholarship 12, 24
foundation of Society of Antiquaries 2, 46, 47–8, 49, 50
minutes written by *44*
Piggott on 40n89
portrait of 33, *34*
royal charter, seeks 47–8, 56, 61–2
Royal Society, membership of 52
social standing 50
Warburton, John 5
Ward, John 79
Ward-Perkins, John 399, 405
Ware (Herts), barrow *see* Youngsbury
Warne, Charles 236
Warner, William 35, 37n12
Warton, Thomas 158
Warwickshire, history of 210
Waterhouse, Edward 31
Watkins Wynn, Sir Charles William 238
Watson, Christopher Knight 212, 213, 214, 218, 223n47
Watson, James 111
Watson, John 83
Way, Albert
Archaeological Journal, editorship 173, 176–7, 178, 192, 252, 253
British Archaeological Association, defects to 259n162
catalogue of collections 211, 220
directorship of Society 210
donations by 214, 218
intellectual network 271, 301n65
letter written to 182, *183*
on prehistory 191, 251, 252, 256
Webb, Philip Carteret 66, 77, 78, 81, 94n10
Webster, Graham 405
Weever, John 26, *27*
Welbeck (Notts), cross *160*
Well (Yorks), mosaic 71n86
Wellington, Dukes of
Arthur 178
Henry 355
Wells (Som), cathedral 96n66, 310
Welwyn Garden City (Herts), burial 406
West, Benjamin 92, 111, 133, 135
painting by *136*
West, James 65
West Kennet (Wilts), excavations 276
Westmacott, Richard 133
Westropp, Hodder 301n65
Whalley Abbey (Lancs), finds from 129, *130*
Wharram Percy (Yorks), fieldwork 412n45
Wharton, Henry 24, 40n89
Whatman, James 37n12, 113
Wheare, Degory 17, 27
Wheathampstead (Herts), excavations 365

Wheeler, Sir R E M
    Animal, Vegetable, or Mineral? 383
    excavations 280, 370
        Caerleon 360
        Caernarfon 360, 377
        France 359, 369
        Lydney 336, 338, 343, 359, 364
        Maiden Castle 359, 367–8
        Verulamium 359, 365–7, 371, 375, 377
    on excavations at Silchester 356
    London Museum, directorship of 359
    at National Museum of Wales 338
    portrait *382*
    presidency 385
        addresses 383, 387, 395, 408–9, 415, 417
        appeals for funds 397–9, 403
    on river gravels 339
Wheeler, Tessa 336, 364, 365, 367, 375
Whitaker, John 83
Whitaker, Revd Thomas Dunham 128–9
White, John 162
White, Robert, portraits by *27, 28, 29, 30*
Whittington, Dick 99
Whittington Court villa (Glos), excavations 399
Whittlesey Mere (Hunts) 331
Wilde, Dr William 241, 252
Wilkins, William 158–9
Willement, Thomas 183
Willetts, Pamela 219–20
Willey, Gordon 385

Williams, John 213
Williams-Ellis, Clough 329, 332, *333*, 334, 341, 343
Williamson, Frances 70n61
Willis, Browne 5, 50
Wilson, Daniel, *Prehistoric Annals of Scotland* 240, 246, 251, 252
Wilson, David 385
Wilson, Richard 79
Wiltshire, barrows 229–32
Winchelsea, Lord 49, 54, 55
Winchester (Hants)
    excavations 371, 398, 399, 400, 406, 412n45, 413n66
    Magdalen Chapel 113, *115*
Winckelmann, Johann Joachim 158
Windsor (Berks)
    castle
        excavations 315
        improvement of 179
        paintings 84, 85, 135, *136*, 162
    St Leonard's Hill, finds 59, 63, *64*
Winterbourne (Berks), cross *160*
Winterton (Lincs), mosaic 71n86, 413n66
Wisbech (Cambs), club 53
Wise, Francis 59
Witham hanging bowl 210
women
    artists 210
    society membership 70n61, 148, 177–8, 221, 392–3, 419
Wood (engraver) 110
Woodchester (Glos), mosaic 71n86, 93, 277

Woodruff, C H 276, 283
Woodstock Manor (Oxon) 309
Woodward, Dr John 23, 24
Wooler, John 310
Woolf, Daniel 6
Woollett, William 111, 114
Woolley, Sir Leonard 363, 385, 387
Wor Barrow (Dorset), excavations 286
Worcestershire 201, 210, 214, 218
Workers Educational Association 383
Wormald, Francis 385, 400
Worsaae, J J A 238, 239–41, 243, 252, 254
Worsley, Sir Richard 158
Wright, James 39n82
Wright, T 187
Wright, Thomas 234–6, 251, 252–3, 256, 296
Wroxeter (Viroconium) (Shrops), excavations 358, 375, 397
Wyatt, James 85, 89–90, 92, 310–13, 322, 431–2

Xanthus (Turkey), excavations 132

York (Yorks)
    Jorvik Viking Centre 390
    St Mary's Abbey 117, *118*
Yorkshire Philosophical Society 177, 248
Yorkshire Post 345
Youngsbury (Herts), excavations 276, 280, 282, 283

Zarnecki, George 385